The Children's Visual
World
Atlas

Published by Fog City Press
Conceived and produced by Weldon Owen Pty Ltd
59 Victoria Street, McMahons Point
Sydney, NSW 2060, Australia
Copyright © 2004 Weldon Owen Inc
Reprinted 2004, 2005 (twice)

Chief Executive Officer John Owen
President Terry Newell
Publisher Lynn Humphries
Creative Director Sue Burk
Vice President International Sales Stuart Laurence
Administrator International Sales Kristine Ravn

Project Editors Angela Handley, Emma Hutchinson
Text Janine Flew, Lynn Humphries, Limelight Press, Margaret McPhee

Design Concept, Cover and Digital Effects John Bull
Designers Melanie Calabretta, Avril Makula, Heather Menzies, Craig Peterson

Maps Map Illustrations
Chief Cartographer Laurie Whiddon
Cartographers Encompass Graphics
Cartographic Consultant Colin Arrowsmith
Information Graphics Andrew Davies
Flags Flag Society of Australia

Editorial Coordinator Jennifer Losco
Production Manager Louise Mitchell
Production Coordinator Monique Layt

ISBN 1 740893 17 4

Colour reproduction by Chroma Graphics (Overseas) Pte Ltd
Printed by Kyodo printing Co. (S'pore) Pte Ltd
Printed in Singapore

A Weldon Owen Production

The Children's Visual
World
Atlas

FOG CITY PRESS

Contents

How to use this atlas

Map Pages

Roanne
Tarare
Saône
Lyon

Illustrations
Illustrations and captions show and describe places, people, wildlife and activities in the area.

Grid reference
The letters and numbers on the border are the key to finding places listed in the gazetteer.

Gazetteer
The gazetteer, starting on page 154, lists a letter and number for each place.

Location map
Continent
Map area

France

🇫🇷 **FRANCE**
POPULATION 60,181,000 • CAPITAL PARIS

🇲🇨 **MONACO**
POPULATION 32,000 • CAPITAL MONACO

Flag and facts
The flag, population and capital city of each country on the map are shown here. The countries are listed by the size of their population.

Feature panel
Feature panels provide more detailed information about topics of interest.

Mont-St-Michel
The abbey of Mont-St-Michel was built in AD 966, and gradually changed over the next thousand years. It stands high on a rocky mound, attached to the mainland by a causeway. When tides are high, Mont-St-Michel becomes an island.

Cave art in Lascaux
Lascaux cave in the Dordogne, in southern France, was discovered in 1940 by four boys and a dog. They explored a hole in the forest and found themselves inside a beautiful painted cave system. There are 600 paintings in Lascaux, dating back 17,000 years. They depict hunting scenes, cattle, horses, deer and extinct animals. The cave is closed to visitors but a nearby replica is a tourist attraction.

1 Great Hall of the Bulls
The walls of this area of the cave seem to come alive with paintings of four aurochs (wild cattle drawn in black outline. Some are 16 feet (5 m) tall and are the largest ice-age artworks.

2 Painted Gallery
This gallery is in a narrow passage off the Great Hall. Horses, bison and deer are crowded together on the wall.

Cave plan

3 Main Gallery
A second passage, to the right of the Great Hall, leads to the Main Gallery. The most impressive painting shows a row of stags swimming. The scene is almost 10 feet (3 m) above the ground. The artist must have used scaffolding.

4 Shaft of the Dead Man
Another passage leads to an area decorated with a scene of a wounded bison that has attacked and killed a man. The bird on a stick may be a spear. The artist made his paints with crushed rock and animal fat.

Bordeaux vineyard
Bordeaux, in France's southwest, is the largest wine-making region in the world. It is famous particularly for its red and sweet white wines. More than 13,000 wine growers in the area produce a third of all France's wine exports.

Paris
The largest city in France began as a small settlement on an island in the Seine River. It became the national capital in AD 987. More than 2 million people live in the center of Paris and another 8 million in its suburbs. The city is a business and industrial center, and one of the world's top tourist destinations. Its most famous landmark, the Eiffel Tower, was built in 1889.

Château de Chambord
Chambord is the most famous castle in the Loire Valley. It was built in the 1500s, in a symmetrical design, and contains 440 rooms, 84 staircases and 365 fireplaces. The French kings, in particular Louis XIV, used it as a retreat but it was so expensive to heat that they went there only in summer.

Mont Blanc, in France, is the highest mountain in the Alps. Its peak stands at 15,771 feet (4,807 m).

Corsica
(to France)

Inside this starburst is a world record held by the area covered by the map, or an important fact about the area.

Regional map
This physical map shows landscape features, cities, towns and roads.

Scale bar
The scale bar makes it possible to calculate distances on the map.

Compass
The compass shows the way the map is facing.

Inset map
This is a place linked to the main map but outside the map area.

THEMATIC MAP

Life zones

CONTINENT OPENER

Europe

CONTINENT COLORS

Europe

North America

South America

Asia

Africa

Oceania

MAP SYMBOLS

Capital city	⬛ **P A R I S**
State capital	● **SYDNEY**
Major city	● **San Francisco**
Town	● Lyon
Point of interest	★ *Mont-St-Michel*
▲ Mountain	—— Major border
▲ Sea mountain	—— State border
▣ Arctic base	•••••• Contested border
+ Pole	Metropolis
Lake	—— Highway
River	—— Main road

Fact File Pages

USING THE LAND | NATURAL FEATURES | PLACES | PEOPLE | TRADITIONS/CULTURE

Quirky fact
This is a snippet of surprising or unusual information about the region.

Categories
The information in the fact file is divided into five categories, marked by blue banners.

Illustrations
Illustrations and photographs support the text entries.

Feature panel
Selected topics of interest are treated in more depth in colored feature panels.

History panel
This provides a timeline of events or a snapshot of a region's history.

Location finder
- Continent
- Map area

Land use image
This provides further information about how the land is used.

Inset map
This is an area linked to the region but outside the area of the main map.

LAND USE

The colors of the map depict the different types of land in the region.

- Forest and woodland
- Arable land
- Grazing
- Arid or marginal

MAP ICONS

These symbols show how the land is used. They include farming, industry, mining and tourism.

- Cereals
- Rice
- Wheat
- Barley
- Corn (maize)
- Flax
- Jute
- Potatoes
- Fruit and vegetables
- Fruit
- Vegetables
- Citrus fruits
- Bananas
- Wine
- Cotton
- Coffee
- Tea
- Beef cattle
- Cocoa
- Tobacco
- Sugarcane
- Sugar beet
- Flowers
- Coconuts
- Groundnuts
- Dates
- Palm oil
- Olives
- Rubber
- Oilseed rape
- Goats
- Reindeer
- Fishing
- Whaling
- Shellfish
- Industrial center
- Mining
- Oil production
- Gas production
- Timber
- Sheep
- Poultry
- Pigs
- Dairy cattle
- Tourism
- Winter sports

FACT FILE STATISTICS

LAND AREA	3,717,813 sq miles (9,629,091 sq km)
OFFICIAL LANGUAGE	English
MAIN RELIGION	Christian
LIFE EXPECTANCY	77 years
LITERACY	97%

This panel contains statistics about the country or region. If the fact file is about a region, the statistics of the countries in the region are combined.

POPULATION

LARGEST CITIES

New York 8,135,000

These diagrams show the population of the main cities in the region. Each figure represents 100,000 people.

URBAN AND RURAL

WHERE PEOPLE LIVE

- Urban
- Rural

| 75% | 25% |

This graph shows the percentage of people who live in urban and rural areas. If there are more than six countries in the region, the graphs show the countries with the highest and lowest percentages in the area and the regional average.

RIVERS AND MOUNTAINS

LONGEST RIVERS

Loire 634 miles (1,020 km)

HIGHEST MOUNTAINS

Mt Logan 19,551 feet (5,959 m)

Mt St Elias 18,009 feet (5,489 m)

Mt Lucania 17,146 feet (5,226 m)

King Peak 16,972 feet (5,173 m)

Where we live

Earth's 6 billion people are not spread evenly around the planet. Most live where resources are plentiful or can easily be obtained by trading. Therefore, few people live in deserts or polar regions, but many live in fertile areas close to energy sources, and near coasts and rivers. As the lights in the photograph below show, the continents of Europe and North America, and parts of Asia, are densely populated. Australia, Africa and South America are less densely populated, and most of their people live along the coast. The River Nile can be seen in Egypt. The image was made by combining information gathered by satellites over a period of nine months.

US–Mexico border
When seen from space, our planet looks very different. This satellite image, which has been artificially colored, clearly shows the contrast between developed and less-developed farmland. At the top, in red, are the gridded and irrigated fields of California's Imperial Valley in the USA, north of the border with Mexico. Below, in blue, are Mexico's less-developed farmlands. The border town of Mexicali-Caliexico is in the center of the photo.

Istanbul, Turkey

In this view of Istanbul (*left*), city areas are blue-green and vegetation is red. Dividing the city is the busy shipping channel of the Bosporus, spanned by two bridges. The image also shows water depth—colder water is a deeper shade of blue.

Tokyo, Japan

Tokyo, with its surrounds, is the largest city in the world. In this view (*right*), the buildings (in blue) spread over a huge distance. The vegetation is colored red. Three rivers can be seen, as well as Tokyo's port area. The block-shaped islands are reclaimed land.

World weather

Since 1960, satellites orbiting high in the sky have sent back to Earth images of land and ocean, clouds and storms. Scientists now rely on these images to monitor the weather and predict how it will change. In the image below, taken from satellites 440 miles (700 km) above Earth, clouds swirl over the landmasses. The tropical region, around the Equator, is less cloudy than the areas to the north and south. The Sahara Desert in northern Africa and the dry lands of the Middle East can be seen, as well as the forests of South America. Greenland is the large white shape at the top. The light blue areas are seas and lakes.

Hurricanes

Hurricanes—also known as cyclones and typhoons—are powerful storms that produce winds of up to 150 miles an hour (250 km/h). These winds, and the heavy rain that follows, can cause enormous damage. Satellite images show hurricanes forming, and scientists can track their progress as they move toward land. This enables them to warn people of the coming danger. This image shows Hurricane Fran as it nears the east coast of the USA in 1996.

El Niño

El Niño is an ocean current that develops off the coast of Peru every year. In some years, it flows much farther south than usual. This changes the temperature of the ocean, and produces extreme weather, such as droughts and flooding rains, over a wide area. These satellite images show El Niño developing in the Pacific Ocean over a six-month period. Landmasses are black and El Niño is the red and white tongue moving westward along the Equator.

1985

1990

Ozone hole

Antarctica

2000

A "hole" in the sky

Ozone is a gas high in the atmosphere that absorbs most of the harmful rays from the Sun, and prevents heat from being lost from Earth. Since the 1980s, the amount of ozone over Antarctica has declined. The dark shades of blue show the growth of the ozone hole since 1985. The 2000 hole was the largest ever recorded—about three times the size of the USA.

Earth's patterns

Photographs from space show things that cannot be seen on land. Many satellite images are artificially colored to make them clearer. They provide a large-scale view of natural events, such as volcanic eruptions, wildfires, dust storms, droughts and floods. They show how our cities are growing, and how our forests are disappearing. Using radar, satellites can "see" below the Sahara Desert to the rocks beneath. The view from space is now a vital tool in agricultural planning and weather forecasting. Satellite images help scientists understand how Earth's climate has changed over millions of years. And, as these pages show, they make interesting patterns.

Coastline, Guinea-Bissau
In this view of the coastline of Guinea-Bissau, in western Africa (*left*), the blue ribbons are rivers. The light blue areas are silt that has been deposited into the Atlantic Ocean at the bottom of the image.

Reservoir, Brazil
The Represa Três Marias winds across southeastern Brazil (*below*). This reservoir was built in 1960 to generate hydroelectric power for the state of Minas Gerais.

Grand Canyon, USA
Snow lies on the north and south rims of the Grand Canyon, Arizona (*above*). The canyon, the largest in the world, was carved out by the Colorado River. The image shows the lack of vegetation around this dramatic landform. The canyon's south rim, on the left of the photograph, is 1 mile (1.6 km) above its floor.

Comet scarring, Sahara
A comet slammed into the Sahara Desert millions of years ago and left the circular scars seen in this image (*left*).

Rain forest, Brazil
Brazil's remaining forest appears as bright red, while dark areas are cleared land, and black and gray patches are recently burned areas (*right*).

Mississippi River, USA
The Mississippi River (*left*) enters the Gulf of Mexico and dumps a load of silt that it has carried on its long journey through the Great Plains. The silt forms a delta at the river's mouth.

Fjords, Norway
Several of Norway's fjords—steep, narrow inlets from the sea—can be seen in this view of the southern part of the country (*right*).

Volcano, New Zealand
The snow-capped peak of volcanic Mt Taranaki (*below*) towers over the surrounding forest. It last erupted in 1755.

Malaspina Glacier, USA
The Malaspina Glacier, shown in light blue, fans out between Icy Bay and Yakutat Bay in Alaska (*right*). The red ridged area is a moraine, or deposit of rocks, that has built up as the glacier moved toward the sea. The moraine prevents the glacier from reaching the ocean, shown as a dark blue area at the bottom of the image.

Planet Earth

Earth is a giant ball of rock, just one of the many bodies that travel around the Sun. It was born about 4.6 billion years ago, when a swirling cloud of gas and dust gradually turned into the solar system. Inside the young Earth, radioactive materials began to decay and heat up. Rocks started to melt, with heavier metals sinking to the center, leaving lighter minerals on top. Eventually, Earth settled into four main layers—a thin rocky crust on the surface; a partly molten layer of rock called the mantle beneath the crust; an outer core of liquid iron and nickel; and an inner core of solid iron and nickel. Reaching temperatures of 5,400°F (3,000°C), the core is still extremely hot. This intense heat drives movements of the surface rocks and forms many of Earth's features.

Birth of a solar system

About 4.6 billion years ago, a cloud of gas and dust was drifting through space. Perhaps triggered by a nearby exploding star, the cloud began to collapse in on itself and rotate. The densest part of the cloud formed a core that grew hotter and larger as its gravity attracted more material. Eventually, this core became the young Sun. Around the Sun, some of the cloud formed a broad disk, called the solar nebula. Particles in the disk collided and stuck together, gradually growing bigger until they became the planets of the solar system.

1. Spinning disk
A cloud of dust and gas starts collapsing in on itself, forming a disk with a hot core. The core eventually becomes the Sun.

Our place in space

In the immensity of space, our planet is a mere speck. Earth orbits the Sun, one of the billions of stars in the Milky Way galaxy. The Milky Way and its companions in the Local Group are just a handful of the universe's 50 billion galaxies.

Key to symbols
- ⬍ Colliding plates
- ⋯⋯ Uncertain boundary
- ⬌ Sliding plates
- ⬍ Spreading plates
- ⬜ Direction of movement

Tectonic puzzle

Earth's rocky crust and the upper part of the mantle form a layer called the lithosphere. The lithosphere is broken up into several tectonic plates, like a giant jigsaw puzzle (above). These plates float on molten rock in the mantle, moving toward, away from, and past each other.

Crust: 3–43 miles (5–69 km) thick

Mantle: 1,800 miles (2,880 km) thick

Outer core: 1,400 miles (2,240 km) thick

Inner core: 750 miles (1,200 km) thick

The Local Group
Our little corner of the universe is occupied by the Local Group, a cluster of about 30 galaxies.

Moving plates

As the hot rocks in Earth's mantle circulate, the tectonic plates above them gradually shift, moving about as fast as fingernails grow. On the surface, we see the results of these movements—valleys and mountains are formed, volcanoes erupt, and the ground rattles in earthquakes.

The Andes
South America's Andes Mountains formed when a plate carrying thin ocean crust slid under a plate of thicker continental crust. This movement pushed up the mountain range and formed volcanoes.

The Himalayas
The collision of two continental plates created the massive Himalayas mountain range in Asia. Because the plates were about as thick as each other, the crusts buckled bird and folded to form the peaks.

The San Andreas Fault
California's San Andreas Fault is the line where two plates—the Pacific and the North American—are sliding past each other. The friction between the two plates often jolts the ground in earthquakes.

2. Colliding particles
Particles in the disk smash into each other and stick together, gradually forming larger bodies.

3. The nine planets
The clumps in the disk keep colliding and building up until they form the nine planets. The solar system has been born.

Sun

Mercury

Uranus

Neptune

Venus

Earth

Mars

Jupiter

Saturn

Pluto

Sizing up the planets

Shown here to scale, all nine planets are dwarfed by the Sun. About 1,400 Earths would fit inside Jupiter, while 900 Jupiters could fit inside the Sun.

The Milky Way
Our galaxy, the Milky Way, is a giant spiral measuring about 100,000 light-years across.

The Great Rift Valley
In East Africa, two continental plates are slowly moving apart and have formed a wide valley known as the Great Rift Valley. Eventually, Africa will split, water will flood in, and a new ocean will form.

The Mid-Atlantic Ridge
The Mid-Atlantic Ridge marks where two ocean plates are separating. Molten rock from the mantle rises through the gap between the plates. When the rock cools, it adds to the underwater ridge.

The solar system
Earth is the third of the nine planets that orbit the Sun. The Sun itself is just one of the Milky Way's 200 billion stars.

Life zones

From steamy tropical rain forests to icy polar regions, Earth is home to a remarkable range of environments. Distinct weather patterns have helped to create this variety. Earth is unevenly heated by the Sun. Areas around the Equator receive intense sunlight all year long, polar regions receive weak sunlight, and the areas in between receive varying amounts of sunlight throughout the year. The circulation of Earth's air and ocean waters around the globe bring wind and rain to particular areas at different times.

The long-term pattern of weather in a region is known as its climate and influences the kind of lifeforms that can survive there. An arid climate, for example, is always hot and dry, creating a desert where only tough, scrubby plants and cacti can grow. Desert animals must be especially hardy.

Earth's environments shelter a staggering number of different plants and animals. So far, scientists have identified almost 2 million species, but they estimate that there are about 14 million in all. Of this total, nearly 8 million are thought to be insects, while fewer than 5,000 are mammals. Together, the land, oceans and atmosphere occupied by living things are called the biosphere.

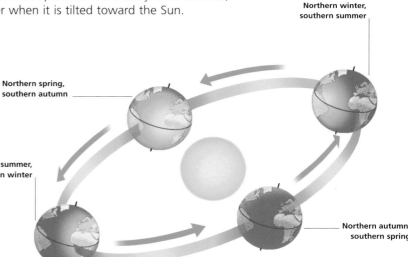

Arctic Circle

Greatest temperature change in a day: 100°F (56°C), from 44°F (6.7°C) to −56°F (−49°C), at Browning, Montana, USA, 1916

Strongest measured wind gust: 231 mph (372 km/h) on Mt Washington, New Hampshire, USA, 1934

Most snow in one year: 1,224 inches (31,102 mm) on Mt Rainier, Washington, USA, 1971–72

NORTH AMERICA

SOUTH AMERICA

Driest place: 0.02 inches (0.5 mm) per year in Quillagua, Atacama Desert, Chile, 1964–2001

Antarctic Circle

Underwater life

While the lifeforms on Earth's land show great variety, many of the world's species are found in water, either in freshwater habitats such as lakes, ponds and rivers, or in the salt water of the oceans. Life in the oceans ranges from microscopic plankton to giant squid. Oceans can be divided into four life zones by water depth.

Mountain Mountain zones are colder, wetter and windier than nearby low-lying areas. Mountain goats move down the slopes when winter comes.

Polar Polar zones are extremely cold and dry all year. They are covered in either low-growing tundra plants or ice. The arctic fox's thick coat keeps it warm.

Sunlight zone
The sunlight zone contains most of the ocean's life, including microscopic plankton; small and large fishes; sharks and rays; and mammals such as seals, dolphins and whales.

0

650 ft (198 m)

3,250 ft (990 m)

Twilight zone
Some sunlight filters through to the twilight zone, but not enough for plants to survive. Many of the fishes contain light-producing bacteria and glow in the dark.

Midnight zone
Sunlight does not reach the midnight zone, a vast mass of dark, cold, slow-moving water. There are fewer lifeforms here than in the waters above.

9,850 ft (3,000 m)

Abyssal zone
The ocean's bottom layer is near freezing and pitch black. In some places, black smokers spew out hot mineral-rich water, which helps mussels, clams and tubeworms to make their own food.

Season to season

Earth takes about 365 days, or one year, to complete one orbit around the Sun. Because Earth is slightly tilted, most regions receive varying amounts of sunlight during the year, which produce seasons. Europe and North America, for example, experience winter when the Northern Hemisphere is tilted away from the Sun, and summer when it is tilted toward the Sun.

Northern winter, southern summer

Northern spring, southern autumn

Northern summer, southern winter

Northern autumn, southern spring

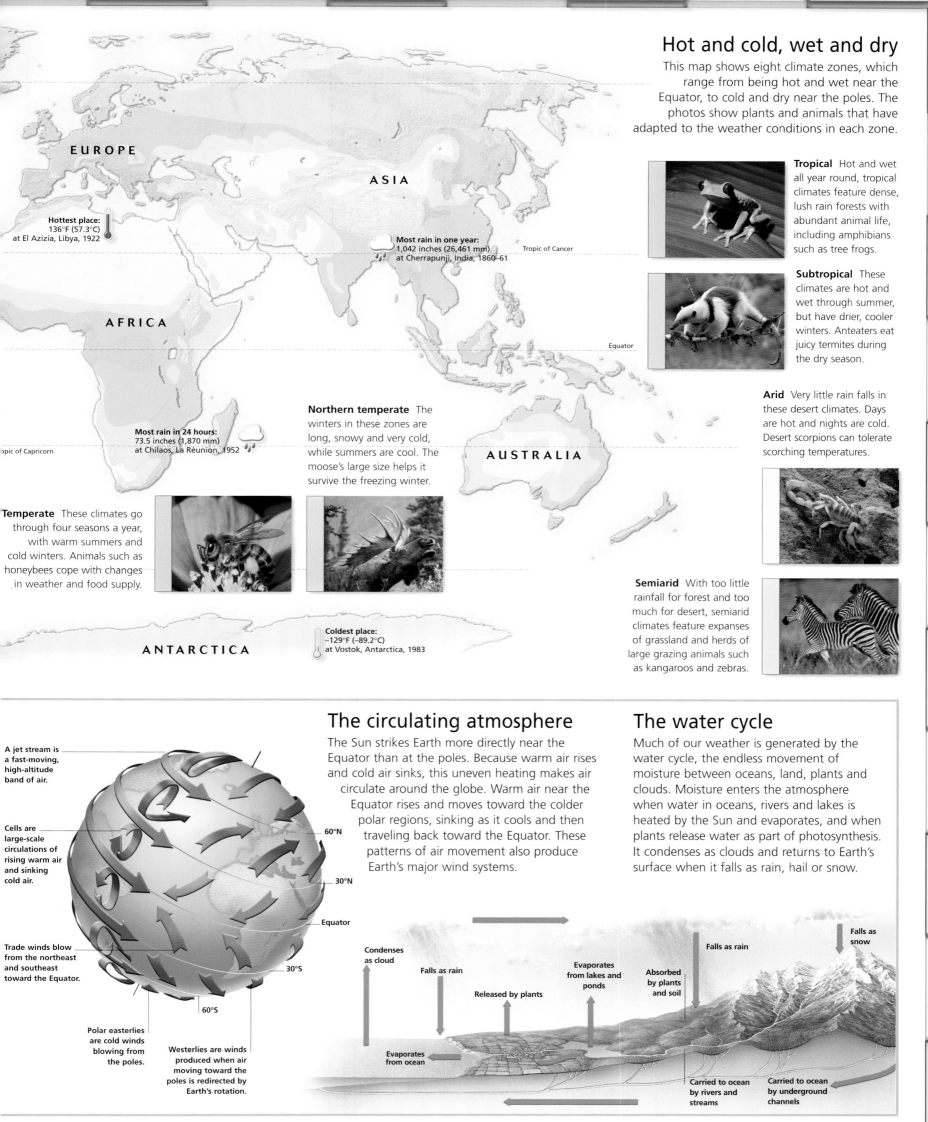

Hot and cold, wet and dry

This map shows eight climate zones, which range from being hot and wet near the Equator, to cold and dry near the poles. The photos show plants and animals that have adapted to the weather conditions in each zone.

EUROPE

ASIA

AFRICA

AUSTRALIA

ANTARCTICA

Hottest place: 136°F (57.3°C) at El Azizia, Libya, 1922

Most rain in one year: 1,042 inches (26,461 mm) at Cherrapunji, India, 1860–61

Tropic of Cancer

Equator

Tropic of Capricorn

Most rain in 24 hours: 73.5 inches (1,870 mm) at Chilaos, La Réunion, 1952

Coldest place: −129°F (−89.2°C) at Vostok, Antarctica, 1983

Tropical Hot and wet all year round, tropical climates feature dense, lush rain forests with abundant animal life, including amphibians such as tree frogs.

Subtropical These climates are hot and wet through summer, but have drier, cooler winters. Anteaters eat juicy termites during the dry season.

Arid Very little rain falls in these desert climates. Days are hot and nights are cold. Desert scorpions can tolerate scorching temperatures.

Northern temperate The winters in these zones are long, snowy and very cold, while summers are cool. The moose's large size helps it survive the freezing winter.

Temperate These climates go through four seasons a year, with warm summers and cold winters. Animals such as honeybees cope with changes in weather and food supply.

Semiarid With too little rainfall for forest and too much for desert, semiarid climates feature expanses of grassland and herds of large grazing animals such as kangaroos and zebras.

The circulating atmosphere

The Sun strikes Earth more directly near the Equator than at the poles. Because warm air rises and cold air sinks, this uneven heating makes air circulate around the globe. Warm air near the Equator rises and moves toward the colder polar regions, sinking as it cools and then traveling back toward the Equator. These patterns of air movement also produce Earth's major wind systems.

A jet stream is a fast-moving, high-altitude band of air.

Cells are large-scale circulations of rising warm air and sinking cold air.

Trade winds blow from the northeast and southeast toward the Equator.

Polar easterlies are cold winds blowing from the poles.

Westerlies are winds produced when air moving toward the poles is redirected by Earth's rotation.

60°N
30°N
Equator
30°S
60°S

The water cycle

Much of our weather is generated by the water cycle, the endless movement of moisture between oceans, land, plants and clouds. Moisture enters the atmosphere when water in oceans, rivers and lakes is heated by the Sun and evaporates, and when plants release water as part of photosynthesis. It condenses as clouds and returns to Earth's surface when it falls as rain, hail or snow.

Condenses as cloud

Falls as rain

Released by plants

Evaporates from lakes and ponds

Absorbed by plants and soil

Falls as rain

Falls as snow

Evaporates from ocean

Carried to ocean by rivers and streams

Carried to ocean by underground channels

The world's people

More than 6 billion people live on our planet, and another 1 million are born every five days. There are now more than 10 times as many people as there were 400 years ago. This incredible population explosion happened because living standards and medical care have improved, allowing people to live longer than ever before. At the same time, birth rates—the number of babies born in each family—stayed high in many parts of the world. Until birth rates fall significantly, the world population will continue to grow, and may reach 10 billion by 2200.

Most of today's increase in population is in developing countries—ones with limited industry and technology. These include most of Asia and Africa, and parts of Central and South America. Many developing countries are finding it difficult to feed and care for their enormous populations. Countries with large industries and advanced technology are known as developed countries. They include Japan, Australia, and much of Europe and North America. Most of their populations have stopped growing, and some are shrinking.

Rich and poor

The gap between the world's rich and poor is growing. Developing countries are home to 75 percent of the world's people, but share just 20 percent of the world's wealth. On average, people in developing countries can expect to have less money, food, medical care, education and access to technology than people in developed countries. These graphs compare living standards in five countries, ranging from one of the world's wealthiest countries, Europe's Norway, to one of the poorest, Africa's Sierra Leone.

Many languages

About 6,000 different languages are spoken today, but more than half the people in the world have one of the 12 languages shown on this chart as their first language. English has fewer than half as many first-language speakers as Mandarin Chinese, but it is spoken by many more people as a second language and is becoming the main world language.

NUMBER OF NATIVE SPEAKERS

Language	Speakers
Mandarin Chinese	874,000,000
Hindi	366,000,000
English	341,000,000
Spanish	340,000,000
Bengali	207,000,000
Portuguese	176,000,000
Russian	167,000,000
Arabic	150,000,000
Japanese	125,000,000
German	100,000,000
Korean	78,000,000
French	77,000,000

Many languages are now endangered. The language of Japan's indigenous people, the Ainu (left), is virtually extinct, with just a handful of elderly speakers remaining. On average, one language is lost every 10 days, and half of the world's 6,000 languages are likely to disappear by 2100.

POPULATION DENSITY

Persons per sq mile	Persons per sq km
Uninhabited	Uninhabited
Less than 2.6	Less than 1
2.6	1
26	10
65	25
130	50
260	100
520	200
1040	400
2080	800
More than 2080	More than 800

World religions

The earliest signs of religious belief date back 60,000 years, and virtually every culture since has followed some kind of religion. There are now hundreds of different religious traditions in the world, but Hinduism, Buddhism, Judaism, Christianity and Islam have had the broadest influence. Hinduism and Buddhism both developed in Asia, while Judaism, Christianity and Islam started in the Middle East.

Islamic mosque

Stained glass window from Christian church

Ganesh, the Hindu god of wisdom

HOW THE WORLD WORSHIPS

- Christianity 33%
- Islam 22%
- Hinduism 15%
- Buddhism 6%
- Chinese traditional 4%
- Non-religious 14%
- Other 3%
- Primal indigenous 3%

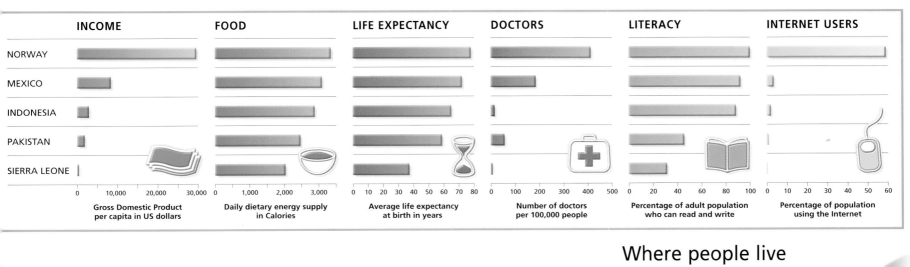

	INCOME	FOOD	LIFE EXPECTANCY	DOCTORS	LITERACY	INTERNET USERS
NORWAY						
MEXICO						
INDONESIA						
PAKISTAN						
SIERRA LEONE						

Gross Domestic Product per capita in US dollars	Daily dietary energy supply in Calories	Average life expectancy at birth in years	Number of doctors per 100,000 people	Percentage of adult population who can read and write	Percentage of population using the Internet

Where people live

The 6 billion people on Earth are spread very unevenly over its landmasses, with China, India and Europe the most crowded areas. People have tended to settle near rivers or the coast. About half of all people now live in cities.

There are now 20 megacities—cities with more than 10 million inhabitants—and 15 of these are in developing countries. As in other megacities, the explosive growth of Calcutta, India, has led to severe overcrowding.

CITY SYMBOLS

- City with 3–5 million people
- City with 5–10 million people
- Megacity with more than 10 million people

* Rhein-Ruhr is an urban region including the cities of Düsseldorf, Essen, Bonn and Cologne

Growing numbers

It took most of human history for the total number of people in the world to reach the billion mark, around 1800. Since then, population growth has sped up, with the sixth billion, achieved in 1999, added in just 12 years. World population is likely to reach 10 billion around the year 2200. About 95 percent of this growth is happening in developing countries, poorer countries with little industry. Asia accounts for 60 percent of the world's people, while Africa has the fastest-growing population.

LARGEST POPULATIONS

China	1,302,200,000
India	1,080,300,000
United States	295,700,000
Indonesia	242,000,000
Brazil	186,100,000
Pakistan	156,700,000
Bangladesh	144,300,000
Russia	143,700,000
Nigeria	140,600,000
Japan	127,400,000
Mexico	106,200,000
Philippines	87,900,000

Geographic comparisons

Largest Islands

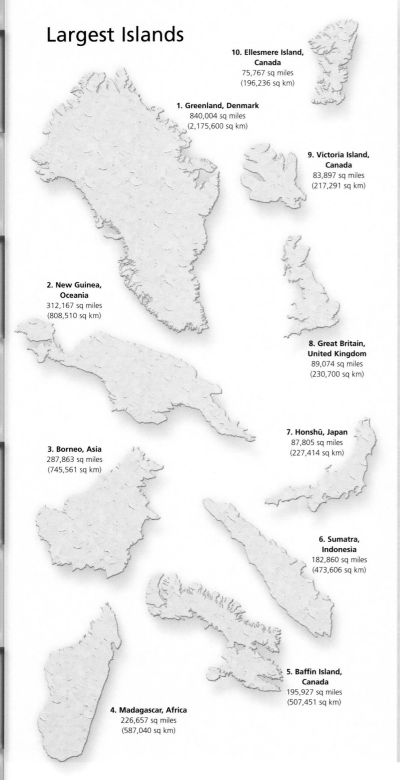

10. Ellesmere Island, Canada
75,767 sq miles
(196,236 sq km)

1. Greenland, Denmark
840,004 sq miles
(2,175,600 sq km)

9. Victoria Island, Canada
83,897 sq miles
(217,291 sq km)

2. New Guinea, Oceania
312,167 sq miles
(808,510 sq km)

8. Great Britain, United Kingdom
89,074 sq miles
(230,700 sq km)

7. Honshū, Japan
87,805 sq miles
(227,414 sq km)

3. Borneo, Asia
287,863 sq miles
(745,561 sq km)

6. Sumatra, Indonesia
182,860 sq miles
(473,606 sq km)

5. Baffin Island, Canada
195,927 sq miles
(507,451 sq km)

4. Madagascar, Africa
226,657 sq miles
(587,040 sq km)

Largest Countries

1. Russia
6,562,115 sq miles
(16,995,800 sq km)

3. United States of America
3,717,813 sq miles
(9,629,091 sq km)

6. Australia
2,941,299 sq miles
(7,617,930 sq km)

7. India
1,147,955 sq miles
(2,973,190 sq km)

Longest Rivers

Murray–Darling, Australia 2,330 miles (3,750 km)

Niger, Africa 2,599 miles (4,184 km)

Mackenzie–Peace–Finlay, North America 2,635 miles (4,241 km)

Lena–Kirenga, Asia 2,734 miles (4,400 km)

Heilong Jiang (Amur)–Argun', Asia 2,744 miles (4,416 km)

Mekong, Asia 2,749 miles (4,425 km)

River Plate–Paraná, South America 2,796 miles (4,500 km)

Congo, Africa 2,900 miles (4,667 km)

Yellow, Asia 3,395 miles (5,464 km)

Yenisey–Angara–Selenga, Asia 3,448 miles (5,550 km)

Ob'–Irtysh, Asia 3,459 miles (5,568 km)

Mississippi–Missouri, North America 3,709 miles (5,969 km)

Yangtze, Asia 3,964 miles (6,380 km)

Amazon, South America 4,049 miles (6,516 km)

Nile, Africa 4,160 miles (6,656 km)

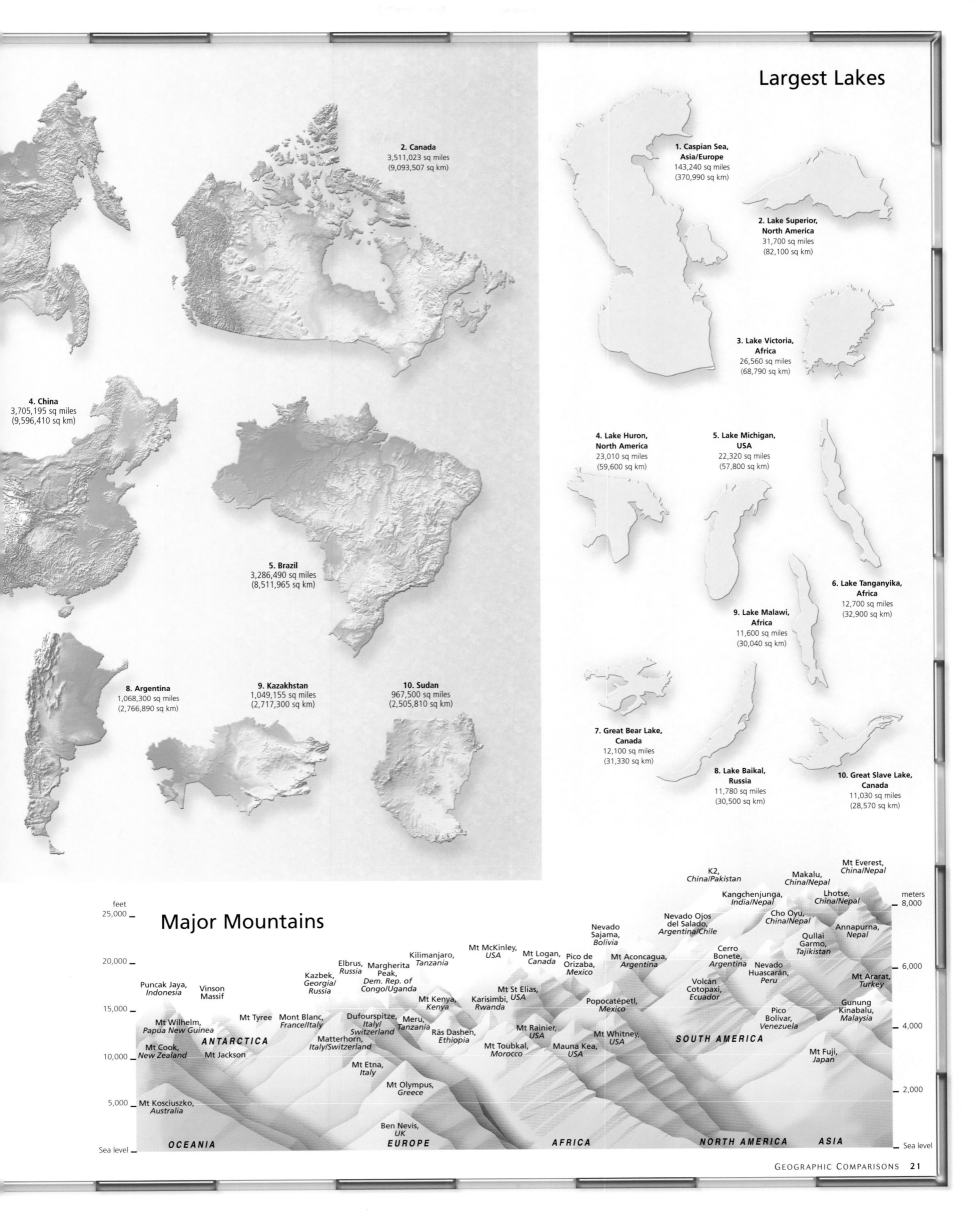

2. Canada
3,511,023 sq miles
(9,093,507 sq km)

4. China
3,705,195 sq miles
(9,596,410 sq km)

5. Brazil
3,286,490 sq miles
(8,511,965 sq km)

8. Argentina
1,068,300 sq miles
(2,766,890 sq km)

9. Kazakhstan
1,049,155 sq miles
(2,717,300 sq km)

10. Sudan
967,500 sq miles
(2,505,810 sq km)

Largest Lakes

1. Caspian Sea, Asia/Europe
143,240 sq miles
(370,990 sq km)

2. Lake Superior, North America
31,700 sq miles
(82,100 sq km)

3. Lake Victoria, Africa
26,560 sq miles
(68,790 sq km)

4. Lake Huron, North America
23,010 sq miles
(59,600 sq km)

5. Lake Michigan, USA
22,320 sq miles
(57,800 sq km)

6. Lake Tanganyika, Africa
12,700 sq miles
(32,900 sq km)

9. Lake Malawi, Africa
11,600 sq miles
(30,040 sq km)

7. Great Bear Lake, Canada
12,100 sq miles
(31,330 sq km)

8. Lake Baikal, Russia
11,780 sq miles
(30,500 sq km)

10. Great Slave Lake, Canada
11,030 sq miles
(28,570 sq km)

Major Mountains

feet
25,000
20,000
15,000
10,000
5,000
Sea level

meters
8,000
6,000
4,000
2,000
Sea level

Mt Everest, *China/Nepal*
K2, *China/Pakistan*
Makalu, *China/Nepal*
Kangchenjunga, *India/Nepal*
Lhotse, *China/Nepal*
Cho Oyu, *China/Nepal*
Nevado Ojos del Salado, *Argentina/Chile*
Annapurna, *Nepal*
Qullai Garmo, *Tajikistan*
Nevado Sajama, *Bolivia*
Mt Aconcagua, *Argentina*
Cerro Bonete, *Argentina*
Mt McKinley, *USA*
Mt Logan, *Canada*
Pico de Orizaba, *Mexico*
Nevado Huascarán, *Peru*
Mt Ararat, *Turkey*
Kilimanjaro, *Tanzania*
Elbrus, *Russia*
Margherita Peak, *Dem. Rep. of Congo/Uganda*
Volcán Cotopaxi, *Ecuador*
Kazbek, *Georgia/Russia*
Popocatépetl, *Mexico*
Gunung Kinabalu, *Malaysia*
Puncak Jaya, *Indonesia*
Vinson Massif
Mt St Elias, *USA*
Karisimbi, *Rwanda*
Pico Bolívar, *Venezuela*
Mt Kenya, *Kenya*
Dufourspitze, *Italy/Switzerland*
Meru, *Tanzania*
Mt Wilhelm, *Papua New Guinea*
Mt Tyree
Mont Blanc, *France/Italy*
Rãs Dashen, *Ethiopia*
Mt Rainier, *USA*
Mt Whitney, *USA*
SOUTH AMERICA
Mt Fuji, *Japan*
ANTARCTICA
Matterhorn, *Italy/Switzerland*
Mt Toubkal, *Morocco*
Mauna Kea, *USA*
Mt Cook, *New Zealand*
Mt Jackson
Mt Etna, *Italy*
Mt Kosciuszko, *Australia*
Mt Olympus, *Greece*
AFRICA
NORTH AMERICA
ASIA
Ben Nevis, *UK*
OCEANIA
EUROPE

The physical world

CIRCUMFERENCE OF EARTH AROUND THE EQUATOR
24,902 miles (40,067 km)

AREA OF SEA
139,782,000 square miles (362,033,000 sq km)

AREA OF LAND ABOVE SEA LEVEL
57,151,000 square miles (148,021,000 sq km)

ARCTIC OCEAN

Queen Elizabeth Islands
Ellesmere Island
Greenland
Greenland Sea
Banks Island
Beaufort Sea
Baffin Bay
Baffin Island
Victoria Island
Great Bear Lake
Brooks Range
Arctic Circle
Yukon
Mackenzie
Great Slave Lake
Hudson Bay
Peninsule d'Ungava
Labrador Sea
Denmark Strait
Iceland
Faroe Islands
Norw
Reindeer Lake
Reykjanes Ridge
Alaska Range
Mt McKinley 20,321ft (6,194m)
Gulf of Alaska
Peace
Lake Athabasca
Canadian Shield
Labrador
Aleutian Islands
Aleutian Trench
Queen Charlotte Islands
Rocky Mountains
Lake Winnipeg
Laurentian Mtns
British Isles

NORTH PACIFIC OCEAN

Vancouver Island
Mt Rainier 14,409ft (4,392m)
NORTH AMERICA
Missouri
Lake Superior
Lake Michigan
Lake Huron
Lake Ontario
Lake Erie
Lake St Lawrence
NORTH ATLANTIC OCEAN
Mont B 15,7 (4,80
Bay of Biscay
Great Basin
Great Plains
North Central Lowlands
Pyrene
Colorado
Arkansas
Plateau
Ohio
Mississippi
Appalachian Mountains
Iberian Peninsula
Rio Grande
Sierra Madre Occidental
Gulf Atlantic Coastal Plain
North American Basin
Bermuda
Azores
Baja California
Gulf of Mexico
Sargasso Sea
Madeira
Canary Basin
Northeast Pacific Basin
Hawaiian Islands
Tropic of Cancer
Guadalupe
The Bahamas
Cape Verde Plateau
Canary Islands
S
Hawaii
Revillagigedo Islands
Yucatan Basin
West Indies
Greater Antilles
Lesser Antilles
Caribbean Sea
Cape Verde Islands
Sierra Madre Oriental
Lake Nicaragua
Demerara Plateau
Mid-Atlantic Ridge
Sah
Niger
Lake Volta
Guatemala Basin
Cocos Ridge
Llanos
Orinoco
Guiana Basin
Guiana Highlands
Mont Can 13,451ft (4, Gulf of G
São T
Galapagos Islands
Chimborazo 20,702ft (6,310m)
Amazon Basin
Japura
Amazon
Equator
Marquesas Islands
Nevado Huascarán 22,205ft (6,768m)
Purus
Madeira
Xingu
Tocantins
SOUTH AMERICA
Ascension
East Pacific Rise
Bauer Basin
Ucayali
Brazil Basin
Cook Islands
Society Archipelago
Tahiti
Tuamotu Archipelago
Galapagos Rise
Peru Basin
Lake Titicaca
Planalto do Mato Grosso
Brazilian Highlands
St Helena
Rarotonga
Polynesia
Tropic of Capricorn
Altiplano
Andes
Mid-Atlantic Ridge
Pitcairn Islands
Sala y Gomez Ridge
Nazca Ridge
Chile Basin
Gran Chaco
Paraguay
Parana
Uruguay
Ilha da Trindade
Easter Island
Peru-Chile Trench
Roggeveen Basin
Mount Aconcagua 22,835ft (6,960m)
Pampas
Rio Grande Rise
Southwest Pacific Basin
Colorado
River Plate
SOUTH PACIFIC OCEAN
Argentine Basin
SOUTH ATLANTIC OCEAN
Falkland Islands
South Georgia
Tierra del Fuego
Cape Horn
Drake Passage
Scotia Sea
South Sandwich Trench
Patagonia
South Shetland Islands
South Sandwich Islands
Southeast Pacific Basin
South Orkney Islands
Antarctic Circle
SOUTHERN OCEAN
Antarctic Peninsula
Ross Sea
Amundsen Sea
Peter I Island
Weddell Sea

N W E S

| 0 miles | | 2000 |
| 0 kilometers | | 2000 |

Oceans and seas
Oceans and seas make up almost 71 percent of Earth's surface. The five oceans are the Pacific, Atlantic, Indian, Arctic and Southern. Beneath these oceans are ridges and trenches, mountain chains, valleys and plains. Currents carry seawater around the globe.

Continents
The land between the oceans is divided into seven main landmasses, or continents—Europe, Asia, North America, South America, Africa, Australia and Antarctica. Europe and Asia form a single landmass called Eurasia, but are treated as separate continents.

Northern Hemisphere

Southern Hemisphere

Polar regions
Centered on the North and South poles, these are the coldest places on Earth. The Arctic, in the north, includes Greenland, parts of Eurasia and North America, and large expanses of ocean. The South Pole is surrounded by the continent of Antarctica.

Hemispheres
The Equator divides Earth into two halves, or hemispheres. Two-thirds of Earth's land, including all of Europe and North America and most of Asia and Africa, is in the Northern Hemisphere. The Southern Hemisphere has much more ocean.

23

Countries of the world

NUMBER OF COUNTRIES	192
NUMBER OF TERRITORIES	65
LONGEST BORDER	USA–Canada 3,987 miles (6,379 km)
LARGEST POPULATION	China 1,286,975,000

ARCTIC OCEAN

Beaufort Sea

Victoria Island

Baffin Island

Baffin Bay

Ellesmere Island

Greenland (to Denmark)

ICELAND

Faroe Isla (to Denmark)

Arctic Circle

USA (ALASKA)

Hudson Bay

CANADA

Gulf of Alaska

Aleutian Islands (to USA)

UNITED KINGDOM

REPUBLIC OF IRELAND

BELG

FRA

NORTH

PACIFIC

OCEAN

UNITED STATES OF AMERICA

NORTH

ATLANTIC

OCEAN

St Pierre and Miquelon (to France)

PORTUGAL

ANDORRA

SPAIN

MO

Azores (to Portugal)

Madeira (to Portugal)

MOROCCO

Canary Islands (to Spain)

ALGE

Tropic of Cancer

Guadalupe (to Mexico)

MEXICO

Gulf of Mexico

THE BAHAMAS

WESTERN SAHARA (occupied by Morocco)

MAURITANIA

MALI

Hawaii (USA)

Revillagigedo Islands (to Mexico)

CUBA

Cayman Is (to UK)

HAITI

DOMINICAN REPUBLIC

Puerto Rico (to USA)

ST KITTS AND NEVIS

ANTIGUA AND BARBUDA

DOMINICA

ST LUCIA

CAPE VERDE

SENEGAL

GAMBIA

BELIZE

JAMAICA

GUATEMALA

HONDURAS

EL SALVADOR

NICARAGUA

COSTA RICA

PANAMA

ST VINCENT & THE GRENADINES

BARBADOS

GRENADA

TRINIDAD AND TOBAGO

GUINEA-BISSAU

GUINEA

SIERRA LEONE

LIBERIA

CÔTE D'IVOIRE

BURKINA FASO

GHA

TO

BEN

Clipperton Island (to France)

VENEZUELA

GUYANA

SURINAME

FRENCH GUIANA

COLOMBIA

EQUA

Galapagos Islands (to Ecuador)

ECUADOR

São Tomé and Prín

SÃO TOMÉ AND PRÍN

0° Equator

KIRIBATI

International Date Line

PERU

BRAZIL

Fernando de Noronha (to Brazil)

Ascension (to UK)

SOUTH

PACIFIC

OCEAN

BOLIVIA

St Helena (to UK)

American Samoa (to USA)

Cook Islands (to NZ)

Tahiti

French Polynesia (to France)

PARAGUAY

Ilha da Trindade (to Brazil)

Tropic of Capricorn

Pitcairn Islands (to UK)

Sala y Gómez (to Chile)

Easter Island (to Chile)

CHILE

ARGENTINA

SOUTH

ATLANTIC

OCEAN

Juan Fernández Islands (to Chile)

URUGUAY

Tristan da Cunha (to UK)

Falkland Islands (to UK)

South Georgia (to UK)

Gough Island (to UK)

South Sandwich Islands (to UK)

South Shetland Islands (to UK)

South Orkney Islands (to UK)

Antarctic Circle

SOUTHERN OCEAN

Peter I Island (to Norway)

Antarctic Peninsula

Weddell Sea

N W E S

| 0 miles | | 2000 |
| 0 kilometers | | 2000 |

Land boundaries
About 150,000 miles (250,000 km) of land boundaries separate the world's countries and territories. These borders may follow landforms, waterways, the edges of traditional territories, or lines of latitude and longitude. Some of them are arbitrary lines.

Maritime boundaries
Many coastal nations have established maritime boundaries, which extend their borders into the ocean. A nation's maritime claim extends 12 nautical miles off the shore, but exclusive fishing and mining zones are generally up to 200 nautical miles offshore.

The world's smallest country, Vatican City, is about the size of 100 football fields. The largest country, Russia, is 39 million times bigger.

ARCTIC OCEAN

Barents Sea

FINLAND

ESTONIA
LATVIA
LITHUANIA
BELARUS

UKRAINE
SLOVAKIA
MOLDOVA
HUNGARY
ROMANIA
SERBIA
BULGARIA
ALBANIA
GREECE
Black Sea

Caspian Sea

Aral Sea

KAZAKHSTAN

RUSSIA

Arctic Circle

Kamchatka Peninsula

Sea of Okhotsk

Bering Sea

Sakhalin

Aleutian Islands (to USA)

Kuril Islands (to Russian Federation)

MONGOLIA

TURKEY
GEORGIA
ARMENIA
AZERBAIJAN
UZBEKISTAN
KYRGYZSTAN
TAJIKISTAN
TURKMENISTAN

CYPRUS
LEBANON
SYRIA
ISRAEL
JORDAN
IRAQ
IRAN
AFGHANISTAN

Mediterranean Sea
Crete

KUWAIT
BAHRAIN
QATAR
UAE

PAKISTAN
NEPAL
BHUTAN

CHINA

NORTH KOREA
SOUTH KOREA

Sea of Japan

JAPAN

NORTH

East China Sea

Ryukyu Islands (to Japan)

PACIFIC

LIBYA
EGYPT

Red Sea

SAUDI ARABIA

OMAN

Arabian Sea

INDIA

BANGLADESH

MYANMAR (BURMA)

LAOS

Hainan

OCEAN

Tropic of Cancer

CHAD
SUDAN
ERITREA
YEMEN
DJIBOUTI
ETHIOPIA

Socotra (to Yemen)

Laccadive Islands (to India)

Bay of Bengal

SRI LANKA

Andaman Islands (to India)

THAILAND

VIETNAM

CAMBODIA

South China Sea

PHILIPPINES

Northern Mariana Islands (to USA)

Wake Atoll (to USA)

Guam (to USA)

MARSHALL ISLANDS

CENTRAL AFRICAN REPUBLIC
UGANDA
KENYA
SOMALIA

Nicobar Islands (to India)

MALDIVES

SEYCHELLES

British Indian Ocean Territory (to UK)

MALAYSIA

BRUNEI

PALAU

FEDERATED STATES OF MICRONESIA

DEMOCRATIC REPUBLIC OF CONGO
RWANDA
BURUNDI
TANZANIA

SINGAPORE

Sumatra

Borneo

Sulawesi

INDONESIA

Java
Bali

New Guinea

PAPUA NEW GUINEA

NAURU

KIRIBATI

Equator 0°

KIRIBATI

ANGOLA
ZAMBIA
MALAWI
COMOROS

Cocos Islands (to Australia)

Christmas Island (to Australia)

EAST TIMOR

SOLOMON ISLANDS

TUVALU

Tokelau Islands (to NZ)

Wallis and Futuna (to France)

SAMOA

MADAGASCAR
MAURITIUS
ZIMBABWE
MOZAMBIQUE

Rodrigues (to Mauritius)

INDIAN

Coral Sea

VANUATU

FIJI

ZAMBIA
BOTSWANA

Réunion (to France)

OCEAN

AUSTRALIA

New Caledonia (to France)

TONGA 20°

Tropic of Capricorn

REPUBLIC OF SOUTH AFRICA
SWAZILAND
LESOTHO

Norfolk Island (to Australia)

Lord Howe Island (to Australia)

Kermadec Islands (to NZ)

Amsterdam Island (to France)

St Paul Island (to France)

North Island

French Southern and Antarctic Territories (to France)

NEW ZEALAND

South Island

Chatham Islands (to NZ)

Prince Edward Islands (to South Africa)

Crozet Islands (to France)

Kerguelen Islands (to France)

Auckland Islands (to NZ)

Bounty Islands (to NZ)

Campbell Island (to NZ)

Heard Island (to Australia)

Macquarie Island (to Australia)

SOUTHERN OCEAN

Antarctic Circle

ANTARCTICA

International Date Line

Territories and dependencies
Some countries govern areas of land outside their borders. These are called territories or dependencies. Some are governed by the land to which they belong. Others receive protection and financial assistance, but have their own government and laws.

New countries
The number of countries in the world has nearly tripled since the end of World War II. In 1946, there were just 74 countries. Most of the new countries were formed when empires broke up or when single countries were divided into more than one nation.

International Date Line
The world is divided into 24 time zones. Time is measured in hours ahead of or behind the time at Greenwich in England. The time is the same throughout each zone, and is usually one hour ahead of, or behind, the neighboring time zones. The International Date Line, an imaginary line from north to south across the Pacific Ocean, marks where one day ends, and another begins.

The Pacific Ocean

Great white shark
The great white shark constantly prowls coastal waters. It eats seals, small whales and other sharks.

Sunfish
When its long back fin breaks the ocean surface, the sunfish can be mistaken for a shark. It is more usual to see the fish lying on its side, warming its flat, almost circular, body with heat from the Sun. The sunfish measures up to 12 feet (3.5 m) long and weighs up to 2 tons (2 t). It eats crustaceans and jellyfishes, and is harmless to humans.

Double canoe
The great ocean voyages of the ancient Polynesians were probably made in double canoes. These canoes were light, fast and stable, and were steered by a long oar used as a rudder. Large double canoes could carry up to 100 people.

Bering Sea
Aleutian Basin
Aleutian Islands
Aleutian Trench
Sea of Okhotsk
Kamchatka Peninsula
Emperor Seamount Chain
Emperor Trough
Chinook Trough
Mendo
Kuril Islands
Kuril Trench
Northwest Pacific Basin
Sea of Japan
Midway Islands
Mu
East China Sea
Hawaiian Isla
Hawaiian R
ASIA
Makarov Seamount
Mid-Pacific Mountains
Taiwan
Ryukyu Trench
Shikoku Basin
Honshu Ridge
Izu Trench
Japan Trench
South Honshu Ridge
Central Basin
Johnston Atoll
Luzon Strait
Luzon
Mariana Islands
East Mariana Basin
Christmas
South China Sea
Philippine Sea
Philippines Trench
Guam
Mariana Trench
MICRONESIA
Central Pacific Basin
Marshall Islands
Philippine Basin
Challenger Deep 35,826ft (10,920m)
Kingman Reef
Palmyra Atoll
Palau Islands
Caroline Islands
Sunda Shelf
Palawan Trough
Celebes Sea
West Caroline Basin
East Caroline Basin
Melanesian Basin
Howland Island
Borneo
Palau Trench
Nauru
Baker Island
Jarvis Island
Greater Sunda Islands
Sumatra
Makassar Strait
Sulawesi
Bismarck Sea
PACIFIC
Java Sea
New Guinea
MELANESIA
Phoenix Islands
Java
Banda Sea
Solomon Islands
Arafura Sea
Wallis and Futuna Islands
Timor Sea
Torres Strait
Coral Sea Basin
Samoa
Cook Island
Gulf of Carpentaria
Great Barrier Reef
Coral Sea
Espiritu Santo
North Fiji Basin
Fiji
P
New Caledonia
Tonga
Tonga Trench
Niue
Raro
AUSTRALIA
Tongatapu Group
Horizon Deep
Ozbourn Seamount
South Fiji Basin
New Caledonia Trough
Lord Howe Rise
Norfolk Island
Kermadec Trench
Louisville Ridge
Lord Howe Island
Kermadec Islands
North Island
Southw
Tasman Sea
Bass Strait
Challenger Plateau
Tasmania
New Zealand
Chatham Rise
Tasman Basin
Chatham Islands
South Tasman Rise
South Island
Bounty Trough
Macquarie Ridge
Campbell Plateau
Bounty Islands
Antipodes Islands
Macquarie Island
SOUTHERN OCEAN
Pacific-Antarc
Balleny Islands
Cape Adare
Iselin Seamount
Ross Sea

Tropic of Cancer
Equator
Tropic of Capricorn
Antarctic Circle

0 miles 1500
0 kilometers 1500

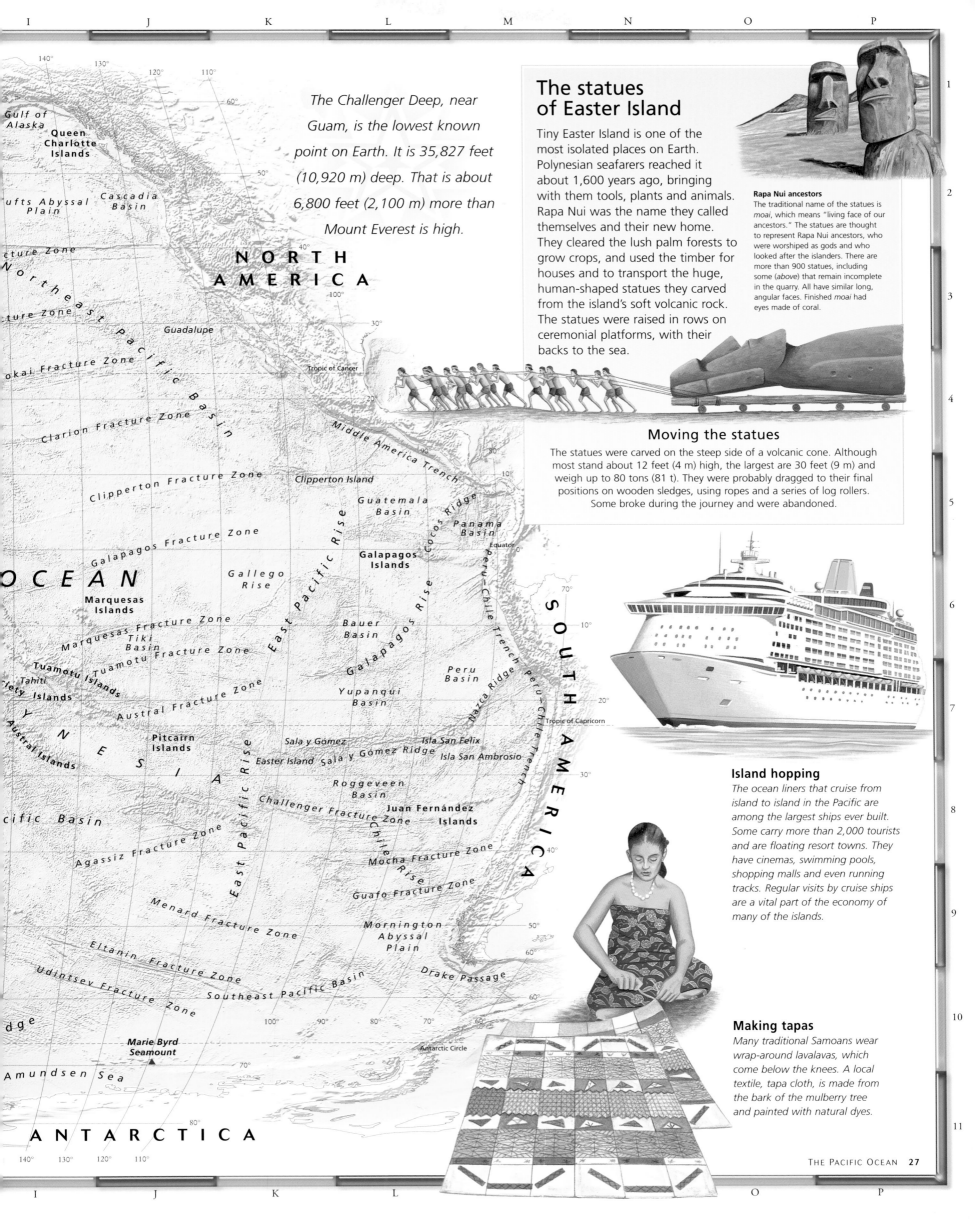

The Challenger Deep, near Guam, is the lowest known point on Earth. It is 35,827 feet (10,920 m) deep. That is about 6,800 feet (2,100 m) more than Mount Everest is high.

The statues of Easter Island

Tiny Easter Island is one of the most isolated places on Earth. Polynesian seafarers reached it about 1,600 years ago, bringing with them tools, plants and animals. Rapa Nui was the name they called themselves and their new home. They cleared the lush palm forests to grow crops, and used the timber for houses and to transport the huge, human-shaped statues they carved from the island's soft volcanic rock. The statues were raised in rows on ceremonial platforms, with their backs to the sea.

Rapa Nui ancestors
The traditional name of the statues is *moai*, which means "living face of our ancestors." The statues are thought to represent Rapa Nui ancestors, who were worshiped as gods and who looked after the islanders. There are more than 900 statues, including some (*above*) that remain incomplete in the quarry. All have similar long, angular faces. Finished *moai* had eyes made of coral.

Moving the statues
The statues were carved on the steep side of a volcanic cone. Although most stand about 12 feet (4 m) high, the largest are 30 feet (9 m) and weigh up to 80 tons (81 t). They were probably dragged to their final positions on wooden sledges, using ropes and a series of log rollers. Some broke during the journey and were abandoned.

Island hopping
The ocean liners that cruise from island to island in the Pacific are among the largest ships ever built. Some carry more than 2,000 tourists and are floating resort towns. They have cinemas, swimming pools, shopping malls and even running tracks. Regular visits by cruise ships are a vital part of the economy of many of the islands.

Making tapas
Many traditional Samoans wear wrap-around lavalavas, which come below the knees. A local textile, tapa cloth, is made from the bark of the mulberry tree and painted with natural dyes.

Map labels:
Gulf of Alaska
Queen Charlotte Islands
Tufts Abyssal Plain
Cascadia Basin
Fracture Zone
Northeast Pacific Basin
Fracture Zone
Guadalupe
Tropic of Cancer
Mokai Fracture Zone
Clarion Fracture Zone
Middle America Trench
NORTH AMERICA
Clipperton Fracture Zone
Clipperton Island
Guatemala Basin
Cocos Ridge
Panama Basin
Galapagos Fracture Zone
Galapagos Islands
Galapagos Rise
OCEAN
Gallego Rise
Equator
Marquesas Islands
East Pacific Rise
Bauer Basin
Peru–Chile Trench
SOUTH AMERICA
Marquesas Fracture Zone
Tiki Basin
Tuamotu Islands
Tuamotu Fracture Zone
Peru Basin
Tahiti
Society Islands
Yupanqui Basin
Nazca Ridge
Austral Islands
Austral Fracture Zone
Tropic of Capricorn
Pitcairn Islands
Sala y Gómez
Isla San Felix
Easter Island
Sala y Gómez Ridge
Isla San Ambrosio
POLYNESIA
East Pacific Rise
Roggeveen Basin
Challenger Fracture Zone
Juan Fernández Islands
Chile Trench
Agassiz Fracture Zone
Mocha Fracture Zone
Mocha Rise
Guafo Fracture Zone
Pacific Basin
Menard Fracture Zone
Mornington Abyssal Plain
Drake Passage
Eltanin Fracture Zone
Southeast Pacific Basin
Udintsev Fracture Zone
Ridge
Marie Byrd Seamount
Antarctic Circle
Amundsen Sea
ANTARCTICA

The Atlantic Ocean

The Titanic

In 1912, on its first voyage, the luxury liner Titanic struck an iceberg and sank. More than 1,400 passengers and crew perished in the icy Atlantic. The ship still lies in water 2½ miles (4 km) deep.

Giant squid

The giant squid lives in the depths of the ocean, and has never been seen alive by humans. It can grow as long as a bus and has eyes as big as basketballs. The two longest tentacles catch food and bring it to the squid's mouth.

Flying fish

CAPE VERDE
POPULATION 412,000 ∗ CAPITAL PRAIA

Water spouts

Water spouts are funnels of whirling spray that form between the surface of the sea and the clouds above. They are common in late summer, when cool air moving over warm water produces strong updrafts.

CAPE VERDE

Santo Antão
Porto Novo
São Vicente
Mindelo
Vila da Ribeira Brava
São Nicolau
Vila da Sal Rei
Sal
Santa Maria
Boa Vista
Maio
Porto Inglês
Vila Nova Sintra
Vila do Tarrafal
Fogo
Brava
São
PRAIA

ATLANTIC OCEAN

Cape Verde

EUROPE
AFRICA
NORTH AMERICA
SOUTH AMERICA

North Sea
Mediterranean Sea
Sardinia
Sicily
Corsica

Greenland
Iceland
Denmark Strait
Faroe–Iceland
Faroe–Shetland
Shetland Islands
British Isles
Ireland

Reykjanes Basin
Irminger Basin
Iceland Basin
Eirik Ridge
Reykjanes Ridge
Iceland Ridge
Mid-Atlantic Ridge
Hatton Ridge
Rockall Trough
Rockall Bank
Goban Spur
Celtic Shelf
Bay of Biscay
Biscay Abyssal Plain
Galicia Bank
Biscay Rise
Azores–Biscay Rise
Tagus Abyssal Plain
Madeira
Monaco Basin
Canary Islands
Cap Vert
Cape Verde Plateau
Cape Verde Islands
Guinea Basin
Gulf of Guinea
São Tomé
Congo Cone
Angola Basin

Northwest Atlantic Mid-Ocean Channel
Charlie-Gibbs Fracture Zone
Hamilton Bank
Newfoundland Basin
Flemish Cap
Grand Banks of Newfoundland
Newfoundland Ridge
Sohm Abyssal Plain
New England Seamounts
Cape Sable
Cape Cod
Cape Hatteras
North American Basin
Bermuda Rise
Bermuda
Blake–Bahama Ridge
Hatteras Abyssal Plain
Nares Abyssal Plain
Sargasso Sea
Oceanographer Fracture Zone
Atlantis Fracture Zone
Kane Fracture Zone
Great Meteor Tablemount
Azores

ATLANTIC OCEAN

Greater Antilles
Jamaica
Lesser Antilles
Puerto Rico Trench
Caribbean Sea
Venezuelan Basin
Colombian Basin
Barracuda Abyssal Plain
Demerara Plateau
Demerara Abyssal Plain
Vema Fracture Zone
Doldrums Fracture Zone
Four North Fracture Zone
Amazon Cone
Ceara Abyssal Plain
Fernando de Noronha
Pernambuco Abyssal Plain
Pernambuco Seamounts
Sierra Leone Basin
Gambia Abyssal Plain
Cape Verde Basin
Sierra Leone Fracture Zone
Saint Paul Fracture Zone
Ascension
St Helena
Bode Verde Fracture Zone
St Helena Fracture Zone
Hotspur Seamount
Ilha da Trindade

Equator
Tropic of Cancer
Tropic of Cancer

The Mid-Atlantic Ridge is the longest mountain range on Earth. It runs beneath the Atlantic, from Iceland to Antarctica. Ascension Island and the Azores are peaks of the range.

Atlantic fishing

About one-third of the world's catch of fishes and shellfishes comes from the Atlantic. Factory ships cruise its rich fishing grounds. They have huge nets to encircle schools of fishes, and power winches to pull in the massive catches.

Whale migration

Most whales spend the summer feeding in the cold waters of the Arctic or the Antarctic. In summer, these waters are rich in tiny shrimplike creatures called krill, which the whales eat. As winter approaches, the whales leave their polar feeding grounds and head into the Atlantic Ocean to tropical seas for the birth of their calves. Many species cover vast distances. They pause frequently to rest and socialize. Most whales do not feed while migrating, and they may lose up to 50 percent of their bodyweight during the trip.

Whale migration routes
Humpback whales make the longest migration. They travel more than 4,300 miles (7,000 km). During this time they live on the energy stored in their blubber.

Atlantic Ocean

Humpback breeding area
Humpback feeding area
Right whale breeding area
Right whale feeding area

Right whale
60 feet (18 m) long

Humpback whale
46 feet (14 m) long

Fin whale
88 feet (27 m) long

Blue whale
110 feet (33.5 m) long

Sperm whale
60 feet (18 m) long

Gray whale
46 feet (14 m) long

N
W E
S

0 miles 1800
0 kilometers 1800

SOUTHERN OCEAN

ANTARCTICA

Namibia Abyssal Plain
Cape Basin
Agulhas Basin
Agulhas Bank
Cape Agulhas
Cape of Good Hope
Tristan da Cunha Fracture Zone
Gough Fracture Zone
Tristan da Cunha
Gough Island
Discovery Seamounts
Agulhas Ridge
Rio Grande Rise
N. Rio Grande
Mid-Atlantic Ridge
Zapiola Seamount
Spiess Seamount
Atlantic–Indian Ridge
Bouvetøya
Shona Ridge
Atlantic–Indian Antarctic Basin
American–Antarctic Ridge
Astrid Ridge
Riiser-Larsen Sea
Lazarev Sea
Maud Rise
Antarctic Circle

Argentine Basin
Argentine Abyssal Plain
Golfo San Matías
Golfo de San Jorge
Falkland Escarpment
Falkland Plateau
Falkland Islands
South Georgia
South Sandwich Trench
South Sandwich Islands
East Scotia Basin
Scotia Sea
Scotia Ridge
South Orkney Islands
West Scotia Ridge
South Shetland Islands
Scotia Ridge
Weddell Abyssal Plain
Weddell Sea
Berkner Island
Ronne Ice Shelf
Alexander Island
Yaghan Basin
Cape Horn
Drake Passage
Antarctic Peninsula
Antarctic Circle

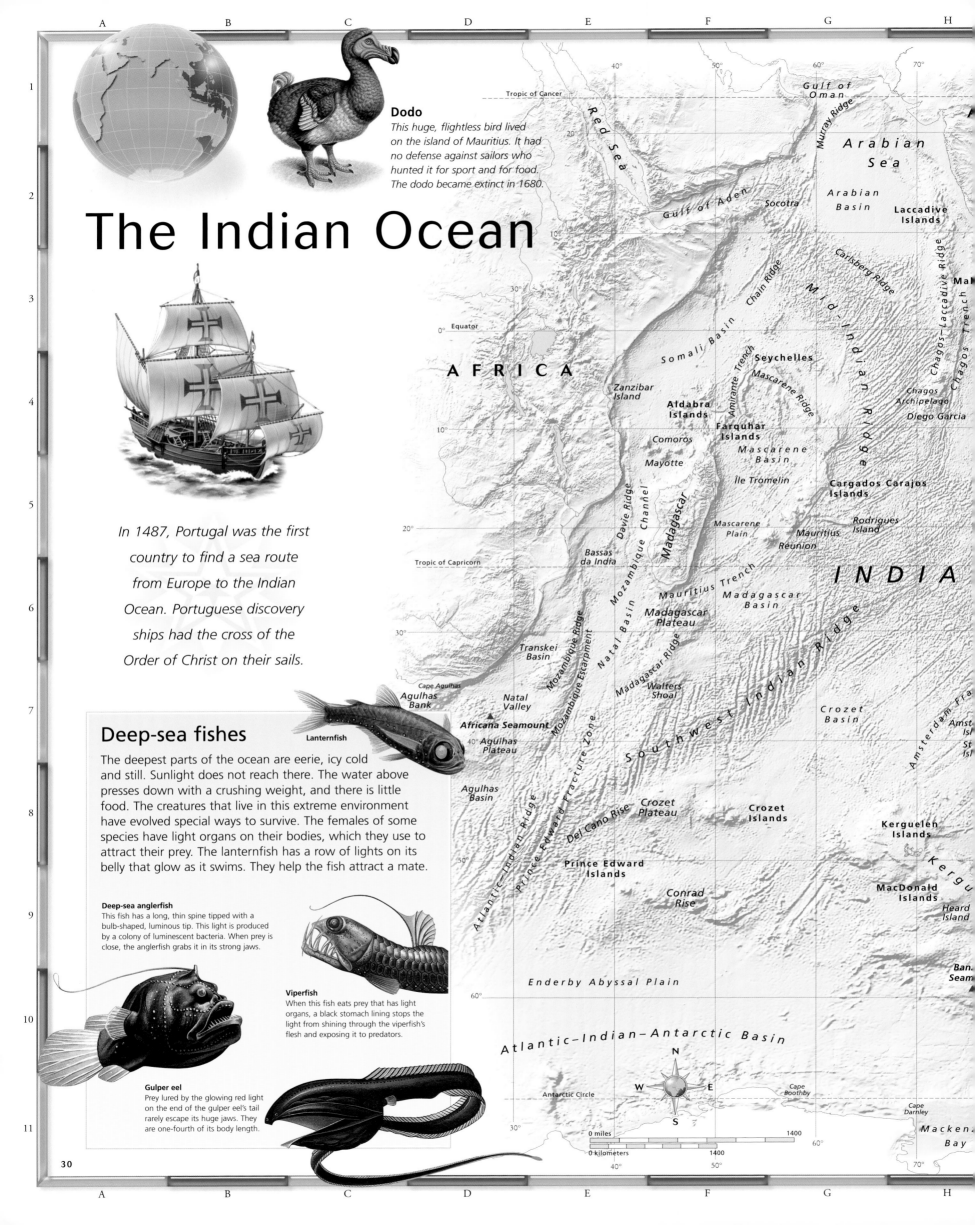

Dodo

This huge, flightless bird lived on the island of Mauritius. It had no defense against sailors who hunted it for sport and for food. The dodo became extinct in 1680.

The Indian Ocean

In 1487, Portugal was the first country to find a sea route from Europe to the Indian Ocean. Portuguese discovery ships had the cross of the Order of Christ on their sails.

Deep-sea fishes

Lanternfish

The deepest parts of the ocean are eerie, icy cold and still. Sunlight does not reach there. The water above presses down with a crushing weight, and there is little food. The creatures that live in this extreme environment have evolved special ways to survive. The females of some species have light organs on their bodies, which they use to attract their prey. The lanternfish has a row of lights on its belly that glow as it swims. They help the fish attract a mate.

Deep-sea anglerfish
This fish has a long, thin spine tipped with a bulb-shaped, luminous tip. This light is produced by a colony of luminescent bacteria. When prey is close, the anglerfish grabs it in its strong jaws.

Viperfish
When this fish eats prey that has light organs, a black stomach lining stops the light from shining through the viperfish's flesh and exposing it to predators.

Gulper eel
Prey lured by the glowing red light on the end of the gulper eel's tail rarely escape its huge jaws. They are one-fourth of its body length.

Tropic of Cancer

Red Sea

Gulf of Oman

Murray Ridge

Arabian Sea

Gulf of Aden

Socotra

Arabian Basin

Laccadive Islands

Chagos–Laccadive Ridge

Mal

Chagos Trench

Carlsberg Ridge

Mid-Indian Ridge

Equator

Somali Basin

Chain Ridge

Seychelles

Chagos Archipelago

Diego Garcia

AFRICA

Zanzibar Island

Aldabra Islands

Amirante Trench

Mascarene Ridge

Mascarene Basin

Farquhar Islands

Comoros

Mayotte

Île Tromelin

Cargados Carajos Islands

Davie Ridge

Mozambique Channel

Madagascar

Mascarene Plain

Mauritius

Réunion

Rodrigues Island

Tropic of Capricorn

Bassas da India

Mozambique Ridge

Natal Basin

Mauritius Trench

Madagascar Basin

INDIA

Transkei Basin

Madagascar Plateau

Madagascar Ridge

Southwest Indian Ridge

Crozet Basin

Amsterdam Fra

Amst Isl

St Isl

Cape Agulhas

Agulhas Bank

Natal Valley

Mozambique Escarpment

Walters Shoal

Africana Seamount

Agulhas Plateau

Atlantic–Indian Ridge

Prince Edward Fracture Zone

Del Cano Rise

Crozet Plateau

Crozet Islands

Kerguelen Islands

Agulhas Basin

Kergu

Prince Edward Islands

MacDonald Islands

Heard Island

Conrad Rise

Ban. Seam

Enderby Abyssal Plain

Atlantic–Indian–Antarctic Basin

N

W E

S

Antarctic Circle

Cape Boothby

Cape Darnley

Macken Bay

0 miles 1400

0 kilometers 1400

Manta ray
Rays are related to sharks. The manta ray grows to 23 feet (7 m) across and is the largest ray in the world. It feeds on plankton, small crustaceans and fishes. Manta rays are harmless to humans.

Pearl diver
Pearls form inside living mollusks in tropical waters. This process occurs naturally but, today, most pearls are specially farmed. A bead is inserted in the pearl oyster shell, and a pearl grows around it. Divers tend the oysters until the pearls are ready to be harvested.

Sea vent
Water heated by volcanic activity beneath the ocean floor bursts up through sea vents. Chimneys sometimes grow around these deep-sea hot springs. They are made of minerals that are contained in the very hot vent water. These minerals form particles on contact with the freezing ocean.

Ganges Cone

Bay of Bengal

Andaman Sea

Andaman Islands

Andaman Basin

Nicobar Islands

ylon ain

Mid-dian asin

Cocos Basin

Ninetyeast Ridge

Investigator Ridge

Sumatra

Java Ridge

Java

Bali

Sumbawa

Timor

Christmas Island

Java Trench 23,376ft (7,125m)

Lombok Basin

North Australian Basin

Timor Sea

Sahul Shelf

Cape Leveque

Cocos Islands

Wharton Basin

Wallaby Plateau

Cuvier Plateau

Exmouth Plateau

Osborn Plateau

OCEAN

East Indiaman Ridge

▲ **Batavia Seamount**

Hartog Ridge

Perth Basin

AUSTRALIA

Broken Plateau

Naturaliste Ridge

Diamantina Deep 21,660ft (6,602m) ▼

Naturaliste Plateau

Cape Leeuwin

Diamantina Fracture Zone

Naturaliste Fracture Zone

Great Australian Bight

South Australian Basin

Bass Strait

King Island

Tasmania

South East Cape

South Australian Plain

Southeast Indian Ridge

Indian–Antarctic Ridge

South Indian Basin

SOUTHERN OCEAN

Indian–Antarctic Basin

eau

Cape Penck

Cape Poinsett

Cape Goodenough

Cape Morse

Fisher Bay

ANTARCTICA

Wilhelm II Land

George V Land

Tropic of Cancer

Equator

Tropic of Capricorn

Antarctic Circle

The polar regions

Polar bear

Beneath its long white fur, a thick layer of fat protects the polar bear from the Arctic's freezing cold. The fat also makes the bear more buoyant when it swims.

Research ship

Lion's mane jellyfish

The lion's mane jellyfish can grow to 8 feet (2.4 m) across. It drifts in Arctic waters, feeding on plankton, fishes, and other jellyfishes that are killed by contact with its trailing tentacles.

NORTH AMERICA

ASIA

EUROPE

St Lawrence Island
Gulf of Anadyr
Norton Sound
Bering Strait
Arctic Circle
Proliv Longa
Wrangel Island
Kolyma
Indigirka
Yana

Brooks Range

Chukchi Sea

Northwind Plain

East Siberian Sea

Mackenzie

Beaufort Sea
Chukchi Abyssal Plain
Chukchi Plateau
Canadian Abyssal Plain

Mendeleyev Ridge

Wrangel Sea

New Siberia Islands

Lena
Olenek

Laptev Sea

Great Slave Lake
Great Bear Lake
Amundsen Gulf
Canada Basin

Limit of permanent ice cap

Banks Island
Victoria Island
McClure Strait
Melville Island
Parry Islands
Queen Elizabeth Islands

ARCTIC OCEAN

Alpha Ridge
Makarov Basin
Lomonosov Ridge
North Pole
Pole Plain
Fram Basin

Nansen Cordillera
Nansen Ridge
Nansen Basin

Limit of permanent ice cap

Severnaya Zemlya
Ozero Taymyr

Kara Sea

Yenisey
Taz
Ostrov Belyy

Boothia Peninsula
Resolute
Devon Island

North Geomagnetic Pole
Ellesmere Island
Cape Columbia
Alert

Wandel Sea

Barents Plain

Franz Josef Land

Novaya Zemlya

Ostrov Vaygach

Hudson Bay
Southampton Island
Melville Peninsula
Foxe Basin
Prince Charles Island
Foxe Peninsula
Baffin Island

Nares Strait
Thule
Ummannaq
Knud Rasmussen Land

Baffin Basin
Baffin Bay

Kong Frederik VIII Land
Station Nord

Nordaustlandet
SVALBARD (to Norway)

Barents Sea

Ostrov Kolguyev

Hudson Strait
Davis Strait
Cape Chidley

Nuussuaq

GREENLAND (to Denmark)

Longyearbyen
Spitsbergen

Barents Trough

Illulissat
Kong Frederik IX Land
Maniitsoq
Dronning Ingrid Land
NUUK ★
Kong Christian IX Land

King Wilhelm Land

Greenland Plain

Nord Kapp

Labrador Sea
Labrador Basin

Gunnbjorn Fjeld
12,139ft (3,700m)
Ittoqqortoormiit
Kap Brewster

Greenland Sea

Kola Peninsula

Ammassalik

Jan Mayen

Norwegian Sea

Kap Farvel

Reykjanes Basin

Denmark Strait

Icelandic Plateau

Arctic Circle

Gulf of Bothnia

40° **Walrus**

Greenland houses

These small, brightly painted wooden houses are home to Inuit families who make their living by hunting seals and fishing.

Reykjanes Ridge

ICELAND

Norwegian Basin

Iceland Basin

Faroe Islands

The Arctic

0 miles   900
0 kilometers   900

Orkney Islands (to UK)
Laurie Island
Orcadas (to Argentina)
Signy (to UK)

ephant Island

rctowski (Poland)
King eorge Island

Joinville Island
Esperanza (Argentina)
Marambio (Argentina)
James Ross Island

Bransfield Strait

nt Island
almer (USA)
dsky (Ukraine)
Faraday (UK)

iscoe Islands

Adelaide Island
Rothera (UK)

Marguerite Bay

Charcot Island
Lataday Island
Smyley Island
Ryberg Peninsula

Bellingshausen Sea

Fletcher Peninsula

Farwell Island

Thurston Island

King Peninsula

Canisteo Peninsula

Bear Peninsula

Martin Peninsula

Carney Island

Siple Island

Russkaya (Russia)

Sulzberger Bay

Jason Peninsula

Larsen Ice Shelf

Antarctic Palmer Land

George VI Sound

Alexander Island

Ellsworth Mountains

Vinson Massif
16,066ft (4,897m)

West Antarctica

Marie Byrd Land

Mt Berlin
11,476ft (3,498m)

Edward VII Peninsula

Roosevelt Island

Wandering albatross

With a wingspan of up to 11 feet (3.5 m), the wandering albatross is the largest flying bird in the world. It spends its life gliding above the Southern Ocean, landing only to feed and breed.

Wandering albatross

Neumayer (Germany)
Sanae (South Africa)
Maitri (India)
Cape Norvegia
Halley (UK)
Belgrano II (Argentina)

Weddell Sea

Ronne Ice Shelf

Berkner Island

Pensacola Mountains

Queen Maud Land

E a s t

Novolazarevskaya (Russia)
Riiser-Larsen Peninsula
Asuka (Japan)
Lützow-Holm Bay
Syowa (Japan)
Mizuho (Japan)
Molodezhnaya (Russia)

Thorshavnheiane

Enderby Land

Law Promontory

Kemp Land

Mawson (Australia)

Mac Robertson Land

Prince Charles Mountains

Cape Darnley

Amery Ice Shelf

Mackenzie Bay

Princess Elizabeth Land

Zhongshan (China)
Davis (Australia)

Davis Sea

Kaiser Wilhelm II Land

ANTARCTICA

South Pole
Amundsen-Scott (USA)

Horlick Mountains

Transantarctic Mountains

Queen Maud Mountains

South Geomagnetic Pole
Vostok (Russia)

Queen Mary Land

Shackleton Ice Shelf

Mirny (Russia)

Mill Island

Bowman Island

Vincennes Bay

Casey (Australia)

Cape Poinsett
Cape Waldron

Mt Kirkpatrick
14,855ft (4,528m)

Ross Ice Shelf

Wilkes Land

Victoria Land

Scott Base (NZ)
Ross Island
McMurdo (USA)

Ross Sea

Adélie Land

Porpoise Bay

George V Land

Dumont d'Urville (France)
Cape Keltie

The Antarctic

0 miles 900
0 kilometers 900

South Pole Station

Since 1975, the 50-foot (16-m) high dome of the South Pole Station has provided year-round shelter to scientists. Now it is slowly disappearing under drifting snow. The replacement building is on stilts and can be raised to keep it above the snow.

Terra Nova Bay (Italy)

Mt Minto
13,665ft (4,165m)

Cape Adare

Leningradskaya (Russia)

Cape Cheetham
Mawson Peninsula
Cape Freshfield
Cape Gray

Dumont d'Urville Sea

SOUTHERN OCEAN

Balleny Islands

Antarctic Circle

The midnight Sun

Earth orbits the Sun at an angle. From late March to late September, the Northern Hemisphere tilts toward the Sun, giving the northern polar regions long hours of daylight. From late October to late February, the same thing happens in the Southern Hemisphere. During these periods, the Sun rises high into the sky and, although it dips toward the horizon, it never sinks below it at the North and South poles. At the summer solstice, when the pole leans most toward the Sun, the entire polar region has several days of total sunlight.

December solstice
northern winter
southern summer

Axis

June solstice
northern summer
southern winter

Axis

The solstices

Each June and December, one pole reaches its maximum tilt toward the Sun, while the other is at its maximum tilt away. These are the solstices.

In midsummer, the Sun never sets in the polar regions

Antarctica is the highest, coldest, driest and windiest continent on Earth. It is also the only continent that has no permanent human population.

Emperor penguins

The largest of all penguins, the emperor penguin lives and breeds on the Antarctic ice. In the fiercely cold winter, a group huddles together for warmth, with each chick perched above the ice on the feet of a parent. The parents take turns to provide food.

NORWEGIAN
Sea

Iceland

Faroe
Islands

Shetland
Islands

Køl

Highlands

Scan

ATLANTIC OCEAN

Outer Hebrides

Ben Nevis
4,406ft
(1,343m)

Orkney
Islands

Atlantic

North
Sea

Skagerrak

Kattegat

Vänern

Vättern

Öl

Jutland

British Isles

Ireland

Irish Sea

Pennines

Fyn

Sjaelland

Bornholm

United Kingdom

Thames

Elbe

Oder

English Channel

Seine

Rhine

Mosel

Hartz
Mountains

Ore Mountains

Bohemian
Forest

Loire

Black
Forest

Danube

Vosges

Jura

Bay of
Biscay

Garonne

Massif
Central

Lake
Geneva

Mont Blanc
15,771ft
(4,807m)

A l p s

Dolomites

Dinar

Po

Apennines

Adriatic Se

Pyrenees

Rhône

Aneto
11,168ft (3,404m)

Ligurian Sea

Corsica

Duero

Ebro

Iberian
Peninsula

Balearic Islands

Minorca

Sardinia

Tyrrhenian Sea

Vesuvius
4,202ft (1,281m)

Sierra Morena

Ibiza

Majorca

Guadalquivir

Sistemas Béticos

Mediterranean Sea

Sicily

Mt Etna
10,902ft (3,323m)

Malta

Novaya Zemlya

Kara Sea

Barents Sea

Ostrov Kolguyev

Inarijärvi

Lappland

Kola Peninsula

White Sea

Pechora

Ural Mountains

Gulf of Bothnia

avian Shield

Northern Dvina

Lake Onega

Kama

Lake Ladoga

Åland

altic Sea

Gulf of Finland

Lake Peipus

Rybinsk Reservoir

Volga

Gulf of Riga

Dnieper

Valdai Hills

Kuybyshev Reservoir

North European Plain

Volga Uplands

istula

Central Russian Uplands

Kiev Reservoir

Dnieper

Tsimlyansk Reservoir

Carpathian Mountains

Dniester

Don

Europe

Great Hungarian Plain

Sea of Azov

Danube

Transylvanian Alps

Crimea

Elbrus 18,510ft (5,642m)

Caspian Sea

Danube

Caucasus

Balkan Mountains

Black Sea

lps

Rhodope Mountains

Sea of Marmara

Pindus Mountains

Aegean Sea

Dodecanese

Peloponnese

nian Sea

Crete

Rhodes

United Kingdom and Ireland

UNITED KINGDOM
POPULATION 60,095,000 ✴ CAPITAL LONDON

IRELAND
POPULATION 3,924,000 ✴ CAPITAL DUBLIN

Stonehenge

The circle of standing stones on Salisbury Plain, in southwestern England, was built between 2900 BC and 1800 BC. While the function of this monument remains unknown, one theory is that the circle formed an astronomical observatory for predicting the best times to plant and harvest.

The first stage
The first builders of Stonehenge laid out a circular bank of earth and a ditch about 380 feet (116 m) in diameter. They raised a huge stone, the Heel Stone, at the entrance.

The second stage
Around 2800 BC, an inner stone circle, the Bluestone Circle, was built. The stone used may have come from another monument.

The third stage
Stonehenge as it looks today was built around 1800 BC. It consists of a ring of 30 stones topped by stone lintels. Within this ring are taller pairs of stones set in a horseshoe shape.

The summer solstice

At sunrise on the summer solstice, which is the longest day of the year, the Sun shines straight through the Heel Stone.

Positioning the stones
Many of the stones were probably brought great distances to the site. Each one was levered into a deep pit with sloping sides, called a posthole.

Pulling the stones upright
A system of ropes was attached to each stone. Because of the immense weight, hundreds of people were needed to pull the stones upright.

Raising the lintels
Each lintel, or cross beam, was shaped to the curve of the circle. A timber scaffold was built so that the lintels could be raised to the top of the stones.

Securing the lintels
A groove carved on the base of each lintel fitted into pegs carved on the top of each stone, ensuring that the two fitted securely together.

Scottish Highland band

Bagpipers traditionally led regiments into battle. The tunes inspired the soldiers and frightened their enemies. The sound of bagpipes carries a long way. Today, military bands of pipers and drummers play on ceremonial occasions.

Loch Ness monster

Loch Ness, in the Scottish Highlands, is the largest freshwater lake in the United Kingdom. It is 788 feet (240 m) deep and about 23 miles (37 km) long. Although many people believe they have seen a monster rather like a dinosaur in the lake, there is still no proof that it exists.

Hadrian's Wall

The emperor Hadrian ordered his army to build and patrol a wall at the northernmost boundary of Roman territory, to keep out invaders. Built between AD 122 and AD 129, near what is now the Scottish border, it extended 73 miles (118 km). Parts of it remain.

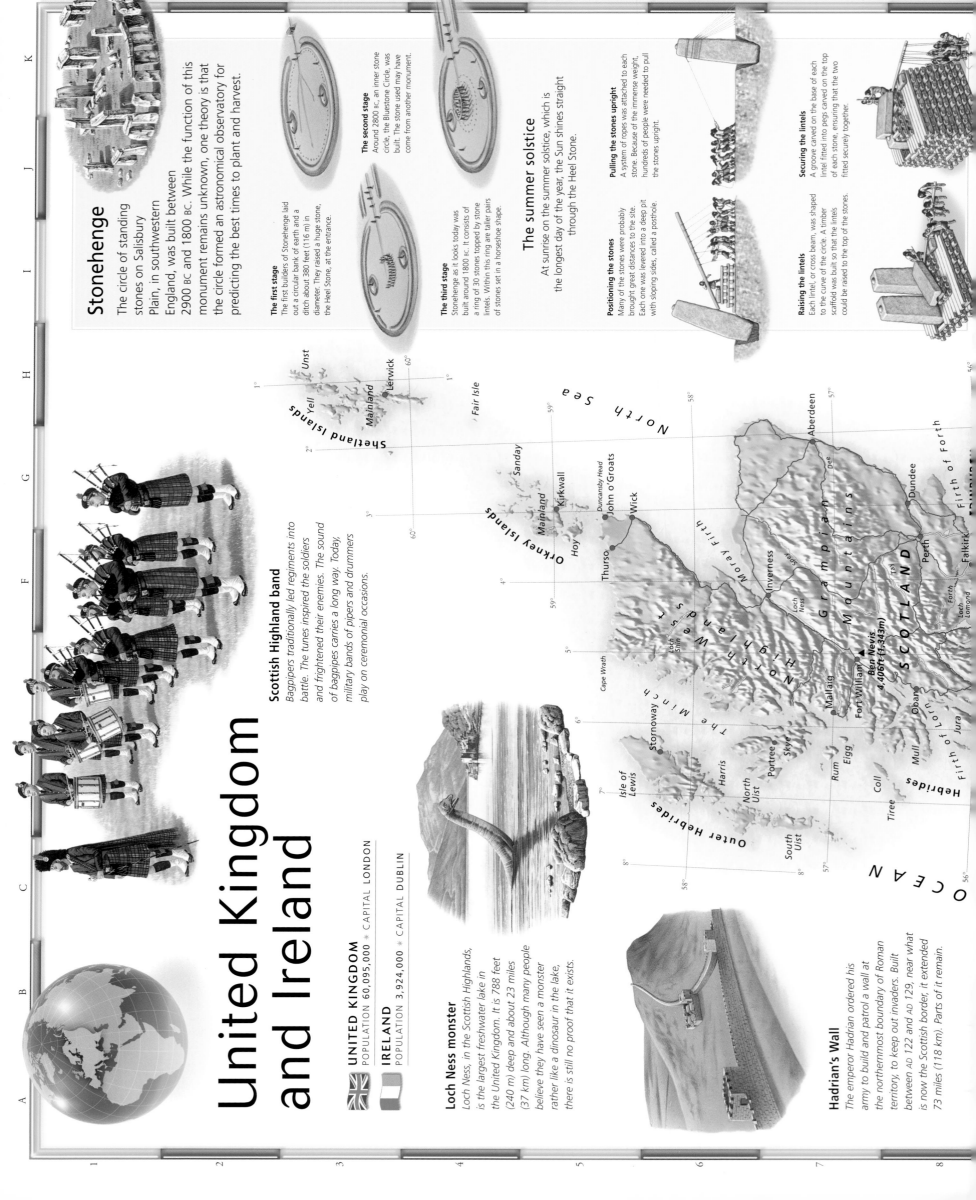

North Sea

OCEAN

Unst
Yell
Mainland
Lerwick
Fair Isle
Shetland Islands

Sanday
Mainland
Kirkwall
Duncansby Head
John o'Groats
Hoy
Orkney Islands
Wick
Thurso

Aberdeen
Dee
Grampian Mountains
Dundee
Firth of Forth
Perth
Falkirk
Forth
Loch Lomond

Inverness
Loch Ness
Spey
Moray Firth

Cape Wrath
Loch Shin
North West Highlands
Ben Nevis 4,406ft (1,343m)
Fort William
Mallaig
Oban
Firth of Lorn
SCOTLAND

Stornoway
The Minch
Isle of Lewis
Harris
North Uist
Portree
Skye
Rum
Eigg
Coll
Mull
Outer Hebrides
Tiree
South Uist
Hebrides

Big Ben
Big Ben is the name of the huge bell in the clock tower of London's Palace of Westminster (also known as the Houses of Parliament). When it was installed in 1858, the bell drowned out people's voices. The angle of the hammer was adjusted to solve the problem.

Eurostar train
These high-speed trains travel between England and the European continent through the Channel Tunnel. The trip from London to Paris takes three hours. Eurostars can travel at speeds up to 186 miles per hour (298 km/h).

Celtic cross, Monasterboice
Carved stone crosses dot the Irish countryside. This one, known as Muiredach's Cross, dates from the AD 900s. It is covered with symbols, patterns and sculptures. Monks erected the crosses in their monasteries.

Between 1845 and 1849, almost a million people died in Ireland when the potato crop failed several years in a row. Potatoes were the main food of the poor. Another 1½ million people emigrated, most to North America.

Fishing trawler

In 1690, the remains of a mammoth were discovered near the present-day Kings Cross Station in London.

United Kingdom and Ireland

UNITED KINGDOM LAND AREA	94,526 sq miles (244,820 sq km)
OFFICIAL LANGUAGE	English
MAIN RELIGION	Christian
LIFE EXPECTANCY	78 years
LITERACY	99%

IRELAND LAND AREA	27,135 sq miles (70,280 sq km)
OFFICIAL LANGUAGE	English
MAIN RELIGION	Christian
LIFE EXPECTANCY	77 years
LITERACY	98%

USING THE LAND

- Forest and woodland
- Arable land
- Grazing

WHERE PEOPLE LIVE

Urban ▮ Rural ▮

UNITED KINGDOM
89% | 11%

IRELAND
59% | 41%

LARGEST CITIES

London 7,465,000

Glasgow 1,101,000

Dublin 1,028,000

Birmingham 969,000

Edinburgh 461,000

Legend
- Cereals
- Potatoes
- Fruit and vegetables
- Sugar beet
- Oilseed rape
- Beef cattle
- Dairy cattle
- Sheep
- Fishing
- Shellfish
- Industrial center
- Mining
- Gas production
- Timber
- Tourism

Black Death

In the late 1340s, the Black Death, a type of bubonic plague, swept through Europe, killing more than a third of the people. By 1348 it had arrived in England. Over the next few centuries, the plague continued to strike, and Londoners fled the city (*above*) with each outbreak. It was finally wiped out by the Great Fire of London in 1666.

NATURAL FEATURES

Lake District ENGLAND
In this beautiful national park in the northern highland area of England (*below*), ice has worn away the land to create valleys and form what are England's largest lakes. The Lake District attracts millions of visitors each year.

Lake District

Norfolk Broads ENGLAND
These shallow, inland waterways, which were caused by peat diggings in the 14th century, crisscross Norfolk. The area is popular with visitors, who hire boats to sail from town to town.

Giant's Causeway NORTHERN IRELAND
This 3-mile (5-km) stretch of basalt columns was formed when molten lava erupted from beneath the sea and cooled very quickly. Some columns are nearly 20 feet (6 m) tall.

Giant's Causeway

Scottish Highlands SCOTLAND
The Scottish Highlands, which make up more than half of Scotland's landmass, have numerous rivers and lochs (lakes). Many native species have died out, but the shaggy-haired Highland cattle (*left*) still wander freely.

Highland cattle

Sheep
Sheep are the United Kingdom's chief livestock. Farming sheep is particularly important in areas such as Wales where the soil is too poor for raising cattle and growing crops.

Glasgow
Edinburgh
Newcastle upon Tyne
Belfast
Leeds
Manchester
DUBLIN
Birmingham
Cardiff
LONDON

Oil mining
Oil was discovered in the United Kingdom under the North Sea in the early 1970s. Extracting it proved difficult. Oil rigs were built to provide a stable surface for drilling into the seabed. By 2001, the United Kingdom had become the 12th-largest oil producer in the world.

The population of Ireland is 95% ethnic Irish.

TRADITIONS AND CULTURE

Wimbledon
Every year since 1877, one of the most famous tennis tournaments in the world has been held at Wimbledon, a suburb of London.

Scottish tartans
Originally hand-woven from woolen material, Scottish tartans are a symbol of Scotland. Items of clothing, especially kilts, are made from different patterns to represent different clans, or families.

Welsh choirs
Almost every town in Wales has a voice choir. There are male, female, mixed and children's choirs, many of which compete in the annual eisteddfod, a festival of music and arts.

St Patrick's Day
Celebrated on 17 March, this day began as a religious holiday to commemorate St Patrick, the patron saint of Ireland. Today, Irish people around the world gather together, wear green clothes and parade through the streets.

Arthurian legends
King Arthur, according to the legends, became king of Britain when he was 15 years old. He married Guinevere and created the knights of the round table. When he went to fight a war in Rome, he left his castle in the care of his nephew Mordred, who betrayed him.

King Arthur fighting Mordred

It's said that if you kiss the Blarney Stone in Ireland, you'll become a clever talker.

The monarchy
The British monarchy is the oldest institution of government in the United Kingdom. James VI of Scotland became the first king of the United Kingdom in 1603. Until the end of the 17th century, the monarch had the right to make and pass legislation, but this is no longer the case. The British monarchy is hereditary—the crown is inherited by the next eligible family member.

Royal carriage

PLACES

London ENGLAND
The Romans chose a small town on the Thames River as their capital in the 1st century AD, and named it Londinium. After being ruled by the Saxons and the Normans, today it is England's capital.

Canterbury Cathedral

Canterbury Cathedral ENGLAND
This cathedral is the seat of the Anglican Church. Archbishop Thomas Becket was murdered there in 1170 and the cathedral is now a site for pilgrims.

Dublin IRELAND
Starting as a permanent Viking settlement in AD 841, Dublin, built on the banks of the River Liffey, is the capital of Ireland and the center of its government.

Edinburgh SCOTLAND
The capital city of Scotland, Edinburgh is a financial, legal and cultural center. Edinburgh Castle stands in the medieval Old Town, once the center of the city.

Roman baths ENGLAND
Ancient Romans spent some leisure time in baths (hot and cold swimming pools), such as those in Bath (*right*). These baths are filled with the water from three natural hot springs.

HISTORY AT A GLANCE

PEOPLE

William Wallace 1270–1305
William Wallace became a hero by leading Scottish resistance to English rule. In 1297, he captured Stirling Castle, but was later defeated by Edward I and executed.

Shakespeare 1564–1616
Recognized as England's greatest dramatist and poet, Shakespeare wrote more than 150 poems and 36 plays. One of his most famous plays is *Romeo and Juliet*.

William Shakespeare

Isaac Newton 1642–1727
Isaac Newton, an influential scientist of the 17th century, invented the reflecting telescope in 1668. Although it was only 6 inches (15 cm) long, it could magnify objects more than 30 times.

Florence Nightingale 1820–1910
In 1854 Florence Nightingale led a group of nurses to work in military hospitals during the Crimean War. Her patients called her the "Lady with the Lamp." After the war, she established a school for nurses in England.

Winston Churchill 1874–1965
A statesman and orator, Churchill was the prime minister of Britain during World War II. His speeches inspired the people during the difficult war years.

The Beatles 1959–70
The Beatles, comprising John Lennon, Paul McCartney, George Harrison and Ringo Starr, were a world-famous rock-and-roll group. They also produced and starred in movies.

The Beatles

Henry VIII
The son of Henry VII and Elizabeth York, Henry VIII (1491–1547) had six wives. Of these, he divorced two and had two beheaded. When the pope refused Henry permission to divorce his first wife, he broke away from the Roman Catholic Church and created the Church of England. His actions aided the Protestant movement in Europe.

Spain and Portugal

Basque folk dancer

The Alhambra

For almost 800 years, from AD 711 until 1492, Spain was ruled by the Islamic Moors. The Alhambra, in Granada, is one of the most beautiful and practical buildings from this period. It was built in the 1300s as a fortress against the Spanish, and was later used as a palace for the sultan and his family. It features cool, airy courtyards and pavilions, trickling fountains and wonderful gardens.

Tower of the Ladies
The oldest decorations in the Alhambra are here, with views into the valley.

Hall of the Two Sisters
This hall is in the center of a series of chambers where the sultan's family lived.

Court of the Lions
A fountain carved with lions stands in the middle of this shaded courtyard.

Mosaic
Decorative patterns of tiles and semi-precious stones are a common feature of Islamic art. The mosaics of the Alhambra are extremely complicated and beautiful.

Court of the Myrtles
This peaceful walkway leads to the throne room.

Azores
(to Portugal)

Corvo · Flores · Graciosa · São Jorge · Nova Lajes · Terceira · Horta · Faial · Pico · Angra do Heroísmo · Ribeira Grande · São Miguel · Ponta Delgada · Santa Maria

ATLANTIC OCEAN

0 miles 125
0 kilometers 125

Madeira
(to Portugal)

Ilha de Porto Santo · Porto Santo · Ilha da Madeira · Câmara de Lobos · Machico · Funchal · Deserta Grande · Ilhas Desertas · Bugio

ATLANTIC OCEAN

0 miles 40
0 kilometers 40

Canary Islands
(to Spain)

Alegranza · Graciosa · Lanzarote · Arrecife · Lobos · Puerto del Rosario · Fuerteventura · Santa Cruz de la Palma · La Palma · San Cristóbal de la Laguna · Santa Cruz de Tenerife · Pico del Teide 12,198ft (3,718m) · La Gomera · Tenerife · Gran Canaria · Las Palmas de Gran Canaria · Pico de las Nieves 6,394ft (1,949m) · El Hierro

ATLANTIC OCEAN

Azores · Madeira · Canary Islands

0 miles 100
0 kilometers 100

Cork trees

One-third of the world's cork oaks grow in Portugal. It takes nearly 60 years before they are mature enough for the cork bark to be harvested.

ATLANTIC OCEAN

PORTUGAL

Cabo Ortegal · Ferrol · Luarca · Avilés · Cabo · A Coruña · Villavicios · Ast · Betanzos · Vilalba · Oviedo · Mie · Santiago del Compostela · Lugo · Ribeira · Lalín · Pontevedra · Ponferrada · Astorga · Vigo · Ourense · Benavente · Cabo Silleiro · Viana do Castelo · Ponte da Barca · Bragança · Tor · Braga · Zamora · Póvoa de Varzim · Matosinhos · Porto · Vila Real · Embalse de Almendra · Vila Nova de Gaia · Ovar · Salamanca · Aveiro · Viseu · Ciudad Rodrigo · Figueira da Foz · Guarda · Béjar · Coimbra · Covilhã · Sis · Alm · Plasencia · 8,504ft (2, · Leiria · Castelo Branco · Tajo · Embalse de Valdecañas · Caldas da Rainha · Cáceres · Trujillo · Cabo Carvoeiro · Torres Novas · Embals · Garcia · Torres Vedras · Santarém · Portalegre · He · del D · Sintra · Elvas · Badajoz · Mérida · Embalse de Orellana · LISBON (LISBOA) · Barreiro · Estremoz · Em · del · Setúbal · Évora · Almendralejo · Cabo Espichel · Alcácer do Sal · Zafra · Sines · Cabo de Sines · Beja · Cortegana · Sierr · Algarve · Seville · Carmor · Huelva · Dos Hermanas · Osu · Cabo de São Vicente · Lagos · Ayamonte · Tavira · Golfo de Cádiz · Marismas del Guadalquivir · Andaluc · Faro · Olhão · Lebrija · Sanlúcar de Barrameda · El Puerto de Santa María · Jerez de la Frontera · Rond · Cádiz · San Fernando · Barbate · Cabo Trafalgar · Algeciras · Gi · Strait of Gibraltar · (to · Ce · Pu · Tanger · Alm · MOROCCO

I J K L M N O P

Bay of Biscay

Mussels

Andalucian horse
Horses from Andalucia in southern Spain are prized for their strength and speed. They are the traditional war horses of Europe and have helped to win many battles.

ta Verde 4°
Llanes
Santander
Cabo Machichaco
na Prieta
ft (2,536m)
Torrelavega
Bilbao
Donostia-
San Sebastián
Tolosa
Reinosa
País Vasco
rica
Pamplona
F R A N C E
43°
Perpignan

Vitoria-Gasteiz
Miranda de Ebro
Estella
Jaca
Aneto
11,168ft (3,404m)
ANDORRA
★ANDORRA LA VELLA
Cabo de Creus

Logroño
Ebro
Huesca
La Seu d'Urgell
Figueras
Ripoll
Girona
42°

Burgos
Calahorra
Barbastro
Cataluña
Vic
Palafrugell
Palamós
Costa Brava

ncia
Lerma
Tudela
Monzón
Balaguer
Cervera
Sabadell
Blanes

Valladolid
Soria
Zaragoza
Lleida
Fraga
Mataró
Barcelona
L'Hospitalet
de Llobregat

dina del
mpo
Aranda de Duero
Medinaceli
Calatayud
Daroca
Valls
El Vendrell
Sitges
Tarragona

Segovia
Central
Sistema Ibérico
Aragón
Alcañiz
Golfo de Sant Jordi
41°

Ávila
Guadalajara
Acalá de Henares
Amposta
Mouth of the Ebro
Sant Carles de la Ràpita

MADRID
Getafe
Embalse de Buendía
Teruel
Vinarós

Sacred Family Church
Barcelona's Sacred Family Church is famous for its strange and original design. It was created by the architect Antoni Gaudi, and although building started in 1883 the church is still not finished.

avera de
Reina
Aranjuez
Tarancón
Cuenca
Castelló de la Plana
Burriana
Golfo de Valencia
Ciudadela
Cap de Formentor
Minorca
40°
Mahón

Toledo
S P A I N
Embalse de Alarcón
Turia
Sagunto
Balearic Islands
Pollença
Majorca
Manacor
Cap des Freu

Meseta
Mota del Cuervo
Júcar
Valencia
Buñol
Palma
Llucmajor
Felanitx

Ciudad Real
Daimiel
Manzanares
La Roda
Albacete
Alginet
Sueca
Cullera
Xátiva
Gandía
Ibiza
Cabrera
Cap de ses Salines

Guadiana
La Solana
Valdepeñas
Almansa
Ontinyent
Denia
Cabo de San Antonio
Cabo de la Nao
Eivissa
39°

Puertollano
Villanueva de los Infantes
Hellín
Villena
Benidorm
Villajoyosa
Formentera

La Carolina
Morena
Beas de Segura
Cieza
Elche
Alicante
Cabo Huertas

toro
Bailén
Linares
Villacarrillo
Orihuela
Costa Blanca
2°

doba
Andújar
Úbeda
Guadalquivir
Huéscar
Murcia
38°

Jaén
Béticos
Sistemas
Lorca
Cartagena
La Unión
Cabo de Palos

Baza
Águilas

Flamenco dancing
Flamenco is the dance of the Spanish Gypsies. Dancers wear shoes with nails driven into the heels and the tips of the soles. The sound the shoes make as the dancer performs is a feature of flamenco, as are clapping, singing and guitar music.

Embalse
e Iznajar
Granada
Guadix
37°

Antequera
Mulhacén
11,421ft (3,481m)
Mediterranean Sea

Málaga
Almería

girola
Cabo Sacratif
Punta de las Entinas

Costa
del Sol
36°

TAR
Mediterranean

N
W E
S

Toledo weapons
For centuries, European kings, knights and soldiers had their weapons forged from Toledo steel. These weapons were the strongest and sharpest in the world.

A vast wild area in southern Spain is home to the highest number of birds of prey in Europe. Among these is the Egyptian vulture. It picks up stones and hurls them to break open the eggs it likes to eat.

Melilla

0 miles   100
0 kilometers   100

1
2
3
4
5
6
7
8
9
10
11

I J K L M N O P

Spain and Portugal

SPAIN	
LAND AREA	194,897 sq miles (504,782 sq km)
OFFICIAL LANGUAGE	Spanish
MAIN RELIGION	Christian
LIFE EXPECTANCY	79 years
LITERACY	97%

PORTUGAL	
LAND AREA	35,672 sq miles (92,391 sq km)
OFFICIAL LANGUAGE	Portuguese
MAIN RELIGION	Christian
LIFE EXPECTANCY	76 years
LITERACY	87%

Portugal's most famous wine is called port—named after Porto, a major seaport.

Cod fishing
Cod is a favorite fish in Portugal. The Bay of Biscay has the most plentiful supplies of cod, tuna and sardines. Supplies have been severely reduced in recent years, causing problems in the local fishing industry. Although fishing is still a way of life for many coastal people, many fishermen have turned to other jobs.

USING THE LAND

Cereals
Citrus fruits
Wine
Fishing
Olives
Beef cattle
Sheep
Industrial center
Mining
Timber
Tourism
Forest and woodland
Arable land
Grazing

Bilbao
ANDORRA LA VELLA
Zaragoza
Barcelona
Porto
MADRID
Valencia
LISBON
Murcia
Seville
Málaga
Cádiz

Olives
More olive oil is produced in Spain than in any other country. Over 1 million tons (1.02 million t) of olives are grown each year, most of which are crushed for olive oil. Olive groves are a common sight all over Spain.

Citrus fruits
The areas around Valencia, Spain, are part of La Huerta, which means "the orchard," because they are bursting with fresh produce. Orange and lemon groves stretch through the countryside.

Saffron farming
Saffron, the aromatic spice ingredient of Spain's famous rice dish, paella, is made from the stigmas of the saffron crocus flower. It takes 250,000 flowers to make just 1 pound (500 g) of saffron.

NATURAL FEATURES

Azores PORTUGAL
This archipelago of nine main islands in three separate groups lies about 1,000 miles (1,600 km) west of Portugal. The islands, formed by volcanic activity and earthquakes, have a subtropical, humid climate in which plants thrive. The island of Pico has the highest point in Portugal, at 7,713 feet (2,351 m).

The Pyrenees SPAIN
Stretching 270 miles (432 km) from the Bay of Biscay to the Mediterranean Sea, this rugged mountain range forms a barrier between Spain and France. During summer, warm air masses from Africa are trapped in the high regions, and cause rainfall to the south.

Mediterranean lynx

Doñana SPAIN
This wetland area south of Seville is Europe's largest nature reserve. Many rare animals roam the area, including the endangered Mediterranean lynx (*above*), fewer than 50 of which exist today. During winter, Doñana is home to thousands of migratory birds. A royal hunting ground for many centuries, it was made a national park in 1969.

Meseta SPAIN
Lying in the dry center of Spain, this high, arid plateau covers about two-thirds of the country and extends into Portugal. Warm air from the Pyrenees settles here, producing long, hot summers. In winter, conditions change and icy winds whip across the wide expanse. Parts of the meseta are mountainous.

La Tomatina

Every August, at the height of the tomato season, the town of Buñol, near Valencia, hosts the biggest food fight in the world. More than 20,000 entrants from Spain and beyond converge on the main street, ready to hurl tomatoes at anyone in sight. Part of a week-long festival, the battle is short-lived— about an hour—but in that time, many truckloads of tomatoes are reduced to pulp.

WHERE PEOPLE LIVE

Urban   Rural

SPAIN
77%   23%

PORTUGAL
63%   37%

LARGEST CITIES

Madrid 3,291,000

Barcelona 1,541,000

Valencia 742,000

Seville 676,000

Zaragoza 646,000

PLACES

Madrid SPAIN
As Spain's capital, Madrid is the focus for industry, business and leisure. It is home to the Prado, a great art museum. King Juan Carlos lives in Madrid in the Royal Palace. Madrid is one of the highest capital cities in Europe.

Guggenheim Museum

Guggenheim Museum SPAIN
This distinctive modern building (above) in Bilbao, designed by the architect Frank O. Gehry, was opened in 1997. With its curving walls clad in thin sheets of titanium, the outside of the museum looks like a huge, free-form ship.

Santiago de Compostela SPAIN
Known as the Town of the Apostle, this university town's name comes from the apostle Saint James, who is buried there. It is the final destination on a popular pilgrimage trail, and has many religious monuments. Impressive processions pass through the streets during Easter week.

PEOPLE

Trajan AD 53–117
The first Roman emperor to be born outside Italy, in what is now Spain, Trajan tried to extend the empire to the east. He improved social welfare and commissioned many new buildings.

Queen Isabella 1451–1504
In 1469, Isabella of Castile married Ferdinand of Aragón, uniting their Catholic kingdoms to form the basis of modern Spain.

Christopher Columbus 1451–1506
This Italian-born sailor left Spain in 1492, in search of western trade routes to India. Three months later, he reached the Americas, not sure where he was. His accidental discovery made Spain a rich and powerful nation.

Vasco da Gama 1460–1524
This Portuguese navigator made three voyages to India (in 1497–99, 1502–03 and 1524), which opened up a new sea route from Europe to Asia and helped to make Portugal a world power.

Évora PORTUGAL
This city, east of Lisbon, was for many years an important military center for the Roman empire. It has also been under Moorish and Spanish control. Ruins of Roman buildings can still be seen throughout the city.

Lisbon PORTUGAL
Lisbon, Portugal's capital, is the country's main seaport. In the 8th century, it was invaded by Moors from Africa, and the city's buildings retain influences from this time. One of the greatest earthquakes ever recorded struck Lisbon in 1755, killing 30,000 people.

Alcazar, Segovia SPAIN
The Alcazar (right) takes its name from the Arabic word for castle. Isabella was crowned there in 1474. Built in the Middle Ages, it was rebuilt after being destroyed by fire in 1862.

The Alcazar at Segovia

Spanish Armada
The Armada was the name given to the Spanish navy under the rule of Phillip II in the 1500s. A flotilla of 130 ships, with 27,000 men on board, set sail to invade Britain in 1588. However, the English navy was better prepared. Using fire ships, it split the Spanish fleet apart and forced the Spaniards to return home in defeat. Spain's reputation as a maritime power was lost forever.

Pablo Picasso 1881–1973
This modern Spanish artist experimented with several different styles in his life. His Cubist period produced masterpieces such as *La Casserole Émailée* (below).

La Casa Mila

Gaudí's Barcelona
The city of Barcelona is adorned with the eye-catching architecture of Spain's most distinctive architect, Antoni Gaudí (1852–1926). Gaudí's buildings combined his love of the natural world with his knowledge of metalwork. The apartment block La Casa Mila (above) was built between 1906 and 1910 in the center of Barcelona. Its ornate roof and curved walls were inspired by the nearby ocean.

Portuguese water dogs were said to have sailed with the Spanish Armada in 1588 as messenger dogs between ships.

TRADITIONS AND CULTURE

Running of the bulls
This tradition is part of an annual festival held each July in Pamplona. As a climax to the 10 days of festivities, six bulls are released into the cobbled streets, behind crowds of young men who dodge the beasts' sharp horns.

Running of the bulls

Spanish food
Small plates of spicy food called tapas are eaten as snacks or appetizers. Rice is a favorite dish in many parts, often prepared with saffron, seafood and meat in paella. A specialty of the Andalucian region, in the south, is gazpacho—a chilled, tomato-based soup.

Jai alai
This game originated in the Basque region and is said to be the fastest ball game in the world. A player must fling the ball from a scooped basket called a *cesta* against a wall. The other player then catches it.

HISTORY AT A GLANCE

Cave painting, Altamira

15,000 BC
Prehistoric people create paintings depicting wild beasts in caves at Altamira, in northern Spain.

218 BC
Romans attack Hannibal's army and gradually move into the area. They remain until AD 409, when they are attacked by the Goths. The Goths rule until AD 711.

AD 711
Moorish Muslims invade southern Spain and Portugal from north Africa. In 1139 they lose control of Portugal and face problems in Spain.

1469
Monarchs Ferdinand and Isabella marry to form one reign, which is the start of modern Spain. By 1492, the Moors are driven out of Spain. The Jews are also expelled.

1492
Christopher Columbus discovers the Americas, and Spain begins to form its empire. The golden age of discovery and cultural activity starts 50 years later and lasts more than 100 years. In 1500, Portugal claims Brazil as a colony.

1561
The first permanent Spanish settlement in the Philippines is founded at Cebu. The Spaniards rule until independence in 1898.

1640
Portugal, a subject of Spain since 1580, gains independence. The country is ruled by kings until it becomes a republic in 1910.

1808–26
The Wars of Independence break out after Latin American countries rebel against the colonial rule imposed by Napoleonic Spain. The Spanish empire rapidly declines: Argentina becomes independent in 1816, Chile in 1817, Peru in 1824 and Bolivia in 1825. Brazil becomes independent from Portugal in 1822.

1926
The republic of Portugal is overthrown in a military coup. The dictator António Salazar is prime minister from 1932 until 1968.

1931
National elections result in overwhelming support for Spain as a republic.

Spanish Civil War

1936
The Spanish Civil War breaks out and military dictator General Franco takes power by 1939. He replaces the Spanish parliament with fascist rule: more than 100,000 are executed.

1974
After Salazar's death in 1970, the virtually bloodless Revolution of the Carnations in Portugal leads to democracy in 1974.

1975
Franco dies and King Juan Carlos I becomes ruler of Spain. He introduces democratic laws with more freedom than under Franco's rule.

Boules player

France

Mont-St-Michel

The abbey of Mont-St-Michel was built in AD 966, and gradually changed over the next thousand years. It stands high on a rocky mound, attached to the mainland by a causeway. When tides are high, Mont-St-Michel becomes an island.

Cave art in Lascaux

Lascaux cave in the Dordogne, in southern France, was discovered in 1940 by four boys and a dog. They explored a hole in the forest and found themselves inside a beautiful painted cave system. There are 600 paintings in Lascaux, dating back 17,000 years. They depict hunting scenes, cattle, horses, deer and extinct animals. The cave is closed to visitors but a nearby replica is a tourist attraction.

1 Great Hall of the Bulls
The walls of this area of the cave seem to come alive with paintings of four aurochs (wild cattle) drawn in black outline. Some are 16 feet (5 m) tall and are the largest ice-age artworks.

2 Painted Gallery
This gallery is in a narrow passage off the Great Hall. Horses, bison and deer are crowded together on the wall.

Cave plan

3 Main Gallery
A second passage, to the right of the Great Hall, leads to the Main Gallery. The most impressive painting shows a row of stags swimming. The scene is almost 10 feet (3 m) above the ground. The artist must have used scaffolding.

4 Shaft of the Dead Man
Another passage leads to an area decorated with a scene of a wounded bison that has attacked and killed a man. The bird on a stick may be a spear. The artist made his paints with crushed rock and animal fat.

Guillemots

Bordeaux vineyard

Bordeaux, in France's southwest, is the largest wine-making region in the world. It is famous particularly for its red and sweet white wines. More than 13,000 wine growers in the area produce a third of all France's wine exports.

UNITED KINGDOM
Folkes
• Brighton

English Chann

Cap de la Hague
Cherbourg
Channel Islands (to UK)
Fécamp
Die
Le Havre
Baie de Seine
Bayeux
Ro
Lou
Év
St-Lô
Caen
Golfe de St-Malo
Granville
Mont-St-Michel
Avranches
Normandy
Morlaix
St-Malo
Dinan
Brest
St-Brieuc
Alençon
Brittany
Rennes
Laval
Le Mans
Quimper
Quimperlé
Vendô
Lorient
Châteaubriant
Vannes
Belle-Île
St-Nazaire
Angers
Tours
La Baule-Escoublac
Loire
Saumur
Nantes
Cholet
Île d'Yeu
Châte
La Roche-sur-Yon
Poitiers
Les Sables-d'Olonne
Île de Ré
Niort
La Rochelle
ATLANTIC OCEAN
Île d'Oléron
Rochefort
Limo
Cognac
FR
Royan
Angoulême
Gironde
Bay of Biscay
Périgueux
Bordeaux
Garonne
Dordogne
Bergera
Marmande
Gascony
Agen
Mont-de-Marsan
Auch
Bayonne
Dax
Biarritz
Orthez
Pau
Tarbes
Lourdes
St-G
SPAIN
Pyrene
Vignemale
10,820ft (3,298m)
ANDORR
ANDORRA L

Notre-Dame Cathedral

Sacre Coeur

Arc de Triomphe

Eiffel Tower

Paris

The largest city in France began as a small settlement on an island in the Seine River. It became the national capital in AD 987. More than 2 million people live in the center of Paris and another 8 million in its suburbs. The city is a business and industrial center, and one of the world's top tourist destinations. Its most famous landmark, the Eiffel Tower, was built in 1889.

Château de Chambord

Chambord is the most famous castle in the Loire Valley. It was built in the 1500s, in a symmetrical design, and contains 440 rooms, 84 staircases and 365 fireplaces. The French kings, in particular Louis XIV, used it as a retreat but it was so expensive to heat that they went there only in summer.

Mont Blanc, in France, is the highest mountain in the Alps. Its peak stands at 15,771 feet (4,807 m).

Monaco Grand Prix

Corsica
(to France)

Mont Blanc
15,771ft (4,807m)

Monte Cinto
8,878ft (2,706m)

Mediterranean Sea

France

LAND AREA	210,669 sq miles (545,630 sq km)
OFFICIAL LANGUAGE	French
MAIN RELIGION	Christian
LIFE EXPECTANCY	79 years
LITERACY	99%

Monaco has been ruled by the Grimaldi dynasty for more than 700 years.

NATURAL FEATURES

Massif Central
This vast and rugged plateau in central and southern France covers almost one-sixth of the country. The higher slopes are forested, and cattle and sheep graze on the lower grasslands.

Corsica
About one-fifth of this mountainous, rocky Mediterranean island is forested with chestnuts, pines and oak trees. The scent of its shrubby underbrush carries for miles, and has given Corsica the name "the scented isle."

Corsican landscape

Normandy beaches
Normandy's shoreline features towering chalk cliffs, golden tourist beaches and elegant resorts. The cliffs of Jobourg are the highest in Europe. Parts of the coast have very swift tides, reaching speeds of 6 miles per hour (10 km/h) in spring.

The Camargue
One of Europe's largest wetlands, this sparsely populated area is known for its free-ranging herds of cattle, horses and bulls (raised for bullfights) and for birds such as flamingoes (*left*). Rice is grown here, and salt is harvested. Nature tourism is a major industry.

USING THE LAND

Forest and woodland

Arable land

Grazing

Arid or marginal

Fishing
Fishing is still a major industry despite its decline over several years as a result of overfishing in the Atlantic Ocean. Recently there has been a move to develop fish farms to make up for the decrease in fish numbers.

Cereals

Potatoes

Fruit and vegetables

Wine

Sugar beet

Beef cattle

Dairy cattle

Sheep

Fishing

Industrial center

Mining

Tourism

Lille

PARIS

Strasbourg

Rennes

Nantes

Dijon

Clermont-Ferrand

Lyon

Bordeaux

Toulouse

MONACO

Nice

Marseille

Perpignan

Ajaccio

Lavender

Lavender is native to the southern Alps, where different varieties grow wild. In the 16th century, the peasants of Provence extracted from it an oil that was used for medicinal purposes. Today, lavender is cultivated for perfumes, soaps and herbal essences.

Wheat
France is one of the world's top five wheat-growing countries. It also exports more food than any other country except the USA.

Tour de France
France's most famous sporting event, the Tour de France, is held over a period of three weeks and covers a grueling 2,200 miles (3,520 km) around the country, ending in the center of Paris. Every year, in summer, more than 150 cyclists compete in this world-famous race.

Dairy farms

Dairy products, such as yogurt and cheese, play a major part in French cuisine and exports. Camembert, a popular soft cheese, has been produced in the lush, fertile fields of Camembert, in Normandy, for more than 200 years.

Nuclear power

France is the world's largest user of nuclear power. Its 58 nuclear reactors generate more than 75 percent of the country's electricity. Nuclear power is produced from the fission, or splitting apart, of the nuclei of atoms. The fuel most widely used in this process is the metal uranium.

WHERE PEOPLE LIVE

Urban	Rural
75%	25%

LONGEST RIVERS

Loire 634 miles (1,020 km)

Rhône 505 miles (813 km)

Seine 485 miles (780 km)

Garonne 357 miles (575 km)

LARGEST CITIES

Paris 2,108,000

Marseille 826,000

Lyon 444,000

Toulouse 417,000

Nice 330,000

Eiffel Tower

Once the tallest structure in the world, the Eiffel Tower was erected as a temporary exhibit for the Centennial Exposition in Paris in 1889 by engineer Alexandre-Gustave Eiffel. When radio was invented, the tower began its long career as an antenna. It carried the first transatlantic radio–telephone call. Each year, about 6 million people visit the tower.

PEOPLE

Joan of Arc 1412–31

Joan of Arc, France's patron saint, led French troops to victory against the English at Orléans in 1429. Captured soon after and accused of witchcraft, she was burned at the stake in 1431.

Victor Hugo 1802–85

The most famous of the French Romantic writers, Victor Hugo is best known for his novels *The Hunchback of Notre Dame* and *Les Misérables*.

Louis Pasteur 1822–95

During his brilliant scientific career, Pasteur invented pasteurization, proved that germs cause many diseases and produced a rabies vaccine. His work provided the basis for a number of branches of science and medicine.

The Water-Lily Pond, by Claude Monet

Claude Monet 1841–1946

One of the great Impressionist artists, Monet is known for his atmospheric paintings of landscapes, water-lilies (*above*) and Rouen Cathedral.

Charles de Gaulle 1890–1970

An outstanding international figure, General de Gaulle became president of the Fifth Republic in 1959, achieving independence for Algeria in 1962. He resigned from office in 1969.

PLACES

Carcassonne

The walled city of Carcassonne lies on the top of a steep bank of the Aude River. It was often besieged in the Middle Ages, and was restored in the 19th century. It has the finest remains of medieval fortifications in Europe.

Carcassonne

Lyon

The Romans founded Lyon in 43 BC, and it later became the capital of Gaul. Today, the city is a center of banking, textiles and pharmaceuticals, but most people associate it with food. It is famed for its fine cuisine, which is sourced from the fertile agricultural land and many vineyards of the region.

The Louvre was formerly the royal family's main residence.

Chartres Cathedral

Chartres Cathedral

The people of Chartres, helped by lavish contributions from the king and nobles, built this cathedral (*above*) in just over 25 years (1195–1220). With its twin west towers, rose windows and figured stained glass, it is one of the finest examples of French Gothic architecture.

Château de Versailles

This palace (*below*) was built between 1668 and 1710 by Louis XIV to display his power and wealth. Set in an immense park, it is more than a quarter of a mile (400 m) long. World War I officially ended here when the Treaty of Versailles was signed in 1919.

Versailles

TRADITIONS AND CULTURE

Perfume and fashion

The French are known for their style and elegance. French perfumes, such as those produced by Chanel, and French fashion designers, such as Pierre Cardin, are famous worldwide.

French cuisine

Good food is essential to the French way of life. The kitchen is the center of the household, and meals are an important part of French leisure activity. Almost every part of France boasts its own ham and wine, and its cheeses are famous all over the world. Nearly every meal is accompanied by bread of some sort, and breakfast often includes a buttery pastry called a croissant.

Croissants

Cafes

Cafes began in the 17th century as places to sample the popular new drinks chocolate and coffee. Le Procope, founded in 1686 in Paris, claims to be the world's oldest coffee house. Writers, artists, intellectuals and students met in cafes to talk and work.

Bastille Day parade (1880)

Bastille Day

Each year on 14 July, parades and ceremonies commemorate the 1789 destruction of the Bastille, the king's prison. At the time, it held only seven prisoners. The fall of the Bastille marks the birth of the French Republic.

Napoleon

Born in Corsica in 1769, Napoleon Bonaparte was a general and reformer of law, education and the army. His goal was the military conquest of Europe. He declared himself emperor of France in 1804, but was forced to abdicate in 1814. He died in exile in 1821 on the island of St Helena.

HISTORY AT A GLANCE

700–500 BC
The Celtic Gauls gradually arrive in France from the north and east.

58–50 BC
Julius Caesar defeats the Gauls and France becomes part of the Roman empire until AD 476, when the Romans lose control of the region to the Franks and Visigoths.

Asterix the Gaul

AD 506
The Franks unite under Clovis, convert to Christianity and grow in power. Their leader, Charlemagne, is crowned the Holy Roman Emperor by the pope in AD 800. By this time, the Franks rule most of Germany, Italy and the Low Countries.

1066
Led by William the Conqueror, the Normans from northern France conquer England, making William the most powerful ruler in France.

1337–1453
England and France fight the Hundred Years' War, an on-and-off struggle over a series of disputes, including who was the rightful king of France. After a great deal of suffering on both sides, the English are eventually driven out of France. France loses nearly a third of its population when plague breaks out in 1348.

1643
Louis XIV—the Sun King—becomes king of France at the age of five and rules until 1715. French culture appears to be at its height.

1685
Religious persecution provokes the emigration of 400,000 Protestant Huguenots.

1789
The French Revolution begins with the storming of the Bastille. Louis XVI and his Austrian queen Marie Antoinette are executed in 1793 after the people rebel against the monarchy. The reign of terror that follows sees thousands of people executed by guillotine. The young republic fights off attacks by Austria and Prussia.

Guillotine

1799
Napoleon Bonaparte comes to power and extends France's territory through much of Europe until he is defeated by England and Prussia at the Battle of Waterloo in 1815. The monarchy is restored until 1848, when another revolution brings in the Second Republic.

Battle of Waterloo

1914–18
World War I devastates France and more than 1.3 million French soldiers die. France fights on the side of the British, Russians, Americans and Italians against Germany, Austria and Turkey.

1939–44
Germany occupies France during World War II. The French resistance works underground to help the Allied powers defeat the Germans. On D-Day—6 June 1944—the largest invasion fleet in history, comprising 156,000 troops and a vast armada of ships, planes and tanks, lands at five beaches on the Normandy coast. This campaign to liberate France is successful within months.

The Low Countries

NETHERLANDS
POPULATION 16,151,000 ✴ CAPITAL AMSTERDAM

BELGIUM
POPULATION 10,289,000 ✴ CAPITAL BRUSSELS

LUXEMBOURG
POPULATION 454,000 ✴ CAPITAL LUXEMBOURG

Land below the sea

A third of the land in the Netherlands is below sea level, including the cities of Amsterdam and Rotterdam. Nearly two-thirds of the population lives below sea level. For centuries, reclaiming land from the sea for housing and farming, and keeping it drained, have been essential to the country's survival. Dikes and canals hold back the sea, and windmills drain the land.

The windmills at Kinderdijk
The Netherlands was once dotted with thousands of working windmills. Kinderdijk, near Rotterdam, has 19 windmills dating from 1740 lined up in long rows. They are still used to pump excess water from reclaimed land and keep it drained.

Afsluitdijk (the barrier dyke)
This 19-mile (30-km) barrier was built in 1932 as part of a project to reclaim 1,274 square miles (3,330 sq km) of land from the Zuider Zee (South Sea). IJsselmeer lake was created at the same time.

The Maaslandkering storm surge barrier
In 1997 the storm surge barrier outside Rotterdam was completed. During a severe storm, two massive gates can be closed to protect the land on either side from floods.

THE LOW COUNTRIES

Dutch trade
For 200 years, starting in the early 1600s, the Dutch had a vast and powerful trading network in the Dutch East Indies (now named Indonesia). Merchant ships carried cargoes of gold to India and on to Asia, using it to buy jade, porcelain, spices, tea, coffee, sugar and tobacco to sell in Europe.

The canals of Amsterdam
The city of Amsterdam was founded in 1275. A network of canals was built to criss-cross the city because the land on which it is built is low and at risk of flooding. Today there are 165 canals and 1,281 bridges. The best way to get around the busy streets is by bicycle.

Clogs

GERMANY

NETHERLANDS

Schiermonnikoog
Eemshaven
Delfzijl
Zuidhorn
Groningen
Haren
Vlagtwedde
Stadskanaal
Borger
Emmen
Coevorden
Assen
Beilen
Hoogeveen
Almelo
Oldenzaal
Hengelo
Enschede
Rijssen
Goor
Haaksbergen
Eibergen
Doetinchem
Winterswijk
Dokkum
Meppel
Staphorst
Zwolle
IJssel
Epe
Deventer
Dieren
Zutphen
Ameland
Leeuwarden
Heerenveen
Wolvega
Steenwijk
Emmeloord
Kampen
Apeldoorn
Barneveld
Ede
Arnhem
Terschelling
Sneek
Joure
Lelystad
Nunspeet
West Frisian Islands
Harlingen
Emmeloord
Almere
Amersfoort
Zeist
Veenendaal
Vlieland
Texel
Schagen
Heerhugowaard
Hoorn
Purmerend
Zaandam
AMSTERDAM
Hilversum
Nieuwegein
Utrecht
Den Helder
Alkmaar
Amstelveen
Haarlem
Zoetermeer
Alphen
Gouda
Sassenheim
Leiden
THE HAGUE ('S-GRAVENHAGE)
Delft
Europoort
Rotterdam

Waddenzee
IJsselmeer
Afsluitdijk
North Sea
Rhine

Mackerel

The brewer's saint

Saint Arnold is the patron saint of Belgian brewers. During a plague in the 11th century, he told people to drink beer instead of water. Many lives were saved. Plague spread when people drank water infected by germs from rats. The high temperature that beer is heated to during production kills germs.

Growing tulips

The Netherlands produces about 9 billion flower bulbs each year, a third of which are tulips. If all these tulip bulbs were placed 4 inches (10 cm) apart, they would circle the Equator seven times. Tulips first grew in Central Asia and were taken to the Netherlands from Turkey. The word tulip comes from the Turkish word for turban.

Bourscheid Castle

This mighty fortress dates from the 10th century. It stands on a hilltop above the Süre River in the Luxembourg Ardennes. The castle was hard to attack because it was protected by a massive ring wall with 11 watchtowers.

Delft china

Merchants from the Dutch East India Company imported porcelain from China in the 1500s. Pottery with blue-and-white handpainted designs became very popular. In the town of Delft, factories produced bowls, plates and vases inspired by the Chinese designs.

Rotterdam, the largest city in the Netherlands, is the busiest port in the world. It is situated on the Maas River. More than 30,000 ships and 110,000 barges visit it every year.

### Map labels

GERMANY
FRANCE
BELGIUM
LUXEMBOURG

BRUSSELS
(BRUSSEL/BRUXELLES)

Flanders
Ardennes

Signal de Botrange 2,277ft (694m)

Oosterschelde, Westerschelde, Schelde, Escaut, Maas, Meuse, Ourthe, Sambre, Süre, Semois, IJzer

Aachen, Venlo, Horst, Helmond, Oirschot, Valkenswaard, Weert, Roermond, Echt, Kinrooi, Bree, Eindhoven, Lommel, Geleen, Heerlen, Maastricht, Vaals, Verviers, Malmédy, Werbomont, Weiswampach, Clervaux, Hosingen, Borscheid, Diekirch, Grevenmacher, Ettelbruck, LUXEMBOURG, Arlon, Aubange, Pétange, Esch-sur-Alzette, Dudelange, Virton, Neufchâteau, Bastogne, Marche-en-Famenne, Ciney, Andenne, Eghezée, Liège, Seraing, Genk, Hasselt, Beringen, Diest, St Truiden, Aarschot, Geel, Turnhout, Heist-op-den-Berg, Lier, Mechelen, Leuven, Tienen, Wavre, Overijse, Braine-l'Alleud, Gembloux, Namur, Charleroi, La Louvière, Courcelles, Binche, Thuin, Erquelinnes, Philippeville, Couvin, Dinant, Mons, Enghien, Halle, Ath, Leuze-en-Hainaut, Peruwelz, Tournai, Mouscron, Kortrijk, Lille, Valenciennes, Waregem, Deinze, Ghent, Aalst, Dendermonde, Melle, Lokeren, St-Niklaas, Antwerp, Brasschaat, Bergen op Zoom, Roosendaal, Breda, Terneuzen, Goes, Middelburg, Vlissingen, Aalter, Roeselare, Torhout, Bruges, Knokke-Heist, Veurne, Oostende, s-Hertogenbosch, Waalwijk, Oosterhout, Tilburg, Geel

0 miles 40
0 kilometers 40

N E S W

The Low Countries

USING THE LAND

	Forest and woodland
	Arable land
	Grazing

NETHERLANDS LAND AREA	16,033 sq miles (41,526 sq km)
OFFICIAL LANGUAGE	Dutch
MAIN RELIGION	Christian
LIFE EXPECTANCY	79 years
LITERACY	99%

BELGIUM LAND AREA	11,780 sq miles (30,510 sq km)
OFFICIAL LANGUAGE	Dutch/French/German
MAIN RELIGION	Christian
LIFE EXPECTANCY	78 years
LITERACY	98%

Luxembourgish is the national language of Luxembourg.

WHERE PEOPLE LIVE

Urban	Rural

BELGIUM
97% — 3%

NETHERLANDS
89% — 11%

Fishing
In the Netherlands, fishing for herring, mackerel and flatfishes is mostly carried out in the North Sea and in some inland fisheries. In Belgium, the fishing industry is suffering because of fishing quotas imposed by the EU. Traditional coastal fishing now plays only a small part in Belgium's economy.

Cereals
Potatoes
Vegetables
Sugar beet
Flowers
Beef cattle
Dairy cattle
Pigs
Gas production
Timber

Groningen
AMSTERDAM
Enschede
Utrecht
The Hague
Rotterdam
Eindhoven
Antwerp
Ghent
BRUSSELS
Liège
LUXEMBOURG

Farming
Cattle are raised on many farms throughout the Netherlands. Dairy cows, especially the black-and-white Holstein and Friesian, are the most popular varieties. The country's fertile polders are perfect for dairy farming.

Sugar beet
Although most farms in the Netherlands are small, their yields are among the world's highest. Leading crops include potatoes and sugar beet (below). Many farmers grow their crops in glasshouses during the winter.

NATURAL FEATURES

Ardennes BELGIUM–LUXEMBOURG
This chain of wooded hills covers 3,860 square miles (10,00 sq km) in northern Luxembourg, southern Belgium and northeast France. Under many of the hills are extensive cave systems, which are just one of the tourist attractions. The Ardennes is Belgium's most heavily forested region and also its least populated.

Beemster Polder
THE NETHERLANDS
Reclaimed in the 17th century from an area that used to be an inland sea, this oldest polder (reclaimed land) in the Netherlands is still divided into the rectangular plots of land that were drawn up in 1612.

Waddenzee
THE NETHERLANDS
This is the part of the North Sea between the Dutch mainland and the West Frisian Islands. Texel, the largest of these islands, is home to more than 300 species of birds, including the Eurasian spoonbill, and many migratory birds. It is one of the most important breeding grounds in Europe.

Eurasian spoonbill

Soignes Forest BELGIUM
Covering an area of about 10,000 acres (4,000 ha), this forest contains five nature reserves. Originally part of the ancient Charbonnière forest of Gaul, in which aurochs and elk roamed, it is known for its lofty beech trees.

Soignes Forest

Cheese markets
Many cheese-producing towns, such as Edam, Gouda and Alkmaar, retain their traditional cheese markets. Large, round balls of cheese are carried from the public weighing house to the cheese market, or *kaasmarkt*, on wooden sledges. The porters dress in white shirts and trousers, and wear leather slings to help them carry the heavy sledge. Gouda and Edam cheeses are world famous.

Edam cheese

LARGEST CITIES

Brussels 984,000

Amsterdam 742,000

Rotterdam 603,000

The Hague 470,000

Antwerp 451,000

Great painters

The 16th and 17th centuries were golden years for painting in Belgium and the Netherlands. The Flemish master Peter Paul Rubens painted for royal families, and is famous for his portraits, such as the *Portrait of a Boy* (*above*). Rembrandt, one of the most gifted Dutch painters, also specialized in portraits, using light and shade for dramatic effect.

TRADITIONS AND CULTURE

Belgian chocolate

Belgium is the world's third-largest producer of chocolates, which are exported all over the world. Some fine chocolate makers still fill and decorate their chocolates by hand.

Wooden shoes

Some Dutch people wear traditional wooden shoes that are shaped like ordinary shoes to help keep their feet warm and dry in the damp. Clogs, the pointy-toed, wooden shoes that are sold as tourist souvenirs, are not worn.

St Nicholas

Each year the people of the Netherlands celebrate the festival of Sinterklaas, or St Nicholas, the patron saint of sailors. On 6 December, the children exchange presents. Over the years, "Sinterklaas" became "Santa Claus."

Elfstedentocht

Also called the "Eleven Cities' Journey," this skating competition takes place on frozen canals that pass through 11 towns in Friesland, covering a distance of 125 miles (200 km).

Moules-frite—mussels with fries—is the national dish of Belgium.

PEOPLE

Desiderius Erasmus 1466–1536

Born in Rotterdam, Erasmus was a thinker and writer of the Renaissance period. He spent his life studying and writing about Christianity.

Abel Tasman c 1603–59

This navigator was chosen by the governor-general of the Dutch East Indies to explore the south Pacific. In 1642 he discovered what is now Tasmania, Australia, naming it Van Diemen's Land for his patron.

Vincent van Gogh 1853–90

Van Gogh's early paintings were mostly of farms and peasants. His later works were of orchards and sunflowers (*left*).

He had a unique brush style and loved to use bright, vivid colors. He is the greatest Dutch painter since Rembrandt.

Sunflowers

Mata Hari 1876–1917

Born in Friesland, Mata Hari's real name was Margarethe Geertruide Zelle. Well known as a dancer, she was accused of being a spy for Germany during World War I and was executed by the French.

Hergé 1907–83

Born in Brussels, Georges Rémi (known as Hergé) was a cartoonist. He created the children's cartoon series *The Adventures of Tintin* (*left*), which tells of the journeys of a boy reporter called Tintin and his white terrier, Snowy.

Anne Frank 1929–45

In 1942, during World War II, Anne Frank and her family hid for two years in an Amsterdam warehouse to avoid capture. Anne kept a diary of her life until taken to Auschwitz.

Anne Frank

PLACES

Amsterdam THE NETHERLANDS

Amsterdam is one of the Netherlands' two capitals (the other is The Hague). It began as a fishing village, and is now a busy port and commercial center.

Amsterdam

City of Luxembourg LUXEMBOURG

The capital of Luxembourg, which is one of Europe's oldest and smallest countries, this city is one of Europe's most important financial centers.

Brussels BELGIUM

Belgium's capital Brussels (*below*) is home to the headquarters of the European Union (EU) and the North Atlantic Treaty Organization (NATO).

Bruges BELGIUM

In the Middle Ages, Bruges was one of the largest and most influential of all European cities. An extensive network of canals runs through the city, which has beautiful gabled buildings and cobblestone streets.

The Hague THE NETHERLANDS

This city is the seat of government of the Netherlands. It is home to the Dutch parliament building and is the official residence of the Dutch royal family.

European Union

The European Union (EU) is an organization of democratic European countries that promotes cooperation among its members. Originally, this cooperation was mostly in the areas of politics, trade and economics, but now it involves such issues as human rights, international security and environmental protection.

HISTORY AT A GLANCE

c 50 BC
Julius Caesar invades the areas now known as the Low Countries. He conquers the land south of the Rhine, but the Frisians north of the Rhine are unconquered.

AD 406–511
Germanic tribes, called the Franks, end Roman rule in the Low Countries. Under Clovis I (king from c 481 to 511) the Franks rule most of Gaul.

AD 713–814
Charles Martel, a Frankish prince, conquers the Frisians and controls the Frankish empire, which reaches its peak between AD 768 and 814 under Charles's grandson, Charlemagne.

AD 925–1350
The Netherlands is ruled by the king of Germany, except for Flanders, which is ruled by France.

1350–1420
The dukes of French Burgundy, such as John the Fearless, become powerful, and the area is called the "Burgundian Netherlands."

John the Fearless

1504
The Low Countries again become part of the Holy Roman Empire.

1579
Seven provinces break away from Spanish rule and form the Union of Utrecht. This union is called the United Provinces of the Netherlands.

1602
The Dutch East India Company is formed and establishes profitable trade routes throughout Europe and East Asia.

1795–1813
The French, led by Napoleon Bonaparte, invade the Netherlands and control the United Provinces.

1814
The Congress of Vienna approves the United Kingdom of the Netherlands, including Belgium and Luxembourg. William I of Orange is king.

Congress of Vienna

1830
Belgians gain their independence after revolting against King William's control. Luxembourg becomes independent nine years later.

1847–48
Belgium and the Netherlands adopt important constitutional reforms.

1940–44
The Germans invade and occupy the Netherlands and Belgium until the end of World War II.

1957
Belgium, France, Italy, Luxembourg, West Germany and the Netherlands form the European Economic Community (EEC) to help free up trade among its members.

1967
The North Atlantic Treaty Organization (NATO) moves its headquarters from France to Belgium.

1992
The members of the European Community sign the Maastricht Treaty, which later establishes the European Union.

2002
Members of the European Union adopt euro notes and coins as their common currency.

Euro

Western Central Europe

GERMANY
POPULATION 82,398,000 ∗ CAPITAL BERLIN

AUSTRIA
POPULATION 8,188,000 ∗ CAPITAL VIENNA

SWITZERLAND
POPULATION 7,319,000 ∗ CAPITAL BERN

LIECHTENSTEIN
POPULATION 33,000 ∗ CAPITAL VADUZ

Switzerland is one of the world's most rugged countries. Mountains make up more than 70 percent of its area.

Barge on Rhine River

Brandenburg Gate
This monumental gateway in Berlin was built between 1788 and 1791. On its top is a statue of a chariot drawn by four horses, representing victory. The gate was damaged in World War II but has since been restored.

Farming
Wheat, barley, corn and sugar beets are grown in the region's richer soils. In the poorer soils of north Germany, rye, oats and potatoes are the main crops.

Car manufacture
The Ruhr valley in Germany is the world's largest car producer after the USA and Japan. German cars are noted for their style and reliability.

Hohensalzburg Castle
This massive fortress dominates the city of Salzburg in Austria. It was built by Archbishop Gebhard in the 11th century to protect the city from

Tugboat
In the North Sea, tugboats bring ships and tankers safely through narrow or shallow waterways, and maneuver them into tight docking bays.

LUXEMBOURG

CZECH REPUBLIC

SLOVAKIA

HUNGARY

AUSTRIA

SLOVENIA

ITALY

SWITZERLAND

LIECHTENSTEIN

FRANCE

Bohemian Forest

Black Forest

Jura

Alps

Alps

Frankfurt am Main

Hof
Bayreuth
Schweinfurt
Bamberg
Aschaffenburg
Würzburg
Erlangen
Nuremberg
Fürth
Regensburg
Landshut
Ingolstadt
Augsburg
Munich
Rosenheim
Passau
Braunau am Inn
Linz
Traun
Wels
Steyr
Amstetten
St. Pölten
Krems an der Donau
Korneuburg
VIENNA (WIEN)
Baden
Wiener Neustadt
Salzburg
Bad Ischl
Hallein
Leoben
Bruck an der Mur
Knittelfeld
Graz
Wolfsberg
Klagenfurt
Villach
Lienz
Grossglockner ▲ 12,457ft (3,797m)

Neuschwanstein Castle
Innsbruck
Zugspitze ▲ 9,721ft (2,963m)
Bregenz
Dornbirn
Feldkirch
VADUZ
Chur
Klosters
Davos
St. Moritz
Bellinzona
Lugano

Hanau
Offenbach
Darmstadt
Mainz
Wiesbaden
Mannheim
Worms
Heidelberg
Ludwigshafen
Speyer
Landau in der Pfalz
Karlsruhe
Heilbronn
Ludwigsburg
Stuttgart
Aalen
Schwäbisch Gmünd
Pforzheim
Tübingen
Reutlingen
Ulm
Kempten
Friedrichshafen
Ravensburg
Konstanz
Lake Constance
Winterthur
Zürich
St Gallen
Zug
Schwyz
Luzern
BERN
Thun
Biel
Bieler See
Lac de Neuchâtel
Fribourg
Lausanne
Montreux
Sion
Brig
Eiger ▲ 13,025ft (3,970m)
Matterhorn ▲ 14,692ft (4,478m)
Geneva
Lake Geneva

Trier
Saarbrücken
Kaiserslautern
Pirmasens
Bad Kreuznach
Freiburg im Breisgau
Offenburg
Baden Baden
Basel (Basle)

Rhine
Main
Neckar
Danube
Mosel
Rhône

N E S W

0 miles   100
0 kilometers   100

0 kilometers   100

Swiss watch
The wristwatch was invented in Switzerland, and the first Swiss watches were made in Geneva in the 16th century. Today, watches and clocks are Switzerland's third-largest export. They are valued for their accuracy.

Matterhorn
On the border between Italy and Switzerland, the Matterhorn stands 14,692 feet (4,478 m) high. It was first climbed on 14 July 1865.

Neuschwanstein Castle

The eccentric King Ludwig II of Bavaria (1845–86) loved ornate, romantic architecture. The design of his fairytale castle of Neuschwanstein in the Bavarian Alps, in Germany, was influenced by the castles of medieval German knights. Building began in 1869, but the castle was unfinished when Ludwig died. Ludwig admired the composer Richard Wagner, and wall paintings throughout the castle depict themes from several of Wagner's operas. Sleeping Beauty's castle in Disneyland, USA, is based on the Neuschwanstein castle.

Ludwig II
Ludwig II, also known as Mad King Ludwig, became king of Bavaria at the age of 18. He preferred to live alone rather than deal with his public duties. He was declared insane and lost the throne in 1886, and drowned soon after.

Ornate carving
Detailed carving, such as that on the four-poster bed in the royal bedroom, took 14 carpenters nearly five years to complete. Murals depicting legends were painted in Ludwig's study. The throne room has a blue dome with golden stars.

Swan
This porcelain swan is one of the many swan images found in the castle. They reflect Ludwig's fascination with classical myths, in which swans were often able to predict the future.

Tim Burners-Lee developed the world wide web in 1989 while working near Geneva.

Western Central Europe

GERMANY LAND AREA	134,836 sq miles (349,223 sq km)
OFFICIAL LANGUAGE	German
MAIN RELIGION	Christian
LIFE EXPECTANCY	78 years
LITERACY	99%

AUSTRIA LAND AREA	31,945 sq miles (82,738 sq km)
OFFICIAL LANGUAGE	German
MAIN RELIGION	Christian
LIFE EXPECTANCY	78 years
LITERACY	98%

SWITZERLAND LAND AREA	15,355 sq miles (39,770 sq km)
OFFICIAL LANGUAGE	German/French/Italian
MAIN RELIGION	Christian
LIFE EXPECTANCY	80 years
LITERACY	99%

WHERE PEOPLE LIVE

Urban	Rural

GERMANY
87% | 13%

SWITZERLAND
68% | 32%

AUSTRIA
65% | 35%

Neanderthals

Named for the Neander Valley near Düsseldorf in Germany, where their remains were discovered in 1856, the Neanderthals lived in Europe between 60,000 and 35,000 years ago. They had a thick brow line and sloping forehead, and were shorter and stockier than other early humans. Their disappearance is a mystery—perhaps it was because they did not develop technology.

USING THE LAND

- Cereals
- Potatoes
- Wine
- Sugar beet
- Beef cattle
- Dairy cattle
- Sheep
- Pigs
- Industrial center
- Mining
- Timber
- Winter sports

- Forest and woodland
- Arable land
- Grazing
- Arid or marginal

Map labels: Kiel, Hamburg, Hannover, BERLIN, Essen, Cologne, Leipzig, Dresden, Frankfurt am Main, Nuremberg, Stuttgart, Basel, Zürich, VADUZ, Innsbruck, Linz, VIENNA, Munich, Salzburg, Graz, Klagenfurt, BERN, Geneva, Lugano

Winter sports
The mountainous landscape of much of this region, as well as the extremely cold winters, make snow- and ice-related sports very popular. Many Germans, Swiss and Austrians love skiing, especially the cross-country style called *langlaufing*. In recent years, snowboarding (*right*) has also become popular.

NATURAL FEATURES

Eisriesenwalt caves AUSTRIA
Discovered in 1879, these huge ice caves in Salzburg have more than 25 miles (40 km) of explored passageways and 39,000 cubic yards (30,000 m³) of ice.

Lake Geneva SWITZERLAND–FRANCE
Lake Geneva is one of the largest and most beautiful lakes in Europe. Sixty percent of its waters belong to Switzerland, the remainder to France. Château de Chillon (*below*) is a fortress built on the shores in the 11th century.

The Alps
Europe's most impressive mountain range extends along Germany's southern border with Austria, into the state of Bavaria. Although the peaks are snow-covered during winter, masses of edelweiss (*left*) blanket the alpine meadows in spring.

The Black Forest GERMANY
Named for its dense growth of spruce and fir trees that let little light into the area, this dramatic forest in southwest Germany has been the backdrop for many magical tales. Pollution, such as acid rain, has recently threatened the forest.

LARGEST CITIES

Berlin 3,387,000

Hamburg 1,731,000

Vienna 1,504,000

Munich 1,238,000

Cologne 970,000

Chemicals
Germany is one of the world's leaders in chemicals production for both the local and export markets. Many corporations are developing measures to ensure that the environment is protected while chemicals are being manufactured.

HIGHEST MOUNTAINS

Monte Rosa massif 15,203 feet (4,634 m)

Dom 14,911 feet (4,545 m)

Weisshorn 14,780 feet (4,505 m)

Taschhorn 14,731 feet (4,490 m)

Classical music

Between 1750 and 1820, Vienna, Austria's capital, was the center of classical music. Two of the most gifted composers from this time were Ludwig van Beethoven (1770–1827), who at the age of 30 began to go deaf, and Wolfgang Amadeus Mozart (1756–91), who died at age 35 at the height of his musical powers. Both relied on the support of wealthy patrons, who provided the funds that enabled them to write music.

Ludwig van Beethoven

PEOPLE

Martin Luther 1483–1546
This German monk and scholar led a split away from the Roman Catholic Church when it did not accept his criticisms. Protestantism grew from this rift.

Gregor Mendel 1822–84
Known as the father of modern genetics, this Austrian monk, and later scientist, discovered why some plants and animals share the same characteristics.

Jean-Henri Dunant 1828–1910
In 1862, this Swiss journalist gathered together 36 people from 14 nations to form the International Red Cross. The Red Cross flag—a red cross on a white background—is the reverse of the Swiss flag.

Albert Einstein 1879–1955
Born in Germany, Einstein, a physicist, became a Swiss citizen in 1901. He published four research papers in 1905, the most influential being on his theory of relativity.

Albert Einstein

Maria von Trapp 1905–87
With her seven stepchildren and husband, this Austrian singer formed the Trapp Family Singers, who sang to audiences the world over. The film *The Sound of Music* is based on Maria's life.

Julie Andrews as Maria in *The Sound of Music*

TRADITIONS AND CULTURE

Oktoberfest
For 16 days during this beer festival in October, beer halls are filled with people drinking steins (*right*) of beer and enjoying oom-pah band music. The festival attracts more than 7 million visitors to Munich.

Fairy tales
Grimms' fairy tales were written by the brothers Grimm—two Germans who collected folktales about kings, magic and talking animals. The tales were often set in the forests and mountains of Germany.

Saint Bernard dog
This shaggy, densely coated dog breed was first reared in the 17th century by monks in the Saint Bernard Monastery, high in the Swiss Alps. Because of the dogs' ability to withstand very cold weather and their excellent sense of direction, they were able to help the guides who led people across the often dangerous Saint Bernard Pass.

PLACES

Berlin GERMANY
This capital city, divided into east and west after World War II but becoming one city again in 1989, began as a trading center in the 13th century. Its most famous landmark is the Brandenberg Gate.

Zurich SWITZERLAND
Situated either side of the Limmat River on Lake Zurich is Switzerland's capital city, a bustling business and cultural center, which earns one-fifth of the national income and has many visitors each year.

Vaduz LIECHTENSTEIN
This small capital city, although wealthy, has an atmosphere more like a village than a thriving center. Liechtenstein Castle, home of the prince, overlooks the city.

Vienna

Lipizzaner horses
This classic horse breed dates from 1580, and is a mix of Spanish, Arabian and Berber. It features in the dressage performances at the Spanish Riding School in Vienna.

Cuckoo clocks
Made in Germany since the 18th century, these decorative clocks (*right*) feature a mechanized cuckoo bird, which appears and sings as the clock strikes. The clock face can also be carved or painted.

Swiss cheese
Switzerland has a thriving dairy industry, and cheese-making is a family tradition that takes great skill. Emmentaler and Gruyère are the most popular varieties. A favorite Swiss dish is fondue, in which cheese is melted in a pot over a gentle flame, and pieces of bread are dipped into the pot.

Gruyère cheese

Liechtenstein is the world's largest exporter of false teeth.

Cologne Cathedral

Cologne Cathedral GERMANY
One of the world's largest Gothic structures, this cathedral is the most visited monument in Germany. Building started in 1248, but the cathedral was not completed until 1880. Its two large towers rise to 515 feet (157 m).

Vienna AUSTRIA
Vienna, on the Danube River, was once the capital of the Holy Roman Empire. It is now known for its architecture, much of which dates from the Habsburg period, and its music. Vienna is the birthplace of the noted composers Franz Schubert, Johann Strauss and Arnold Schoenberg.

AD 962
King Otto of Saxony rules the Holy Roman Empire as the first Holy Roman Emperor.

1200s
Three German cantons (districts) combine to form the Swiss Federation. More join over time. Zurich joins in 1351.

1278
Robert de Habsburg begins the Habsburg dynasty after taking control of Austria. By the 1500s this dynasty dominates most of Europe.

1455
Johann Gutenberg produces the Gutenberg Bible, the first European book printed with movable type.

Gutenberg Bible

1517
Martin Luther speaks out against the Roman Catholic Church. The Reformation follows. Luther establishes the Protestant Church.

1529
Ottoman Turks besiege Vienna but fail to take over the city.

1618–48
Protestants start the Thirty Years War as a protest against the Habsburg Holy Roman emperors. The Treaty of Westphalia ends the war.

1713
Liechtenstein becomes a principality under the Holy Roman Empire and gains independent sovereignty 150 years later.

1781
Joseph II of Austria abolishes serfdom in the Austrian empire.

1871
Prussian leader Otto von Bismarck forms the new German empire. The Victory column is built two years later in Berlin to commemorate unification and past victories.

Victory column

1914–18
Germany is defeated in World War I by the Allies and becomes a republic.

1933
Adolf Hitler leads the Nazi party into power. The following year Hitler gains total control and imposes his rule on the German people.

1938
Under Hitler's direction, tanks move into Vienna and occupy the city. Austria unites with Germany.

Adolf Hitler

1939–45
World War II occurs between Germany and the Allied forces. Millions of Jews are killed by Nazis during the Holocaust. Many German cities are bombed by the Allies. Germany is defeated and divided into East and West.

1961–89
The Berlin Wall separates the two halves of Berlin into East and West, and isolates West Berlin. The wall comes down in 1989, following the collapse of communism. Germany reunites.

Italy

Football players

ITALY
POPULATION 57,998,000 * CAPITAL ROME

MALTA
POPULATION 400,000 * CAPITAL VALLETTA

SAN MARINO
POPULATION 28,000 * CAPITAL SAN MARINO

VATICAN CITY
POPULATION 911 * CAPITAL VATICAN CITY

The Colosseum of Rome

In AD 72 the Roman emperor Vespasian began building a massive amphitheater (theater in the round). It took eight years to complete. The arena was used for the cruel and bloody gladiatorial games, the Romans' favorite popular entertainment. More than 5,000 animals and gladiators died in the opening 123 days of celebration.

Awning
An enormous canvas was attached to the top in the summer.

Size and capacity
The Colosseum is four stories high with 80 entrances. It could seat 50,000 spectators.

Under the floor
The gladiators and animals were kept in chambers underneath the arena's wooden floor until their performance began.

Arches
There are 80 arches on every floor, each separated by columns.

The Colosseum today
After 400 years the arena fell into disuse. Today, thousands of tourists visit the ruins every year.

Program of events

The arena of the Colosseum was sometimes flooded for mock sea battles. Wild animal hunts also took place. A setting of hills, trees and small lakes was created to make the event more realistic. The fights of the gladiators were the main attraction.

Villa Capra

Andrea Palladio designed the Villa Capra in Vicenza in 1566. It was based on the architecture of ancient Greece and Rome. Squares, circles and rectangles were combined to create a formal building that became the model for many stately homes throughout Europe.

Carnevale celebrations

Carnevale is held each year in February. This tradition dates from the 14th century. People wear bright costumes and enjoy parades and masked balls. Venice is famous for its carnevale masks. Many depict characters from Italian folktales.

Vatican City, where the Pope lives, is the smallest country in the world. It is so small that it takes less than an hour to walk

SLOVENIA
CROATIA
SWITZERLAND
AUSTRIA
FRANCE
MONACO

Adriatic Sea
Ligurian Sea
Gulf of Genoa
Gulf of Venice
Mediterranean Sea

Mont Blanc 15,771ft (4,807m)
Monte Rosa 15,203ft (4,634m)
Sion
Nice
San Remo
Ventimiglia
Imperia
Mondovì
Cuneo
Susa
Rivoli
Turin
Alba
Asti
Biella
Vercelli
Novara
Savona
Alessandria
Piacenza
Pavia
Como
Varese
Lake Maggiore
Lake Como
Bergamo
Monza
Milan
Cremona
Mantova
Brescia
Lake Garda
Edolo
Trento
Bolzano
Merano
Bressanone
Cortina d'Ampezzo
Tarvisio
Gemona del Friuli
Udine
Trieste
Pordenone
Treviso
Vicenza
Padova
Verona
Rovigo
Venice
Chioggia
Po Delta
Comacchio
Ferrara
Modena
Carpi
Parma
Reggio nell'Emilia
Massa
Carrara
La Spezia
Viareggio
Livorno
Pisa
Lucca
Pistoia
Prato
Florence
Arezzo
Siena
Empoli
Bologna
Imola
Faenza
Forlì
Cesena
Ravenna
Rimini
SAN MARINO
Fano
Ancona
Città di Castello
Perugia
Lago Trasimeno
Civitanova Marche
Isola di Capraia
Tuscany
Dolomites
Northern Plain
Apennines
Arno
Po

Pope's ceremonial headdress

Red mullet

Pompei
In AD 79, Mount Vesuvius, near Naples, erupted. The people of the city of Pompei looked up to see a tower of thick black smoke. Ash 20 feet (6 m) deep quickly covered the city. More than 1,600 years later, the city was unearthed and its secrets were revealed.

Octopus

Cruise ship

Scooter transport
In 1946, the first commercially successful motor scooter was made in Italy. Called the Vespa (Latin for wasp), it is still popular. Scooters are easy to drive in crowded cobbled streets.

Sardinian woman

Sardines

Michelangelo's David
In 1501, the artist Michelangelo was commissioned to create a monument to represent the city of Florence. Three years later, the famous statue was finished. Carved from a single piece of marble, it shows the biblical hero David just before he defeats the giant Goliath.

Italy

LAND AREA	113,522 sq miles (294,020 sq km)
OFFICIAL LANGUAGE	Italian
MAIN RELIGION	Christian
LIFE EXPECTANCY	79 years
LITERACY	98%

USING THE LAND

NATURAL FEATURES

Blue Grotto
On a clear day, the waters of this huge underground cave on the shore of the island of Capri reflect a beautiful deep blue. In Roman times, the grotto was a water monument for Emperor Tiberius, but it lay unused until the 1800s because local fishermen believed that it was haunted by evil spirits.

Sicily and Sardinia
These two Italian islands are off Italy's west coast. Sicily lies at the southern tip and Sardinia sits between Naples and Rome. Sicily has a mix of fine beaches and local historical treasures while Sardinia's windswept coastline is popular for fishing and water sports.

Dolomites
These majestic mountains, made of dolomite limestone, lie near the Austrian border on the edge of the Alps, in the northwest of Italy. Eighteen of the peaks rise to more than 10,000 feet (3,050 m).

Appennines
This steep mountain range extends for 860 miles (1,376 km) like a backbone down the center of Italy, between the east and west coasts. Most of Italy's rivers have their source in this range.

WHERE PEOPLE LIVE

Urban		Rural
67%		33%

LARGEST CITIES

Rome 2,453,000

Milan 1,180,000

Naples 991,000

Turin 855,000

Palermo 651,000

Mount Etna
Perched above the Sicilian town of Catania, Mount Etna is one of the world's most active volcanoes. Eruptions have occurred for more than 2.5 million years. Lava flows destroy villages and farmland every few years, and smaller eruptions happen even more often. Etna's name comes from the Greek for "I burn."

PEOPLE

Marco Polo 1254–1324
Born in Venice, Marco Polo set sail for China in 1271. He completed his journey by camel along the Silk Road and spent time in the emperor Kublai Khan's court. He did not return to Italy for 24 years.

Leonardo da Vinci 1452–1519
A brilliant inventor, engineer, architect, scientist and artist, da Vinci was a leading figure of the Renaissance. He designed flying machines, such as the one below, based on his belief that humans could fly. His paintings, such as *Mona Lisa* and *The Last Supper*, are masterpieces.

Leonardo's flying machine

Galileo Galilei 1564–1642
Mathematician, astronomer, scientist: this genius made sense of the world by inventing the telescope, through which he viewed the planets.

Maria Montessori 1870–1952
Maria Montessori, Italy's first female medical student and later, a teacher, paved the way for a new way of teaching—the Montessori method.

Benito Mussolini 1883–1945
Prime minister from 1922 to 1943 and founder of fascism, this dictator carried out many social reforms and public works, but abolished democracy and banned trade unions and the free press.

Map legend
- Cereals
- Rice
- Vegetables
- Citrus fruits
- Wine
- Olives
- Beef cattle
- Dairy cattle
- Sheep
- Fishing
- Industrial center
- Tourism

- Forest and woodland
- Arable land
- Grazing
- Arid or marginal

Map labels: Turin, Milan, Venice, Genoa, SAN MARINO, Florence, ROME, Naples, Bari, Cagliari, Palermo, VALLETTA

Fruit and vegetables
Olive oil, garlic and tomatoes are a tasty basis for many of Italy's dishes. The country produces olives and vegetables of a very high quality. This is due to its Mediterranean climate of hot, dry summers and cool winters.

Winemaking
Different grape varieties are grown for wine throughout Italy. Tuscany's Chianti region is highly productive, while white frascati grapes are grown in the Lazio region around Rome.

Fishing
The waters of the Mediterranean Sea are home to sardines, tuna and anchovies. Fishing is an important industry for Italy.

St Peter's Basilica VATICAN CITY
Each year, tourists flock to St Peter's Basilica (*above*). Built between 1506 and 1615, it is the church of the popes and a pilgrimage site for Roman Catholics. In front of it is a vast colonnaded square in which crowds gather to hear the pope speak.

Rome ITALY
Set on seven hills around the Tiber River, Rome is a thriving blend of ancient traditions and modern lifestyle. Italy's capital, it attracts millions of visitors who walk the city in search of its architectural treasures and appreciate its lively, buzzing atmosphere. Its attractions include ancient sites such as the Pantheon and the ruins of the Forum.

Milan ITALY
This northern city is a center of fashion, showcased each year at the Milan Fashion Show. Italian designers such as Miuccia Prada and Giorgio Armani are known all over the world.

Valletta MALTA
This seaport, Malta's capital, has been ruled by many different powers over the centuries. Once an important naval base, it was heavily bombed in World War II.

The Leaning Tower of Pisa
The most unusual feature of this bell tower in Pisa is its lean. Building stopped shortly after it began in 1173 as the subsiding ground below the tower caused it to tilt. Almost 200 years later, it was finally completed to a height of 180 feet (55 m), with 294 steps leading to the top. The bells in the tower are no longer rung, and concrete now supports the foundations under the ground.

Naples ITALY
Italy's most densely populated city, the seaport of Naples sits on the west coast's Bay of Naples, close to possible earthquake and volcano activity.

Florence ITALY
Florence is the cultural heart of Italy, showcasing such architectural marvels as the imposing Duomo (*below*). A center of the Renaissance, the city is home to the Uffizi gallery, which displays Italy's rich heritage of art. Notable Florentines include Michelangelo, Leonardo da Vinci, Galileo, Machiavelli, Dante and the city's most famous rulers, the Medici family.

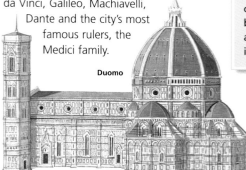
Duomo

TRADITIONS AND CULTURE

Pinocchio
This world-famous story of the wooden boy puppet who comes to life was written by Carlo Collodi and first published in 1890. Pinocchio learns about life through his adventures. His nose grows whenever he tells a lie.

Pinocchio

The Renaissance
In the 14th century there was a rebirth in art and classical knowledge, first in northern Italy and then throughout Europe. Ancient Greek thought was rediscovered and people began to view the world differently. There were great advances in art, science, literature and architecture. Michelangelo, one of the greatest Renaissance painters, brought a realism to art not seen before. His masterpiece, a series of frescoes painted on the ceiling of the Vatican's Sistine Chapel (*below*), took five years to complete.

Venice
This city consists of 118 small islands, linked by waterways and bridges, including the famous Rialto Bridge (*above*). In the 14th century, Venice was Europe's greatest seaport, and it is still a major Italian port today. Cars are banned from most of the city; water transport is provided by gondolas, vaporettos and power boats. Floods frequently bring the city to a halt. Industries include boatbuilding, textiles, furniture and glassworking. Tourism is an important source of income.

San Marino is the smallest republic in Europe and the oldest republic in the world.

Football (soccer)
Football is Italy's national sport. Most cities have their own first-grade teams, and some import highly paid players from other countries to play for them. Matches attract huge crowds.

Italian tastes
Italian people love their food. Their favorites are pizza (*right*) and pasta, which are both made from a dough of wheat grain mixed with water. There are hundreds of pasta varieties, from long spaghetti to small ravioli, served with many different sauces. Another favorite is Italian ice cream, or gelato.

Pizza

Italian design
Italian firms such as Alessi and Cappellini are known for their stylish and innovative designs, particularly in the areas of homewares, furniture and cars. Italy encourages good design through its design schools and exhibitions.

Alessi bottle opener

Opera
This combination of singing and drama originated in Italy in the 16th century. Italian operas include Verdi's *Rigoletto* and Puccini's *Tosca*. Famous modern opera singers include Luciano Pavarotti.

HISTORY AT A GLANCE
ANCIENT ROME

BEGINNINGS
According to legend, the city of Rome was founded in 753 BC by Romulus and Remus, twins who were raised by a wolf. The city-state was ruled by kings, until the final one, Tarquin the Cruel, was defeated in 509 BC by the Etruscans.

Romulus and Remus

THE REPUBLIC 509–27 BC
Two elected consuls ruled instead of the former kings. The consuls were advised by a council called the Senate, composed of wealthy citizens. During the 6th century BC, Rome became more powerful and by 275 BC controlled all of Italy. In the Punic Wars (264–146 BC), Rome fought Carthage for control of the Mediterranean and won. Further battles against Greece, Syria, Egypt and Macedonia were also successful.

JULIUS CAESAR
In 49 BC, as a popular general during the Roman Republic period, Julius Caesar led his army to victory over England and Germany. He made himself dictator of Rome and was murdered on 15 March 44 BC, known as the "ides of March."

THE EMPIRE 27 BC – AD 476
Rome's first emperor, Augustus, was Julius Caesar's nephew. He was crowned in 27 BC. The Roman empire continued to grow until it reached its largest point under Trajan (ruled AD 98–117). Rome ruled most of western Europe, including Britain, northern Africa and the Mediterranean Basin. However, the empire grew weaker and eventually split into two, with its eastern capital in Constantinople in 395. The fall of Rome was completed in 476 when Germanic tribes overran the city. The eastern empire continued until 1453, when the Ottomans captured Constantinople.

THE ARMY
The backbone of Rome's empire was its army—the most advanced and well-organized army of the ancient world. It was divided into 60 units, or legions, of foot soldiers, called legionaries. Each legion contained about 5,000 men. The army conquered many lands, expanding Rome's territory. Military life was harsh, but retired soldiers were given money or land to farm.

Roman soldiers

ROMAN ACHIEVEMENTS
The Romans invented concrete, which made it possible to build large, strong structures such as domed roofs and arched bridges. Roman roads were paved, and were known for their durability and straightness. Aqueducts supplied cities with water for public lavatories, fountains and bathhouses. The water flowed gently from a higher level to a lower one. Tiers of arches supported the pipes across steep valleys. Rome had an extensive and efficient sewerage system that was not bettered until the late 19th century.

Roman aqueduct

Southeastern Europe

Diocletian's palace
This massive palace on the Adriatic coast in Split, Croatia, was built for the Roman emperor Diocletian in the late 3rd century AD. The palace is set out like a Roman fort, and now forms the city center.

Folk dancing
Ranging from simple, quick steps and gentle turns to lively jumping, traditional folk dances are enjoyed throughout Romania. Music and loud shouts accompany the dancers.

Greek evzones guards

The dalmatian is a breed of dog named for the Adriatic coastal region of Dalmatia, its first known home. These dogs once ran beside horsedrawn carriages to frighten highwaymen.

Rural life
Farming methods are changing as more country people move to the cities to find work. However, in some areas, the traditional way of life continues.

ROMANIA
POPULATION 22,272,000 • CAPITAL BUCHAREST

GREECE
POPULATION 10,666,000 • CAPITAL ATHENS

SERBIA AND MONTENEGRO
POPULATION 10,665,000 • CAPITAL BELGRADE

BULGARIA
POPULATION 7,538,000 • CAPITAL SOFIA

CROATIA
POPULATION 4,422,000 • CAPITAL ZAGREB

BOSNIA–HERZEGOVINA
POPULATION 3,990,000 • CAPITAL SARAJEVO

ALBANIA
POPULATION 3,582,000 • CAPITAL TIRANA

MACEDONIA
POPULATION 2,063,000 • CAPITAL SKOPJE

SLOVENIA
POPULATION 1,936,000 • CAPITAL LJUBLJANA

Greek temples

The rock of the Acropolis, with its magnificent marble temples, stands high above the city of Athens, in Greece. The Greeks built temples in honor of their gods, so that the gods would live among them and protect them. The Parthenon is the largest temple on the Acropolis. It was built between 447 and 431 BC in the Doric style of architecture, and is dedicated to the goddess Athena. Parts of its exterior were once brightly painted in gold, red and blue.

Statue of Athena
A huge statue of Athena, the goddess of wisdom, stood in the Parthenon. It was made of wood and covered in ivory and gold. The statue no longer exists.

Parthenon frieze
Carved panels around the top of the Parthenon represent an annual procession to honor Athena's birth. Many panels are now in London's British Museum.

Ancient Greek architecture
Greek architects built in three styles, called orders. The simplest and most admired was the Doric. Corinthian developed from the Ionic and was the most ornate.

Doric
The column is thick. The wide section at the top, called the capital, is plain.

Ionic
The column is thinner. It has a capital with two wide spirals, called volutes.

Corinthian
The column is elaborate. The capital is decorated with acanthus leaves.

Illusions in stone
Greek architects used geometry and visual tricks, called optical illusions, to ensure that their temples were pleasing and harmonious. For example, if steps are built flat, from a distance they will appear to sag in the middle. Similarly, if columns are built straight up and down, from a distance they appear to bulge outward. To correct these problems, all horizontal lines in the temples curve slightly upward, and all vertical lines curve slightly inward.

Sunflowers
Sunflowers are grown throughout Eastern Europe. The seeds are used for birdfeed and as a snack for humans. Oil is extracted for cooking.

Meteora
Meteora, meaning "suspended in air," is the site of 24 monasteries built on top of huge rocks near Larisa, Greece. Building began in the late 1300s. At first, the monks climbed up ladders to the top. Steps and paths were built in the 1920s.

Greek islands
There are more than 2,000 islands off the coast of Greece. Santorini, in the Aegean Sea, was blasted apart 3,500 years ago by a violent volcanic eruption. According to legend, the island is the lost city of Atlantis.

Albania is the only European country in which most of the population is Muslim.

Southeastern Europe

LAND AREA	291,034 sq miles (753,774 sq km)
LARGEST COUNTRY	Romania
SMALLEST COUNTRY	Slovenia
MAIN RELIGION	Christian
LIFE EXPECTANCY	74 years
LITERACY	96%

NATURAL FEATURES

Mt Olympus GREECE
The mythological home of the Greek gods, the peak of this mountain—Mytikas—reaches almost 10,000 feet (3,050 m) into the air. Its rocky summit is often called "the throne of Zeus."

Dalmatian coast
CROATIA–SLOVENIA
This 200-mile (320-km) coastline, along the Adriatic Sea, is dotted with spectacular rocky cliffs and ancient towns. Mljet Island, one of several islands off this coast, has a saltwater lake in its lush national park.

Black Sea BULGARIA–ROMANIA
This body of water, which forms the coastline of Bulgaria and Romania, is said to have been named for the blackness of its water during winter. In summer, it is a popular resort for beachgoers.

Lake Ohrid MACEDONIA–ALBANIA
Two-thirds of this lake is Macedonian territory and the rest is Albanian. Fish species from the prehistoric Tertiary period have survived here, making the lake a museum of living fossils.

Tara River Canyon
SERBIA–MONTENEGRO
This is the second-largest canyon in the world. It is 50 miles (80 km) long and up to ¾-mile (1.2 km) deep. Wild boar and goats live on its stony slopes.

Wild boar

USING THE LAND

Forest and woodland	Cereals	Sugar beet	Sheep
Arable land	Fruit	Flowers	Pigs
Grazing	Citrus fruits	Olives	Fishing
	Wine	Beef cattle	Industrial center
	Tobacco	Dairy cattle	Mining
			Oil production
			Gas production
			Timber

Roses
Bulgaria produces nearly two-thirds of the world's rose oil, or attar. The Kazanluk rose, from Bulgaria's Kazanluk Valley, has the most pungent aroma and is used in the manufacture of high-quality perfumes.

LARGEST CITIES

Bucharest 1,897,000

Belgrade 1,290,000

Sofia 1,085,000

Athens 762,000

Zagreb 682,000

Olives
Greece is the world's largest exporter of olive oil. Olive groves grow in the north and south. Once planted, an olive tree takes about six years to bear fruit. At harvest time, its branches are hit with poles, and the olives fall off into huge nets. The oil (above) that comes from the first pressing of the fruit is called extra virgin and is the best quality.

Knossos
About 2,000 years ago, the Minoan people of Crete built palaces for their kings. The largest of these, at Knossos, was the palace of King Minos, and may once have been the home of more than 30,000 people. Its main rooms were decorated with colorful frescoes. The palace burned down around 1400 BC and its ruins were discovered in 1894. To the Minoans, bulls were symbols of power, and statues of bulls' heads (above) were found in the ruins.

Grapes

Slovenia is a wine-growing country whose people have been growing grapes for thousands of years. The oldest grapevine in Europe grows at Maribor in Slovenia and is thought to be more than 400 years old. This vine alone yields approximately 35 to 55 pounds (16 to 25 kg) of grapes each year, which is enough to make about 100 bottles of wine. The Greeks were the first Europeans to produce wine, probably learning how to do so from the Phoenicians.

WHERE PEOPLE LIVE

	Urban		Rural	

REGION
54%			46%

Most urban: BULGARIA
69%			31%

Most rural: ALBANIA
39%			61%

Map labels: Maribor, LJUBLJANA, Rijeka, ZAGREB, Osijek, Banja Luka, Split, SARAJEVO, Mostar, BELGRADE, Niš, Podgorica, Priština, SKOPJE, TIRANA, Cluj-Napoca, Timişoara, Braşov, BUCHAREST, Constanţa, Ruse, Varna, SOFIA, Plovdiv, Burgas, Thessaloniki, Larisa, Patra, ATHENS, Irakleiou

TRADITIONS AND CULTURE

Iliad and *Odyssey*
These two epic poems, written by the Greek poet Homer, tell the story of the Trojan War—a battle between Greece and Troy, in Asia Minor. The two poems are the earliest surviving examples of Greek literature.

Greek vase

Roma people
In the villages of Romania, these Gypsies perform their traditional folk music and dancing. Although little of their history is written down, their past is remembered through story-telling, usually in the Gypsy language called Romany.

Wagons at a Roma camp

Festivals
Many festivals are held throughout the year in southeastern Europe. In Bulgaria, at the *Martenitsa*, tiny red and white trims are tied to clothes to celebrate winter's end and the start of summer. For Greek Easter, red eggs are exchanged as gifts.

Macedonian folk music
The folk music of Macedonia has Turkish and Bulgarian influences. It is always linked to dancing. In the villages, the men play traditional instruments such as the *gaida*, or bagpipe, to accompany the folk dances.

Olympic Games
The Olympic Games have taken place since ancient Greek times, when they were held over five days every four years at Olympia, to honor the god Zeus. The best all-round athlete had to succeed in five events—discus and javelin throwing, running, jumping and wrestling. Chariot racing was the most popular event for the spectators.

Discus thrower

PLACES

Dubrovnik CROATIA
This capital city, on the Dalmatian coast, was founded by Roman refugees in the 7th century. In the 1991–92 civil war, much of the city was destroyed by shell fire, but many of its historic buildings have now been restored.

Mostar BOSNIA–HERZOGOVINA
This medieval town is set in the Neretva River's valley. Its name means "bridge," for the 16th-century bridge that was destroyed in the shelling raids of the 1990s. Mostar is now divided into Muslim and Croat areas.

Bucharest ROMANIA
The tree-lined boulevards of this capital city have taken their inspiration from Paris. Monasteries and churches are clustered into the back streets of the city, and on a small island in Snagov Lake, to the city's north, is the supposed tomb of Dracula.

Predjama Castle

Predjama Castle SLOVENIA
Perched on a steep cliff, this stately castle sits at the entrance to a huge cave. Castle treasure, dating back to the 16th century when the legendary knight Erasmus of Predjama lived, has been found during recent restoration of the site.

Rhodes GREECE
The city of Rhodes, founded in 408 BC, is capital of the island of the same name. The city was home to the Colossus of Rhodes, a massive statue and one of the Seven Wonders of the World. The Old Town in the city is the oldest inhabited medieval town in Europe.

Shipka Memorial Church BULGARIA
The five golden domes of this huge church, built in 1902 after the Russo-Turkish war, tower over Shipka village. The church is dedicated to Russian leader Alexander Nevsky. Its crypt is the resting place for soldiers lost in battle.

Shipka Memorial Church

PEOPLE

Archimedes c 290–212 BC
This Greek inventor is famous for his discovery that the force weighing down on a submerged object is equal to the weight of the fluid the object displaces. He was also skilled in astronomy, mathematics and mechanics.

Constantin Brancusi 1876–1957
This Romanian sculptor is known for the dramatic, yet simple, lines and shapes in his work, made from bronze or wood. He designed a memorial (*left*) in Tirgu Jui Memorial Park in Romania, which gives the effect of an endless column.

Josip Tito 1892–1980
Born in Croatia, this revolutionary statesman led the former country of Yugoslavia (now Slovenia) from 1943 to 1980 under communist rule. He disagreed with many of Stalin's severe communist ideas.

Dracula
The legend of Dracula was inspired by the 15th-century Romanian prince Vlad Tepesset, also known as Vlad the Impaler. This brutal ruler led his people in raids against the Turks and punished his captured enemies harshly. He died in battle in 1476.

Dracula's castle

Mother Teresa 1910–97
Born in Macedonia, this nun dedicated her life to helping the sick and poor in Calcutta, India. She first went to India in 1928 and, in 1950, set up the Missionaries of Charity, which now has more than 450 centers around the world.

Mother Teresa

HISTORY AT A GLANCE
ANCIENT GREECE

GREEK MYTHOLOGY
The ancient stories about Greek gods and goddesses, and their adventures with magic and monsters, are among the best known in the world. Zeus was the king of gods and Hercules, the son of Zeus, was the most popular hero. In one of his feats, Hercules strangled the Nemean lion, then wore its skin as a cloak. Many of the gods were depicted in artworks (*above*).

GREEK THINKERS
Some of the greatest philosophers, or thinkers, of all time were from ancient Greece. They tried to work out how people should live and how the world worked. Socrates' ideas were about goodness, known as ethics. Plato, one of Socrates' students, developed a theory of ideals. Aristotle was taught by Plato. Pythagoras' theories have formed the basis for many of today's scientific understandings.

ATHENS
Spreading out from the Acropolis, a rocky hill that created natural protection from enemies, Athens had become the most powerful city-state by 500 BC. Athens is known as the birthplace of democracy, as its free male citizens were able to vote for the city's leaders .

SPARTA
The city-state of Sparta was established in the 10th century BC. Spartan warriors were known to be tough and strong in battle, and they fought to increase their territory. All Spartan men were soldiers, while girls were trained for outdoor life.

Temple of Apollo at Delphi

DELPHI
The ancient Greeks often received advice from oracles, or representatives of the gods. Apollo offered advice from his temple at Delphi by speaking through the most honored oracle, the Pythia. A road led up to Apollo's temple, lined with buildings that were filled with gifts for him.

PERSIAN WARS
The Persians, from the area in western Asia now known as Iran, tried to take over many of the Greek city-states to gain more power. They captured the state of Ionia but were fought off by soldiers of the Greek army, called hoplites, in the Battle of Marathon. The account of the Persian War, where the historian Herodotus interviewed survivors, was the first accurate written record of history.

Hoplite

ALEXANDER THE GREAT 356–323 BC
After King Philip II of Macedonia died in 337 BC, his son Alexander reigned. This young leader decided to conquer the Persian territories and beyond, creating the largest empire the world had ever seen. He was clever and courageous and his cavalry of 5,000 horsemen had great respect for him. He died at 32, which fragmented his empire and brought his era to an end.

Tobogganing

A toboggan is a long, flat-bottomed sled made of thin boards curved up at the front. The curved runners of the sled move easily over snow and ice. Tobogganing is a popular sport during the cold winters of Eastern Europe.

Eastern Europe

UKRAINE
POPULATION 48,055,000 * CAPITAL KIEV

POLAND
POPULATION 38,623,000 * CAPITAL WARSAW

BELARUS
POPULATION 10,322,000 * CAPITAL MINSK

CZECH REPUBLIC
POPULATION 10,249,000 * CAPITAL PRAGUE

HUNGARY
POPULATION 10,045,000 * CAPITAL BUDAPEST

SLOVAKIA
POPULATION 5,430,000 * CAPITAL BRATISLAVA

MOLDOVA
POPULATION 4,440,000 * CAPITAL CHISINAU

LITHUANIA
POPULATION 3,593,000 * CAPITAL VILNIUS

LATVIA
POPULATION 2,349,000 * CAPITAL RIGA

ESTONIA
POPULATION 1,409,000 * CAPITAL TALLINN

Gdańsk shipyards

Gdańsk, a port on the Baltic Sea, was once Poland's most prosperous city. In the 1980s, the shipyards were the base of the trade union group called Solidarity, which successfully opposed the communist government.

Astronomical clock

Prague's astronomical clock, on a wall of the city's town hall, was built in 1410. It includes an astrolabe (an early scientific instrument for measuring time), signs of the zodiac, sculptures and moving figures of the 12 apostles.

Budapest parliament

One of the largest parliament buildings in the world overlooks the Danube River in Budapest. It was built between 1884 and 1902, and has 691 rooms and more than 12 miles (19 km) of corridors.

The Estonian islands in the Gulf of Finland are a resting place for hundreds of species of birds migrating from the north to the Baltic Sea.

Wildcat

Latvian folk dancers
Latvia proudly maintains its traditional folk songs and dances. One kind of folk song, called daina, tells stories that date back many hundreds of years.

Tallinn

Tallinn, on the Gulf of Finland, is the capital of Estonia. The city started as a Danish fort in 1219. It became a thriving trade center in the mid-1300s, and merchants from around Europe sold their goods in its busy marketplace. Tallinn's medieval buildings, such as St Olaf's church and the town hall, are among the best preserved in Europe. The city is now a commercial fishing port.

Built to protect

Wealthy cities like Tallinn were often threatened by invaders. Dating from the 16th century, the imposing wall surrounding Tallinn's Old Town protected its citizens from enemies.

St Olaf's church
St Olaf's spire is a Tallinn landmark. The church, built in the 12th century, was the tallest in medieval Europe.

Watchtowers
There are 26 watchtowers. Soldiers armed with crossbows stood guard in them.

The town wall
Tallinn's massive wall was the strongest in Northern Europe.

Harvesting wheat
Wheat is grown throughout Eastern Europe. In some countries, such as Ukraine and Belarus, where there are many small farms, much of the work is done by hand.

Cossack dancer
The Cossacks are a group of people who live north of the Black Sea. They are known for their lively folk dances, which include athletic jumps, kicks and balancing acts.

Eastern Europe

LAND AREA	594,413 sq miles (1,539,522 sq km)
LARGEST COUNTRY	Ukraine
SMALLEST COUNTRY	Moldova
MAIN RELIGION	Christian
LIFE EXPECTANCY	71 years
LITERACY	88%

USING THE LAND

- Cereals
- Flax
- Potatoes
- Vegetables
- Wine
- Sugar beet
- Flowers
- Dairy cattle
- Sheep
- Pigs
- Fishing
- Industrial center
- Mining
- Oil production
- Gas production
- Timber

Forest and woodland
Arable land
Grazing

Grapes are Moldova's largest crop. Forty-five miles (72 km) of tunnels store wine underground in the town of Cricova.

Beer
The people of the Czech Republic drink more beer than any other country in the world. Plzen, the largest city in the Bohemian–Moravian highlands, is a manufacturing center famous for brewing beer. The city's breweries use locally grown hops (*left*) to produce a pale beer called Pilsner. Pilsner beers are now popular throughout the world.

Amber
The Baltic States—Lithuania, Estonia and Latvia—have the world's largest supply of amber, the fossilized gum or resin from ancient trees. It is used to make ornaments and jewelry. Insects can sometimes be seen inside lumps of amber (*above*). They were trapped as the resin oozed from the tree.

Sweet peppers
Peppers (*left*) are the main crop in some regions of Hungary, especially in the fertile district between Szeged and Kalocsa near the Danube River. Hungarians grow red peppers to make a seasoning called paprika, which is used in the dish Hungarian goulash.

(Map labels: TALLINN, Tartu, RĪGA, Liepāja, Daugavpils, Šiauliai, Klaipėda, Vitsyebsk, VILNIUS, MINSK, Mahilyow, Gdańsk, Hrodna, Baranavichy, Homyel', Szczecin, Bydgoszcz, Poznań, WARSAW, Brest, Sumy, Łódź, Wrocław, Radom, KIEV, Kharkiv, PRAGUE, Katowice, Kraków, Plzeň, Ostrava, L'viv, Khmel'nyts'kyy, Dnipropetrovs'k, Donets'k, Brno, Košice, BRATISLAVA, Győr, BUDAPEST, Debrecen, CHIŞINĂU, Odesa, Pécs, Szeged, Simferopol')

WHERE PEOPLE LIVE

Urban | Rural

REGION
65% | 35%

Most urban: CZECH REPUBLIC
75% | 25%

Most rural: MOLDOVA
46% | 54%

Chernobyl

In April 1986, an explosion and fire in the Chernobyl nuclear power plant, Ukraine, released huge amounts of radiation into the air. This poisoned food and water supplies, and caused health problems in Ukraine and surrounding areas. The pink in the image above shows how far the radioactivity had spread around the Northern Hemisphere by the tenth day after the explosion.

NATURAL FEATURES

Courland Lagoon LITHUANIA
Courland Lagoon, or Kursky Zaliv, is 56 miles (90 km) long and 28 miles (45 km) wide. It is separated from the Baltic Sea by the Courland Spit, a strip of sand dunes that is classified as a UNESCO World Heritage Site.

Bialowieza Forest POLAND–BELARUS
This nature reserve along the borders of Poland and Belarus is administered by both nations. The forest is home to many animals, such as lynx, boar, tarpan horses and a large herd of rare European bison called wisent (*below*).

Tatra mountains POLAND–SLOVAKIA
The Tatras, the highest of the central Carpathian Mountains, mark part of the border between Poland and Slovakia. Forests of spruce and firs thrive in the alpine climate. The chamois (*left*) lives in the high mountains, and is hunted for its skin, which is made into soft leather.

Chamois

Danube River
The second-longest river in Europe, the Danube flows through nine countries from southern Germany through eastern Europe to the Black Sea. It is a transport route for agricultural and industrial freight. Chemical pollution in the Danube has affected its wildlife and the water supply of farmlands on its banks.

LONGEST RIVERS

Danube 1,770 miles (2,850 km)

Dnieper 1,420 miles (2,285 km)

Vistula 651 miles (1,047 km)

Western Dvina 632 miles (1,020 km)

LARGEST CITIES

Kiev 2,581,000

Warsaw 2,200,000

Budapest 1,730,000

Brest 1,476,000

Kharkiv 1,418,000

PLACES

Warsaw POLAND
Located on the Vistula River in the center of Poland, Warsaw is Poland's capital and its largest city. The Old Town, built in the 13th century, is a mix of architectural styles and cobbled streets. Much of the city had to be rebuilt after World War II.

Bratislava SLOVAKIA
Bratislava, Slovakia's capital, is dominated by its huge castle that stands 300 feet (90 m) above the Danube. This was once the home of the Austrian royal family. Modern Bratislava is a center for learning, a transport hub and river port.

St Stephen's crown
When Stephen was crowned king of Hungary in AD 1000, he received a jeweled crown from Pope Sylvester II. That crown forms part of what is now called the Hungarian Holy Crown, held as a national treasure and relic. Stephen was made the patron saint of Hungary, and his crown is a symbol of Hungarian nationhood.

St Sophia's Cathedral UKRAINE
Completed in 1037, this is the oldest church in Kiev, the capital of Ukraine. It had fallen into ruin by the 13th century and was rebuilt between 1685 and 1707.

Budapest HUNGARY
The capital of Hungary, this city is divided by the Danube, with Buda on the east and Pest on the west. Buda is the city's historical heart and Pest is its economic, commercial and political center.

Riga LATVIA
Founded by German crusaders in 1201 and now the capital of Latvia, Riga is a shipping center. Its art nouveau buildings are among the finest in Europe.

Prague CZECH REPUBLIC
One of the oldest cities in Europe, Prague is situated on the Vltava River. It is the capital city, business hub and cultural center of the Czech Republic, and is known for its historic buildings.

Prague

Copernicus
Nicolaus Copernicus was born in Poland in 1473. An astronomer, physician and economist, he proposed the idea that Earth and other planets in the solar system revolved around the Sun. Until then, people believed that Earth was the center of the universe and everything revolved around it. He died in 1543, just after his theory was published.

Copernican solar system

PEOPLE

Attila the Hun c AD 406–53
In 434, Attila became king of the Huns. He united them and ruled their kingdom in present-day Hungary. He conquered lands from the Baltic to the Caspian Sea but failed to keep them under his control.

Frédéric Chopin 1810–49
Polish-born Frédéric Chopin gave his first public piano concert at the age of eight, and by 15 was composing music. He composed more than 200 pieces of music for the solo piano.

Rain by Marc Chagall

Marc Chagall 1887–1985
Born in present-day Belarus, Chagall moved to Paris in 1910. He is known for his unusual, dreamlike paintings, in which his figures sometimes float upside down. He was also a printmaker and stage designer.

Pope John Paul II born 1920
In 1978, Polish-born Karol Wojtyla became the first non-Italian pope since 1522 and took the name Pope John Paul II. He has visited more countries than any other pope in history.

Martina Navratilova born 1956
Born in Prague, Navratilova became a US citizen in 1981. She is one of the world's top women's tennis players, and has won a record 167 singles championships.

HISTORY AT A GLANCE
KEY EVENTS SINCE 1918

1918–20
Poland fights Russia, winning the Battle of Warsaw and gaining independence in 1920. Hungary, Estonia, Belarus, Latvia, Ukraine, Lithuania and Czechoslovakia also gain their independence in this period.

1938–39
Nazi Germany annexes first Sudetenland, the German-speaking part of Czechoslovakia, then the rest of Czechoslovakia. It then invades Poland, which leads the UK to declare war on Germany.

Polish cavalry (1939)

1939–45
The Soviet Union and Germany either invade or annex Estonia, Belarus, Latvia, Lithuania, Ukraine, Moldova (then part of Bessarabia) and Czechoslovakia. World War II breaks out.

1945–46
The victory of the Allies leads to the Soviet Union annexing western Ukraine, Estonia, part of Poland, western Belarus and part of Bessarabia (now Moldova). Poland regains some territory from Germany and Warsaw begins to rebuild.

1956
Hungary revolts against the Soviet Union. The revolt is put down by Soviet troops, who execute many of the revolution's leaders. The Soviets form a new government with János Kádár as prime minister.

Demonstration in Prague

1989
Protests, now known as the "velvet revolution," are held in Czechoslovakia to end communist rule. After nearly a decade of struggle, the Polish Solidarity campaign for independence is successful, and the first free elections are held. The border with Austria reopens.

1991
Moldova, Estonia, Lithuania, Latvia, Ukraine and Belarus gain their independence. Soviet forces withdraw from Czechoslovakia, and the country prepares to divide politically.

1993
Czechoslovakia forms two independent countries—the Czech Republic and Slovakia. Michal Kovac is elected president of Slovakia, and Vaclav Havel becomes president of the Czech Republic.

1999
Vaira Vike-Freiberga is elected president of Latvia, and becomes Eastern Europe's first female president. Hungary, the Czech Republic and Poland join as members of NATO.

Vaira Vike-Freiberga

2002
The European Union invites Hungary, Poland, Latvia, Lithuania, Estonia, Slovakia and the Czech Republic to join in 2004. Lithuania agrees to close Ignalina nuclear power station.

TRADITIONS AND CULTURE

Midsummer's Eve LATVIA
This important festival in Latvia, also called St John's Eve, celebrates the middle of summer on 23–24 June. People light bonfires, sing and dance. They feast on special foods, such as caraway cheese and barley beer.

Puppetry CZECH REPUBLIC
A Czech tradition since medieval times, puppetry entertained and educated children. Czech puppeteers also used puppets to comment on the social and political concerns of the people. Puppetry remains very popular today.

Bohemian crystal CZECH REPUBLIC
Since the 15th century, the region of Bohemia in the western Czech Republic has manufactured Bohemian crystal. This is some of the world's finest and most expensive glassware.

Painted eggs UKRAINE
Exchanging hand-painted, decorated eggs as gifts has been an Easter tradition in Ukraine for centuries. Painting the eggs coincides with the arrival of spring. They are a symbol of rebirth, or the creation of new life.

Cowboys HUNGARY
Hungarian cowboys, or *csikósok*, manage herds of horses and cattle on the plains and grasslands of Hungary. They are admired for their skills on horseback.

Northern Europe

Iceland is known as the land of ice and fire. In just over 1,000 years, it has had more than 30 volcanic eruptions. One-third of all the lava that has erupted on land since 1500 has come from Iceland.

SWEDEN
POPULATION 8,878,000 ✳ CAPITAL STOCKHOLM

DENMARK
POPULATION 5,384,000 ✳ CAPITAL COPENHAGEN

FINLAND
POPULATION 5,191,000 ✳ CAPITAL HELSINKI

NORWAY
POPULATION 4,546,000 ✳ CAPITAL OSLO

ICELAND
POPULATION 281,000 ✳ CAPITAL REYKJAVÍK

Reindeer

Reindeer, or caribou, travel great distances in search of food. They use their long antlers to scrape away snow to expose the grasses on which they feed. Reindeer have four toes on each foot, which they spread out to keep their balance on soft snow.

Puffin

Skiing

People have used skis as a form of winter transport for thousands of years. Today, they mostly use them for sport. Ski sports include ski-jumping, slalom and downhill racing.

Breaking the ice

An icebreaker has a special steel hull to help it rise up on thick polar ice and then crush down through it. Powerful engines propel the ship up and forward.

Iceland

ICELAND

Greenland Sea
Arctic Circle
Akureyri
Langjökull Hofsjökull
Vatnajökull
Hvannadalshnúkur
6,952ft (2,119m)
ATLANTIC OCEAN
REYKJAVÍK
Keflavík

0 miles 100
0 kilometers 100

RUSSIA
Arctic Circle
Kuhmo
Kajaani
Suomussalmi
Oulujoki
Kuusamo
Oulu
Hailuoto
Raahe
Kemijärvi
Rovaniemi
Kemi
Ivalo
Inarijärvi
Karigasniemi
Kaamanen
Tana Bru
Sodankylä
Kittilä
Kemijoki
Ounasjoki
Tornio
Kolari
Muonio
Kiruna
Jukkasjärvi
Tornealven
Kebnekaise
6,926ft (2,111m)
Gällivare
Boden
Luleå
Piteå
Skellefteå
Lycksele
Vilhelmina
Arvidsjaur
Jokkmokk
Storuman
Mosjøen
Mo i Rana
Vega
Sømna
Namsos
Vikna
Namsen

Barents Sea
Varanger Fjord
Kirkenes
Lakse Fjord
Lakselv
Porsangen
North Cape
Magerøya
Alta
Søroya
Karesuando
Lapland
Arnøya
Ringvassøy
Kvaløya
Tromsø
Senja
Harstad
Narvik
Vesterålen
Lofoten
Vest Fjord
Fauske
Bodø

ARCTIC OCEAN

Konkämäeno

How fjords are formed

During the last ice age, most of the region now known as Norway was covered by immensely thick layers of ice, called glaciers. As these glaciers moved forward, their mighty weight cut deep, U-shaped channels into the river valleys. When the climate warmed, the ice melted and the sea rose, filling the coastal channels to form thousands of steep inlets, or fjords.

The ice age: 18,000 years ago

Glaciers covering Northern Europe ground down mountains and created thousands of islands and deep lakes, as well as fjords.

NORTHERN EUROPE

ARCTIC OCEAN

Polar ice cap

Northern Europe
18,000 years ago

The size of fjords

Some fjords are so deep that whales can swim in them. Sogne Fjord is the largest fjord in Norway. It stretches 127 miles (203 km) inland. Its walls rise as high as 4,291 feet (1,309 m) in places.

How glaciers form

Snow collects in a thick layer in the mountains. Its weight is so great that the snow is packed tight, forming a glacier that slowly slides downhill.

Bedrock

Glacier

Meltwater

Little Mermaid

This bronze sculpture overlooks the sea near Copenhagen. It is the national symbol of Denmark and was inspired by Hans Christian Andersen's tale of a mermaid who fell in love with a prince she saved from drowning.

Mallard duck

N
W — E
S

0 miles 160
0 kilometers 160

Northern Europe

| Forest and woodland |
| Arable land |
| Grazing |
| Arid or marginal |

REYKJAVÍK

SWEDEN LAND AREA	173,732 sq miles (449,964 sq km)
OFFICIAL LANGUAGE	Swedish
MAIN RELIGION	Christian
LIFE EXPECTANCY	80 years
LITERACY	99%

DENMARK LAND AREA	16,639 sq miles (43,094 sq km)
OFFICIAL LANGUAGE	Danish
MAIN RELIGION	Christian
LIFE EXPECTANCY	77 years
LITERACY	99%

FINLAND LAND AREA	130,128 sq miles (337,030 sq km)
OFFICIAL LANGUAGE	Finnish
MAIN RELIGION	Christian
LIFE EXPECTANCY	78 years
LITERACY	99%

NORWAY LAND AREA	125,182 sq miles (324,220 sq km)
OFFICIAL LANGUAGE	Norwegian
MAIN RELIGION	Christian
LIFE EXPECTANCY	79 years
LITERACY	99%

Reykjavík in Iceland is the world's northernmost capital. At midnight, you can see the Sun go down.

Trondheim

Bergen

OSLO

Gothenburg

Århus

COPENHAGEN

Oulu

Umea

Turku   HELSINKI

STOCKHOLM

Fishing
The waters of Northern Europe are full of both freshwater and saltwater fishes. Salmon, trout and perch are found in the inland rivers and lakes, while mackerel, cod and herring live in coastal waters. Norway is one of the world's leading fishing countries, and has fish farms for salmon and trout in the fjord areas.

Timber
Much of Northern Europe is forested with coniferous, or cone-bearing, trees, including spruce and pine. Deciduous trees, such as birch, are grown in the southern regions. The timber from these forests is produced largely for export.

NATURAL FEATURES

Lake Vänern SWEDEN
This inland lake, the largest in Sweden and dating back to 6500 BC, is situated near the Göta Canal, an inland waterway connecting Stockholm and Gothenberg.

Aurora borealis
Auroras are streaks or curtains of colored light, caused when electrically charged particles from the Sun collide with Earth's atmosphere. The aurora borealis, or northern lights, is especially bright near the Arctic Circle. It can be seen many times a year in Northern Europe.

Arctic fox

Lappland
Pine and spruce trees cover most of this region, which takes in parts of Sweden, Norway, Russia and Finland. Lappland falls within the Arctic Circle and is home to animals such as the Arctic fox, whose coat changes color with the seasons.

Åland Islands FINLAND
Thousands of islands lie in Finland's Coastal Islands region—one of its four geographic areas. Although most of them are uninhabited, about 80 of the 6,500 islands in the Åland group, off the southwest coast, are home to Swedish-speaking Finns. In this group, the island of Åland is the largest.

Cereals	Fishing
Sugar beet	Industrial center
Beef cattle	Mining
Sheep	Oil production
Pigs	Gas production
Reindeer	Timber

LARGEST CITIES

Stockholm 1,265,000

Copenhagen 1,101,000

Oslo 799,000

Helsinki 591,000

Gothenburg 510,000

WHERE PEOPLE LIVE

| Urban | | Rural |

DENMARK	85%	15%
SWEDEN	83%	17%
NORWAY	75%	25%
FINLAND	67%	33%

Tollund Man

In 1950, two brothers from the small village of Tollund on Denmark's Jutland Peninsula, while digging up peat, discovered a well-preserved body from about 2,000 years ago. The peat covering Tollund Man was removed, revealing that he wore a pointed hat, tied under his chin.

Sami people

These traditional people live mainly in Lappland, which stretches across northern Norway, Sweden and Finland into the western part of Russia. They are the only people in Northern Europe allowed to herd reindeer, and many are now involved in fishing and handicrafts.

PEOPLE

Saint Bridget c 1303–73
The patron saint of Sweden, Saint Bridget is the most celebrated saint of Northern Europe. She founded the Brigittine order of nuns and monks, and helped sick and poor people.

Hans Christian Andersen 1805–75
The stories of this Danish fairy-tale writer often had characters who went through hard times in their search for happiness. One of Andersen's most famous tales is *The Ugly Duckling*.

Edvard Munch
1863–1944
This Norwegian artist created paintings, such as *The Scream* (right), which usually showed extremes of emotion. He moved to Paris in 1889 and learned from great French artists such as Paul Gauguin.

Roald Amundsen 1872–1928
In 1911, this Norwegian explorer, in an expedition with four others, was the first person to reach the South Pole. He was also the first to fly over the North Pole.

ABBA

ABBA 1973–83
In 1974, this Swedish pop music band won the Eurovision Song Contest. For the next six years, they topped music charts the world over with one hit after another.

TRADITIONS AND CULTURE

Nobel Prize
Annual prizes in literature, science and peace are awarded by the Nobel Foundation, which was established in 1900 using funds from Alfred Nobel, the Swedish inventor of dynamite.

Saunas
Many Swedish and Finnish people have saunas about once a week. They lie or sit on wooden slats in a hot, enclosed room, then plunge into cold water.

Runes
These are the characters, made up of sticks, in the Viking alphabet. Stones were carved with runic letters and stories in memory of events.

Trolls
These odd creatures are part of Norway's rich folklore. In early tales, trolls were very large creatures who turned to stone if they went out in the sun. The nokken is a water spirit troll and the hulder troll is female.

The *Kalevala*
Elias Lönnrot compiled this Finnish national epic from ancient spoken poetry he collected in Finland and Karelia. It was published in 1835.

Legoland, built with more than 45 million Lego bricks, is Denmark's most visited attraction.

PLACES

Reykjavík ICELAND
This lively capital city, founded in AD 874, was a small fishing village until the 20th century. It was a naval base in World War II. Today it is a fishing port and home to half of Iceland's industries.

Copenhagen DENMARK
Mostly situated on the east coast of Zealand, this thriving city is Denmark's center for industry, education and culture.

Helsinki FINLAND
Much of this city was rebuilt after fire destroyed it in the 19th century. The Helsinki Cathedral, a grand, domed building, was one of the main projects.

Bergen waterfront

Bergen NORWAY
As Norway's second-largest city and one of the country's chief ports, Bergen is a center for manufacture and trade. The waterfront is lined with wharves from the 13th century.

Stockholm SWEDEN
This picturesque city, Sweden's capital, is a blend of old and new. Its Old Town reflects the Middle Ages, sitting alongside modern life in the rest of the city.

Kronborg Castle DENMARK
This noble castle in Elsinore provided the setting for Hamlet's home in Shakespeare's play. It is one of Northern Europe's most renowned buildings.

Stavkirks

These wooden places of worship, known as stave churches, were built in Norway about 1,000 years ago after the Vikings converted to Christianity. They have high-pitched roofs and are decorated with a mix of Viking and Christian symbols. Dragons (a Viking symbol) often appear at the ends of the gables and crosses (a Christian symbol) are placed at the doors and windows.

Stavkirk in Vikøyri, built in 1130

HISTORY AT A GLANCE
THE VIKINGS

Viking pendants, worn in battle

NORSE MYTHS
Many myths and legends evolved during Viking times. The Vikings believed in gods and goddesses who lived in a place called Asgard. Each god had its own characteristics—Thor was the god of thunder and was very strong; Odin was the god of wisdom and war, and had magic powers; and Frey, a fertility god, had a boat in which all the gods could travel.

VIKING RAIDS
Between the 8th and 11th centuries, fierce Vikings from Norway, Sweden and Denmark, in search of more territory, metals and slaves, raided the far-flung lands of Europe and even North America. They were clever traders and craftsmen who told wonderful stories.

LONGSHIPS
The Vikings were skilled navigators who traveled in longships. The wooden hull was built from 16 overlapping planks. A carved figure, often a dragon, sat at the prow, or front, of the ship.

Viking longship

WEAPONS
A Viking warrior valued his weapons greatly. With his ax, shield and spear at his side, he was armed for any battle. Shields were usually wooden with an iron center to protect the warrior's hand, and the ax, made from iron, had engraved silver patterns on it.

HOUSES
Timber, straw or stone was used to make long, narrow houses, called longhouses. Early in the Viking age, houses did not have windows and were dark but, later, animal bladders were stretched across openings in the wall to let in some light. A hearth was always in the center.

BURIALS
Viking graves were often marked out in the shape of boats. Before Christianity, possessions were buried with the body for use in the next life. According to legend, dead warriors were taken by women to Valhalla—the Viking heaven.

Leif Eriksson sighting America

EXPLORERS
The Vikings were great adventurers, keen to explore lands near and far. In AD 982, Erik the Red discovered Greenland after he left Iceland in search of a new land. Leif Eriksson, one of Eric's sons, is thought to have been the first Viking to land in North America. Harald Haardraade, a member of the Byzantine fighting Vikings called the Varangian Guard, was the last Viking to land in England. The last of the warrior Viking kings, he was killed in battle in 1066.

ARCTIC OCEAN

Queen Elizabeth Islands

Parry Island

Melville Island

Bathurst Island

Banks Island

Prince o Wales Isla

Victoria Island

Chukchi Sea

Beaufort Sea

Bering Strait

Brooks Range

Great Bear Lake

Mackenzie

Bering Sea

Mt McKinley
20,321ft (6,194m)

Yukon

Alaska ▲ Range

Mackenzie Mountains

Great Slave Lake

Aleutian Islands

Aleutian Range

Lake Athabasca

Gulf of Alaska

Coast Mountains

Peace

Reindeer Lake

Saskatchewan

R O C K Y

Lake Manitoba

PACIFIC OCEAN

Mt Rainier
14,409ft (4,392m) ▲

Cascade Range

Coast Ranges

Columbia

M o u n t a i n s

G r e a

Snake

Great Salt Lake

Sierra Nevada

G r e a t

B a s i n

Mt Whitney
14,495ft (4,418m) ▲

Mt Elbert ▲
14,432ft (4,399m)

▲ Death Valley
–282ft (–86m)

Colorado

C o l o r a d o

P l a t e a u

Mojave Desert

Colorado

Grand Canyon

Sonoran Desert

B a j a   C a l i f o r n i a

Gulf of California

S i e r r a   M a d r e   O c c i d e n t a l

Rio Grande

S i e r r a   M a d r e   O r i e n t a l

Volcan Popocate
17,837ft (5,4.

Sierra Madr

esmere
sland

on Island
rset

Greenland

Baffin Bay

Baffin Island

Melville
Peninsula

Davis Strait

Foxe
Basin

Hudson Strait

Péninsule
d'Ungava

Labrador
Sea

Hudson
Bay

Labrador

anadian Shield

peg

Reservoir
Manicouagan

Laurentian Mountains

Newfoundland

Lake
Nipigon

Lake Superior

Nova
Scotia

Great Lakes

Lake
Huron

Central Lowlands

Lake
Michigan

Lake Ontario

Lake Erie

ATLANTIC OCEAN

ns

Missouri

Ohio

pl

Appalachian Mountains

Arkansas

Mississippi

Gulf–Atlantic Coastal Plain

s

North America

Mississipi
Delta

The Bahamas

West Indies

Gulf of Mexico

Cuba

Greater Antilles

Leeward Islands

Yucatan
Peninsula

co de Orizaba
,405ft (5,610m)

Caribbean Sea

Lesser Antilles

ur

Lake
Nicaragua

sthmus of Panama

Canada

Ice hockey

Snow geese

Huge flocks of snow geese fly over Canada each year as they migrate to California for the winter. They gather in an area near the Beaufort Sea to fatten up for their flight.

CANADA
POPULATION 32,207,000 • CAPITAL OTTAWA

Inuit hunter

The territory of Nunavut covers about one-fifth of Canada and is the homeland of the Inuit people. Snowmobiles make it easier to travel across this vast area.

Salmon fishing

Pacific salmon are caught on Canada's west coast, and most are canned for export. Fishing is also an important industry on Canada's east coast.

Wheat harvesting

The prairies of central Canada are among the world's richest farming regions. Cereals, fruit and vegetables are some of the main crops. Ranching is also common on the prairies.

Gray jay

### Map labels

ARCTIC OCEAN
Beaufort Sea
Queen Elizabeth Islands
Ellesmere Island
Nares Strait
Axel Heiberg Island
Melville Island
Devon Island
Lancaster Sound
Somerset Island
Brodeur Peninsula
Viscount Melville Sound
Stefansson Island
Prince of Wales Island
Boothia Peninsula
Gulf of Boothia
Banks Island
Passage Point
Prince Albert Peninsula
Storkerson Peninsula
McClintock Channel
Igloo
Amundsen Gulf
Uluqsaqtuuk
Victoria Island
Collinson Peninsula
Simpson Peninsula
Mackenzie Bay
Cape Dalhousie
Cape Parry
Wollaston Peninsula
King William Island
Pelly Bay
Ikaahuk
Tuktoyaktuk
Aklavik
Inuvik
Cambridge Bay
Gjoa Haven
Repulse Bay
Arctic Circle
Mackenzie
Fort Good Hope
Norman Wells
Great Bear Lake
Napaktulik Lake
NUNAVUT
Contwoyto Lake
Aberdeen Lake
Baker Lake
Mayo
Back
YUKON TERRITORY
Mt Logan 19,550ft (5,959m)
Haines Junction
WHITEHORSE
NORTHWEST TERRITORIES
Aylmer Lake
Dubawnt Lake
USA (ALASKA)
Fort Providence
Fort Liard
Great Slave Lake
YELLOWKNIFE
Mt Fairweather 15,322ft (4,670m)
JUNEAU
Hay River
Fort Nelson
Rocky Mountains
Slave
BRITISH COLUMBIA
Peace
Lake Athabasca
Wollaston Lake
Churchill
Cape Chu
CAN
Cape Knox
ALBERTA
Fort St John
Reindeer Lake
Prince Rupert
Peace River
Fort McMurray
Thompson
Queen Charlotte Islands
Prince George
Grande Prairie
Lesser Slave Lake
Athabasca
SASKATCHEWAN
MANITOBA
Flin Flon
Queen Charlotte Sound
Mt Robson 12,972ft (3,954m)
North Saskatchewan
The Pas
Cedar Lake
Lake Winnipeg
Port Hardy
Mt Waddington 13,261ft (4,042m)
EDMONTON
Camrose
Prince Albert
Melfort
Cape Cook
Red Deer
North Battleford
Saskatoon
Lake Winnipegosis
Dauphin
Vancouver Island
Kamloops
Banff
Lake Winnipegosis
Nanaimo
Vernon
Kelowna
Calgary
Kindersley
Yorkton
Lake Manitoba
Selkirk
Rennie
Vancouver
Abbotsford
Lethbridge
Medicine Hat
Swift Current
REGINA
Brandon
Portage la Prairie
WINNIPEG
Cape Flattery
Weyburn
Ke
VICTORIA
Seattle
UNITED STATES OF AMERICA
Fran
PACIFIC OCEAN

0 miles 500
0 kilometers 500

N
W E
S

Corythosaurus

Dinosaurs from Canada's past

About 75 million years ago, dinosaurs roamed along the gullies and rivers of southern Alberta. Ten million years later, the dinosaurs vanished. In 1909, a rancher reported that he had discovered dinosaur bones on his property. Today that property is part of the Dinosaur Provincial Park. Up to 250 dinosaur skeletons of 36 different species have been found there. They can be seen in more than 30 museums all round the world.

Ankylosaurus
This dinosaur used its massive tail club to protect itself.

Albertosaurus
This dinosaur's name means "Alberta lizard." It grew to 26 feet (8 m) long.

Fossil foot
This fossil foot of *Albertosaurus* shows its powerful clawed toes.

Parasaurolophus
This dinosaur probably used the long crest on its head to signal to other dinosaurs.

Triceratops
This bulky, slow-moving dinosaur was a plant eater. It grew to 30 feet (9 m) long.

Container shipping
Canada is the world's largest supplier of wood products, but its factories also produce many kinds of industrial goods. About 90 percent of Canada's exports are sent to the USA.

The Bay of Fundy, between New Brunswick and Nova Scotia, has the highest tides in the world. The difference between high and low tide can be as large as a three-story building.

Beaver

CN Tower, Toronto
The CN Tower, a telecommunications hub, rises high above the city of Toronto. When it was built in 1976, it was the world's tallest building.

GREENLAND
(to Denmark)
75°
70°

Baffin Bay

Davis Strait

Arctic Circle
65°

Kangeeak Point
Cape Dyer

Cumberland Peninsula
Cape Mercy
Cumberland Sound

Prince Charles Island
Nettilling Lake
Amadjuak Lake

Foxe Basin

60°

Labrador Sea

Foxe Peninsula

IQALUIT

Resolution Island

55°

Hudson Strait
Cape Labrador

Cap Hopes Advance
Akpatok Island

Ivujivik

Péninsule d'Ungava

Ungava Bay

Mansel Island

Nain

Cartwright

Ottawa Islands

Inukjuak

Labrador

NEWFOUNDLAND AND LABRADOR

Cape Bauld
50°

Kuujjuaq

Smallwood Reservoir
Happy Valley Goose Bay

Churchill

Gander
ST JOHN'S

Belcher Islands

QUEBEC

Newfoundland

Corner Brook

45°

 severn

Réservoir la Grande Trois
Réservoir Manicouagan
Lac Caniapiscau

Natashquan
Île d'Anticosti
Gulf of St Lawrence

ST PIERRE & MIQUELON
(to France)

James Bay

Réservoir la Grande Deux

Sept-Îles
Gaspé

Cape Breton Island

55°

Akimiski Island

Eastmain
Lac Mistassini

Baie Comeau
Matane

PRINCE EDWARD ISLAND
Prince Edward Island

Glace Bay

Sydney

ATLANTIC OCEAN

Attawapiskat

Nottaway
Périboncq

Chibougamau

Rivière du-Loup
Cambellton
NEW BRUNSWICK
Moncton

CHARLOTTETOWN

New Glasgow
Truro

HALIFAX

Albany

Harricana
Moose
Lac Saint-Jean
Jonquière
Chicoutimi

60°

Moosonee

ONTARIO

Val-d'Or

FREDERICTON
St John
NOVA SCOTIA

Lake Nipigon

Kapuskasing

Kirkland Lake
Réservoir Cabonga

La Tuque
Trois-Rivières
Victoriaville
QUÉBEC

Bay of Fundy
Liverpool

Timmins

Joliette
Sorel
Drummondville
Sherbrooke

Yarmouth

Marathon

North Bay
Pembroke
OTTAWA
Montreal
St Jean sur-Richelieu-
Cornwall

Gulf of Maine

65°

Thunder Bay
Wawa
Sudbury
Lake Nipissing

pigon
Sault Ste Marie

Owen Sound
Orillia
Peterborough

Lake Superior

Oshawa
TORONTO
Kitchener
Niagara Falls
St Catharines
Buffalo
Lake Ontario

70°

Lake Michigan
Lake Huron

London
Sarnia
Lake Erie
Rochester

Detroit
Erie

Windsor

Cleveland

Milwaukee
Chicago

90°
85°
80°
75°

Canada

LAND AREA	3,511,023 sq miles (9,093,507 sq km)
OFFICIAL LANGUAGE	English/French
MAIN RELIGION	Christian
LIFE EXPECTANCY	80 years
LITERACY	97%

- Forest and woodland
- Arable land
- Grazing
- Arid or marginal

Maple syrup
The maple trees that grow throughout Canada are the source for this much-loved sweet treat. At the end of winter, a special tap, or spigot, is pushed into the trunk of the maple tree and the sticky sap drips into a bucket that hangs from the spigot. The sap is then boiled to produce the sugary syrup.

USING THE LAND

- Cereals
- Fruit and vegetables
- Fruit
- Beef cattle
- Fishing
- Industrial center
- Mining
- Oil production
- Gas production
- Timber
- Tourism
- Winter sports

Cod fishing
The shallow waters of Newfoundland's continental shelf, particularly the Grand Banks, were once teeming with cod. When Cabot discovered the area in 1497 he called it "the land of cod." European fishermen migrated to the area soon after to fish the waters. Today, supplies are much reduced as a result of overfishing.

Explorers

Explorers from England and France, in search of the New World, were among the first Europeans to land on Canada's shores. John Cabot was England's first arrival and Frenchman Jacques Cartier soon followed. After several attempts, Henry Hudson (*above*) discovered Hudson Bay for England in 1610, two years after Samuel de Champlain had founded the city of Québec.

Map labels: Iqaluit, Whitehorse, Yellowknife, Churchill, St John's, Edmonton, Saskatoon, Québec, Halifax, Calgary, Winnipeg, Thunder Bay, Montreal, OTTAWA, Vancouver, Toronto

NATURAL FEATURES

Hudson Bay
This inland sea on Canada's northern boundary is linked by channels and straits to both the Atlantic and Arctic oceans. Its coastal marshes provide a wetland habitat for an array of unique animals, notably bird species.

Nunavut
Established as Inuit territory in 1999, Nunavut (*below*), meaning "our people," is in the eastern Arctic region. The Inuit have claim to native land in this region, which includes Baffin and Ellesmere islands.

Rocky Mountains
This string of mountain ranges stretches for 3,000 miles (4,800 km) from the Yukon in Canada, down through the USA to Mexico. Banff National Park, home of the Moraine Lake, is in the Canadian Rockies.

Moraine Lake

The prairies
These flat, fertile, treeless grasslands east of the Rockies—which seem to stretch forever—now contain 75 percent of Canada's farmland, although they were once home to roaming buffalo herds.

St Lawrence River
The waters of Lake Ontario—one of the Great Lakes—flow into this river. The icy river supports a population of about 650 beluga whales.

Beluga whale

Forty percent of Toronto's population was born overseas— UNESCO voted it the world's most diverse city.

Wheat
This grain crop—Canada's largest agricultural export—is ideally suited to the natural grassland areas of the prairies. Two-thirds of Canadian wheat is grown in the Saskatchewan province. Once harvested, the grain is pooled, then stored in tall structures called silos (*above*), which dot the landscape.

WHERE PEOPLE LIVE

Urban	Rural
77%	23%

HIGHEST MOUNTAINS

Mt Logan 19,551 feet (5,959 m)	Mt Lucania 17,146 feet (5,226 m)
Mt St Elias 18,009 feet (5,489 m)	King Peak 16,972 feet (5,173 m)

LARGEST CITIES

Toronto 4,559,000

Montreal 3,264,000

Vancouver 1,883,000

Calgary 943,000

Ottawa 864,000

PLACES

Québec City
Situated above the mighty St Lawrence River, this capital city of Québec province has a predominantly French lifestyle, and over 90 percent of the population speaks French. Its Old Town is filled with classic 18th- and 19th-century houses.

Château Frontenac, Québec City

Vancouver
This busy port is Canada's contact point for trade with Japan and the East. Canada Place Pavilion overlooks the harbor, and the city's coastal setting, framed by hills and mountains, is ideal for outdoor sports.

St John's
Established in 1528 after John Cabot's discovery of its harbor, this city was the first British colony outside England, and is the oldest city in North America. It is where the Trans-Canada Highway starts.

Parliament building
Ottawa's parliament building (*above*), built in the mid-19th century and overlooking the Ottawa River, is the seat of Canada's government.

Dawson
During the gold rush of the late 1800s, this town (*below*) in the Klondike region was home to 40,000 people; now only about 2,000 people live there. Buildings from the gold rush have been preserved.

Basketball was invented in 1891 by James Naismith, a Canadian teacher, to occupy his students.

TRADITIONS AND CULTURE

Curling
Curling, one of Canada's most popular winter sports, is played on ice. Team members compete to slide a smooth, round stone toward a mark, called a tee.

Totem poles
These tall cedar poles depicting totems, or storytelling symbols, of different tribes were carved by native peoples, such as the Tlingits, of North America.

Tlingit totem pole

Calgary Stampede
Every July, this huge 10-day rodeo in Calgary attracts cowboys who compete in a range of horse- and bull-racing events. In the chuckwagon-racing event (*above*), introduced in 1925, cowboys sit on a wagon behind teams of four horses and race around a track.

Inuit carvings
The Inuit have carved sculptures from stone and other materials for thousands of years. Today, the carvings are sold to collectors around the world.

Dog mushing
This activity, in which people travel across snow-covered land on sleds pulled by teams of dogs, is a competitive sport in Canada and Alaska. Huskies are used as they are intelligent and adapt well to cold conditions.

Buffalo jump
For almost 6,000 years, the native people of the North American Plains hunted buffalo by forcing them to run over a cliff, then collecting their carcasses. At Alberta, the Head-Smashed-In Buffalo Jump, named for a boy who was crushed by the falling beasts, has been declared a World Heritage Site by UNESCO.

Huskies

Canadian Mounties
The Royal Canadian Mounted Police, called the Mounties, was established in 1873 to maintain order between new settlers and native people in Canada's northwest. The Mounties rode horses, wore distinctive red jackets and flat-brimmed hats, and, as legend goes, "always got their man." Today, they patrol in cars and ride horses only on special occasions.

PEOPLE

Laura Secord 1775–1868
In 1813, during the Battle of Beaver Dams, this courageous woman trekked through the wilds for 18 hours to inform the British that the USA intended to attack and take over Niagara Peninsula. Her news saved this territory.

Norman Bethune 1890–1939
Born in Ontario, this dedicated doctor pioneered many medical procedures, particularly in blood transfusions, that changed the lives of the sick. He worked with soldiers in China, and devised a public health system for Canada.

Joe Shuster 1914–92
This talented artist, who moved from Canada to Ohio, USA, in 1923, teamed up with writer Jerry Siegel to create *Superman*, one of the world's most successful comic strips.

Shuster's Superman

Pierre Trudeau 1919–2000
First elected as Canada's prime minister in 1968, and in power for 16 years, this progressive politician led the country through some of its most challenging times.

Jim Carrey born 1962
This internationally renowned actor is known for his comedy antics and impersonations, as well as character acting.

Jim Carrey in *The Mask*

HISTORY AT A GLANCE

c 20,000 BC
The first inhabitants, ancestors of the Inuit, come to Alaska from Asia via the Bering Strait.

AD 1000
Led by Leif Eriksson, the Vikings start to colonize the Newfoundland coast, but not permanently.

1497
John Cabot, an Italian–British explorer, reaches and names Newfoundland, claiming it for Britain.

1534
Jacques Cartier explores the Gulf of St Lawrence, then discovers the St Lawrence River and claims Canada for France.

Jacques Cartier

1605
The first European colony is established by France at Port Royal, Nova Scotia. Samuel de Champlain founds Québec three years later.

1663
Canada, known as New France, becomes a province of France.

1670
King Charles II of England allows the Hudson Bay Company to trap animals. Trade, especially in fur, is encouraged between England and Canada.

1754
Britain and France fight in the French and Indian War. France gives up Québec to Britain.

1759
Battle of the Plains of Abraham is fought outside Québec City and France is defeated by Britain. By 1763, the whole of Canada is in Britain's hands.
Québec soldier

1793
Alexander Mackenzie travels overland to reach the west coast of Canada—the Pacific Ocean. He is the first European to do so.

1846
The Oregon Treaty confirms Canada's northwest borders with the USA. The Dominion of Canada is established 21 years later.

1885
Canadian Pacific Railway is completed, creating a link across the country.

Canadian Pacific Railway

1949
Newfoundland becomes the newest province. Canada is a founding member of NATO.

1968
The Québec Party is formed, sparking independence for the province.

1989
Britain transfers all power relating to Canada in British law back to Canada.

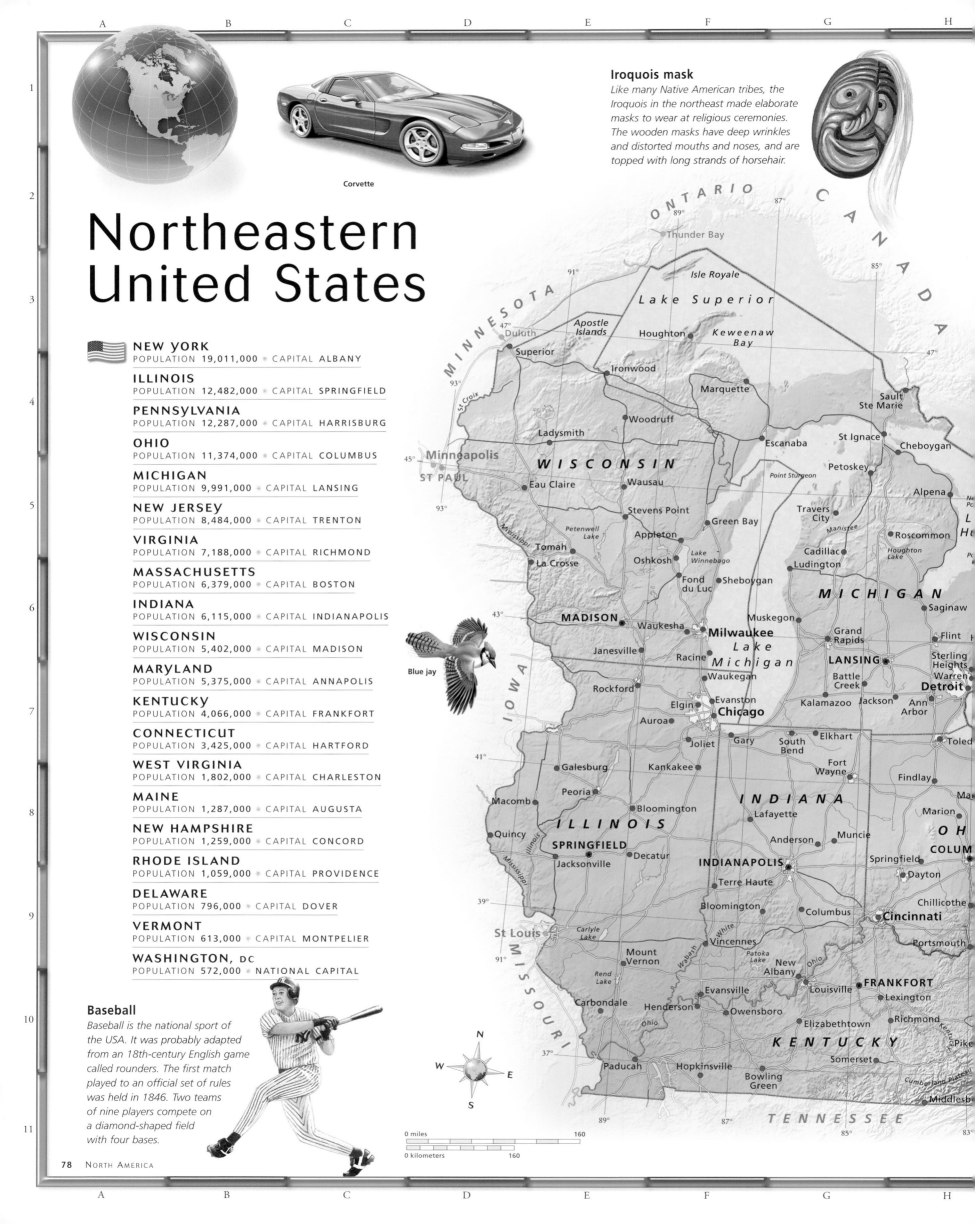

Corvette

Iroquois mask
Like many Native American tribes, the Iroquois in the northeast made elaborate masks to wear at religious ceremonies. The wooden masks have deep wrinkles and distorted mouths and noses, and are topped with long strands of horsehair.

Northeastern United States

NEW YORK
POPULATION 19,011,000 • CAPITAL ALBANY

ILLINOIS
POPULATION 12,482,000 • CAPITAL SPRINGFIELD

PENNSYLVANIA
POPULATION 12,287,000 • CAPITAL HARRISBURG

OHIO
POPULATION 11,374,000 • CAPITAL COLUMBUS

MICHIGAN
POPULATION 9,991,000 • CAPITAL LANSING

NEW JERSEY
POPULATION 8,484,000 • CAPITAL TRENTON

VIRGINIA
POPULATION 7,188,000 • CAPITAL RICHMOND

MASSACHUSETTS
POPULATION 6,379,000 • CAPITAL BOSTON

INDIANA
POPULATION 6,115,000 • CAPITAL INDIANAPOLIS

WISCONSIN
POPULATION 5,402,000 • CAPITAL MADISON

MARYLAND
POPULATION 5,375,000 • CAPITAL ANNAPOLIS

KENTUCKY
POPULATION 4,066,000 • CAPITAL FRANKFORT

CONNECTICUT
POPULATION 3,425,000 • CAPITAL HARTFORD

WEST VIRGINIA
POPULATION 1,802,000 • CAPITAL CHARLESTON

MAINE
POPULATION 1,287,000 • CAPITAL AUGUSTA

NEW HAMPSHIRE
POPULATION 1,259,000 • CAPITAL CONCORD

RHODE ISLAND
POPULATION 1,059,000 • CAPITAL PROVIDENCE

DELAWARE
POPULATION 796,000 • CAPITAL DOVER

VERMONT
POPULATION 613,000 • CAPITAL MONTPELIER

WASHINGTON, DC
POPULATION 572,000 • NATIONAL CAPITAL

Blue jay

Baseball
Baseball is the national sport of the USA. It was probably adapted from an 18th-century English game called rounders. The first match played to an official set of rules was held in 1846. Two teams of nine players compete on a diamond-shaped field with four bases.

0 miles 160
0 kilometers 160

New York City

The largest city in the USA stands at the mouth of the Hudson River and is an important seaport. Named New York in 1664, it is a center of world trade and finance, art, entertainment and fashion. The city has long been seen as a place of opportunity and has attracted migrants from all over the world.

Statue of Liberty
This statue, erected in 1886, is an international symbol of refuge and democracy.

Empire State Building
The architect's aim was to make this skyscraper, built in 1931, look like a pencil.

Chrysler Building
This steel-framed tower was built in 1930 in the ornate Art Deco style.

Brooklyn Bridge

Woodchuck

Traditional farmhouse
Farmhouses in New England, an area extending from the state of Maine to Albany, New York, are of simple design. Made of timber, they are often shaped like a box, with a steep roof so that snow slides off in winter.

Lobster fishing
The lobster industry is important to the economy of the state of Maine. The cold waters of New England's shoreline are an ideal habitat for lobsters. Their dark shells turn red when cooked.

The *Mayflower*
In 1620, the Pilgrim Fathers sailed from England aboard the Mayflower. They arrived at what is now Plymouth, Massachusetts, and founded one of the first permanent European settlements.

Philadelphia in Pennsylvania was the capital city of the USA from 1790 to 1800. It was here that the Declaration of Independence was proclaimed.

Niagara Falls
Niagara Falls creates a boundary between the USA and Canada. It is made up of two large waterfalls and one small one. The American Falls are about 1,000 feet (300 m) long; the Horseshoe Falls on the Canadian side are twice as long.

CANADA

QUÉBEC

ONTARIO

NEW BRUNSWICK

Madawaska

Presque Isle

Houlton

Chésuncook Lake

Moosehead Lake

Mt Katahdin
5,269ft (1,606m)

MAINE

Bangor

Bar Harbor
Mount Desert Island

St Lawrence

Montréal

Longueuil

Sherbrooke

Newport

Lake Champlain

Plattsburgh

Mt Washington
6,293ft (1,918m)

MONTPELIER

Adirondack Mountains

Mt Marcy
5,344ft (1,629m)

Watertown

NEW HAMPSHIRE

AUGUSTA

Brunswick

Portland

Biddeford

VERMONT

Lebanon

Laconia

CONCORD

Portsmouth

TORONTO

Lake Ontario

Oneida Lake

Hamilton

Rochester

St Catherines

Niagara Falls

Buffalo

NEW YORK

Finger Lakes

Catskill Mountains

Manchester

Nashua

Lowell

Worcester

ALBANY

MASSACHUSETTS

BOSTON

Pittsfield

Springfield

Plymouth

Cape Cod

Orleans

Syracuse

Schenectady

Troy

Utica

Glens Falls

Lake Erie

Erie

Dunkirk

Olean

Ithaca

Elmira

Binghamton

Kingston

Jamestown

Mansfield

HARTFORD

Warwick

PROVIDENCE

New Bedford

CONNECTICUT

Newport

RHODE ISLAND

Nantucket

Nantucket Island

Ashtabula

Cleveland

Warren

Meadville

Scranton

Wilkes Barre

Milford

Middletown

Waterbury

New Haven

Bridgeport

Montauk Point

Youngstown

Williamsport

PENNSYLVANIA

Paterson

Stamford

Yonkers

Long Island

Canton

Altoona

State College

Allentown

Reading

Jersey City

Newark

Elizabeth

New York

Pittsburgh

Carlisle

HARRISBURG

Lancaster

TRENTON

Philadelphia

Wheeling

Uniontown

York

Wilmington

NEW JERSEY

esville

Clarksburg

Cumberland

Hagerstown

MARYLAND

DOVER

DELAWARE

Parkersburg

Spruce Knob
4,859ft (1,481m)

Baltimore

Arlington

ANNAPOLIS

WEST VIRGINIA

Alexandria

WASHINGTON, DC

Albans

Harrisonburg

Fredericksburg

Salisbury

LESTON

Staunton

Charlottesville

Assateague Island

ckley

VIRGINIA

RICHMOND

Bluestone Lake

Petersburg

Cape Charles

Hampton

Norfolk

Bluefield

Roanoke

Newport News

Portsmouth

Virginia Beach

NORTH CAROLINA

ATLANTIC OCEAN

Gulf of Maine

Chesapeake Bay

Potomac

Ohio

Appalachian Mountains

New England Mountains

Hudson

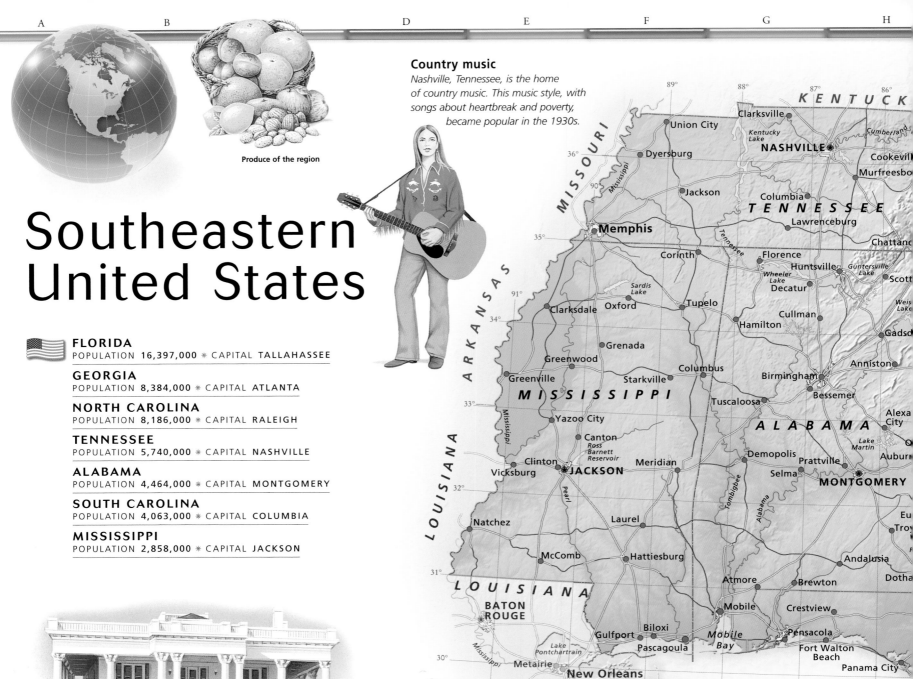

Country music
Nashville, Tennessee, is the home of country music. This music style, with songs about heartbreak and poverty, became popular in the 1930s.

Produce of the region

Southeastern United States

FLORIDA
POPULATION 16,397,000 ✳ CAPITAL TALLAHASSEE

GEORGIA
POPULATION 8,384,000 ✳ CAPITAL ATLANTA

NORTH CAROLINA
POPULATION 8,186,000 ✳ CAPITAL RALEIGH

TENNESSEE
POPULATION 5,740,000 ✳ CAPITAL NASHVILLE

ALABAMA
POPULATION 4,464,000 ✳ CAPITAL MONTGOMERY

SOUTH CAROLINA
POPULATION 4,063,000 ✳ CAPITAL COLUMBIA

MISSISSIPPI
POPULATION 2,858,000 ✳ CAPITAL JACKSON

Plantation mansion
In the early 1800s, wealthy plantation owners in the southern states built large, elegant homes inspired by classical Greek architecture. These mansions featured imposing covered porches with pillars, sweeping staircases and huge ballrooms. They were often painted white.

In 1803, the USA paid France US$15 million for 828,000 square miles (2,144,500 sq km) of land west of the Mississippi River. This Louisiana Purchase, as it was called, doubled the nation's size.

Mississippi steamboat
The Mississippi is the largest river in North America and one of the world's busiest commercial waterways. Steam-powered boats carried building and farm goods, food and people along the river throughout the 1900s. Today, paddle-wheelers are tourist boats.

Cotton farming
The USA is one of the world's largest cotton producers. Cotton plantations were established in the southern states in the early 1800s. The invention of machinery for harvesting and cleaning the cotton revolutionized the industry in the mid-1800s and reduced the need for human labor.

0 miles 140
0 kilometers 140

VIRGINIA

Cumberland Plateau

84° 83° 82° 81° 80° 79° 78° 77° 76°

Johnson City
Bristol
Winston Salem
Greensboro
Henderson
Elizabeth City
36°
Knoxville
Durham
High Point
Rocky Mount
Roanoke Island
Ashville
▲ Mt Mitchell 6,683ft (2,037m)
Lake Norman
RALEIGH
Greenville
Hatteras Island

NORTH CAROLINA

Pamlico Sound
Cape Hatteras

Gastonia
Goldsboro
New Bern
Raleigh Bay 35°
veland
Charlotte
Fayetteville
Havelock
Greenville
Rock Hill
Laurinburg
Jacksonville
Cape Lookout
Spartanburg
Lumberton

Lake Sidney Lanier
Hartwell Lake
Gainesville
Greenwood
Florence
Onslow Bay
3
34°

SOUTH CAROLINA

ATLANTA
Athens
Richard B. Russell Lake
Lake Murray
COLUMBIA
Sumter
Wilmington
Decatur
Clark Hill Reservoir
Long Bay
Cape Fear
78°

GEORGIA
Augusta
Orangeburg
Lake Marion
Myrtle Beach
76°
Lake Oconee
Santee
Lake Moultrie
Savannah
Lake Sinclair
Milledgeville
33°
Macon
Cape Romain
ibus
Dublin
Statesboro
Mount Pleasant
Charleston
Cordele
Savannah
Altamaha
Ocmulgee
32°
Albany
Tifton
79°
Bainbridge
Waycross
Brunswick
Lake Seminole
Valdosta
31°
Thomasville
TALLAHASSEE
Jacksonville

ATLANTIC OCEAN

Lake City
St Augustine
30°
84°
Apalachee Bay
Gainesville
29°
29°
Ocala
Lake George
Daytona Beach
Deltona
Orlando
Cape Canaveral
Kissimmee
Melbourne
28°
Tampa
Lakeland
28°
Clearwater
St Petersburg
Largo
FLORIDA
Tampa Bay
Sarasota
83°
Fort Pierce
27°
Lake Okeechobee
27°
Port Charlotte
West Palm Beach
Charlotte Harbor
Fort Myers
Sanibel Island
Cape Coral
Boca Raton
Everglades
Pompano Beach
Naples
Fort Lauderdale
Hollywood
26°
Hialeah
Miami
26°
Ten Thousand Islands
Cape Romano
Miami Beach
Kendall
82°
Key Largo
Cape Sable
Key Largo
25°
25°
Florida Bay
Florida Keys
Straits of Florida
Marquesas Keys
Key West
80°
81°
80°

Alligator

American football

American football is a combination of rugby and soccer. It developed in schools and colleges during the 1860s and is now the nation's favorite winter game. Football is a strenuous body-contact sport involving running, tackling and passing the ball.

Kennedy Space Center

The John F. Kennedy Space Center was built by NASA (National Aeronautics and Space Administration) at Cape Canaveral, Florida, as the launch site for United States' space flights. The first flight with an astronaut on board took off in 1961. In 1969, Apollo 11 flew astronauts to the Moon for the first time. The space shuttle, the first reusable spacecraft, first flew in 1981. The shuttle has an orbiter space-plane, booster rockets and an external fuel tank.

Flight of the space shuttle

The empty external fuel tank is dropped.

The rocket boosters fall away.

Takeoff

Space shuttle is prepared for takeoff.

The orbiter's engines propel it into orbit.

A satellite is launched from the payload bay.

The engines fire to begin the shuttle's descent.

It glows red as it plunges through the atmosphere.

The orbiter glides down toward the runway.

Touchdown

Thermal tiles
Tiles cover the orbiter to protect it from intense heat as it re-enters the atmosphere.

Flight deck
The space shuttle can carry up to eight people. The orbiter is controlled by its commander and pilot.

Robot arm
A robot arm inside the orbiter moves satellites and experiments into and out of the bay.

Rocket thrusters
Powerful thrusters in the nose and tail are fired to change the orbiter's position.

Central United States

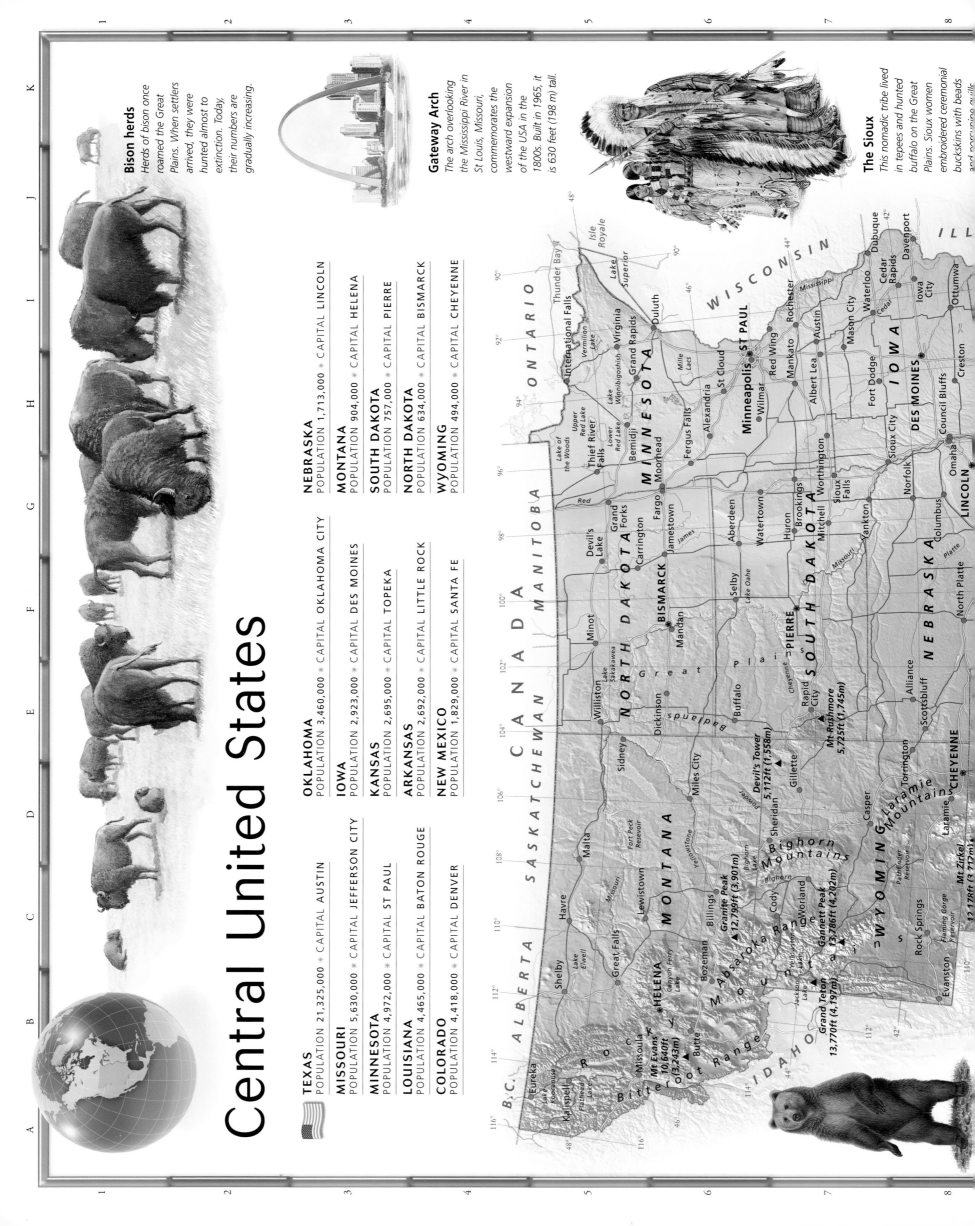

Bison herds

Herds of bison once roamed the Great Plains. When settlers arrived, they were hunted almost to extinction. Today, their numbers are gradually increasing.

Gateway Arch

The arch overlooking the Mississippi River in St Louis, Missouri, commemorates the westward expansion of the USA in the 1800s. Built in 1965, it is 630 feet (198 m) tall.

The Sioux

This nomadic tribe lived in tepees and hunted buffalo on the Great Plains. Sioux women embroidered ceremonial buckskins with beads and porcupine quills.

TEXAS
POPULATION 21,325,000 ✳ CAPITAL AUSTIN

MISSOURI
POPULATION 5,630,000 ✳ CAPITAL JEFFERSON CITY

MINNESOTA
POPULATION 4,972,000 ✳ CAPITAL ST PAUL

LOUISIANA
POPULATION 4,465,000 ✳ CAPITAL BATON ROUGE

COLORADO
POPULATION 4,418,000 ✳ CAPITAL DENVER

OKLAHOMA
POPULATION 3,460,000 ✳ CAPITAL OKLAHOMA CITY

IOWA
POPULATION 2,923,000 ✳ CAPITAL DES MOINES

KANSAS
POPULATION 2,695,000 ✳ CAPITAL TOPEKA

ARKANSAS
POPULATION 2,692,000 ✳ CAPITAL LITTLE ROCK

NEW MEXICO
POPULATION 1,829,000 ✳ CAPITAL SANTA FE

NEBRASKA
POPULATION 1,713,000 ✳ CAPITAL LINCOLN

MONTANA
POPULATION 904,000 ✳ CAPITAL HELENA

SOUTH DAKOTA
POPULATION 757,000 ✳ CAPITAL PIERRE

NORTH DAKOTA
POPULATION 634,000 ✳ CAPITAL BISMARCK

WYOMING
POPULATION 494,000 ✳ CAPITAL CHEYENNE

Satellite dishes

The Very Large Array telescope in the desert near Socorro, New Mexico, consists of 27 large dish antennas. They are ideally sited to receive radio emissions from the universe because there is no interference from city lights and noise.

Texas oil

Nearly a fourth of all the oil produced in the USA comes from Texan fields. Some are small, privately owned operations that produce just a few barrels a day. The first major oil discovery in Texas was made in 1901. About 56 percent of the nation's oil is imported.

Carlsbad Caverns

Carlsbad Caverns National Park, in New Mexico, is a spectacular maze of chambers deep underground that covers 73 square miles (189 sq km). The caverns were carved out over thousands of years by rain seeping into limestone. The dissolved limestone was deposited by the dripping water onto floors and ceilings, and slowly formed stalagmites and other elaborate shapes.

Straw-shaped formations

Stalactite
Some stalactites are long and pointed. Others grow into the shape of huge chandeliers.

Pillar
A pillar forms when a stalactite and a stalagmite meet.

Stalagmite
The width of a stalagmite depends on the height of the fall of the dissolved limestone.

10,000 years

5,000 years

1,000 years

Cross section of a stalactite
The center of a stalactite is the first layer in its formation.

Cave entrance

More tornadoes occur in the USA than in any other country. Around 750 of these spinning columns of air strike each year, most of them in the Great Plains.

Jazz music

The city of New Orleans was the birthplace of jazz in the late 1800s. Jazz is a combination of music styles, including blues and ragtime. Jazz musicians love improvising, to give a unique interpretation of a piece of music.

Western United States

CALIFORNIA
POPULATION 34,501,000 ✳ CAPITAL SACRAMENTO

WASHINGTON
POPULATION 5,988,000 ✳ CAPITAL OLYMPIA

ARIZONA
POPULATION 5,307,000 ✳ CAPITAL PHOENIX

OREGON
POPULATION 3,473,000 ✳ CAPITAL SALEM

UTAH
POPULATION 2,270,000 ✳ CAPITAL SALT LAKE CITY

NEVADA
POPULATION 2,106,000 ✳ CAPITAL CARSON CITY

IDAHO
POPULATION 1,321,000 ✳ CAPITAL BOISE

HAWAII
POPULATION 1,224,000 ✳ CAPITAL HONOLULU

ALASKA
POPULATION 635,000 ✳ CAPITAL JUNEAU

Frontier wagon trail

The tallest tree in the world is a coast redwood in California called the Stratosphere Giant. It is more than 369 feet (112 m) tall.

Bald eagle
In 1782, a team of judges chose the bald eagle as the national bird of the United States of America. They liked its fierce expression, and preferred it to its rival in the competition, the wild turkey.

Silicon Valley
In the early 1980s, an area in the San Jose and Santa Clara valleys in California became a center for high-technology industries. Silicon is a material used in electronic equipment such as computers.

Wind turbines
Wind is an important source of energy. Turbines harness the power of wind for electricity. About 1 percent of electricity in California is generated by wind.

Moose

RUSSIA

Beaufort Sea

ALASKA
Mt McKinley 20,321ft (6,194m)
Brooks Range
Alaska Range
Yukon
Arctic Circle
Bering Strait
Bering Sea
St Lawrence Island
Nunivak Island
Pribilof Islands
Umnak Island
Aleutian Islands
Shumagin Islands
Gulf of Alaska
Kodiak Island
Kodiak
Anchorage
Fairbanks
Nome
Barrow
Prudhoe Bay
JUNEAU
Sitka
PACIFIC OCEAN

CANADA
YUKON TERRITORY

0 miles 400
0 kilometers 400

Alaska

CANADA
BRITISH COLUMBIA
VICTORIA
Vancouver
Vancouver Island
Burnaby
Victoria

MONTANA

IDAHO
Borah Peak
Challis
Weiser
Ontario

WASHINGTON
OLYMPIA
Seattle
Bellevue
Tacoma
Bremerton
Auburn
Everett
Mt Vernon
Oak Harbor
Bellingham
Port Angeles
Cape Flattery
Mt Rainier 14,409ft (4,392m)
Wenatchee
Ellensburg
Yakima
Othello
Pasco
Kennewick
Walla Walla
Pullman
Spokane
Moscow
Lewiston
Sandpoint
Lake Pend Oreille
Lake Coeur d'Alene
Columbia Basin
Lake Chelan
Franklin D Roosevelt Lake
Banks Lake
Omak
Columbia
Snake
Columbia

OREGON
SALEM
Portland
Vancouver
Longview
Kelso
Chehalis
Centralia
Aberdeen
Astoria
Cape Disappointment
Lincoln City
Newport
Corvallis
Albany
Lebanon
Eugene
Springfield
McMinnville
Newberg
Bend
Redmond
Madras
The Dalles
Pendleton
Hermiston
La Grande
Baker
Mt Jefferson 10,499ft (3,200m)
Willamette
Columbia
Clearwater
Hell's Canyon

Puget Sound

PACIFIC OCEAN

Golden Gate Bridge

This suspension bridge across San Francisco Bay opened in 1937. Forty painters and 18 metal-workers work full time to maintain it, and 118,000 commuters cross it each day.

Disneyland

The first Disney theme park opened in California in 1955. One million people visited in the first six months. Sleeping Beauty's castle at the entrance was modeled on a castle in Germany.

Alaska was bought by the USA from Russia in 1867 for US$7,200,000.

United States of America

LAND AREA	3,717,813 sq miles (9,629,091 sq km)
OFFICIAL LANGUAGE	English
MAIN RELIGION	Christian
LIFE EXPECTANCY	77 years
LITERACY	97%

USING THE LAND

- Forest and woodland
- Arable land
- Grazing
- Arid or marginal

Anchorage
Juneau

Oranges
More oranges are harvested yearly in the USA than any other fruits. Florida, the center of the citrus-growing industry, produces one-third of all US citrus fruits. Most of the oranges from Florida are made into juice, while most of the oranges from California are for eating.

NATURAL FEATURES

Yellowstone National Park
Yellowstone, the world's first national park, was set up in 1872 and spreads across three states. It covers 3,468 square miles (8,982 sq km) and features about 10,000 natural springs, or geysers (*left*). Grizzly bears, bison and moose wander freely around the park.

Old Faithful

Mt McKinley
At 20,321 feet (6,194 m), Mt McKinley is the highest mountain in North America. It is part of the long Alaska Range and is a major attraction in the Denali National Park. Its peak is often shrouded in cloud, especially during summer.

Monument Valley
Situated on the border between Arizona and Utah, Monument Valley (*above*) is owned and managed by the Navajo people. It is famous for its unique rock formations and remnants of volcanoes.

Great Lakes
The Great Lakes—Michigan, Huron, Ontario, Superior and Erie—are the world's largest group of freshwater lakes. Together they make up 18 percent of Earth's fresh surface water.

Grand Canyon
Formed over the last 6 million years, as the Colorado River slowly cuts through layers of rock, the Grand Canyon in northwestern Arizona is the world's largest canyon. It is 285 miles (456 km) long, 1 mile (1.6 km) deep and up to 18 miles (29 km) wide. In 1919, the canyon became a national park.

LARGEST CITIES

New York 8,135,000

Los Angeles 3,901,000

Chicago 2,888,000

Houston 2,072,000

Philadelphia 1,483,000

- 🌾 Cereals
- Corn (maize)
- Fruit and vegetables
- 🍎 Fruit
- Citrus fruits
- Wine
- Cotton
- Tobacco
- Sugarcane
- Soybeans
- Groundnuts
- 🐄 Beef cattle
- Sheep
- Fishing
- Shellfish
- ⚙️ Industrial center
- ⛏️ Mining
- Oil production
- 🌲 Timber
- Tourism
- Winter sports

Seattle, Helena, Minneapolis, Detroit, Boston, Chicago, New York, Philadelphia, WASHINGTON, DC, Salt Lake City, San Francisco, Denver, Nashville, Las Vegas, Santa Fe, Oklahoma City, Atlanta, Los Angeles, Dallas, New Orleans, Houston, Miami

Honolulu

WHERE PEOPLE LIVE

Urban	Rural
77%	23%

PLACES

Washington, DC
Named for George Washington, America's first president, Washington, DC is the capital of the USA. The city was designed for that purpose before it was built. It is home to the Capitol building, where both houses of Congress meet, and the White House, where the president lives and works.

Capitol building, Washington, DC

Honolulu
The capital city and main port of Hawaii, Honolulu is the only US city located in the tropics, the only US city with a royal palace (Iolani Palace) and the only US city with an equal blend of western, Asian and Polynesian influences.

Cliff Palace

Cliff Palace
About 1,000 years ago, the Anasazi people began to build high stone dwellings along canyon walls in southwestern Colorado. Cliff Palace, the largest of these dwellings, contains more than 200 rooms.

San Francisco
Famous for the Golden Gate Bridge and its cable cars, San Francisco was almost destroyed by an earthquake in 1906. In its bay is the former prison Alcatraz, now open for tourists.

Statue of Liberty
A gift from France to the USA, the Statue of Liberty has stood on Liberty Island in New York City harbor since 1886. The copper statue is 151 feet (46 m) high, with a 12-story spiral staircase inside, which leads to a public observation area in the statue's crown. To the USA, the statue is a symbol of freedom and democracy.

TRADITIONS AND CULTURE

Thanksgiving Day
For almost 400 years, Americans have observed Thanksgiving Day on the fourth Thursday in November. What began as a religious event is now a family day set aside to give thanks for blessings received.

Halloween
On 31 October every year, Americans celebrate the festival of Halloween, when children wear costumes, go trick-or-treating and make jack-o'-lanterns out of pumpkins.

Halloween jack-o'-lantern

Cheerleaders
Beginning in 1898 at the University of Minnesota, cheerleading had become popular across the nation by 1920. Cheerleaders dance and lead the spectators to support their team with chants and cheers at athletic events, especially basketball and football games.

Rap music
Rap music in America developed first in New York City. It is a form of music that is spoken quickly to match the rhythm. It is particularly popular with African-American teenagers. Some rap music has been criticized for its violent lyrics.

Hollywood
Hollywood, a district of Los Angeles, is known as the movie capital of the world. The first film studio was built there in 1911 and within a year, 15 others had sprung up. The late 1920s saw the first production of sound films, and by the 1930s movies, such as *Gone with the Wind* (1939), were being produced on a grand scale. Hollywood is also famous for "The Strip"—a section of shops, nightclubs and restaurants along Sunset Boulevard.

PEOPLE

Sitting Bull c 1834–90
Born in what is present-day South Dakota, Sitting Bull was a medicine man, and by around 1867 was leader of all the Sioux Indians. His advice before the battle of Little Bighorn resulted in victory for the Sioux.

Annie Oakley 1860–1926
Annie Oakley was a sharpshooter who starred in Buffalo Bill's traveling Wild West show for more than 16 years. Firing from the back of a galloping horse was one of her special skills.

Annie Oakley

Wright brothers
In 1903, Wilbur and Orville Wright successfully flew the world's first power-driven plane in North Carolina. The plane, which the brothers had invented, flew 852 feet (260 m) and managed to stay in the air for 59 seconds.

Martin Luther King 1929–68
Martin Luther King was a Baptist minister and a leader of the civil rights movement. His policy of nonviolent protest won him the Nobel Peace Prize in 1964. After his assassination, he became only the second American whose birthday is honored by a public holiday.

Elvis Presley 1935–77
Born in Tupelo, Mississippi, Elvis Presley was one of the world's greatest stars of rock music. He began his singing career in 1954, and his concert style and music divided people. Some towns even banned his shows. Elvis sold more than 1 billion records and starred in 33 films.

HISTORY AT A GLANCE

1607
English ships, under the command of Captain Christopher Newport, land and establish a permanent colony at Jamestown, Virginia.

1620
English pilgrims seeking religious freedom arrive on the *Mayflower* at Plymouth, Massachusetts.

1775–81
The War of Independence begins at Lexington, Massachusetts, when the American colonists rebel against the English soldiers. War lasts for six years.

Battle of Lexington

1789
George Washington becomes the first president of the new USA. He supports the new constitution, which sets out the country's laws.

1836
Texan soldiers fighting for their independence from Mexico hold off the Mexicans for 13 days at the Alamo, a mission in San Antonio, Texas.

The Alamo

1861–65
The Civil War is fought when the South withdraws from the USA. The North wins the war, keeps the states united, and ends slavery.

1870s
Wars are fought between Native Americans and the white colonists. These frontier wars lead to the loss of many lives on both sides.

1920–33
Laws are in place for 13 years prohibiting the manufacture and sale of alcoholic drinks.

1929–39
Business slumps worldwide after stock values in the USA fall. The Great Depression ends when industries get a boost because of World War II.

1941
The Japanese invade Pearl Harbor, bringing the USA into World War II. The war ends in 1945 when the USA drops atomic bombs on Japan.

1954
The Supreme Court rules against racial segregation in public schools and meets enormous resistance from white people.

1964–73
The Vietnam War is fought when the USA opposes North Vietnam's invasion of the South. The cold war between the communist and non-communist nations eases.

1969
First people on the moon, Neil Armstrong and Edwin Aldrin, land the Apollo 11 module, *Eagle*.

Footprint on the moon

1991 and 2003
In 1991, the USA leads a war against Iraq, which has invaded Kuwait. In 2003, the USA again fights Iraq and ends the reign of Saddam Hussein.

Mexico

![MEXICO flag]
MEXICO
POPULATION 104,908,000 * CAPITAL MEXICO CITY

Monarch butterflies
The monarch butterfly is a long-distance traveler. Each year, tens of millions of these colorful butterflies fly up to 2,500 miles (4,000 km) from Canada and the east coast of the USA to spend the winter in Mexico.

Cattle rancher
Only about one-fifth of Mexico is suitable for farming. The northern part is hot and dry, and cattle ranching is the main activity there. Mexico has large supplies of oil and is the world's biggest supplier of silver.

Piñata
A piñata is a papier-mâché container filled with toys and sweets. At Mexican celebrations, a piñata is hung from the ceiling or a tree branch, and children take turns trying to break it open with a stick to get the treats.

Traditional dancers
Folk dances and music are popular at fiesta time. Many of the dances performed today are based on Indian dances from before the Spanish conquest of Mexico.

The cardón cactus is the world's largest cactus. It grows in the deserts of the Baja California peninsula. Some are nearly 70 feet (21 m) high. These plants can live for more than 300 years.

San Diego
Tijuana
Mexicali
San Luis
Río Colorado
Ensenada
UNITED STATE
El Pas
Ciuda
Juáre
Cerro de La Encantada
10,157ft (3,096m)
Nogales
Agua Prieta
El Bárreal
Caborca
Cananea
Cabo San Quintín
Magdalena
Nuevo Casas
Grandes
Isla Guadalupe
Cumpas
El Suec
Isla Ángel
de la Guarda
Chihu
Hermosillo
Cuauhtém
Isla Cedros
Rosarito
Bahía
Sebastián
Vizcaíno
Isla
Tiburón
Sonora
Empalme
Punta Eugenia
Guerrero
Negro
Guaymas
Esperanza
Ciudad
Obregón
Navojoa
Huatabampo
Punta Rosa
Loreto
San Blas
Los Mochis
Guasave
Guamúchil
Cabo San Lázaro
Bahía La Paz
Culiacán
Isla Santa Margarita
La Paz
El Dorado
Tropic of Cancer
Santa Genoveva
7,894ft (2,406m)
Mazatlán
Cabo San Lucas
Cabo San Lucas
Escu
Islas Marías
Pun
Cabo C
PACIFIC OCEAN

Gulf of California

Baja California

Sierra San Pedro Mártir

Conquistador

The conquistadors were the Spanish soldiers who invaded Mexico in the 16th century. Spain ruled Mexico from 1521, when the Aztec empire fell, until 1821, when Mexico became independent.

Teotihuacán—City of the Gods

On a high plateau about 30 miles (50 km) northeast of Mexico City are the ruins of what was once one of the largest cities in the world. For about 900 years Teotihuacán dominated the area around it. The city was at its peak around AD 600, when 150,000 people lived there. It was the capital of one of the earliest civilizations in the region and was an important center for religious ceremonies. The city was well planned and laid out on a grid system. Rising above its plazas, temples and palaces were the Pyramid of the Moon and the Pyramid of the Sun.

Mosaic mask
Masks were important in Teotihuacán. They were probably worn for ceremonies and were sometimes put over the faces of people who had died.

Pyramid of the Sun
This was the largest building in the city and is the third-largest pyramid in the world.

Avenue of the Dead
This wide road divided the city into sections. It was probably used for colorful processions.

Housing
The center of Teotihuacán was for religious ceremonies; the people lived on the outskirts.

Pyramid of the Moon
Like all the city's buildings, this massive pyramid was built with the use of simple stone tools.

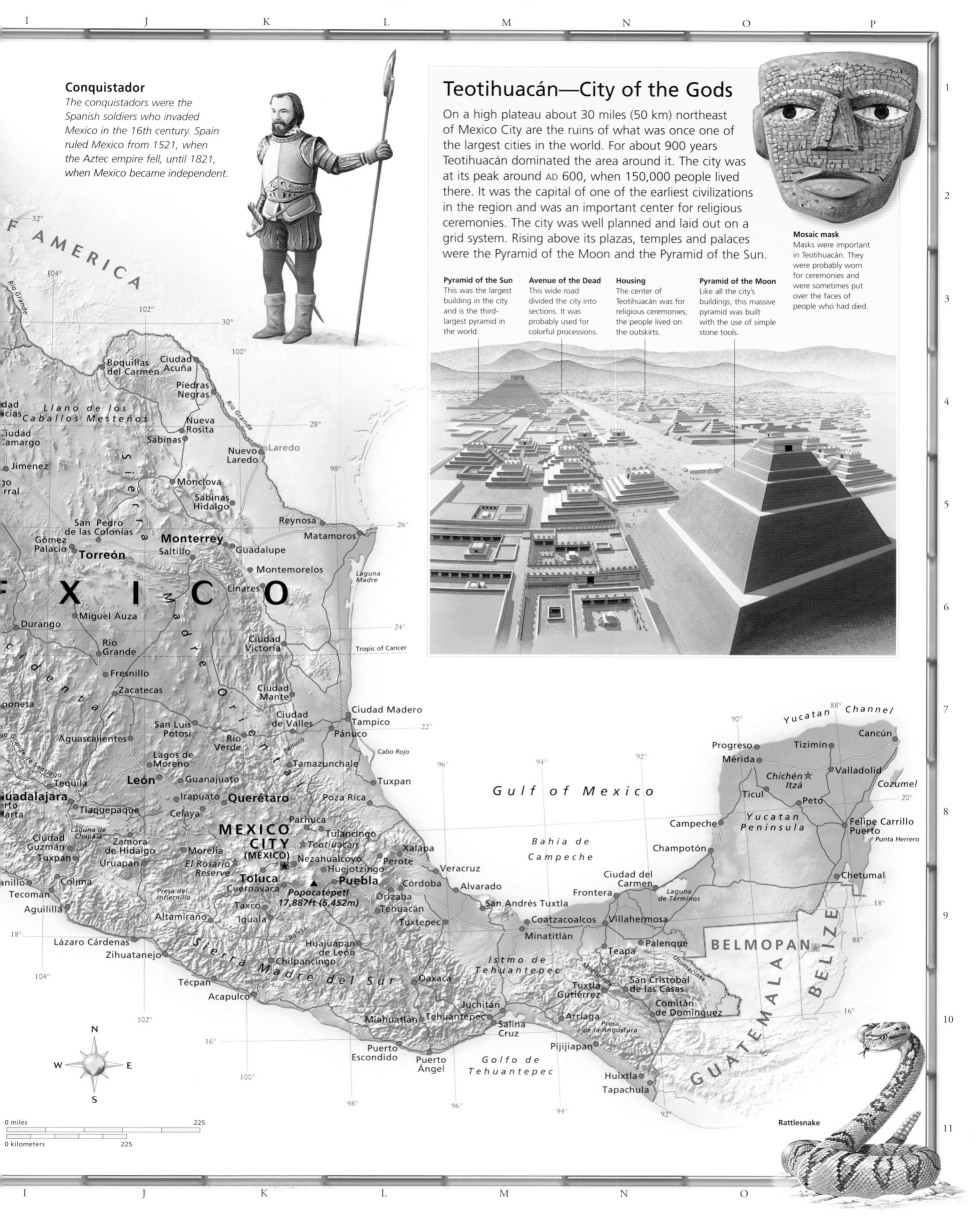

Rattlesnake

0 miles · 225
0 kilometers · 225

N · W · E · S

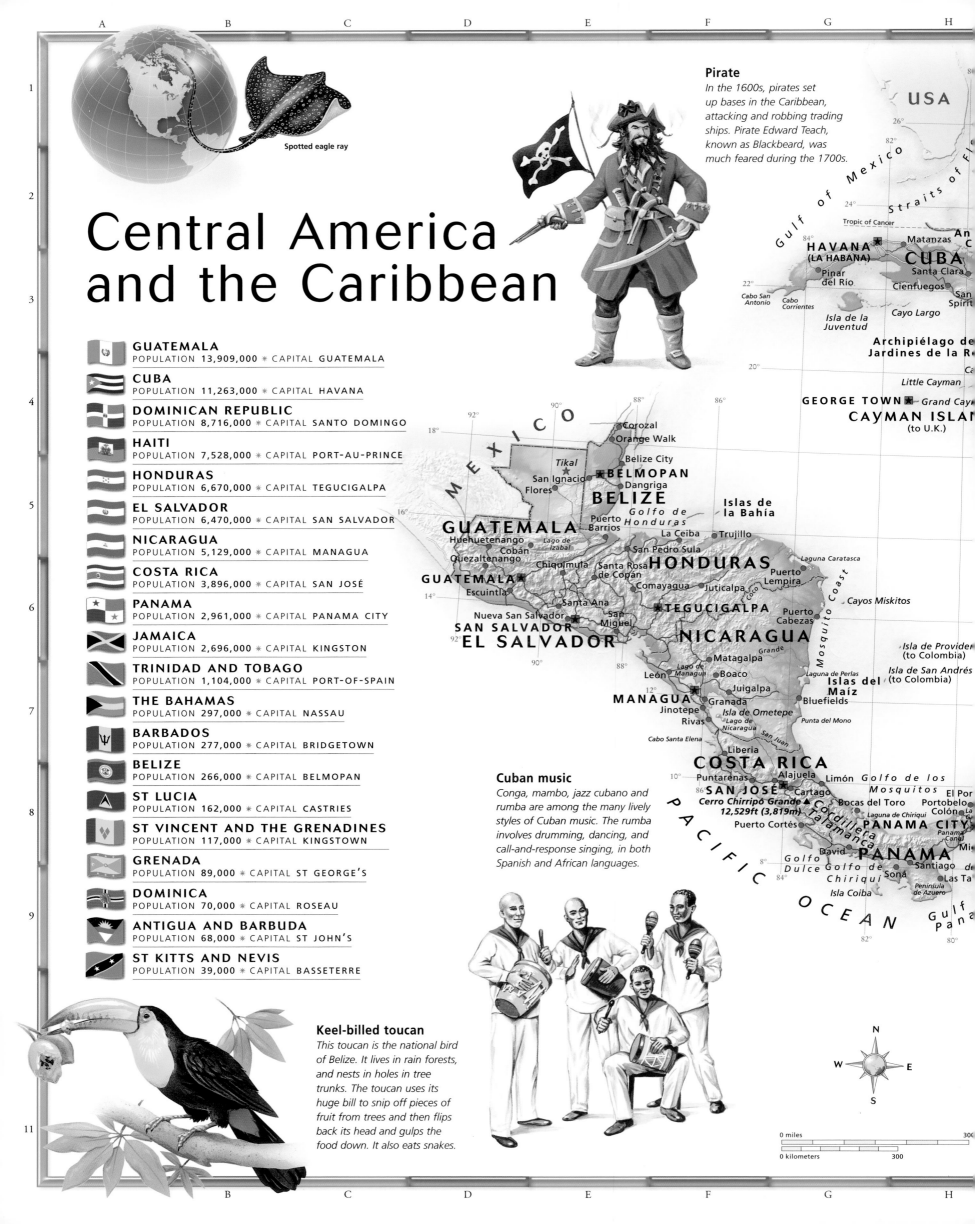

Central America and the Caribbean

Spotted eagle ray

Pirate
In the 1600s, pirates set up bases in the Caribbean, attacking and robbing trading ships. Pirate Edward Teach, known as Blackbeard, was much feared during the 1700s.

GUATEMALA
POPULATION 13,909,000 ∗ CAPITAL GUATEMALA

CUBA
POPULATION 11,263,000 ∗ CAPITAL HAVANA

DOMINICAN REPUBLIC
POPULATION 8,716,000 ∗ CAPITAL SANTO DOMINGO

HAITI
POPULATION 7,528,000 ∗ CAPITAL PORT-AU-PRINCE

HONDURAS
POPULATION 6,670,000 ∗ CAPITAL TEGUCIGALPA

EL SALVADOR
POPULATION 6,470,000 ∗ CAPITAL SAN SALVADOR

NICARAGUA
POPULATION 5,129,000 ∗ CAPITAL MANAGUA

COSTA RICA
POPULATION 3,896,000 ∗ CAPITAL SAN JOSÉ

PANAMA
POPULATION 2,961,000 ∗ CAPITAL PANAMA CITY

JAMAICA
POPULATION 2,696,000 ∗ CAPITAL KINGSTON

TRINIDAD AND TOBAGO
POPULATION 1,104,000 ∗ CAPITAL PORT-OF-SPAIN

THE BAHAMAS
POPULATION 297,000 ∗ CAPITAL NASSAU

BARBADOS
POPULATION 277,000 ∗ CAPITAL BRIDGETOWN

BELIZE
POPULATION 266,000 ∗ CAPITAL BELMOPAN

ST LUCIA
POPULATION 162,000 ∗ CAPITAL CASTRIES

ST VINCENT AND THE GRENADINES
POPULATION 117,000 ∗ CAPITAL KINGSTOWN

GRENADA
POPULATION 89,000 ∗ CAPITAL ST GEORGE'S

DOMINICA
POPULATION 70,000 ∗ CAPITAL ROSEAU

ANTIGUA AND BARBUDA
POPULATION 68,000 ∗ CAPITAL ST JOHN'S

ST KITTS AND NEVIS
POPULATION 39,000 ∗ CAPITAL BASSETERRE

Cuban music
Conga, mambo, jazz cubano and rumba are among the many lively styles of Cuban music. The rumba involves drumming, dancing, and call-and-response singing, in both Spanish and African languages.

Keel-billed toucan
This toucan is the national bird of Belize. It lives in rain forests, and nests in holes in tree trunks. The toucan uses its huge bill to snip off pieces of fruit from trees and then flips back its head and gulps the food down. It also eats snakes.

0 miles 300
0 kilometers 300

### Map labels
USA
Gulf of Mexico
Straits of Fl...
Tropic of Cancer
HAVANA (LA HABANA)
Matanzas
An...
CUBA
Santa Clara
Pinar del Río
Cienfuegos
San...
Cabo San Antonio
Cabo Corrientes
Cayo Largo
Isla de la Juventud
Cayo...
Spirit...
Archipiélago de Jardines de la R...
Little Cayman
GEORGE TOWN
Grand Cay...
CAYMAN ISLAN...
(to U.K.)

MEXICO
Corozal
Orange Walk
Belize City
Tikal
San Ignacio
Flores
BELMOPAN
Dangriga
BELIZE
Islas de la Bahía
GUATEMALA
Golfo de Honduras
Puerto Barrios
La Ceiba
Trujillo
Huehuetenango
Lago de Izabal
Cobán
San Pedro Sula
HONDURAS
Laguna Caratasca
Quezaltenango
Chiquimula
Santa Rosa de Copán
Puerto Lempira
GUATEMALA
Escuintla
Comayagua
Juticalpa
Coco
Mosquito Coast
Cayos Miskitos
Santa Ana
TEGUCIGALPA
Nueva San Salvador
San Miguel
Puerto Cabezas
SAN SALVADOR
NICARAGUA
Isla de Providen... (to Colombia)
EL SALVADOR
Matagalpa
Grande
Isla de San Andrés (to Colombia)
León
Lago de Managua
Boaco
Laguna de Perlas
Islas del Maíz
MANAGUA
Juigalpa
Bluefields
Jinotepe
Granada
Isla de Ometepe
Rivas
Lago de Nicaragua
San Juan
Punta del Mono
Cabo Santa Elena
Liberia
COSTA RICA
Puntarenas
Alajuela
Limón
Golfo de los Mosquitos
El Por...
SAN JOSÉ
Cartago
Bocas del Toro
Portobelo
Colón
Cerro Chirripó Grande 12,529ft (3,819m)
Puerto Cortés
Cordillera de Talamanca
PANAMA CITY
Panama Canal
Mi...
PACIFIC OCEAN
David
PANAMA
Santiago
de
Golfo Dulce
Golfo de Chiriquí
Soná
Las Ta...
Península de Azuero
Isla Coiba
Gulf Pana...

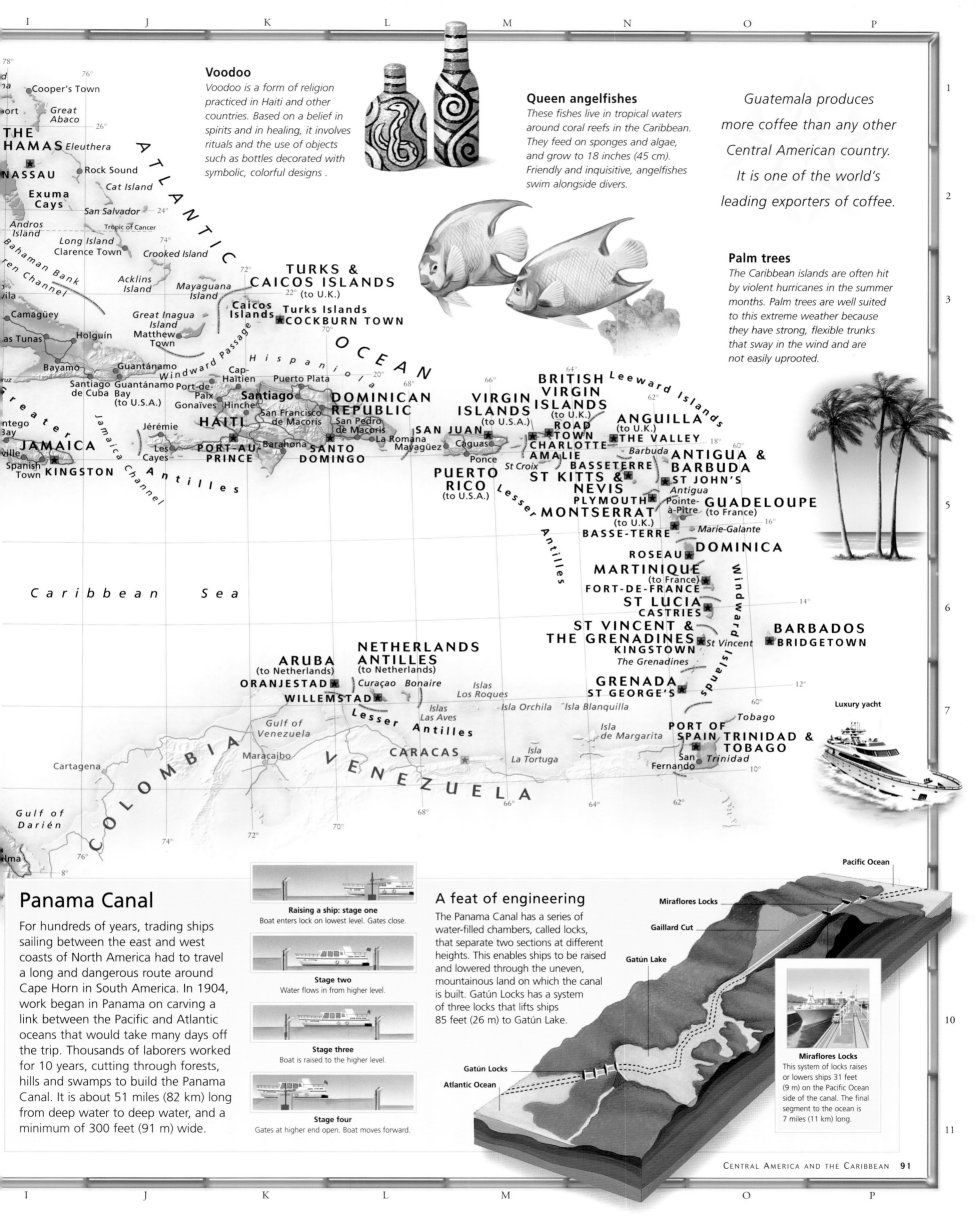

I J K L M N O P

1

2

3

5

6

7

10

11

Voodoo

Voodoo is a form of religion practiced in Haiti and other countries. Based on a belief in spirits and in healing, it involves rituals and the use of objects such as bottles decorated with symbolic, colorful designs .

Queen angelfishes

These fishes live in tropical waters around coral reefs in the Caribbean. They feed on sponges and algae, and grow to 18 inches (45 cm). Friendly and inquisitive, angelfishes swim alongside divers.

Guatemala produces more coffee than any other Central American country. It is one of the world's leading exporters of coffee.

Palm trees

The Caribbean islands are often hit by violent hurricanes in the summer months. Palm trees are well suited to this extreme weather because they have strong, flexible trunks that sway in the wind and are not easily uprooted.

Luxury yacht

### Map labels

Cooper's Town
Great Abaco
76°
78°
THE
HAMAS *Eleuthera*
NASSAU
Rock Sound
Cat Island
Exuma Cays
Andros Island
San Salvador
24°
Tropic of Cancer
Long Island
Clarence Town
Crooked Island
74°
Bahaman Bank
Camagüey
Holguín
as Tunas
Bayamo
72°
Acklins Island
Mayaguana Island
TURKS & CAICOS ISLANDS
22° (to U.K.)
Caicos Islands
Turks Islands
★COCKBURN TOWN
70°
Great Inagua Island Matthew Town
ATLANTIC
OCEAN
Guantánamo
Santiago de Cuba
Guantánamo Bay (to U.S.A.)
Windward Passage
Cap-Haïtien
Port-de-Paix
Hispaniola
20°
Puerto Plata
68°
66°
Leeward Islands
BRITISH VIRGIN ISLANDS (to U.K.)
64°
VIRGIN ISLANDS (to U.S.A.)
62°
ANGUILLA (to U.K.)
★THE VALLEY
18°
60°
Greater
Santiago
Gonaïves
Hinche
San Francisco de Macoris
DOMINICAN REPUBLIC
ROAD TOWN
ANTIGUA & BARBUDA
Jérémie
HAITI
San Pedro de Macoris
SAN JUAN
CHARLOTTE AMALIE
★ST JOHN'S
Barbuda
Jamaica Channel
Les Cayes
PORT-AU-PRINCE
Barahona
SANTO DOMINGO
La Romana
Mayagüez
C?guas
St Croix
BASSETERRE
ST KITTS & NEVIS
Antigua
Pointe-à-Pitre
GUADELOUPE (to France)
JAMAICA
Spanish Town
KINGSTON
Antilles
Ponce
PUERTO RICO (to U.S.A.)
Lesser Antilles
PLYMOUTH
MONTSERRAT (to U.K.)
BASSE-TERRE
16°
Marie-Galante
ROSEAU ★
DOMINICA
MARTINIQUE (to France)
FORT-DE-FRANCE
Windward Islands
Caribbean Sea
ST LUCIA
CASTRIES
14°
ST VINCENT & THE GRENADINES
KINGSTOWN *St Vincent*
BARBADOS
★BRIDGETOWN
The Grenadines
ARUBA (to Netherlands)
ORANJESTAD ✴
NETHERLANDS ANTILLES (to Netherlands)
Curaçao *Bonaire*
WILLEMSTAD ✴
Islas Los Roques
GRENADA
ST GEORGE'S
12°
60°
Islas Las Aves
Isla Orchila *Isla Blanquilla*
Tobago
Lesser Antilles
Gulf of Venezuela
COLOMBIA
Maracaibo
VENEZUELA
CARACAS ★
Isla La Tortuga
Isla de Margarita
PORT OF SPAIN
TRINIDAD & TOBAGO
San Fernando *Trinidad*
10°
62°
64°
66°
Cartagena
Gulf of Darién
8°
74°
72°
70°
68°
66°
64°
62°
76°

Panama Canal

For hundreds of years, trading ships sailing between the east and west coasts of North America had to travel a long and dangerous route around Cape Horn in South America. In 1904, work began in Panama on carving a link between the Pacific and Atlantic oceans that would take many days off the trip. Thousands of laborers worked for 10 years, cutting through forests, hills and swamps to build the Panama Canal. It is about 51 miles (82 km) long from deep water to deep water, and a minimum of 300 feet (91 m) wide.

Raising a ship: stage one
Boat enters lock on lowest level. Gates close.

Stage two
Water flows in from higher level.

Stage three
Boat is raised to the higher level.

Stage four
Gates at higher end open. Boat moves forward.

A feat of engineering

The Panama Canal has a series of water-filled chambers, called locks, that separate two sections at different heights. This enables ships to be raised and lowered through the uneven, mountainous land on which the canal is built. Gatún Locks has a system of three locks that lifts ships 85 feet (26 m) to Gatún Lake.

Pacific Ocean
Miraflores Locks
Gaillard Cut
Gatún Lake
Gatún Locks
Atlantic Ocean

Miraflores Locks
This system of locks raises or lowers ships 31 feet (9 m) on the Pacific Ocean side of the canal. The final segment to the ocean is 7 miles (11 km) long.

CENTRAL AMERICA AND THE CARIBBEAN **91**

Sapodilla, a Central American plant, produces chicle, the gum in most chewing gum.

Mexico, Central America and the Caribbean

LAND AREA	1,024,715 sq miles (2,654,000 sq km)
LARGEST COUNTRY	Mexico
SMALLEST COUNTRY	St Kitts-Nevis
MAIN RELIGION	Christian
LIFE EXPECTANCY	70 years
LITERACY	87%

NATURAL FEATURES

Soufrière Hills MONTSERRAT
In July 1995, this volcano began erupting and spitting out lava. The volcanic activity still continues, and has destroyed almost half of Montserrat.

Las Baulas COSTA RICA
This national park, which covers about 4 sq miles (10 sq km) of swamps and beaches, was founded in 1995 to protect endangered wildlife species, especially leatherback turtles, which nest there each year.

Leatherback turtle

Baja peninsula

Baja peninsula MEXICO
This is the world's longest peninsula. Its extremely arid land supports some hardy lizards, such as the gila monster and the Mexican beaded lizard. More than 120 species of cactus thrive there.

Lake Nicaragua NICARAGUA
This freshwater lake is the largest in Central America. It is home to the slow-moving bull shark, which is one of the most frequent attackers of humans.

Belize's reefs BELIZE
Parallel to the coastline, and fringed by tiny islands called cays, Belize's barrier reef is famous for its sponges, coral and fishes. Just beyond is Lighthouse Reef, with its underwater cave, the Blue Hole.

Blue Hole, Lighthouse Reef, Belize

USING THE LAND

- Corn (maize)
- Fruit
- Bananas
- Cotton
- Coffee
- Sugarcane
- Beef cattle
- Fishing
- Shellfish
- Industrial center
- Mining
- Oil production
- Tourism

- Forest and woodland
- Arable land
- Grazing
- Arid or marginal

Corn
Corn has been grown in Mexico for the last 7,000 years. It is one of Mexico's most important commercially grown crops, and more than half of Mexico's farmland is used for its cultivation. Tortillas, the flat bread that most Mexicans eat every day, are made from corn flour.

There are more Spanish speakers in Mexico than any other country.

Bananas
Bananas are especially important in Honduras, which is one of the poorest countries in the Western Hemisphere. Grown along the northern lowlands near the Caribbean Sea, they are a leading source of income.

Tijuana · La Paz · Guadalajara · Monterrey · MEXICO CITY · Puebla · Acapulco · Mérida · HAVANA · GUATEMALA · SAN SALVADOR · BELMOPAN · TEGUCIGALPA · MANAGUA · SAN JOSÉ · PANAMA CITY · PORT-AU-PRINCE · KINGSTON · SANTO DOMINGO · SAN JUAN · PORT OF SPAIN

Cigars
Cigars from Havana, Cuba, are famous as being among the finest in the world, and exporting them is one of Cuba's best sources of foreign revenue. The choicest tobacco comes from western Cuba. The highest-quality cigars are rolled by hand.

The quetzal

This beautiful jungle bird lives in the dense rain forests of Central America. The male is especially brightly colored, with a long, green, feathered tail that can add up to 3 feet (90 cm) to its length. The Aztecs believed the quetzal to be a symbol of freedom because it dies in captivity. Anyone caught killing a quetzal could be sentenced to death. Today, the quetzal is the national emblem of Guatemala, and appears on its flag and postage stamps.

Resplendent quetzal

LARGEST CITIES

Mexico City 8,750,000

Havana 2,359,000

Santo Domingo 2,241,000

Guadalajara 1,672,000

Puebla 1,371,000

WHERE PEOPLE LIVE

Urban		Rural

REGION
54% · 46%

Most urban: THE BAHAMAS
88% · 12%

Most rural: ST KITTS-NEVIS
34% · 66%

Blue agave
This plant is cultivated in Mexico. It produces a sweet sap, which is fermented to make a mild alcoholic drink called pulque. Pulque is then distilled and made into a stronger drink called tequila. Tequila, Mexico's national drink, is named for the town in which it was first made.

PLACES

Havana CUBA
The capital and largest city in Cuba, Havana is also its commercial and industrial center. The old colonial city includes the Spanish governor's palace and the 18th-century Havana Cathedral.

Colonial architecture, Havana

Mexico City MEXICO
Built on the ruins of Tenochtitlán in the 16th century, this city is one of the most populated urban areas in the world. It is home to Mexico's government and is its industrial and business center. Its cathedral (*below*) forms part of the main square.

Temple of the Magician MEXICO
In Uxmal lie the ruins of the Mayan Temple of the Magician (*below*), named

for the legend of a boy who built the temple in one night. The Mayans often built a new temple over an old one. This one has been built five separate times.

Antigua GUATEMALA
Built in the 16th century, Antigua, the capital of Guatemala in colonial days, was badly damaged by an earthquake in 1773. It is a city of old, historic buildings, although many of them are now preserved only as ruins.

San Juan PUERTO RICO
The second-oldest city in the Americas, San Juan is Puerto Rico's main seaport. In the early 16th century it was a walled city and the site of Spanish fortifications, many of which have been restored and are tourist attractions today.

The smallest bird in the world is the bee hummingbird, from Cuba.

PEOPLE

Montezuma 1466–1520
An Aztec emperor who extended Aztec land to include most of south-central Mexico, Montezuma was captured by Hernán Cortés in 1519. He was killed in 1520 when the Aztecs rebelled.

Hernán Cortés

Sent by the Spanish governor of Cuba in 1519 to explore the coast of Mexico, Cortés spent the next two years conquering central and southern Mexico. By 1521, Cuauhtémoc, the last Aztec emperor, had surrendered to Cortés, and the Aztec empire became a Spanish colony. When Cortés took over Tenochtitlán, the Aztec capital, he tore down all the buildings.

Frida Kahlo 1907–54
This Mexican painter is famous for her

brightly colored self-portraits, which reflected her tragic life. Kahlo taught herself to paint after she was severely injured in a traffic accident in 1925.

Fidel Castro born c 1926
Largely unchallenged as leader of Cuba since 1959, Castro has a poor relationship with the USA. However, he has improved Cuba's health and education standards.

Bob Marley 1945–81
Marley was a Jamaican musician and composer who popularized reggae music—a mix of native styles, rock and soul, with lyrics about social and political problems.

TRADITIONS AND CULTURE

Spirit dances GUATEMALA
A number of the Guatemalan folk dances re-enact old spiritual rituals and historical events. The Dance of the Conquistadores depicts the fierce battles between the Guatemalans and Hernán Cortés.

Calypso music TRINIDAD AND TOBAGO
The West Indies is the home of calypso music—a lively style of music, with lyrics that express the mood and beliefs of the people. The Carnival in Trinidad is the most important musical event of the year. Bands and dancers fill the streets.

Day of the Dead MEXICO
In this festival, Mexicans remember their loved ones who have died. Families have feasts for the living next to the graves of the dead, and children exchange toy skeletons or dolls to honor them.

Chilies
Mexicans are very fond of chilies, and grow more than 100 varieties. Chilies range in color from green to red and black. The most common is the jalapeño chili, which is very hot.

Mayan sun calendar

Early calendars
Mayans were one of the first people to develop a reliable system of measuring the passing of time. They used two main systems for counting days which, when used together, produced a 52-year cycle called the Calendar Round. The first system was a 260-day year, and the second was a 365-day year, based on the orbit of Earth around the Sun.

HISTORY AT A GLANCE
GREAT CIVILIZATIONS

Aztec gold mask

OLMECS 1150–800 BC
The Olmecs were the first people to develop an advanced culture in Mexico. They lived near the rivers and swamps in southeast Mexico, in what are now the states of Veracruz and Tabasco. They devised their own way of writing and counting, and worked out a basic calendar. They carved huge stone heads with flat faces, wearing a type of helmet, to honor their gods, warriors and kings. An important Olmec settlement was found at La Venta, leading some historians to believe that Olmec culture began there.

Olmec head

MAYANS AD 250–900
The Mayans were the most advanced of all the Native American peoples. They settled in villages and developed agriculture in southern Mexico, Guatemala and northern Belize. They built stone cities, palaces and temple pyramids decorated with fine carvings. Religion played a large part in the life of the Mayans. Priests climbed the stairs of the pyramids and performed ceremonies in the temple at the top, offering sacrifices—animal and human—to their gods. The Mayans developed a system of picture writing, or hieroglyphics, and made paper from the bark of wild fig trees.

Mayan temple, Tikal, Guatemala

TOLTECS 900–1200
These were a warrior people who invaded central Mexico from the north, burning the city of Teotihuacán, one of the most important cultural centers in Mexico. The Toltecs were craftspeople, skilled in intricate sculptures, such as this huge carved statue of a soldier (*right*). They worshiped many gods, in particular, Quetzalcóatl, the Feathered Serpent, whose image (a snake crowned with quetzal feathers) adorns many of the buildings at Chichén Itzá and Tula.

Toltec carved stone column

AZTECS 1428–1521
The Aztecs came from the northwest and built their capital, Tenochtitlán (now Mexico City), in the Valley of Mexico. They had one of the most advanced cultures in the Americas, and created art, sculpture, poetry and music. They were deeply religious, and their religion affected every aspect of their lives. They worshiped more than 120 gods—nearly every event, day, month and city had its own special god. The Aztecs built many huge temples and elaborate sculptures to worship their gods. They especially honored Huitzilopochtli, a fierce god to whom they sacrificed thousands of people every year.

Caribbean Sea

Gulf of
Darién

Punta Gallinas

Lake
Maracaibo

Orinoco

La Gr
Saba

Gulf of
Panama

Cordillera Occidental

Cordillera Central

Magdalena

Cordillera Oriental

Llanos

G u i a n a
Highlands

Negro

▲ Volcán Cotopaxi
19,344ft (5,896m)

Putumayo

A m a z o n

Gulf of
Guayaquil

Chimborazo
20,702ft
(6,310m)

▲

Marañón

Ucayali

B a s i n

Madei

Punta
Pariñas

Nevado Huascarán
22,205ft (6,768m)

▲

A
n
d
e
s

Lake
Titicaca

Altiplano

P A C I F I C   O C E A N

A
t
a
c
a
m
a

D
e
s
e
r
t

A
n
d
e
s

Gra
Chac

Mt Aconcagua
22,835ft (6,960m)

▲

Pamp

Negro

P
a
t
a
g
o
n
i
a

Chico

Golfo de
San Jorge

Deseado

Golfo de
Penas

Bahía
Grande

Tierra del
Fuego

Cape Horn

Tumuc-Humac
Mountains

Amazon

Xingu

Araguaia

Tocantins

Planalto da
Borborema

Cabo de
São Roque

São Francisco

Planalto
do Mato
Grosso

Paraguay

B r a z i l i a n
H i g h l a n d s

Paraná

Serra
Geral

Serra do Mar

Uruguay

...tamia

Lagoa dos
Patos

Lagoa Mirim

River Plate

South America

Falkland
slands

South
Georgia

Northern South America

Peacock dancer, Rio de Janeiro

BRAZIL
POPULATION 182,033,000 ✳ CAPITAL BRASÍLIA

COLOMBIA
POPULATION 41,662,000 ✳ CAPITAL BOGOTÁ

PERU
POPULATION 28,410,000 ✳ CAPITAL LIMA

VENEZUELA
POPULATION 24,655,000 ✳ CAPITAL CARACAS

ECUADOR
POPULATION 13,710,000 ✳ CAPITAL QUITO

GUYANA
POPULATION 702,000 ✳ CAPITAL GEORGETOWN

SURINAME
POPULATION 435,000 ✳ CAPITAL PARAMARIBO

Galapagos Islands
(to Ecuador)

PACIFIC OCEAN

Galapagos

Isla Pinta
Isla Marchena
Isla Genovesa
Volcán Wolf 5,600ft (1,707m)
Equator
Volcán Darwin 4,199ft (1,280m)
Isla San Salvador
Volcán La Cumbre 5,075ft (1,547m)
Isla Santa Cruz
Isla Fernandina
Puerto Ayora
Isla San Cristóbal
Cerro Azol 5,541ft (1,689m)
Isla Isabela
Isla Santa Fé
Puerto Villamil
Puerto Baquerizo Moreno
Isla Santa Maria
Isla Española

0 miles 60
0 kilometres 60

Marine iguanas
These iguanas live only on the Galapagos Islands. They dive into the ocean for food and then warm up on the rocks.

Jivaro hunter
The Jivaro people live in the rain forests of Ecuador. They hunt monkeys and birds by shooting matchstick-thin darts from their blowguns.

Yanomami woman
About 19,000 Yanomami people live along the Brazil–Venezuela border. They live in small villages, grouped by families, and are trying to keep their traditional crafts and way of life.

Reed boat, Lake Titicaca

Lake Titicaca is in the Andes mountains between Peru and Bolivia. It is the highest navigable lake in the world— 12,506 feet (3,810 m) above sea level.

N
W E
S

0 miles 600
0 kilometers 600

## Map labels

Caribbean Sea
ARUBA (to Netherlands)
NETHERLANDS ANTILLES (to Netherlands)
GRENADA
TRINIDAD & TOBAGO
Santa Marta
Ríohacha
Coro
Maiquetia
CARACAS
Cumaná
Maturín
Barranquilla
Maracaibo
Valencia
Barcelona
Cartagena
Valledupar
Lake Maracaibo
Barquisimeto
PANAMA CITY
Montería
Sincelejo
Mérida
Barinas
San Fernando de Apure
Ciudad Bolívar
Ciudad Guayana
PANAMA
Cúcuta
San Cristóbal
Apure
Orinoco
Embalse de Guri
Gulf of Panama
Bucaramanga
VENEZUELA
GUY
Medellín
Puerto Carreño
Guiana Highlands
Quibdó
Cabo Corrientes
Tunja
Puerto Ayacucho
Pereira
Manizales
Meta
Orinoco
Lether
Armenia
BOGOTÁ
Villavicencio
Punta Chirambirá
Ibagué
Llanos
Guaviare
Boa Vista
Buenaventura
Palmira
Neiva
COLOMBIA
San José del Guaviare
Branco
Cali
Popayán
Nevado del Huila 18,865ft (5,750m)
Mitú
Vaupés
Florencia
Pasto
Mocoa
Caquetá
Esmeraldas
Bahía de Mania
Ibarra
Napo
Içana
Negro
Re de
Equator
QUITO
Japurá
Manta
ECUADOR
Napo
Portoviejo
Ambato
Riobamba
Içá
Amazon Basin
Manaus
Guayaquil
Cuenca
Tigre
Iquitos
Amazon
Tefé
Machala
Loja
Coari
Punta Pariñas
Juruá
Sullana
PERU
Purus
Piura
Chachapoyas
Moyobamba
Ucayali
Madiera
Punta Negro
Tarapoto
Chiclayo
Cajamarca
Pucallpa
Porto Velho
Trujillo
Purus
Río Branco
B
Chimbote
Nevado Huascarán 22,205ft (6,768m)
Alto Purús
Cerro de Pasco
Huacho
A
Madre de Dios
Huancayo
Machu Picchu
Callao
LIMA
Cuzco
Puerto Maldonado
Ayacucho
Abancay
BOLIVIA
Peninsula Paracas
Ica
Nevado Coropuna 21,079ft (6,425m)
Juliaca
Lake Titicaca
Punta Santa Maria
Puno
LA PAZ
Arequipa
PACIFIC OCEAN
Mollendo
Tacna
Arica
CHILE

Quechua Indian

About 45 percent of Peru's people are Indians, and most of these are Quechua. Their ancestors were the Incas who once ruled Peru.

Amazon ferry

The Amazon

The mighty Amazon River flows from the highlands of Peru through Brazil to the coast near Macapá. Dense tropical rain forest surrounds the river and its many tributaries. Here, trees can grow as tall as 20-story buildings to reach sunlight. More kinds of animals live in these jungles than anywhere else on Earth. At least 1,500 kinds of birds fly above the forest and up to 3,000 kinds of fishes swim in the rivers. Lizards and snakes slither along the ground. More than 800 types of mammals—including the world's largest group of bats—and countless insects are all at home in the Amazon.

Layers of life

High above the ground is the rain-forest canopy. Its tall trees and vines are home to birds and monkeys. The middle forest is more sheltered. Many birds also live here, along with reptiles and thousands of insects. The forest floor is cool, damp and dark. Ferns, fungi and saplings grow here, providing shelter and food for animals that live on the ground.

Kinkajou

Toucan

Tamandua
The tamandua is a skilled climber in its search for ants, termites and bees.

Jaguar
A jaguar is on the watch for prey. This powerful big cat is at risk because of rain-forest clearing.

Palla's long-tongued bat
Bats of many kinds are found in the Amazon rain forest. They feed on insects, fruits and nectar.

Bushmaster snake
Snakes thrive on the rain-forest floor. The bushmaster is the largest poisonous snake in the Americas. It grows to 10 feet (3 m).

Bird-eating spider
The bird-eating spider is a giant: it can be as wide as 11 inches (28 cm).

Hoatzin
The hoatzin is an unusual bird—it eats only leaves. Fifteen percent of all known bird species live in the Amazon rain forest.

Rio de Janeiro

Rio de Janeiro—home to 7 million people—is Brazil's most famous city. It was named in January 1502 by the Portuguese explorer Gaspar de Lemos, who mistook its huge bay for a river and called it Rio de Janeiro (River of January). The mountain Corcovado rises straight up from the city and is topped by a huge statue, Christ the Redeemer.

Christ the Redeemer

Sugarloaf Mountain

Copacabana Beach

Guanabara Bay

### Map labels

ATLANTIC OCEAN

ORGETOWN
w Amsterdam
PARAMARIBO
Moengo
poera
ssor Van
tein Meer
RINAME
FRENCH GUIANA
(to France)
Kourou
CAYENNE
Cabo Orange
Cabo Norte
Mouths of the Amazon
Macapá
Baía de Marajó
Equator
Ilha de Marajó
Belém
Castanhal
Baía de São Marcos
arintins
Santarém
São Luís
Parnaíba
Amazon
Santa Inês
Sobral
Fortaleza
uba
Tapajós
Maranhão
Iriri
Bacabal
Teresina
Mossoró
Marabá
Imperatriz
Natal
Araguaína
Carolina
Picos
Iguatu
João Pessoa
Redenção
Juàzeiro do Norte
Campina Grande
Recife
Manuel
Xingu
Palmas
Juàzeiro
Arapiraca
Maceió
Gurupi
Barragem de Sobradinho
São Francisco
Aracaju
AZIL
Mato Grosso
Barragem de São Simão
Feira de Santana
Camaçari
Salvador
Cuiabá
Vitória da Conquista
Itabuna
Ilhéus
Rondonópolis
BRASÍLIA
Brazilian Highlands
Montes Claros
Teófilo Otôni
Ponta da Baleia
antal
Anápolis
Goiânia
Rio Verde
Represa São Simão
Represa Três Marias
umbá
Uberlândia
Uberaba
Patos de Minas
Governador Valadares
Campo Grande
Represa Porto Primavera
São José do Rio Preto
Ipatinga
Colatina
Linhares
ourados
Franca
Poços de Caldas
Belo Horizonte
Serra
Vitória
Araçatuba
Ribeirão Preto
Barbarena
Juiz de Fora
Cachoeiro do Itapemirim
Marília
Bauru
Limeira
Campos dos Goytacazes
Londrina
Piracicaba
Nova Iguaçu
Macaé
São Gonçalo
of Capricorn
Maringá
Campinas
São Paulo
Rio de Janeiro
Represa de Itaipu
Ponta Grossa
Santos
Tropic of Capricorn
Foz do Iguaçu
Curitiba
Iguaço Falls
Joinville
NTINA
Chapecó
Uruguai
Lages
Florianópolis
Santa Maria
Passo Fundo
Caxias do Sul
Novo Hamburgo
Canoas
Bagé
Porto Alegre
URUGUAY
Pelotas
Lagoa dos Patos
Rio Grande
Lagoa Mirim
Lagoa Mangueira

Southern South America

Andean condor
This bird is a type of vulture. It is one of two animals that appear on the national coat of arms of Chile. The Andean condor ranges from the Pacific coast to the high Andes in search of the dead animals on which it feeds. It has a wingspan of 10 feet (3 m).

ARGENTINA
POPULATION 38,741,000 ★ CAPITAL BUENOS AIRES

CHILE
POPULATION 15,665,000 ★ CAPITAL SANTIAGO

BOLIVIA
POPULATION 8,586,000 ★ CAPITAL LA PAZ

PARAGUAY
POPULATION 6,037,000 ★ CAPITAL ASCUNCIÓN

URUGUAY
POPULATION 3,413,000 ★ CAPITAL MONTEVIDEO

Llamas
Llamas are related to the camel. They are domesticated animals and are used to carry goods in mountainous regions in Bolivia, Chile and Argentina. They are also farmed for their meat, wool and hides.

The Andes extends down western South America and is the longest continuous mountain chain in the world. It has 13 peaks more than 20,000 feet (6,100 m) high, and many active volcanoes.

Bolivian dress
The Aymara are one of the native peoples of Bolivia. They weave textiles to make colorful ponchos and shawls. The women wear bowler hats. Married women wear their hats straight, and unmarried ones tip them to one side.

Jesuit mission
Jesuits are a Roman Catholic order of religious men known for missionary and educational work. In the 1600s, Jesuits went to Bolivia and set up religious settlements called missions. The church buildings, such as the one at Concepción, were often built of rare timbers, decorated with ornate carving.

### Map labels

BRAZIL

BOLIVIA
PARAGUAY
PERU

PACIFIC OCEAN

Cascavel
Foz do Iguaçu
Eldorado
Posadas
Represa de Itaipú
Iguaçú Falls
Pedro Juan Caballero
Concepción
Paraguay
San Lorenzo
ASUNCIÓN
Villarrica
San Juan Bautista
Encarnación
Corrientes
Pilar
Filadelfia
Ibarreta
Formosa
Pozo Colorado
Las Lomitas
Bermejo
Resistencia
Presidencia Roque
Bahía Negro
Puerto Suárez
San Matías
San Ignacio
Robore
Concepción
Santa Cruz
Camiri
Yacuiba
Bermejo
San Salvador de Jujuy
Salta
San Miguel de Tucumán
La Banda
Santiago del Estero
Cafayate
Metán
Nevado de Cachi 22,047ft (6,720m)
San Pedro de Atacama
Nevado Ojos del Salado 22,664ft (6,908m)
Volcán Llullaillaco 22,057ft (6,723m)
Volcán Licancábur 19,426ft (5,920m)
Chuquicamata
Calama
Tupiza
Villazón
Tarija
Villa Montes
SUCRE
Potosí
Uyuni
Villa Martín
Salar de Uyuni
Salar de Coipasa
Lago de Poopó
Oruro
Huanuni
Cochabamba
Punata
Montero
Concepción
Magdalena
Negro
San Miguel
Mamoré
Trinidad
Laguna San Luis
Laguna Rogaguado
San Borja
Riberalta
Beni
Madre de Dios
Río Branco
Lake Titicaca
Juliaca
Tacna
Arica
Iquique
Lagunas
Pica
Putre
Nevado Sajama 21,463ft (6,542m)
LA PAZ
Atacama Desert
Antofagasta
Tocopilla
Taltal
Chañaral
Caldera
Copiapó
Punta Jorjino
Salinas Grandes
Salar de Atacama
Puna de Atacama
Pilcomayo
Chaco
Bermejo Viejo

Tropic of Capricorn

Atacama Desert

The Atacama Desert is the driest place on Earth. Rain has never been recorded in some parts. The desert extends about 600 miles (1,000 km) from northern Chile to the adjacent Peruvian Desert. It is bordered by the Pacific Ocean on one side and the Andes mountains on the other. The land is made up of salt basins, sand and lava flows, and is so rugged that it has been compared to the surface of the Moon.

Rainfall

A passing shower may occur only a few times each century in some parts of the Atacama Desert. In general, there is so little rain that it can hardly be measured.

Fog-catcher nets
Fog catchers are used in very dry areas where there is frequent fog. As the fog passes through the nets, beads of moisture are trapped and drip down into pipes. The pipes carry this water to villages for use in homes and on farms.

Fog-catcher nets

Coastal deserts

Frequent fog and cold water along the shore are common features of coastal deserts. The Pacific Ocean waters on the coast of the Atacama Desert are chilled by the cold Humboldt Current that flows north from Antarctica. Onshore winds are normally warm and moist, bringing rain, but in this region, they are cooled by the cold current. This lowers the rate of evaporation from the water's surface, reduces moisture, produces fogs, and makes the desert even drier.

Low-latitude winds

High-latitude winds

Cold current

Cold water

Tango dancers

The tango is a passionate dance and type of music that originated during the mid-1800s in the poor districts of Buenos Aires, Argentina. The dance mixes long pauses with rapid, stylized moves.

Orca

Pampas

In Argentina, there are vast areas of grass-covered plains called pampas. These support millions of beef cattle. From the mid-1800s, skilled horsemen called gauchos lived a nomadic life roaming the pampas. Today, they live and work on cattle farms.

South America

LAND AREA	6,731,004 sq miles (17,433,220 sq km)
LARGEST COUNTRY	Brazil
SMALLEST COUNTRY	Suriname
MAIN RELIGION	Christian
LIFE EXPECTANCY	72 years
LITERACY	93%

Anchovies
Peru is one of the top five fishing countries in the world, and anchovies are the main catch. Recent supplies have been affected by overfishing, and the seasonal changes to ocean currents called the El Niño effect. Most of the anchovies are dried to produce fish meal, which is sold for livestock feed.

USING THE LAND

- Forest and woodland
- Arable land
- Grazing
- Arid or marginal

- Cereals
- Fruit
- Citrus fruits
- Bananas
- Wine
- Cotton
- Coffee
- Cocoa
- Sugarcane
- Soybeans
- Rubber
- Beef cattle
- Sheep
- Fishing
- Shellfish
- Industrial center
- Mining
- Oil production
- Timber
- Tourism

Silver and tin
In 1545, huge silver deposits were found at Potosí, Bolivia, and it soon became the richest source of silver in the world. After four centuries of mining, the mine was largely exhausted. Tin has since become Bolivia's most important mineral.

Tomatoes and potatoes are originally from South America.

CARACAS, BOGOTÁ, GEORGETOWN, PARAMARIBO, CAYENNE, QUITO, Guayaquil, Macapá, Belém, Manaus, Trujillo, Fortaleza, LIMA, Recife, Arequipa, LA PAZ, BRASÍLIA, SUCRE, Salvador, SÃO PAULO, Rio de Janeiro, ASUNCIÓN, Córdoba, Porto Alegre, SANTIAGO, BUENOS AIRES, MONTEVIDEO, Bahía Blanca, Puerto Montt, Stanley, Punta Arenas

Potatoes
Potatoes grow wild in the Chilean highlands. Sliced, dried potato, called *chuño*, which was eaten centuries ago by the Incas, is still eaten today. It can be stored for months for later use.

NATURAL FEATURES

Moreno Glacier ARGENTINA
Moreno Glacier, at the southern tip of the Andes, is 30 miles (50 km) long and 2 miles (3 km) wide. Named for the naturalist Francisco Moreno, it is the largest glacier in Patagonia and the only one not decreasing in size.

Moreno Glacier

Salar de Uyuni BOLIVIA
The Salar (salt pan) de Uyuni was once a prehistoric lake. Today, it covers 4,680 square miles (12,120 sq km) of the Bolivian altiplano, or high plains. When it rains, the salt pan fills with a layer of water and shines like a mirror.

The Pantanal BRAZIL
Covering an area of 50,000 square miles (129,500 sq km), the Pantanal in western Brazil is the world's largest wetland. It sustains huge flocks of birds, as well as anacondas, crocodiles, deer and giant river otters.

Iguaçu Falls

Iguaçu Falls ARGENTINA–BRAZIL
These spectacular falls on the Argentine border with Brazil include 275 separate waterfalls, some of which drop 262 feet (80 m). The surrounding subtropical rain forest is home to howler monkeys, jaguars and tapirs.

Torres del Paine CHILE
The Torres (towers) del Paine are three jagged granite peaks that rise more than 6,560 feet (2,000 m) above the surrounding plain in Patagonia. The earliest was formed about 12 million years ago. Glaciers flow from the peaks.

Torres del Paine

Blue-footed booby

Galapagos Islands

About 600 miles (960 km) off the coast of Ecuador, the Galapagos Islands are home to many unique plants and animals. Some species of animals and birds, such as the blue-footed booby, are found only on these islands. The Galapagos tortoise, the world's largest living tortoise, can survive for up to 200 years—longer than any other animal.

WHERE PEOPLE LIVE

	Urban	Rural	

REGION	
73%	27%

Most urban: URUGUAY	
91%	9%

Most rural: PARAGUAY	
55%	45%

LARGEST CITIES

Buenos Aires 11,928,000

São Paulo 10,333,000

Lima 8,380,000

Bogotá 6,982,000

PLACES

La Paz BOLIVIA
At an altitude of 12,500 feet (3,812 m) at its center, La Paz, the administrative capital of Bolivia, is the highest capital city in the world. This hub of Bolivian commerce lies in a valley surrounded by Altiplano (high plains).

Cartagena COLOMBIA
Founded in 1533, Cartagena was once a slave port. Although the Spanish built forts to ward off British and French attacks, they were unsuccessful—in the 17th and 18th centuries Spain built the largest defense system in South America.

Machu Picchu
The Incas built this city on a ridge 50 miles (80 km) from Cuzco, in southern Peru, in the mid-1400s. They abandoned it 100 years later, and it was not rediscovered until 1911. The site is a 2-square-mile (5-sq-km) complex of granite buildings and plazas surrounded by farm terraces. It was probably a royal estate or religious center.

National Congress, Brasília

Brasília BRAZIL
The construction of Brasília, the capital of Brazil, began on an almost barren site in 1956. The city, complete with parks and artificial lakes, was laid out to a plan that, from the air, some say resembles a bow and arrow and others say a bird in flight.

Buenos Aires ARGENTINA
Buenos Aires was founded in the 16th century and became the capital of Argentina in the 18th century. More than a third of Argentina's people live in the city and its suburbs. Buenos Aires has a large number of theaters and museums.

Paramaribo SURINAME
This city, the capital of Suriname, was settled by the French around 1640. It became a British colony in 1651 and, in a deal in 1667, Britain swapped it for present-day New York, which was then owned by the Dutch.

Dutch colonial buildings

TRADITIONS AND CULTURE

Maté tea
Maté tea is made in a gourd (*below*) from a herb called yerba mate, and sipped through a metal straw called a *bombilla*. Groups of people often drink the tea together, passing the gourd and straw from person to person.

Gauchos
Gauchos are cowboys of the pampas of Argentina and Chile. Centuries ago, they led a tough, independent life. Now they work on ranches and are no longer self-reliant, but they still value their strength and independence.

Gauchos

Amazon peoples
People have lived in the Amazon rain forest for at least 10,000 years. They obtain a small amount of their food by hunting and gathering, but most of their food is harvested from small agricultural plots. Their traditional way of life is today threatened by the destruction of much of the rain forest.

Apus
People in parts of Peru have combined their traditional beliefs with Christianity. They worship apus, or spirits of the mountains, by marking the apu's home, such as a hill or a stream, with a type of Christian cross.

Hallaca
This traditional Christmas dish in Venezuela consists of a corn or maize dough filled with meat and seasonings, wrapped in a banana leaf and steamed. It is eaten after mass on Christmas Eve.

Amazon animals
The anaconda (*above*), which kills its prey by squeezing until it suffocates, is found in the Amazon River. It can reach 30 feet (9 m) in length. The goliath bird-eating spider, the largest in the world, lives in rain-forested regions. It eats young birds, frogs and even bats. When threatened, it makes a loud hissing noise by rubbing its legs together. The world's heaviest rodent, the capybara, is also a rain-forest dweller. It can weigh up to 145 pounds (65 kg).

PEOPLE

Atahuallpa c 1502–33
Atahuallpa was the last ruler of the Inca. In 1532, after a five-year struggle, he was captured by the Spaniards, who asked the Incas for a huge ransom for his release. Although the ransom was paid, Atahuallpa was executed in 1533.

Bernardo O'Higgins 1776–1842
A revolutionary leader who fought to achieve Chile's independence from Spain, O'Higgins became the director of Chile in 1817. However, he was unpopular and resigned in 1823.

Simón Bolívar 1783–1830
Bolívar (*right*), born in Venezuela, was called "the Liberator" for his role in helping several South American nations to gain independence. The country of Bolivia was named in his honor.

Eva Perón 1919–52
Known also as Evita, Eva was the popular wife of Juan Perón, the president of Argentina. She gained women the right to vote in 1947 and provided financial assistance to the poor.

Eva Perón

Pelé born 1940
Brazilian-born Pelé is a world-famous soccer player and the only player to have played in four World Cup championships. In 1999, Pelé was named the athlete of the century by the National Olympics Committee.

HISTORY AT A GLANCE
GREAT CIVILIZATIONS

Moche ear ornament

NAZCA
The Nazca people lived in southern Peru from about 200 BC to AD 600. They are best known for their distinctive pottery, which was decorated with bright, multicolored images of humans and animals, and for the huge depictions of animals and shapes they made on the desert floor. No one knows why these "Nazca lines" were created.

MOCHE
Moche was the main civilization on the north coast of Peru from the 1st to the 8th century. Two well-known remnants of this civilization are the Temple of the Sun and the Temple of the Moon. In 1987, tombs filled with treasures were found near Sipán. The most famous tomb is thought to contain the Lord of Sipán, a Moche warrior-priest.

Kalasasaya temple, Tiwanaku

TIWANAKU AND HUARI
These two civilizations held power in the south-central Andes from the 1st to the 9th century. The Tiwanaku built temples and pyramids south of Lake Titicaca. The Huari people established their city in the Ayacucho Basin. Huari buildings have not survived, but remnants of their pottery have been found.

CHIMÚ AND CHINCHA
The Chimú people appeared in the 10th century in the Moche Valley and built the city of Chan Chan as their capital. They dug irrigation canals to supply water to the city and their crops. Chincha, on the south coast of Peru, was a rich desert kingdom. It was a powerful commercial center that was brought under Inca control.

Inca statue

THE INCAS
The Incas were a group of tribes that lived around Cuzco in southern Peru. By the 13th century they began to expand, and in the 15th century were well established. At its height, the Inca empire was the largest in the Americas, extending 2,500 miles (4,000 km) from Colombia and Equador south to Chile and Argentina. In 1532, the empire fell to the Spanish conquistador Francisco Pizarro, who had with him only 167 men.

Francisco Pizarro

ARCT

Kara Sea

North Siber
Lowlan

Ural Mountains

West Siberian Plain

Ob'

Irtysh

Yenisey

Altai Mountai

Caspian
Depression

Kazakhskiy
Plain

Black Sea

Caucasus

Aral
Sea

Lake
Balkhash

Anatolia

Caspian Sea

Ustyurt
Plateau

Turan Lowland

Tien Shan

Cyprus

Karakum
Desert

Tarim Basin

Taklimakan Desert

Kunlun Shan

Quil

Syrian
Desert

Tigris

Iranian
Plateau

Hindu Kush

Plateau of
Tibet

An Nafūd

Euphrates

Zagros
Mountains

Indus

Himalaya

Mt Everest
29,035ft (8,850m)

Red Sea

Persian Gulf

Thar Desert

Gangetic Plain

Brahmaputra

Arabian
Peninsula

Gulf of
Oman

Ganges

Rubʿ al Khālī

Indian
Subcontinent

Chin Hills

Irrawaddy

Gulf of Aden

Socotra

Arabian
Sea

Western Ghats

Deccan
Plateau

Eastern Ghats

Bay of
Bengal

Laccadive
Islands

Laccadive Sea

Andaman
Islands

Andaman
Sea

Maldives

Sri Lanka

Nicobar
Islands

INDIAN OCEAN

CEAN

vernaya
mlya

New Siberia
Islands

East
Siberian
Sea

Laptev Sea

Bering Strait

Gulf of Anadyr

Khrebet Cherskogo

Kamchatka Peninsula

entral
berian
ateau

Varkhoyanskiy Khrebet

Lena

i b e r i a

Kirenga

Stanovoy
Khrebet

Sea of
Okhotsk

Lake
Baikal

Heilong Jiang (Amur)

Sakhalin

Argun

Mongolian
Plateau

Manchurian
Plain

Sikhote-Alin'

Sea
of

Kuril Islands

obi Desert

Yellow

Yellow

Bo
Hai

Korea
Bay

Japan

Hokkaidō

Korean
Peninsula

Yellow
Sea

Honshū

Great Plain
of China

Korea Strait

Shikoku

Sichuan
Basin

Yangtze

East
China
Sea

Kyūshū

Ryukyu Islands

Yangtze

Taiwan Strait

Asia

Taiwan

Hainan

Luzon

Philippine
Sea

PACIFIC OCEAN

Khorat
Plateau

Mindoro

Philippines

Samar

Indochina
Peninsula

South

Palawan

Panay

China

Negros

Cebu

Gulf of
hailand

Sea

Sulu
Sea

Mindanao

Malay
ninsula

Celebes
Sea

lt of Malacca

Greater Sunda Islands

umatra

Borneo

Moluccas

New
Guinea

Malay Archipelago

Sulawesi

Banda
Sea

Java Sea
Flores

Arafura
Sea

Java

Sea

Lesser Sunda Islands

Timor

Timor

Sea

Russia

Nenets' camp
The Nenets live in the far northwest region of Russia. They are hunters and reindeer herders. Each season, when the reindeer migrate, the Nenets set up tents and cover them with animal skins for warmth.

RUSSIA
POPULATION **144,526,000** ＊ CAPITAL **MOSCOW**

St Basil's Cathedral
This ornate cathedral in Moscow was built by Czar Ivan the Terrible. Work began in 1554. When first built, the cathedral was painted white. The eight colorful domes are shaped rather like onions to shed heavy snow and rain.

Russia is the largest country in the world. It covers two-thirds of Asia and one-third of Europe, and has 11 time zones. Russia was once part of a much larger country called the Soviet Union.

Wolf

Sturgeon
Up to 90 percent of the world's sturgeon comes from the Caspian Sea. The giant sturgeon grows to 19 feet (6 m) long and can live for 150 years. Sturgeon roe, or eggs, is called caviar. It is an expensive delicacy.

Siberian timber house
The homes of wealthy Siberians in the early 1800s were built of timber. Some of the finest are in Irkutsk, near Lake Baikal. They have shuttered windows and ornate decoration.

Franz Josef Land

Novaya Zemlya

Kara Sea

Ostrov Belyy

Barents Sea

Ostrov Kolguyev

Pechorskoye More

Ostrov Vaygach

Yamal Peninsula

Gydanskiy Peninsula

North Cape

Arctic Circle

FINLAND

Murmansk

Kandalaksha

Kola Peninsula

White Sea

Severodvinsk

Arkhangel'sk

Vorkuta

ESTONIA

Gulf of Finland

St Petersburg

Lake Ladoga

Petrozavodsk

Lake Onega

LATVIA

Pskov

Velikiye Novgorod

Cherepovets

Velikiye Luki

Smolensk

Tver'

Vologda

Rybinsk

BELARUS

Kaluga

Yaroslavl'

Bryansk

MOSCOW (MOSKVA)

Vladimir

Syktyvkar

Ukhta

Orel

Tula

Kolomna

Novomoskovsk

Nizhniy Novgorod

Kirov

UKRAINE

Kursk

Ryazan'

Arzamas

Yoshkar-Ola

Solikamsk

Belgorod

Lipetsk

Michurinsk

Cheboksary

Glazov

Berezniki

Staryy Oskol

Voronezh

Tambov

Saransk

Kazan'

Izhevsk

Perm'

Serov

Penza

Ul'yanovsk

Kuznetsk

Naberezhnyye Chelny

Sarapul

Nizhniy Tagil

Donets'k

Saratov

Syzran'

Tol'yatti

Neftekamsk

Pervoural'sk

Yekaterinburg

Surgut

Nizhnevartovsk

Sea of Azov

Engel's

Balakovo

Samara

Oktyabr'skiy

Ufa

Kamensk-Ural'skiy

Rostov-na-Donu

Volga

Sterlitamak

Zlatoust

Tyumen'

Tobol'sk

Novorossiysk

Shakhty

Volgograd

Miass

Chelyabinsk

Krasnodar

Maykop

Armavir

Elista

Ural'sk

Orenburg

Magnitogorsk

Kurgan

Sochi

Nevinnomyssk

Stavropol

Pyatigorsk

Nal'chik

Astrakhan'

Orsk

Petropavlovsk

Omsk

Cherkessk

Elbrus 18,510ft (5,642m)

Caspian Depression

Atyrau

Tomsk

Black Sea

GEORGIA

Groznyy

Caspian Sea

KAZAKHSTAN

Achinsk

T'BILISI

Makhachkala

Kemerovo

Krasnoyarsk

AZERBAIJAN

Caucasus

Novosibirsk

Kiselevsk

Novokuznetsk

Abakan

Barnaul

BAKU (BAKI)

Biysk

Rubtsovsk

Semipalatinsk

Zapadnyy

Gora Belukha 14,783ft (4,506m)

Ural Mountains

West Siberian Plain

R U S S

Ob

Irtysh

Yenisey

Taz

Obskaja Guba

Baydaratskaya Guba

Noril'sk

Life in the last ice age

The last ice age was at its coldest 18,000 years ago. Because of the extreme cold, only large animals that had adapted to the climate survived. Frozen remains, and paintings on the walls of caves, reveal what these creatures were like. Many ice-age animals died out as the climate became warmer.

Woolly rhinoceros
This animal had two prominent nose horns. The longer front one extended more than 40 inches (104 cm).

Cave bear
This animal got its name from its habit of sleeping in a cave during winter. It had a large head and very powerful front legs.

Musk ox
The huge musk ox still lives in Greenland and Canada. It is related to the goat.

Early hunter
Humans hunted ice-age animals for their meat and skins. People on the Russian plain lived in huts made of mammoth bones.

Woolly mammoth
This huge animal belonged to the same family as the elephant. It stood about 10 feet (3 m) tall at the shoulder and had curved tusks of about the same length. Its woolly coat protected it from the cold.

Shaman
A shaman is a spiritual leader and healer. Some Central Asian nomadic peoples have followed a religion called Shamanism for hundreds of years.

Mining
Coal mining has been an important industry in Russia for more than 150 years. Oil, gas, diamonds, zinc and silver are also mined.

Ostrov Komsomolets
Ostrov Oktyabr'skoy Revolyutsii
Ostrov Bol'shevik
Severnaya Zemlya
Cape Chelyuskin
Ozero Taymyr
Severo-Sibirskaya Nizmennost'
ARCTIC OCEAN
Laptev Sea
New Siberia Islands
Ostrov Kotel'nyy
Ostrov Novaya Sibir'
Ostrov Bol'shoy Lyakhovskiy
Ostrov Bol'shoy Begichev
East Siberian Sea
Wrangel Island
Chuckchi Sea
Bering Strait
Arctic Circle
Chukotskiy Peninsula
U.S.A.
Sevenyy Anyuyskiy Khrebet
Anadyr'
Bering Sea
Khatanga
Olenek
Lena
Yana
Indigirka
Kolyma
Omolon
Verkhoyanskiy Khrebet
Khrebet Cherskogo
Khrebet Kolymskiy
Yukagirskoye Ploskogor'ye
Koryakskiy Khrebet
Central Siberian Plateau
Vilyuyskoye Vodokhranilishche
Nizhnyaya Tunguska
Mirnyy
Vilyuy
Amga
Aldan
Yakutsk
Okhotsk
Magadan
Zaliv Shelikhova
Ostrov Karaginskiy
Sopka Klyuchevskaya 15,584ft (4,750m)
Kamchatka Peninsula
Petropavlovsk-Kamchatskiy
RUSSIA
SIBERIA
Angara
Ust'-Ilimsk
...atsk
Bratskoye Vodokhranilishche
Usol'ye-Sibirskoye
Angarsk
Irkutsk
Ulan-Ude
Lake Baikal
Stanovoye Nagor'ye
Chita
Stanovoy Khrebet
Khrebet Dzhugdzhur
Tynda
Zeyskoye Vodokhranilishche
Shantarskiye Ostrova
Sea of Okhotsk
Ostrov Paramushir
Ostrov Onekotan
Kuril Islands
Ostrov Urup
Ostrov Iturup
Ostrov Kunashir
(administered by Russian Federation; claimed by Japan)
MONGOLIA
Manzhouli
CHINA
Komsomol'sk-na-Amure
Blagoveshchensk
Khabarovsk
Birobidzhan
Amur
Hegang
Jiamusi
Jixi
Mudanjiang
Ussuriysk
Vladivostok
Nakhodka
Sakhalin
Tatarskiy Proliv
Sikhote-Alin'
Yuzhno-Sakhalinsk
PACIFIC OCEAN
Hokkaidō
Kushiro
Sapporo
Sea of Japan
JAPAN

0 miles 600
0 kilometers 600
N W E S

Russia

LAND AREA	6,562,115 sq miles (16,995,800 sq km)
OFFICIAL LANGUAGE	Russian
MAIN RELIGION	Christian
LIFE EXPECTANCY	73 years
LITERACY	99%

NATURAL FEATURES

Siberian tiger

Russian steppe
The Russian steppe is a vast, low-lying plain in southern Russia. Much of the plain lies less than 650 feet (200 m) above sea level. The natural vegetation includes grasses, mosses, lichen and trees.

Ural Mountains
These mountains divide European Russia from Siberia, and form the traditional border between Europe and Asia. The Urals extend from the Arctic Circle south for 1,550 miles (2,500 km) to the arid region near the Kazakhstan border.

Russian taiga
An area of coniferous forest, lakes, bogs and rivers in northern Russia, the taiga is home to many small mammals as well as moose, wolves and the rare Siberian tiger.

Lake Baikal
Formed more than 25 million years ago, Lake Baikal, in Siberia, is the oldest and deepest lake in the world. More than 1 mile (1,620 m) deep, it holds one-fifth of Earth's freshwater supplies. Home to more than 1,200 native plant and animal species, it is threatened by industrial wastewater pollution.

Tunguska meteorite
On 30 June 1908, a huge area of the forest in Tunguska, in a remote part of Siberia, was destroyed by an enormous fireball. Many scientists believe it was the largest meteorite to fall to Earth in the last 2,000 years. No fragments of it were left behind.

USING THE LAND

Natural resources
Russia has enormous deposits of iron, coal, oil and natural gas (left). However, two-thirds of the country's oil and natural gas deposits are in Siberia, which is a long way from the major population centers. Siberia's harsh climate makes it difficult to extract them.

- Forest and woodland
- Arable land
- Grazing
- Arid or marginal

Lake Baikal

- Cereals
- Potatoes
- Beef cattle
- Reindeer
- Fishing
- Industrial center
- Mining
- Oil production
- Gas production
- Timber

St Petersburg · MOSCOW · Nizhniy Novgorod · Volgograd · Stavropol' · Yekaterinburg · Omsk · Novosibirsk · Irkutsk · Yakutsk · Magadan · Anadyr' · Petropavlovsk-Kamchatskiy · Vladivostok

Russia is the largest country in the world.

LARGEST CITIES

Moscow 11,247,000

St Petersburg 4,645,000

Novosibirsk 1,435,000

Yekaterinburg 1,300,000

Nizhniy Novgorod 1,269,000

HIGHEST MOUNTAINS

Elbrus 18,510 feet (5,642 m)
Dykhtau 17,073 feet (5,204 m)
Sopka Klyuchevskaya 15,584 feet (4,750 m)
Gora Belukha 14,783 feet (4,506 m)

WHERE PEOPLE LIVE

Urban	Rural
77%	23%

Reindeer farms
Reindeer provide food and livelihood for many ethnic communities in Russia. More than 200 reindeer farms raise 2.4 million animals across the northern half of Russia, mostly in Siberia. Farming has been affected by wolves, and by oil, gas and mineral exploration.

Forestry
Russia contains the largest tracts of forests on Earth and produces one-fifth of the world's softwood. However, Russia's forests and timber industry are now threatened by a high level of illegal logging and a decrease in the use of wood by neighboring countries.

PEOPLE

Ivan the Terrible 1530–84
Ivan IV became the first czar (emperor) of Russia in 1547. Balanced against his political reform and territorial expansion was the fact that he instituted a reign of terror among the Russian nobility, killing thousands of people.

Catherine the Great 1729–96
Catherine II became czarina (empress) of Russia in 1796 as a result of a coup in which her husband (Peter the Great) was murdered. She successfully waged war against Turkey and Poland, increasing Russia's territory. During her reign, Russia enjoyed a period of stability.

Leo Tolstoy 1828–1910
One of the world's literary masters, Leo Tolstoy had a strong belief in the virtues of the simple peasant life—a belief that was reflected in his work. His most famous novel is *War and Peace*, an epic tale about Russia's struggle against France in the Napoleonic Wars.

Peter Tchaikovsky 1840–93
The compositions of the classical composer Peter Tchaikovsky are still played in concerts all over the world. His works include the ballets *Swan Lake* and *The Nutcracker*.

Grigory Rasputin 1871–1916

Born a Siberian peasant, this priest and mystic exerted a great deal of influence over the family of Czar Nicholas II and the court. Scandals surrounding Rasputin led to his murder by a group of nobles.

Trans-Siberian railroad
Stretching almost one-fourth of the way around the globe, the Trans-Siberian railroad is the longest rail system in the world. The journey from Moscow to Vladivostok makes 92 stops, takes eight days and covers 5,778 miles (9,244 km). The railroad was built between 1891 and 1904, in the reign of Alexander III.

TRADITIONS AND CULTURE

Icon painting
Icons are small religious images. Russia developed its own style of icon painting in the 15th century, using local saints and backgrounds. The icons illustrate legends, parables or rites of the Russian Orthodox Church. Painted icons are noted for their bright colors, including gold, and emphasis on strong outlines.

Matryoshka dolls
Also called "nesting dolls," these brightly painted, hollow wooden dolls are shaped so that they fit inside one another. They are an example of traditional Russian folk art. Sometimes matryoshka dolls represent a whole family, with some sets including more than 12 dolls.

Fabergé eggs
Created by Russian goldsmith and jeweler Peter Fabergé, these Easter eggs are his finest work. Fabergé made the first egg in 1884 as an Easter present for Czar Alexander III to give to his wife—thus beginning a tradition in the royal family. Each ornate jeweled egg contained an elaborate surprise gift for the czarina.

Russian ballet
Russia's ballet schools have produced many of the world's greatest ballet dancers, such as Rudolph Nureyev and Anna Pavlova. The Bolshoi Ballet, meaning "great ballet" in Russian, in Moscow is one of the world's leading ballet companies.

Troika rides
Far from being a thing of the past, horse-drawn sleighs in winter (and carriages in summer) are becoming more popular in Russia, not just as a novelty ride, but as transport for well-to-do business people and politicians.

Lenin
Born Vladimir Ilyich Ulyanov in 1870, Lenin founded the Communist Party, led the Russian Revolution and created the Soviet state, the world's first communist regime. His aim was to create a classless society ruled by workers, soldiers and peasants. He died in 1924 and people visit his tomb in the Kremlin, where his body is preserved.

PLACES

The Kremlin MOSCOW
This is a large walled area in the center of Moscow (*below*). Built in 1156 and much enlarged since, the Kremlin is the seat of the Russian government and the center of the Russian Orthodox Church. It also has magnificent palaces and churches that are open to the public.

The Kremlin

Velikiy Novgorod
This northwestern city is one of the oldest in Russia. It was a thriving cultural and trading center in medieval times. With its many fine historic buildings, it is a popular tourist destination.

Vladivostok
This major port and naval base is located on a peninsula in the Sea of Japan. Its name means "rule the East." Founded in 1860 as a military outpost, it was closed to foreigners during the Cold War.

St Petersburg
This city, built in 1703 by Peter the Great, is the second-largest city in Russia. For 200 years up to 1918, it was Russia's capital city. St Petersburg is a major industrial and commercial center and its port, although frozen for part of the year, is one of the largest in the world. Constructed in the 18th century for Catherine the Great as her winter palace, the Hermitage Museum (*below*) is the largest museum and art gallery in Russia.

Hermitage Museum, St Petersburg

HISTORY AT A GLANCE
RUSSIA SINCE 1917

Russian Revolution poster

RUSSIAN REVOLUTION
Czar Nicholas II was a poor leader in World War I, and his government collapsed in 1917. The Bolsheviks seized power in October of that year and brought Russia under communist control, with Lenin as leader. After a series of wars, the communists formed the Union of Soviet Socialist Republics (USSR), or Soviet Union, in 1922.

JOSEPH STALIN
By 1928, Stalin had assumed sole power over the USSR and remained as dictator until his death in 1953. He centralized industries and set up state farms. His rule was noted for its harshness.

WORLD WAR II
In 1941, Germany invaded the USSR and encircled the city of Leningrad. After much suffering, the Soviets broke the siege in 1944. At the end of the war, the USSR occupied much of eastern Europe.

The Battle of Leningrad memorial

COLD WAR
The so-called cold war between the USSR and the USA climaxed in October 1962, with the Cuban missile crisis—the USA's discovery of Soviet missiles in Cuba. Nuclear war was averted.

YURI GAGARIN
On 12 April 1961, this Soviet cosmonaut became the first man in space. Flying at a maximum altitude of 187 miles (299 km) in the Vostok I spacecraft, Gagarin orbited Earth once before landing. He never flew into space again.

Yuri Gagarin

POLITICAL REFORM
Mikhail Gorbachev, president of the USSR (1990–91), was a reformer within the Communist Party who worked to decentralize power in the USSR and improve ties with the USA.

BREAKUP OF THE USSR
Gorbachev's quest for openness (*glasnost*) and restructuring (*perestroika*) led to the breakup of the USSR and ended its control of eastern Europe. The USSR ceased to exist on 31 December 1991.

RUSSIAN FEDERATION
Russia faced many problems as it tried to become more democratic and develop a freer economy. In 1994, Russia invaded Chechnia to reassert its control over its former territory. In 2000, Vladimir Putin became president.

Western Asia

Whirling dervishes

Library at Ephesus
Ephesus, in western Turkey, was part of the Roman empire. In about AD 151, a two-storied library was built there for the public to use. Most libraries at that time were privately owned. Books were in the form of hand-written papyrus rolls. Copies were made by people called scribes.

Sheep farming
Farmers in Turkey raise sheep for their milk, meat, wool and hides. The wool of the fat-tailed carpet breeds is used to make rugs. Very fast, agile Anatolian shepherd dogs guard the sheep. They ward off predators and defend property.

TURKEY
POPULATION 68,109,000 ✳ CAPITAL ANKARA

AZERBAIJAN
POPULATION 7,831,000 ✳ CAPITAL BAKU

GEORGIA
POPULATION 4,934,000 ✳ CAPITAL T'BILISI

ARMENIA
POPULATION 3,326,000 ✳ CAPITAL YEREVAN

CYPRUS
POPULATION 772,000 ✳ CAPITAL NICOSIA

Trojan horse
Troy was an ancient city in what is now Turkey. According to legend, after 10 years of war between Greece and Troy, the Greeks hid soldiers inside a huge wooden horse, and left it at the gates of Troy. Intrigued, the Trojans took it into the city. The Greek soldiers emerged and defeated Troy.

Citrus farming
Groves of lemons, grapefruit and oranges thrive on the many small citrus farms in Cyprus. The hot summers and mild, rainy winters provide ideal conditions for their cultivation.

Map labels:

BULGARIA
GREECE
Edirne
Kirklareli
Igneada Burnu
Çorlu
Tekirdağ
Istanbul
Gebze
Saros Körfezi
Gökçeada
Gallipoli Peninsula
Dardanelles
Marmara
Sea of Marmara
Çanakkale
Ayvacik
Balikesir
Bozüyük
Bilecik
Bursa
Eskişehir
Kütahya
Akhisar
Izmir Körfezi
Manisa
Bornova
Izmir
Uşak
Afyon
Ödemiş
Kusadasi Körfezi
Aydin
Söke
Denizli
Tavas
Burdur
Isparta
Beyşehir Gölü
Egirdir Gölü
Akşehir
Anatolia
Cihanbeyli
Güllük Körfezi
Bodrum
Muğla
Gökova Körfezi
Marmaris
Dalaman
Antalya
Aegean Sea
Rhodes
Megisti (to Greece)
Kaş
Yardimci Burnu
Antalya Körfezi
Alanya
Manavgat
Mut
Anamur
Incekum Burnu
Silifke
Mediterranean Sea
Sardines
Keryneia
NICOSIA
CYPRUS
Lemesos
Lárnaka
Cape Greko
Ammóchostos
TURKISH REPUBLIC OF NORTHERN CYPRUS (Recognized only by Turkey)
Cape Apostolos Andreas
Black Sea
Kerempe Burnu
Cide
Inebolu
Ince Burnu
Sinop Burnu
Sinop
Gerze
Bafra Burnu
Bafra
Bartin
Zonguldak
Pazarbaşi Burnu
Baba Burnu
Karabük
Kastamonu
Civa Burnu
Sams
Gerede
Bolu
Çerkeş
Çankiri
Merzifon
ANKARA
Kalecik
Alaca
Çorum
Tokat
Kizilirmak
Kirikkale
Polatli
Sorgun
Boğazliyan
Şarkişla
TUR
Kulu
Bünyan
Tuz Gölü
Nevşehir
Kayseri
Aksaray
Cappadocia
Niğde
Konya
Karaman
Ereğli
Kahramanmara
Adana
Ceyhan
Tarsus
Mersin
Iskenderun
Osmani
Iskenderun Körfezi
Antioch
Kirikh
Al Ládhiqíyah
Sakarya

Kurdish people

Kurds live in Turkey, Armenia, Iran, Iraq and Syria. They have no homeland of their own and their attempts to gain political independence have been crushed many times. Most Kurds are Muslims. They farm and herd sheep.

Rock formations of Cappadocia

An unusual landscape has formed at Cappadocia in central Turkey, as a result of lava eruptions from the now-extinct Mt Erciyes. Over centuries, wind and rain eroded the volcanic rock into strange, pointed formations. Early Christians made homes and churches in caves cut into the soft rock. Inside, they hid from their enemies.

Fresco
The walls of many of the cave churches are covered in paintings called frescoes. They are colorful, detailed representations of events from the Bible.

Sochi

RUSSIA

Sokhumi

Caucasus

Kazbek
16,558ft (5,047m)

Oni

Tebulosmt'a
14,741ft (4,493m)

Tqibuli

Chiat'ura

GEORGIA

Sturgeon

Anchovies

P'ot'i

Samtredia

Khashuri

Gori

Xaçmaz

Caspian

Bat'umi

Akhalts'ikhe

T'BILISI

Rust'avi

Säki

Bazardüzü Daği
14,652ft (4,466m)

Mingäçevir
Su Anbari

Black

Sea

Hopa

Kür

Mingäçevir

Sumqayit

Mastağa

Fener
Burnu

Artvin

Gyumri

Vanadzor

Ganca

AZERBAIJAN

BAKU
(BAKI)

Giresun

Trabzon

Rize

Of

Coruh

Hrazdan

Sevana
Lich

Yevlax

Äli Bayramli

Kars

ARMENIA

Ağdam

Xankändi

Muğan
Düzü

Sarikamiş

YEREVAN

Salyan

Refahiye

Aşkale

Pasinler

Aras

Artashat

Goris

Kür

Erzincan

Erzurum

Mt Ararat
16,945ft (5,165m)

Kapan

Länkäran

Kemah

Euphrates

Ağri

Doğubeyazit

AZERBAIJAN

Naxçivan

Murat

Patnos

Ardabīl

Bingöl

Süphan Daglari
13,314ft (4,058m)

Erciş

IRAN

Elaziğ

Keban
Baraji

Muş

Lake Van

Muradiye

Van

Malatya

Dicle
Baraji

Tatvan

Silvan
Baraji

Bitlis

Turquoise

E Y

Diyarbakir

Batman

Ilisu
Baraji

Siirt

Kurdistan

Tigris

Şirnak

iyaman

Siverek

Mardin

The Caspian Sea, a saltwater lake between Asia and Europe, is the largest inland expanse of water in the world. It is 750 miles (1,200 km) long and 270 miles (432 km) wide.

Aratürk
Baraji

Nusaybin

ntep

Kiziltepe

IRAQ

Al Qāmishli

SYRIA

Baku oil fields

Baku, on the Caspian Sea, is built on top of vast oil reserves. In the late 1900s, the city was supplying half the world's oil. Today, production is declining because the area has become severely polluted.

Turkish carpets

Turkey is famous for its beautiful handwoven carpets. Each carpet-producing region uses designs and colors that are unique to that area. The craftspeople often incorporate symbols into the design that relate to their own family history.

N
W E
S

0 miles   140
0 kilometers   140

Central Asia

PAKISTAN
POPULATION 150,695,000 ✴ CAPITAL ISLAMABAD

AFGHANISTAN
POPULATION 28,717,000 ✴ CAPITAL KABUL

UZBEKISTAN
POPULATION 25,982,000 ✴ CAPITAL TASHKENT

KAZAKHSTAN
POPULATION 16,764,000 ✴ CAPITAL ASTANA

TAJIKISTAN
POPULATION 6,864,000 ✴ CAPITAL DUSHANBE

KYRGYZSTAN
POPULATION 4,893,000 ✴ CAPITAL BISHKEK

TURKMENISTAN
POPULATION 4,776,000 ✴ CAPITAL ASHGABAT

The Aral Sea is an environmental disaster area. Harmful irrigation practices have turned two-thirds of the sea into desert over 30 years. The fishing industry is now in ruins.

Bactrian camel train
The two-humped bactrian camel can travel for four days without water. These camels have been used since ancient times to transport goods across the deserts of Central Asia.

Stranded fishing boats, Aral Sea

The Silk Road

The Silk Road is one of the most important trade routes in history. It was not a single road, but a network of shorter routes that linked scattered oasis settlements and market towns. From about 130 BC, goods from China were taken across the vast continent of Asia to the shores of the Mediterranean. Traders battled along the edges of deserts and braved dangerous mountain passes. Sometimes, camel trains were attacked by bandits. As well as goods, ideas, skills and religion also moved along the routes. Buddhism reached China from India in this way. The Silk Road declined in importance when a sea route from Europe to Asia was discovered in the late 15th century.

— Silk Road ■ Central Asia

Trading along the Silk Road

Few merchants ever traveled the full length of the route. Most covered just part of the journey, trading their wares for products from other countries, then returning home. Goods moved slowly and changed hands many times. Camel trains heading toward China carried gold, ivory, gems and glass.

Goods from Asia
Traders from Asia carried silk, furs, ceramics, jade and finely worked objects of bronze. Even in Roman times small quantities of Chinese goods were reaching Europe.

Uzbek clothing
The traditional layered clothing of the women of Uzbekistan is made from a multicolored silk fabric known as "the king of satins." Jewelry included a tiara with delicate pendants that followed the curve of the eyebrows.

Registan Square
This square in the ancient city of Samarkand, in Uzbekistan, was once a marketplace for traders traveling the Silk Road. Majestic Islamic buildings dating from the 14th century line the square.

I J K L M N O P

RUSSIA

KAZAKHSTAN

Petropavlovsk
Kostanay
Rudnyy
Tobol
Kokshetau
Shchuchinsk
Pavlodar
Rubtsovsk
★ ASTANA
Arkalyk
Temirtau
Ust'-Kamenogorsk
Zyryanovsk
Karabutak
Karaganda
Semipalatinsk
Georgiyevka
Ozero Tengiz
Ozero Zaysan
Satpayev
Zhezkazgan
Chelkar
MONGOLIA
Mugodzhary
Aral'sk
Aral Sea
Lake Balkhash
Tacheng
CHINA
Sarysu
Kyzylorda
Betpak-Dala
Ile
Taldykorgan
Ozero Sasykkol
Ozero Alakol'
Peski Muyunkum
Saryozek
Kapchagayskoye Vodokhranilishche
ostyurt Plateau
Turkestan
Almaty
Nukus
Kyzylkum Desert
Syrdar'ya
Taraz
Kara-Balta
★ **BISHKEK**
Karakol
UZBEKISTAN
Shymkent
Talas
Kirghiz Range
Ysyk-Köl
Balykchy
ashkhovuz
Urgench
KYRGYZSTAN
Naryn
Tien Shan
Chirchik
Tash-Kömur
Jalal-Abad
TASHKENT ★
Yangiyul
Andizhan
Osh
Ozero Aydarkul'
Kokand
Fergana
Navoi
Gulistan
Khujand
Dzhizak
Uroteppa
Bukhara
Kattakurgan
Samarkand
Zarafshon
Qarokul
Pamirs
CHINA
Chardzhev
Karshi
TAJIKISTAN
Guzar
K2 28,251ft (8,611m) claimed by India
RKMENISTAN
Denau
★ **DUSHANBE**
Murghob
★ **ASHGABAT**
Amudar'ya
Termez
Feyzabad
Khorugh
Tedzhen
Mary
Bayramaly
Andkhvoy
Konduz
Kokcha
Gilgit
Karakoram
Yeloten
Mazar-e Sharif
Baghlan
Hindu Kush
IRAN
Meymaneh
Sar-e Pol
Mongora
Qal'eh-ye Now
AFGHANISTAN
Charikar
Asadabad
Mardan
Abbottabad
Chaghcharan
KABUL ★ (KĀBUL)
Jalalabad
Khyber Pass
Wah ★ **ISLAMABAD**
Herat
Shahrak
Peshawar
Rawalpindi
Ghazni
Gardez
Jhelum
Jammu
Farah
Zarghun Shahr
Mianwali
Khushab
Gujrat
Gujranwala
Qalat
Sargodha
Chiniot
Shekhupura
Helmand
Arghandab
Dera Ismail Khan
Lahore
Kandahar
Registan
Faisalabad
Zaranj
Dasht-i Margow
Dera Ghazi Khan
Sahiwal
Okara
Sulaiman Range
Ravi
Deh Shu
Helmand
Quetta
Multan
Muzaffargarh
Dalbandin
Thar Desert
Sutlej
PAKISTAN
Bahawalpur
Indus
INDIA
Rahimyar Khan
Central Makran Range
Shikarpur
Larkana
Sukkur
Khairpur
Dasht
Turbat
Pasni
Nawabshah
Mirpur Khas
Hyderabad
Gwadar
Sonmiani Bay
Karachi
Gulf of Oman
Mouths of the Indus

Snow leopard
The snow leopard lives high in the rocky mountains of Central Asia where its fur markings help it blend into its surroundings. It is a secretive, solitary animal. Snow leopards are an endangered species.

Cotton farming
Uzbekistan is the world's fifth-largest producer of cotton. The crop depends on irrigated water diverted from the Aral Sea. The fluffy white fiber that bursts out of the seedpods, or cotton bolls, is picked by hand. About three-quarters of the crop is exported.

Yurt housing
Nomadic herders of Kazakhstan's flat, treeless areas, called steppes, live in round tents called yurts. They consist of a collapsible frame of poles covered with felt. An opening in the domed roof lets out smoke from the stove.

Turkmenistan horse
Turkmenistan horses have been valued for more than 2,000 years for their elegance, strength, speed and endurance. Buccephalus, the horse of Alexander the Great, was one of this ancient breed.

N W E S

0 miles 400
0 kilometers 400

The city of Kandahar in Afghanistan was founded by Alexander the Great in the 4th century BC.

Western and Central Asia

Opium poppies
Opium poppies, used to make drugs such as morphine and codine, are grown widely in Afghanistan. Sap from the seedpods is often traded illegally, and is used to produce the banned drug, heroin.

LAND AREA	2,435,424 sq miles (6,307,720 sq km)
LARGEST COUNTRY	Kazakhstan
SMALLEST COUNTRY	Cyprus
MAIN RELIGION	Muslim
LIFE EXPECTANCY	64 years
LITERACY	88%

- Forest and woodland
- Arable land
- Grazing
- Arid or marginal

USING THE LAND

- Cereals
- Rice
- Wheat
- Fruit and vegetables
- Fruit
- Citrus fruits
- Wine
- Cotton
- Tobacco
- Sugar beet
- Dates
- Beef cattle
- Sheep
- Fishing
- Industrial center
- Mining
- Oil production
- Gas production

Map labels: Petropavlovsk, Ust'-Kamenogorsk, ASTANA, Ural'sk, Aktyubinsk, Kyzylorda, BISHKEK, Istanbul, Izmir, ANKARA, Trabzon, T'BILISI, YEREVAN, BAKU, Dashkhovuz, TASHKENT, Adana, NICOSIA, ASHGABAT, DUSHANBE, Herãt, KABUL, ISLAMABAD, Kandahãr, Lahore, Quetta, Hyderabad, Karachi

NATURAL FEATURES

Kazakhstan steppes KAZAKHSTAN
Steppes, or flat, grassy plains, cover most of Kazakhstan's north—about half of this country's total area. Farmers raise sheep and cattle in some parts.

Pammukale TURKEY
These chalk-coated cliffs look like a frozen waterfall. Calcium-rich spring waters flow over the cliffs to form pools, overhangs, stalactites and other formations.

Tien Shan
These largely unexplored, snow-capped mountains run for 1,500 miles (2,410 km) between Kazakhstan, Kyrgyzstan and China, along the steppe's southern edge.

North Anatolian Fault TURKEY
This fault, or deep crack in Earth's surface, runs from the Sea of Marmara to Lake Van. Shifting land either side of the fault can cause earthquakes, most recently in 1999, when more than 18,000 people died.

Mt Ararat TURKEY
As Turkey's highest mountain, the summit of this imposing landmark is 16,945 feet (5,165 m) above sea level. A glacier stretches down its northern face. The mountain is thought to be the resting place of Noah's Ark, referred to in the Old Testament of the Bible.

Khyber Pass
The Khyber Pass links Pakistan and Afghanistan through the Hindu Kush mountains. It is 33 miles (53 km) long. Invading armies have used it as a passage for centuries. The pass was well defended, and ancient fortresses and watchtowers still stand. It is walled by steep cliffs, and narrows to less than 10 feet (3 m) in parts.

Wheat
Wheat, which is grown extensively throughout this region, is used to make flat bread. The bread is sometimes cooked in a clay oven under the ground (*above*). Regional varieties include *nan*, *pide* and *chapatti*. *Jelabi* is an Afghan sweet bread that is deep-fried and coated in sugar syrup. Rice and other cereals are also grown in Western and Central Asia.

"Stan" at the end of a country's name means country.

WHERE PEOPLE LIVE

	Urban			Rural	

REGION
48% — 52%

Most urban: TURKEY
74% — 26%

Most rural: AFGHANISTAN
20% — 80%

Watermelons
In spring, snow from the Tien Shan mountains melts, providing water for irrigation. The fertile valleys of Kazakhstan are excellent for growing fruit crops, such as watermelons and citrus fruits.

LARGEST CITIES

Karachi 10,809,000

Istanbul 9,631,000

Lahore 5,904,000

Ankara 3,544,000

Hagia Sophia

Hagia Sophia, in Istanbul, Turkey, is one of the most spectacular examples of domed architecture in the world. It was built as a Christian church in the 6th century, in the Byzantine period. From 1453 until the 1930s, Hagia Sophia was used as a mosque. Many of its features—from the intricate mosaics and fountain, to the minarets (tall towers) built on each corner—are from this period. Today, it is used as a museum.

PEOPLE

Ismail al-Bukhari AD 810–870
This Arabic scholar wrote a book of sayings of the prophet Muhammad. Muslims believe it is second in value only to their holy book, the Koran.

Öz Beg ruled 1312–41
As khan, or ruler, of the Golden Horde—an area under Mongol rule—Öz Beg adopted Islam as his religion. The Uzbek people derive their name from his.

Timur the Great 1336–1405
Some say this Mongol ruler, known as Tamerlane in Europe, was one of history's most bloodthirsty tyrants, while others believe he was wise and just. Today, pilgrims and tourists flock to his tomb in Samarkand.

Roxelana died 1558
Chosen from the sultan's harem as his favorite, Roxelana became the wife of the Ottoman ruler Süleyman, and advised him on political and social matters.

Mustafa Kemal Atatürk 1881–1938
This military hero became Turkey's first president and prime minister in 1923, after he led a nationalist movement to abolish Ottoman rule.

Mustafa Kemal Atatürk

Imran Khan born 1952
This world-class Pakistani cricketer first captained his country's cricket team in 1982. He is now a politician.

PLACES

Kabul AFGHANISTAN
Afghanistan's capital, Kabul, has been under constant attack over the centuries. Following Soviet occupation in the 1980s, civil war broke out, with warlords fighting for control of the city. From 1996 to 2002, Kabul was controlled by the repressive Taliban.

Istanbul TURKEY
Called Constantinople until its capture by the Ottomans in the 15th century, Istanbul is Turkey's grandest city. Much of its architecture is from Byzantine times.

Samarkand UZBEKISTAN
Samarkand, Uzbekistan's second-largest city, is also one of the world's oldest. Its culture is a blend of Iranian, Indian and Mongolian traditions.

Badshahi Mosque PAKISTAN
This 5,000-seat mosque (*below*) at Lahore is the largest in the Indian subcontinent. Its enclosed central space and beautiful pool are typical of Islamic architecture.

Tool artifacts

Mohenjo-daro PAKISTAN
The ruins of this ancient city lie on the banks of the Indus River. The well-planned city was built around 3000 BC, with buildings made from unbaked mud bricks. It was the largest city of the ancient Indus civilization.

Topkapi harem

In the 15th century, part of Turkey's Topkapi Palace (*above*) was home to a group of women chosen to look after the *padishah*, or ruler. Women in the Topkapi harem lived in the palace for life, and were forbidden to leave. At times, there were several thousand women in the harem.

TRADITIONS AND CULTURE

Shari'a law
Often called Islamic law, this legal system has been inspired by religious traditions and writings, notably the Koran. Many of the laws relate to worship, politics, criminal acts and family life.

Buzkashi
In this regional sport, players compete on horseback to bring an animal carcass into a scoring circle. *Buzkashi* means "goat grabbing."

An imam, or Muslim leader

Hamam
These are traditional baths Turkish men and women still visit regularly. Bathers go through three stages—they lie on hot marble, making them sweat, then have a body massage, followed by a drink.

In Greek mythology, the goddess Aphrodite was born in the waves of Cyprus.

Islamic art
Islamic art is brightly colored, with strong patterns and shapes. Calligraphy, or decorative handwriting, and geometric patterns (*above*) are typical features of this style. Islamic designs decorate ceramics, glass, textiles, metalwork and woodwork.

Grand Bazaar
This shopping market in Istanbul's center, which started as just a few stalls in the 15th century, now contains 4,000 shops stretching through 60 streets. Everything from leather and carpets to sweets and spices (*below*) is for sale.

Constantinople

AD 330
The emperor Constantine I renames Byzantium as Constantinople and makes it the capital of the Eastern Roman and Byzantine empires. The city becomes the new financial and political center and remains powerful for the next 1,000 years, but slowly declines by the 12th century.

1401
The Safavid dynasty in Persia is founded by Shah Ismail I. In the years to come, wars are fought between the Safavids and Ottoman Turks.

1453
The Ottoman Turks, headed by Sultan Mehmet, capture Constantinople. During Mehmet's reign, the Grand Bazaar is redeveloped, which improves the city's economy. The architectural masterpiece, the Topkapi Palace, is built.

1457
The Ottomans rename the city of Constantinople as Istanbul, and declare it the capital of their growing empire. Five years later, the Ottoman Turks take over Bosnia.

1520
Süleyman I, known as Süleyman the Magnificent because of his successes in expanding the empire, is crowned ruler over the Ottoman empire. Art and architecture expand during his reign.

Süleyman the Magnificent

1522
The Turks capture the Greek Island of Rhodes in the Aegean Sea and by 1524 it becomes part of the Ottoman empire.

1526
The Turks invade Hungary in the Battle of Mohacs. The battle lasts only two hours and the Turks gain victory, claiming Hungary for the Ottomans.

1529
The Turks fail to capture the city of Vienna, capital of Austria. The Ottoman empire shows signs of losing power.

1571
The Turks are defeated at the Battle of Lepanto, a huge sea battle fought off the coast of Greece between a Turkish and a Christian fleet.

1590
The Turks and Persians make peace after years of fighting with each other. Shortly after this, the Ottoman empire starts to decline.

1909
The last of the 36 Ottoman sultans, Muhammed Vahiduddin starts his reign. His rule ends in 1922 after Mustafa Kemal Atatürk abolishes the Muslim rank of sultan and founds the Republic of Turkey in 1924.

Muhammed Vahiduddin

Desert oasis

The Middle East

IRAN
POPULATION 68,279,000 * CAPITAL TEHRAN

IRAQ
POPULATION 24,683,000 * CAPITAL BAGHDAD

SAUDI ARABIA
POPULATION 24,294,000 * CAPITAL RIYADH

YEMEN
POPULATION 19,350,000 * CAPITAL ŞAN'Ā'

SYRIA
POPULATION 17,586,000 * CAPITAL DAMASCUS

ISRAEL
POPULATION 6,117,000 * CAPITAL JERUSALEM

JORDAN
POPULATION 5,460,000 * CAPITAL AMMĀN

LEBANON
POPULATION 3,728,000 * CAPITAL BEIRUT

OMAN
POPULATION 2,807,000 * CAPITAL MUSCAT

UNITED ARAB EMIRATES
POPULATION 2,485,000 * CAPITAL ABU DHABI

KUWAIT
POPULATION 2,183,000 * CAPITAL KUWAIT

QATAR
POPULATION 817,000 * CAPITAL DOHA

BAHRAIN
POPULATION 667,000 * CAPITAL AL MANĀMAH

Dead Sea
This landlocked sea, between Israel and Jordan, contains large amounts of salt. This makes the water dense so that people can float in it without even trying.

The world's largest known reserves of oil are in the Middle East. Saudi Arabia, Iraq, Iran, the United Arab Emirates and Kuwait are among the world's leading oil producers.

Jerusalem's holy sites

Jerusalem is one of the holiest cities in the world. Within its boundaries are sites central to the beliefs of the Jewish, Christian and Islamic faiths. Jews consider Jerusalem a holy city because it was the religious center and capital of the ancient Israelite nation. For Christians, it is the place where Jesus Christ taught and was crucified. Muslims believe that Muhammad, the founder of Islam, rose to heaven from Jerusalem. Over the centuries, followers of these faiths have often disagreed about who controls Jerusalem, and conflicts have occurred as a result.

Jewish rabbi

Western Wall
This wall is all that remains of the Jewish Temple destroyed by the Romans in AD 70. It is the Jews' holiest site. They pray here and leave prayers on pieces of paper between the stones.

Temple Mount
Muslims believe Muhammad was lifted to heaven from the rock that lies directly beneath the golden dome. It is one of the most sacred Islamic sites. Jews believe the rock is the place where Abraham prepared to sacrifice his son, Isaac.

Church of the Holy Sepulchre
This church is built over the site where many Christians believe Jesus Christ was crucified. It is said to contain the sepulchre (tomb) where he was buried. The building dates from 1149, the time of Crusades.

Muslim praying

Christian nun

Hunting with falcons
This is a traditional sport in Saudi Arabia. Young, preferably female, wild falcons are trained to kill prey and return it to their handler. A leather glove protects the handler's arm from sharp talons.

### Map labels

Mediterranean Sea

Antioch
Al Lādhiqīyah
Idlib
Hamāh
Tārtūs
Tripoli
Hims
LEBANON
BEIRUT
(BAYRŪT)
Soûr   Saïda
Haifa   Nazareth
ISRAEL   Irbid
Tel Aviv-Jaffa   Nablus
JERUSALEM
Gaza
EGYPT
Be'er Sheva
CAIRO
(EL QÂHIRA)   Suez
Suez Canal
Sinai
Negev   JORDAN
Ma'ān
Wadi Rum
Elat   Al 'Aqabah
Jabal al Lawz
8,461ft (2,579m)
Tabūk
Hurghada
Rās Karkūmā
Nile
Rās Abū Madd
Tropic of Cancer
Rās Barīdī
Yanbu' al Baḥr
Jedda
Nubian Desert
SUDAN
Port Sudan
Suakin
ERITR
Massa
ASMARA

Antioch
Ale
Ar R
SYR
Pa
Ba'albek
DAMASCUS
(DIMASHQ)
As Suwayd
Az Zarqā'
Jericho
AMMĀN
Kāf
At Tubayd

SYR

Rābie

Mar

35°
35°
30°
30°
30°
25°
20°
15°

I J K L M N O P

1
2
3
4
5
6
7
8
9
10
11

YEREVAN
ARMENIA AZERBAIJAN
TURKMENISTAN
Caspian Sea
ASHGABAT
Khvoy Tabrīz Ardabīl
Bandar-e Anzalī
Gonbad-e Kavūs
Bojnūrd
Quchan
Orūmīyeh Marāgheh
Rasht
Gorgān
Sabzevār Mashhad
Al Qāmishlī Dahūk
Kūh-e Hājī Ebrāhīm 11,811ft (3,600m)
Zanjān
Bābol Sārī
Amol
Semnān
Neyshābūr
Hasakah Mosul Arbīl
Kūh-e Chehel Chashmeh 10,377ft (3,163m)
Qazvīn
Karaj
Torbat-e Heydarīyeh
Torbat-e Jām
Dayr az Zawr As Sulaymānīyah
Kirkūk
Sanandaj
TEHRAN (TEHRĀN)
Hamadān
Qom
Daryācheh-ye Namak
Dasht-e Kavir
Rāwah Buhayrat ath Tharthār Tikrīt
Kermānshāh
Malāyer
Arāk
Kāshān
IRAQ
Al Muqdādīyah Borūjerd
IRAN
Bīrjand
Ar Ramādī BAGHDAD (BAGHDĀD)
Khorramābād
Khomeynīshahr
Eşfahān
Karbalā Al Fallūjah Buhayrat ar Razāzah Dezful Najafābād
Iranian
Daryācheh-ye Sīstān
Al Hillah Al Kūt Yazd
Plateau
Hāmūn-e Helmand
An Najaf Al 'Amārah Masjed Soleymān Dasht-e Lut
Rafsanjān
Ar Rutbah As Samāwah An Nāşirīyah Ahvāz
Kermān Zāhedān
Sūq ash Shuyūkh Baṣra Ābādān
Kūh-e Ilazārān 14,501ft (4,420m)
Shīrāz Daryācheh-ye Bakhtegān Sīrjan Bam Jīroft
Al Labbah KUWAIT Borāzjān Fasa Jahrom
Daryācheh-ye Tashk
Hāmūn-e Jaz Mūriān
KUWAIT (AL KUWAYTĪ)
Būshehr
Īrānshahr
Al Jahrah Al Farwānīyah
Ḥafar al Bāṭin
Bandar-e 'Abbās
Rafḥā' Ad Dahnā Rās Tanāqib Makran
Buraydah Rās az Zawr Al Jubayl
Al Khaşab
Chabahār
Hā'il Al Majma'ah Ad Dammām BAHRAIN Ras al Khaimah Makran Coast
'Afif AL MANĀMAH QATAR Sharjah Gulf of Oman
Al Hufūf DOHA (AD DAWHAH) Dubai Şuḥār
RIYADH (AR RIYĀD) ABU DHABI Al 'Ayn MUSCAT (MASQAT)
Ţā'if Ḥaraḍh As Salamīyah Al Hajar al Gharbī Ar Rustāq Tropic of Cancer
UNITED ARAB EMIRATES Ibrī Nazwá
Al Bāḥah Qal'at Bishah As Sulayyil OMAN
Jabal Sawdá' 10,279ft (3,133m) Rub' al Khālī Al Khalīf
Khamīs Abha Khalīj Maşīrah
Najrān Rās al Madrakah
SAUDI ARABIA
Jiddat al Harāsis Dawhat Şawqirah
Jīzān Ramlat Dahm Zufār Rās Sawqirah
Thamarīt Khalīj al Halānīyāt Rās Sharbithāt
Ḥajjah SAN'Ā' Ramlat as Sab'atayn Al Mahrah Jabal al Qamar Şalālah Rās Naws
Rās 'Īsā Ḥaḍramawt Ghubbat al Qamar Rās Fartak
Al Ḥudaydah Dhamār YEMEN
Jabal Taqar 10,138ft (3,090m) Ibb Arabian Sea
Ta'izz Al Baydā' Say'ūn Al Mukallā Rās al Kalb
Zinjibār Socotra (to Yemen)
Aden
ETHIOPIA DJIBOUTI DJIBOUTI Gulf of Aden
SOMALIA Berbera

TURKEY
Lake Urmia
Tigris
Euphrates
Zagros Mountains
Persian Gulf
Strait of Hormuz
Kopet Dag
AFGHANISTAN
PAKISTAN

N E W S

0 miles   400
0 kilometers   400

Burj Al Arab
At 1,053 feet (321 m) high, the Burj Al Arab hotel in Dubai, in the United Arab Emirates, is the tallest hotel in the world. It is the shape of a billowing sail, and stands on an artificial island.

Muslim dress
As part of their religion, Muslim women wear modest clothes that cover all their body except for their face and hands. The headscarf is called a hijab.

Winged sphinx
Huge sculptures of mythical creatures guarded palace entrances in ancient Assyria (now Iraq). These beasts, some with five legs, had the strength of a bull, the speed of an eagle and the intelligence of a human.

The Middle East

LAND AREA	1,971,313 sq miles (5,105,677 sq km)
LARGEST COUNTRY	Iran
SMALLEST COUNTRY	Bahrain
MAIN RELIGION	Muslim
LIFE EXPECTANCY	73 years
LITERACY	78%

NATURAL FEATURES

Elburz and Zagros mountains IRAN
There are two mountain ranges in Iran, the Zagros and the Elburz. Mt Damavand, at more than 18,638 feet (5,681 m) above sea level, is Iran's highest peak. It is an almost extinct volcano, which still spouts occasional plumes of gas.

Mt Damavand

Mesopotamia IRAQ
Mesopotamia (from a Greek word that means "between the rivers") was the site of the world's earliest civilizations, from about 10,000 BC. It lay between the Tigris and Euphrates rivers. The northern region had a mild climate and fertile land, while the southern had lush, marshy areas.

Arz el Rab LEBANON
Arz el Rab, or Cedars of the Lord, is the oldest cedar grove in Lebanon. The mountains were once covered with cedar trees, since cut down over the centuries.

Wadi Rum JORDAN
This wadi, or river valley, is unusual for its deep, pinkish sands covered in small shrubs, and its occasional enormous rock formations, called *jebels,* that rise up into the sky, making the wadi look rather like the surface of the Moon.

USING THE LAND

- Forest and woodland
- Arable land
- Grazing
- Arid or marginal

- Rice
- Wheat
- Fruit
- Citrus fruits
- Cotton
- Coffee
- Dates
- Sheep
- Goats
- Fishing
- Industrial center
- Oil production
- Gas production

Frankincense
Thousands of years ago, frankincense was used for religious ceremonies and embalming. It comes from a small tree that is common in the southern part of Arabia. The bark is scraped off (*left*) and eventually a gum, frankincense, oozes out. Today, it is used in incense and perfumes.

Grain
Wheat, millet and barley are the main grain crops of the Middle East. The greatest problem is the lack of water but the area suitable for growing these crops has been extended by irrigation. Small crops are even planted in moist wadis (river valleys) in the desert.

WHERE PEOPLE LIVE

Urban		Rural

REGION
76% 24%

Most urban: KUWAIT
97% 3%

Most rural: YEMEN
24% 76%

The Crusades

In the 11th century, Palestine was under the control of the Muslims. In 1095, Pope Urban II joined with the Byzantine emperor to recapture the Holy Land (Palestine) from the Muslims for the Christians. For almost 200 years, until 1294, the armies of eight separate crusades raided Palestine. In periods of peace, the crusaders were accepted and entertained by the Muslims (*above*).

Oil
The Middle East has some of the world's largest and most productive oilfields. The most important are in Saudi Arabia, Iran, Iraq and Kuwait. Kuwait is the second-largest oil producer (Saudi Arabia is the largest) in the Middle East. During the 1991 Gulf War, the Iraqis set fire to many of the oil wells and oil refineries in Kuwait (*above*).

LARGEST CITIES

Tehran 8,068,000

Baghdad 5,949,000

Riyadh 3,823,000

Jeddah 2,818,000

Mashhad 2,082,000

TRADITIONS AND CULTURE

Damascus souks

Souks, or market stalls, are a common sight in the old section of Damascus, Syria. Famous for their crafts, the souks sell fine damask tapestries, glassware and carvings inlaid with mother-of-pearl.

Kibbutzim

These are groups of farms in Israel in which the owners share the work, the decision-making, the food and the earnings in return for the work they do for the community.

Camel racing

Camel races are popular in Saudi Arabia. Every year, more than 2,000 camels and riders compete in the grueling King's Cup Camel Race in Riyadh.

Camel racing

Over 95 percent of Saudi Arabia is desert. The Rub' al Khāli desert is known as the Empty Quarter.

Five pillars of Islam

Mecca, in Saudi Arabia, is the holiest city of Islam. One of the five duties (or pillars) of faith for Muslims is that they make a pilgrimage to Mecca (a hajj, *above*) at least once in their lifetime.

Birthplace of religions

The Middle East is the birthplace of three of the world's major religions: Christianity, Judaism and Islam. Judaism, which began in the area around 2000 BC, is the world's oldest major religion. Christianity, based on the teachings of Jesus Christ around 2,000 years ago, also reveres some of Judaism's scriptures as holy. Islam arose in the 7th century from the teachings of the prophet Muhammad.

PLACES

Jericho ISRAEL

The ancient walled city of Jericho was first settled around 8350 BC. Now situated in the West Bank area, Jericho was handed over to Palestinian control in 1994 after years of unrest.

Petra JORDAN

Once a wealthy trading center, the city of Petra (*left*) was carved from red sandstone cliffs more than 2,000 years ago. It seems to have been abandoned at some time in the 6th century.

Baghdad IRAQ

The capital of Iraq and its largest city, Baghdad is situated near the Tigris River. The site has been settled since ancient times, and Baghdad was once one of the world's richest cities. Much of the city has been destroyed by recent wars.

Mecca SAUDI ARABIA

Every year, millions of Muslims make the pilgrimage to Mecca, the birthplace of Muhammad, to pray. Muslims think of Mecca as their homeland and even when they are elsewhere in the world, they face in the direction of Mecca to pray.

Esfahan IRAN

One of the largest cities in Iran, Esfahan is famous for its mosques, such as the 17th-century Royal Mosque, now called Masjid-e Iman, its medieval Islamic architecture and its public gardens.

Royal Mosque

PEOPLE

Solomon c 1000 BC

Solomon, son of King David, was the third king of ancient Israel. He was known as a wise and clever king who established peace and unity in Israel.

King Solomon

Harun Al-Rashid AD 766–809

A ruler of the Abbasid dynasty, Harun Al-Rashid supported the arts, literature, mathematics and medicine. The capital, Baghdad, flourished under his rule.

Saladin 1138–93

Saladin, a Muslim sultan, captured Jerusalem from the Christians in 1187. The English king Richard the Lionheart fought against him in the Third Crusade, which ended in a truce in 1192.

Ibn Saud 1880–1953

From 1902, when he first attacked Riyadh, Ibn Saud's aim was to unify Arabia. He achieved this in 1932, when he brought tribal conflicts under control and became the king of Arabia.

Ayatollah Khomeini 1900–89

In 1979, this Muslim leader took control of Iran from the king and changed its government to an Islamic republic. Khomeini was its first leader.

Flying carpet

Arabian Nights

Also called *The Thousand and One Nights*, this collection of almost 200 folktales first appeared around the year AD 800. The stories tell of the heroic and romantic adventures of well-known characters, such as Sinbad the Sailor, Aladdin and Ali Baba. These tales have been collected from several countries, including Arabia, India, Egypt and Persia.

HISTORY AT A GLANCE
ANCIENT MESOPOTAMIA

c 5000 BC
Tribes, probably from Arabia, begin to settle into village life along the banks of the Tigris and Euphrates rivers—the area called Mesopotamia.

c 3000 BC
The Sumerians, an advanced culture whose inventions include writing, a calendar, systems of measurement and the wheel, live in this area.

c 2340 BC
Sargon of Agade, a military ruler from central Mesopotamia, conquers Syria and the Sumer, forming the kingdom of Akkad, the first nation–state in world history.

c 1760 BC
King Hammurabi, of the Amorite dynasty, establishes Babylon as an important trading center and the capital of Mesopotamia. He introduces laws, called the Code of Hammurabi, which are carved into a black stone called a stela (*right*).

Hammurabi

c 1600 BC
The Hittites, a people from an area that is now part of Turkey, sweep down into Babylon, conquer and plunder the city, and bring the dynasty of Hammurabi to an end.

c 1240 BC
The Assyrians, a people from the northern part of what is now Iraq, decide to expand into Babylon. After a series of battles, Hittite power collapses and the Assyrians control Babylon.

c 1200 BC
One of the oldest epics in world literature, *The Epic of Gilgamesh*, is written, telling the tale of Gilgamesh, a powerful king in ancient Sumeria.

c 1155 BC
The Assyrians create a unified empire by installing Assyrian rulers in each capital they conquer.

706–681 BC
Sennacherib succeeds his father, Sargon II, as king of Assyria. He makes Nineveh the capital city, and sets up a library of thousands of clay tablets of technical and scientific writings. In 689, he destroys the city of Babylon.

612 BC
The Medes, a people from Iran, join forces with the Babylonians to destroy the Assyrian empire.

Ishtar Gate

605–562 BC
King Nebuchadnezzar II captures Jerusalem and controls the southern area of Mesopotamia. He rebuilds Babylon and fortifies it with walls. One of its eight gates is the Ishtar Gate (*above*), named after Ishtar, goddess of love and war.

539 BC
The Persian king, Cyrus the Great, and his soldiers (*right*), incorporate Babylon into the rapidly growing Persian empire. Persia rules much of the Middle East until it is conquered by Alexander the Great.

331 BC
Macedonian general Alexander the Great conquers Babylon, ruling until his death in 323.

Persian soldier

Southern Asia

INDIA POPULATION 1,049,700,000 * CAPITAL NEW DELHI

BANGLADESH POPULATION 138,448,000 * CAPITAL DHAKA

NEPAL POPULATION 26,470,000 * CAPITAL KATHMANDU

SRI LANKA POPULATION 19,742,000 * CAPITAL COLOMBO

BHUTAN POPULATION 2,140,000 * CAPITAL THIMPHU

MALDIVES POPULATION 330,000 * CAPITAL MALE

Indian elephants

The Indian, or Asian, elephant is smaller than the African elephant. It is a strong, calm animal that can carry people, logs and food.

Indian dancer

Dancing takes place at festivals throughout India. Some dances tell stories or are associated with a particular religion. This dancer in Jaipur, in Rajasthan, is celebrating Holi, the festival that welcomes spring and honors elephants.

The Himalayas

The Himalayas extend more than 1,600 miles (2,600 km) from northern Pakistan, through Kashmir and northern India, across Tibet and Nepal and into Bhutan. Although the mountains are known as the Himalayas, they are three separate ranges. The Great Himalaya range includes Mount Everest. Nearly a third of the world's mammal species live in the Himalayas. They include the snow leopard and the red panda. Rhododendrons bloom on the lower slopes and there are more than 250 species of orchids.

EURASIAN PLATE

INDIA today

Equator

INDIAN OCEAN

Sri Lanka

"INDIA" landmass

- 10 million years ago
- 38 million years ago
- 55 million years ago
- 71 million years ago

On the move
The continents are carried along by Earth's tectonic plates. The plates are moving up to 8 inches (20 cm) per year in some places.

How the Himalayas were formed

The Himalayas were formed by the collision of two tectonic plates. The Indian Plate and the Eurasian Plate started on their collision course about 60 million years ago.

Continents in collision
One continent pushes over the top of the other and the rocks start to crumple and fold.

Rising mountains
Peaks are thrust upward as pressure continues. Fossils from the seabed move to the top of the mountains.

Growing sideways
Some land is pushed outward, so the mountain range then extends sideways.

Taj Mahal

The Taj Mahal near Agra, in northern India, was built in the mid-1600s by Mughal emperor Shah Jahan as a monument to his favorite wife. It is made of white marble and decorated with jewels and carvings.

The largest, most famous sapphire in the world was discovered in Sri Lanka more than 300 years ago. Surprisingly, it is called the Star of India.

CHINA

Mishmi Hills

Dibrugarh   Tinsukia

BHUTAN
*THIMPHU

Kula Kangri
24,783ft (7,554m)

Mt Everest
29,035ft (8,850m)
*KATHMANDU

NEPAL

Annapurna
26,545ft (8,091m)

Dhangadhi   Dhangadhi

Bahraich
Ghat

CHINA

(Administered by China, claimed by India)

(Administered by China, claimed by India)

(Administered by China, claimed by India)

(Administered by China, claimed by India)

K2
28,251ft (8,611m)

Karakoram Range

Ladakhe

Jammu and Kashmir

Line of control

Srinagar

H i m a l a y a s

Haldwani   Moradabad
Rampur   Pilibhit
Bareilly   Budaun   Sitapur
Haridwar   Shahjahanpur
Muzaffarnagar   Aligarh
Meerut   Hathras   Fatehgarh
Ghaziabad   NEW   Budaun
DELHI   Firozabad
Faridabad   Mathura

CHINA

Pathankot
Hoshiarpur
Jalandhar
Ludhiana
Chandigarh
Dun   Dehra
Dun
Patiala
Karnal
Saharanpur

Amritsar
Jammu
Jhelum

Gujranwala

Lahore

Abohar
Ganganagar   Moga   Bathinda
Sirsa   Hisar
Bhiwani   Rohtak

PAKISTAN

ISLAMABAD
*

Hindu Kush

Bikaner
Sikar
Rajasthan   Jaipur

Thar Desert

Delhi

Tea pickers
India grows about 30 percent of the world's tea and is the largest producer. Women pick the tea by hand. Only the top two leaves and bud are used.

Stilt fishermen
On Sri Lanka's south coast, fishermen wade out into the water each morning and climb tall wooden poles. They perch precariously on bamboo crossbars, high above the surf, and spend hours fishing.

The Maldives has over 1,200 islands, but only about 80 are open to foreigners.

Bhutan is the only country with a national park formed to protect the yeti.

Southern Asia

INDIA	
TOTAL AREA	1,147,955 sq miles (2,973,190 sq km)
OFFICIAL LANGUAGE	English, Hindu and others
MAIN RELIGION	Hinduism
LIFE EXPECTANCY	63 years
LITERACY	59%

BANGLADESH	
TOTAL AREA	51,703 sq miles (133,910 sq km)
OFFICIAL LANGUAGE	Bangla (Bengali)
MAIN RELIGION	Muslim
LIFE EXPECTANCY	61 years
LITERACY	43%

NEPAL	
TOTAL AREA	52,819 sq miles (136,800 sq km)
OFFICIAL LANGUAGE	Nepali
MAIN RELIGION	Hinduism
LIFE EXPECTANCY	59 years
LITERACY	41%

SRI LANKA	
TOTAL AREA	24,996 sq miles (64,740 sq km)
OFFICIAL LANGUAGE	Sinhala
MAIN RELIGION	Buddhism
LIFE EXPECTANCY	72 years
LITERACY	92%

BHUTAN	
TOTAL AREA	18,147 sq miles (47,000 sq km)
OFFICIAL LANGUAGE	Dzongkha
MAIN RELIGION	Buddhism
LIFE EXPECTANCY	53 years
LITERACY	42%

One-fifth of the world's people live in Southern Asia.

WHERE PEOPLE LIVE

Urban — Rural

INDIA
28% / 72%

BANGLADESH
24% / 76%

SRI LANKA
23% / 77%

NEPAL
12% / 88%

BHUTAN
7% / 93%

USING THE LAND

Forest and woodland
Arable land
Grazing
Arid or marginal

Map labels: Srinagar, Delhi, NEW DELHI, KATHMANDU, THIMPHU, Varanasi, DACCA, Calcutta, Chittagong, Ahmadabad, Mumbai, Hyderabad, Chennai, COLOMBO

Map key:
- Cereals
- Rice
- Jute
- Cotton
- Tea
- Groundnuts
- Rubber
- Beef cattle
- Goats
- Fishing
- Industrial center
- Mining
- Tourism

LARGEST CITIES

Mumbai 12,623,000

Delhi 10,401,000

Dacca 9,363,000

Calcutta 4,853,000

HIGHEST MOUNTAINS

Kangchenjunga 28,169 feet (8,586 m)
Mt Everest 29,035 feet (8,850 m)
Lhotse 27,940 feet (8,516 m)
Makalu 27,765 feet (8,462 m)

Rice
Rice is grown throughout Southern Asia and is the largest single crop of Sri Lanka. Much rice cultivation is still performed by hand (below). A variety of long-grained rice called basmati, grown in northern India, is prized for its light, fluffy texture and delicate aroma. More than half the world's people depend on rice for survival.

Jute
Jute is a strong, fibrous plant used in rope, mats and sacking. Jute is one of Bangladesh's greatest income sources, and its largest export crop. However, the production of synthetic fibers is now threatening this industry's future.

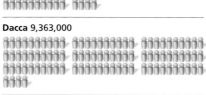

NATURAL FEATURES

Thar Desert INDIA
Also known as the Great Indian Desert, the Thar covers 74,000 square miles (192,000 sq km) in northwest India. High winds erode the desert's sand dunes into constantly changing forms.

The Sundarbans INDIA–BANGLADESH
One of the largest mangrove swamps on Earth, the Sundarbans span the border between India and Bangladesh on the Bay of Bengal. They are home to rare species of animals, such as the Bengal tiger (below) and the Indian python.

Ladakh

Ladakh KASHMIR
The remote region of Ladakh, often called the Land of High Passes, lies across the disputed Kashmir Valley in the rainshadow of the Indian Himalayas. High plains and deep valleys dominate the landscape. It is one of the highest and driest regions in the world.

Mt Everest NEPAL
Located in the Himalayas on the border between Nepal and Tibet, Mt Everest is the highest point on Earth. The ultimate challenge for any mountain climber is to reach its summit, a steep and rugged area 29,035 feet (8,850 m) above sea level.

Bengal tiger

Shiva

Hindu gods

Hindus believe that their gods, even though they appear in separate forms, are part of one supreme god, Brahman. The three most important gods reflect the circle of life. First is Brahma, the creator of the world; then Vishnu, the preserver of the existing world; and finally, Shiva, the destroyer of the world.

PEOPLE

The Buddha c 566–486 BC
Siddhartha Gautama, founder of the Buddhist religion and known as the Buddha, began life as a Hindu. Dissatisfied with many Hindu teachings, he searched for spiritual answers and received "enlightenment," after which he taught about the true nature of the world.

Akbar 1542–1605
The grandson of the Mughal founder Babur, Akbar (*right*) was the greatest of India's Mughal emperors. He tolerated all religions and supported the arts.

Mahatma Gandhi 1869–1948
Called the Mahatma, or great soul, Gandhi helped to gain India's independence from Britain in 1947. Later, as head of the Indian National Congress, he led peaceful protests in an effort to unify the country. He was shot dead by a Hindu rebel.

Tenzing Norgay 1914–86
After six failed attempts, Tenzing Norgay, a Sherpa from Nepal, joined Edmund Hillary to become the first to conquer Mt Everest and return, in May 1953.

Indira Gandhi 1917–84
The first female prime minister of India, Indira Gandhi led her country twice, from 1966 to 1967, and from 1980 until she was assassinated by her guards in 1984. She supported social changes that improved the lives of many Indians.

PLACES

Mumbai INDIA
Located on an island connected by bridges to the mainland, Mumbai, India's largest city, provides much of the country's wealth through its port trade and film industry. In contrast, many of its citizens are poor and homeless.

Meenakshi Temple INDIA
Towering above the heart of Madurai is this temple complex (*below*), built

by the Nayaks in the 16th century. Towers carved with mythical figures enclose the main shrine, which honors the god Shiva and his wife Meenakshi.

Colombo SRI LANKA
The administrative capital of Sri Lanka, Colombo was founded in the mid-1300s at the mouth of the Kelani River. Many of Colombo's buildings date from its 450 years of European colonization.

Golden Temple

Golden Temple INDIA
This holiest of Sikh shrines (*above*) stands in the middle of a pool of water at Amritsar. It was built by Guru Arjun, one of the 10 Sikh gurus, and houses his original writings on the Sikh faith.

Thimpu BHUTAN
Located in the heart of the Himalayas, this small Buddhist city is the capital of the kingdom of Bhutan. Buildings constructed in the traditional Bhutanese style dominate the skyline.

Kathmandu NEPAL
The capital of Nepal, Kathmandu has a rich architectural heritage from several religions. This Buddhist temple, the Bodhnath Stupa (*left*), looks like a mandala from above, and is the largest of its kind.

TRADITIONS AND CULTURE

Tsechus BHUTAN
These annual festivals are held to celebrate Buddhism's arrival in Bhutan. Dancers wearing silk costumes and animal masks (*right*) act out traditional legends in the streets.

Sacred cows
For Hindus, many of whom live in southern Asia, cows are sacred beasts. No Hindu eats beef, and cows are free to roam.

Varanasi ghats INDIA
In Varanasi, India's most holy city, the ghats, or steps, of the Ganges River attract millions of pilgrims who bathe in the river's sacred waters. First light is the most blessed time to bathe.

Bollywood INDIA
Mumbai has the largest film industry in the world, producing about 800 films a year. Watching Bollywood films is one of the most popular pastimes for Southern Asians.

Kandy perahera SRI LANKA
Decorated elephants and hundreds of dancers take part in the 10-day perahera Buddhist festival, at Kandy. The sacred tooth, a relic of the Buddha, is displayed.

Sikhism INDIA
This religion, founded by Guru Nanak in the 15th century, combines Hindu and Islamic beliefs. Nine gurus succeeded Nanak and each added his mark to the Sikh faith, now followed by millions.

Indian cobra
Found in the rain forests, rice paddies and cultivated fields of India, the Indian cobra is highly venomous. When threatened, the snake rises up and spreads its neck vertebrae (*above*). To attack, the cobra "spits" by pressing on its venom glands, forcing venom out through its fangs. It can spit venom over 6½ feet (2 m).

THE MUGHALS 1526–1857
Babur (*above*), a Muslim leader from Afghanistan, founded the Mughal dynasty. Babur's grandson Akbar, a ruler at 15, brought more power and strength to the empire and formed his own religion. Shah Jahan, the grandson of Akbar, developed art and architecture, and created the Taj Mahal. The dynasty slowly declined after his rule, and was ended by Britain in 1857.

RIVAL STATES
As the Mughal empire became less powerful, other countries tried to take control of India. Portuguese seaman Vasco de Gama was the first European to land there, in Calicut in 1498, and Dutch, French and British ships arrived soon after. The Portuguese set up a factory in Goa and took control of Indian trade during the 16th century. Britain then gained trading control through the East India Company, set up in 1600.

SPICE TRADE
In the 17th century, trading companies were set up by other Europeans keen to trade with India for silk and spices. The British East India Company took spices, and later silks, back to England. France also competed for trade.

Indian spice market

THE BRITISH RAJ
In 1756, the prince of Bengal tried to regain power from the English. A year later, Britain, led by Robert Clive, won the Battle of Plassey, and took over the rule of Bengal and India. In 1858, Indian rule passed to the British crown. Many British people went to India and lived as they would in their homeland. In 1947, Britain agreed to release India from its control and it became independent.

Indians served the British during the Raj

SINCE INDEPENDENCE
Once India gained independence, Pakistan, a Muslim nation, wanted to split away. Riots broke out, and millions were killed as they tried to flee the unrest in the "partition" of India. Kashmir joined India, which has caused warring with Pakistan ever since. In 1971, with the support of India's army, East Pakistan gained independence from Pakistan and formed Bangladesh. In 1950, India became a democratic republic and is now governed by a coalition, or joint, government, headed by its own prime minister.

Southeast Asia

Shadow puppet

Indonesian puppet masters play out traditional stories using puppets made from buffalo or goat skin. The moving puppets cast large shadows onto a screen. The puppet master operates the arms with rods, and speaks all the voices.

Inlay Lake

The fishing people who live by the shallow waters of Inlay Lake, in Myanmar, have a unique rowing style. They use a single oar, powered by one leg.

INDONESIA
POPULATION 234,893,000 ✳ CAPITAL JAKARTA

PHILIPPINES
POPULATION 84,620,000 ✳ CAPITAL MANILA

VIETNAM
POPULATION 81,625,000 ✳ CAPITAL HANOI

THAILAND
POPULATION 64,265,000 ✳ CAPITAL BANGKOK

MYANMAR (BURMA)
POPULATION 42,511,000 ✳ CAPITAL RANGOON

MALAYSIA
POPULATION 23,093,000 ✳ CAPITAL KUALA LUMPUR

CAMBODIA
POPULATION 13,125,000 ✳ CAPITAL PHNOM PENH

LAOS
POPULATION 5,922,000 ✳ CAPITAL VIENTIANE

SINGAPORE
POPULATION 4,609,000 ✳ CAPITAL SINGAPORE

EAST TIMOR
POPULATION 998,000 ✳ CAPITAL DILI

BRUNEI
POPULATION 358,000 ✳ CAPITAL BANDAR SERI BEGAWAN

Buddhist monk

Becak taxi

These cycle taxis are common in the small towns and rural areas of Indonesia. They take people to school and to market, and also carry goods. They were once popular in large cities, but were banned because they caused traffic jams.

Thai dancers

Elaborately costumed dancers perform plays depicting Thai myths and religious stories. The dancers' faces are either masked or expressionless. Emotions are communicated through hand and body movements. These performances were originally seen only in the royal courts.

The merlion is the symbol of Singapore, the busiest port in Southeast Asia. It is half-fish, to pay tribute to Singapore's beginnings as a fishing village.

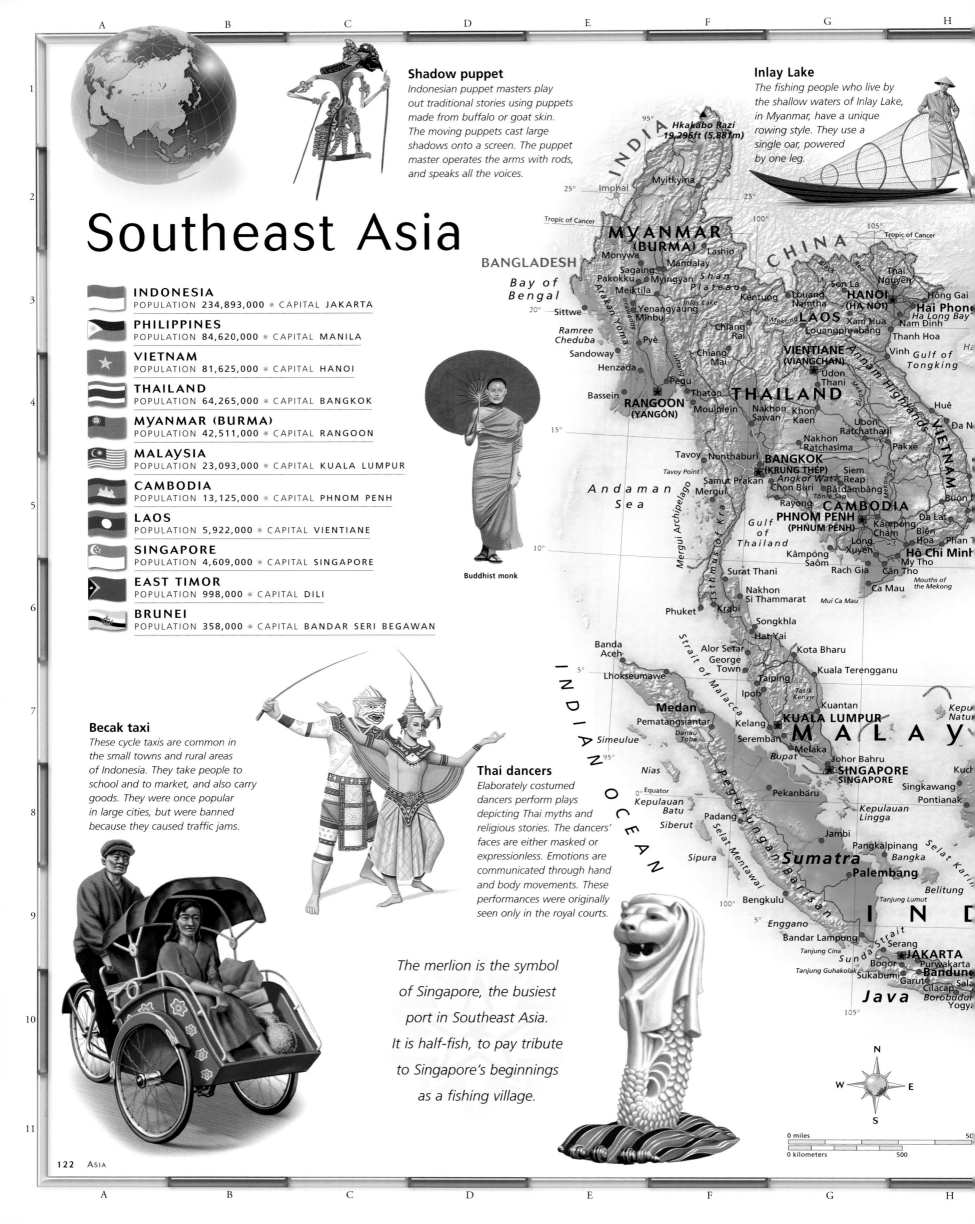

### Map labels

INDIA

CHINA

Hkakabo Razi
19,295ft (5,881m)

Imphal
Myitkyina

MYANMAR
(BURMA)

BANGLADESH

Monywa
Lashio
Sagaing
Mandalay
Pakokku
Myingyan
Shan
Plateau
Meiktila
Thai
Nguyen

Bay of
Bengal

Sittwe
Yenangyaung
Minbu
Chiang
Rai
Xam Hua
Louangphrabang

Ramree
Cheduba

Sandoway
Chiang
Mai

Henzada
Pegu
Thaton

Bassein
RANGOON
(YANGÔN)
Moulmein

THAILAND

Louang
Namtha

HANOI
(HA NÔI)
Hông Gai
Ha Long Bay
Nam Dinh
Thanh Hoa
Vinh
Gulf of
Tongking
Da Na

LAOS

VIENTIANE
(VIANGCHAN)
Udon
Thani

Hai Phong

Huê

Nakhon
Sawan
Khon
Kaen
Ubon
Ratchathani
Pakxe

Tavoy
Nonthaburi
Nakhon
Ratchasima

Tavoy Point
Samut Prakan
BANGKOK
(KRUNG THEP)
Angkor Wat
Siem
Reap
Chon Buri
Bàtdâmbâng

Mergui
Tônlé Sap
Rayong
CAMBODIA

Andaman
Sea

Gulf
of
Thailand
PHNOM PENH
(PHNUM PÉNH)
Kâmpóng
Cham

Kâmpóng
Saôm
Long
Xuyên

Da Lat
Biên
Hoa
Phan

Hô Chi Minh

Surat Thani
Rach Gia
Cân Tho

Nakhon
Si Thammarat
Mui Ca Mau
Ca Mau
Mouths of
the Mekong

Phuket
Krabi
Songkhla

Hat Yai

Banda
Aceh
Alor Setar
George
Town
Kota Bharu

Lhokseumawe
Taiping
Kuala Terengganu

Ipoh
Tasik
Kenyir
Kuantan

Medan
Kelang
KUALA LUMPUR

Pematangsiantar
MALAY

Simeulue
Danau
Toba
Seremban
Melaka

Bupat
Johor Bahru

Nias
SINGAPORE
SINGAPORE
Singkawang

Pekanbaru
Kepulauan
Batu
Pontianak

Padang
Siberut
Kepulauan
Lingga

Jambi
Pangkalpinang
Bangka

Sipura
Sumatra
Palembang

Bengkulu
Belitung
Tanjung Lumut
IND

Enggano

Bandar Lampung
Serang
JAKARTA

Tanjung Cina
Sunda
Strait
Bogor
Purwakarta

Tanjung Guhakolak
Sukabumi
Bandun
Garut

Java
Cilacap
Borobudur
Yogya

Tropic of Cancer
Tropic of Cancer

INDIAN OCEAN

Equator

0 miles   500
0 kilometers   500

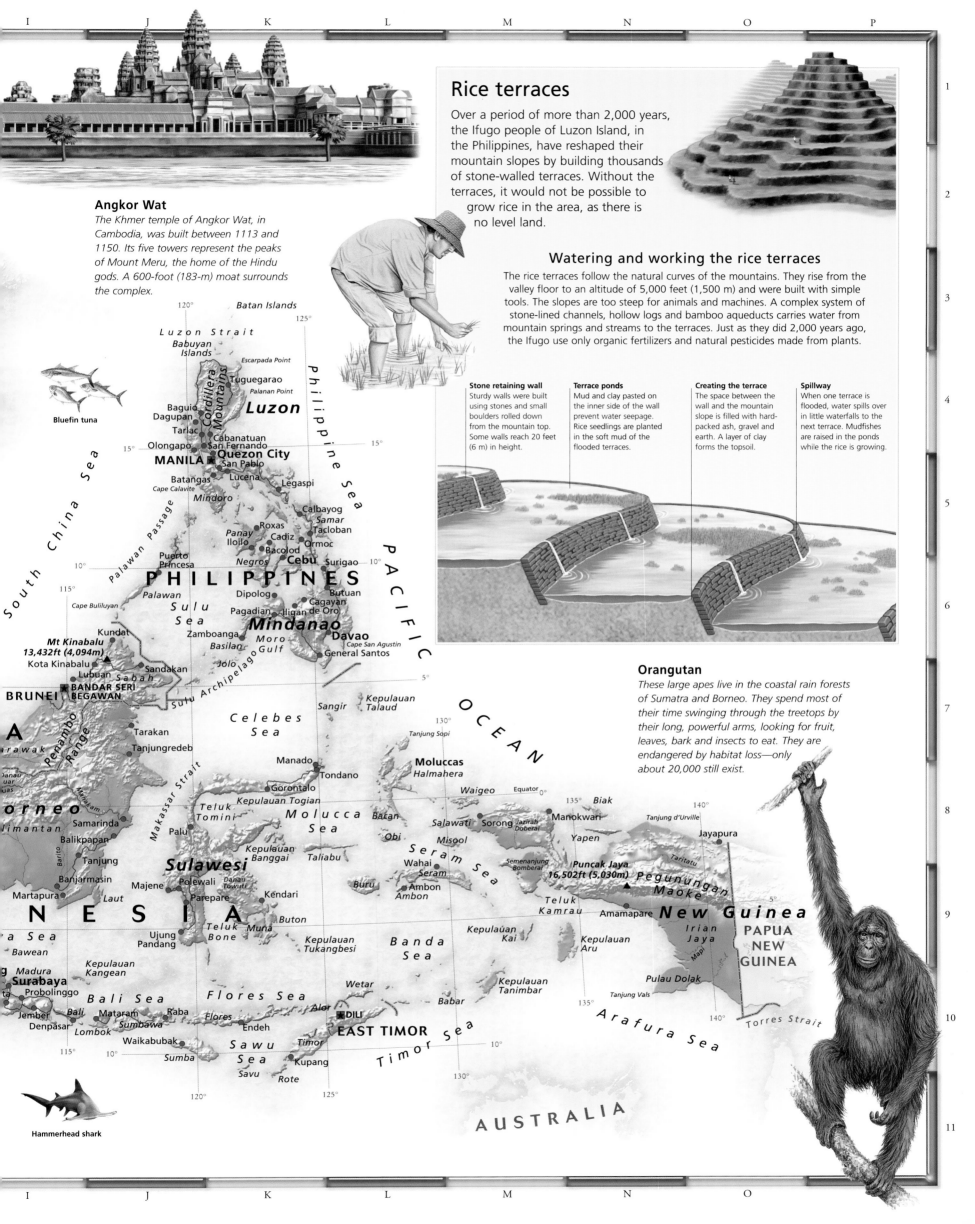

Angkor Wat

The Khmer temple of Angkor Wat, in Cambodia, was built between 1113 and 1150. Its five towers represent the peaks of Mount Meru, the home of the Hindu gods. A 600-foot (183-m) moat surrounds the complex.

Rice terraces

Over a period of more than 2,000 years, the Ifugo people of Luzon Island, in the Philippines, have reshaped their mountain slopes by building thousands of stone-walled terraces. Without the terraces, it would not be possible to grow rice in the area, as there is no level land.

Watering and working the rice terraces

The rice terraces follow the natural curves of the mountains. They rise from the valley floor to an altitude of 5,000 feet (1,500 m) and were built with simple tools. The slopes are too steep for animals and machines. A complex system of stone-lined channels, hollow logs and bamboo aqueducts carries water from mountain springs and streams to the terraces. Just as they did 2,000 years ago, the Ifugo use only organic fertilizers and natural pesticides made from plants.

Stone retaining wall
Sturdy walls were built using stones and small boulders rolled down from the mountain top. Some walls reach 20 feet (6 m) in height.

Terrace ponds
Mud and clay pasted on the inner side of the wall prevent water seepage. Rice seedlings are planted in the soft mud of the flooded terraces.

Creating the terrace
The space between the wall and the mountain slope is filled with hard-packed ash, gravel and earth. A layer of clay forms the topsoil.

Spillway
When one terrace is flooded, water spills over in little waterfalls to the next terrace. Mudfishes are raised in the ponds while the rice is growing.

Orangutan

These large apes live in the coastal rain forests of Sumatra and Borneo. They spend most of their time swinging through the treetops by their long, powerful arms, looking for fruit, leaves, bark and insects to eat. They are endangered by habitat loss—only about 20,000 still exist.

Bluefin tuna

Hammerhead shark

**Map labels:**

Batan Islands
120°
Luzon Strait
Babuyan Islands
125°
Escarpada Point
Tuguegarao
Cordillera Mountains
Palanan Point
Baguio
Luzon
Dagupan
Tarlac
15°
Olongapo
Cabanatuan
San Fernando
MANILA
Quezon City
San Pablo
Batangas
Lucena
Legaspi
Cape Calavite
Mindoro
Calbayog
Samar
Roxas
Panay
Cadiz
Tacloban
Iloilo
Bacolod
Ormoc
10°
Puerto Princesa
Negros
Cebu
Surigao
Palawan Passage
PHILIPPINES
115°
Dipolog
Butuan
Cape Buliluyan
Palawan
Sulu Sea
Pagadian
Cagayan de Oro
Iligan
Kundat
Zamboanga
Mindanao
Davao
Mt Kinabalu 13,432ft (4,094m)
Basilan
Moro Gulf
Cape San Agustin
Kota Kinabalu
Jolo
General Santos
Lubuan
Sabah
Sandakan
5°
BRUNEI
BANDAR SERI BEGAWAN
Sulu Archipelago
Kepulauan Talaud
Sangir
Penambo Range
Tarakan
Celebes Sea
Tanjung Sopi
Tanjungredeb
130°
Manado
Moluccas
Halmahera
Waigeo
Equator 0°
135°
Biak
Tondano
Salawati
Sorong
Jazirah Doberai
Manokwari
Gorontalo
Kepulauan Togian
Bacan
Obi
Misool
Yapen
140°
Tanjung d'Urville
Samarinda
Teluk Tomini
Palu
Molucca Sea
Jayapura
Balikpapan
Kepulauan Banggai
Taliabu
Seram Sea
Puncak Jaya 16,502ft (5,030m)
Pegunungan Maoke
Tanjung Vals
Tanjung
Sulawesi
Wahai
Seram
Semenanjung Bomberai
New Guinea
Banjarmasin
Majene
Polewali
Danau Towuti
Buru
Ambon
Teluk Kamrau
Amamapare
Irian Jaya
PAPUA NEW GUINEA
Martapura
Parepare
Kendari
Ambon
5°
NESIA
Laut
Teluk Bone
Buton
Kepulauan Kai
Kepulauan Aru
Mapi
Ujung Pandang
Muna
Banda Sea
Kepulauan Tukangbesi
Pulau Dolak
Bawean
Madura
Kepulauan Kangean
Wetar
Surabaya
Kepulauan Tanimbar
Probolinggo
Bali Sea
Flores Sea
Alor
Babar
Arafura Sea
Jember
Bali
Mataram
Raba
Flores
DILI
135°
140°
Denpasar
Lombok
Sumbawa
Endeh
EAST TIMOR
Timor Sea
Torres Strait
Waikabubak
Sawu Sea
Timor
10°
Sumba
Kupang
130°
Savu
Rote
120°
125°

AUSTRALIA

South China Sea
Palawan passage
Philippine Sea
PACIFIC OCEAN
Makassar Strait
Sulu Sea
Celebes Sea
Molucca Sea
Seram Sea
Banda Sea
Flores Sea
Bali Sea
Timor Sea
Arafura Sea
Sawu Sea

There are more than 13,000 islands in the Indonesian archipelago.

Southeast Asia

LAND AREA	1,689,703 sq miles (4,376,310 sq km)
LARGEST COUNTRY	Indonesia
SMALLEST COUNTRY	Singapore
MAIN RELIGION	Muslim
LIFE EXPECTANCY	70 years
LITERACY	76%

The small country of Brunei became rich when oil was discovered in 1929. The Sultan of Brunei owns the largest fleet of Rolls Royce cars in the world.

WHERE PEOPLE LIVE

Urban — Rural

REGION
43% — 57%

Most urban: SINGAPORE
100%

Most rural: CAMBODIA
16% — 84%

USING THE LAND

Forest and woodland

Arable land

Grazing

Arid or marginal

Timber
Timber is a prized resource in Southeast Asia, but its logging (*left*) has led to serious environmental problems in countries such as Thailand, Myanmar and Malaysia. Careless and often illegal logging has destroyed forests. Many species of animals have therefore lost their habitats and some may become extinct.

Krakatoa

In 1883, Krakatoa, a volcano on a small Indonesian island, erupted. The noise from the explosion was heard as far away as Australia and Japan. Several tsunamis (giant tidal waves) killed thousands of people—the largest killed 36,000. A steamship called the *Berouw* (*above*) was swept inland 1½ miles (2.4 km) by the force of one of the waves.

NATURAL FEATURES

Irian Jaya
Occupying the western half of New Guinea, Irian Jaya is an area of high mountains and dense rain forests. It is home to many animals, including the tree kangaroo, and the Arfak butterflies, which are found only in this region.

Tree kangaroo

Spice Islands
Lying between Sulawesi and New Guinea, the Spice Islands (Moluccas Islands) were the only source of spices, such as cloves, nutmeg and pepper, from the early 1500s to the late 1800s.

Lake Tonle Sap CAMBODIA
During the wet season, Lake Tonle Sap, the largest inland lake in Southeast Asia, floods. When the water subsides, the farmland is covered with rich, fertile soil.

Ha Long Bay VIETNAM

Ha Long Bay, or the Bay of the Descending Dragon, includes more than 1,600 rocky islands whose limestone cliffs are full of alcoves, caves and tunnels.

LARGEST CITIES

Manila 10,330,000

Jakarta 8,988,000

Bangkok 6,709,000

Rangoon 4,455,000

Map legend

- Rice
- Tobacco
- Coconuts
- Palm oil
- Rubber
- Beef cattle
- Fishing
- Shellfish
- Industrial center
- Mining
- Oil production
- Gas production
- Timber
- Tourism

### Map labels

Mandalay, HANOI, Louangphrabang, Chiang Mai, VIENTIANE, RANGOON, Đa Nẵng, Tavoy, BANGKOK, Bătdâmbâng, PHNOM PENH, Hồ Chi Minh, Phuket, Hat Yai, MANILA, Cebu, Davao, BANDAR SERI BEGAWAN, KUALA LUMPUR, SINGAPORE, Padang, Palembang, JAKARTA, Surabaya, Denpasar, Banjarmasin, Ujung Pandang, Ambon, DILI, Jayapura

Fruits
An amazing variety of fruits are grown in the plantations of Southeast Asia. Tropical fruits, such as pineapples (*left*), bananas, melons and mangoes, are sold at local markets. Some countries, including Vietnam and Malaysia, export fruits to other countries, often in canned form.

PLACES

Jakarta INDONESIA
Jakarta, situated on the island of Java, was settled in the 5th century. It is the capital of Indonesia, its largest city and its industrial and commercial center.

Rangoon MYANMAR
Rangoon is the political center of Myanmar. Located on the Ayeyarwady delta, it is also a major trading port and industrial city.

Ho Chi Minh VIETNAM
Formerly called Saigon, this is the largest city in Vietnam. The busy streets are filled with people, market stalls and traffic. Its architecture is a mix of French colonial and Asian.

Getting around Ho Chi Minh

Grand Palace BANGKOK
Built in 1782, this palace on the east bank of the Choa Phraya River was the home of the Thai royal family until the late 1800s. It is now used for ceremonial purposes.

Borobodur INDONESIA
This is the largest Buddhist monument in the world. It was built on the island of Java in the 700s and 800s, and is shaped like a pyramid, with a square base and five tiers topped with three circular terraces.

Komodo dragon
The Komodo dragon is the biggest lizard in the world. It is an excellent swimmer and moves freely between several Indonesian islands. It can grow up to 10 feet (3 m) and weigh up to 200 pounds (90 kg). It has strong, thick legs with sharp claws, fanglike teeth and a lashing tail. Despite its size, it moves fast and can kill deer, goats and wild boar.

The Petronas Towers, 1,483 feet (452 m) high, in Kuala Lumpur, Malaysia, are the tallest buildings in the world.

TRADITIONS AND CULTURE

White elephants
In ancient times, the kings of Siam (now Thailand) and Burma (Myanmar) valued and protected these animals because they believed that they would bring them peace, power and riches.

Balinese festivals
Many Balinese festivals are based on religious traditions and feature elaborate costumes (*below*). Galungan, or Balinese New Year, begins on the first day of the Hindu calendar year and lasts for 10 days. Villages honor dead ancestors and celebrate good defeating evil.

Stilt villages
In many countries in Southeast Asia, houses are built up on stilts. In some regions, this is because the houses are built over water, but in others, it is to provide shelter and living quarters underneath for the farm animals, such as pigs, chicken and water buffalo.

Stilt village

Ceremonial silks
For centuries, Thai people have been weaving silk that is famous worldwide. The colors and patterns have symbolic meanings and the silks are worn in ceremonies. Thai silk is printed by a process called silk-screen printing.

Islamic traders
Arab merchants brought Islam to Southeast Asia in the 7th century. By the 13th century, sailing in ships called dhows (*above*), these Muslim sailors had set up a spice-trading network across Asia. Muhammad, the prophet and founder of Islam, had himself been a merchant, so Islamic merchants were well respected as honest traders.

PEOPLE

King Mongkut 1804–68
Also known as Rama IV, Thailand's King Mongkut was a Buddhist monk for 27 years before becoming king. In 1862, he hired a British governess to teach his children English. The musical *The King and I* was based on her journals.

Tunku Abdul Rahman 1903–90
Rahman, the prime minister of Malaya from 1957 to 1963, led the movement to set up the independent country of Malaysia. He then became Malaysia's prime minister from 1963 to 1970.

King Norodom Sihanouk born 1922
Born in Cambodia, Sihanouk became king in 1941 when he was 18. In 1955, he gave up his throne to form a political party and become prime minister. After many years of political unrest, Sihanouk became king again in 1993.

Aung San Suu Kyi born 1945
Aung San helped found the National League for Democracy and was awarded the Nobel Peace Prize in 1991 for her work toward democracy for Myanmar.

Aung San Suu Kyi

Xanana Gusmão born 1946
Gusmão, a former guerilla leader who fought against Indonesian rule, and was imprisoned for it, was elected president of East Timor in 2002.

C 1,600,000 BC
Humanlike people live in Java. They are about 5 feet (150 cm) tall, with large eyebrow ridges, a heavy jaw, a small chin and a thick skull.

C 2100 BC
Humans live in Ban Chiang, a settlement in the Udon Thani province in Thailand. They cultivate rice and raise animals for food. They also make and use metal tools.

Pagan palace

AD 1044
King Anawratha comes to the throne of Burma and rules from its capital, Pagan. Over the next 13 years he defeats the Mon, who are an Austro-Asian people, and unifies Burma.

1350
King Ramathibodi I founds the new kingdom of Ayutthaya in Thailand. He sets up his capital on an island near the Chao Phraya River just north of present-day Bangkok. He unifies the people and establishes a legal system. The kingdom lasts until 1767.

Ayutthayan Buddha

1595–98
The first Dutch trading missions arrive in Indonesia and, several years later, the powerful Dutch East India Company is founded.

1782
King Rama I becomes king of Thailand. He is the first of the Chakri dynasty, which rules Thailand today. He moves the court to Bangkok, turning it from a small village to a royal city.

1959
The island of Singapore, previously a colony of Britain, gains self-government for its internal affairs. Britain remains responsible for its defense and foreign affairs.

Vietnam War

1965–73
The USA joins the South Vietnamese in their efforts to prevent the North Vietnamese and South Vietnamese rebels from taking over Vietnam. The USA is involved for eight years, the longest war in which it has taken part.

1967
Suharto takes over from Sukarno as president of Indonesia. He makes peace with Malaysia and helps form the Association of Southeast Asian States (ASEAN), which promotes trade and cooperation with western countries.

1975–79
Cambodia is ravaged by the dictator Pol Pot, the leader of the Khmer Rouge soldiers. Temples and mosques are destroyed, and thousands of Cambodians are tortured, executed and buried.

2002
East Timor, which has been ruled by force by Indonesia since 1975, becomes independent, elects Xanana Gusmão as president and joins the United Nations.

Eastern Asia

Tibet, in southwest China, is known as "the roof of the world." The Himalayas, on the border between Tibet and Nepal, are Earth's highest mountains.

Traditional costume, Mongolia

CHINA
POPULATION 1,286,975,000 ✳ CAPITAL BEIJING

SOUTH KOREA
POPULATION 48,289,000 ✳ CAPITAL SEOUL

TAIWAN
POPULATION 22,603,000 ✳ CAPITAL TAIPEI

NORTH KOREA
POPULATION 22,466,000 ✳ CAPITAL PYONGYANG

MONGOLIA
POPULATION 2,712,000 ✳ CAPITAL ULAANBAATAR

The Great Wall of China

For thousands of years, the people of China built walls along their northern frontier. They all had one purpose: to keep Mongolian tribes from invading China's farmlands. The first wall—known as the Long Wall—was built between 217 and 208 BC by Emperor Qin Shi Huangdi, and stretched for 1,800 miles (2,900 km), with 25,000 watchtowers along its length.

Today's wall, snaking like a dragon through northern China's mountains and plains, is the fourth one. Emperor Zhu Yuanzhang ordered work to begin in 1368, and building continued for almost 300 years until 1644. The wall was made of earth rammed between stone and brick, with watchtowers, gateways and forts along the way.

CHINA

Length
The Great Wall of China is the longest structure ever built. The main wall and its branches are about 4,000 miles (6,400 km) long.

China's first emperor, Qin Shi Huangdi

Building the wall
Millions of prisoners, soldiers and peasants were forced to work on the wall. So many of them died that the wall has been called "the world's longest graveyard."

Defending the wall
Archers on each tower could cover half the distance between them. This meant that enemy soldiers storming the wall were never out of arrow range.

Chinese lion dance
The lion dance is about 2,000 years old, and is part of Chinese New Year and other festivals. Two dancers are inside the lion costume. One handles the head; the other plays the body and the tail. Three musicians accompany the lion.

Map labels:
KAZAKHSTAN · Altay · Altai · Ozero Zaysan · Karamay · Yining · Changji · Bogda Feng 17,864ft (5,44...) · Ürümqi · Bogda S... · Turpan · KYRGYZSTAN · Tian Shan · Aksu · Korla · Bosten Hu · Kuruktag · TAJIKISTAN · Kashi · Tarim He · Lop Nur · AFGHANISTAN · Kongur Shan 25,325ft (7,719m) · Shache · Yarkant He · Tarim Basin · Taklimakan Desert · PAKISTAN · (Administered by China, claimed by India) · Hotan · Altun Shan · K2 28,251ft (8,611m) · (Line of Control) · Kunlun Shan · (Administered by China, claimed by India) · Mutztag Feng 25,338ft (7,723m) · Ulan Ul Hu · (Administered by China, claimed by India) · INDIA · Gar · Tibet · Plateau of Tibet · Siling · Tangra Yumco · Gangdise Shan · Himalayas · Zhari Namco · Nam Co · Nago... · Nyainq... · NEPAL · Xigaze · Lhasa · Yamzho Yumco · Ny... · Mt Everest 29,035ft (8,850m) · KATHMANDU · THIMPHU · BHUTAN · IND...

Mongol roundup

Herdsmen from Mongolia round up their horses. Many people living in this harsh land are nomadic herders.

Korean drum dancer

Strength and acrobatic skills are needed to play the drums and dance at the same time.

Taiwanese industry

Taiwan has a thriving manufacturing industry. It produces textiles, cars, clothes and electronic products.

Hong Kong tram

More than 160 colorful double-decker trams rattle slowly through Hong Kong's bustling streets. They are powered by electricity and carry almost a quarter of a million people each day.

RUSSIA

Hövsgöl Nuur

Hyargas Nuur

ngom

Altay

Bayanhongor

Hangayn Nuruu

MONGOLIA

Erdenet

Darhan

★ULAANBAATAR

Öndörhaan

Choybalsan

Govi Altayn Nuruu

Dalandzadgad

Gobi Desert

Ejin Qi

Badain Jaran Desert

Yümen

Qilian Shan

Qinghai Hu

Jinchang

Shizuishan

Lang Shan

Inner Mongolia

Hohhot

Baotou

Datong

Huai'an

Jining

Zhangjiakou

Yinchuan

Wuhai

Wuzhong

Yulin

Yellow

Xining

Lanzhou

CHINA

Yan'an

Gyaring Hu

Tianshui

Tongchuan

Changzhi

Linfen

Taiyuan

Yangquan

Handan

Xingtai

Anyang

Xinxiang

Jiaozuo

Luoyang

Zhengzhou

Kaifeng

Zhuxian

Zhuzhou

Uldz

Manzhouli

Yakeshi

Hailar

Hulun Nur

Zalantun

Tahe

Heihe

Blagoveshchensk

Khabarovsk

Yichun

Hegang

Shuangyashan

Jiamusi

Qiqihar

Tieli

Daqing

Anda

Jixi

Harbin

Lake Khanka

Baicheng

Mudanjiang

Manchuria

Changchun

Jilin

Ussuriysk

Tongliao

Siping

Liaoyuan

Yanji

Vladivostok

Dunhua

Tieling

Tonghua

Baishan

Ch'ŏngjin

Fuxin

Fushun

Shenyang

Kanggye

Kimch'aek

Liaoyang

Jinzhou

Anshan

Haicheng

Hamhŭng

Yingkou

Dandong

Sinŭiju

NORTH KOREA

Chengde

Qinhuangdao

P'YŎNGYANG ★

Wŏnsan

Chifeng

Namp'o

Sariwŏn

Kaesŏng

Tangshan

Dalian

Korea Bay

Ch'unch'ŏn

★SEOUL (SŎUL)

BEIJING ★

Tianjin

Baoding

Bo Hai

Yantai

Inch'ŏn

Suwon

Taejŏn

Shijiazhuang

Cangzhou

Dongying

Zibo Weifang

Chŏnju

Taegu

Ulsan

P'ohang

Jinan

SOUTH KOREA

Kwangju

Pusan

Xintai

Qingdao

Sunch'ŏn

Yellow Sea

Zaozhuang

Xuzhou

Lianyungang

JAPAN

Korea Strait

Shangqiu

Suqian

Hongze Hu

Hualyin

Suzhou

Bengbu

Yangzhou

Huainan

Nantong

Xuchang

Pingdingshan

Xi'an

Baoji

Xianyang

Sanmenxia

Nanyang

Xinyang

Hefei

Changzhou

Changshu

Nanjing

Zhenjiang

Wuxi

Suzhou Shanghai

Mouth of the Yangtze

Hanzhong

Ankang

Shiyan

Suizhou

Xiangfan

Wuhu

Huzhou Jiaxing

Hangzhou

30°

Guangyuan

Jingmen

Wuhan

Anqing

Shaoxing

Ningbo

Daba Shan

Yichang

Huangshi

Jingdezhen

Jinhua

Mianyang

Three Gorges Dam

Jingsha

Jingzhou

Jiujiang

Taizhou

East China Sea

Chengdu

Nanchong

Sichuan Basin

Yueyang

Poyang Hu

Shangrao

Wenzhou

Leshan

Neijiang

Changde

Dongting Hu

Yiyang

Zigong

Chongqing

Nanchang

Linchuan

Yibin

Changsha

Luzhou

Xiangtan

Zhuzhou

Nanping

Zunyi

Loudi

Pingxiang

Ji'an

Kaili

Shaoyang

Hengyang

Sanming

Fuzhou

Guiyang

Anshun

Duyun

Yong'an

TAIPEI (T'AIPEI) ★

Panzhihua

Dongchuan

Guilin

Ganzhou

Longyan

Quanzhou

T'aoyüan

Hsinchu

Dali

Shaoguan

Zhangzhou

Xiamen

T'aichung

Hualien

Tropic of Cancer

Baoshan

Kunming

Liuzhou

Wuzhou

Chaozhou

Changhua

Chiai

TAIWAN

Kaiyuan

Shantou

T'ainan

P'ingtung

Gejiu

Nanning

Yulin

Guangzhou

Dongguan

Kaohsiung

MYANMAR

Foshan

Shenzhen

Jiangmen

Hong Kong

VIETNAM

Macau

Beihai

Maoming

South China Sea

HANOI (HA NOI)

Zhanjiang

LAOS

Hai Phong

Gulf of Tongking

Xuwen

Hainan Strait

Haikou

Hainan

Da Hinggan Ling (Greater Khingan Range)

Xiao Hinggan Ling

Zhangguangcai Ling

Sea of Japan

Yangtze

Hengduan Shan

Taiwan Strait

Amdo Jagbarwa 546ft (7,756m)

0 miles   400
0 kilometers   400

Eastern Asia

CHINA	
LAND AREA	3,705,195 sq miles (9,596,410 sq km)
OFFICIAL LANGUAGE	Chinese/Mandarin
MAIN RELIGION	Buddhist/Taoist
LIFE EXPECTANCY	72 years
LITERACY	86%

SOUTH KOREA	
LAND AREA	37,911 sq miles (9,596,410 sq km)
OFFICIAL LANGUAGE	Korean
MAIN RELIGION	Christian
LIFE EXPECTANCY	75 years
LITERACY	98%

TAIWAN	
LAND AREA	12,456 sq miles (32,260 sq km)
OFFICIAL LANGUAGE	Mandarin
MAIN RELIGION	Buddhist/Taoist
LIFE EXPECTANCY	76 years
LITERACY	86%

NORTH KOREA	
LAND AREA	46,491 sq miles (120,410 sq km)
OFFICIAL LANGUAGE	Korean
MAIN RELIGION	Buddhist
LIFE EXPECTANCY	70 years
LITERACY	99%

MONGOLIA	
LAND AREA	600,543 sq miles (1,555,400 sq km)
OFFICIAL LANGUAGE	Khalkha Mongol
MAIN RELIGION	Buddhist
LIFE EXPECTANCY	63 years
LITERACY	99%

LARGEST CITIES

Seoul 9,552,000

Shanghai 9,111,000

Beijing 6,696,000

Tianjin 4,384,000

USING THE LAND

- Cereals
- Rice
- Tea
- Sugarcane
- Soybeans
- Beef cattle
- Sheep
- Pigs
- Fishing
- Industrial center
- Mining
- Oil production
- Timber
- Forest and woodland
- Arable land
- Grazing
- Arid or marginal

Tea plantations
During the 17th century, European traders came to China's coast to buy tea and other goods. Today, Chinese tea remains popular. Plantations in more than 20 provinces grow crops for local use and for export.

NATURAL FEATURES

Plateau of Tibet CHINA
This high, flat and dry region in southwest China, north of the Himalayas, is the largest plateau in the world. It is home to Tibetan farmers, who keep yaks (*right*) for meat and dairy products.

Yellow River CHINA
The name of this river comes from the yellow silt that gathers on its bed as it flows downstream. Because its floods cause so much damage, the Yellow River is also called "China's Sorrow."

Gobi Desert MONGOLIA–CHINA
Vast areas of the Gobi Desert are covered in rugged, bare rock, with little vegetation. The desert stretches across 500,000 square miles (1,300,000 sq km).

Guilin CHINA
Tourists flock to this scenic area in Guangxi province to see its unusual limestone mountain peaks, known as karst formations. These landscapes have inspired artists and poets for centuries.

Guilin mountains

Rice paddies
Rice, China's main crop, is grown in flooded fields called paddies. The seeds are sown elsewhere, and once the rice shoots appear, women plant them out into the paddies. When the rice stalks are ripe, they are harvested. The grains are shaken from the stalks and left to dry in the sun. Water buffalo are sometimes used to plow the rice fields.

WHERE PEOPLE LIVE

	Urban	Rural
SOUTH KOREA	81%	19%
TAIWAN	69%	31%
NORTH KOREA	60%	40%
MONGOLIA	58%	42%
CHINA	32%	68%

LONGEST RIVERS

Yangtze (Chang Jiang) 3,964 miles (6,380 km)

Yellow (Huang He) 3,395 miles (5,464 km)

Lancang Jiang (Mekong) 2,749 miles (4,425 km)

Heilong Jiang (Amur) 1,786 miles (2,874 km)

Three Gorges Dam

A massive dam is being built across the Yangtze River at Sandouping. Work began in 1993, and when complete, water from the dam will generate hydroelectricity to power China's industries. The water will flood an area the size of Singapore, washing away the homes of more than a million people, and destroying historic sites and magnificent scenery.

TRADITIONS AND CULTURE

Tai chi
Each morning, people all over China start their day outdoors with a series of gentle movements that they believe will help develop their mind, body and spirit. Tai chi started in the 3rd century AD.

Moon Festival
At this mid-autumn festival during the eighth full moon of the Chinese lunar year, people let off loud fireworks when the moon appears, and eat moon cakes (*left*).

Woodblock printing
People in Eastern Asia invented the first form of printing in the 8th century. They carved characters from printed blocks, covered them with ink, and pressed the inked block onto paper.

There are 300 million bicycles in China, and people need a licence to ride one.

Dragon boat racing
As part of the Dragon Boat Festival, celebrated in Taiwan as well as China, long, decorated boats race on waterways to commemorate the death of the poet Chu Yuan, who drowned in 299 BC. Rice dumplings are served on the day.

Dragon boat

Chinese art
For centuries, Chinese painters have created landscapes using ink and brush on silk or paper. Plants and animals, combined with calligraphy, are popular subjects for scrolls, fans or folded albums.

PEOPLE

Confucius 551–479 BC
The values of this great thinker and teacher still form part of the Chinese way of life. Although he lived 2,500 years ago, his ideas on the family, school and nation are respected throughout China.

Zhang Heng AD 78–139
This Chinese mathematician and astronomer invented a seismoscope (*right*), for recording earthquakes. A ball fell out of a dragon's mouth into a frog's mouth when an earthquake occurred, making a loud noise, which woke the emperor.

Genghis Khan 1162–1227
One of the great Mongol leaders, Genghis Khan brought together the tribes of central Asia in 1209, and was crowned lord of all. His grandson was Kublai Khan.

Mao Zedong 1893–1976
The son of a peasant, Mao Zedong was a revolutionary leader. As head of the People's Republic of China, formed in 1949, Chairman Mao led China for almost 30 years under communist rule.

Dalai Lama born 1935
This spiritual leader of Tibet, now the 14th, has lived in exile in India since 1959. His title means "Ocean of Wisdom." In 1989, he received the Nobel Peace Prize.

Giant pandas
The number of giant pandas in China has dropped to 700 because the fountain bamboo forests that provide their food are being cleared for housing. These bears live in Sichuan province in central China.

Terra-cotta warriors
In 1974, workers in Shaanxi province, China, discovered a pit of life-size pottery statues. Emperor Qin Shi Huangdi had ordered the terra-cotta warriors to be made so that they could protect him after his death. In one pit, 7,000 soldiers and 600 horses, originally painted in bright colors, were found. Although they were made from molds, no two faces are the same.

Koumiss, the national drink of Mongolia, is made from fermented mare's milk.

PLACES

Shanghai CHINA
Shanghai, on the Huangpu River, was first settled in AD 1000. This thriving port is China's chief industrial and commercial city, and has long been a center for foreign investment and trade.

The Forbidden City CHINA
The emperor once lived behind the walls of this elaborate complex, whose intricate features date from the Ming dynasty. Today, tourists are able to enter the area and walk around its grounds.

The Forbidden City

Seoul SOUTH KOREA
South Korea's capital, Seoul, is a modern city on the Han River. Many businesses have their headquarters in the center and the streets bustle with a quarter of the nation's population.

Potala Palace TIBET
This traditional home of the Dalai Lama, or priest-king, of Tibet sits on a rocky hill above the city of Lhasa. The 1,000-room palace was built in the 17th century.

Potala Palace

HISTORY AT A GLANCE
THE CHINESE DYNASTIES

XIA c 2205–c 1700 BC
People are living in communities and use tools by the time this first dynasty develops, but few records exist. Yu, a Xia emperor, builds the first of China's canals.

SHANG 1600–1050 BC
The Shang dynasty overthrows the Xia. People use bronze for the first time, for tools and pottery. The Shang develop a 12-month, 360-day calendar.

Bronze Shang pot

ZHOU 1050–221 BC
Local armies fight for land, with much bloodshed. Confucianism develops. Iron is used and ox-drawn plows, crossbows and irrigation are invented.

QIN 221–207 BC
The ruler of the Qin state overthrows the Zhou ruler. Local states are destroyed and unified into one nation. The word China comes from "Qin."

HAN 206 BC – AD 220
The country is run by a new national civil service, based on the teachings of Confucius. Factories produce silk, cloth, paper and farm tools.

JIN AD 265–420
Two Jin dynasties emerge—northern and southern—under the rule of the Emperor Sima Yan. China cannot maintain its unity.

SUI AD 581–618
China is reunified after three centuries of disunity. The Great Wall is rebuilt and planning for the Grand Canal begins. Defeat by the Turks causes this short dynasty to collapse.

Fashions from the Tang dynasty

TANG AD 618–907
A lively emperor brings a new age of prosperity and opportunity in art and culture. Paper money is introduced and Buddhism becomes popular.

LIAO AD 907–1125
China disintegrates during these years, following attacks from the north. Many areas fall into foreign hands. The south divides into small states.

SONG AD 960–1279
The country is once again united. Cities grow. This is a golden age for architecture, craft, science, painting and learning.

YUAN 1206–1368
Kublai Khan sets up the Mongol emperors in Beijing to rule the Silk Road. The Chinese resent their Mongol invaders.

MING 1368–1644
The ideals of the Tang and Song dynasties return under Zhou Yuanzhang. This is a time of stability and order.

The last emperor

QING 1644–1911
The Manchus seize China. The empire gradually weakens and the Manchus are overthrown. Still a child, Pu Yi is the last emperor of China.

MODERN CHINA 1949
After civil war, China becomes a communist regime and is renamed the People's Republic of China. Industry and agriculture are modernized.

Japan

JAPAN
POPULATION 127,214,000 ★ CAPITAL
TOKYO

Earthquakes and volcanoes

Earth's crust is broken into pieces, called tectonic plates, that constantly move around. When a thick plate rides up over a thinner plate, the thinner one is forced down into the layer between Earth's crust and its core, a process called subduction. On the surface, volcanoes and earthquakes occur. There are three tectonic plates beneath Japan, and regular, sometimes devastating, earthquakes and volcanic eruptions take place on land.

The Ring of Fire

Japan sits on the Ring of Fire (in red). This chain includes more than half Earth's volcanoes and is the source of more than half its earthquakes.

Equator

JAPAN

PACIFIC OCEAN

Ring of Fire

Double trouble

Japan lies on both the Pacific and the Philippine plates. The Pacific Plate moves 4 inches (10 cm) each year. The Philippine Plate moves at half that speed. These two plates cause many of Japan's earthquakes and volcanoes.

Pacific Plate

Eurasian Plate

JAPAN

Kobe • **Tokyo**

Philippine Plate

How volcanoes form

Forces deep within Earth cause magma to burst through the crust and spit ash and fire.

Mid-ocean ridge
When plates under the ocean are pushed apart, magma rises through the gap. It cools and hardens to form a series of ridges on the ocean floor.

Ocean crust

Magma upwelling

Island arc volcano
When two plates with ocean crust collide, island arc volcanoes form.

Direction of plate movement

Trench

Magma upwelling

Hot-spot volcano
Sometimes, magma from a spot deep in the mantle forces its way through a weak spot in the middle of a plate to form a series of hot-spot volcanoes.

Continental volcano
When thin ocean crust meets thicker continental crust, the thin crust slides under the thicker one. This process forms a line of volcanoes.

Magma chamber
As magma rises from the mantle, it collects in the crust in large pockets called magma chambers.

Japanese cranes
These large wading birds are a symbol of loyalty and good luck. They make a loud sound like a bugle and are famous for their spectacular courtship dances and the great care they take of their young.

Japanese macaques
These animals, also called Japanese snow monkeys, live in the mountains of northern Honshū. The area is snow-covered for more than half the year. Japanese macaques keep warm by sitting in groups in hot volcanic springs.

RUSSIA

Kuril Islands

(Administered by Russian Federation claimed by Japan)

Ostrov Iturup

Ostrov Kunashir

RUSSIA

Sakhalin

Sea of Okhotsk

La Pérouse Strait

Sōya-wan

Wakkanai

Rebun-tō

Rishiri-tō

Teshio

Asahikawa

Nemuro-kaikyō

Nosapu-misaki

Nemuro

Shari

Shiretoko-misaki

Abashiri

Kitami

Kussharo-ko

Kushiro

Hokkaidō

Asahi-dake
7,513ft (2,290m)

Obihiro

Tokkachi

Horoshirir-dake
6,732ft (2,052m)

Tomakomai

Muroran

Esan-misaki

Hakodate

Tsugaru-kaikyō

Uchiura-wan

Ishikari-wan

Otaru

Ebetsu

Sapporo

Shikotsu-ko

Toya-ko

Shakotan-misaki
Kamui-misaki

Benkei-misaki

Okushiri-tō

Shiriya-zaki

Ōma-zaki

Mutsu-wan

Aomori

Hirosaki

Henashi-zaki

Nyūdō-zaki

Akita

Hachinohe

Towada-ko

Morioka

Iwate-san
6,696ft (2,041m)

Yamagata

Mogami

Sendai

Sakata

Tsuruoka

Sendai-wan

Ishinomaki

Kinka-san

Fukushima

Niigata

Sadoga-shima

J A P A N

P A C I F I C   O C E A N

Tokyo and its surrounding cities have the largest population of any urban center in the world. More than 31 million people live there.

Tokyo city hall

Robot technology

Japan is a world leader in robotics. Asimo, a humanoid robot made of tin, is 47 inches (119 cm) tall. It responds to spoken commands.

The gateway, or torii, at the Itsukushima Buddhist shrine on an island near Hiroshima, is a boundary between the sacred world of the shrine and the outside world. Gates such as this stand at the front of most Japanese shrines.

Samurai

The samurai were warriors. They lived according to a strict code of discipline and loyalty to their master. Only samurai could carry swords, and wealthy landlords hired them to protect their property. The samurai class was abolished in 1868.

Horyuji temple

This complex of Buddhist temples near Nara was built in about AD 700. The temples, with their delicate, complicated detailing, are the oldest surviving wooden buildings in the world. The pagoda stands on the place where important Buddhist relics are buried.

Pearl divers

Bluefin tuna

Ryukyu Islands

Japan

LAND AREA	144,689 sq miles (374,744 sq km)
OFFICIAL LANGUAGE	Japanese
MAIN RELIGION	Shinto/Buddhism
LIFE EXPECTANCY	81 years
LITERACY	99%

Japan has an average of 546 residents per square mile (337 per sq km)—one of the world's highest population densities.

WHERE PEOPLE LIVE

Urban	Rural
79%	21%

Rice plantations
About half the country's farmland is planted with rice, Japan's main food. Japan has abundant rainfall and many rivers that can be used for irrigation, allowing rice to be cultivated in paddies—fields that have been submerged under 2–4 inches (5–10 cm) of water. Farmers harvest their crops quickly with efficient machinery.

Map legend:
- Forest and woodland
- Arable land
- Rice
- Fruit
- Tobacco
- Beef cattle
- Fishing
- Industrial center
- Winter sports

Fruit and vegetables
Although four-fifths of the country is mountainous, and the soils are poor, Japan grows a wide variety of crops, including tomatoes, strawberries, cherries and carrots. Because of the limited amount of suitable farming land, Japanese farms are very small—seldom more than 2 acres (1 ha)—and every usable piece of land is planted.

Map labels: Sapporo, Sendai, TOKYO, Yokohama, Nagoya, Kyōto, Ōsaka, Hiroshima, Fukuoka, Nakamura, Kagoshima

Fishing
Since earliest times, the Japanese have relied on the sea and waterways for food. Deep-sea fishes, such as mackerel and tuna, are plentiful. However, to keep up with the demand for freshwater species, such as trout and eel, fish farms have been developed. Seaweed is also part of many Japanese dishes—fishermen gather kelp along Hokkaido's coast, and laver seaweed, or *nori*, is grown in Kyushu.

LARGEST CITIES

Tokyo 8,274,000

Yokohama 3,517,000

Ōsaka 2,596,000

Nagoya 2,195,000

Sapporo 1,856,000

Earthquake damage

Earthquakes
Japan experiences about 1,000 mostly minor Earth tremors each year. In 1923, an earthquake in the Tokyo–Yokohama area killed 140,000 people. The 1995 Kobe quake lasted only 20 seconds, but caused US$200 billion worth of damage and killed more than 5,000 people.

Mt Fuji
This volcano, which last erupted in 1707, is the highest peak in Japan, at 12,388 feet (3,776 m). Its name means "everlasting life." Regarded as sacred, it is a place of pilgrimage and the subject of many paintings and poems.

Mt Fuji

Ryukyu islands
This archipelago of 55 islands—some flat and built from coral, others mountainous and volcanic—extends 400 miles (640 km). Agriculture is the main occupation. The main crops are rice, sweet potatoes, sugar and pineapples. The islanders have their own language.

Shirakami mountains
This uninhabited, mountainous area in northern Honshū contains Japan's last beech forest. Many plants and animals are found here, including the Asiatic bear.

Asiatic bear

Bullet train
The first section of the *Shinkansen*—a high-speed electric rail line between Tokyo and Fukuoka—opened in 1964. About 250 "bullet trains" operate along the line daily. On some sections they can reach speeds of 160 miles (260 km) per hour. The fastest trains can complete the 664-mile (1,062-km) trip in less than seven hours.

Great Buddha

Erected in 1252, this 37-foot (11-m) tall bronze statue is in the grounds of Kotokuin Temple in Kamakura. The wooden building that once housed it was destroyed by a tsunami in 1495. Today, more than 96 million people follow Buddhism, which came to Japan from China in the 6th century. This Buddha faces the ocean, thought to be an ideal place to meditate.

PEOPLE

Murasaki Shikibu AD 978–1014
This Japanese noblewoman created *The Tale of Genji*—one of the world's first novels. The story was painted on a scroll, with intricately detailed illustrations. She also kept a diary of her life at court.

Toyotomi Hideyoshi 1536–98
The son of a peasant, Hideyoshi rose to be a samurai, then a feudal lord. He conquered Japan and unified the country after more than a century of warfare.

The Great Wave Off Kanagawa

Katsushika Hokusai 1760–1849
This artist produced thousands of artworks by printing from carved wood blocks. His series "Thirty-six Views of Mount Fuji," which includes *The Great Wave Off Kanagawa*, is famous.

Emperor Hirohito 1901–89
Japan's longest-reigning monarch, Hirohito oversaw dramatic changes in Japan, through an era of military expansion that ended with defeat in World War II, to the country's emergence as an economic superpower.

TRADITIONS AND CULTURE

Cherry blossoms
The brief season of Japan's national flower, the cherry blossom, is eagerly awaited each spring. Many poems have been written about these flowers. During World War II, they symbolized the soldiers who died in the war. In peacetime, they represent the start of the school year.

Shinto
Shinto is an ancient Japanese religion, based on the worship of spirits. There are more than 80,000 Shinto shrines in Japan. Before entering a shrine to pay their respects to the spirits, people wet their fingertips and rinse out their mouth.

Tea ceremony
This ancient ceremony takes great skill and concentration. The host prepares the tea in silence, then serves it to guests with delicate sweets. The ceremony signifies calm and self-discipline.

Hari-kiri, or seppuku, is a traditional form of ritual suicide.

PLACES

Tokyo
Tokyo, Japan's largest city, was founded in 1457 as the fortified town of Edo. In 1868, it became the capital and was renamed Tokyo. This bustling, crowded city is where much of the nation's political, economic and social activity takes place, and is home to one-fourth of the nation's people.

Kyoto
Founded in AD 794, Kyoto was the capital and home of the emperor's family for more than 1,000 years. A center of Buddhism and traditional culture, it is known for its historic temples and gardens, schools of tea ceremony and flower arranging, museums, geisha houses, artisans, theaters and festivals.

Golden Pavilion, Kyoto

Theater
Japan has three main types of traditional theater. Noh plays are short, with more symbolism than action. Lively Kabuki plays combine music, dance and mime with elaborate staging and costuming. Bunraku is a sophisticated form of puppet theater.

Noh mask

Rock gardens
The 2,000-year-old Japanese art of rock gardening follows strict rules to create serene spaces through harmony of the various elements. The patterns have spiritual and symbolic significance.

Sumo wrestling

Sumo wrestling, the national sport, is a popular spectacle in Japan. Following centuries-old rules and rituals, the two opponents, who eat special food to bulk up their size, use their strength and weight to try to knock each other out of a ring.

Hiroshima
On 6 August 1945, the USA dropped an atomic bomb on Hiroshima. Some 70,000 people died instantly or soon after the blast; a similar number died later of radiation sickness. The Atomic Bomb Dome (*above*) was one of the few buildings not completely destroyed. The city has been rebuilt, and is now a center of the peace movement.

Atomic Bomb Dome

Osaka
Japan's second city, Osaka has long been a cultural center, and has several universities. Its castle was built in the 16th century by the warlord Toyotomi Hideyoshi. Today, the city is a financial center with a busy port. Its industries include machinery, chemicals, metal production, textiles, paper and printing.

HISTORY AT A GLANCE

Jamon pottery

13,000 BC
Hunters and gatherers form the Jamon period. The first pottery is created.

300 BC
Settlers from Southeast Asia and Korea arrive, bringing their knowledge of rice-farming.

AD 500
The Yamato period starts. *Daimyo* (rulers) take control of large areas.

AD 710
The Nara period starts. Later this century, Japanese culture evolves, with a new writing system. Buddhism becomes the state religion.

AD 794
Kyoto is built as the new capital city. It remains Japan's principal city for more than 1,000 years.

1185
After defeating the Taira family, Minamoto Yoritomo establishes a rival government and becomes the first shogun.

1274
The Mongols invade Japan. A "divine wind" (kamikaze) sinks their ships and they retreat. A second Mongol invasion also fails.

1542
The first Europeans arrive in search of spices and silk to trade. Missionaries spread the Christian faith. Firearms are introduced.

Imperial Palace

1590
After a series of wars, Toyotomi Hideyoshi unifies Japan and takes control. Guns are banned and the samurai gain status.

1600
The Tokugama period starts. Edo (Tokyo) becomes the new capital. All foreigners are expelled from 1637—only the Dutch and Chinese are allowed to trade from Nagasaki. Christianity is banned in 1614.

1868
Emperor Meiji is made head of state and moves to Tokyo. A period of rapid modernization begins. Japan's national pride grows.

Zero plane

1941
Japan launches a surprise attack on Pearl Harbor and fights the USA and Allies in World War II.

1945
Japan surrenders after the USA drops atomic bombs over Hiroshima and Nagasaki.

1997
After a period of rapid growth, the Japanese economy enters a severe recession.

Cap Blanc

Strait of
Gibraltar

Atlas Mountains

Grand Erg
Occidental

Grand Erg
Oriental

Al Hamâdah
al Hamrâ

Canary
Islands

Hammada
du Drâa

'Erg Chech

S   a   h   a

Hoggar

Tibes

Adrar des
Ifôghas

Massif
de l'Aïr

Ténéré
du
Tafassâsset

Niger

Lake
Chad

Cap
Vert

Sénégal

S   a   h   e   l

Cape Verde
Islands

Fouta
Djallon

White Volta

Black Volta

Benue

Dorsale Camerounaise

Lac de
Buyo

Lake
Volta

Slave Coast

Mouths of
the Niger

Mont Cameroun
13,451ft (4,100m)

Cong

Ivory Coast

Gold Coast

Gulf of Guinea

Isla de Bioco

São Tomé

ATLANTIC   OCEAN

Huíla
Plateau

Namib Desert

Oran

Cape of
Good Hope

Mediterranean Sea

Libyan
Desert

Qattâra
Depression

Nile
Delta

Sinai

a

Nile

Eastern Desert

Western Desert

Nubian
Desert

Red Sea

Massif
Ennedi

Marra
Plateau

Blue Nile

White Nile

Gulf of Aden

Rās Xaafuun

Lake
Tana

Ethiopian

Highlands

Ahmar
Mountains

Horn of
Africa

Ubangi

Mendebo
Mountains

Great Rift Valley

Shebeli

ngo

Lake
Albert

Lake
Turkana

Basin

Lake
Victoria

▲ Mt Kenya
17,057ft (5,199m)

Serengeti
Plain

Great Rift Valley

East African
Plateau

▲
Kilimanjaro
19,331ft (5,892m)

Pemba Island

Africa

Lake
Tanganyika

Zanzibar Island

ateau
Kasai

INDIAN   OCEAN

Lake
Malawi

Comoros
Islands

Zambezi

Lake
Kariba

Zambezi

Mozambique Channel

Okavango
Delta

Madagascar

alahari
Basin

alahari
Desert

Limpopo

has

Drakensberg

Great Karoo
le Karoo

Northern Africa

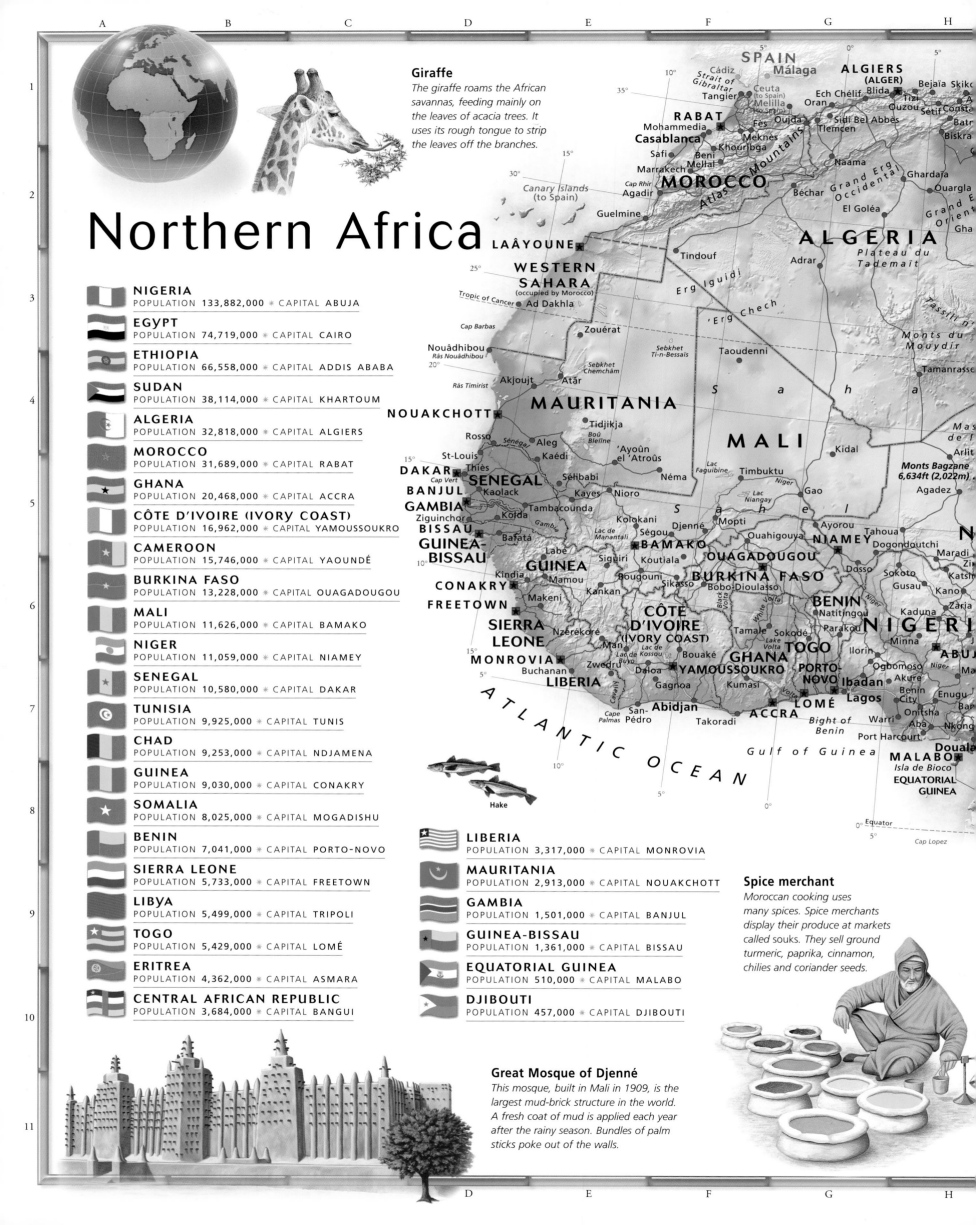

Giraffe

The giraffe roams the African savannas, feeding mainly on the leaves of acacia trees. It uses its rough tongue to strip the leaves off the branches.

NIGERIA
POPULATION 133,882,000 * CAPITAL ABUJA

EGYPT
POPULATION 74,719,000 * CAPITAL CAIRO

ETHIOPIA
POPULATION 66,558,000 * CAPITAL ADDIS ABABA

SUDAN
POPULATION 38,114,000 * CAPITAL KHARTOUM

ALGERIA
POPULATION 32,818,000 * CAPITAL ALGIERS

MOROCCO
POPULATION 31,689,000 * CAPITAL RABAT

GHANA
POPULATION 20,468,000 * CAPITAL ACCRA

CÔTE D'IVOIRE (IVORY COAST)
POPULATION 16,962,000 * CAPITAL YAMOUSSOUKRO

CAMEROON
POPULATION 15,746,000 * CAPITAL YAOUNDÉ

BURKINA FASO
POPULATION 13,228,000 * CAPITAL OUAGADOUGOU

MALI
POPULATION 11,626,000 * CAPITAL BAMAKO

NIGER
POPULATION 11,059,000 * CAPITAL NIAMEY

SENEGAL
POPULATION 10,580,000 * CAPITAL DAKAR

TUNISIA
POPULATION 9,925,000 * CAPITAL TUNIS

CHAD
POPULATION 9,253,000 * CAPITAL NDJAMENA

GUINEA
POPULATION 9,030,000 * CAPITAL CONAKRY

SOMALIA
POPULATION 8,025,000 * CAPITAL MOGADISHU

BENIN
POPULATION 7,041,000 * CAPITAL PORTO-NOVO

SIERRA LEONE
POPULATION 5,733,000 * CAPITAL FREETOWN

LIBYA
POPULATION 5,499,000 * CAPITAL TRIPOLI

TOGO
POPULATION 5,429,000 * CAPITAL LOMÉ

ERITREA
POPULATION 4,362,000 * CAPITAL ASMARA

CENTRAL AFRICAN REPUBLIC
POPULATION 3,684,000 * CAPITAL BANGUI

LIBERIA
POPULATION 3,317,000 * CAPITAL MONROVIA

MAURITANIA
POPULATION 2,913,000 * CAPITAL NOUAKCHOTT

GAMBIA
POPULATION 1,501,000 * CAPITAL BANJUL

GUINEA-BISSAU
POPULATION 1,361,000 * CAPITAL BISSAU

EQUATORIAL GUINEA
POPULATION 510,000 * CAPITAL MALABO

DJIBOUTI
POPULATION 457,000 * CAPITAL DJIBOUTI

Hake

Spice merchant

Moroccan cooking uses many spices. Spice merchants display their produce at markets called souks. They sell ground turmeric, paprika, cinnamon, chilies and coriander seeds.

Great Mosque of Djenné

This mosque, built in Mali in 1909, is the largest mud-brick structure in the world. A fresh coat of mud is applied each year after the rainy season. Bundles of palm sticks poke out of the walls.

Pyramids of Giza

The pyramids were built about 2500 BC as tombs for the mummified bodies of Egypt's pharaohs. They were guarded by a massive sphinx, cut out of rock. A sphinx is a mythological creature with a lion's body and a human's head. The largest of the three huge pyramids was built for Pharaoh Khufu and is made of more than 2 million blocks of stone averaging 2½ tons (2.5 t) each. It was the world's tallest building for about 4,000 years.

Inside the Great Pyramid
1 King's chamber
2 Queen's chamber
3 Underground chamber
4 Grand gallery
5 Entrance

A technical marvel

The pyramids are extraordinary examples of engineering and craftsmanship. Thousands of workers dragged huge limestone blocks up ramps. They placed them so precisely that even a playing card cannot be slotted between them.

Food in Somalia

Sorghum, millet and corn are grown in Somalia. These grains are either cooked in a clay pot over hot ashes to make a thin porridge, or ground into flour for pancakes.

Felucca

A felucca is a narrow, fast sailing boat used on the Nile River and the Mediterranean Sea off the coast of Egypt. It has a tall, triangular sail longer than the boat.

The Nile is the longest river in the world. It travels 4,160 miles (6,656 km) from its most remote headstream in Burundi, southern Africa, to the Mediterranean Sea.

Tuareg tribesman

The Tuareg live in Mali, in the Sahara Desert. They are nomads who herd camels and goats. The Tuareg are sometimes referred to as the blue men of the desert because their robes are dyed indigo blue, and the dye stains their skin.

0 miles 600
0 kilometers 600

Northern Africa

LAND AREA	6,482,026 sq miles (16,788,371 sq km)
LARGEST COUNTRY	Algeria
SMALLEST COUNTRY	Cape Verde Islands
MAIN RELIGION	Muslim
LIFE EXPECTANCY	52 years
LITERACY	53%

USING THE LAND

- Wheat
- Citrus fruits
- Wine
- Cotton
- Coffee
- Cocoa
- Sugarcane
- Groundnuts
- Dates
- Olives
- Beef cattle
- Sheep
- Goats
- Fishing
- Industrial center
- Mining
- Oil production
- Gas production
- Tourism

- Forest and woodland
- Arable land
- Grazing
- Arid or marginal

Suez Canal
In 1869, the Suez Canal was opened, joining the Red Sea, which lies to the east of Egypt, with the Mediterranean Sea, which lies to the north. This shortened the distance for ships moving between Europe and Asia. The canal took 11 years to build and is one of the busiest waterways in the world.

Grinding millet
Africa is becoming one of the world's leading producers of millet. Much is used within the continent—each African eats an average of 44 pounds (20 kg) of millet grain each year. Millet stalks are valuable as livestock feed, building material and fuel.

Cacao beans
Cacao beans are the seeds inside the pods of the cacao tree. All chocolate products, including cocoa, are made from cacao beans. Most of the world's cacao beans come from forests on the west coast of Africa, especially Ghana, Nigeria and Côte d'Ivoire.

Liberia and Ethiopia are the only countries in Africa that have never been colonized.

Map labels: ALGIERS, TUNIS, RABAT, Casablanca, TRIPOLI, Banghāzī, Alexandria, CAIRO, LAÂYOUNE, Aswân, NOUAKCHOTT, Port Sudan, DAKAR, BANJUL, BISSAU, BAMAKO, NIAMEY, KHARTOUM, ASMARA, OUAGADOUGOU, NDJAMENA, DJIBOUTI, CONAKRY, FREETOWN, ABUJA, ADDIS ABABA, YAMOUSSOUKRO, PORTO-NOVO, MONROVIA, ACCRA, LOMÉ, Lagos, Abidjan, MALABO, YAOUNDÉ, BANGUI, MOGADISHU

Gelada

NATURAL FEATURES

Sinai Desert EGYPT
The Sinai Desert is in northeastern Egypt, east of the Suez Canal and the Gulf of Suez. It is a barren area, but it does have a number of oases, such as Wadi Ferain in the southwest, which has been used by the Bedouin for thousands of years.

Atlas Mountains MOROCCO–TUNISIA

These mountains are made up of three ranges that run from the northeast to the southwest and extend for 1,200 miles (2,000 km). The land between the mountains and the coast is fertile.

Ethiopian highlands ETHIOPIA
Covering two-thirds of the country and divided by the Great Rift Valley, the highlands have the country's richest farmland. A wide variety of animals live in the highlands—the gelada baboon is found only in this region.

Jungle CÔTE D'IVOIRE
Côte d'Ivoire is on the west coast of Africa along the Gulf of Guinea. Almost one-third of the country is a densely forested tropical jungle. The region's elephants are threatened because their habitat is being destroyed and animals are being killed to supply the ivory market.

Sahara Desert
The Sahara is the largest desert in the world. It stretches across more than half of northern Africa, from the Atlantic Ocean to the Red Sea. Its rocky plains are barren and not suitable for farming. Most of the Saharan people are nomads who move their herds of camels, sheep and goats around to take advantage of available water and pasture land.

Cassava
Cassava, the starchy root of a small shrub, grows well in the hot climates of western Africa. The bark of the root is peeled off, the juice squeezed out and the remaining pulp is baked to make flat cakes. Cassava can also be dried and deep-fried, or fermented and made into an alcoholic drink. Cassava is also known as manioc or yuca.

WHERE PEOPLE LIVE

Urban	Rural

REGION
42% — 58%

Most urban: LIBYA
87% — 13%

Most rural: ETHIOPIA
17% — 83%

Aswan High Dam

Before the Aswan High Dam was completed in 1970, Egyptian farmers depended on the River Nile to water their crops. The dam now provides Egypt with regular water supplies, but its construction was difficult. In the 1960s, Abu Simbel (*below*), the temple of Ramses II, had to be moved to save it from the rising waters.

TRADITIONS AND CULTURE

Musical storytelling ALGERIA

The Berbers of Algeria (*below*) use music and song to tell stories and record their history. They play their many instruments, including various kinds of drums, at traditional festivals and weddings.

Dinka people SUDAN

These are a group of closely related cattle-herding peoples living in central Africa. The women plant and raise most of the crops and the men are responsible for the goats, sheep and cattle.

Tribal religions

Followers of tribal religions worship spirits that they believe are in all living things. These spirits communicate through shamans (priests), who honor them in rituals.

Minarets

A minaret is a tall tower attached to a mosque. A *muezzin*, or crier, calls the followers of Islam to prayer five times each day from the balcony of the minaret.

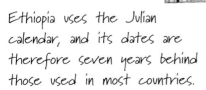

Ethiopia uses the Julian calendar, and its dates are therefore seven years behind those used in most countries.

PLACES

Cairo EGYPT

Cairo, the capital of Egypt, is one of the oldest cities in Africa and among the world's most crowded. Its noisy and colorful streets have a mix of mosques, monuments, museums and bazaars.

Timbuktu MALI

Timbuktu began as a nomad camp in 1100, and later became a trading post for merchants crossing the Sahara. Today, the city is a center of Islamic learning.

Carthage TUNISIA

Carthage, founded in the 8th century BC, was one of the greatest cities and busiest seaports of ancient times. It was destroyed by the Romans in 146 BC.

Lalibela churches ETHIOPIA

These 11 churches, carved out of rock in the 13th century, were named for King Lalibela of the Zagwe dynasty. They are joined by a maze of tunnels and passages.

Nomadic Wodaabe people have male beauty contests.

PEOPLE

Queen of Sheba c 1000 BC

The Queen of Sheba features in the traditional stories of Muslims and Christians, but her homeland is not known. Ethiopians claim that their first emperor, Menelik I, was the son of the Queen of Sheba and King Solomon of Israel.

Hannibal c 287–c 183 BC

The Carthaginian general Hannibal led his army across the Alps by elephant in 218 BC to fight his enemies, the Romans. Many years later, he poisoned himself rather than surrender to Rome.

Ibn Batuta c AD 303–c 377

Born in Tangier, Morocco, Arab traveler and author Ibn Batuta visited western Africa, western Europe and Asia. He journeyed for 29 years recording his travels in his book *Rihla* (Journey).

Leptis Magna LIBYA

Originally a Phoenician port, Leptis Magna became part of the Roman empire in 111 BC. Its ruined buildings show that it was once a large and bustling city.

Leptis Magna

Marrakech MOROCCO

Marrakech, on the plains below the Atlas Mountains, was founded in 1062 by the Almoravid dynasty as the capital of its empire. It became one of Islam's great cities and today is a popular tourist resort, famous for its bazaars.

Liberia

Liberia, a small country on the west coast, is Africa's oldest republic. It was founded in 1822 by freed slaves from the USA, but today most of its people are native Africans. The name Liberia means "free land." Less than 4 percent of the land can be farmed, but there are rich reserves of iron ore.

Freed slave

Haile Selassie 1892–1975

Haile Selassie became emperor of Ethiopia in 1930 and set about modernizing his country. After a military rebellion, he was removed from power in 1974.

Kofi Annan born 1938

Kofi Annan was born in Kumasi, Ghana, and studied in the USA and Switzerland. He joined the United Nations in 1962 and was head of its peacekeeping department from 1993 to 1995. In 1997, he became the seventh Secretary General of the United Nations.

Kofi Annan

HISTORY AT A GLANCE
ANCIENT EGYPT

The Sphinx

RIVER NILE
Life in ancient Egypt revolved around the River Nile. Every year the river flooded its banks, watering the land and leaving behind rich, fertile soil in which the people grew crops.

PHARAOHS
Ancient Egyptians believed that their rulers, the pharaohs, were god-kings. They believed the pharaohs could control the weather, their crops and even Egypt's success in war and trade.

GODS AND GODDESSES
Ancient Egyptians worshiped hundreds of gods and goddesses. Some, such as the sun-god Re, were honored as great gods throughout the country, but others were recognized only in particular regions. Many gods appeared in animal form.

Gods and goddesses

HIEROGLYPHICS
The ancient Egyptians used hieroglyphics, a form of writing in which picture symbols represented objects, people, and even ideas and sounds.

PAPYRUS
Papyrus is a water plant. Egyptians sliced the stems to make paper. When one layer was placed on another, the plant's juices glued them together.

MUMMIES
A mummy is a dead body that has been dried out to stop it from decaying. The bodies were preserved by a special embalming process and stored inside a decorated coffin or case.

Mummy case

SPHINXES
The Egyptians built sphinxes to guard their temples or tombs. They usually had a human head (as a sign of intelligence) and a lion's body (as a sign of strength).

NEFERTITI
Nefertiti, an Egyptian queen of the 14th century BC, was the wife of the pharaoh Akhenaton. With her husband, she established a new religion based on Sun worship.

TUTANKHAMEN
Tutankhamen (*right*) was pharaoh of Egypt from about 1347 to 1339 BC. In 1922, his tomb containing thousands of golden treasures was discovered near Luxor.

CLEOPATRA
Cleopatra became queen of Egypt in 51 BC. She was the last pharaoh to rule Egypt. She was clever and ambitious, and was supported in battle by two Roman generals, Mark Antony and Julius Caesar.

Wildlife safari

Southern Africa

DEMOCRATIC REPUBLIC OF CONGO
POPULATION 56,625,000 * CAPITAL KINSHASA

SOUTH AFRICA
POPULATION 42,769,000 * CAPITAL PRETORIA

TANZANIA
POPULATION 35,922,000 * CAPITAL DODOMA

KENYA
POPULATION 31,639,000 * CAPITAL NAIROBI

UGANDA
POPULATION 25,633,000 * CAPITAL KAMPALA

MOZAMBIQUE
POPULATION 17,479,000 * CAPITAL MAPUTO

MADAGASCAR
POPULATION 16,980,000 * CAPITAL ANTANANARIVO

ZIMBABWE
POPULATION 12,577,000 * CAPITAL HARARE

MALAWI
POPULATION 11,651,000 * CAPITAL LILONGWE

ANGOLA
POPULATION 10,766,000 * CAPITAL LUANDA

ZAMBIA
POPULATION 10,307,000 * CAPITAL LUSAKA

RWANDA
POPULATION 7,810,000 * CAPITAL KIGALI

BURUNDI
POPULATION 6,096,000 * CAPITAL BUJUMBURA

CONGO
POPULATION 2,954,000 * CAPITAL BRAZZAVILLE

NAMIBIA
POPULATION 1,927,000 * CAPITAL WINDHOEK

LESOTHO
POPULATION 1,862,000 * CAPITAL MASERU

BOTSWANA
POPULATION 1,573,000 * CAPITAL GABORONE

GABON
POPULATION 1,322,000 * CAPITAL LIBREVILLE

MAURITIUS
POPULATION 1,210,000 * CAPITAL PORT LOUIS

SWAZILAND
POPULATION 1,161,000 * CAPITAL MBABANE

COMOROS
POPULATION 633,000 * CAPITAL MORONI

SÃO TOMÉ AND PRINCIPE
POPULATION 176,000 * CAPITAL SÃO TOMÉ

SEYCHELLES
POPULATION 80,000 * CAPITAL VICTORIA

Fang mask
The Fang tribespeople mainly live in the hot, humid rain forests of Gabon. The spiritual leader of each village wears ceremonial masks to bring good health and prosperity to the tribe.

Herero woman
Various tribes form the Herero group and speak a common language. They live in Namibia. In the late 19th century, Herero women were encouraged by German missionaries to dress in the style of clothing then worn in Europe. Their distinctive clothes remain much the same today.

Mountain gorilla
This gorilla inhabits forests in the mountains of Rwanda and Uganda. It lives in family groups led by one or two males, and eats bamboo shoots. It is now endangered.

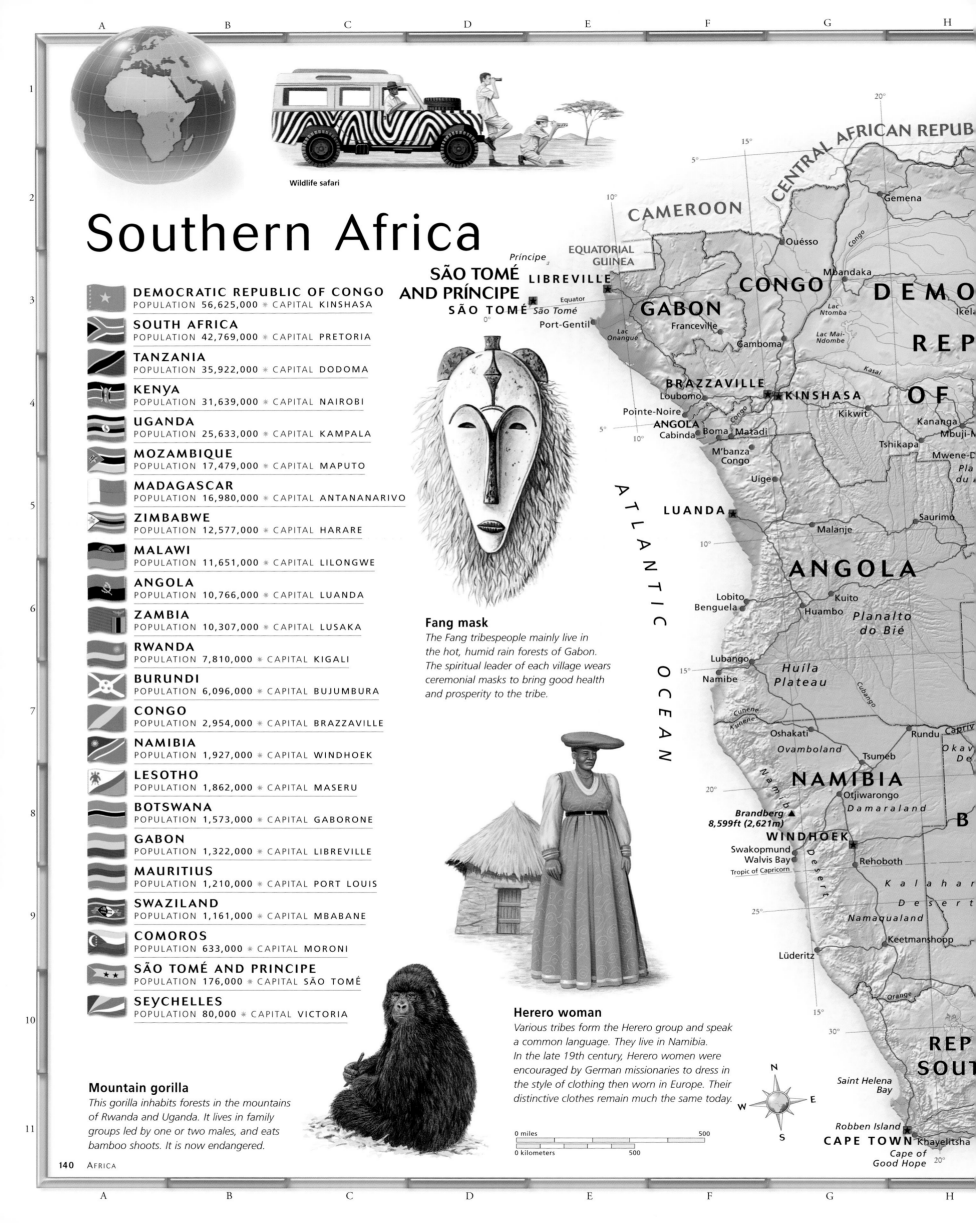

Map labels: CENTRAL AFRICAN REPUBLIC, CAMEROON, Ouésso, Gemena, Mbandaka, EQUATORIAL GUINEA, Príncipe, SÃO TOMÉ AND PRÍNCIPE, SÃO TOMÉ, São Tomé, LIBREVILLE, CONGO, GABON, Franceville, Port-Gentil, Lac Onangue, Lac Ntomba, Ikel, Lac Mai-Ndombe, Kasai, DEMOCRATIC REPUBLIC OF, BRAZZAVILLE, Loubomo, KINSHASA, Pointe-Noire, Kikwit, Kananga, ANGOLA, Cabinda, Boma, Matadi, Mbuji-M, Tshikapa, Mwene-, M'banza Congo, Uige, LUANDA, Malanje, Saurimo, ANGOLA, Lobito, Benguela, Kuito, Huambo, Planalto do Bié, Lubango, Namibe, Huíla Plateau, Cubango, Cunene, Kunene, Oshakati, Ovamboland, Rundu, Capriv, Tsumeb, Okav, De, NAMIBIA, Otjiwarongo, Damaraland, Brandberg ▲ 8,599ft (2,621m), B, WINDHOEK, Swakopmund, Walvis Bay, Rehoboth, Tropic of Capricorn, Kalahar, Desert, Namaqualand, Keetmanshoop, Lüderitz, ATLANTIC OCEAN, Saint Helena Bay, REP SOUT, Robben Island, CAPE TOWN, Khayelitsha, Cape of Good Hope, Namib Desert, Orange

0 miles 500
0 kilometers 500

The Serengeti migration

The Serengeti is Tanzania's largest and oldest national park. Millions of zebra, gazelles and wildebeest graze on its vast plains. The animals migrate each year, trekking up to 1,900 miles (3,040 km) for food and water.

1 December to April
The herds begin trekking at the end of the rainy season, when there is plenty to eat. Traveling in a clockwise direction, they head from the woodlands out onto the Serengeti's grassy plains. Eighty percent of wildebeest females give birth between late January and mid March.

2 May
Stinging, hot winds start to blow, and food on the plains begins to disappear.

3 June
The animals move north toward woodlands.

4 July to October
Columns of wildebeest and other animals gather from all over the plains to cross the Mara River north into Kenya. More than a million wildebeest cross, though many drown in the crush. The herds remain in Masai-Mara reserve in Kenya until the rains begin again.

5 November
The trek back to the plains of the Serengeti starts.

Kenya
Mara River
Tanzania
Serengeti National Park
■ Migration route

Coffee growing
Coffee is grown in many countries in Southern Africa, including Uganda, Kenya and Tanzania. The ripe, red fruit of the coffee plant is called a cherry.

Zulu warrior
The Zulu people of South Africa were once feared because of their fighting skills. Today, many Zulus live and work in cities.

The Ngorongoro Crater, in Tanzania, is the world's largest unflooded caldera—a crater produced when a volcano collapses. It was formed around 2,500,000 years ago

African elephant

Southern Africa

USING THE LAND

- Forest and woodland
- Arable land
- Grazing
- Arid or marginal

Kenya has the world's youngest population. The average age is 18 years.

Rubber
The people of the Democratic Republic of Congo cut into the bark of the rubber tree to drain off the fluid that is made into rubber. This is called tapping. Some species of rubber trees grow only in the Democratic Republic of Congo. Rubber is one of the country's main exports. However, the use of synthetic rubber has led to a decline in demand.

Vanilla beans
Vanilla beans are harvested from the vanilla plant, which is a tropical orchid that takes about three years to flower. The world's leading producer of vanilla beans is the island of Madagascar.

LAND AREA	4,281,904 sq miles (11,090,080 sq km)
LARGEST COUNTRY	Democratic Republic of Congo
SMALLEST COUNTRY	Seychelles
MAIN RELIGION	Christian
LIFE EXPECTANCY	45 years
LITERACY	66%

NATURAL FEATURES

Congo River
The Congo, the fifth-longest river in the world, flows through western central Africa. People along its banks rely on the river for transport and trade.

Mt Kilimanjaro TANZANIA
Kilimanjaro is Africa's highest mountain. Although it is near the Equator in Tanzania, its summit is always covered in snow. It was once an active volcano.

Mt Kilimanjaro

Kalahari Desert
Most of the large Kalahari Desert is in Botswana, but it also extends to Namibia and South Africa. Although little rain falls, trees and grasses grow in the desert.

Victoria Falls
Victoria Falls forms part of the border between Zambia and Zimbabwe. The falls are fed by the Zambezi River. Their local name, *mosi-oa-tunya*, means "smoke that thunders" because the water can be heard 10 miles (16 km) away.

Ngorongoro Crater TANZANIA
The Ngorongoro Crater, at the eastern edge of the Serengeti Plain, is home to more than 30,000 animals. The crater has a constant supply of spring water.

SÃO TOMÉ · LIBREVILLE · KAMPALA · KIGALI · NAIROBI · BUJUMBURA · BRAZZAVILLE · KINSHASA · DODOMA · Zanzibar · Dar es Salaam · LUANDA · Lubumbashi · MORONI · LILONGWE · Namibe · LUSAKA · HARARE · ANTANANARIVO · Beira · WINDHOEK · GABORONE · PRETORIA · MAPUTO · Johannesburg · MBABANE · Bloemfontein · MASERU · Durban · Cape Town · Port Elizabeth

- Corn (maize)
- Citrus fruits
- Wine
- Cotton
- Coffee
- Tea
- Cocoa
- Tobacco
- Beef cattle
- Sheep
- Fishing
- Industrial center
- Mining
- Oil production
- Timber

Great Rift Valley

The Great Rift Valley cuts across the entire length of Kenya, and extends north into Ethiopia and south into Tanzania. Millions of years ago, the land slowly moved apart, creating the valley. The area is rich in fossils, and is famous for the discovery of the bones of an early human, nicknamed Lucy, who lived 3 million years ago.

Reconstruction of Lucy

Boyoma Falls in the Democratic Republic of Congo has the world's greatest waterfall flow.

WHERE PEOPLE LIVE

Urban — Rural

REGION
36% — 64%

Most urban: GABON
80% — 20%

Most rural: RWANDA
6% — 94%

Diamond mining
South Africa's diamond mining industry began in 1867 with the discovery of a single diamond on the banks of the Orange River. Today, South Africa produces 9 percent of the world's diamonds, and exports 90 percent of what it mines. It is the world's fifth-largest rough diamond producer.

LARGEST CITIES

Kinshasa 6,790,000

Cape Town 2,984,000

Dar es Salaam 2,538,000

Durban 2,531,000

Nairobi 2,504,000

PLACES

Cape Town SOUTH AFRICA
Cape Town is South Africa's oldest city and legislative capital. It was the first white settlement in South Africa, founded in 1652. Set between the coast and Table Mountain, Cape Town is a shipping and commercial center.

Stone Town TANZANIA
In historical Stone Town, on Zanzibar Island, African and Arabic cultures are brought together in a mix of cathedrals, mosques, temples and houses built in the 19th century on the island.

Stone Town

Nairobi KENYA
The capital of Kenya, Nairobi is a center of trade, industry, business and tourism, and one of the largest cities in Africa. It is home to several museums of African history, art and natural history.

Source of the Nile
For hundreds of years, explorers were puzzled about the starting point of the world's longest river, the Nile. In 1862, John Hanning Speke discovered that its primary source is Lake Victoria, whose waters rise from the Ruvironza River in the mountains of Burundi. The River Nile flows northward through a total of eight African countries from central Africa to the Mediterranean Sea.

Robben Island SOUTH AFRICA
Used for more than 400 years as a prison, Robben Island is best known for two ex-prisoners: anti-apartheid activists Nelson Mandela and Walter Sisulu.

Great Zimbabwe ZIMBABWE
This city, built by the Shona people in the 1100s, was once the center of a great empire. Its structures were made from stones put together without mortar.

PEOPLE

Shaka c 1787–1828
The son of a Zulu chieftain, Shaka was a fierce warrior. When his father died, Shaka took over the Zulu clan. Under his leadership, the Zulus established one of Africa's most powerful empires.

Louis Leakey 1893–1976
Archaeologist Louis Leakey and his wife Mary discovered fossils believed to be early human beings that lived in Africa about 2 million years ago. They found these fossils (called hominids) in Olduvai Gorge in Tanzania.

Nelson Mandela born 1918
After working as a lawyer, Mandela joined the African National Congress in 1944. He organized protests against the government and was sentenced to life in prison in 1964. Mandela was released in 1990, and in 1994 he became South Africa's first black president.

Christiaan Barnard 1922–2001
Born in South Africa, Christiaan Barnard was a heart surgeon in Cape Town. He pioneered open-heart surgery, and in 1967 became the first surgeon to transplant a human heart from one person to another.

TRADITIONS AND CULTURE

Chokwe masks
Masks once played an important role in the rituals of the Chokwe people of the Democratic Republic of Congo. Today, they are used mostly for entertainment.

Masai people
The Masai are a nomadic people who live in the grasslands of southern Kenya and northern Tanzania. Their daily life centers around the herding of cattle. Families and their herds live together in a compound known as a *kraal*.

San people of the Kalahari
The San live in the Kalahari region of Botswana and Namibia. In the past, the San survived by hunting animals with bows and snares, and gathering desert berries and insects. Today, few of them follow this traditional way of life.

San hunters

Zionist church
About 6 million people in southern Africa are followers of this faith, which combines the teachings of Christianity with traditional African beliefs and forms of worship such as dancing.

Animals of Madagascar
The forests of Madagascar, an island off the east coast of Africa, are home to an amazing variety of animals. Many species of birds, reptiles, insects and mammals exist only on this island. The best known are the lemurs, which have survived there for 58 million years. There are more than 20 species, ranging in size from the 11-inch (29-cm) mouse lemur to the 3-foot (90-cm) indri. Many are now endangered.

Ring-tailed lemur

Elephants can walk under water by sticking their trunks up in the air above the water like a snorkel.

HISTORY AT A GLANCE
SOUTH AFRICA

1488
Portuguese explorer Bartholomew Diaz rounds the Cape of Good Hope and calls it the "Cape of Storms" because of the terrible weather.

1652
The Dutch East India Company establishes a settlement at the Cape to supply its ships sailing between the East Indies and the Netherlands.

Dutch East India crest

1779
First war between the Xhosa tribe, who had been tending cattle and raising crops at the Cape since the 1500s, and the British and Dutch settlers.

1795
Britain annexes the Cape for the first time and many of the Afrikaner (Dutch-supporting) settlers go north to gain freedom from British rule.

1852
Afrikaners in the Transvaal gain independence from Britain. Shortly afterward, the Afrikaners establish the Orange Free State, one of the four provinces of the Union of South Africa.

1879
After many fierce battles, the Zulu kingdom finally loses its independence and is defeated by the British armies.

1880
The first Boer War between the British and the Afrikaners begins. The Afrikaners are victorious.

The second Boer War

1899–1902
The second Boer War, also called the South African War, takes place between the British and the Afrikaners. Although the Afrikaners fight fiercely, the British defeat them, and the Transvaal and the Orange Free State become British colonies.

1950
A policy of segregation, called apartheid, is implemented. People are officially classified into four distinct racial groups: black, white, colored and Asian.

Apartheid sign

1961
South Africa leaves the Commonwealth of Nations and becomes a republic. The African National Congress (ANC) begins to use weapons in its protests against the government.

1990
Nelson Mandela is released from prison; negotiations begin on voting rights for blacks.

1994
The ANC wins the first election after apartheid is abolished and Nelson Mandela becomes president. After an absence of 20 years, South Africa rejoins the United Nations.

1999
The ANC wins the general elections and Thabo Mbeki takes over as president.

Mariana Islands

Agrihan
Pagan
Alamagan
Guguan

Anatahan
Saipan
Tinian
Rota
Guam

M
I
C
R
O

Hall
Islands

Chuuk
Islands

Caroline Islands

Yap

Palau
Islands

Admiralty Islands

Bismarck Sea

New Ireland

New Britain

M
E
L

Sol

New
Guinea

Mt Wilhelm
14,793ft (4,509m)

Bougainville

Chois

Arafura
Sea

Torres Strait

Cape
York

Solom
Sea

Melville
Island

Timor
Sea

Bathurst
Island

Arnhem
Land

Gulf of
Carpentaria

Kimberley

Barkly Tableland

Bartle Frere
5,322ft (1,622m)

Coral
Sea

Great Barrier Reef

Tanami
Desert

Great Dividing Range

Barrow
Island

Pilbara

North
West Cape

Great Sandy
Desert

Mt Zell
5,023ft (1,531m)

Simpson
Desert

Fraser
Island

Mt Meharry
4,111ft (1,253m)

A U S T R A L I A

Gibson
Desert

Mt Woodroffe
4,708ft (1,435m)

Lake
Eyre

Great
Artesian
Basin

INDIAN OCEAN

Great Victoria
Desert

Nullarbor Plain

Cape
Leeuwin

Great Australian Bight

Flinders
Ranges

Darling

Lachlan

Murray

Great Dividing Range

Kangaroo
Island

Mt Kosciuszko
7,310ft (2,228m)

King
Island

Bass Strait

Flinders
Island

Mt Ossa
5,305ft (1,617m)

Tasmania

S O U T H E R N   O C E A N

Australia and Papua New Guinea

AUSTRALIA
POPULATION 19,732,000 ✳ CAPITAL CANBERRA

PAPUA NEW GUINEA
POPULATION 5,296,000 ✳ CAPITAL PORT MORESBY

Red kangaroo

Bird-of-paradise
Birds-of-paradise live in the forests of Papua New Guinea. To attract a mate, male birds gather in the treetops and call loudly, dance and display their long, brightly colored tail feathers. Female birds are drab and have short feathers.

Iron ore mining
Australia is one of the world's largest producers of iron ore. Most comes from the Hamersley Range, in Western Australia. The massive trucks that cart iron ore are too big for public roads and never leave the mine.

Dugongs

Aboriginal dancers
Aboriginal Australians use dancing to express their beliefs and represent their lives. Some of the dances tell the stories of the Dreamtime—the time of the creation of all things. These dances and stories have been handed down by tribal elders over thousands of years.

Uluru rises 2,844 feet (867 m) above sea level and measures nearly 6 miles (9.5 km) around its base. It is the largest monolith (single piece of rock) in the world.

Arafura Sea

Timor Sea

Melville Island
Cobourg Peninsula
Gou... Islan...
Bathurst Island
Van Diemen Gulf
DARWIN
Palmerston
Kakadu ☆ National P...
Arnh... Lan...
Cape Ford
Pine Creek
Katherine
Joseph Bonaparte Gulf
Daly
Daly Wat...

Bonaparte Archipelago
Wyndham
Kununurra
Kimberley Plateau
Lake Argyle
Top Springs

Cape Leveque
King Sound
King Leopold Ranges
Bungle Bungles
Fitzroy
Victoria
Ord

INDIAN OCEAN

Broome
Fitzroy Crossing
Halls Creek
Tanami Desert
Tennant Creek

Eighty Mile Beach

Dampier
Port Hedland
Great Sandy Desert
Percival Lakes
Lake Gregory
Lake White
Lake Mackay
NORTHERN TERRITORY

Barrow Island
Onslow
North West Cape
Exmouth
Hamersley Range
Newman
Lake Disappointment
Gibson Desert
Lake Neale
Lake Amadeus
MacDonnell Ranges
Al... Spr...
A U S T R...
▲ Uluru (Ayers 2,844ft (867m...

Tropic of Capricorn
Lake MacLeod
WESTERN AUSTRALIA

Gascoyne
Carnarvon
Lake Carnegie
Great Victoria Desert
Coo... P...

Dirk Hartog Island
Shark Bay
Denham
Murchison
Meekatharra
Lake Wells

Lake Austin
Mount Magnet
Lake Noondie
Lake Ballard
Lake Carey
Lake Minigwal
SOUTH AUSTRAL...

Geraldton
Dongara
Lake Barlee
Lake Moore
Coolgardie
Kalgoorlie
Lake Lefroy
Lake Cowan
Nullarbor Plain
Eucla
Tarco...
Penong

Moora
Northam
Norseman
Balladonia
Great Australian Bight
Ell...

PERTH
Fremantle
Mandurah
Brookton
Wagin
Esperance
Ravensthorpe

Bunbury
Busselton
Augusta
Albany
SOUTHERN OCEAN

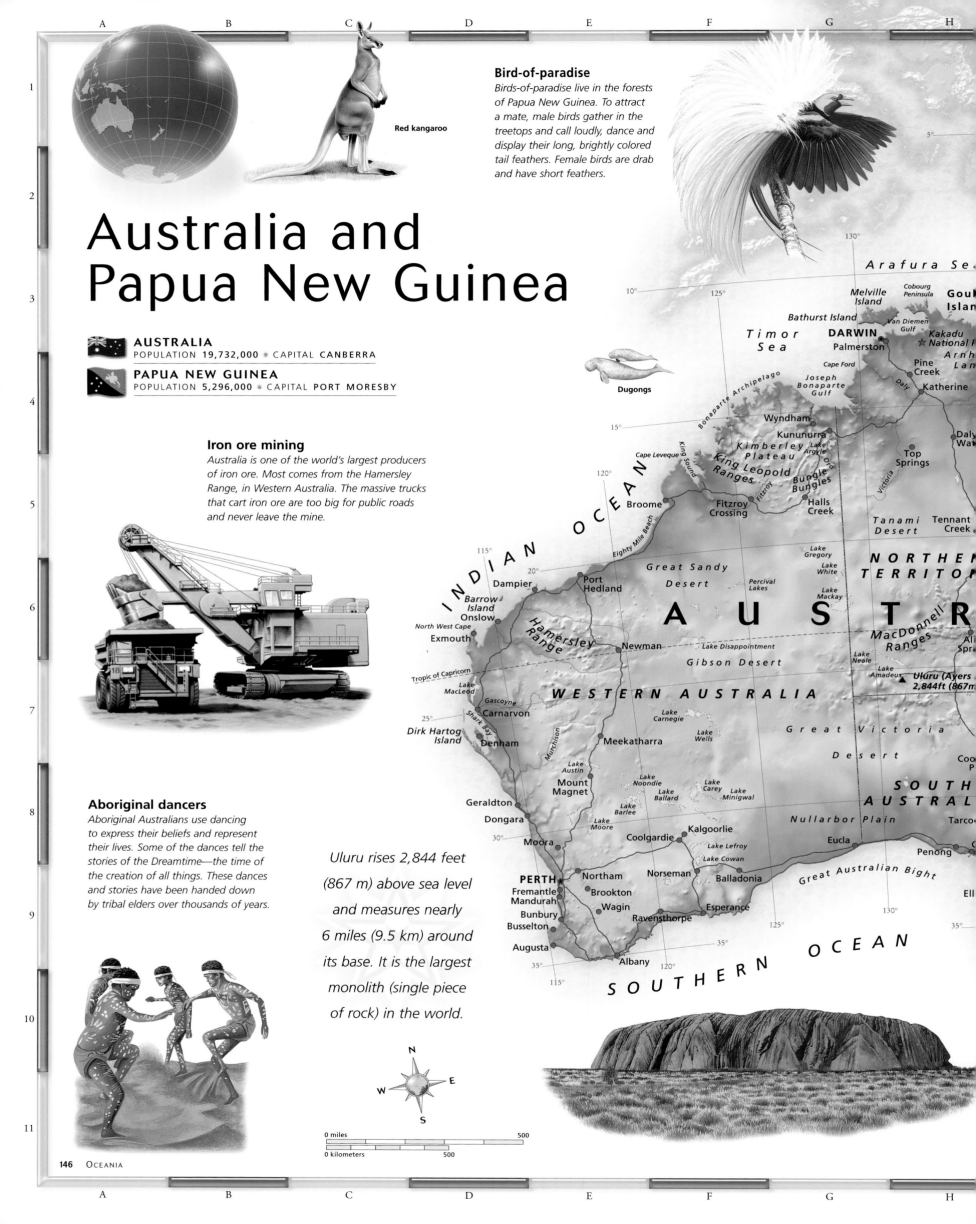

0 miles 500
0 kilometers 500

The Great Barrier Reef

Queensland's Great Barrier Reef consists of about 3,000 separate coral reefs. It runs parallel to the coast for 1,250 miles (2,000 km), and is the largest structure in the world made by living creatures.

Bleached coral
Live coral is colored by tiny algae that live in its outer tissues. It casts these off when conditions are poor.

Bluelines
Triggerfish
Bannerfish
Parrotfish
Moorish idol
Angelfish
Groper
Crown-of-thorns starfish
Clownfish
Lionfish

Surf lifesavers

Droving cattle
On many outback properties, drovers, or cattle herders, muster and yard cattle on four-wheel-drive bikes, known as quads. Hard-working cattle dogs play a vital role in rounding up beasts that stray from the herd.

Sydney
Australia's largest city, Sydney, is built around a natural harbor. Sydney Tower, the city's tallest building, rises 1,000 feet (305 m) above the commercial center. The Sydney Harbor Bridge is the largest single-arch steel bridge in the world. Nearby, the graceful shells of the Opera House contrast with the lush green of the botanic gardens.

### Map labels

INDONESIA

New Guinea
Vanimo
Wewak
Cape Girgir
Sepik
Central Range
Mt Wilhelm 14,793ft (4,509m)
Mt Hagen
Goroka
Lae
Cape Cretin
Bulolo
Daru
Gulf of Papua
Fly
Lake Murray

Admiralty Islands
Lorengau
St Matthias Group
Bismarck Archipelago
Kavieng
Bismarck Sea
Karkar Island
Madang
New Ireland
Kimbe
Rabaul
New Britain
Crater Point
Bougainville
Arawa

PAPUA NEW GUINEA

Solomon Sea
Popondetta
Cape Nelson
D'Entrecasteaux Islands

Louisiade Archipelago
Cape Siri

Torres Strait
Prince of Wales Island
Cape York

Vessel Islands
Cape Arnhem
pe Shield
andt
ote
Gulf of Carpentaria
Cape Grenville
Cape York Peninsula
Cape Melville

Sir Edward Pellew Group
Wellesley Islands
y Tableland
Burketown

Coral Sea

Cooktown
Cairns
Mareeba
Innisfail
Hinchinbrook Island
Townsville

Great Barrier Reef

Great Dividing Range

Normanton
Mitchell
Norman
Leichhardt
Flinders
Burdekin

Mount Isa
Cloncurry
Hughenden

QUEENSLAND
LIA

Whitsunday Group

Winton
Clermont
Warginburra Peninsula
Mackay

Longreach
Barcaldine
Emerald
Springsure
Rockhampton
Tropic of Capricorn

Blackall
Gladstone
Bundaberg
Biloela
Fraser Island
Maryborough
Gympie
Murgon
Miles
Sunshine Coast
Dalby
BRISBANE

Charleville
Mitchell
Roma
Cunnamulla
St George
Toowoomba
Warwick
Gold Coast
Surfers Paradise
Lismore

Bollon
Dirranbandi
Ballina
Coffs Harbour
Armidale

mpson Desert

Bourke
Walgett
Narrabri
Tamworth
Muswellbrook
Taree

NEW SOUTH WALES

Darling
Wilcannia
Nyngan
Dubbo
Macquarie
Lachlan
Parkes
Orange
Newcastle

Broken Hill
Ivanhoe
Bathurst

Lake Eyre North
Lake Blanche
Eyre uth
Marree
Lake Torrens
Lake Frome

Flinders Ranges

Port Augusta
Peterborough
Griffith
SYDNEY
Wollongong
Goulburn

Port Pirie
Mildura
Wagga Wagga
Albury
CANBERRA
AUSTRALIAN CAPITAL TERRITORY

Gawler
ADELAIDE
Murray Bridge
Tailem Bend
Keith
Bendigo
Wangaratta
VICTORIA
Mt Kosciuszko 7,310ft (2,228m)

angaroo land
Naracoorte
Horsham
Ballarat
Sunbury
Melton
Geelong
MELBOURNE
Bairnsdale
Moe Sale

Mount Gambier
Warrnambool

Tasman Sea

King Island
Bass Strait
Flinders Island

Marrawah
Burnie
Devonport
Launceston
Queenstown
TASMANIA
HOBART
Maria Island
Bruny Island
South East Cape

Murray
Lach'lan
Macquarie

On the Aboriginal flag, the color black represents the people, red is the land, and yellow represents the Sun.

Australia and Papua New Guinea

AUSTRALIA LAND AREA	2,941,299 sq miles (7,617,930 sq km)
OFFICIAL LANGUAGE	English
MAIN RELIGION	Christian
LIFE EXPECTANCY	80 years
LITERACY	99%

PAPUA NEW GUINEA LAND AREA	174,850 sq miles (452,860 sq km)
OFFICIAL LANGUAGE	English
MAIN RELIGION	Christian
LIFE EXPECTANCY	64 years
LITERACY	66%

LARGEST CITIES

Sydney 4,306,000
ᵻᵻᵻᵻᵻᵻᵻᵻᵻ ᵻᵻᵻᵻᵻᵻᵻᵻᵻ ᵻᵻᵻᵻᵻᵻᵻᵻᵻ ᵻᵻᵻᵻᵻᵻᵻᵻᵻ ᵻᵻᵻ

Melbourne 3,660,000
ᵻᵻᵻᵻᵻᵻᵻᵻᵻ ᵻᵻᵻᵻᵻᵻᵻᵻᵻ ᵻᵻᵻᵻᵻᵻᵻᵻᵻ ᵻᵻᵻᵻᵻᵻᵻ

Brisbane 1,553,000
ᵻᵻᵻᵻᵻᵻᵻᵻᵻ ᵻᵻᵻᵻᵻᵻ

Perth 1,394,000
ᵻᵻᵻᵻᵻᵻᵻᵻᵻ ᵻᵻᵻᵻ

Adelaide 1,093,000
ᵻᵻᵻᵻᵻᵻᵻᵻᵻ ᵻ

NATURAL FEATURES

Lake Eyre AUSTRALIA
This usually dry salt lake in the Simpson Desert fills with water only a few times each century, after heavy rains. Millions of birds gather around the lake to breed.

Tasmanian forests AUSTRALIA
The dense forests of the Tasmanian wilderness contain some of the world's oldest living plants. The Tasmanian tiger roamed the forests until last century.

Highlands PAPUA NEW GUINEA
The Southern Highlands have spectacular natural scenery. The Baiyer Wildlife Sanctuary is in the Western Highlands and Mt Wilhelm lies in the Eastern Highlands.

Cereals
Wine
Coffee
Sugarcane

Coconuts
Palm oil
Rubber
Beef cattle

Sheep
Fishing
Industrial center
Mining

Oil production
Gas production
Timber
Tourism

Forest and woodland
Arable land
Grazing
Arid or marginal

Rabaul
PORT MORESBY
Darwin

Cairns
Alice Springs
Brisbane
Perth
Adelaide
Sydney
CANBERRA
Melbourne
Hobart

New Guinea, the second largest island in the world, has over 750 languages—more than any other country.

Sugarcane
Queensland produces most of Australia's sugarcane, grown on more than 6,000 farms for export as well as local use. Raw sugar comes from the juice inside the cane, which is extracted after the long stalks (above) are harvested and stripped of leaves. Ethanol, a renewable fuel, is produced from sugarcane waste.

Gold
This precious metal, discovered in Victoria and New South Wales in 1851, brought gold seekers from all over the world in search of their fortune. Today, Australia is the world's third-largest gold-mining country, with more than 300 tons (300 t) mined annually.

Bungle Bungles AUSTRALIA
These massive rock domes in Western Australia formed 350 million years ago. Their distinctive orange and black bands are best seen from the air. Pools and gorges lie among the domes.

Kakadu National Park AUSTRALIA
Lagoons and billabongs, or waterholes, are a common sight in the Kakadu National Park in Australia's Northern Territory. Much of the land in the park, which supports many animals and birds, floods every year for several months.

Waterlilies at Kakadu

WHERE PEOPLE LIVE

Urban — Rural

AUSTRALIA	
85%	15%

PAPUA NEW GUINEA	
17%	83%

LONGEST RIVERS

Murray 1,566 miles (2,520 km)

Murrumbidgee 979 miles (1,575 km)

Darling 864 miles (1,390 km)

Lachlan 851 miles (1,370 km)

Koala and baby

Australian wildlife

Australia is home to two unusual groups of animals. Marsupials are mammals that carry their newborn in a pouch. Koalas, kangaroos and wombats are the most common marsupials. Kangaroos have strong hind legs and can bound along at great speed. Monotremes—platypus and echidnas—are unique animals that lay eggs. When the eggs hatch, they feed their young with milk.

PLACES

Parliament House AUSTRALIA

This modern concrete building, with its imposing flagpole, was opened in 1988 in Canberra, Australia's capital city. It is the seat of national government.

Parliament House

Melbourne AUSTRALIA

This cosmopolitan city, established in 1835, holds several world-renowned sporting events each year, including the Melbourne Cup horse race and the Australian Open tennis grand slam.

Adelaide AUSTRALIA

Named for Queen Adelaide in 1836, this small Australian city hosts the nation's most popular arts festival every two years. The city is surrounded by hills.

Darwin AUSTRALIA

This tropical city in the Northern Territory is Australia's closest point to Southeast Asia. In 1974, Cyclone Tracy devastated the city and it had to be rebuilt.

Sydney Opera House

Jutting into Sydney's harbor, this unique structure, with its curved sail-like roofs, has become one of Australia's most famous landmarks. In 1958, the designs of Danish architect Jørn Utzon were chosen from more than 200 competition entries, and work on the Opera House began. It took 15 years to complete. Musicians and actors from all over the world perform in its theaters and concert halls.

Port Moresby PAPUA NEW GUINEA

Local business people and foreigners populate this city, the largest in Papua New Guinea. The parliament building is in the style of a traditional spirit house.

Coober Pedy AUSTRALIA

Most buildings in this opal-mining town are underground, often in unused mines. Temperatures are so hot for much of the year that people prefer to live, and sometimes work, underground.

Underground house, Coober Pedy

PEOPLE

Captain Arthur Philip 1738–1814

As captain of the British fleet that landed on Australian soil in 1788, and first governor, Arthur Philip chose Sydney Cove as the site of a convict settlement.

Caroline Chisholm 1808–77

Called "the immigrants' friend," Caroline Chisholm set up quarters for 11,000 homeless convict women who came to Australia. She found work for many of these women on farms.

Ned Kelly 1854–80

This Victorian bushranger from an Irish convict family stole money from banks and animals from farms. He was found guilty of his crimes in 1880, and was hanged in Melbourne jail. He wore a metal face shield and suit of armor (right) to disguise himself, as well as for protection.

Ned Kelly

Sir Donald Bradman 1908–2001

Regarded as one of the best cricketers in the world, "the Don" (right) scored a batting average of 99.94. He played for Australia in 52 test matches over 20 years.

Edward Mabo 1936–92

This Aboriginal rights activist, in the Mabo decision of 1993, convinced the High Court of Australia to rule that ownership of land by Australian Aborigines before European settlement should be legally recognized.

Sir Michael Somare born 1936

This politician was the leader of Papua New Guinea's fight for independence. He became the country's first prime minister after independence in 1975. Over 10 years, the "big chief," as he was called, was twice voted into office, then out again.

TRADITIONS AND CULTURE

Sing-sings PAPUA NEW GUINEA

Dance, music and drama are combined at cultural festivals, called sing-sings. People wear elaborate costumes, and display carved masks outside spirit houses to protect the community. One tribe, the mudmen of Asaro (right), wear huge clay masks to imitate dead people in their dances.

Aboriginal art AUSTRALIA

The earliest Aboriginal paintings have been found in caves, drawn with yellow ocher and charcoal. Artists from different areas use a variety of styles, including dots (below), to create pictures that tell stories of their lives.

Aboriginal dot painting

Beaches

Most Australians live near the coast, so the beach is a popular destination for many families, especially at Christmas time. Ocean waves can be dangerous so surf lifesavers patrol the beach to keep swimmers safe.

Surf lifesavers

Four of the world's five deadliest snakes are found in Australia. The inland taipan is 50 times more venomous than the Indian cobra.

The Royal Flying Doctor Service

The outback

Australia is a vast country. People who live in the remote and sparsely populated outback areas rely on distance services to link them with the rest of the country. Doctors and nurses of the Royal Flying Doctor Service visit their outback patients by air. Many outback children are educated by lessons from the correspondence school or by two-way radio via the School of the Air.

HISTORY AT A GLANCE

C 50,000 BC
Aborigines arrive in Australia from New Guinea by crossing a land bridge. They occupy Fraser Cave, on the southern tip of Tasmania, about 30,000 years later.

Aboriginal tools

C 8000–6000 BC
New Guinea separates from Australia. Tribes develop in New Guinea's high mountain valleys.

AD 1688
William Dampier lands on the northwest coast of Australia in his ship *Cygnet*—the first European to land on Australian soil. Almost 100 years later, Captain James Cook lands at Botany Bay on the east coast and claims it for Britain.

1788
The First Fleet, of 11 ships carrying 1,500 convicts and soldiers, arrives in Sydney Cove.

1851
Gold is discovered in Victoria and New South Wales, and the gold rush begins.

Convicts

1868
The last convicts are sent from Britain. They arrive in Western Australia. Free settlers migrate to Australia and the population grows.

1884
Britain annexes the southeast of New Guinea and Germany controls the northeast. Australia takes over the British area 20 years later.

1901
The six British colonies of Australia join to form a single federation of states, to be governed as one nation—the Commonwealth of Australia.

1914–18
Australia fights for Britain in World War I, along with New Zealand soldiers. They become known as ANZACs.

1921
German New Guinea comes under the control of Australia.

1939–45
Britain declares war on Germany, and Australia supports Britain in World War II. Japan occupies New Guinea from 1942 to 1945.

1975
Papua New Guinea gains its independence from Australia. Michael Somare is its first prime minister.

2000
Sydney hosts the Olympic Games. Sprinter Cathy Freeman wins a gold medal for Australia.

Cathy Freeman

New Zealand and the Pacific Islands

Brown kiwi

The kiwi cannot fly. Instead, it has strong legs for running, kicking and burrowing. Nostrils at the end of its long beak help it to sniff out insects to eat.

Parliament House

New Zealand's Parliament House is in Wellington. The circular building behind, known as the Beehive, contains the offices of government ministers.

NEW ZEALAND
POPULATION 3,951,000 * CAPITAL WELLINGTON

FIJI
POPULATION 869,000 * CAPITAL SUVA

SOLOMON ISLANDS
POPULATION 509,000 * CAPITAL HONIARA

VANUATU
POPULATION 199,000 * CAPITAL PORT VILA

SAMOA
POPULATION 178,000 * CAPITAL APIA

FEDERATED STATES OF MICRONESIA
POPULATION 108,000 * CAPITAL PALIKIR

TONGA
POPULATION 108,000 * CAPITAL NUKU'ALOFA

KIRIBATI
POPULATION 99,000 * CAPITAL TARAWA

MARSHALL ISLANDS
POPULATION 56,000 * CAPITAL MAJURO

PALAU
POPULATION 20,000 * CAPITAL KOROR

NAURU
POPULATION 13,000 * CAPITAL YAREN

TUVALU
POPULATION 11,000 * CAPITAL FUNAFUTI

Farming

Lush pastures grow in New Zealand's rich volcanic soil. They support large numbers of sheep, deer and cattle. Meat, wool and dairy products are the main exports.

Tiki

The tiki is a Maori fertility symbol. Tiki are carved from nephrite, a hard stone similar to jade that can be found on New Zealand's South Island.

Traditional house, Solomon Islands

Conch shell blower

### Map labels

Three Kings Island
North Cape
Cape Reinga
Great Exhibition Bay
Cape Karikari
Ahipara Bay
Awanui
Bay of Islands
Cape Brett
Tauroa Point
Poor Knights Islands
Whangarei
Dargaville
Great Barrier Island
Warkworth
Colville Channel
North Head
Hauraki Gulf
Helensville
Takapuna
Colville
Waitakere
Auckland
Manukau Harbour
Manukau
Coromandel Peninsula
Waiuku
Pukekohe
Thames
Mayor Island
White Island
Cape Runaway
Matakaoa Point
Paeroa
Waihi
Motiti Island
Morrinsville
Hamilton
Tauranga
Bay of Plenty
East Cape
Ruatoria
Cambridge
Lake Rotorua
Whakatane
Albatross Point
Otorohanga
Rotorua
Lake Tarawera
Opotiki
Tirua Point
Te Kuiti
Tokoroa
Murupara
North Island
Lake Taupo
Ohura
Taupo
Gisborne
New Plymouth
Mt Ruapehu 9,176ft (2,797m)
Wairoa
Poverty Bay
Stratford
Hawera
Waiouru
Hawke Bay
Napier
Mahia Peninsula
South Taranaki Bight
Taihape
Hastings
Cape Kidnappers
NEW ZEALAND
Wanganui
Waipawa
Cape Farewell
Farewell Spit
Woodville
Golden Bay
D'Urville Island
Palmerston North
Cape Turnagain
Wekakura Point
Tasman Bay
Otaki
Cook Strait
Upper Hutt
Masterton
Nelson
Porirua
Lake Wairarapa
Richmond
Picton
Lower Hutt
WELLINGTON
Karamea Bight
Blenheim
Cape Palliser
Westport
Buller
Cape Campbell
Cape Foulwind
Wairau
Clarence
Reefton
Grey
Springs Junction
Clarence
Greymouth
Clarence
Kaikoura
Kaikoura Peninsula
Hokitika
South Island
Spy Glass Point
Ross
Otira
Rangiora
Pegasus Bay
Franz Josef Glacier
Oxford
Kaiapoi
Fox Glacier
Christchurch
Mt Cook 12,316ft (3,754m)
Rakaia
Cascade Point
Lake Tekapo
Banks Peninsula
Awarua Point
Lake Pukaki
Ashburton
Fairlie
Canterbury Plains
Lake Ohau
Canterbury Bight
Milford Sound
Timaru
Wanaka
Lake Wanaka
Lake Hawea
Waimate
Queenstown
Waitaki
Oamaru
Cromwell
Hampden
Lake Wakatipu
Alexandra
Shag Point
Lake Te Anau
Clutha
Lake Manapouri
Taieri
Port Chalmers
Otago Peninsula
Resolution Island
Lumsden
Dunedin
West Cape
Winton
Cape Providence
Gore
Kaitangata
Mataura
Puysegur Point
Balclutha
Bluff
Invercargill
Foveaux Strait
Codfish Island
Ruapuke Island
Mason Bay
Halfmoon Bay
Stewart Island
South West Cape

PACIFIC OCEAN

Tasman Sea

Southern Alps

Fiordland

Equator
YAREN
NAURU
SOLOMON ISLANDS
HONIARA
Guadalcanal
Santa Cruz Is.
Ndeni
Espíritu Santo
VANUA
Malakula
Éfaté
NEW CALEDONIA (to France)
Loyalty Is.
New Caledonia
NOUMÉA
Tropic of Capricorn

N W E S

0 miles 160
0 kilometers 160

FEDERATED STATES OF MICRONESIA

10°
135° Colonia ●Yap
Ngajangel Uithi Gaferut
Palau Ngulu Faraulep West Hall
★ Sorol Woleai Fayu Ulul Fayu Islands
KOROR Eaurupik Elato Pulap Nomwin
Ifalik Pulawat Weno Chuuk Oroluk PALIKIR ★ Kolonia
Pulusuk Islands Pohnpei Mwokil Pingelap
Caroline Islands Losap Negetik Atoll Kosrae
Namoluk Nukuoro Tofol
5°
Pulo Anna PALAU Mortlock
Merir Islands

0 miles 300
0 kilometers 300

Maug Islands
20° 146° 20°
Asuncion

NORTHERN MARIANA ISLANDS (to USA)
Agrihan
18° Pagan 18°
Alamagan
Guguan
Anatahan
16° 16°

SAIPAN
San Jose Saipan
Tinian
14° Rota 14°
HAGÁTÑA
GUAM
Guam (to USA)

166° 168° 170° 172°
12° Bikar 12°
Bikini Rongelap Atoll Rongrik Utrik
Ailinginae PACIFIC OCEAN Ailuk Mejit
Wotho Likiep Island
10° Ujae Kwajalein Wotje 10°
Lae Ratak Chain Maloelap
Ralik Chain Namu Aur
8° Jabwat 8°
166° Ailinglaplap Majuro Arno
MARSHALL MAJURO ★
ISLANDS Mili
6° Jaluit 6°
Namorik Kili Island Knox
168° 170° 172°
Ebon

0 miles 150
0 km 150

0 miles 150
0 km 150

Copra making
Copra is the meat of ripe coconuts that has been scraped out and dried in the sun. It is sold for processing into coconut oil. The oil is used in margarine, salad oils, soaps and cosmetics.

Frangipani flowers

Mariana Islands
Marshall Islands
Micronesia
Pacific Islands

New Zealand is in an active volcanic zone, with geysers, hot springs and pools of boiling mud. The greatest concentration of thermal activity is at Rotorua.

Spear fishing
Polynesians eat a lot of seafood. The men fish with nets, lines and spears. Women and children gather crabs and shellfish.

Gilbert Islands
RIKI
175° 180° 175° 170° 165°
P o l y Northern Line Islands
International Date Line n e 5° 5°
KIRIBATI s Christmas Island
Kanton i KIRIBATI 150°
SOUTH Equator 0°
Orona a
Phoenix Islands PACIFIC
TUVALU Central Line Islands 5°
TOKELAU OCEAN
Funafuti ISLANDS International Date Line
VAIAKU (to New Zealand)
WALLIS AND AMERICAN 145° 140° 135°
FUTUNA ISLANDS SAMOA SAMOA Nuku Hiva
(to France) Wallis (to USA) Northern Cook Islands 10° Hiva Oa
MATÁ'UTU Savai'i APIA ★ Tutuila Marquesas Islands
Futuna Upolu PAGO COOK Southern Line
Niua Group PAGO ISLANDS Islands Tuamotu Archipelago
Vanua Levu (to New Zealand) Îles Sous le Vent 15°
Viti NIUE Bora-Bora
Levu (to New Zealand) Raiatea
SUVA Niue ALOFI Southern Moorea ★ Tahiti
FIJI NUKU'ALOFA Cook Islands Society Archipelago PAPEETE Groupe Actéon
★ Tongatapu Rarotonga FRENCH POLYNESIA 20° 130°
Eua AVARUA (to France) Gambier Islands PITCAIRN
TONGA Austral Islands ISLANDS
175° 180° 175° 170° 165° 160° (to UK)
155° Pitcairn Henderson
25° Island Island 25°
140° 135° 130°

0 miles 900
0 kilometers 900

N
W E
S

In 1893, New Zealand became the first country to grant women the right to vote.

New Zealand and the Pacific Islands

LAND AREA	128,126 sq miles (331,846 sq km)
LARGEST COUNTRY	New Zealand
SMALLEST COUNTRY	Nauru
MAIN RELIGION	Christian
LIFE EXPECTANCY	68 years
LITERACY	89%

The word "maori" means local, or original, people. White settlers were called "paheka."

Kiwifruit
First called a Chinese gooseberry after its place of origin, but now named after New Zealand's national bird, this delicious fruit is mainly grown near the Bay of Plenty in the north. The fruit, which grows on a vine, needs sunny conditions and rich soil to grow. New Zealand is the world's leading producer of kiwifruit.

NATURAL FEATURES

Yasawa Islands FIJI
This chain of coral islands, protected by reefs, lies off the northwest coast of Fiji's main island, Viti Levu. Beaches of white sand fringe the islands (*below*).

Wood and paper products
New Zealand is one of the largest paper and wood producers in the Pacific region. Kauri trees (*above*), which take more than 1,000 years to mature, were plentiful in New Zealand before European settlement, but are now protected because of years of logging. Many smaller islands in the Pacific region grow coconut trees for wood, copra (dried coconut meat) and palm oil production.

Tahitian mountains FRENCH POLYNESIA
The volcanic mountains of Tahiti run along the island's north and south coasts. The dense tropical rain forests that cover the mountains have provided inspiration for artists such as Paul Gauguin.

Milford Sound

Milford Sound NEW ZEALAND
These deep, fjordlike waterways (*above*), in South Island, are the final destination for trampers on the Milford Track, a famous walking trail through spectacular mountains and river valleys.

Tongariro National Park
NEW ZEALAND
In the center of New Zealand's North Island lies a Maori sacred area, situated on several active volcanoes, notably Mt Ruapehu (*left*), which erupted in 1995.

USING THE LAND

	Forest and woodland
	Arable land
	Grazing
	Arid or marginal

Auckland

Hamilton

Napier

WELLINGTON

Wellington is the southernmost national capital in the world.

Christchurch

Queenstown

Dunedin

Invercargill

	Cereals
	Fruit
	Wine
	Beef cattle
	Dairy cattle
	Sheep
	Pigs
	Fishing
	Industrial center
	Timber
	Tourism

Dairy food
New Zealand is the world's largest exporter of butter and cheese. Most dairy foods are exported, as more goods are produced than the small population needs. New Zealand's rich soils and grasslands provide fodder for the country's herds of cattle.

LARGEST CITIES

Auckland 374,000

Christchurch 340,000

Wellington 166,000

Hamilton 143,000

Dunedin 106,000

WHERE PEOPLE LIVE

Urban	Rural

REGION
49% — 51%

Most urban: NAURU
100%

Most rural: SOLOMON ISLANDS
19% — 81%

Tourism

Millions of tourists are attracted to the South Pacific islands each year, because of their beautiful beaches, coral reefs teeming with fishes and relaxed lifestyle. Most countries in the region rely on the income tourism brings. However, the high number of tourists can cause environmental problems, both on land and in the sea. Clean, fresh water is often in short supply, and an increased demand from visitors can reduce the amount available for local islanders.

Flightless birds

Several birds of New Zealand cannot fly. Before European settlement, the Maoris hunted the giant moa (*above*) to extinction. The kiwi, New Zealand's national bird, is like a hen but has stumps instead of wings. Flightless species of parrots include the kea, kaka and kakapo.

PEOPLE

Fletcher Christian 1764–93
Christian led the crew of the *Bounty* in a mutiny against Captain Bligh in 1789, and sailed for Pitcairn Island in the Pacific. His descendants still live there.

Te Rauparaha c 1768–1849
This fearless warrior and Maori chief signed the Treaty of Waitangi in 1840. New Zealand's rugby teams perform his haka (war song) before their matches.

Ernest Rutherford 1871–1937
Many call this New Zealand-born scientist the father of nuclear physics. He received world recognition for his discoveries relating to nuclear atoms.

Queen Salote Tupou III 1900–65
Queen Salote ruled the Kingdom of Tonga from 1918 until her death in 1965. She improved health and education, and helped to develop national pride.

Sir Edmund Hillary born 1919
This mountain climber from Auckland, New Zealand, made several attempts to climb the world's highest peak, Mt Everest. With the Sherpa Tenzing Norgay, he was first to reach the summit in May 1953.

Jonah Lomu born 1975
Jonah Lomu was a player in New Zealand's rugby team from 1994 to 2002. He played 63 international test matches in his 73 games.

TRADITIONS AND CULTURE

Family life SAMOA
In Samoa, the *aiga* (extended family) is all important. Each village is comprised of several *aiga*. The larger the extended family, the more important it is and the more influence it has in village affairs.

Maori culture NEW ZEALAND
As part of their traditional ceremonies, Maori men chant loudly in a haka, while women in traditional dress (*below*) perform a dance with twirling balls, called *poi*. The striking patterns painted on their faces are symbolic of the tattoos their ancestors wore.

PLACES

Sky Tower AUCKLAND
This striking structure in Auckland, New Zealand, is the tallest building in the Southern Hemisphere. It towers more than 1,075 feet (328 m) above the ground.

Queenstown NEW ZEALAND
Queenstown is a popular ski resort on Lake Wakatipu, South Island, nestled below the Remarkables mountain range. Breathtaking scenery surrounds the town.

Port Vila VANUATU
Vanuatu's capital, Port Vila, lies on the southwest coast of the island of Efate. The city's daily markets and bustling harbor attract many visitors.

Jean-Marie Tjibaou Cultural Center NOUMEA
This structure (*below*) was built on Tina Peninsula, Noumea, in 2000. It was designed by architect Renzo Piano and the unusual shapes reflect the traditional buildings of the local Kanak people.

War clubs MELANESIA
During the 18th and 19th centuries, warriors carried clubs to fight the enemy. A throwing club was strapped to the waist and thrown in battle. A bladed club was used to cut down the enemy. A chief's club, however, was ornamental.

Village chieftains SOUTH PACIFIC
As the village leader and part of a council of chiefs, the chieftain is responsible for the problems that arise in his community and has authority over the people.

Tramping NEW ZEALAND
Keen walkers from all over the world head for the many tracks in New Zealand to go tramping through the country's spectacular natural landscape. The summer months from November to April are the best times to tramp.

Royal Palace TONGA
This stately waterfront palace (*above*), built in 1867 in the capital Nuku'alofa, on the island of Tongatapu, is home to the royal family of Tonga.

Papeete FRENCH POLYNESIA
Papeete is the chief port of the island of Tahiti, and capital of French Polynesia. The lifestyle of this city is a lively mix of French, Polynesian and Chinese cultures.

Cook's voyages

Captain James Cook set sail from England three times between 1768 and 1779 on scientific expeditions to the South Pacific. On his first trip, he charted the coastlines of Tahiti, New Zealand and eastern Australia, claiming them as part of Britain. On his later trips he visited Tonga and many more Pacific islands. He was the first captain to give his crew fresh fruit to prevent the disease, scurvy.

Cook's ship *Endeavour*

HISTORY AT A GLANCE

40,000 BC
Early peoples begin to inhabit the island chains of the Pacific Ocean region.

4000 BC
Sea vessels are developed, which makes travel between island chains possible. Expert navigators follow the paths of birds to find new islands.

Double-hulled canoe used for exploration

AD 1000
Most Pacific islands are inhabited, and the first Maori settle in New Zealand.

1513
Spanish conquistador Vasco Nuñez de Balboa is the first European to sight the Pacific Ocean, on his voyage from Panama.

1560s
Alvaro de Mendana discovers the Marquesas Islands. He lands on the Solomon Islands, naming them for the biblical King Solomon.

1606
Pedro Fernandez de Quiros, from Portugal, discovers the Cook Islands and the New Hebrides.

1642
Dutch explorer Abel Tasman is the first European to sight New Zealand. He visits the mainland. More than 100 years later, James Cook maps the New Zealand coastline.

1818
The musket wars start in New Zealand, between British settlers and the Maori.

1840
The Treaty of Waitangi is signed between the Maori and British. The treaty protected Maori rights if they sold their land to the British. New Zealand becomes a British colony.

Treaty House, Waitangi

1843–72
The Maori wars, also known as the land wars, flare up in New Zealand over issues arising from the Treaty of Waitangi.

1893
Social reforms are introduced in New Zealand, including the suffrage (right to vote) for women.

1941–45
Parts of World War II are fought in the Pacific region. At the end of the war, the USA begins to test its nuclear weapons on Bikini atoll.

1962
Western Samoa (now Samoa) becomes the first independent Pacific nation. Eight years later, Fiji and Tonga gain independence from Britain.

1985
The Treaty of Rarotonga declares the South Pacific a nuclear-free zone. New Zealand bans all nuclear trade.

1995
The Waikato-Raupatu Claims Settlement Act for Maori land claims is passed.

Nuclear testing

Gazetteer

How to use the gazetteer

This gazetteer is a geographical index of places in this atlas. To find the city of Agra in India, for example, look up its name in the gazetteer.

The entry reads: **118** **D8** **Agra**, India

The number 118 indicates that Agra appears on the map on page 118. The reference D8 tells you that it can be found in square D8. Turn to page 118. Trace down from the letter D at the top of the page (or up from the letter D on the bottom of the page) and then across from the number 8 on the side of the page. You will find Agra within the square where the letter and number intersect.

The symbols below are used to indicate the geographic feature of each entry.

≈ **Bay**
Includes bays and gulfs

⊠ **Channel**
Includes channels, straits and passages

□ **Country**

▣ **Dependent Territory**
Internal administrative region, province or state
eg Scotland, Falkland Islands, Manitoba, Queensland

▲ **Desert**
Includes sand dune features

⠿ **Geographic Area**
Includes regions eg Costa Blanca, Tuscany

▶ **Headland**
Includes headlands, points, capes, peninsulas and sand spits

⚲ **Island**
Includes atolls

⚵ **Island Group**

⌇ **Lake**
Includes reservoirs

▲ **Mountain**
Includes individual mountains and volcanoes

⛰ **Mountain Range**

▣ **National Capital**

⊙ **Ocean**

◇ **Physical Feature**
Includes plains, moors, wetlands, plateaus, peat bogs, mudflats, swamps and marshes

▬ **Polar Base**

↘ **River**
Includes deltas, rivers, waterfalls, estuaries

⊋ **Sea**

★ **Special Feature**

⌂ **State Capital**

■ **Underwater Feature**
Includes seamounts, reefs, abyssal plains

A name without a symbol indicates a town or city

Abbreviations

UNITED STATES OF AMERICA
Alabama	AL
Alaska	AK
Arizona	AZ
Arkansas	AR
California	CA
Colorado	CO
Connecticut	CT
Delaware	DE
District of Columbia	DC
Florida	FL
Georgia	GA
Guam	GU
Hawaii	HI
Idaho	ID
Illinois	IL
Indiana	IN
Iowa	IA
Kansas	KS
Kentucky	KY
Louisiana	LA
Maine	ME
Maryland	MD
Massachusetts	MA
Michigan	MI
Minnesota	MN
Mississippi	MS
Missouri	MO
Montana	MT
Nebraska	NE
Nevada	NV
New Hampshire	NH
New Jersey	NJ
New Mexico	NM
New York	NY
North Carolina	NC
North Dakota	ND
Ohio	OH
Oklahoma	OK
Oregon	OR
Pennsylvania	PA
Puerto Rico	PR
Rhode Island	RI
South Carolina	SC
South Dakota	SD
Tennessee	TN
Texas	TX
Utah	UT
Vermont	VT
Virginia	VA
Virgin Islands	VI
Washington	WA
West Virginia	WV
Wisconsin	WI
Wyoming	WY

CANADA
Alberta	AB
British Columbia	BC
Manitoba	MB
New Brunswick	NB
Newfoundland	NL
Northwest Territory	NT
Nova Scotia	NS
Nunavut	NU
Ontario	ON
Prince Edward Island	PE
Québec	QC
Sasketchewan	SK
Yukon Territory	YT

AUSTRALIA
Australian Capital Territory	ACT
New South Wales	NSW
Northern Territory	NT
Queensland	QLD
South Australia	SA
Tasmania	TAS
Victoria	VIC
Western Australia	WA

A

40	F 1	A Coruña, Spain
52	B 8	Aachen, Germany
53	E 10	Aalen, Germany
49	E 11	Aalst, Belgium
49	C 11	Aalter, Belgium
49	F 11	Aarschot, Belgium
136	H 7	Aba, Nigeria
115	K 4	Ābādān, Iran
104	H 9	Abakan, Russia
96	F 7	Abancay, Peru
130	I 2	Abashiri, Japan
45	I 2	Abbeville, France
74	D 10	Abbotsford, BC, Canada
111	L 8	Abbottabad, Pakistan
137	J 6	Abéché, Chad
36	G 7	Aberdeen, United Kingdom
82	G 6	Aberdeen, SD, United States
84	C 6	Aberdeen, WA, United States
74	G 6	Aberdeen Lake, NU, Canada ⌇
37	F 12	Aberystwyth, United Kingdom
115	I 9	Abhā, Saudi Arabia
136	F 7	Abidjan, Côte d'Ivoire
83	F 12	Abilene, TX, United States
118	C 7	Abohar, India
82	B 6	Absaroka Range, MT/WY, United States ⛰
115	M 6	Abu Dhabi, United Arab Emirates ▣
115	I 3	Abū Kamāl, Syria
136	H 6	Abuja, Nigeria ▣
41	J 5	Acalá de Henares, Spain
89	I 7	Acaponeta, Mexico
89	K 10	Acapulco, Mexico
136	G 7	Accra, Ghana ▣
104	H 9	Achinsk, Russia
57	H 14	Acireale, Italy
91	J 3	Acklins Island, The Bahamas ⚲
115	J 5	Ad Dahnā', Saudi Arabia ▲
136	E 3	Ad Dakhla, Western Sahara
115	K 6	Ad Dammām, Saudi Arabia
115	K 4	Adana, Turkey
109	G 9	Adana, Turkey
137	M 6	Addis Ababa, Ethiopia ▣
119	B 16	Addu Atoll, Maldives ⚲
147	I 9	Adelaide, SA, Australia ⌂
33	I 3	Adelaide Island, Antarctica ⚲
33	N 7	Adélie Land, Antarctica ⠿
115	J 10	Aden, Yemen
79	K 6	Adirondack Mountains, NY, United States ⛰
109	I 9	Adiyaman, Turkey
147	K 1	Admiralty Islands, Papua New Guinea ⚵
119	D 12	Adoni, India
136	G 3	Adrar, Algeria
56	G 7	Adriatic Sea, Europe ⊋
61	H 11	Aegean Sea, Greece/Turkey ⊋
111	K 7	Afghanistan, Asia □
137	N 8	Afgooye, Somalia
115	I 7	'Afif, Saudi Arabia
30	D 7	Africana Seamount, Indian Ocean ■
48	G 5	Afsluitdijk, Netherlands ◇
108	E 8	Afyon, Turkey
136	H 5	Agadez, Niger
136	F 2	Agadir, Morocco
119	I 9	Agartala, India
27	I 9	Agassiz Fracture Zone, Pacific Ocean ■
109	N 7	Ağdam, Azerbaijan
45	J 10	Agde, France
44	H 9	Agen, France
61	G 11	Agiokampos, Greece
61	H 11	Agios Efstratios, Greece ⚲
61	I 13	Agios Kirykos, Greece
118	D 8	Agra, India
108	L 7	Ağri, Turkey
57	G 15	Agrigento, Italy
151	L 3	Agrihan, Northern Mariana Islands ⚲
57	H 11	Agropoli, Italy
88	G 3	Agua Prieta, Mexico
89	J 7	Aguascalientes, Mexico
41	K 9	Águilas, Spain
89	I 9	Aguililla, Mexico
30	C 7	Agulhas Bank, Indian Ocean ■
30	D 8	Agulhas Basin, Indian Ocean ■
30	D 7	Agulhas Plateau, Indian Ocean ■
29	I 10	Agulhas Ridge, Atlantic Ocean ■
150	E 1	Ahipara Bay, New Zealand ≈
119	B 10	Ahmadabad, India
119	C 11	Ahmadnagar, India
115	K 4	Ahvāz, Iran
61	F 12	Aigio, Greece
151	M 3	Ailinginae, Marshall Islands ⚲
151	N 4	Ailinglaplap, Marshall Islands ⚲
151	N 3	Ailuk, Marshall Islands ⚲
45	L 10	Aix-en-Provence, France
119	J 9	Aizawl, India
130	H 8	Aizu-Wakamatsu, Japan
45	N 11	Ajaccio, Corsica
137	J 2	Ajdābiyā, Libya
118	C 8	Ajmer, India
85	I 15	Ajo, AZ, United States
131	E 11	Akashi, Japan
109	L 5	Akhalts'ikhe, Georgia
108	C 7	Akhisar, Turkey
75	J 8	Akimiski Island, NU, Canada ⚲
130	H 7	Akita, Japan
136	E 4	Akjoujt, Mauritania
74	D 5	Aklavik, NT, Canada
119	D 10	Akola, India
75	J 6	Akpatok Island, NU, Canada ⚲
61	H 11	Akra Akrathos, Greece ▶
61	G 11	Akra Drepano, Greece ▶
61	G 14	Akra Maleas, Greece ▶
61	G 11	Akra Paliouri, Greece ▶
61	F 14	Akra Tainaro, Greece ▶
79	I 8	Akron, OH, United States
108	G 8	Aksaray, Turkey
108	E 8	Akşehir, Turkey
126	F 4	Aksu, China
110	H 5	Aktau, Kazakhstan
111	I 3	Aktyubinsk, Kazakhstan
136	H 7	Akure, Nigeria
68	C 5	Akureyri, Iceland
115	K 4	Al 'Amārah, Iraq
114	G 4	Al 'Aqabah, Jordan
115	M 6	Al 'Ayn, United Arab Emirates
115	I 8	Al Bāḥah, Saudi Arabia
115	J 10	Al Baydā', Yemen
137	J 2	Al Baydā', Libya
115	I 3	Al Fallujah, Iraq
115	K 5	Al Farwāniyah, Kuwait
115	M 6	Al Hajar'al Gharbī, Oman ⛰
114	H 4	Al Ḥamād, Jordan/Saudi Arabia ◇
115	I 2	Al Ḥasakah, Syria
115	J 4	Al Hijāz, Saudi Arabia ⠿
115	J 4	Al Ḥillah, Iraq
115	I 10	Al Ḥudaydah, Yemen
115	K 6	Al Hufūf, Saudi Arabia
115	K 5	Al Jahrah, Kuwait
115	I 4	Al Jawf, Saudi Arabia
137	J 4	Al Jawf, Libya
115	K 5	Al Jubayl, Saudi Arabia
115	N 8	Al Khalif, Oman
115	M 6	Al Khaṣab, Oman
137	I 2	Al Khums, Libya
115	J 4	Al Kūt, Iraq
115	I 4	Al Labbah, Saudi Arabi ◇
114	H 2	Al Lādhiqīyah, Syria
115	L 9	Al Mahrah, Yemen ⛰
115	J 6	Al Majma'ah, Saudi Arabia
115	L 6	Al Manāmah, Bahrain ▣
115	K 10	Al Mukallā, Yemen
115	K 3	Al Muqdādiyah, Iraq
115	I 2	Al Qāmishlī, Syria
80	G 4	Alabama, United States ▣
80	G 5	Alabama, United States ↘
108	G 7	Alaca, Turkey
90	G 8	Alajuela, Costa Rica
151	L 4	Alamagan, Northern Mariana Islands ⚲
85	G 12	Alamo, NV, United States
83	D 12	Alamogordo, NM, United States
83	D 10	Alamosa, CO, United States
69	G 11	Åland, Finland
69	G 11	Ålands Hav, Finland ⊠
109	E 10	Alanya, Turkey
84	J 5	Alaska, United States ▣
84	I 6	Alaska Peninsula, AL, United States ▶

B

Page	Grid	Name
99	G 11	Bahía Blanca, Argentina
89	M 8	Bahía de Campeche, Mexico ≈
96	D 4	Bahía de Mania, Ecuador ≈
99	F 15	Bahía Grande, Argentina ≈
88	G 6	Bahía La Paz, Mexico ≈
98	I 6	Bahia Negro, Paraguay
88	E 4	Bahia Sebastian Vizcaino, Mexico ≈
137	M 6	Bahir Dar, Ethiopia
118	F 8	Bahraich, India
115	L 6	Bahrain, Asia □
97	J 4	Baía de Marajó, Brazil ≈
97	K 4	Baía de São Marcos, Brazil ≈
60	G 5	Baia Mare, Romania
127	N 3	Baicheng, China
44	G 3	Baie de Seine, France ≈
75	L 8	Baie-Comeau, QC, Canada
41	I 8	Bailén, Spain
81	I 6	Bainbridge, GA, United States
151	I 7	Bairiki, Kiribati
147	K 10	Bairnsdale, VIC, Australia
127	O 4	Baishan, China
88	E 3	Baja California, Mexico ►
84	F 8	Baker, OR, United States
26	G 6	Baker Island, Pacific Ocean
74	H 6	Baker Lake, NU, Canada
85	E 13	Bakersfield, CA, United States
109	P 6	Baku, Azerbaijan
41	M 3	Balaguer, Spain
104	C 7	Balakovo, Russia
64	F 10	Balaton, Hungary
150	C 10	Balclutha, New Zealand
41	N 7	Balearic Islands, Spain
123	I 10	Bali, Indonesia
123	J 10	Bali Sea, Indonesia ≈
108	C 7	Balikesir, Turkey
123	J 8	Balikpapan, Indonesia
23	I 4	Balkan Mountains, Europe ▲
146	F 9	Balladonia, WA, Australia
147	J 10	Ballarat, VIC, Australia
33	N 8	Balleny Islands, Antarctica
147	L 8	Ballina, NSW, Australia
83	F 12	Ballinger, TX, United States
89	K 9	Balsas, Mexico
65	J 9	Bălți, Moldova
23	I 3	Baltic Sea, Europe ≈
79	K 9	Baltimore, MD, United States
111	M 5	Balykchy, Kyrgyzstan
115	M 5	Bam, Iran
136	E 5	Bamako, Mali
137	J 7	Bambari, Central African Republic
53	F 9	Bamberg, Germany
136	H 7	Bamenda, Cameroon
119	C 9	Banas, India
122	E 6	Banda Aceh, Indonesia
123	L 9	Banda Sea, Indonesia ≈
122	G 9	Bandar Lampung, Indonesia
123	I 7	Bandar Seri Begawan, Brunei
115	M 5	Bandar-e 'Abbās, Iran
115	K 2	Bandar-e Anzali, Iran
122	H 10	Bandung, Indonesia
74	I 8	Banff, AB, Canada
119	D 13	Bangalore, India
137	J 2	Banghāzī, Libya
122	H 8	Bangka, Indonesia
122	F 5	Bangkok, Thailand
119	H 9	Bangladesh, Asia □
37	F 12	Bangor, United Kingdom
79	O 5	Bangor, ME, United States
137	J 7	Bangui, Central African Republic
137	K 7	Bani, Central African Republic
123	J 9	Banjarmasin, Indonesia
136	D 5	Banjul, Gambia
74	F 4	Banks Island, NT, Canada
84	E 6	Banks Lake, WA, United States
150	E 8	Banks Peninsula, New Zealand ►
119	H 10	Bankura, India
30	H 10	Banzare Seamount, Southern Ocean
127	M 5	Baoding, China
127	K 7	Baoji, China
127	I 9	Baoshan, China
127	L 5	Baotou, China
115	J 3	Ba'qūbah, Iraq
61	D 9	Bar, Serbia and Montenegro
79	O 5	Bar Harbor, ME, United States
91	K 4	Barahona, Dominican Republic
65	I 5	Baranavichy, Belarus
97	K 8	Barbacena, Brazil
91	O 6	Barbados, North America □
41	M 3	Barbastro, Spain
40	H 10	Barbate, Spain
91	N 4	Barbuda, Antigua and Barbuda
147	K 6	Barcaldine, QLD, Australia
41	N 4	Barcelona, Spain
96	G 2	Barcelona, Venezuela
119	H 10	Barddhaman, India
118	E 8	Bareilly, India
32	E 8	Barents Plain, Arctic Ocean
32	F 8	Barents Sea, Arctic Ocean ≈
32	F 8	Barents Trough, Arctic Ocean
57	J 10	Bari, Italy
96	F 2	Barinas, Venezuela
119	I 10	Barisal, Bangladesh
123	I 8	Barito, Indonesia
146	H 4	Barkly Tableland, NT, Australia ⸬
60	I 6	Bârlad, Romania
45	K 4	Bar-le-Duc, France
57	I 10	Barletta, Italy
104	G 9	Barnaul, Russia
48	H 8	Barneveld, Netherlands
37	F 14	Barnstaple, United Kingdom
96	F 2	Barquisimeto, Venezuela
28	E 6	Barracuda Fracture Zone, Atlantic Ocean
97	K 6	Barragem de Sobradinho, Brazil
96	E 1	Barranquilla, Colombia
40	E 7	Barreiro, Portugal
37	D 13	Barrow, Ireland
84	J 4	Barrow, AL, United States
146	D 6	Barrow Island, WA, Australia
37	G 10	Barrow-in-Furness, United Kingdom
85	F 14	Barstow, CA, United States
108	F 5	Bartin, Turkey
83	H 10	Bartlesville, OK, United States
65	J 5	Barysaw, Belarus
53	C 12	Basel, Switzerland
123	K 6	Basilan, Philippines
37	H 14	Basingstoke, United Kingdom
115	K 4	Basra, Iraq
147	J 10	Bass Strait, VIC, Australia ✕
56	E 5	Bassano del Grappa, Italy
30	E 6	Bassas da India, France
122	E 4	Bassein, Myanmar
91	N 5	Basseterre, St Kitts and Nevis
91	N 5	Basse-Terre, Guadeloupe
45	N 10	Bastia, Corsica
49	H 14	Bastogne, Belgium
83	J 11	Bastrop, LA, United States
136	H 8	Bata, Equatorial Guinea
123	K 3	Batan Islands, Philippines
123	J 5	Batangas, Philippines
31	J 6	Batavia Seamount, Indian Ocean
122	G 5	Bătdâmbâng, Cambodia
37	G 14	Bath, United Kingdom
118	C 7	Bathinda, India
147	K 9	Bathurst, NSW, Australia
146	G 3	Bathurst Island, NT, Australia
109	K 9	Batman, Turkey
136	H 1	Batna, Algeria
83	J 12	Baton Rouge, LA, United States
119	F 15	Batticaloa, Sri Lanka
78	G 7	Battle Creek, MI, United States
109	K 6	Bat'umi, Georgia
27	L 6	Bauer Basin, Pacific Ocean
97	J 8	Bauru, Brazil
52	I 8	Bautzen, Germany
53	F 11	Bavaria, Germany ⸬
88	G 3	Bavispe, Mexico
123	I 9	Bawean, Indonesia
31	I 2	Bay of Bengal, Indian Ocean ≈
41	J 1	Bay of Biscay, France/Spain ≈
75	L 9	Bay of Fundy, NS, Canada ≈
150	E 1	Bay of Islands, New Zealand ≈
150	G 4	Bay of Plenty, New Zealand ≈
91	I 4	Bayamo, Cuba
127	J 4	Bayanhongor, Mongolia
104	F 5	Baydaratskaya Guba, Russia ≈
137	N 7	Baydhabo, Somalia
44	G 3	Bayeux, France
44	F 10	Bayonne, France
111	J 7	Bayramaly, Turkmenistan
53	G 9	Bayreuth, Germany
41	J 9	Baza, Spain
109	N 6	Bazardüzü Dağl, Azerbaijan ▲
85	I 9	Bear Lake, ID/UT, United States
33	J 5	Bear Peninsula, Antarctica ►
41	J 8	Beas de Segura, Spain
32	G 5	Beaufort Sea, Arctic Ocean ≈
83	I 13	Beaumont, TX, United States
45	K 6	Beaune, France
45	I 3	Beauvais, France
136	G 2	Béchar, Algeria
79	I 10	Beckley, WV, United States
114	G 4	Be'ér Sheva', Israel
83	G 14	Beeville, TX, United States
127	L 10	Beihai, China
127	M 5	Beijing, China
48	J 5	Beilen, Netherlands
141	K 8	Beira, Mozambique
114	G 3	Beirut, Lebanon
60	F 6	Beiuş, Romania
40	F 8	Beja, Portugal
136	H 1	Bejaïa, Algeria
40	H 5	Béjar, Spain
64	G 10	Békéscsaba, Hungary
65	I 5	Belarus, Europe □
75	J 8	Belcher Islands, NU, Canada ✕
137	N 7	Beledweyne, Somalia
97	J 4	Belém, Brazil
37	E 10	Belfast, United Kingdom
45	L 5	Belfort, France
119	C 12	Belgaum, India
49	C 12	Belgium, Europe □
104	B 6	Belgorod, Russia
61	E 7	Belgrade, Serbia and Montenegro
33	L 2	Belgrano II, Antarctica
122	H 9	Belitung, Indonesia
90	E 5	Belize, North America □
90	E 5	Belize City, Belize
119	D 12	Bellary, India
44	C 5	Belle-Île, France
84	D 6	Bellevue, WA, United States
84	D 5	Bellingham, WA, United States
33	J 4	Bellingshausen Sea, Southern Ocean ≈
53	D 14	Bellinzona, Switzerland
90	E 5	Belmopan, Belize
97	K 8	Belo Horizonte, Brazil
82	H 5	Bemidji, MN, United States
36	E 7	Ben Nevis, United Kingdom ▲
40	H 5	Benavente, Spain
84	D 8	Bend, OR, United States
147	J 10	Bendigo, VIC, Australia
127	M 7	Bengbu, China
122	G 9	Bengkulu, Indonesia
140	F 6	Benguela, Angola
98	F 4	Beni, Bolivia
136	F 2	Beni Mellal, Morocco
41	M 7	Benidorm, Spain
136	G 6	Benin, Africa □
136	H 7	Benin City, Nigeria
130	K 8	Benkei-misaki, Japan ►
85	J 16	Benson, AZ, United States
131	C 13	Beppu, Japan
137	N 6	Berbera, Somalia
137	I 7	Berbérati, Central African Republic
45	I 2	Berck, France
65	N 9	Berdyans'k, Ukraine
65	N 9	Berdyans'ka Kosa, Ukraine ►
64	H 10	Berettyóújfalu, Hungary
104	E 7	Berezniki, Russia
56	C 7	Bergamo, Italy
69	A 11	Bergen, Norway
49	E 9	Bergen op Zoom, Netherlands
44	H 4	Bergerac, France
52	C 8	Bergisch Gladbach, Germany
26	H 1	Bering Sea, Pacific Ocean ≈
32	D 4	Bering Strait, Arctic Ocean ✕
49	G 10	Beringen, Belgium
85	C 12	Berkeley, CA, United States
33	K 3	Berkner Island, Antarctica
52	H 6	Berlin, Germany
98	G 2	Bermejo, Argentina
98	H 7	Bermejo, Argentina
98	H 7	Bermejo Viejo, Argentina
28	D 5	Bermuda, United Kingdom ◨
28	D 5	Bermuda Rise, Atlantic Ocean
53	C 13	Bern, Switzerland
137	I 7	Bertoua, Cameroon
36	G 8	Berwick-upon-Tweed, United Kingdom
45	L 5	Besançon, France
80	L 5	Bessemer, AL, United States
40	F 2	Betanzos, Spain
111	K 4	Betpak-Dala, Kazakhstan ◇
109	L 9	Beyşehir Gölü, Turkey
45	J 10	Béziers, France
119	C 13	Bhadravati, India
119	G 9	Bhagalpur, India
119	C 10	Bharuch, India
119	H 10	Bhatpara, India
119	B 10	Bhavnagar, India
119	F 10	Bhilai, India
136	H 1	Blida, Algeria
119	C 9	Bhilwara, India
119	F 12	Bhimavaram, India
118	E 8	Bhind, India
119	C 11	Bhiwandi, India
118	D 8	Bhiwani, India
119	D 10	Bhopal, India
119	G 11	Bhubaneshwar, India
119	D 10	Bhusawal, India
118	H 8	Bhutan, Asia □
123	N 8	Biak, Indonesia
64	H 6	Biała Podlaska, Poland
64	H 5	Białystok, Poland
44	F 10	Biarritz, France
119	C 11	Bid, India
119	D 11	Bidar, India
79	N 6	Biddeford, ME, United States
53	B 12	Biel, Switzerland
52	C 7	Bielefeld, Germany
53	B 12	Bieler See, Switzerland
56	B 5	Biella, Italy
64	G 8	Bielsko- Biała, Poland
122	H 5	Biên Hoa, Vietnam
83	F 12	Big Spring, TX, United States
82	C 6	Bighorn, WY, United States
82	C 6	Bighorn Lake, MT, United States
82	D 6	Bighorn Mountains, MT/WY, United States ▲
136	G 7	Bight of Benin, Africa ≈
61	B 7	Bihać, Bosnia-Herzegovina
119	F 12	Bihar Sharif, India
119	C 12	Bijapur, India
61	D 7	Bijeljina, Bosnia-Herzegovina
118	C 8	Bikaner, India
151	N 2	Bikar, Marshall Islands
151	M 2	Bikini, Federated States of Micronesia
65	K 8	Bila Tserkva, Ukraine
119	F 10	Bilaspur, India
41	J 2	Bilbao, Spain
108	D 7	Bilecik, Turkey
82	C 6	Billings, MT, United States
147	L 7	Biloela, QLD, Australia
80	F 6	Biloxi, MS, United States
49	E 13	Binche, Belgium
79	L 7	Binghamton, NY, United States
108	J 8	Bingöl, Turkey
137	I 3	Birāk, Libya
118	G 8	Biratnagar, Nepal
115	N 3	Bīrjand, Iran
37	G 11	Birkenhead, United Kingdom
37	H 12	Birmingham, United Kingdom
80	G 4	Birmingham, AL, United States
105	M 10	Birobidzhan, Russia
85	K 16	Bisbee, AZ, United States
28	H 3	Biscay Abyssal Plain, Atlantic Ocean
33	I 3	Biscoe Islands, Antarctica
111	L 5	Bishkek, Kyrgyzstan
136	H 1	Biskra, Algeria
82	F 6	Bismarck, ND, United States
147	K 1	Bismarck Archipelago, Papua New Guinea
26	E 6	Bismarck Sea, Pacific Ocean ≈
136	D 5	Bissau, Guinea Bissau
60	H 5	Bistrița, Romania
108	K 8	Bitlis, Turkey
61	F 10	Bitola, Macedonia
57	J 10	Bitonto, Italy
85	A 5	Bitteroot Range, MT, United States ▲
131	F 11	Biwa-ko, Japan
104	G 9	Biysk, Russia
137	I 1	Bizerte, Tunisia
61	C 6	Bjelovar, Croatia
122	G 3	Black, Vietnam
53	C 12	Black Forest, Germany ⸬
85	E 10	Black Rock Desert, NV, United States ▲
23	J 3	Black Sea, Europe ≈
136	F 6	Black Volta, Burkina Faso
147	K 7	Blackall, QLD, Australia
85	I 9	Blackfoot, ID, United States
37	G 11	Blackpool, United Kingdom
37	C 13	Blackwater, Ireland
61	G 9	Blagoevgrad, Bulgaria
105	L 10	Blagoveshchensk, Russia
28	C 5	Blake-Bahama Ridge, Atlantic Ocean
41	O 3	Blanes, Spain
141	K 8	Blantyre, Malawi
150	E 7	Blenheim, New Zealand
136	H 1	Blida, Algeria
141	I 10	Bloemfontein, South Africa
37	C 9	Bloody Foreland, Ireland ►
78	E 8	Bloomington, IL, United States
78	F 9	Bloomington, IN, United States
23	J 5	Blue Nile, Africa
79	I 10	Bluefield, VI, United States
90	G 7	Bluefields, Nicaragua
79	I 10	Bluestone Lake, WV, United States
150	B 11	Bluff, New Zealand
127	M 5	Bo Hai, China ≈
96	H 3	Boa Vista, Brazil
28	B 8	Boa Vista, Cape Verde
90	F 7	Boaco, Nicaragua
136	F 6	Bobo-Dioulasso, Burkina Faso
141	M 8	Boby, Madagascar ▲
81	L 10	Boca Raton, LA, United States
90	G 8	Bocas del Toro, Panama
52	C 7	Bochum, Germany
28	G 8	Bode Verde Fracture Zone, Atlantic Ocean
68	H 7	Boden, Sweden
68	E 6	Bodo, Norway
109	C 9	Bodrum, Turkey
83	J 12	Bogalusa, LA, United States
108	G 7	Boğazliyan, Turkey
126	H 4	Bogda Feng, China ▲
126	H 4	Bogda Shan, China ▲
122	H 9	Bogor, Indonesia
96	F 3	Bogotá, Colombia
64	E 8	Bohemia, Czech Republic ⸬
64	D 8	Bohemian Forest, Czech Republic/Germany ⸬
84	G 8	Boise, ID, United States
115	M 2	Bojnürd, Iran
69	A 12	Bokna Fjord, Norway ≈
98	F 5	Bolivia, South America □
45	K 9	Bollene, France
69	F 10	Bollnäs, Sweden
147	K 7	Bollon, QLD, Australia
56	E 7	Bologna, Italy
37	G 11	Bolton, United Kingdom
108	G 6	Bolu, Turkey
56	E 4	Bolzano, Italy
140	F 4	Boma, Democratic Republic of Congo
91	L 7	Bonaire, Netherlands Antilles ◨
146	F 4	Bonaparte Archipelago, WA, Australia
118	I 8	Bongaigaon, India
45	N 11	Bonifacio, Corsica
52	C 8	Bonn, Germany
137	O 6	Boosaaso, Somalia
74	G 4	Boothia Peninsula, NU, Canada ►
89	J 4	Boquillas del Carmen, Mexico
151	M 10	Bora-Bora, French Polynesia
84	H 8	Borah Peak, ID, United States ▲
69	D 13	Borås, Sweden
115	L 5	Borāzjān, Iran
44	G 8	Bordeaux, France
48	J 5	Borger, Netherlands
69	F 13	Borgholm, Sweden
69	E 11	Borlänge, Sweden
123	I 8	Borneo, Asia
69	E 15	Bornholm, Denmark
108	C 8	Bornova, Turkey
122	H 10	Borobudur, Indonesia ✱
49	I 14	Borscheid, Luxembourg
115	K 3	Borūjerd, Iran
61	C 7	Bosanska Dubica, Bosnia-Herzegovina
61	C 7	Bosanska Gradiška, Bosnia-Herzegovina
61	C 7	Bosnia-Herzegovina, Europe □
108	D 6	Bosporus, Turkey ✕
137	J 7	Bossangoa, Central African Republic
126	G 4	Bosten Hu, China
79	N 6	Boston, MA, United States
61	G 9	Botevgrad, Bulgaria
60	I 5	Botoşani, Romania
140	H 8	Botswana, Africa □
52	B 7	Bottrop, Germany
136	E 4	Boû Bleïne, Mauritania
136	F 6	Bouaké, Côte d'Ivoire
137	I 7	Bouar, Central African Republic
147	L 2	Bougainville, Papua New Guinea
136	E 6	Bougouni, Mali
85	G 13	Boulder City, NV, United States
45	I 1	Boulogne-sur-Mer, France
26	G 9	Bounty Islands, New Zealand
26	G 9	Bounty Trough, Pacific Ocean
45	K 7	Bourg-en-Bresse, France
45	I 6	Bourges, France
147	K 8	Bourke, NSW, Australia

≈ Bay   ⧗ Channel   □ Country   ◨ Dependent Territory   ▲ Desert   ⸬ Geographic Area   ► Headland   Island   Island Group   Lake   ▲ Mountain

37	H 14	Bournemouth, United Kingdom
29	I 11	Bouvetøya, Atlantic Ocean ⚓
78	F 11	Bowling Green, KY, United States
33	P 5	Bowman Island, Antarctica ⚓
141	I 3	Boyoma Falls, Democratic Republic of Congo
82	B 6	Bozeman, MT, United States
108	D 7	Bozüyük, Turkey
33	I 2	Brabant Island, Antarctica ⚓
61	C 8	Brač, Croatia
37	H 11	Bradford, United Kingdom
40	F 4	Braga, Portugal
40	G 3	Bragança, Portugal
119	I 9	Brahmanbaria, Bangladesh
119	G 11	Brahmapur, India
23	L 5	Brahmaputra, Asia ⌇
60	J 7	Brăila, Romania
49	E 12	Braine-l'Alleud, Belgium
96	H 4	Branco, Brazil ⌇
140	E 8	Brandberg, Namibia ▲
52	G 6	Brandenburg, Germany
74	G 10	Brandon, MB, Canada
33	I 2	Bransfield Strait, Antarctica ≋
97	J 7	Brasília, Brazil ▪
60	H 6	Braşov, Romania
49	E 10	Brasschaat, Belgium
64	F 9	Bratislava, Slovakia ▪
105	I 9	Bratsk, Russia
105	I 9	Bratskoye Vodokhranilishche, Russia ⌇
53	H 11	Braunau am Inn, Austria
52	E 6	Braunschweig, Germany
28	A 8	Brava, Cape Verde ⚓
85	G 15	Brawley, CA, United States
96	H 5	Brazil, South America ▫
29	G 9	Brazil Basin, Atlantic Ocean ▬
22	F 7	Brazilian Highlands, South America ▲
83	G 12	Brazos, TX, United States ⌇
140	F 4	Brazzaville, Congo ▪
49	F 9	Breda, Netherlands
49	H 11	Bree, Belgium
53	E 12	Bregenz, Austria
52	D 6	Bremen, Germany
52	D 5	Bremerhaven, Germany
84	D 6	Bremerton, WA, United States
52	D 5	Bremervörde, Germany
83	H 13	Brenham, TX, United States
56	D 5	Brescia, Italy
56	E 4	Bressanone, Italy
65	I 6	Brest, Belarus
44	D 4	Brest, France
80	G 6	Brewton, AL, United States
45	L 8	Briançon, France
79	M 7	Bridgeport, RI, United States
91	O 6	Bridgetown, Barbados ▪
53	C 13	Brig, Switzerland
85	I 10	Brigham City, UT, United States
37	I 14	Brighton, United Kingdom
57	K 11	Brindisi, Italy
147	L 7	Brisbane, QLD, Australia ⌂
37	G 14	Bristol, United Kingdom
81	J 1	Bristol, TN, United States
37	F 14	Bristol Channel, United Kingdom ≋
74	D 7	British Columbia, Canada ▫
91	N 4	British Virgin Islands, United Kingdom ▫
44	E 4	Brittany, France ▒
45	I 8	Brive-la-Gaillarde, France
64	F 8	Brno, Czech Republic
74	H 4	Brodeur Peninsula, NU, Canada
147	J 8	Broken Hill, NSW, Australia
31	I 6	Broken Plateau, Indian Ocean ▬
82	G 7	Brookings, SD, United States
85	C 9	Brookings, OR, United States
22	C 2	Brooks Range, North America ▲
146	E 9	Brookton, WA, Australia
146	F 5	Broome, WA, Australia
83	F 12	Brownfield, TX, United States
83	G 15	Brownsville, TX, United States
83	G 12	Brownwood, TX, United States
53	J 12	Bruck an der Mur, Austria
49	C 10	Bruges, Belgium
123	I 7	Brunei, Asia ▫
81	K 6	Brunswick, GA, United States
79	N 5	Brunswick, ME, United States
147	K 11	Bruny Island, TAS, Australia ⚓
49	E 11	Brussels, Belgium ▪
104	C 6	Bryansk, Russia
96	F 2	Bucaramanga, Colombia
136	E 7	Buchanan, Liberia

60	I 7	Bucharest, Romania
64	G 9	Budapest, Hungary
118	E 3	Budaun, India
96	E 3	Buenaventura, Colombia
99	G 10	Buenos Aires, Argentina ▪
79	J 6	Buffalo, NY, United States
82	E 6	Buffalo, SD, United States
64	H 6	Bug, Poland/Ukraine ⌇
40	D 10	Bugio, Portugal
115	J 3	Buḥayrat ar Razāzah, Iraq ⚓
115	I 3	Buḥayrat ath Tharthār, Iraq ⚓
141	J 4	Bujumbura, Burundi ▪
141	I 3	Bukavu, Democratic Republic of Congo
111	J 6	Bukhara, Uzbekistan
141	I 8	Bulawayo, Zimbabwe
61	J 9	Bulgaria, Europe ▫
150	D 7	Buller, New Zealand ⌇
147	K 2	Bulolo, Papua New Guinea
146	E 9	Bunbury, WA, Australia
147	L 7	Bundaberg, QLD, Australia
146	G 5	Bungle Bungles, WA, Australia ▲▲
131	C 13	Bungo-suidō, Japan ≋
141	J 2	Bunia, Democratic Republic of Congo
41	L 6	Buñol, Spain
108	H 8	Bünyan, Turkey
122	H 5	Buôn Mê Thuột, Vietnam
115	J 6	Buraydah, Saudi Arabia
85	E 14	Burbank, CA, United States
147	K 5	Burdekin, QLD, Australia ⌇
109	D 9	Burdur, Turkey
61	J 9	Burgas, Bulgaria
41	J 3	Burgos, Spain
45	J 6	Burgundy, France ▒
119	D 10	Burhanpur, India
147	I 5	Burketown, QLD, Australia
136	F 6	Burkina Faso, Africa ▫
147	K 11	Burnie, TAS, Australia
84	E 8	Burns, OR, United States
41	M 6	Burriana, Spain
108	D 6	Bursa, Turkey
123	L 9	Buru, Indonesia ⚓
141	J 4	Burundi, Africa ▫
115	L 5	Būshehr, Iran
146	E 9	Busselton, WA, Australia
141	I 2	Buta, Democratic Republic of Congo
123	K 9	Buton, Indonesia ⚓
82	B 6	Butte, MT, United States
123	L 6	Butuan, Philippines
60	I 7	Buzău, Romania
65	K 6	Byarezina, Belarus ⌇
64	F 5	Bydgoszcz, Poland
64	G 7	Bytom, Poland

C

122	G 6	Ca Mau, Vietnam
123	K 4	Cabanatuan, Philippines
140	F 4	Cabinda, Angola
99	F 15	Cabo Buen Tiempo, Argentina ▶
40	E 6	Cabo Carvoeiro, Portugal ▶
96	E 3	Cabo Corrientes, Colombia ▶
88	H 8	Cabo Corrientes, Mexico ▶
90	G 3	Cabo Corrientes, Cuba ▶
40	I 1	Cabo Cruz, Cuba ▶
41	O 3	Cabo de Creus, Spain ▶
41	M 7	Cabo de la Nao, Spain ▶
41	L 8	Cabo de Palos, Spain ▶
40	H 1	Cabo de Penas, Spain ▶
41	M 7	Cabo de San Antonio, Spain ▶
40	F 9	Cabo de Santa Maria, Portugal ▶
40	E 9	Cabo de São Vincente, Portugal ▶
40	E 8	Cabo de Sines, Portugal ▶
99	G 13	Cabo Dos Bahías, Argentina ▶
40	E 7	Cabo Espichel, Portugal ▶
40	E 2	Cabo Fisterra, Spain ▶
41	L 7	Cabo Huertas, Spain ▶
41	J 1	Cabo Machichaco, Spain ▶
97	J 3	Cabo Norte, Brazil ▶
97	J 3	Cabo Orange, Brazil ▶
40	F 1	Cabo Ortegal, Spain ▶
99	E 15	Cabo Pilar, Chile ▶
99	G 16	Cabo Quilán, Chile ▶
89	L 7	Cabo Rojo, Mexico ▶
41	J 10	Cabo Sacratif, Spain ▶
90	G 3	Cabo San Antonio, Cuba ▶
99	G 16	Cabo San Diego, Argentina ▶
88	F 6	Cabo San Lázaro, Mexico ▶

88	G 7	Cabo San Lucas, Mexico ▶
88	G 7	Cabo San Lucas, Mexico ▶
88	E 3	Cabo San Quintín, Mexico ▶
90	F 7	Cabo Santa Elena, Costa Rica ▶
40	E 3	Cabo Silleiro, Spain ▶
40	G 10	Cabo Trafalgar, Spain ▶
99	G 14	Cabo Tres Puntas, Argentina ▶
99	F 15	Cabo Vírgenes, Argentina ▶
88	F 3	Caborca, Mexico
97	L 8	Cachoeiro do Itapemirim, Brazil
78	G 5	Cadillac, MI, United States
40	G 10	Cádiz, Spain
123	K 5	Cadiz, Philippines
44	G 3	Caen, France
98	G 3	Cafayate, Argentina
123	K 6	Cagayan de Oro, Philippines
57	B 12	Cagliari, Italy
91	M 4	Caguas, Puerto Rico
45	I 9	Cahors, France
65	K 11	Cahul, Moldova
91	K 3	Caicos Islands, Turks and Caicos Islands ⚓
147	K 4	Cairns, QLD, Australia
137	L 3	Cairo, Egypt ▪
96	E 5	Cajamarca, Peru
57	J 12	Calabria, Italy ▒▒
99	E 15	Calafate, Argentina
41	K 3	Calahorra, Spain
45	I 1	Calais, France
98	F 7	Calama, Chile
41	K 4	Calatayud, Spain
123	K 5	Calbayog, Philippines
119	H 10	Calcutta, India
40	E 6	Caldas da Rainha, Portugal
98	E 8	Caldera, Chile
99	F 13	Caleta Olivia, Argentina
74	E 9	Calgary, AB, Canada
96	E 3	Cali, Colombia
119	C 14	Calicut, India
85	D 14	California, United States ▫
96	E 6	Callao, Peru
57	J 11	Caltanissetta, Italy
122	H 5	Cam Ranh, Vietnam
97	L 7	Camaçari, Brazil
91	I 3	Camagüey, Cuba
40	G 2	Câmara de Lobos, Portugal
45	K 10	Camargue, France ◇
75	L 8	Cambellton, NB, Canada
122	G 6	Cambodia, Asia ▫
45	J 2	Cambrai, France
37	F 13	Cambrian Mountains, United Kingdom ▲▲
37	I 13	Cambridge, United Kingdom
150	F 4	Cambridge, New Zealand
79	I 8	Cambridge, OH, United States
74	G 5	Cambridge Bay, NU, Canada
137	I 8	Cameroon, Africa ▫
98	G 6	Camiri, Bolivia
85	I 14	Camp Verde, AZ, United States
23	G 9	Campbell Island, Oceania ⚓
26	G 9	Campbell Plateau, Pacific Ocean ▬
89	O 8	Campeche, Mexico
97	M 5	Campina Grande, Brazil
97	J 9	Campinas, Brazil
97	I 8	Campo Grande, Brazil
57	H 10	Campobasso, Italy
97	L 8	Campos dos Goytacazes, Brazil
74	F 9	Camrose, AB, Canada
122	G 6	Cần Thơ, Vietnam
74	C 5	Canada, North America ▫
32	C 5	Canada Abyssal Plain, Arctic Ocean ▬
83	F 10	Canadian, TX, United States ⌇
32	C 4	Canadian Basin, Arctic Ocean ▬
22	D 2	Canadian Shield, North America ▒▒
108	B 6	Çanakkale, Turkey
88	G 3	Cananea, Mexico
40	A 10	Canary Islands, Spain ▶
22	G 4	Canary Islands, Africa ⚓
147	L 9	Canberra, ACT, Australia ▪
89	P 7	Cancún, Mexico
127	M 5	Cangzhou, China
33	J 5	Canisteo Peninsula, Antarctica ▶
108	F 6	Cankiri, Turkey
45	M 10	Cannes, France
97	J 10	Canoas, Brazil
37	J 14	Canterbury, United Kingdom
150	D 9	Canterbury Bight, New Zealand ≋
150	D 9	Canterbury Plains, New Zealand ▒▒

80	E 4	Canton, MS, United States
79	I 8	Canton, OH, United States
83	F 11	Canyon, TX, United States ▶
82	B 6	Canyon Ferry Lake, MT, United States
136	D 3	Cap Barbas, Western Sahara ▶
41	O 5	Cap de Formentor, Spain ▶
44	F 2	Cap de la Hague, France ▶
41	O 6	Cap de ses Salines, Spain ▶
41	O 6	Cap des Freu, Spain ▶
75	J 6	Cap Hopes Advance, QC, Canada ▶
136	D 5	Cap Vert, Senegal ▶
33	M 7	Cape Adare, Antarctica ▶
23	I 8	Cape Agulhas, Africa ▶
108	G 10	Cape Apostolos Andreas, Cyprus ▶
147	I 3	Cape Arnhem, NT, Australia ▶
29	J 9	Cape Basin, Atlantic Ocean ▬
75	M 7	Cape Bauld, NL, Canada ▶
85	B 9	Cape Blanco, OR, United States ▶
30	F 11	Cape Boothby, Antarctica ▶
75	M 8	Cape Breton Island, NS, Canada ⚓
150	E 1	Cape Brett, New Zealand ▶
150	E 7	Cape Campbell, New Zealand ▶
81	L 8	Cape Canaveral, FL, United States ▶
79	L 10	Cape Charles, VI, United States ▶
33	M 7	Cape Cheetham, Antarctica ▶
105	J 4	Cape Chelyuskin, Russia ▶
32	B 8	Cape Chidley, Canada ▶
119	E 12	Cape Chirala, India ▶
74	H 7	Cape Churchill, MB, Canada ▶
79	N 7	Cape Cod, MA, United States ▶
32	D 7	Cape Columbia, Canada ▶
119	D 15	Cape Comorin, India ▶
74	C 9	Cape Cook, BC, Canada ▶
81	K 10	Cape Coral, FL, United States ▶
147	K 2	Cape Cretin, Papua New Guinea ▶
74	E 4	Cape Dalhousie, NT, Canada ▶
30	G 11	Cape Darnley, Antarctica ▶
84	C 7	Cape Disappointment, WA, United States ▶
75	J 4	Cape Dyer, NU, Canada ▶
150	D 6	Cape Farewell, New Zealand ▶
81	M 3	Cape Fear, NC, United States ▶
84	C 5	Cape Flattery, WA, United States ▶
146	G 4	Cape Ford, NT, Australia ▶
150	D 7	Cape Foulwind, New Zealand ▶
33	N 7	Cape Freshfield, Antarctica ▶
147	K 1	Cape Girgir, Papua New Guinea ▶
31	L 11	Cape Goodenough, Antarctica ▶
33	O 7	Cape Gray, Antarctica ▶
108	G 11	Cape Greko, Cyprus ▶
147	J 3	Cape Grenville, QLD, Australia ▶
81	O 2	Cape Hatteras, NC, United States ▶
22	F 9	Cape Horn, South America ▶
150	E 1	Cape Karikari, New Zealand ▶
33	O 7	Cape Keltie, Antarctica ▶
150	G 5	Cape Kidnappers, New Zealand ▶
74	C 8	Cape Knox, BC, Canada ▶
75	K 6	Cape Labrador, NL, Canada ▶
31	K 7	Cape Leeuwin, Australia ▶
146	F 5	Cape Leveque, WA, Australia ▶
81	N 3	Cape Lookout, NC, United States ▶
147	J 4	Cape Melville, QLD, Australia ▶
85	B 10	Cape Mendocino, CA, United States ▶
75	J 5	Cape Mercy, NU, Canada ▶
31	L 11	Cape Morse, Antarctica ▶
147	L 3	Cape Nelson, Papua New Guinea ▶
33	L 1	Cape Norvegia, Antarctica ▶
140	H 11	Cape of Good Hope, South Africa ▶
150	F 7	Cape Palliser, New Zealand ▶
136	E 7	Cape Palmas, Côte d'Ivoire/Liberia ▶
74	E 4	Cape Parry, NT, Canada ▶
31	I 11	Cape Penck, Antarctica ▶
31	K 11	Cape Poinsett, Antarctica ▶
150	A 10	Cape Providence, New Zealand ▶
150	D 1	Cape Reinga, New Zealand ▶
81	L 4	Cape Romain, SC, United States ▶
81	K 10	Cape Romano, FL, United States ▶
150	G 3	Cape Runaway, New Zealand ▶
28	E 4	Cape Sable, North America ▶
81	K 11	Cape Sable, FL, United States ▶
123	L 6	Cape San Agustin, Philippines ▶
147	I 4	Cape Shield, NT, Australia ▶
147	M 3	Cape Siri, Papua New Guinea ▶
74	H 8	Cape Tatnam, MB, Canada ▶

140	H 11	Cape Town, South Africa ▪
150	E 5	Cape Turnagain, New Zealand ▶
28	A 7	Cape Verde, Africa ▶
28	G 6	Cape Verde Basin, Atlantic Ocean ▬
28	G 6	Cape Verde Islands, Atlantic Ocean ▬
28	G 5	Cape Verde Plateau, Atlantic Ocean ▬
33	P 6	Cape Waldron, Antarctica ▶
36	E 5	Cape Wrath, United Kingdom ▶
147	I 3	Cape York, QLD, Australia ▶
147	J 4	Cape York Peninsula, QLD, Australia ▶
91	K 4	Cap-Haïtien, Haiti
57	A 11	Capo Caccia, Italy ▶
57	C 13	Capo Carbonara, Italy ▶
57	J 13	Capo Colonna, Italy ▶
57	C 11	Capo Comino, Italy ▶
57	B 10	Capo del Falcone, Italy ▶
57	B 12	Capo della Frasca, Italy ▶
57	H 15	Capo delle Correnti, Italy ▶
57	H 13	Capo di Milazzo, Italy ▶
57	C 11	Capo di Monte Santu, Italy ▶
57	G 14	Capo Gallo, Italy ▶
57	I 12	Capo Palinuro, Italy ▶
57	J 13	Capo Rizzuto, Italy ▶
57	F 14	Capo San Vito, Italy ▶
57	K 12	Capo Santa Maria di Leuca, Italy ▶
57	H 15	Capo Scaramia, Italy ▶
57	B 13	Capo Spartivento, Italy ▶
57	I 13	Capo Vaticano, Italy ▶
108	G 8	Cappadocia, Turkey ▒▒
57	G 11	Capri, Italy ⚓
140	H 7	Caprivi Strip, Namibia ▒▒
96	E 4	Caquetá, Colombia ⌇
119	K 14	Car Nicobar, India ⚓
60	G 8	Caracal, Romania
96	G 1	Caracas, Venezuela ▪
78	E 10	Carbondale, IL, United States
45	I 10	Carcassonne, France
37	G 14	Cardiff, United Kingdom ⌂
37	F 12	Cardigan Bay, United Kingdom ≋
60	F 5	Carei, Romania
30	G 5	Cargados Carajos Islands, Mauritius ⚓
37	G 10	Carlisle, United Kingdom
79	K 8	Carlisle, PA, United States
37	D 12	Carlow, Ireland
83	E 12	Carlsbad, NM, United States
30	F 2	Carlsberg Ridge, Indian Ocean ▬
78	E 9	Carlyle Lake, IL, United States ⌇
40	H 8	Carmona, Spain
146	D 7	Carnarvon, WA, Australia ⚓
33	J 6	Carney Island, Antarctica ⚓
137	I 7	Carnot, Central African Republic
97	K 5	Carolina, Brazil
151	J 1	Caroline Islands, Federated States of Micronesia ⚓
23	I 3	Carpathian Mountains, Europe ▲▲
56	D 6	Carpi, Italy
56	D 7	Carrara, Italy
37	A 13	Carrauntuohil, Ireland ▲
82	F 5	Carrington, ND, United States
85	I 11	Carson City, NV, United States ⌂
41	L 8	Cartagena, Spain
96	E 2	Cartagena, Colombia
90	G 8	Cartago, Costa Rica
91	O 6	Castries, St Lucia ▪
57	E 12	Castro, Chile
57	I 12	Castrovillari, Italy
91	J 2	Cat Island, The Bahamas ⚓
41	N 3	Cataluña, Spain ▒▒
97	J 4	Castanhal, Brazil
41	M 6	Castelló de la Plana, Spain
45	I 10	Castelnaudary, France
40	G 6	Castelo Branco, Portugal
98	G 8	Catamarca, Argentina
57	H 14	Catania, Italy

▲▲ Mountain Range   ▪ National Capital   ⚓ Ocean   Physical Feature   ▬ Polar Base   ⌇ River   ⚓ Sea   ★ Special Feature   ⌂ State Capital   ▬ Underwater Feature

GAZETTEER 157

57 J 13 **Catanzaro**, Italy
79 L 7 **Catskill Mountains**, NY, United States ▲
96 E 2 **Cauca**, Colombia ⤴
23 J 4 **Caucasus**, Asia/Europe ▲
99 E 10 **Cauquenes**, Chile
136 E 7 **Cavally**, Côte d'Ivoire/Libya ⤴
97 J 10 **Caxias do Sul**, Brazil
97 J 3 **Cayenne**, French Guiana ♣
90 H 4 **Cayman Brac**, Cayman Islands ⚑
90 H 4 **Cayman Islands**, United Kingdom
90 H 3 **Cayo Largo**, Cuba ⚑
90 G 6 **Cayos Miskitos**, Nicaragua ⚑
28 F 7 **Ceara Abyssal Plain**, Atlantic Ocean
123 K 6 **Cebu**, Philippines
82 I 7 **Cedar**, IA, United States ⤴
85 I 12 **Cedar City**, UT, United States
74 G 9 **Cedar Lake**, MB, Canada ⤴
82 I 7 **Cedar Rapids**, IA, United States
146 H 8 **Ceduna**, SA, Australia
89 J 4 **Celaya**, Mexico
26 D 5 **Celebes Sea**, Pacific Ocean
60 B 6 **Celje**, Slovenia
52 E 6 **Celle**, Germany
37 D 14 **Celtic Sea**, Ireland/United Kingdom
28 H 3 **Celtic Shelf**, Atlantic Ocean
137 J 7 **Central African Republic**, Africa
26 D 4 **Central Basin**, Pacific Ocean
151 M 8 **Central Line Islands**, Kiribati
22 D 4 **Central Lowlands**, North America
111 J 10 **Central Makran Range**, Pakistan ▲
26 G 5 **Central Pacific Basin**, Pacific Ocean
147 J 1 **Central Range**, Papua New Guinea
23 K 2 **Central Siberian Plateau**, Asia
85 D 10 **Central Valley**, CA, United States
84 D 6 **Centralia**, WA, United States
57 I 10 **Cerignola**, Italy
108 F 6 **Cerkeş**, Turkey
99 E 14 **Cerro Arenales**, Chile ▲
96 A 7 **Cerro Azol**, Galapagos Islands ▲
90 G 8 **Cerro Chirripó Grande**, Costa Rica ▲
88 E 2 **Cerro de La Encantada**, Mexico ▲
96 E 6 **Cerro de Pasco**, Peru
99 E 14 **Cerro Murallón**, Argentina/Chile ▲
99 E 15 **Cerro Paine**, Chile ▲
99 E 13 **Cerro San Valentín**, Chile ▲
99 F 10 **Cerro Tupungato**, Argentina/Chile ▲
41 N 3 **Cervera**, Spain
56 F 7 **Cesena**, Italy
64 E 8 **České Budějovice**, Czech Republic
40 H 10 **Ceuta**, Spain
109 H 9 **Ceyhan**, Turkey
30 H 4 **Ceylon Plain**, Indian Ocean
115 N 6 **Chābahār**, Iran
96 E 5 **Chachapoyas**, Peru
137 I 5 **Chad**, Africa
111 J 8 **Chaghcharān**, Afghanistan
30 G 4 **Chagos Archipelago**, Indian Ocean
30 H 4 **Chagos Trench**, Indian Ocean
30 G 4 **Chagos-Laccadive Ridge**, Indian Ocean
30 F 3 **Chain Ridge**, Indian Ocean
61 G 12 **Chalkida**, Greece
26 E 5 **Challenger Deep**, Pacific Ocean
27 K 8 **Challenger Fracture Zone**, Pacific Ocean
26 G 8 **Challenger Plateau**, Pacific Ocean
84 H 4 **Challis**, ID, United States
45 K 6 **Chalon-sur-Saône**, France
45 K 3 **Châlons-en-Champagne**, France
45 L 7 **Chambéry**, France
45 M 7 **Chamonix-Mont-Blanc**, France
89 O 4 **Champotón**, Mexico
98 E 8 **Chañaral**, Chile
80 F 7 **Chandeleur Islands**, LA, United States
118 D 7 **Chandigarh**, India
85 I 15 **Chandler**, AZ, United States
119 E 11 **Chandrapur**, India
127 N 4 **Changchun**, China
127 L 8 **Changde**, China
127 N 9 **Changhua**, Taiwan
126 G 4 **Changji**, China
127 L 8 **Changsha**, China

127 N 7 **Changshu**, China
127 L 6 **Changzhi**, China
127 M 7 **Changzhou**, China
61 G 14 **Chania**, Greece
37 G 16 **Channel Islands**, United Kingdom
85 E 15 **Channel Islands**, CA, United States
37 K 14 **Channel Tunnel**, United Kingdom/France
127 M 10 **Chaozhou**, China
97 J 9 **Chapecó**, Brazil
33 J 3 **Charcot Island**, Antarctica ⚑
111 J 6 **Chardzhev**, Turkmenistan
111 K 7 **Chārīkār**, Afghanistan
49 F 13 **Charleroi**, Belgium
81 L 4 **Charleston**, SC, United States
79 I 10 **Charleston**, WV, United States
147 K 3 **Charleville**, QLD, Australia
45 K 3 **Charleville-Mézières**, France
28 F 3 **Charlie-Gibbs Fracture Zone**, Atlantic Ocean
81 K 2 **Charlotte**, NC, United States
91 M 4 **Charlotte Amalie**, Virgin Islands
81 J 9 **Charlotte Harbor**, FL, United States ≈
79 J 10 **Charlottesville**, VI, United States
75 M 8 **Charlottetown**, PE, Canada
45 I 4 **Chartres**, France
44 G 5 **Châteaubriant**, France
45 I 5 **Châteaudun**, France
45 I 6 **Châteauroux**, France
45 J 3 **Château-Thierry**, France
44 H 6 **Châtellerault**, France
26 G 9 **Chatham Islands**, New Zealand
26 G 9 **Chatham Rise**, Pacific Ocean
80 H 3 **Chattanooga**, TN, United States
45 K 4 **Chaumont**, France
119 E 14 **Chavakachcheri**, Sri Lanka
104 D 6 **Cheboksary**, Russia
78 H 4 **Cheboygan**, MI, United States
122 E 3 **Cheduba**, Myanmar ⚑
84 C 6 **Chehalis**, WA, United States
111 I 3 **Chelkar**, Kazakhstan
64 H 7 **Chelm**, Poland
37 J 13 **Chelmsford**, United Kingdom
37 H 13 **Cheltenham**, United Kingdom
104 E 8 **Chelyabinsk**, Russia
52 G 8 **Chemnitz**, Germany
127 M 5 **Chengde**, China
127 J 8 **Chengdu**, China
119 E 13 **Chennai**, India
44 G 3 **Cherbourg**, France
104 D 5 **Cherepovets**, Russia
65 L 8 **Cherkasy**, Ukraine
104 B 8 **Cherkessk**, Russia
65 L 6 **Chernihiv**, Ukraine
65 I 9 **Chernivtsi**, Ukraine
65 K 7 **Chernobyl**, Ukraine
64 H 4 **Chernyakhovsk**, Russia
79 K 9 **Chesapeake Bay**, United States ≈
79 N 4 **Chesuncook Lake**, ME, United States ⤴
89 P 9 **Chetumal**, Mexico
82 D 8 **Cheyenne**, WY, United States
82 E 7 **Cheyenne**, SD, United States ⤴
127 N 10 **Chiai**, Taiwan
122 F 4 **Chiang Mai**, Thailand
122 F 3 **Chiang Rai**, Thailand
109 L 5 **Chiat'ura**, Georgia
131 I 10 **Chiba**, Japan
75 K 9 **Chibougamau**, QC, Canada
78 F 7 **Chicago**, IL, United States
89 O 8 **Chichén Itzá**, Mexico ✳
96 D 5 **Chiclayo**, Peru
99 F 13 **Chico**, Argentina ⤴
85 D 11 **Chico**, CA, United States
75 K 9 **Chicoutimi**, QC, Canada
57 G 9 **Chieti**, Italy
127 M 4 **Chifeng**, China
88 H 4 **Chihuahua**, Mexico
83 F 11 **Childress**, TX, United States
99 E 11 **Chile**, South America
99 E 13 **Chile Chico**, Chile
27 L 8 **Chile Rise**, Pacific Ocean
99 E 11 **Chillán**, Chile
78 H 9 **Chillicothe**, OH, United States
89 K 9 **Chilpancingo**, Mexico
96 E 6 **Chimbote**, Peru
141 J 7 **Chimoio**, Mozambique
127 I 6 **China**, Asia
141 I 6 **Chingola**, Zambia

141 J 7 **Chinhoyi**, Zimbabwe
111 L 8 **Chiniot**, Pakistan
26 G 2 **Chinook Trough**, Pacific Ocean
56 F 6 **Chioggia**, Italy
61 I 12 **Chios**, Greece
61 I 12 **Chios**, Greece ⚑
141 J 6 **Chipata**, Zambia
90 E 6 **Chiquimula**, Guatemala
111 L 5 **Chirchik**, Uzbekistan
65 K 10 **Chişinău**, Moldova ▲
105 J 10 **Chita**, Russia
119 D 13 **Chitradurga**, India
119 I 10 **Chittagong**, Bangladesh
119 E 13 **Chittoor**, India
141 J 7 **Chitungwiza**, Zimbabwe
99 G 11 **Choele Choel**, Argentina
44 G 6 **Cholet**, France
141 I 7 **Choma**, Zambia
64 D 7 **Chomutov**, Moldova
122 G 5 **Chon Buri**, Thailand
127 O 4 **Ch'ŏngjin**, North Korea
127 K 8 **Chongqing**, China
127 O 6 **Chŏnju**, South Korea
127 L 3 **Choybalsan**, Mongolia
150 D 8 **Christchurch**, New Zealand
23 M 7 **Christmas Island**, Australia ⚑
150 L 7 **Christmas Island**, Kiribati ⚑
26 L 7 **Christmas Ridge**, Pacific Ocean
99 F 12 **Chubut**, Argentina ⤴
105 O 3 **Chuckchi Sea**, Russia
131 C 12 **Chūgoku-sanchi**, Japan ▲
32 D 5 **Chukchi Abyssal Plain**, Arctic Ocean
32 D 5 **Chukchi Plateau**, Arctic Ocean
32 D 5 **Chukchi Sea**, Arctic Ocean
105 O 4 **Chukotskiy Peninsula**, Russia ▶
85 F 15 **Chula Vista**, CA, United States
127 O 5 **Ch'unch'ŏn**, South Korea
127 O 5 **Ch'ungju**, South Korea
98 E 6 **Chuquicamata**, Chile
53 D 8 **Chur**, Switzerland
74 H 7 **Churchill**, MB, Canada
74 H 8 **Churchill**, NL, Canada ⤴
75 L 7 **Churchill**, MB, Canada ⤴
151 L 1 **Chuuk Islands**, Federated States of Micronesia
65 K 10 **Ciadir Lunga**, Moldova
108 F 5 **Cide**, Turkey
64 H 5 **Ciechanów**, Poland
91 I 3 **Ciego de Ávila**, Cuba
90 H 3 **Cienfuegos**, Cuba
41 K 8 **Cieza**, Spain
108 F 8 **Cihanbeyli**, Turkey
122 H 10 **Cilacap**, Indonesia
78 G 9 **Cincinnati**, OH, United States
49 G 13 **Ciney**, Belgium
57 J 12 **Cirà Marina**, Italy
56 F 8 **Città di Castello**, Italy
89 J 3 **Ciudad Acuña**, Mexico
96 G 2 **Ciudad Bolívar**, Venezuela
89 I 4 **Ciudad Camargo**, Mexico
89 K 7 **Ciudad de Valles**, Mexico
89 N 9 **Ciudad del Carmen**, Mexico
89 I 4 **Ciudad Delicias**, Mexico
96 H 2 **Ciudad Guayana**, Venezuela
89 I 8 **Ciudad Guzmán**, Mexico
88 H 2 **Ciudad Juárez**, Mexico
89 L 7 **Ciudad Madero**, Mexico
89 K 7 **Ciudad Mante**, Mexico
88 G 4 **Ciudad Obregón**, Mexico
41 I 7 **Ciudad Real**, Spain
40 G 5 **Ciudad Rodrigo**, Spain
89 K 6 **Ciudad Victoria**, Mexico
41 P 5 **Ciudadela**, Spain
108 H 6 **Civa Burnu**, Turkey ▶
56 G 8 **Civitanova Marche**, Italy
57 E 9 **Civitavecchia**, Italy
150 E 7 **Clarence**, New Zealand
150 E 7 **Clarence**, New Zealand ⤴
91 J 3 **Clarence Town**, The Bahamas
27 I 4 **Clarion Fracture Zone**, Pacific Ocean
81 J 4 **Clark Hill Reservoir**, GA, United States ⤴
79 I 9 **Clarksburg**, WV, United States
80 E 3 **Clarksdale**, MS, United States
80 G 1 **Clarksville**, TN, United States
83 E 10 **Clayton**, NM, United States
85 C 11 **Clear Lake**, CA, United States ⤴
85 D 9 **Clear Lake Reservoir**, CA, United States ⤴
81 J 8 **Clearwater**, FL, United States

84 G 7 **Clearwater**, United States ⤴
147 K 6 **Clermont**, QLD, Australia
45 J 7 **Clermont-Ferrand**, France
49 I 14 **Clervaux**, Luxembourg
81 I 2 **Cleveland**, TN, United States
79 I 7 **Cleveland**, OH, United States
80 E 5 **Clinton**, MS, United States
27 I 5 **Clipperton Fracture Zone**, Pacific Ocean
27 K 5 **Clipperton Island**, Pacific Ocean ⚑
147 J 5 **Cloncurry**, QLD, Australia
37 C 12 **Clonmel**, Ireland
83 E 11 **Clovis**, NM, United States
60 G 6 **Cluj-Napoca**, Romania
150 C 10 **Clutha**, New Zealand ⤴
37 F 9 **Clyde**, United Kingdom ⤴
85 C 10 **Coast Ranges**, CA/OR/WA, United States ▲
75 I 6 **Coats Island**, NU, Canada ⚑
89 M 9 **Coatzacoalcos**, Mexico
90 G 6 **Cobán**, Guatemala
146 H 3 **Cobourg Peninsula**, NT, Australia ▶
98 F 5 **Cochabamba**, Bolivia
119 D 14 **Cochin**, India
99 F 14 **Cochrane**, Chile
91 K 3 **Cockburn Town**, Turks Islands and Caicos
90 F 6 **Coco**, Honduras/Nicaragua ⤴
119 J 13 **Coco Channel**, India
31 I 4 **Cocos Basin**, Indian Ocean
31 I 5 **Cocos Islands**, Australia
27 I 5 **Cocos Ridge**, Pacific Ocean
150 B 11 **Codfish Island**, New Zealand ⚑
82 C 7 **Cody**, WY, United States
84 G 6 **Coeur d'Alene**, ID, United States
48 J 6 **Coevorden**, Netherlands
147 L 8 **Coffs Harbour**, NSW, Australia
44 G 7 **Cognac**, France
99 E 13 **Coihaique**, Chile
119 D 14 **Coimbatore**, India
40 F 5 **Coimbra**, Portugal
97 L 3 **Colatina**, Brazil
37 J 13 **Colchester**, United Kingdom
89 I 9 **Colima**, Mexico
36 D 7 **Coll**, United Kingdom ⚑
74 G 4 **Collinson Peninsula**, NU, Canada ▶
45 M 4 **Colmar**, France
52 B 8 **Cologne**, Germany
96 E 3 **Colombia**, South America
28 C 6 **Colombian Basin**, Atlantic Ocean
119 E 15 **Colombo**, Sri Lanka
99 H 10 **Colón**, Argentina
90 H 8 **Colón**, Panama
151 J 1 **Colonia**, Federated States of Micronesia
22 E 8 **Colorado**, South America ⤴
83 D 9 **Colorado**, United States
85 H 13 **Colorado**, United States ⤴
88 E 2 **Colorado**, Mexico ⤴
85 F 14 **Colorado Desert**, CA, United States ▲
22 D 4 **Colorado Plateau**, North America
83 D 9 **Colorado Springs**, CO, United States
80 G 2 **Columbia**, TN, United States
81 K 3 **Columbia**, SC, United States
83 I 9 **Columbia**, MO, United States
84 E 6 **Columbia**, United States ⤴
84 F 6 **Columbia Basin**, WA, United States
84 F 8 **Columbia Plateau**, ID/OR, United States ▲
80 F 4 **Columbus**, MS, United States
81 I 5 **Columbus**, GA, United States
78 G 9 **Columbus**, IN, United States
78 H 8 **Columbus**, OH, United States
82 G 8 **Columbus**, NE, United States
150 F 3 **Colville**, New Zealand
150 F 2 **Colville Channel**, New Zealand
56 C 5 **Como**, Italy
90 E 6 **Comayagua**, Honduras
99 E 9 **Combarbalá**, Chile
89 N 10 **Comitán de Domínguez**, Mexico
56 C 5 **Como**, Italy
99 F 13 **Comodoro Rivadavia**, Argentina
141 M 6 **Comoros**, Africa
45 J 3 **Compiègne**, France
136 F 6 **Conakry**, Guinea
99 E 11 **Concepción**, Chile
98 H 5 **Concepción**, Bolivia
98 I 7 **Concepción**, Paraguay
99 I 9 **Concepción del Uruguay**, Argentina

88 H 4 **Conchos**, Mexico ⤴
79 M 6 **Concord**, NH, United States
85 C 12 **Concord**, CA, United States
99 I 9 **Concordia**, Argentina
23 I 6 **Congo**, Africa ⤴
140 G 2 **Congo**, Congo/Democratic Republic of Congo ⤴
23 I 6 **Congo Basin**, Africa
28 I 7 **Congo Cone**, Atlantic Ocean
79 M 7 **Connecticut**, United States
30 E 9 **Conrad Rise**, Southern Ocean
60 J 8 **Constanţa**, Romania
136 H 1 **Constantine**, Algeria
74 F 6 **Contwoyto Lake**, NU, Canada ⤴
83 I 10 **Conway**, AR, United States
146 H 7 **Coober Pedy**, SA, Australia
151 L 9 **Cook Islands**, New Zealand
150 E 6 **Cook Strait**, New Zealand
80 H 2 **Cookeville**, TN, United States
147 K 4 **Cooktown**, QLD, Australia
146 F 8 **Coolgardie**, WA, Australia
91 I 1 **Cooper's Town**, The Bahamas
84 C 8 **Coos Bay**, OR, United States
69 C 14 **Copenhagen**, Denmark ♣ ▲
98 E 8 **Copiapó**, Chile
99 E 9 **Coquimbo**, Chile
60 H 8 **Corabia**, Romania
26 F 7 **Coral Sea**, Pacific Ocean
26 E 6 **Coral Sea Basin**, Pacific Ocean
81 I 5 **Cordele**, GA, United States
40 G 3 **Cordillera Cantabrica**, Spain ▲
123 K 4 **Cordillera Mountains**, Philippines ▲
90 G 8 **Cordillera Talamanca**, Costa Rica/Panama ▲
41 I 8 **Córdoba**, Spain
99 G 9 **Córdoba**, Argentina
89 L 9 **Córdoba**, Mexico
61 D 11 **Corfu**, Greece ⚑
80 F 3 **Corinth**, MS, United States
61 G 12 **Corinth Canal**, Greece
37 B 13 **Cork**, Ireland
108 C 6 **Çorlu**, Turkey
75 M 7 **Corner Brook**, NL, Canada
75 K 10 **Cornwall**, ON, Canada
96 F 1 **Coro**, Venezuela
150 F 3 **Coromandel Peninsula**, New Zealand ▶
90 E 4 **Corozal**, Belize
83 G 14 **Corpus Christi**, TX, United States
98 I 8 **Corrientes**, Argentina
45 N 9 **Corsica**, France ⚑
83 H 12 **Corsicana**, TX, United States
40 G 8 **Cortegana**, Spain
56 F 4 **Cortina d'Ampezzo**, Italy
108 J 7 **Çoruh**, Turkey ⤴
108 G 7 **Çorum**, Turkey
97 I 8 **Corumbá**, Brazil
84 C 8 **Corvallis**, OR, United States
40 A 8 **Corvo**, Portugal ⚑
45 J 5 **Cosne-cours-sur-Loire**, France
41 L 8 **Costa Blanca**, Spain ⣿
41 O 4 **Costa Brava**, Spain ⣿
41 I 10 **Costa del Sol**, Spain ⣿
90 G 8 **Costa Rica**, North America
40 H 1 **Costa Verde**, Spain
45 L 10 **Côte d'Azur**, France ⣿
136 F 6 **Côte d'Ivoire**, Africa
52 I 7 **Cottbus**, Germany
82 H 8 **Council Bluffs**, IA, United States
49 E 13 **Courcelles**, Belgium
49 E 14 **Couvin**, Belgium
37 H 13 **Coventry**, United Kingdom
40 G 5 **Covilhã**, Portugal
89 P 8 **Cozumel**, Mexico ⚑
82 C 8 **Craig**, CO, United States
60 G 8 **Craiova**, Romania
85 D 9 **Crater Lake**, OR, United States ⤴
147 L 2 **Crater Point**, Papua New Guinea ▶
37 I 14 **Crawley**, United Kingdom
56 D 6 **Cremona**, Italy
61 A 7 **Cres**, Croatia ⚑
85 C 9 **Crescent City**, CA, United States
82 H 8 **Creston**, IA, United States
80 H 6 **Crestview**, FL, United States
61 H 15 **Crete**, Greece ⚑
61 B 7 **Crikvenica**, Croatia
65 M 11 **Crimea**, Ukraine ▶
61 D 6 **Croatia**, Europe
150 C 9 **Cromwell**, New Zealand
91 J 3 **Crooked Island**, The Bahamas ⚑
57 J 12 **Crotone**, Italy

≈ Bay　✕ Channel　□ Country　▣ Dependent Territory　▲ Desert　⣿ Geographic Area　▶ Headland　⚑ Island　⚋ Island Group　⤴ Lake　▲ Mountain

Page	Grid	Name
37	I 14	Croydon, United Kingdom
30	G 7	Crozet Basin, Indian Ocean
23	J 9	Crozet Islands, Antarctica
30	E 8	Crozet Plateau, Indian Ocean
88	H 4	Cuauhtémoc, Mexico
90	H 3	Cuba, North America
23	I 7	Cubango, Africa
96	F 2	Cúcuta, Colombia
119	E 14	Cuddalore, Sri Lanka
119	E 13	Cuddapah, India
41	K 5	Cuenca, Spain
96	E 4	Cuenca, Ecuador
89	K 9	Cuernavaca, Mexico
97	I 7	Cuiabá, Brazil
88	H 6	Culiacán, Mexico
41	L 7	Cullera, Spain
80	G 3	Cullman, AL, United States
96	G 2	Cumaná, Venezuela
80	H 1	Cumberland, United States
79	J 9	Cumberland, MD, United States
75	J 4	Cumberland Peninsula, NU, Canada
81	I 2	Cumberland Plateau, United States
75	J 5	Cumberland Sound, NU, Canada
88	G 3	Cumpas, Mexico
140	F 7	Cunene, Angola
56	A 7	Cuneo, Italy
147	K 7	Cunnamulla, QLD, Australia
91	L 7	Curaçao, Netherlands Antilles
99	E 10	Curicó, Chile
97	J 9	Curitiba, Brazil
99	F 11	Cutral-Co, Argentina
119	G 11	Cuttack, India
31	J 6	Cuvier Plateau, Indian Ocean
52	D 5	Cuxhaven, Germany
96	F 7	Cuzco, Peru
61	H 13	Cyclades, Greece
108	F 11	Cyprus, Asia
64	E 7	Czech Republic, Europe
64	G 7	Częstochowa, Poland
64	F 5	Człuchów, Poland
60	I 8	Cǎlǎraşi, Romania

D

Page	Grid	Name
127	M 3	Da Hinggan Ling, China
122	H 5	Đa Lat, Vietnam
122	H 4	Đa Nẵng, Vietnam
127	K 7	Daba Shan, China
64	G 7	Dąbrowa Górnicza, Poland
119	I 9	Dacca, Bangladesh
123	J 4	Dagupan, Philippines
115	I 2	Dahūk, Iraq
41	J 7	Daimiel, Spain
131	G 11	Daiō-zaki, Japan
136	D 5	Dakar, Senegal
109	D 9	Dalaman, Turkey
127	K 4	Dalandzadgad, Mongolia
111	J 9	Dalbandin, Pakistan
147	L 7	Dalby, QLD, Australia
80	H 1	Dale Hollow Lake, TN, United States
127	J 9	Dali, China
127	N 5	Dalian, China
83	H 12	Dallas, TX, United States
84	D 7	Dalles, The, OR, United States
61	A 7	Dalmatia, Croatia
136	E 7	Daloa, Côte d'Ivoire
81	I 3	Dalton, GA, United States
146	H 4	Daly, NT, Australia
146	H 4	Daly Waters, NT, Australia
140	G 8	Damaraland, Namibia
114	H 3	Damascus, Syria
146	E 6	Dampier, WA, Australia
123	I 8	Danau Luar, Indonesia
122	F 7	Danau Toba, Indonesia
123	K 9	Danau Towuti, Indonesia
127	N 5	Dandong, China
90	E 5	Dangriga, Belize
23	I 3	Danube, Europe
127	N 3	Daqing, China
141	L 5	Dar es Salaam, Tanzania
119	G 9	Darbhanga, India
108	B 6	Dardanelles, Turkey
137	K 6	Darfur, Sudan
150	E 2	Dargaville, New Zealand
127	K 3	Darhan, Mongolia
23	N 8	Darling, Australia
37	H 10	Darlington, United Kingdom
53	D 9	Darmstadt, Germany
137	K 2	Darnah, Libya
41	K 4	Daroca, Spain
37	F 15	Dartmoor, United Kingdom
147	J 3	Daru, Papua New Guinea
146	G 3	Darwin, NT, Australia
115	L 4	Daryācheh-ye Bakhtegan, Iran
115	L 3	Daryācheh-ye Namak, Iran
115	N 4	Daryācheh-ye Sīstān, Iran
115	L 4	Daryācheh-ye Tashk, Iran
111	I 5	Dashkhovuz, Turkmenistan
111	I 11	Dasht, Pakistan
115	L 3	Dasht-e Kavīr, Iran
115	M 3	Dasht-e Lut, Iran
111	I 11	Dasht-i Margow, Afghanistan
127	L 5	Datong, China
65	J 3	Daugavpils, Latvia
74	G 9	Dauphin, MB, Canada
119	D 13	Davangere, India
123	L 6	Davao, Philippines
82	J 8	Davenport, IA, United States
90	G 8	David, Panama
30	E 6	Davie Ridge, Indian Ocean
33	P 4	Davis, Australia
75	J 4	Davis Strait, Canada/Greenland
53	E 13	Davos, Switzerland
115	N 8	Dawḩat Şawqirah, Oman
44	G 10	Dax, France
115	I 2	Dayr az Zawr, Syria
78	H 9	Dayton, OH, United States
81	K 7	Daytona Beach, FL, United States
83	I 12	De Ridder, LA, United States
114	G 4	Dead Sea, Israel/Jordan
85	F 13	Death Valley, CA, United States
64	G 9	Debrecen, Hungary
80	G 3	Decatur, AL, United States
81	I 4	Decatur, GA, United States
78	E 8	Decatur, IL, United States
23	L 5	Deccan Plateau, Asia
36	G 7	Dee, United Kingdom
111	J 9	Deh Shū, Afghanistan
118	E 7	Dehra Dun, India
49	C 11	Deinze, Belgium
60	G 5	Dej, Romania
30	E 8	Del Cano Rise, Indian Ocean
83	F 13	Del Rio, TX, United States
85	E 13	Delano, CA, United States
79	L 9	Delaware, United States
48	E 8	Delft, Netherlands
48	K 4	Delfzijl, Netherlands
118	D 8	Delhi, India
52	D 6	Delmenhorst, Germany
85	I 11	Delta, UT, United States
81	K 8	Deltona, FL, United States
28	E 6	Demerara Abyssal Plain, Atlantic Ocean
28	E 6	Demerara Plateau, Atlantic Ocean
83	C 12	Deming, NM, United States
140	G 3	Democratic Republic of Congo, Africa
80	G 5	Demopolis, AL, United States
48	F 5	Den Helder, Netherlands
111	K 6	Denau, Uzbekistan
49	E 11	Dendermonde, Belgium
146	D 7	Denham, WA, Australia
41	M 7	Denia, Spain
108	D 8	Denizli, Turkey
69	C 14	Denmark, Europe
32	C 10	Denmark Strait, Greenland/Iceland
123	I 10	Denpasar, Indonesia
83	G 11	Denton, TX, United States
147	L 3	D'Entrecasteaux Islands, Papua New Guinea
83	D 9	Denver, CO, United States
137	J 5	Dépression du Mourdi, Chad
83	D 9	Dera Ghazi Khan, Pakistan
111	L 9	Dera Ismail Khan, Pakistan
37	H 12	Derby, United Kingdom
61	C 7	Derventa, Bosnia-Herzegovina
82	H 8	Des Moines, IA, United States
99	F 9	Desaguadero, Argentina
40	D 9	Deserta Grande, Portugal
65	K 7	Desna, Ukraine
52	G 7	Dessau, Germany
52	D 7	Detmold, Germany
78	H 7	Detroit, MI, United States
60	G 6	Deva, Romania
48	I 7	Deventer, Netherlands
82	G 5	Devil's Lake, ND, United States
82	D 6	Devil's Tower, WY, United States
74	H 3	Devon Island, NU, Canada
147	J 11	Devonport, TAS, Australia
119	D 10	Dewas, India
115	K 3	Dezfūl, Iran
115	J 10	Dhamār, Yemen
118	E 8	Dhangadhi, India
118	G 8	Dharan, Nepal
119	C 12	Dharwad, India
119	C 10	Dhule, India
31	J 7	Diamantina Deep, Indian Ocean
31	J 7	Diamantina Fracture Zone, Indian Ocean
118	J 8	Dibrugarh, India
82	E 6	Dickinson, ND, United States
108	J 8	Dicle Baraji, Turkey
61	I 10	Didymoteicho, Greece
30	G 4	Diego Garcia, United Kingdom
49	I 14	Diekirch, Luxembourg
44	H 2	Dieppe, France
48	I 8	Dieren, Netherlands
49	G 11	Diest, Belgium
137	I 6	Diffa, Niger
45	L 9	Digne-les-Baines, France
45	J 8	Digoin, France
45	K 5	Dijon, France
123	L 10	Dili, East Timor
119	H 9	Dinajpur, Bangladesh
44	H 4	Dinan, France
49	F 13	Dinant, Belgium
119	D 14	Dindigul, India
37	A 13	Dingle Bay, Ireland
123	K 6	Dipolog, Philippines
137	N 6	Dirē Dawa, Ethiopia
146	D 7	Dirk Hartog Island, WA, Australia
147	K 8	Dirranbandi, QLD, Australia
29	I 10	Discovery Seamounts, Atlantic Ocean
79	K 9	District of Columbia, United States
109	J 9	Diyarbakir, Turkey
136	F 5	Djenné, Mali
137	N 6	Djibouti, Africa
137	N 6	Djibouti, Djibouti
23	I 3	Dnieper, Europe
65	K 9	Dniester, Moldova/Ukraine
65	M 8	Dniprodzerzhyns'k, Ukraine
65	M 8	Dnipropetrovs'k, Ukraine
65	K 10	Dnistrov'ky Lyman, Ukraine
61	D 7	Doboj, Bosnia-Herzegovina
61	J 8	Dobrich, Bulgaria
61	I 13	Dodecanese, Greece
83	F 10	Dodge City, KS, United States
141	K 4	Dodoma, Tanzania
48	I 8	Doetinchem, Netherlands
131	H 8	Dōgo, Japan
136	G 5	Dogondoutchi, Niger
108	L 7	Doğubeyazit, Turkey
115	L 6	Doha, Qatar
48	I 4	Dokkum, Netherlands
28	F 6	Doldrums Fracture Zone, Atlantic Ocean
45	L 6	Dôle, France
56	E 5	Dolomites, Italy
99	I 10	Dolores, Uruguay
69	C 10	Dombås, Norway
98	E 8	Domeyko, Chile
91	O 5	Dominica, North America
91	L 4	Dominican Republic, North America
61	F 12	Domokos, Greece
23	J 3	Don, Europe
37	H 11	Doncaster, United Kingdom
37	C 10	Donegal, Ireland
37	B 10	Donegal Bay, Ireland
65	O 9	Donets'k, Ukraine
146	F 4	Dongara, WA, Australia
127	J 9	Dongchuan, China
127	M 10	Dongguan, China
137	L 4	Dongola, Sudan
127	N 7	Dongtai, China
127	L 8	Dongting Hu, China
127	M 6	Dongying, China
41	K 1	Donostia-San Sebastián, Spain
44	G 8	Dordogne, France
49	F 9	Dordrecht, Netherlands
53	C 13	Dornbirn, Austria
68	F 8	Dorotea, Sweden
52	C 7	Dortmund, Germany
40	H 9	Dos Hermanas, Spain
136	G 6	Dosso, Niger
80	H 5	Dothan, AL, United States
136	H 7	Douala, Cameroon
37	F 10	Douglas, United Kingdom
85	K 16	Douglas, AZ, United States
97	I 8	Dourados, Brazil
37	J 14	Dover, United Kingdom
79	L 9	Dover, DE, United States
131	D 11	Dōzen, Japan
29	C 11	Drake Passage, Atlantic Ocean/Pacific Ocean
23	I 8	Drakensberg, Africa
61	H 10	Drama, Greece
69	C 11	Drammen, Norway
52	H 8	Dresden, Germany
60	F 7	Drobeta-Turnu Severin, Romania
32	B 9	Dronning Ingrid Land, Greenland
75	L 9	Drummondville, QC, Canada
74	H 10	Dryden, ON, Canada
115	M 6	Dubai, United Arab Emirates
65	K 10	Dubăsari, Moldova
65	K 9	Dubăsari Vodokhranilishche, Moldova
74	G 6	Dubawnt Lake, NU, Canada
147	K 8	Dubbo, NSW, Australia
37	D 11	Dublin, Ireland
81	J 5	Dublin, GA, United States
61	B 8	Dubrovnik, Croatia
82	I 7	Dubuque, IA, United States
49	I 15	Dudelange, Luxembourg
37	H 12	Dudley, United Kingdom
40	H 4	Duero, Spain
61	B 8	Dugi Otok, Croatia
52	B 8	Duisburg, Germany
99	G 9	Dulce, Argentina
61	I 8	Dulovo, Bulgaria
82	I 6	Duluth, MN, United States
83	E 10	Dumas, TX, United States
33	O 7	Dumont d'Urville, France
119	J 14	Duncan Passage, India
36	G 5	Duncansby Head, United Kingdom
37	D 11	Dundalk, Ireland
36	G 8	Dundee, United Kingdom
150	C 10	Dunedin, New Zealand
37	J 14	Dungeness, United Kingdom
127	O 4	Dunhua, China
45	I 1	Dunkerque, France
79	J 7	Dunkirk, NY, United States
61	G 9	Dupnista, Bulgaria
89	I 6	Durango, Mexico
141	J 10	Durban, South Africa
52	B 8	Düren, Germany
119	F 10	Durg, India
119	H 10	Durgapur, India
37	H 10	Durham, United Kingdom
81	L 2	Durham, NC, United States
61	D 10	Durrës, Albania
150	E 6	D'Urville Island, New Zealand
111	K 6	Dushanbe, Tajikistan
52	B 8	Düsseldorf, Germany
127	K 9	Duyun, China
80	F 2	Dyersburg, TN, United States
111	K 6	Dzhizak, Uzbekistan
52	H 6	Eberswalde-Finow, Germany
130	H 4	Ebetsu, Japan
151	N 5	Ebon, Marshall Islands
41	K 3	Ebro, Spain
136	G 1	Ech Chélif, Algeria
49	I 11	Echt, Luxembourg
40	H 8	Écija, Spain
96	D 4	Ecuador, South America
48	H 8	Ede, Netherlands
37	G 10	Eden, United Kingdom
36	G 8	Edinburgh, United Kingdom
65	J 9	Edineţ, Moldova
108	C 5	Edirne, Turkey
74	E 9	Edmonton, AB, Canada
56	D 5	Edolo, Italy
33	L 6	Edward VII Peninsula, Antarctica
48	J 4	Eemshaven, Netherlands
150	H 10	Éfaté, Vanuatu
64	G 9	Eger, Hungary
69	A 12	Egersund, Norway
49	F 12	Eghezée, Belgium
108	E 8	Eğirdir Gölü, Turkey
137	K 3	Egypt, Africa
48	J 8	Eibergen, Netherlands
53	C 13	Eiger, Switzerland
36	D 7	Eigg, United Kingdom
146	E 5	Eighty Mile Beach, WA, Australia
49	H 10	Eindhoven, Netherlands
28	E 3	Eirik Ridge, Atlantic Ocean
52	E 8	Eisenach, Germany
41	N 7	Eivissa, Spain
127	J 5	Ejin Qi, China
88	H 3	El Barreal, Mexico
85	F 15	El Cajon, CA, United States
85	G 15	El Centro, CA, United States
88	H 6	El Dorado, Mexico
137	L 2	El Giza, Egypt
136	G 2	El Goléa, Algeria
40	A 11	El Hierro, Spain
137	L 2	El Mansûra, Egypt
137	L 3	El Minya, Egypt
137	L 6	El Obeid, Sudan
83	D 12	El Paso, TX, United States
90	H 8	El Porvenir, Panama
40	G 9	El Puerto de Santa María, Spain
89	K 9	El Rosario Reserve, Mexico
90	E 6	El Salvador, North America
88	H 3	El Sueco, Mexico
41	N 4	El Vendrell, Spain
114	G 4	Elat, Israel
151	K 1	Elato, Federated States of Micronesia
108	J 8	Elazığ, Turkey
52	F 5	Elbe, Czech Republic/Germany
64	G 5	Elbląg, Poland
104	B 8	Elbrus, Russia
115	K 2	Elburz Mountains, Iran
41	L 8	Elche, Spain
98	J 8	Eldorado, Argentina
141	K 3	Eldoret, Kenya
141	K 1	Elemi Triangle, Kenya
83	C 11	Elephant Butte Reservoir, NM, United States
33	I 1	Elephant Island, Antarctica
91	I 2	Eleuthera, The Bahamas
78	F 7	Elgin, IL, United States
104	B 8	Elista, Russia
79	L 8	Elizabeth, NJ, United States
81	N 1	Elizabeth City, NC, United States
78	G 10	Elizabethtown, KY, United States
78	G 7	Elkhart, IN, United States
84	E 6	Ellensburg, WA, United States
74	H 1	Ellesmere Island, NU, Canada
146	H 9	Elliston, SA, Australia
33	J 4	Ellsworth Land, Antarctica
33	K 4	Ellsworth Mountains, Antarctica
79	K 7	Elmira, NY, United States
52	E 5	Elmshorn, Germany
85	I 15	Eloy, AZ, United States
27	I 9	Eltanin Fracture Zone, Pacific Ocean
40	G 7	Elvas, Portugal
85	G 11	Ely, NV, United States
79	I 8	Elyria, OH, United States
41	K 6	Embalse de Alarcón, Spain
40	H 4	Embalse de Almendra, Spain
41	J 5	Embalse de Buendía, Spain
41	J 5	Embalse de Cíjara, Spain
40	H 6	Embalse de García Sola, Spain
96	H 2	Embalse de Guri, Venezuela
41	I 9	Embalse de Iznajar, Spain

▲▲ Mountain Range　　National Capital　　Ocean　　Physical Feature　　Polar Base　　River　　Sea　　★ Special Feature　　State Capital　　Underwater Feature

≈ Bay ✕ Channel ▣ Country ▭ Dependent Territory ▲ Desert ⠿ Geographic Area ▶ Headland ⌕ Island ⌕⌕ Island Group ⌣ Lake ▲ Mountain

160

82　D 7　Gillette, WY, United States
85　D 12　Gilroy, CA, United States
108　I 6　Giresun, Turkey
41　O 3　Girona, Spain
44　G 7　Gironde, France
150　G 4　Gisborne, New Zealand
56　G 8　Giulianova, Italy
60　I 8　Giurgiu, Romania
74　G 5　Gjoa Haven, NU, Canada
69　D 11　Gjøvik, Norway
75　M 8　Glace Bay, NS, Canada
147　L 6　Gladstone, QLD, Australia
69　D 11　Glåma, Norway
36　F 8　Glasgow, United Kingdom
104　D 6　Glazov, Russia
85　I 15　Glendale, AZ, United States
79　L 6　Glens Falls, NY, United States
64　F 7　Gliwice, Poland
85　J 15　Globe, AZ, United States
37　G 13　Gloucester, United Kingdom
119　C 12　Goa, India
28　H 3　Goban Spur, Atlantic Ocean
23　M 4　Gobi Desert, Asia
127　K 4　Gobi Desert, Mongolia
119　E 11　Godavari, India
99　F 10　Godoy Cruz, Argentina
49　D 9　Goes, Netherlands
97　J 7　Goiânia, Brazil
108　B 6　Gökçeada, Turkey
109　C 9　Gökova Körfezi, Turkey
69　C 11　Gol, Norway
147　L 7　Gold Coast, QLD, Australia
150　E 6　Golden Bay, New Zealand
81　M 2　Goldsboro, NC, United States
137　I 2　Golfe de Gabès, Tunisia
44　F 3　Golfe de St-Malo, France
45　J 11　Golfe du Lion, France
40　G 9　Golfo de Cádiz, Spain
90　G 9　Golfo de Chiriqui, Panama
90　F 5　Golfo de Honduras, Honduras
90　H 8　Golfo de los Mosquitos, Panama
99　G 13　Golfo de San Jorge, Argentina
41　N 4　Golfo de Sant Jordi, Spain
89　M 10　Golfo de Tehuantepec, Mexico
41　M 7　Golfo de Valencia, Spain
57　G 10　Golfo di Gaeta, Italy
90　G 8　Golfo Dulce, Costa Rica
29　E 10　Golfo San Matias, Argentina
141　J 3　Goma, Democratic Republic of Congo
89　I 5　Gómez Palacio, Mexico
91　K 4　Gonaïves, Haiti
115　M 2　Gonbad-e Kavus, Iran
137　M 6　Gonder, Ethiopia
119　E 10　Gondia, India
48　J 7　Goor, Netherlands
85　D 9　Goose Lake, CA, United States
104　G 10　Gora Belukha, Russia
118　F 8　Gorakhpur, India
61　D 8　Goražde, Bosnia-Herzegovina
150　C 10　Gore, New Zealand
115　M 2　Gorgân, Iran
109　L 5　Gori, Georgia
109　N 7　Goris, Armenia
52　I 8　Görlitz, Germany
61　E 8　Gornji Milanovac, Serbia and Montenegro
147　K 2　Goroka, Papua New Guinea
123　K 8　Gorontalo, Indonesia
111　I 4　Gory Mugodzhary, Kazakhstan
104　H 6　Goryna Putorana, Russia
64　E 5　Gorzów Wielkopolski, Poland
52　E 7　Goslar, Germany
61　B 7　Gospić, Croatia
61　E 9　Gostivar, Macedonia
52　E 8　Gotha, Germany
69　D 13　Gothenburg, Sweden
69　G 13　Gotland, Sweden
131　A 14　Gotō-rettō, Japan
61　G 10　Gotse Delchev, Bulgaria
52　E 7　Göttingen, Germany
48　F 8　Gouda, Netherlands
29　G 10　Gough Fracture Zone, Atlantic Ocean
29　H 10　Gough Island, Atlantic Ocean
147　K 9　Goulburn, NSW, Australia
146　H 3　Goulburn Islands, NT, Australia
97　K 8　Governador Valadares, Brazil
127　I 4　Govi Altayn Nuruu, Mongolia
119　F 9　Govind Ballash Pant Sagar, India
98　H 8　Goya, Argentina
57　G 16　Gozo, Malta

40　D 10　Graciosa, Spain
40　B 9　Graciosa, Portugal
61　D 7　Gradačac, Bosnia-Herzegovina
36　F 7　Grampian Mountains, United Kingdom
40　B 11　Gran Canaria, Spain
98　G 7　Gran Chaco, Argentina/Paraguay
41　J 9　Granada, Spain
90　F 7　Granada, Nicaragua
91　I 1　Grand Bahama, The Bahamas
28　E 4　Grand Banks of Newfoundland, Atlantic Ocean
85　H 13　Grand Canyon, AZ, United States
90　H 4　Grand Cayman, Cayman Islands
137　I 5　Grand Erg de Bilma, Niger
136　G 2　Grand Erg Occidental, Algeria/Tunisia
136　H 2　Grand Erg Oriental, Algeria/Tunisia
82　G 5　Grand Forks, ND, United States
83　C 9　Grand Junction, CO, United States
78　G 6　Grand Rapids, MI, United States
82　H 5　Grand Rapids, MN, United States
82　B 7　Grand Teton, WY, United States
98　G 6　Grande, Bolivia
90　F 7　Grande, Nicaragua
141　M 6　Grande Comore, Comoros
74　E 8　Grande Prairie, AB, Canada
82　C 6　Granite Peak, MT, United States
83　C 11　Grants, NM, United States
85　C 9　Grants Pass, OR, United States
44　G 4　Granville, France
53　J 12　Graz, Austria
91　I 1　Great Abaco, The Bahamas
146　G 9　Great Australian Bight, SA, Australia
90　H 2　Great Bahaman Bank, The Bahamas
150　F 2　Great Barrier Island, New Zealand
147　J 3　Great Barrier Reef, QLD, Australia
85　F 11　Great Basin, NV, United States
74　E 6　Great Bear Lake, NT, Canada
83　F 9　Great Bend, KS, United States
119　J 15　Great Channel, India
119　J 13　Great Coco Island, India
23　N 8　Great Dividing Range, Australia
150　E 1　Great Exhibition Bay, New Zealand
82　B 5　Great Falls, MT, United States
91　J 3　Great Inagua Island, The Bahamas
28　G 5　Great Meteor Tablemount, Atlantic Ocean
119　K 15　Great Nicobar, India
37　I 12　Great Ouse, United Kingdom
23　M 4　Great Plain of China, Asia
22　D 4　Great Plains, North America
23　I 4　Great Rift Valley, Africa
85　I 10　Great Salt Lake, UT, United States
85　H 11　Great Salt Lake Desert, UT, United States
137　J 3　Great Sand Sea, Egypt/Libya
146　F 6　Great Sandy Desert, WA, Australia
74　F 7　Great Slave Lake, NT, Canada
146　G 7　Great Victoria Desert, SA/WA, Australia
37　K 12　Great Yarmouth, United Kingdom
141　J 8　Great Zimbabwe, Zimbabwe
91　I 4　Greater Antilles, Caribbean Sea
61　G 11　Greece, Europe
82　D 8　Greeley, CO, United States
85　J 11　Green, United States
78　F 5　Green Bay, WI, United States
85　J 11　Green River, UT, United States
32　C 8　Greenland, Denmark
32　D 9　Greenland Plain, Arctic Ocean
32　D 9　Greenland Sea, Arctic Ocean
81　L 2　Greensboro, NC, United States
80　E 4　Greenville, MS, United States
81　J 3　Greenville, SC, United States
81　M 2　Greenville, NC, United States
83　H 11　Greenville, TX, United States
80　E 4　Greenwood, MS, United States
81　J 3　Greenwood, SC, United States
147　J 5　Gregory Range, QLD, Australia
52　H 4　Greifswald, Germany
80　F 3　Grenada, MS, United States
91　N 7　Grenada, North America

91　O 7　Grenadines, The, St Vincent and the Grenadines
45　L 8　Grenoble, France
49　J 15　Grevenmacher, Luxembourg
150　D 7　Grey, New Zealand
150　D 7　Greymouth, New Zealand
81　I 4　Griffin, GA, United States
147　K 9　Griffith, NSW, Australia
37　I 11　Grimsby, United Kingdom
48　J 4　Groningen, Netherlands
147　I 4　Groote Eylandt, NT, Australia
56　E 8　Grosseto, Italy
53　G 12　Grossglockner, Austria
151　O 10　Groupe Actéon, French Polynesia
104　B 8　Groznyy, Russia
64　G 5　Grudziądz, Poland
41　J 5　Guadalajara, Spain
89　I 8　Guadalajara, Mexico
150　I 8　Guadalcanal, Solomon Islands
41　I 8　Guadalquivir, Spain
27　J 3　Guadalupe, Pacific Ocean
89　K 5　Guadalupe, Mexico
83　D 12　Guadalupe Peak, TX, United States
91　O 5　Guadeloupe, France
41　I 7　Guadiana, Spain
41　J 9　Guadix, Spain
27　L 9　Guafo Fracture Zone, Pacific Ocean
99　I 9　Gualeguaychú, Argentina
151　L 5　Guam, United States
88　H 5　Guamúchil, Mexico
89　J 8　Guanajuato, Mexico
127　K 7　Guangyuan, China
127　M 10　Guangzhou, China
91　J 4　Guantánamo, Cuba
91　J 4　Guantánamo Bay, United States
40　G 5　Guarda, Portugal
88　G 5　Guasave, Mexico
90　D 6　Guatemala, Guatemala
90　E 5　Guatemala, North America
27　L 5　Guatemala Basin, Pacific Ocean
96　F 3　Guaviare, Colombia
96　D 6　Guayaquil, Ecuador
88　F 4　Guaymas, Mexico
115　I 4　Gudayyidat 'Ar'ar, Saudi Arabia
119　E 12　Gudivada, India
136　E 2　Guelmine, Morocco
45　I 7　Guéret, France
37　G 16　Guernsey, United Kingdom
88　E 4　Guerrero Negro, Mexico
151　L 4　Guguan, Northern Mariana Islands
22　E 6　Guiana Highlands, South America
37　I 14　Guildford, United Kingdom
127　L 9　Guilin, China
136　D 6　Guinea, Africa
28　I 7　Guinea Basin, Atlantic Ocean
136　D 5　Guinea-Bissau, Africa
127　K 9　Guiyang, China
111　M 8　Gujranwala, Pakistan
111　M 8　Gujrat, Pakistan
119　D 12　Gulbarga, India
30　E 2　Gulf of Aden, Indian Ocean
84　J 6　Gulf of Alaska, AL, United States
32　D 3　Gulf of Anadyr, Russia
114　G 5　Gulf of Aqaba, Asia
74　G 4　Gulf of Boothia, NU, Canada
69　G 10　Gulf of Bothnia, Finland
88　E 2　Gulf of California, Mexico
147　I 4　Gulf of Carpentaria, QLD, Australia
61　F 12　Gulf of Corinth, Greece
91　I 8　Gulf of Darién, Panama/Colombia
104　C 4　Gulf of Finland, Europe
64　G 4　Gulf of Gdańsk, Poland/Russia
56　C 7　Gulf of Genoa, Italy
22　t c　Gulf of Guinea, Africa
119　A 9　Gulf of Kachchh, India
119　B 10　Gulf of Khambhat, India
79　N 6　Gulf of Maine, United States
119　D 15　Gulf of Mannar, India/Sri Lanka
22　D 4　Gulf of Mexico, Mexico/United States

57　G 11　Gulf of Naples, Italy
115　M 6　Gulf of Oman, Iran/Oman
96　D 2　Gulf of Panama, Colombia/Panama
147　K 2　Gulf of Papua, Papua New Guinea
65　I 2　Gulf of Riga, Estonia/Latvia
57　H 11　Gulf of Salerno, Italy
137　J 2　Gulf of Sirte, Libya
75　M 8　Gulf of St Lawrence, Canada
137　L 3　Gulf of Suez, Egypt
57　J 12　Gulf of Taranto, Italy
122　F 5　Gulf of Thailand, Cambodia/Thailand
122　H 4　Gulf of Tongking, China/Vietnam
56　F 6　Gulf of Venice, Italy/Slovenia
22　D 4　Gulf-Atlantic Coastal Plain, North America
80　F 6　Gulfport, MS, United States
111　K 6　Gulistan, Uzbekistan
109　C 9　Güllük Körfezi, Turkey
141　J 2　Gulu, Uganda
119　D 9　Guna, India
32　C 9　Gunnbjørn Fjeld, Greenland
119　D 12　Guntakal, India
80　H 3　Guntersville Lake, AL, United States
119　E 12　Guntur, India
141　K 7　Gurué, Mozambique
108　I 8　Gürün, Turkey
97　J 6　Gurupi, Brazil
136　H 6　Gusau, Nigeria
64　H 4　Gusev, Russia
131　J 16　Gushikawa, Japan
52　D 7　Gütersloh, Germany
118　I 8　Guwahati, India
96　H 2　Guyana, South America
111　K 6　Guzar, Uzbekistan
111　J 11　Gwadar, Pakistan
119　D 9　Gwalior, India
141　J 7　Gweru, Zimbabwe
127　I 7　Gyaring Hu, China
104　H 7　Gydanskiy Peninsula, Russia
147　L 7　Gympie, QLD, Australia
64　F 9　Győr, Hungary
109　L 6　Gyumri, Armenia

H

122　H 3　Ha Long Bay, Vietnam
48　J 7　Haaksbergen, Netherlands
65　I 1　Haapsalu, Estonia
48　F 7　Haarlem, Netherlands
131　I 12　Hachijō-jima, Japan
130　H 6　Hachinohe, Japan
119　B 15　Hadhdhunmathi Atoll, Maldives
115　K 10　Hadramawt, Yemen
37　G 9　Hadrian's Wall, United Kingdom
115　J 5　Ḥafar al Bāţin, Saudi Arabia
151　K 5　Hagåtña, Guam
52　C 8　Hagen, Germany
79　K 9　Hagerstown, MD, United States
48　E 8　Hague, The, Netherlands
122　H 3　Hai Phong, Vietnam
127　N 5　Haicheng, China
114　G 3　Haifa, Israel
127　L 11　Haikou, China
115　I 5　Ḥā'il, Saudi Arabia
127　M 2　Hailar, China
68　I 8　Hailuoto, Finland
127　L 11　Hainan, China
127　L 11　Hainan Strait, China
74　C 6　Haines Junction, YT, Canada
91　K 4　Haiti, North America
115　J 9　Ḥajjah, Yemen
130　H 5　Hakodate, Japan
137　M 4　Halaib Triangle, Egypt/Sudan
69　D 12　Halden, Norway
118　E 7　Haldwani, India
150　B 11　Halfmoon Bay, New Zealand
37　H 11　Halifax, United Kingdom
75　M 9　Halifax, NS, Canada
151　L 1　Hall Islands, Federated States of Micronesia
52　G 7　Halle, Germany
49　E 12　Halle, Belgium
53　H 12　Hallein, Austria
33　L 2　Halley, United Kingdom

146　G 5　Halls Creek, WA, Australia
123　L 8　Halmahera, Indonesia
69　D 14　Halmstad, Sweden
131　C 12　Hamada, Japan
115　K 3　Hamadān, Iran
114　H 2　Ḥamāh, Syria
131　G 11　Hamamatsu, Japan
69　D 11　Hamar, Norway
119　F 16　Hambantota, Sri Lanka
52　E 5　Hamburg, Germany
69　I 11　Hämeenlinna, Finland
52　D 7　Hameln, Germany
146　D 6　Hamersley Range, WA, Australia
127　O 5　Hamhŭng, North Korea
127　I 4　Hami, China
37　F 9　Hamilton, United Kingdom
150　F 4　Hamilton, New Zealand
80　G 3　Hamilton, AL, United States
28　E 3　Hamilton Bank, Atlantic Ocean
52　C 7　Hamm, Germany
150　D 10　Hampden, New Zealand
79　L 10　Hampton, VI, United States
115　N 4　Hāmūn Helmand, Iran
115　N 5　Hāmūn-e Jaz Mūriān, Iran
53　D 9　Hanau, Germany
127　M 6　Handan, China
127　I 3　Hangayn Nuruu, Mongolia
127　N 8　Hangzhou, China
69　I 11　Hanko, Finland
82　I 8　Hannibal, MO, United States
52　E 6　Hannover, Germany
69　E 14　Hanöbukten, Sweden
122　H 3　Hanoi, Vietnam
127　K 7　Hanzhong, China
119　H 10　Haora, India
75　L 7　Happy Valley Goose Bay, NL, Canada
127　I 3　Har Nuur, Mongolia
127　I 3　Har Us Nuur, Mongolia
115　K 6　Haraḍh, Saudi Arabia
141　J 7　Harare, Zimbabwe
127　N 3　Harbin, China
48　J 5　Haren, Netherlands
137　N 6　Härer, Ethiopia
137　N 6　Hargeysa, Somalia
118　E 7　Haridwar, India
64　F 8　Harířov, Czech Republic
48　G 5　Harlingen, Netherlands
83　G 14　Harlingen, TX, United States
84　E 8　Harney Basin, OR, United States
85　E 9　Harney Lake, OR, United States
69　F 9　Härnösand, Sweden
115　I 6　Ḥarrat Rahaṭ, Saudi Arabia
75　J 9　Harricana, Canada
36　D 6　Harris, United Kingdom
79　K 8　Harrisburg, PA, United States
79　J 10　Harrisonburg, VI, United States
37　H 11　Harrogate, United Kingdom
69　F 5　Harstad, Norway
79　M 7　Hartford, CT, United States
31　J 7　Hartog Ridge, Southern Ocean
81　J 3　Hartwell Lake, GA, United States
37　J 13　Harwich, United Kingdom
49　G 11　Hasselt, Belgium
37　J 14　Hastings, United Kingdom
150　G 5　Hastings, New Zealand
122　F 6　Hat Yai, Thailand
60　G 7　Haţeg, Romania
118　D 8　Hathras, India
28　D 5　Hatteras Abyssal Plain, Atlantic Ocean
81　O 2　Hatteras Island, NC, United States
80　F 6　Hattiesburg, MS, United States
28　G 3　Hatton Ridge, Atlantic Ocean
69　A 11　Haugesund, Norway
69　B 11　Haukeligrend, Norway
69　J 10　Haukivesi, Finland
150　F 3　Hauraki Gulf, New Zealand
90　G 3　Havana, Cuba
81　M 3　Havelock, NC, United States
82　C 5　Havre, MT, United States
85　A 16　Hawaii, United States
85　A 14　Hawaii, HI, United States
85　B 14　Hawaiian Islands, HI, United States
26　G 4　Hawaiian Ridge, Pacific Ocean
150　E 5　Hawera, New Zealand
150　G 5　Hawke Bay, New Zealand
85　E 12　Hawthorne, NV, United States

▲▲ Mountain Range　■ National Capital　◎ Ocean　Physical Feature　▬ Polar Base　River　≈ Sea　✱ Special Feature　State Capital　■ Underwater Feature

≈ Bay   ⊒ Channel   □ Country   ▣ Dependent Territory   ▲ Desert   ⋮⋮ Geographic Area   ▶ Headland   🏝 Island   ⚌ Island Group   🝪 Lake   ▲ Mountain

91 J4 Jamaica Channel, Caribbean Sea
122 G8 Jambi, Indonesia
82 G6 James, ND, United States
75 J8 James Bay, ON, Canada
33 I2 James Ross Island, Antarctica
79 J7 Jamestown, NY, United States
82 G6 Jamestown, ND, United States
118 C6 Jammu, India
118 D6 Jammu and Kashmir, Asia
119 B10 Jamnagar, India
119 G10 Jamshedpur, India
32 D9 Jan Mayen, Norway
78 E6 Janesville, WI, United States
130 G7 Japan, Asia
26 E3 Japan Trench, Pacific Ocean
96 G4 Japurá, Brazil/Columbia
22 E6 Japurá, South America
91 J4 Jari, Brazil
26 H5 Jarvis Island, Pacific Ocean
33 J2 Jason Peninsula, Antarctica
64 F8 Jastrzębie-Zdrój, Poland
119 F9 Jaunpur, India
122 G10 Java, Indonesia
31 J4 Java Ridge, Indian Ocean
123 I9 Java Sea, Indonesia
31 K5 Java Trench, Indian Ocean
137 O7 Jawhar, Somalia
123 O8 Jayapura, Indonesia
123 M8 Jazirah Doberai, Indonesia
114 H7 Jeddah, Saudi Arabia
83 I9 Jefferson City, MO, United States
65 I3 Jēkabpils, Latvia
64 E7 Jelenia Góra, Poland
65 I3 Jelgava, Latvia
123 I10 Jember, Indonesia
52 F8 Jena, Germany
91 J4 Jérémie, Haiti
40 G9 Jerez de la Frontera, Spain
114 G4 Jericho, Israel
37 H16 Jersey, United Kingdom
79 L8 Jersey City, NJ, United States
114 G4 Jerusalem, Israel
119 H10 Jessore, Bangladesh
119 E9 Jhansi, India
119 L8 Jhelum, Pakistan
127 O3 Jiamusi, China
127 M9 Ji'an, China
127 M10 Jiangmen, China
127 L6 Jiaozuo, China
127 N7 Jiaxing, China
115 M8 Jiddat al Ḩarāsīs, Oman
64 E8 Jihlava, Czech Republic
127 O4 Jilin, China
137 M7 Jima, Ethiopia
89 I5 Jiménez, Mexico
127 M6 Jinan, China
127 J5 Jinchang, China
127 M8 Jingdezhen, China
127 M8 Jingmen, China
127 L8 Jingsha, China
127 L8 Jingzhou, China
127 N8 Jinhua, China
127 L5 Jining, China
127 M6 Jining, China
141 K3 Jinja, Uganda
90 F7 Jinotepe, Nicaragua
127 N5 Jinzhou, China
115 N5 Jiroft, Iran
127 M8 Jiujiang, China
127 O3 Jixi, China
115 I9 Jīzān, Saudi Arabia
97 M5 João Pessoa, Brazil
118 C8 Jodhpur, India
69 K9 Joensuu, Finland
131 G9 Jōetsu, Japan
141 I9 Johannesburg, South Africa
36 G5 John o'Groats, United Kingdom
81 J1 Johnson City, TN, United States
26 H4 Johnston Atoll, Pacific Ocean
122 G7 Johor Bahru, Malaysia
97 J9 Joinville, Brazil
33 I2 Joinville Island, Antarctica
68 G7 Jokkmokk, Sweden
78 F7 Joliet, IL, United States
75 K9 Joliette, QC, Canada
75 K9 Jolo, Philippines
65 I4 Jonava, Lithuania
83 J10 Jonesboro, AR, United States
69 E13 Jönköping, Sweden
75 K9 Jonquière, QC, Canada
83 H10 Joplin, MO, United States

114 H4 Jordan, Asia
136 H6 Jos, Nigeria
146 H4 Joseph Bonaparte Gulf, WA, Australia
48 H5 Joure, Netherlands
27 M8 Juan Fernandez Islands, Pacific Ocean
97 L6 Juàzeiro, Brazil
97 L5 Juázeiro do Norte, Brazil
137 L7 Juba, Sudan
137 N8 Juba, Somalia
41 K6 Júcar, Spain
89 M10 Juchitán, Mexico
90 F7 Juigalpa, Nicaragua
97 K8 Juiz de Fora, Brazil
68 G6 Jukkasjarvi, Sweden
96 G7 Juliaca, Peru
119 B10 Junagadh, India
84 K6 Juneau, AL, United States
99 H10 Junín, Argentina
36 E8 Jura, United Kingdom
53 B12 Jura, France/Switzerland
65 I3 Jūrmala, Latvia
96 G5 Juruá, Brazil
90 F6 Juticalpa, Honduras
69 C14 Jutland, Denmark
69 I10 Jyväskylä, Finland

K

126 E5 K2, China/Pakistan
68 I5 Kaamanen, Finland
111 K8 Kabul, Afghanistan
141 I6 Kabwe, Zambia
141 J7 Kadoma, Zimbabwe
136 H6 Kaduna, Nigeria
136 E5 Kaédi, Mauritania
137 I6 Kaélé, Cameroon
127 O5 Kaesŏng, North Korea
114 H4 Kâf, Saudi Arabia
141 I7 Kafue, Zambia
131 B15 Kagoshima, Japan
85 C15 Kahoolawe, HI, United States
109 H9 Kahramanmaraş, Turkey
150 D8 Kaiapoi, New Zealand
127 M7 Kaifeng, China
150 E7 Kaikoura, New Zealand
150 E7 Kaikoura Peninsula, New Zealand
127 K9 Kaili, China
85 C15 Kailua, HI, United States
33 N4 Kaiser Wilhelm II Land, Antarctica
53 C10 Kaiserslautern, Germany
150 C11 Kaitangata, New Zealand
127 J10 Kaiyuan, China
68 I8 Kajaani, Finland
146 H3 Kakadu National Park, NT, Australia
65 M9 Kakhovs'ke Vodoskhovyshche, Ukraine
119 F12 Kakinada, India
23 I7 Kalahari Desert, Africa
61 G10 Kalamaria, Greece
61 F13 Kalamata, Greece
78 G7 Kalamazoo, MI, United States
108 F7 Kalecik, Turkey
146 F8 Kalgoorlie, WA, Australia
123 I8 Kalimantan, Indonesia
64 G4 Kaliningrad, Russia
64 H4 Kaliningrad, Russia
82 A5 Kalispell, MT, United States
64 F6 Kalisz, Poland
69 F14 Kalmar, Sweden
104 C6 Kaluga, Russia
61 I11 Kalymnos, Greece
61 I13 Kalymnos, Greece
131 H10 Kamakura, Japan
105 O8 Kamchatka Peninsula, Russia
104 F7 Kamensk-Ural'skiy, Russia
141 I5 Kamina, Democratic Republic of Congo
74 D9 Kamloops, BC, Canada
141 J3 Kampala, Uganda
48 H6 Kampen, Netherlands
122 G5 Kâmpóng Cham, Cambodia
122 G5 Kâmpóng Saôm, Cambodia
130 G4 Kamui-misaki, Japan
65 J9 Kam"yanets'-Podil's'kyy, Ukraine

140 H4 Kananga, Democratic Republic of Congo
131 F10 Kanazawa, Japan
119 E13 Kanchipuram, India
111 K9 Kandahār, Afghanistan
104 D4 Kandalaksha, Russia
119 E15 Kandy, Sri Lanka
28 E5 Kane Fracture Zone, Atlantic Ocean
85 B15 Kaneohe, HI, United States
147 I9 Kangaroo Island, SA, Australia
75 J4 Kangeeak Point, NU, Canada
127 O4 Kanggye, North Korea
78 F8 Kankakee, IL, United States
136 E6 Kankan, Guinea
136 H6 Kano, Nigeria
118 E8 Kanpur, India
83 F9 Kansas, United States
83 G9 Kansas, KS, United States
83 H9 Kansas City, MO, United States
104 H9 Kansk, Russia
151 K8 Kanton, Kiribati
141 I9 Kanye, Botswana
127 N10 Kaohsiung, Taiwan
136 D5 Kaolack, Senegal
52 H4 Kap Arkona, Germany
32 D9 Kap Brewster, Greenland
32 B10 Kap Farvel, Greenland
109 N7 Kapan, Armenia
111 M4 Kapchagayskoye Vodokhranilishche, Kazakhstan
64 F10 Kaposvár, Hungary
123 I8 Kapuas, Indonesia
75 J9 Kapuskasing, ON, Canada
32 F7 Kara Sea, Arctic Ocean
111 L5 Kara-Balta, Kyrgyzstan
108 F6 Karabük, Turkey
111 I3 Karabutak, Kazakhstan
111 K11 Karachi, Pakistan
111 L5 Karaganda, Kazakhstan
115 L2 Karaj, Iran
111 M5 Karakol, Kyrgyzstan
118 D5 Karakoram Range, Asia
23 J4 Karakum Desert, Asia
109 F9 Karaman, Turkey
126 G3 Karamay, China
150 D7 Karamea Bight, New Zealand
115 J3 Karbalā', Iraq
61 F11 Karditsa, Greece
119 B14 Kardiva Channel, Maldives
61 H10 Kärdzhali, Bulgaria
68 H5 Karesuando, Finland
68 I5 Karigasniemi, Finland
119 E11 Karimnagar, India
147 K1 Karkar Island, Papua New Guinea
61 B6 Karlovac, Croatia
61 H9 Karlovo, Bulgaria
64 D7 Karlovy Vary, Czech Republic
69 E12 Karlskoga, Sweden
69 E14 Karlskrona, Sweden
53 D10 Karlsruhe, Germany
69 E12 Karlstad, Sweden
118 D7 Karnal, India
61 J14 Karpathos, Greece
61 J14 Karpathos, Greece
61 F12 Karpenisi, Greece
108 L6 Kars, Turkey
111 J6 Karshi, Uzbekistan
61 H12 Karystos, Greece
109 D10 Kaş, Turkey
23 I6 Kasai, Africa
141 J5 Kasama, Zambia
141 J3 Kasese, Uganda
115 L3 Kāshān, Iran
126 E4 Kashi, China
131 I9 Kashima-nada, Japan
61 J14 Kasos, Greece
137 M5 Kassala, Sudan
52 E8 Kassel, Germany
108 G6 Kastamonu, Turkey
61 F11 Kastoria, Greece
131 G11 Kasugai, Japan
131 I9 Kasumiga-ura, Japan
61 F11 Katerini, Greece
146 H4 Katherine, NT, Australia
119 B10 Kathiawar Peninsula, India
118 G8 Kathmandu, Nepal
119 H9 Katihar, India
64 F7 Katowice, Poland
136 H6 Katsina, Nigeria

111 K6 Kattakūrgan, Uzbekistan
69 D13 Kattegat, Denmark
85 B14 Kauai, HI, United States
65 I4 Kaunas, Lithuania
61 F10 Kavadarci, Macedonia
61 H10 Kavala, Greece
147 L1 Kavieng, Papua New Guinea
131 H10 Kawasaki, Japan
136 E5 Kayes, Mali
108 G8 Kayseri, Turkey
111 J3 Kazakhstan, Asia
104 D7 Kazan', Russia
61 H9 Kazanluk, Bulgaria
109 L4 Kazbek, Georgia
61 H13 Kea, Greece
82 F8 Kearney, NE, United States
108 J8 Keban Baraji, Turkey
68 G6 Kebnekaise, Sweden
137 N7 K'ebri Dehar, Ethiopia
64 G10 Kecskemét, Hungary
65 I4 Kėdainiai, Lithuania
140 G9 Keetmanshoop, Namibia
61 E12 Kefallonia, Greece
68 B6 Keflavik, Iceland
69 I9 Keitele, Finland
147 I9 Keith, SA, Australia
131 J14 Kekeroma-jima, Japan
64 G9 Kékes, Hungary
122 F7 Kelang, Malaysia
108 I7 Kelkit, Turkey
74 D9 Kelowna, BC, Canada
84 D7 Kelso, WA, United States
108 I7 Kemah, Turkey
104 H9 Kemerovo, Russia
68 I7 Kemi, Finland
68 I6 Kemijärvi, Finland
68 I6 Kemijoki, Finland
33 O2 Kemp Land, Antarctica
53 E12 Kempten, Germany
81 L10 Kendall, FL, United States
123 K9 Kendari, Indonesia
111 I5 Keneurgench, Turkmenistan
84 E7 Kennewick, WA, United States
74 H10 Kenora, ON, Canada
78 G10 Kentucky, United States
78 H10 Kentucky, United States
80 G1 Kentucky Lake, TN, United States
122 F3 Kentung, Myanmar
141 K2 Kenya, Africa
119 B14 Kepulauan Aru, Indonesia
123 N9 Kepulauan Banggai, Indonesia
123 K8 Kepulauan Batu, Indonesia
122 F8 Kepulauan Kai, Indonesia
123 M9 Kepulauan Kangean, Indonesia
123 I9 Kepulauan Lingga, Indonesia
122 G8 Kepulauan Natuna, Indonesia
122 H7 Kepulauan Talaud, Indonesia
123 L7 Kepulauan Tanimbar, Indonesia
123 M10 Kepulauan Togian, Indonesia
123 K8 Kepulauan Tukangbesi, Indonesia
61 G13 Keratea, Greece
65 N10 Kerch, Ukraine
108 F5 Kerempe Burnu, Turkey
30 G8 Kerguelen Islands, France
30 G8 Kerguelen Plateau, Indian Ocean
141 K3 Kericho, Kenya
61 E11 Kerkyra, Greece
26 G8 Kermadec Trench, Pacific Ocean
115 M4 Kermān, Iran
115 K3 Kermanshah, Iran
83 G13 Kerrville, TX, United States
108 F11 Keryneia, Cyprus
69 I10 Keuruu, Finland
78 F3 Keweenaw Bay, MI, United States
81 K11 Key Largo, FL, United States
81 L10 Key Largo, FL, United States
81 K11 Key West, FL, United States
105 M10 Khabarovsk, Russia
111 K10 Khairpur, Pakistan
115 M9 Khalīj al Ḩalānīyāt, Oman
115 N8 Khalīj Maşirah, Oman
115 I8 Khamīs, Saudi Arabia
119 D10 Khandwa, India
119 H10 Kharagpur, India
65 N7 Kharkiv, Ukraine
137 L5 Khartoum, Sudan
137 L5 Khashuri, Georgia
61 H9 Khaskovo, Bulgaria
105 I6 Khatanga, Russia

140 H11 Khayelitsha, South Africa
65 L10 Kherson, Ukraine
65 J8 Khmel'nyts'kyy, Ukraine
115 L3 Khomeynīshahr, Iran
122 G4 Khon Kaen, Thailand
115 K3 Khorramābād, Iran
111 L7 Khorugh, Tajikistan
136 F2 Khouribga, Morocco
105 L7 Khrebet Cherskogo, Russia
105 L9 Khrebet Dzhugdzhur, Russia
105 M7 Khrebet Kolymskiy, Russia
111 K6 Khujand, Tajikistan
119 I10 Khulna, Bangladesh
111 L8 Khushab, Pakistan
115 J1 Khvoy, Iran
111 L8 Khyber Pass, Afghanistan/Pakistan
61 E10 Kičevo, Macedonia
136 G4 Kidal, Mali
37 G13 Kidderminster, United Kingdom
52 E4 Kiel, Germany
64 G7 Kielce, Poland
52 E4 Kieler Bay, Germany
65 K7 Kiev, Ukraine
141 J3 Kigali, Rwanda
141 J4 Kigoma, Tanzania
85 C15 Kihei, HI, United States
131 E12 Kii-suidō, Japan
131 K14 Kikai, Japan
131 K14 Kikai-jima, Japan
61 E6 Kikinda, Serbia and Montenegro
140 G4 Kikwit, Democratic Republic of Congo
151 N4 Kili Island, Marshall Islands
141 K4 Kilimanjaro, Tanzania
37 C12 Kilkenny, Ireland
37 B13 Killarney, Ireland
83 G12 Killeen, TX, United States
37 F9 Kilmarnock, United Kingdom
141 K5 Kilosa, Tanzania
147 L2 Kimbe, Papua New Guinea
141 I10 Kimberley, South Africa
146 F4 Kimberley Plateau, WA, Australia
127 O4 Kimch'aek, North Korea
74 F9 Kindersley, SK, Canada
136 D6 Kindia, Guinea
33 I2 King George Island, Antarctica
147 J10 King Island, TAS, Australia
146 F4 King Leopold Ranges, WA, Australia
33 J5 King Peninsula, Antarctica
146 F4 King Sound, WA, Australia
32 C8 King Wilhelm Land, Greenland
74 G5 King William Island, NU, Canada
37 J12 King's Lynn, United Kingdom
85 H14 Kingman, AZ, United States
26 H5 Kingman Reef, Pacific Ocean
79 L7 Kingston, NY, United States
90 I4 Kingston, Jamaica
37 I11 Kingston upon Hull, United Kingdom
91 O6 Kingstown, St Vincent and the Grenadines
83 G14 Kingsville, TX, United States
130 I8 Kinka-san, Japan
49 H10 Kinrooi, Belgium
140 G4 Kinshasa, Democratic Republic of Congo
37 E9 Kintyre, United Kingdom
111 L5 Kirghiz Range, Kazakhstan/Kyrgyzstan
151 J8 Kiribati, Pacific Ocean
109 H10 Kirikhan, Turkey
108 G7 Kirikkale, Turkey
68 J4 Kirkenes, Norway
75 J9 Kirkland Lake, ON, Canada
108 C5 Kirklareli, Turkey
82 I8 Kirksville, MO, United States
115 J2 Kirkūk, Iraq
36 G5 Kirkwall, United Kingdom
104 D6 Kirov, Russia
65 K9 Kirovohrad, Ukraine
68 G6 Kiruna, Sweden
141 I3 Kisangani, Democratic Republic of Congo
131 I10 Kisarazu, Japan
104 G9 Kiselevsk, Russia
131 E12 Kishiwada, Japan
137 O8 Kismaayo, Somalia
131 G10 Kiso-sanmyaku, Japan
81 K8 Kissimmee, FL, United States

▲▲ Mountain Range　　🏛 National Capital　　⌇ Ocean　　Physical Feature　　▬ Polar Base　　🏞 River　　🌊 Sea　　★ Special Feature　　⌂ State Capital　　◼ Underwater Feature

141 K 3 Kisumu, Kenya
131 B 13 Kita-Kyūshū, Japan
141 K 2 Kitale, Kenya
130 I 3 Kitami, Japan
75 J 10 Kitchener, ON, Canada
68 I 6 Kitinen, Finland
68 I 6 Kittilä, Finland
141 I 6 Kitwe, Zambia
108 G 7 Kizilirmak, Turkey
109 J 9 Kiziltepe, Turkey
64 E 7 Kladno, Czech Republic
53 I 13 Klagenfurt, Austria
64 H 4 Klaipėda, Lithuania
85 D 9 Klamath Falls, OR, United States
61 C 7 Ključ, Bosnia-Herzegovina
53 E 13 Klosters, Switzerland
61 B 8 Knin, Croatia
53 I 12 Knittelfeld, Austria
49 C 10 Knokke-Heist, Belgium
151 N 4 Knox, Marshall Islands
81 J 2 Knoxville, TN, United States
32 C 7 Knud Rasmussen Land, Greenland
131 E 11 Kōbe, Japan
53 C 9 Koblenz, Germany
131 D 13 Kōchi, Japan
84 I 6 Kodiak, AL, United States
84 J 6 Kodiak Island, AL, United States
131 H 10 Kōfu, Japan
65 J 1 Kohtla- Järve, Estonia
111 L 6 Kokand, Uzbekistan
111 L 7 Kokcha, Afghanistan
69 H 9 Kokkola, Finland
111 K 2 Kokshetau, Kazakhstan
104 E 4 Kola Peninsula, Russia
68 H 6 Kolari, Finland
136 D 5 Kolda, Senegal
119 C 12 Kolhapur, India
119 A 15 Kolhumadulu Atoll, Maldives
136 E 5 Kolokani, Mali
104 C 6 Kolomna, Russia
151 M 1 Kolonia, Federated States of Micronesia
141 I 5 Kolwezi, Democratic Republic of Congo
105 M 6 Kolyma, Russia
131 F 11 Komaki, Japan
131 F 10 Komatsu, Japan
61 H 10 Komotini, Greece
105 M 9 Komsomol'sk-na-Amure, Russia
111 K 7 Kondūz, Afghanistan
32 C 9 Kong Christian IX Land, Greenland
32 C 8 Kong Frederik IX Land, Greenland
32 D 8 Kong Frederik VIII Land, Greenland
69 C 11 Kongsberg, Norway
69 D 11 Kongsvinger, Norway
126 E 5 Kongur Shan, China
64 F 6 Konin, Poland
61 E 11 Konitsa, Greece
61 D 8 Konjic, Bosnia-Herzegovina
68 G 5 Könkämäeno, Sweden
65 L 7 Konotop, Ukraine
53 D 12 Konstanz, Germany
109 F 9 Konya, Turkey
60 A 6 Koper, Slovenia
115 M 1 Kopet Dag, Iran
61 E 10 Korçë, Albania
127 N 5 Korea Bay, North Korea
127 O 7 Korea Strait, South Korea
61 G 13 Korinthos, Greece
130 I 8 Kōriyama, Japan
126 G 4 Korla, China
53 K 11 Korneuburg, Austria
141 L 4 Korogwe, Tanzania
151 I 1 Koror, Palau
65 K 7 Korosten', Ukraine
49 C 11 Kortrijk, Belgium
105 O 6 Koryakskiy Khrebet, Russia
131 B 14 Koshiki-kaikyō, Japan
61 E 9 Kosovska Mitrovica, Serbia and Montenegro
151 M 2 Kosrae, Federated States of Micronesia
111 J 2 Kostanay, Kazakhstan
137 L 6 Kosti, Sudan
65 N 8 Kostyantynivka, Ukraine
64 F 4 Koszalin, Poland
119 D 9 Kota, India
122 G 6 Kota Bharu, Malaysia

123 J 7 Kota Kinabalu, Malaysia
69 J 11 Kotka, Finland
61 D 9 Kotor, Serbia and Montenegro
137 I 6 Koumra, Chad
97 J 3 Kourou, French Guiana
136 F 6 Koutiala, Mali
69 J 11 Kouvola, Finland
65 I 7 Kovel, Ukraine
61 F 11 Kozani, Greece
131 H 11 Kōzu-shima, Japan
122 F 6 Krabi, Thailand
61 E 8 Kragujevac, Serbia and Montenegro
64 G 7 Kraków, Poland
61 E 8 Kraljevo, Serbia and Montenegro
65 N 8 Kramators'k, Ukraine
60 A 6 Kranj, Slovenia
104 B 7 Krasnodar, Russia
104 H 9 Krasnoyarsk, Russia
65 O 8 Krasnyy Luch, Ukraine
52 B 8 Krefeld, Germany
65 M 8 Kremenchuk, Ukraine
65 L 8 Kremenchuts'ka Vodoskhovyshche, Ukraine
53 J 11 Krems an der Donau, Austria
119 D 12 Krishna, India
119 H 9 Krishnanagar, India
119 D 13 Krishnaraja Sagara, India
69 B 12 Kristiansand, Norway
69 E 14 Kristianstad, Sweden
69 C 9 Kristiansund, Norway
61 A 7 Krk, Croatia
60 B 6 Krško, Greece
61 F 8 Kruševac, Serbia and Montenegro
65 M 9 Kryvyy Rih, Ukraine
122 G 7 Kuala Lumpur, Malaysia
122 G 7 Kuala Terengganu, Malaysia
122 G 7 Kuantan, Malaysia
122 H 8 Kuching, Malaysia
131 B 16 Kuchino-shima, Japan
119 A 15 Kuda Huvadu Channel, Maldives
115 J 2 Kūh-e Chehel Chashmeh, Iran
115 J 2 Kūh-e Ḩājī Ebrāhīm, Iraq
115 M 4 Kūh-e Ilazārān, Iran
68 J 7 Kuhmo, Finland
140 G 6 Kuito, Angola
61 E 9 Kukës, Albania
118 I 3 Kula Kangri, Bhutan
108 F 8 Kulu, Turkey
131 B 13 Kumamoto, Japan
61 F 9 Kumanovo, Macedonia
136 F 7 Kumasi, Ghana
136 H 7 Kumba, Cameroon
119 E 14 Kumbakonam, India
131 J 16 Kume-jima, Japan
52 G 5 Kummerower See, Germany
137 I 6 Kumo, Nigeria
123 J 6 Kundat, Malaysia
140 F 7 Kunene, Namibia
69 D 13 Kungsbacka, Sweden
23 K 4 Kunlun Shan, Asia
127 J 2 Kunming, China
146 G 4 Kununurra, WA, Australia
69 J 9 Kuopio, Finland
123 L 10 Kupang, Indonesia
109 M 6 Kür, Azerbaijan/Turkey
131 D 12 Kurashiki, Japan
109 L 9 Kurdistan, Turkey
131 D 12 Kure, Japan
104 E 8 Kurgan, Russia
105 N 10 Kuril Islands, Russia
26 E 2 Kuril Trench, Pacific Ocean
119 D 12 Kurnool, India
131 B 15 Kuro-shima, Japan
104 C 6 Kursk, Russia
126 G 4 Kuruktag, China
131 B 13 Kurume, Japan
110 H 5 Kuryk, Kazakhstan
108 B 8 Kusadasi Körfezi, Turkey
130 J 3 Kushiro, Japan
130 J 3 Kussharo-ko, Japan
108 D 7 Kütahya, Turkey
97 J 10 K'ut'aisi, Georgia
61 C 7 Kutina, Croatia
75 K 6 Kuujjuaq, QC, Canada
68 J 7 Kuusamo, Finland
115 K 4 Kuwait, Asia
115 K 5 Kuwait, Kuwait
104 C 7 Kuznetsk, Russia
68 F 4 Kvaløya, Norway
151 M 3 Kwajalein, Marshall Islands
127 O 6 Kwangju, South Korea
61 H 12 Kymi, Greece

131 E 10 Kyōga-misaki, Japan ▶
131 F 11 Kyōto, Japan
111 L 5 Kyrgyzstan, Asia □
61 G 14 Kythira, Greece
61 H 13 Kythnos, Greece
131 B 13 Kyūshū, Japan
61 F 9 Kyustendil, Bulgaria
65 K 7 Kyyivs'ke Vodoskhovyshche, Ukraine
104 H 10 Kyzyl, Russia
111 J 5 Kyzylkum Desert, Uzbekistan ▲
111 J 4 Kyzylorda, Kazakhstan

L

98 G 8 La Banda, Argentina
44 F 5 La Baule-Escoublac, France
41 J 8 La Carolina, Spain
90 F 5 La Ceiba, Honduras
78 E 6 La Crosse, WI, United States
40 B 11 La Gomera, Spain
84 F 7 La Grande, OR, United States
83 E 10 La Junta, CO, United States
99 E 9 La Ligua, Chile
49 E 12 La Louvière, Belgium
57 C 10 La Maddalena, Italy
40 A 10 La Palma, Spain
91 I 8 La Palma, Panama
98 F 5 La Paz, Bolivia
88 G 6 La Paz, Mexico
130 G 1 La Pérouse Strait, Japan
99 I 10 La Plata, Argentina
98 F 8 La Rioja, Argentina
44 G 7 La Rochelle, France
44 G 7 La Roche-sur-Yon, France
41 K 7 La Roda, Spain
91 L 4 La Romana, Dominican Republic
99 E 9 La Serena, Chile
41 N 3 La Seu, Spain
41 J 7 La Solana, Spain
56 C 7 La Spezia, Italy
75 K 9 La Tuque, QC, Canada
41 L 8 La Unión, Spain
136 E 3 Laâyoune, Western Sahara ■
136 E 5 Labé, Guinea
75 K 6 Labrador, NL/QC, Canada
32 B 9 Labrador Basin, Arctic Ocean
32 B 9 Labrador Sea, Arctic Ocean
75 K 7 Lac Caniapiscau, QC, Canada
136 E 6 Lac de Buyo, Côte d'Ivoire
136 F 6 Lac de Kossou, Côte d'Ivoire
137 I 7 Lac de Ladgo, Cameroon
136 E 5 Lac de Manantali, Mali
53 B 13 Lac de Neuchâtel, Switzerland
136 F 5 Lac Faguibine, Mali
140 G 3 Lac Mai-Ndombe, Democratic Republic of Congo
75 K 8 Lac Mistassini, QC, Canada
136 F 5 Lac Niangay, Mali
140 G 3 Lac Ntomba, Democratic Republic of Congo
140 G 3 Lac Onangue, Gabon
75 K 9 Lac Saint-Jean, QC, Canada
74 H 9 Lac Seul, ON, Canada
141 I 5 Lac Upemba, Democratic Republic of Congo/Uganda
30 G 2 Laccadive Islands, India
147 J 9 Lachlan, NSW, Australia
79 M 6 Laconia, NH, United States
60 J 7 Lacul Razim, Romania
60 J 7 Lacul Sinoie, Romania
118 D 6 Ladakh, India/Pakistan
78 D 4 Ladysmith, WI, United States
147 K 2 Lae, Papua New Guinea
151 M 3 Lae, Marshall Islands
78 F 8 Lafayette, IN, United States
83 J 13 Lafayette, LA, United States
97 J 10 Lages, Brazil
99 E 14 Lago Argentino, Argentina
99 E 13 Lago Buenos Aires, Argentina
141 J 6 Lago de Cahora Bassa, Mozambique
90 E 5 Lago de Izabal, Guatemala
90 F 7 Lago de Managua, Nicaragua
90 F 7 Lago de Nicaragua, Nicaragua
98 F 5 Lago de Poopó, Bolivia
99 F 16 Lago Fagnano, Argentina
90 H 8 Lago Gatún, Panama

99 E 13 Lago General Carrera, Chile
99 E 12 Lago Llanquihué, Chile
99 G 9 Lago Mar Chiquita, Argentina
99 F 13 Lago Musters, Argentina
99 E 12 Lago Nahuel Huapi, Argentina
99 E 14 Lago San Martin, Argentina
97 J 10 Lagoa dos Patos, Brazil
97 I 11 Lagoa Mangueira, Brazil
97 I 11 Lagoa Mirim, Brazil/Uruguay
40 E 9 Lagos, Portugal
136 G 7 Lagos, Nigeria
89 J 7 Lagos de Moreno, Mexico
90 G 6 Laguna Caratasca, Honduras
89 J 8 Laguna de Chapala, Mexico
90 G 8 Laguna de Chiriqui, Panama
90 G 7 Laguna de Perlas, Nicaragua
89 N 9 Laguna de Terminos, Mexico
89 L 6 Laguna Madre, Mexico
98 F 4 Laguna Rogaguado, Bolivia
98 G 4 Laguna San Luis, Bolivia
98 E 6 Lagunas, Chile
85 C 15 Lahaina, HI, United States
111 M 9 Lahore, Pakistan
69 I 10 Lahti, Finland
137 N 6 Lake Abbe, Djibouti/Ethiopia
85 E 9 Lake Abert, OR, United States
141 J 2 Lake Albert, Democratic Republic of Congo/Uganda
146 G 7 Lake Amadeus, NT, Australia
146 G 4 Lake Argyle, WA, Australia
74 F 7 Lake Athabasca, AB/SK, Canada
146 E 8 Lake Austin, WA, Australia
105 I 10 Lake Baikal, Russia
111 M 4 Lake Balkhash, Kazakhstan
146 F 8 Lake Ballard, WA, Australia
141 J 5 Lake Bangweulu, Zambia
146 E 8 Lake Barlee, WA, Australia
147 I 8 Lake Blanche, SA, Australia
57 E 9 Lake Bolsena, Italy
79 M 5 Lake Champlain, Canada/United States
83 I 13 Lake Charles, LA, United States
84 E 5 Lake Chelan, WA, United States
81 J 7 Lake City, FL, United States
56 C 5 Lake Como, Italy
53 D 12 Lake Constance, Europe
146 F 8 Lake Cowan, WA, Australia
146 F 6 Lake Disappointment, WA, Australia
37 G 10 Lake District, United Kingdom
141 J 3 Lake Edward, Democratic Republic of Congo/Uganda
82 B 5 Lake Elwell, MT, United States
79 I 7 Lake Erie, Canada/United States
147 I 7 Lake Eyre North, SA, Australia
147 I 8 Lake Eyre South, SA, Australia
147 I 8 Lake Frome, SA, Australia
147 I 8 Lake Gairdner, SA, Australia
56 D 5 Lake Garda, Italy
53 B 13 Lake Geneva, Italy/Switzerland
81 K 7 Lake George, FL, United States
146 G 5 Lake Gregory, WA, Australia
85 H 14 Lake Havasu City, AZ, United States
150 C 9 Lake Hawea, New Zealand
78 H 5 Lake Huron, Canada/United States
141 I 7 Lake Kariba, Zambia/Zimbabwe
127 P 3 Lake Khanka, China/Russia
82 A 5 Lake Koocanusa, MT, United States
104 C 4 Lake Ladoga, Russia
146 F 8 Lake Lefroy, WA, Australia
146 G 6 Lake Mackay, WA, Australia
146 D 7 Lake MacLeod, WA, Australia
56 B 5 Lake Maggiore, Italy/Switzerland
150 B 10 Lake Manapouri, New Zealand
74 H 9 Lake Manitoba, MB, Canada
96 F 2 Lake Maracaibo, Venezuela
81 K 4 Lake Marion, SC, United States
80 H 4 Lake Martin, AL, United States
85 H 13 Lake Mead, AZ/NV, United States
78 F 6 Lake Michigan, Canada/United States
146 F 8 Lake Minigwal, WA, Australia
146 E 8 Lake Moore, WA, Australia
81 L 4 Lake Moultrie, SC, United States
147 J 2 Lake Murray, Papua New Guinea
81 K 3 Lake Murray, SC, United States

141 J 5 Lake Mweru, Democratic Republic of Congo/Zambia
137 L 4 Lake Nasser, Egypt
146 G 6 Lake Neale, NT, Australia
75 I 9 Lake Nipigon, ON, Canada
75 J 10 Lake Nipissing, ON, Canada
146 E 8 Lake Noondie, WA, Australia
81 K 2 Lake Norman, NC, United States
137 L 4 Lake Nuba, Egypt/Sudan
141 K 6 Lake Nyasa, Africa
82 F 6 Lake Oahe, SD, United States
81 J 4 Lake Oconee, GA, United States
83 I 9 Lake of the Ozarks, MO, United States
82 H 5 Lake of the Woods, Canada/United States
150 C 9 Lake Ohau, New Zealand
61 E 10 Lake Ohrid, Albania/Macedonia
81 K 9 Lake Okeechobee, FL, United States
104 D 5 Lake Onega, Russia
79 K 6 Lake Ontario, Canada/United States
83 I 11 Lake Ouachita, AR, United States
84 F 8 Lake Owyhee, OR, United States
65 J 1 Lake Peipus, Estonia/Russia
84 G 6 Lake Pend Oreille, ID, United States
85 J 13 Lake Powell, AZ/UT, United States
61 E 10 Lake Prespa, Europe
150 C 9 Lake Pukaki, New Zealand
150 F 4 Lake Rotorua, New Zealand
82 E 5 Lake Sakakawea, ND, United States
61 D 9 Lake Scutari, Albania/Serbia and Montenegro
81 I 6 Lake Seminole, GA, United States
81 I 3 Lake Sidney Lanier, GA, United States
81 J 4 Lake Sinclair, GA, United States
78 H 7 Lake St Clair, Canada/United States
78 E 3 Lake Superior, Canada/United States
85 E 11 Lake Tahoe, CA/NV, United States
141 J 4 Lake Tanganyika, Africa
150 G 4 Lake Tarawera, New Zealand
150 F 4 Lake Taupo, New Zealand
150 B 10 Lake Te Anau, New Zealand
150 C 8 Lake Tekapo, New Zealand
96 G 7 Lake Titicaca, Bolivia/Peru
147 I 8 Lake Torrens, SA, Australia
56 F 8 Lake Trasimeno, Italy
141 K 2 Lake Turkana, Kenya
115 J 1 Lake Urmia, Iran
108 L 8 Lake Van, Turkey
141 J 3 Lake Victoria, Africa
136 G 6 Lake Volta, Ghana
150 F 6 Lake Wairarapa, New Zealand
150 B 10 Lake Wakatipu, New Zealand
150 C 9 Lake Wanaka, New Zealand
146 F 1 Lake Wells, WA, Australia
146 G 6 Lake White, WA, Australia
78 F 5 Lake Winnebago, WI, United States
82 H 5 Lake Winnibigoshish, MN, United States
74 H 9 Lake Winnipeg, MB, Canada
74 G 9 Lake Winnipegosis, MB, Canada
81 K 8 Lakeland, FL, United States
83 D 9 Lakewood, CO, United States
68 I 3 Lakse Fjord, Norway
68 H 4 Lakselv, Norway
137 M 6 Lalibela, Ethiopia
40 F 2 Lalín, Spain
57 I 13 Lamezia, Italy
61 F 12 Lamia, Greece
85 C 15 Lanai, HI, United States
127 I 8 Lancang, China
79 K 8 Lancaster, PA, United States
85 F 14 Lancaster, CA, United States
74 G 4 Lancaster Sound, NU, Canada
53 C 10 Landau in der Pfalz, Germany
37 G 15 Land's End, United Kingdom
53 G 11 Landshut, Germany
127 K 5 Lang Shan, China
68 B 6 Langjökull, Iceland ◇
45 K 5 Langres, France
109 O 8 Länkäran, Azerbaijan

≈ Bay   ✕ Channel   □ Country   ▣ Dependent Territory   ▲ Desert   ▦ Geographic Area   ▶ Headland   🏝 Island   🏝 Island Group   ⬩ Lake   ▲ Mountain

78	G 7	Lansing, MI, United States 🏛
40	C 10	Lanzarote, Spain 🏔
127	J 6	Lanzhou, China
45	J 3	Laon, France
122	G 3	Laos, Asia 🔲
69	J 10	Lappeenranta, Finland
68	G 6	Lappland, Finland ⊞
32	F 6	Laptev Sea, Arctic Ocean 🌊
69	H 9	Lapua, Finland
57	G 9	L'Aquila, Italy
82	D 8	Laramie, WY, United States
82	D 7	Laramie Mountains, MT/WY, United States 🔺
83	G 14	Laredo, TX, United States
81	J 9	Largo, FL, United States
61	F 11	Larisa, Greece
111	K 10	Larkana, Pakistan
108	F 11	Lárnaka, Cyprus
33	J 2	Larsen Ice Shelf, Antarctica ◇
69	C 12	Larvik, Norway
83	D 12	Las Cruces, NM, United States
99	F 9	Las Heras, Argentina
98	H 7	Las Lomitas, Argentina
40	C 11	Las Palmas de Gran Canaria, Spain
90	H 9	Las Tablas, Panama
91	I 3	Las Tunas, Cuba
85	G 13	Las Vegas, NV, United States
122	F 3	Lashio, Myanmar
61	C 9	Lastovo, Croatia 🏔
33	J 3	Lataday Island, Antarctica 🏔
57	F 10	Latina, Italy
119	D 11	Latur, India
65	I 3	Latvia, Europe 🔲
147	K 11	Launceston, TAS, Australia
80	F 5	Laurel, MS, United States
75	K 9	Laurentian Mountains, NL/QC, Canada 🔺
57	I 11	Lauria, Italy
33	J 1	Laurie Island, Argentina 🏔
81	L 3	Laurinburg, NC, United States
53	B 13	Lausanne, Switzerland
123	J 9	Laut, Indonesia 🏔
44	G 5	Laval, France
33	P 2	Law Promontory, Antarctica ▶
80	G 2	Lawrenceburg, TN, United States
83	G 11	Lawton, OK, United States
29	I 12	Lazarev Sea, Atlantic Ocean 🌊
89	J 9	Lázaro Cárdenas, Mexico
44	H 3	Le Havre, France
44	H 5	Le Mans, France
79	M 6	Lebanon, NH, United States
84	C 8	Lebanon, OR, United States
114	H 3	Lebanon, Asia 🔲
40	G 9	Lebrija, Spain
99	E 11	Lebu, Chile
57	K 11	Lecce, Italy
37	B 13	Lee, Ireland 🔊
37	H 11	Leeds, United Kingdom
48	H 4	Leeuwarden, Netherlands
91	N 4	Leeward Islands, Caribbean Sea 🏖
61	E 12	Lefkada, Greece
61	E 12	Lefkada, Greece 🏔
61	E 11	Lefkimmi, Greece
123	K 5	Legaspi, Philippines
64	F 6	Legnica, Poland
37	H 12	Leicester, United Kingdom
147	I 5	Leichhardt, QLD, Australia 🔊
48	F 8	Leiden, Netherlands
52	E 7	Leine, Germany 🔊
52	G 8	Leipzig, Germany
40	E 6	Leiria, Portugal
69	A 11	Leirvik, Norway
69	E 11	Leksand, Sweden
48	H 7	Lelystad, Netherlands
108	F 11	Lemesos, Cyprus
105	K 5	Lena, Russia 🔊
33	N 7	Leningradskaya, Russia ⬛
53	I 12	Leoben, Austria
40	H 2	León, Spain
89	J 8	León, Mexico
90	F 7	León, Nicaragua
137	I 2	Leptis Magna, Libya ✦
45	J 8	Le-Puy-en-Velay, France
41	J 3	Lerma, Spain 🔊
61	I 13	Leros, Greece 🏔
36	H 3	Lerwick, United Kingdom
91	H 4	Les Cayes, Haiti
44	F 6	Les Sables-d'Olonne, France
61	I 12	Lesbos, Greece 🏔
127	J 8	Leshan, China
61	F 9	Leskovac, Serbia and Montenegro
141	I 10	Lesotho, Africa 🔲

91	M 5	Lesser Antilles, Caribbean Sea 🏖
74	E 8	Lesser Slave Lake, AB, Canada 🔊
64	F 6	Leszno, Poland
74	E 10	Lethbridge, AB, Canada
96	H 3	Lethem, Guyana
49	F 11	Leuven, Belgium
49	D 12	Leuze-en-Hainaut, Belgium
61	G 12	Levadeia, Greece
52	B 8	Leverkusen, Germany
84	F 7	Lewiston, ID, United States
82	C 5	Lewistown, MT, United States
78	G 10	Lexington, KY, United States
82	F 8	Lexington, NE, United States
126	H 8	Lhasa, China
122	F 7	Lhokseumawe, Indonesia
41	N 4	L'Hospitalet de Llobregat, Spain
127	N 6	Lianyungang, China
127	N 4	Liaoyang, China
127	N 4	Liaoyuan, China
83	F 10	Liberal, KS, United States
64	E 7	Liberec, Czech Republic
90	F 7	Liberia, Costa Rica
136	E 7	Liberia, Africa 🔲
140	E 3	Libreville, Gabon 🔳
137	I 3	Libya, Africa 🔲
137	K 3	Libyan Desert, Egypt/Libya 🔺
137	K 2	Libyan Plateau, Egypt/Libya ◇
65	I 5	Lida, Belarus
69	D 12	Lidköping, Sweden
53	E 13	Liechtenstein, Europe 🔲
49	H 12	Liège, Belgium
53	G 13	Lienz, Austria
64	H 3	Liepāja, Latvia
49	F 11	Lier, Belgium
37	D 11	Liffey, Ireland 🔊
56	B 8	Ligurian Sea, France/Italy 🌊
85	B 15	Lihue, HI, United States
141	I 5	Likasi, Democratic Republic of Congo
151	M 3	Likiep, Marshall Islands 🏔
45	J 2	Lille, France
69	D 10	Lillehammer, Norway
141	K 6	Lilongwe, Malawi 🔳
96	E 7	Lima, Peru ⭐
99	F 12	Limay, Argentina 🔊
99	F 11	Limay Mahuida, Argentina
97	J 8	Limeira, Brazil
37	B 12	Limerick, Ireland
61	G 12	Limni, Greece
61	H 11	Limnos, Greece 🏔
44	H 7	Limoges, France
90	G 8	Limón, Costa Rica
45	I 10	Limoux, France
141	I 8	Limpopo, Botswana/Mozambique 🔊
41	J 8	Linares, Spain
89	K 6	Linares, Mexico
127	M 8	Linchuan, China
37	I 12	Lincoln, United Kingdom
82	G 8	Lincoln, NE, United States 🏛
84	C 7	Lincoln City, OR, United States
97	I 2	Linden, Guyana
61	J 14	Lindos, Greece
37	G 11	Lindow Moss, United Kingdom ◇
127	L 6	Linfen, China
97	L 8	Linhares, Brazil
69	E 12	Linköping, Sweden
53	I 11	Linz, Austria
57	H 14	Lipari Islands, Italy 🏖
104	C 6	Lipetsk, Russia
52	C 7	Lippstadt, Germany
141	J 2	Lira, Uganda
40	E 7	Lisbon, Portugal
147	L 8	Lismore, NSW, Australia
64	H 4	Lithuania, Europe 🔲
119	J 14	Little Andaman, India 🏔
90	H 4	Little Cayman, Cayman Islands 🏔
85	J 13	Little Colorado, United States, United States 🔊
119	K 15	Little Nicobar, India 🏔
83	I 11	Little Rock, AR, United States 🏛
127	L 10	Liuzhou, China
37	G 11	Liverpool, United Kingdom
75	M 9	Liverpool, NS, Canada
141	I 7	Livingstone, Zambia
61	C 8	Livno, Bosnia-Herzegovina
56	D 8	Livorno, Italy
61	E 12	Lixouri, Greece
37	E 15	Lizard Point, United Kingdom ▶
60	B 6	Ljubljana, Slovenia
69	E 12	Ljungby, Sweden
69	E 10	Ljusnan, Sweden 🔊

41	I 1	Llanes, Spain
89	I 4	Llano de los Caballos Mesteños, Mexico ◇
83	E 12	Llano Estacado, United States, United States ◇
96	F 3	Llanos, Colombia ⊞
41	M 4	Lleida, Spain
41	O 6	Llucmajor, Spain
140	F 6	Lobito, Angola
40	C 10	Lobos, Spain 🏔
36	F 8	Loch Lomond, United Kingdom 🔊
36	F 7	Loch Ness, United Kingdom 🔊
36	F 8	Loch Shin, United Kingdom 🔊
85	D 12	Lodi, CA, United States
64	G 6	Łódź, Poland
68	C 5	Lofoten, Norway 🏔
85	I 10	Logan, UT, United States
41	K 3	Logroño, Spain
45	I 5	Loire, France 🔊
96	C 6	Loja, Ecuador
49	D 11	Lokeren, Belgium
69	D 15	Lolland, Denmark 🏔
99	I 10	Lomas de Zamora, Argentina
123	I 10	Lombok, Indonesia 🏔
31	K 5	Lombok Basin, Southern Ocean 🔺
136	G 7	Lomé, Togo 🔳
49	G 10	Lommel, Belgium
32	D 7	Lomonosov Ridge, Arctic Ocean 🔺
85	E 14	Lompoc, CA, United States
64	H 5	Łomża, Poland
37	I 13	London, United Kingdom 🔳
75	J 11	London, ON, Canada
37	D 9	Londonderry, United Kingdom
97	J 9	Londrina, Brazil
81	L 4	Long Bay, NC/SC, United States ≈
85	E 15	Long Beach, CA, United States
79	M 8	Long Island, NY, United States 🏔
91	J 2	Long Island, The Bahamas 🏔
122	G 5	Long Xuyên, Vietnam
147	J 6	Longreach, QLD, Australia
83	I 12	Longview, TX, United States
84	C 7	Longview, WA, United States
127	M 9	Longyan, China
32	E 8	Longyearbyen, Savlbard
45	L 6	Lons-le-Saunier, France
37	A 12	Loop Head, Ireland ▶
126	H 5	Lop Nur, China 🔊
41	K 8	Lorca, Spain
26	F 7	Lord Howe Rise, Pacific Ocean 🔳
147	K 1	Lorengau, Papua New Guinea
88	F 5	Loreto, Mexico
44	E 5	Lorient, France
83	D 10	Los Alamos, NM, United States
99	E 11	Los Ángeles, Chile
85	E 14	Los Ángeles, CA, United States
88	G 5	Los Mochis, Mexico
99	E 9	Los Vilos, Chile
151	L 1	Losap, Federated States of Micronesia 🏔
122	G 3	Louang Namtha, Laos
122	G 3	Louangphrabang, Laos
140	F 4	Loubomo, Congo
127	L 9	Loudi, China
37	C 10	Lough Allen, Ireland 🔊
37	B 10	Lough Conn, Ireland 🔊
37	B 11	Lough Corrib, Ireland 🔊
37	B 12	Lough Derg, Ireland 🔊
37	B 11	Lough Mask, Ireland 🔊
37	D 10	Lough Neagh, United Kingdom 🔊
37	C 11	Lough Ree, Ireland 🔊
147	L 3	Louisiade Archipelago, Papua New Guinea 🏔
83	I 13	Louisiana, United States 🔲
78	G 10	Louisville, IN, United States
26	G 7	Louisville Ridge, Pacific Ocean 🔳
44	G 10	Lourdes, France
44	H 3	Louviers, France
61	H 8	Lovech, Bulgaria
82	D 8	Loveland, CO, United States
79	N 6	Lowell, MA, United States
150	F 6	Lower Hutt, New Zealand
37	C 10	Lower Lough Erne, United Kingdom 🔊
82	H 5	Lower Red Lake, MN, United States 🔊
150	H 10	Loyalty Islands, New Caledonia 🏖
61	D 7	Loznica, Serbia and Montenegro
140	F 5	Luanda, Angola 🔳
141	I 6	Luanshya, Zambia
40	G 1	Luarca, Spain
140	F 7	Lubango, Angola
83	E 11	Lubbock, TX, United States

52	E 5	Lübeck, Germany
52	F 5	Lübecker Bay, Germany ≈
64	H 7	Lublin, Poland
123	I 7	Lubuan, Malaysia
141	I 6	Lubumbashi, Democratic Republic of Congo
56	D 7	Lucca, Italy
123	K 5	Lucena, Philippines
118	E 8	Lucknow, India
140	G 9	Lüderitz, Namibia
118	D 7	Ludhiana, India
78	G 6	Ludington, MI, United States
69	E 11	Ludvika, Sweden
53	D 10	Ludwigsburg, Germany
53	D 10	Ludwigshafen, Germany
83	H 12	Lufkin, TX, United States
53	D 14	Lugano, Switzerland
40	G 2	Lugo, Spain
60	F 7	Lugoj, Romania
65	O 8	Luhans'k, Ukraine
68	H 7	Luleå, Sweden
68	G 7	Luleälven, Sweden 🔊
81	L 3	Lumberton, NC, United States
150	B 10	Lumsden, New Zealand
69	D 14	Lund, Sweden
52	E 5	Lüneburg, Germany
127	L 7	Luoyang, China
141	I 6	Lusaka, Zambia 🔳
52	G 7	Lutherstadt Wittenberg, Germany
37	I 13	Luton, United Kingdom
65	I 7	Luts'k, Ukraine
33	O 1	Lützow-Holm Bay, Antarctica ≈
141	I 4	Luvua, Democratic Republic of Congo 🔊
49	I 15	Luxembourg, Luxembourg
49	H 15	Luxembourg, Europe 🔲
137	L 3	Luxor, Egypt
53	C 13	Luzern, Switzerland
127	K 8	Luzhou, China
123	K 4	Luzon, Philippines 🏔
26	D 4	Luzon Strait, Pacific Ocean ⚡
65	I 8	L'viv, Ukraine
68	G 8	Lycksele, Sweden
37	G 15	Lyme Bay, United Kingdom ≈
45	K 7	Lyon, France
65	O 8	Lysychans'k, Ukraine

M

114	G 4	Ma'ān, Jordan
49	H 9	Maas, Netherlands 🔊
49	H 11	Maastricht, Luxembourg
33	O 3	Mac Robertson Land, Antarctica ⊞
97	K 8	Macaé, Brazil
97	J 4	Macapá, Brazil
127	M 10	Macau, China
99	H 15	Macbride Head, Falkland Islands ▶
30	G 9	MacDonald Islands, Australia 🏖
146	G 6	MacDonnell Ranges, NT, Australia 🔺
61	F 10	Macedonia, Europe 🔲
97	M 6	Maceió, Brazil
141	K 3	Machakos, Kenya
96	D 5	Machala, Ecuador
40	D 9	Machico, Portugal
119	F 12	Machilipatnam, India
141	J 6	Machinga, Malawi
96	F 6	Machu Picchu, Peru ⭐
147	K 6	Mackay, QLD, Australia
22	D 2	Mackenzie, North America 🔊
74	D 4	Mackenzie Bay, NT/YT, Canada ≈
74	D 5	Mackenzie Mountains, Canada 🔺
78	E 8	Macomb, IL, United States
57	B 11	Macomer, Italy
45	K 7	Mâcon, France
81	I 4	Macon, GA, United States
147	K 8	Macquarie, NSW, Australia 🔊
26	F 9	Macquarie Island, Australia 🏔
26	F 10	Macquarie Ridge, Pacific Ocean 🔳
141	M 9	Madagascar, Africa 🔲
30	E 6	Madagascar Basin, Indian Ocean 🔳
30	E 6	Madagascar Plateau, Indian Ocean 🔳
30	E 7	Madagascar Ridge, Indian Ocean 🔳
147	K 2	Madang, Papua New Guinea
79	N 3	Madawaska, NB, United States
40	C 8	Madeira, Portugal 🏔
22	E 6	Madeira, South America 🔊
85	E 12	Madera, CA, United States

96	H 5	Madiera, Bolivia/Brazil 🔊
78	E 6	Madison, WI, United States 🏛
84	D 8	Madras, OR, United States
96	F 6	Madre de Dios, Bolivia/Peru 🔊
41	J 5	Madrid, Spain 🔳
123	I 10	Madura, Indonesia 🏔
119	D 14	Madurai, India
131	H 9	Maebashi, Japan
141	L 5	Mafia Island, Tanzania 🏔
105	N 7	Magadan, Russia
98	G 4	Magdalena, Bolivia
96	E 3	Magdalena, Colombia 🔊
88	G 3	Magdalena, Mexico
88	F 3	Magdalena, Mexico 🔊
52	F 7	Magdeburg, Germany
68	H 3	Mageroya, Norway 🏔
57	K 11	Maglie, Italy
104	E 8	Magnitogorsk, Russia
141	M 7	Mahajanga, Madagascar
123	I 8	Mahakam, Indonesia 🔊
119	D 12	Mahbubnagar, India
150	G 5	Mahia Peninsula, New Zealand ▶
65	K 5	Mahilyow, Belarus
41	P 6	Mahón, Spain
37	J 14	Maidstone, United Kingdom
137	I 6	Maiduguri, Nigeria
53	D 9	Main, Germany 🔊
79	N 4	Maine, United States 🔲
36	F 5	Mainland, United Kingdom 🏔
36	G 3	Mainland, United Kingdom 🏔
53	D 9	Mainz, Germany
28	B 8	Maio, Cape Verde 🏔
96	G 1	Maiquetía, Venezuela
33	M 1	Maitri, India ⬛
61	E 9	Maja Jezercë, Albania 🔺
123	J 9	Majene, Indonesia
41	O 6	Majorca, Spain 🏔
151	N 4	Majuro, Marshall Islands 🔳
151	N 4	Majuro, Marshall Islands 🏔
32	D 7	Makarov Basin, Arctic Ocean 🔳
26	F 4	Makarov Seamount, Pacific Ocean 🔳
61	C 8	Makarska, Croatia
123	J 9	Makassar Strait, Indonesia ⚡
110	H 3	Makat, Kazakhstan
136	D 6	Makeni, Sierra Leone
104	B 9	Makhachkala, Russia
115	N 5	Makran, Iran 🔊
115	N 6	Makran Coast, Iran ⊞
136	H 7	Makurdi, Nigeria
136	H 7	Malabo, Equatorial Guinea 🔳
65	J 4	Maladzyechna, Belarus
41	I 9	Málaga, Spain
137	L 6	Malakal, Sudan
150	H 10	Malakula, Vanuatu 🏔
123	I 10	Malang, Indonesia
140	G 5	Malanje, Angola
108	I 8	Malatya, Turkey
141	J 6	Malawi, Africa 🔲
23	M 6	Malay Peninsula, Asia ▶
115	K 3	Malāyer, Iran
122	G 7	Malaysia, Asia 🔲
119	A 15	Maldives, Asia 🔲
119	B 14	Male, Maldives 🔳
119	B 14	Male Atoll, Maldives 🏔
119	D 11	Malegaon, India
84	E 8	Malheur Lake, OR, United States 🔊
136	F 4	Mali, Africa 🔲
36	E 7	Mallaig, United Kingdom
49	I 13	Malmédy, Belgium
69	D 14	Malmö, Sweden
151	N 3	Maloelap, Marshall Islands 🏔
57	H 16	Malta, Europe 🔲
82	D 5	Malta, MT, United States
57	H 15	Malta Channel, Italy/Malta ⚡
69	E 11	Malung, Sweden
98	G 4	Mamoré, Bolivia 🔊
136	E 6	Mamou, Guinea
136	E 6	Man, Côte d'Ivoire
41	O 6	Manacor, Spain
123	K 8	Manado, Indonesia
90	F 7	Managua, Nicaragua 🔳
109	E 9	Manavgat, Turkey
114	H 2	Manbij, Syria
37	G 11	Manchester, United Kingdom
79	M 6	Manchester, NH, United States
127	N 3	Manchuria, China ▶
23	M 3	Manchurian Plain, Asia ◇
122	F 3	Mandalay, Myanmar
82	F 6	Mandan, ND, United States
91	I 4	Mandeville, Jamaica
146	E 9	Mandurah, WA, Australia

Legend: ▲▲ Mountain Range   🔳 National Capital   🌊 Ocean   Physical Feature   ▬ Polar Base   🔊 River   🌊 Sea   ★ Special Feature   🏛 State Capital   🔳 Underwater Feature

119	D 13	Mandya, India
57	I 10	Manfredonia, Italy
119	C 13	Mangalore, India
83	G 9	Manhattan, KS, United States
32	B 9	Maniitsoq, Greenland
123	J 5	Manila, Philippines
108	C 8	Manisa, Turkey
78	G 5	Manistee, United States
74	H 8	Manitoba, Canada
96	E 3	Manizales, Colombia
82	H 7	Mankato, MN, United States
119	E 15	Mannar, Sri Lanka
53	D 10	Mannheim, Germany
123	M 8	Manokwari, Indonesia
45	L 9	Manosque, France
141	J 5	Mansa, Zambia
75	I 6	Mansel Island, NU, Canada
37	H 12	Mansfield, United Kingdom
78	H 8	Mansfield, OH, United States
79	K 7	Mansfield, PA, United States
96	D 4	Manta, Ecuador
56	D 6	Mantova, Italy
150	F 3	Manukau, New Zealand
150	F 3	Manukau Harbour, New Zealand
41	J 7	Manzanares, Spain
89	I 9	Manzanillo, Mexico
127	M 2	Manzhouli, China
137	I 5	Mao, Chad
127	L 10	Maoming, China
123	O 9	Mapi, Indonesia
141	J 9	Maputo, Mozambique
99	I 11	Mar del Plata, Argentina
97	J 5	Marabá, Brazil
96	F 1	Maracaibo, Venezuela
136	H 5	Maradi, Niger
115	J 2	Marāgheh, Iran
33	I 2	Marambio, Argentina
96	E 6	Marañón, Peru
75	I 10	Marathon, ON, Canada
40	H 10	Marbella, Spain
52	D 8	Marburg, Germany
49	G 13	Marche-en- Famenne, Belgium
111	L 8	Mardan, Pakistan
109	J 9	Mardin, Turkey
147	K 5	Mareeba, QLD, Australia
37	J 13	Margate, United Kingdom
141	J 3	Margherita Peak, Democratic Republic of Congo/Uganda
33	I 3	Marguerite Bay, Antarctica
147	K 11	Maria Island, TAS, Australia
151	L 4	Mariana Islands, Northern Mariana Islands
26	E 5	Mariana Trench, Pacific Ocean
60	B 6	Maribor, Greece
33	K 5	Marie Byrd Land, Antarctica
27	J 10	Marie Byrd Seamount, Pacific Ocean
91	O 5	Marie-Galante, Guadeloupe
81	I 3	Marietta, GA, United States
64	H 4	Marijampolė, Lithuania
97	J 8	Marilia, Brazil
97	J 9	Maringá, Brazil
78	H 8	Marion, OH, United States
40	G 9	Marismas del Guadalquivir, Spain
61	H 9	Maritsa, Bulgaria
65	O 9	Mariupol', Ukraine
44	H 9	Marmande, France
108	C 6	Marmara, Turkey
109	C 9	Marmaris, Turkey
141	N 6	Maromokotro, Madagascar
137	I 6	Maroua, Cameroon
27	I 6	Marquesas Fracture Zone, Pacific Ocean
151	N 8	Marquesas Islands, French Polynesia
81	J 11	Marquesas Keys, FL, United States
78	F 4	Marquette, MI, United States
136	E 2	Marrakech, Morocco
147	J 11	Marrawah, TAS, Australia
147	I 8	Marree, SA, Australia
137	K 2	Marsa Matrûh, Egypt
141	L 2	Marsabit, Kenya
57	F 14	Marsala, Italy
45	L 10	Marseille, France
83	J 13	Marsh Island, LA, United States
83	I 12	Marshall, TX, United States
151	M 4	Marshall Islands, Pacific Ocean
123	I 9	Martapura, Indonesia
33	J 5	Martin Peninsula, Antarctica
91	O 6	Martinique, United States
111	J 7	Mary, Turkmenistan
147	L 7	Maryborough, QLD, Australia
79	K 9	Maryland, United States
141	J 3	Masaka, Uganda
30	F 5	Mascarene Basin, Indian Ocean
30	F 5	Mascarene Plain, Indian Ocean
30	F 4	Mascarene Ridge, Indian Ocean
141	I 10	Maseru, Lesotho
115	N 2	Mashhad, Iran
115	K 4	Masjed Soleymān, Iran
150	B 11	Mason Bay, New Zealand
82	I 7	Mason City, IA, United States
56	D 7	Massa, Italy
79	M 6	Massachusetts, United States
45	J 8	Massif Central, France
136	H 4	Massif de l'Aïr, Niger
109	P 6	Mastağa, Azerbaijan
150	F 6	Masterton, New Zealand
141	J 8	Masvingo, Zimbabwe
140	F 4	Matadi, Democratic Republic of Congo
90	F 7	Matagalpa, Nicaragua
150	H 3	Matakaoa Point, New Zealand
89	L 5	Matamoros, Mexico
75	L 8	Matane, QC, Canada
90	H 2	Matanzas, Cuba
119	E 16	Matara, Sri Lanka
123	J 10	Mataram, Indonesia
41	O 4	Mataró, Spain
131	D 11	Matsue, Japan
131	G 10	Matsumoto, Japan
131	F 11	Matsusaka, Japan
131	C 12	Matsuyama, Japan
53	C 14	Matterhorn, Italy/Switzerland
91	J 3	Matthew Town, The Bahamas
96	H 2	Maturín, Venezuela
119	F 9	Mau, India
29	H 12	Maud Rise, Atlantic Ocean
64	H 3	Maùeikiai, Lithuania
151	K 2	Maug Islands, Northern Mariana Islands
85	C 15	Maui, HI, United States
140	H 8	Maun, Botswana
85	C 15	Mauna Kea, HI, United States
85	C 16	Mauna Loa, HI, United States
136	E 4	Mauritania, Africa
30	F 5	Mauritius, Mauritius
141	O 8	Mauritius, Africa
30	E 6	Mauritius Trench, Indian Ocean
33	P 2	Mawson, Australia
33	N 7	Mawson Peninsula, Antarctica
91	J 3	Mayaguana Island, The Bahamas
91	L 4	Mayagüez, Puerto Rico
104	B 7	Maykop, Russia
74	D 6	Mayo, YT, Canada
150	G 3	Mayor Island, New Zealand
141	M 6	Mayotte, France
57	F 14	Mazara del Vallo, Italy
111	K 7	Mazār-e Sharīf, Afghanistan
88	H 7	Mazatlán, Mexico
54	H 6	Mazowiecki, Poland
65	K 6	Mazyr, Belarus
141	J 9	Mbabane, Swaziland
141	K 2	Mbale, Uganda
140	G 3	Mbandaka, Democratic Republic of Congo
140	F 5	M'banza Congo, Angola
141	J 3	Mbarara, Uganda
141	J 5	Mbeya, Tanzania
140	H 4	Mbuji-Mayi, Democratic Republic of Congo
83	H 11	McAlester, OK, United States
83	G 14	McAllen, TX, United States
83	E 12	McCamey, TX, United States
74	G 4	McClintock Channel, NU, Canada
32	C 6	McClure Strait, Canada
80	E 6	McComb, MS, United States
83	F 9	McCook, NE, United States
84	C 7	McMinnville, OR, United States
33	M 6	McMurdo, United States
79	J 7	Meadville, PA, United States
114	H 4	Mecca, Saudi Arabia
49	F 11	Mechelen, Belgium
52	F 4	Mecklenburger Bay, Germany
122	F 7	Medan, Indonesia
96	E 2	Medellín, Colombia
85	C 9	Medford, PR, United States
74	F 7	Medicine Hat, AB, Canada
114	H 6	Medina, Saudi Arabia
41	I 4	Medina del Campo, Spain
41	K 4	Medinaceli, Spain
23	I 4	Mediterranean Sea, Europe
146	E 7	Meekatharra, WA, Australia
122	F 3	Meiktila, Myanmar
151	N 3	Mejit Island, Marshall Islands
137	M 5	Mek'elē, Ethiopia
136	F 1	Meknès, Morocco
23	M 5	Mekong, Asia
122	G 7	Melaka, Malaysia
26	H 3	Melanesian Basin, Pacific Ocean
147	J 10	Melbourne, VIC, Australia
81	K 8	Melbourne, FL, United States
74	G 9	Melfort, SK, Canada
41	J 11	Melilla, Spain
65	N 10	Melitopol', Ukraine
49	D 11	Melle, Belgium
69	D 7	Mellerud, Sweden
99	J 9	Melo, Uruguay
147	J 10	Melton, VIC, Australia
45	I 4	Melun, France
146	G 3	Melville Island, NT, Australia
74	F 3	Melville Island, NT/NU, Canada
74	H 5	Melville Peninsula, NU, Canada
80	F 2	Memphis, TN, United States
27	J 9	Menard Fracture Zone, Pacific Ocean
45	J 9	Mende, France
32	D 6	Mendeleyev Ridge, Arctic Ocean
26	H 3	Mendocino Fracture Zone, Pacific Ocean
99	F 10	Mendoza, Argentina
48	I 6	Meppel, Netherlands
56	E 4	Merano, Italy
85	D 12	Merced, CA, United States
99	G 10	Mercedes, Argentina
99	I 10	Mercedes, Uruguay
98	I 8	Mercedes, Argentina
122	F 6	Mergui, Myanmar
122	F 6	Mergui Archipelago, Myanmar
40	G 7	Mérida, Spain
96	F 2	Mérida, Venezuela
89	O 8	Mérida, Mexico
80	F 5	Meridian, MS, United States
151	I 2	Merir, Palau
37	G 13	Mersey, United Kingdom
109	G 10	Mersin, Turkey
37	G 13	Merthyr Tydfil, United Kingdom
141	L 3	Meru, Kenya
108	E 8	Merzifon, Turkey
85	I 15	Mesa, AZ, United States
41	I 6	Meseta, Spain
99	H 9	Mesopotamia, Argentina/Uruguay
57	I 14	Messina, Italy
141	I 9	Messina, South Africa
96	F 3	Meta, Colombia/Venezuela
83	J 13	Metairie, LA, United States
98	G 7	Metán, Argentina
61	F 11	Meteora, Greece
61	C 8	Metković, Croatia
61	I 11	Metsovo, Greece
45	L 3	Metz, France
49	G 12	Meuse, Belgium
88	E 2	Mexicali, Mexico
89	N 9	Mexico, North America
89	K 8	Mexico City, Mexico
111	J 7	Meymaneh, Afghanistan
89	N 9	Mezcalapa, Mexico
89	L 10	Miahuatlán, Mexico
81	L 10	Miami, FL, United States
81	L 10	Miami Beach, FL, United States
111	L 8	Mianwali, Pakistan
127	K 8	Mianyang, China
104	E 8	Miass, Russia
78	G 6	Michigan, United States
104	C 6	Michurinsk, Russia
29	H 10	Mid-Atlantic Ridge, Atlantic Ocean
49	D 9	Middelburg, Netherlands
27	K 4	Middle America Trench, Pacific Ocean
119	J 13	Middle Andaman, India
78	H 11	Middlesboro, VI, United States
37	H 10	Middlesbrough, United Kingdom
79	L 7	Middletown, NY, United States
30	H 4	Mid-Indian Basin, Indian Ocean
30	F 3	Mid-Indian Ridge, Indian Ocean
26	F 4	Mid-Pacific Mountains, Pacific Ocean
26	G 3	Midway Islands, United States
40	H 2	Mieres, Spain
64	G 4	Mierzeja Helska, Poland
89	I 6	Miguel Auza, Mexico
131	I 11	Mikura-jima, Japan
56	C 5	Milan, Italy
147	J 9	Mildura, VIC, Australia
147	K 7	Miles, QLD, Australia
82	D 6	Miles City, MT, United States
79	L 7	Milford, PA, United States
150	B 9	Milford Sound, New Zealand
151	N 4	Mili, Marshall Islands
33	P 5	Mill Island, Antarctica
82	H 6	Mille Lacs, MN, United States
81	J 4	Milledgeville, GA, United States
61	G 13	Milos, Greece
37	I 13	Milton Keynes, United Kingdom
78	F 6	Milwaukee, WI, United States
89	M 9	Minatitlán, Mexico
122	E 3	Minbu, Myanmar
36	E 6	Minch, The, United Kingdom
52	D 6	Minden, Germany
123	J 5	Mindoro, Philippines
123	K 6	Mindanao, Philippines
28	A 7	Mindelo, Cape Verde
136	H 6	Minna, Nigeria
82	H 6	Minneapolis, MN, United States
82	G 6	Minnesota, United States
41	J 2	Minorca, Spain
82	F 5	Minot, ND, United States
65	J 5	Minsk, Belarus
118	J 7	Mishmi Hills, India
33	P 4	Mirny, Russia
105	J 8	Mirnyy, Russia
111	K 10	Mirpur Khas, Pakistan
64	G 9	Miskolc, Hungary
123	L 8	Misool, Indonesia
137	I 2	Mişrātah, Libya
22	D 4	Mississippi, North America
80	E 4	Mississippi, United States
82	B 5	Missoula, MT, United States
22	D 3	Missouri, North America
83	I 9	Missouri, United States
147	K 7	Mitchell, QLD, Australia
147	J 4	Mitchell, QLD, Australia
82	G 7	Mitchell, SD, United States
131	I 9	Mito, Japan
96	F 5	Mitú, Colombia
131	I 11	Miyake-jima, Japan
131	C 14	Miyakonojō, Japan
131	C 14	Miyazaki, Japan
37	A 13	Mizen Head, Ireland
33	N 2	Mizuho, Japan
61	C 9	Mljet, Croatia
68	E 7	Mo i Rana, Norway
85	J 11	Moab, UT, United States
80	G 6	Mobile, AL, United States
80	G 6	Mobile Bay, AL, United States
27	L 9	Mocha Fracture Zone, Pacific Ocean
96	E 4	Mocoa, Colombia
141	K 7	Mocuba, Mozambique
56	D 6	Modena, Italy
85	D 12	Modesto, CA, United States
57	H 15	Modica, Italy
147	K 10	Moe, VIC, Australia
97	I 3	Moengo, Suriname
52	B 7	Moers, Germany
118	C 7	Moga, India
137	N 8	Mogadishu, Somalia
130	H 7	Mogami, Japan
136	F 1	Mohammedia, Morocco
141	L 6	Mohéli, Comoros
131	B 13	Mojikō, Japan
69	B 9	Molde, Norway
65	J 9	Moldova, Europe
141	I 9	Molepolole, Botswana
57	J 10	Molfetta, Italy
53	H 13	Möll, Austria
96	F 7	Mollendo, Peru
65	N 10	Molochnyy Lyman, Ukraine
33	O 2	Molodezhnaya, Russia
85	C 15	Molokai, HI, United States
26	H 4	Molokai Fracture Zone, Pacific Ocean
61	G 12	Molos, Greece
123	K 8	Molucca Sea, Indonesia
123	L 8	Moluccas, Indonesia
141	L 4	Mombasa, Kenya
69	D 15	Møn, Denmark
45	M 9	Monaco, Monaco
45	M 9	Monaco, Europe
28	G 4	Monaco Basin, Atlantic Ocean
37	D 11	Monasterboice, Ireland
52	B 8	Mönchengladbach, Germany
89	J 5	Monclova, Mexico
75	L 9	Moncton, NB, Canada
56	B 7	Mondovì, Italy
137	J 6	Mongo, Chad
127	J 3	Mongolia, Asia
111	L 7	Mongora, Pakistan
141	I 6	Mongu, Zambia
85	E 12	Mono Lake, CA, United States
83	J 12	Monroe, LA, United States
136	E 7	Monrovia, Liberia
49	D 13	Mons, Belgium
45	M 7	Mont Blanc, France/Italy
61	G 8	Montana, Bulgaria
82	C 6	Montana, United States
45	J 5	Montargis, France
45	I 9	Montauban, France
79	M 7	Montauk Point, NY, United States
45	L 5	Montbéliard, France
44	G 9	Mont-de-Marsan, France
57	G 9	Monte Carno, Italy
99	I 9	Monte Caseros, Argentina
45	N 10	Monte Cinto, Corsica
56	B 5	Monte Rosa, Italy
91	I 3	Montego Bay, Jamaica
45	K 9	Montélimar, France
89	K 6	Montemorelos, Mexico
85	C 13	Monterey, CA, United States
85	C 12	Monterey Bay, CA, United States
96	E 2	Montería, Colombia
98	G 5	Montero, Bolivia
89	K 5	Monterrey, Mexico
97	K 7	Montes Claros, Brazil
99	I 10	Montevideo, Uruguay
80	G 5	Montgomery, AL, United States
45	I 7	Montluçon, France
41	I 8	Montoro, Spain
79	M 5	Montpelier, VT, United States
45	J 10	Montpellier, France
75	K 10	Montréal, QC, Canada
53	B 13	Montreux, Switzerland
83	C 9	Montrose, CO, United States
136	H 5	Monts Bagzane, Niger
136	H 3	Monts du Mouydir, Algeria
141	I 5	Monts Mitumba, Democratic Republic of Congo
91	N 5	Montserrat, United Kingdom
44	F 4	Mont-St-Michel, France
122	E 3	Monywa, Myanmar
56	C 5	Monza, Italy
41	M 3	Monzón, Spain
146	E 8	Moora, WA, Australia
151	M 10	Moorea, French Polynesia
82	G 6	Moorhead, MN, United States
75	J 9	Moose, Canada
79	N 4	Moosehead Lake, ME, United States
75	J 9	Moosonee, ON, Canada
136	F 5	Mopti, Mali
69	E 11	Mora, Sweden
118	E 8	Moradabad, India
64	F 8	Moraua, Czech Republic
61	F 8	Morava, Serbia and Montenegro
36	F 6	Moray Firth, United Kingdom
89	J 8	Morelia, Mexico
118	D 8	Morena, India
130	I 6	Morioka, Japan
44	E 4	Morlaix, France
27	L 9	Mornington Abyssal Plain, Pacific Ocean
123	K 6	Moro Gulf, Philippines
136	F 2	Morocco, Africa
141	K 4	Morogoro, Tanzania
141	M 8	Morondava, Madagascar
141	M 6	Moroni, Comoros
150	F 3	Morrinsville, New Zealand
151	L 2	Mortlock Islands, Federated States of Micronesia
84	F 6	Moscow, WA, United States

≈ Bay   ⋈ Channel   ☐ Country   ▣ Dependent Territory   ▲ Desert   ⁝⁝⁝ Geographic Area   ▶ Headland   🏝 Island   🏝 Island Group   ↘ Lake   ▲ Mountain

N

104	C 6	Moscow, Russia ■
53	C 9	Mosel, Europe ╮
141	K 4	Moshi, Tanzania
68	E 7	Mosjøen, Norway
90	G 7	Mosquito Coast, Nicaragua ◇
69	D 12	Moss, Norway
97	L 5	Mossoró, Brazil
64	D 7	Most, Czech Republic
61	C 8	Mostar, Bosnia-Herzegovina
115	I 2	Mosul, Iraq
41	J 6	Mota del Cuervo, Spain
150	G 3	Motiti Island, New Zealand ⊥
150	G 4	Motu, New Zealand ╮
45	J 6	Moulins, France
122	F 4	Moulmein, Myanmar
137	I 7	Moundou, Chad
99	F 9	Mt Aconcagua, Argentina/Chile ▲
108	M 7	Mt Ararat, Turkey ▲
33	K 6	Mt Berlin, Antarctica ▲
150	C 8	Mt Cook, New Zealand ▲
79	O 5	Mount Desert Island, ME, United States ⊥
57	H 14	Mt Etna, Italy ▲
82	B 6	Mt Evans, MT, United States ▲
118	H 8	Mt Everest, China/Nepal ▲
74	C 7	Mt Fairweather, BC, Canada ▲
131	H 10	Mt Fuji, Japan ▲
147	I 10	Mount Gambier, SA, Australia
147	J 2	Mt Hagen, Papua New Guinea
83	D 9	Mt Harvard, CO, United States ▲
147	I 5	Mount Isa, QLD, Australia
84	D 7	Mt Jefferson, OR, United States ▲
85	F 11	Mt Jefferson, NV, United States ▲
79	N 4	Mt Katahdin, ME, United States ▲
141	K 3	Mt Kenya, Kenya ▲
123	J 6	Mt Kinabalu, Malaysia ▲
33	M 5	Mt Kirkpatrick, Antarctica ▲
147	K 10	Mt Kosciuszko, NSW, Australia ▲
74	C 6	Mt Logan, YT, Canada ▲
146	E 8	Mount Magnet, WA, Australia
79	L 6	Mt Marcy, NY, United States ▲
85	I 11	Mt Marvine, UT, United States ▲
84	J 5	Mt McKinley, AL, United States ▲
33	M 7	Mt Minto, Antarctica, ▲
81	J 2	Mt Mitchell, NC, United States ▲
61	F 11	Mt Olympus, Greece ▲
81	L 4	Mount Pleasant, SC, United States
84	D 6	Mt Rainier, WA, United States ▲
74	E 9	Mt Robson, BC, Canada ▲
150	F 5	Mt Ruapehu, New Zealand ▲
82	E 7	Mt Rushmore, SD, United States ▲
85	D 10	Mt Shasta, CA, United States ▲
78	E 9	Mount Vernon, IL, United States
84	D 5	Mt Vernon, WA, United States
74	D 9	Mt Waddlington, BC, Canada ▲
79	M 5	Mt Washington, NH, United States ▲
85	F 13	Mt Whitney, CA, United States ▲
147	K 1	Mt Wilhelm, Papua New Guinea ▲
83	C 10	Mt Wilson, CO, United States ▲
82	D 8	Mt Zirkel, CO, United States ▲
85	G 9	Mountain Home, ID, United States
49	C 12	Mouscron, Belgium
41	M 5	Mouth of the Ebro, Spain ╮
127	N 7	Mouth of the Yangtze, China ╮
97	J 4	Mouths of the Amazon, Brazil ╮
119	H 10	Mouths of the Ganges, Bangladesh
119	F 12	Mouths of the Godavari, India ╮
111	K 11	Mouths of the Indus, Pakistan ╮
119	E 12	Mouths of the Krishna, India ╮
122	H 6	Mouths of the Mekong, Vietnam ╮
96	E 5	Moyobamba, Peru
141	J 8	Mozambique, Africa □
141	L 9	Mozambique Channel, Madagascar/Mozambique ⇄
30	D 7	Mozambique Escarpment, Indian Ocean ⬛
30	D 7	Mozambique Ridge, Indian Ocean ⬛
141	J 6	Mpika, Zambia
141	L 5	Mtwara, Tanzania
127	O 3	Mudanjiang, China
141	I 6	Mufulira, Zambia
109	O 7	Muğan Düzü, Azerbaijan ◇
109	C 9	Muğla, Turkey
122	G 6	Mui Ca Mau, Vietnam ►
64	H 9	Mukacheve, Ukraine
119	B 15	Mulakatholhu Atoll, Maldives ⊥
41	J 9	Mulhacén, Spain ▲
45	M 5	Mulhouse, France
36	D 8	Mull, United Kingdom ⊥
37	C 11	Mullingar, Ireland
111	L 9	Multan, Pakistan
119	B 11	Mumbai, India
123	K 9	Muna, Indonesia ⊥
78	G 8	Muncie, IN, United States
119	G 9	Munger, India
53	F 11	Munich, Germany
52	C 7	Münster, Germany
68	H 6	Muonio, Finland
114	H 4	Muqāţ, Jordan
108	L 8	Muradiye, Turkey
108	K 7	Murat, Turkey ╮
146	E 7	Murchison, WA, Australia
41	L 8	Murcia, Spain
80	H 2	Murfreesboro, TN, United States
111	L 6	Murghob, Tajikistan
147	L 7	Murgon, QLD, Australia
52	G 5	Müritz, Germany ⌐
104	E 4	Murmansk, Russia
130	H 4	Muroran, Japan
131	E 13	Muroto-zaki, Japan ►
147	J 9	Murray, NSW/VIC, Australia ╮
147	J 9	Murray Bridge, SA, Australia
26	H 3	Murray Fracture Zone, Pacific Ocean ⬛
30	G 2	Murray Ridge, Indian Ocean ⬛
150	G 4	Murupara, New Zealand
119	E 9	Murwara, India
137	I 3	Murzūq, Libya
108	K 8	Muş, Turkey
61	K 9	Musala, Bulgaria ▲
115	N 6	Muscat, Oman ■
78	G 6	Muskegon, MI, United States
83	H 10	Muskogee, OK, United States
141	K 3	Musoma, Tanzania
147	L 8	Muswellbrook, NSW, Australia
109	F 10	Mut, Turkey
141	J 7	Mutare, Zimbabwe
130	H 5	Mutsu-wan, Japan ≈
126	G 6	Mutztag Feng, China ▲
111	L 9	Muzaffargarh, Pakistan
118	D 7	Muzaffarnagar, India
119	G 9	Muzaffarpur, India
141	J 3	Mwanza, Tanzania
140	H 5	Mwene-Ditu, Democratic Republic of Congo
151	M 2	Mwokil, Federated States of Micronesia ⊥
122	H 6	My Tho, Vietnam
122	F 2	Myanmar, Asia □
122	F 3	Myingyan, Myanmar
122	F 2	Myitkyina, Myanmar
65	L 10	Mykolayiv, Ukraine
61	H 13	Mykonos, Greece
61	H 13	Mykonos, Greece ⊥
61	H 11	Myrina, Greece
81	L 4	Myrtle Beach, SC, United States
65	M 11	Mys Ayya, Ukraine ►
65	M 11	Mys Khersones, Ukraine ►
119	D 13	Mysore, India
61	I 11	Mytilini, Greece
141	K 6	Mzuzu, Malawi
136	G 2	Naama, Algeria
104	D 7	Naberezhnyye Chelny, Russia
114	G 3	Nāblus, Israel
141	L 6	Nacala, Mozambique
119	C 10	Nadiad, India
61	G 13	Nafplio, Greece
131	G 9	Nagano, Japan
131	G 9	Nagaoka, Japan
119	E 12	Nagarjuna Sagar, India ╮
131	B 14	Nagasaki, Japan
119	D 15	Nagercoil, India
131	J 15	Nago, Japan
131	F 11	Nagoya, Japan
119	D 10	Nagpur, India
126	H 7	Naggu, China
64	F 10	Nagykanizsa, Hungary
131	J 16	Naha, Japan
75	K 6	Nain, NL, Canada
141	K 3	Nairobi, Kenya ■
141	K 3	Naivasha, Kenya
115	L 3	Najafābād, Iran
115	J 9	Najrān, Saudi Arabia
131	D 13	Nakamura, Japan
131	B 16	Nakano-shima, Japan ⊥
105	M 11	Nakhodka, Russia
122	F 5	Nakhon Ratchasima, Thailand
122	F 4	Nakhon Sawan, Thailand
122	F 6	Nakhon Si Thammarat, Thailand
141	K 3	Nakuru, Kenya
104	B 8	Nal'chik, Russia
126	H 7	Nam Co, China ⌐
122	H 3	Nam Đinh, Vietnam
140	G 9	Namaqualand, Namibia ◇
140	F 7	Namib Desert, Namibia ▲
140	F 7	Namibe, Angola
140	G 8	Namibia, Africa □
29	J 9	Namibia Abyssal Plain, Atlantic Ocean ⬛
127	I 8	Namjagbarwa, China ▲
151	L 2	Namoluk, Federated States of Micronesia ⊥
151	M 4	Namorik, Marshall Islands ⊥
84	F 8	Nampa, ID, United States
127	O 5	Namp'o, North Korea
141	L 7	Nampula, Mozambique
68	D 8	Namsos, Norway
151	M 3	Namu, Marshall Islands ⊥
49	F 13	Namur, Belgium
74	D 9	Nanaimo, BC, Canada
127	K 8	Nanchang, China
127	K 8	Nanchong, China
45	L 4	Nancy, France
119	D 11	Nanded, India
119	E 12	Nandyal, India
127	N 7	Nanjing, China
127	K 10	Nanning, China
127	N 9	Nanping, China
32	E 7	Nansen Basin, Arctic Ocean ⬛
32	D 8	Nansen Cordillera, Arctic Ocean ▲
44	F 6	Nantes, France
127	N 7	Nantong, China
79	N 7	Nantucket, MA, United States
79	N 7	Nantucket Island, MA, United States ⊥
127	L 7	Nanyang, China
85	C 12	Napa, CA, United States
74	F 5	Napaktulik Lake, NU, Canada ⌐
150	G 11	Napier, New Zealand
57	G 11	Naples, Italy
81	K 10	Naples, FL, United States
96	E 4	Napo, Ecuador/Peru ╮
131	J 7	Nara, Japan
147	I 10	Naracoorte, SA, Australia
45	J 10	Narbonne, France
28	D 5	Nares Abyssal Plain, Atlantic Ocean ⬛
74	H 2	Nares Strait, NU, Canada/Greenland ⌐
64	H 6	Narew, Poland ╮
23	K 5	Narmada, Asia ╮
147	K 8	Narrabri, NSW, Australia
65	J 1	Narva, Estonia
65	J 1	Narva laht, Estonia ≈
68	F 5	Narvik, Norway
111	M 5	Naryn, Kyrgyzstan
119	C 11	Nashik, India
79	M 6	Nashua, NH, United States
80	H 2	Nashville, TN, United States ⎍
91	I 2	Nassau, The Bahamas ■
97	M 5	Natal, Brazil
30	F 4	Natal Basin, Indian Ocean ⬛
30	D 7	Natal Valley, Indian Ocean ⬛
75	L 8	Natashquan, QC, Canada
80	E 5	Natchez, MS, United States
83	I 12	Natchitoches, LA, United States
136	G 6	Natitingou, Benin
31	J 7	Naturaliste Fracture Zone, Indian Ocean ⬛
31	K 7	Naturaliste Plateau, Southern Ocean ⬛
150	H 8	Nauru, Pacific Ocean □
65	K 4	Navapolatsk, Belarus
111	J 6	Navoi, Uzbekistan
88	G 5	Navojoa, Mexico
119	B 10	Navsari, India
111	K 10	Nawabshah, Pakistan
109	M 7	Naxşivan, Azerbaijan
61	H 13	Naxos, Greece
61	I 13	Naxos, Greece ⊥
114	G 3	Nazareth, Israel
27	M 7	Nazca Ridge, Pacific Ocean ⬛
131	K 14	Naze, Japan
137	N 6	Nazrēt, Ethiopia
115	N 7	Nazwá, Oman
137	J 7	Ndélé, Central African Republic
137	I 6	Ndjamena, Chad ■
141	J 6	Ndola, Zambia
110	H 6	Nebitdag, Turkmenistan
82	F 8	Nebraska, United States □
82	F 8	Nebraska City, NE, United States
53	D 10	Neckar, Germany ╮
99	H 11	Necochea, Argentina
104	E 7	Neftekamsk, Russia
151	M 2	Negetik Atoll, Federated States of Micronesia ⊥
114	G 4	Negev, Israel ▲
119	E 15	Negombo, Sri Lanka
99	G 11	Negro, Argentina ╮
96	G 9	Negro, Bolivia/Brazil ╮
123	K 6	Negros, Philippines ⊥
127	K 8	Neijiang, China
96	E 3	Neiva, Colombia
137	L 6	Nek'emtē, Ethiopia
119	E 13	Nellore, India
150	E 6	Nelson, New Zealand
74	H 8	Nelson, Canada ╮
136	F 5	Néma, Mauritania
64	H 4	Nemunas, Lithuania ╮
130	J 3	Nemuro, Japan
130	J 2	Nemuro-kaikyō, Japan ≈
118	F 8	Nepal, Asia □
61	C 9	Neretva, Bosnia-Herzegovina ╮
61	H 10	Nestos, Greece ╮
48	F 6	Netherlands, Europe □
91	L 6	Netherlands Antilles, Netherlands □
75	J 5	Nettilling Lake, NU, Canada ⌐
52	H 5	Neubrandenburg, Germany
49	H 14	Neufchâteau, Belgium
33	L 1	Neumayer, Germany ▬
52	E 4	Neumünster, Germany
99	F 11	Neuquén, Argentina
99	F 11	Neuquén, Argentina ╮
53	F 12	Neuschwanstein Castle, Germany ★
52	B 8	Neuss, Germany
53	C 9	Neuwied, Germany
85	F 11	Nevada, United States □
96	F 7	Nevado Coropuna, Peru ▲
98	F 7	Nevado de Cachi, Argentina ▲
96	E 3	Nevado del Huila, Colombia ▲
96	E 6	Nevado Huascarán, Peru ▲
98	F 8	Nevado Ojos del Salado, Argentina/Chile ▲
98	F 5	Nevado Sajama, Bolivia ▲
45	J 6	Nevers, France
104	B 8	Nevinnomyssk, Russia
108	G 8	Nevşehir, Turkey
78	G 9	New Albany, IN, United States
97	I 2	New Amsterdam, Guyana
79	N 7	New Bedford, MA, United States
81	M 2	New Bern, NC, United States
147	L 2	New Britain, Papua New Guinea ⊥
75	L 9	New Brunswick, Canada □
150	G 10	New Caledonia, France □
26	F 7	New Caledonia Trough, Pacific Ocean ⬛
118	D 8	New Delhi, India, ■
79	M 7	New England, United States ◇
28	D 4	New England Seamounts, Atlantic Ocean ⬛
75	M 8	New Glasgow, NS, Canada
123	N 9	New Guinea, Asia/Oceania ⊥
79	M 5	New Hampshire, United States □
79	M 7	New Haven, CT, United States
83	J 13	New Iberia, LA, United States
147	L 1	New Ireland, Papua New Guinea ⊥
79	L 9	New Jersey, United States □
83	C 11	New Mexico, United States □
83	K 13	New Orleans, LA, United States
150	E 5	New Plymouth, New Zealand
105	K 4	New Siberia Islands, Russia ⊥
147	K 8	New South Wales, Australia □
79	J 7	New York, United States □
79	L 8	New York, NY, United States
150	E 5	New Zealand, Pacific Ocean □
79	L 8	Newark, NJ, United States
84	C 7	Newberg, OR, United States
37	H 14	Newbury, United Kingdom
147	L 8	Newcastle, NSW, Australia
37	H 9	Newcastle upon Tyne, United Kingdom
75	M 7	Newfoundland, NL, Canada □
75	L 6	Newfoundland and Labrador, Canada □
28	E 4	Newfoundland Ridge, Atlantic Ocean ⬛
146	E 6	Newman, WA, Australia
37	H 14	Newport, United Kingdom
79	M 5	Newport, VT, United States
79	N 7	Newport, RI, United States
84	C 8	Newport, OR, United States
79	K 10	Newport News, VI, United States
83	G 9	Newton, KS, United States
115	N 2	Neyshābūr, Iran
89	K 8	Nezahualcóyo, Mexico
151	I 1	Ngajangel, Palau ⊥
137	I 7	Ngaoundéré, Cameroon
151	J 1	Ngulu, Federated States of Micronesia ⊥
122	H 5	Nha Trang, Vietnam
79	J 6	Niagara Falls, Canada/United States
75	K 10	Niagara Falls, ON, Canada
136	G 5	Niamey, Niger ■
122	F 8	Nias, Indonesia ⊥
90	F 6	Nicaragua, North America □
45	M 10	Nice, France
119	J 15	Nicobar Islands, India □
108	F 11	Nicosia, Cyprus ■
48	G 8	Nieuwegein, Netherlands
109	G 9	Niğde, Turkey
22	H 5	Niger, Africa ╮
136	H 5	Niger, Africa □
136	G 6	Nigeria, Africa □
130	G 8	Niigata, Japan
131	D 12	Niihama, Japan
85	A 15	Niihau, HI, United States ⊥
131	H 11	Nii-jima, Japan ⊥
48	H 8	Nijmegen, Netherlands
65	M 9	Nikopol', Ukraine
61	D 9	Nikšić, Serbia and Montenegro
119	A 15	Nilandhoo Atoll, Maldives ⊥
23	I 4	Nile, Africa ╮
45	K 9	Nîmes, France
31	I 6	Ninetyeast Ridge, Indian Ocean ⬛
127	N 8	Ningbo, China
136	E 5	Nioro, Mali
44	G 7	Niort, France
75	I 10	Nipigon, ON, Canada
61	F 8	Niš, Serbia and Montenegro
151	J 9	Niua Group, Tonga ⇄
26	H 7	Niue, Niue ⊥
151	K 10	Niue, New Zealand □
119	E 11	Nizamabad, India
104	G 7	Nizhnevartovsk, Russia
104	D 6	Nizhniy Novgorod, Russia
104	E 7	Nizhniy Tagil, Russia
105	I 7	Nizhnyaya Tunguska, Russia ╮
136	H 7	Nkongsamba, Cameroon
131	C 14	Nobeoka, Japan
131	I 10	Noda, Japan
85	J 16	Nogales, AZ, United States
88	G 3	Nogales, Mexico
131	I 10	Nojima-zaki, Japan ►
69	I 10	Nokia, Finland
84	I 4	Nome, AL, United States
151	L 1	Nomwin, Federated States of Micronesia ⊥
122	F 5	Nonthaburi, Thailand
32	E 9	Nord Kapp, Norway ►
32	E 8	Nordaustlandet, Svalbard ⊥
52	F 7	Nordhausen, Germany
52	E 7	Nordhorn, Germany
79	L 10	Norfolk, VI, United States
82	G 8	Norfolk, NE, United States
104	H 6	Noril'sk, Russia
147	J 5	Norman, QLD, Australia ╮
83	G 11	Norman, OK, United States
74	E 5	Norman Wells, NT, Canada
44	G 4	Normandy, France ◇
147	J 5	Normanton, QLD, Australia
69	F 12	Norrköping, Sweden
69	G 11	Norrtälje, Sweden
146	F 9	Norseman, WA, Australia
28	D 5	North American Basin, Atlantic Ocean ⬛
119	J 13	North Andaman, India ⊥
31	K 5	North Australian Basin, Southern Ocean ⬛
74	F 9	North Battleford, SK, Canada
75	J 10	North Bay, ON, Canada
68	I 3	North Cape, Norway ►
150	E 1	North Cape, New Zealand ►
81	K 4	North Carolina, United States □
82	E 5	North Dakota, United States □
22	H 3	North European Plain, Europe ◇
26	G 7	North Fiji Basin, Pacific Ocean ⬛
37	K 13	North Foreland, United Kingdom ►

▲ Mountain Range   ■ National Capital   ☺ Ocean   Physical Feature   ▬ Polar Base   ╮ River   ⌐ Sea   ★ Special Feature   ⎍ State Capital   ⬛ Underwater Feature

Page	Ref	Name
52	D 3	North Frisian Islands, Germany
32	C 7	North Geomagnetic Pole, Arctic Ocean ◇
150	E 2	North Head, New Zealand ▶
119	B 15	North Huvadhu Atoll, Maldives
150	F 4	North Island, New Zealand
127	O 5	North Korea, Asia □
119	A 14	North Maalhosmadulu Atoll, Maldives
119	B 13	North Miladunmadulu Atoll, Maldives
82	F 8	North Platte, NE, United States
78	H 5	North Point, MI, United States ▶
32	D 6	North Pole, Arctic Ocean
74	F 9	North Saskatchewan, Canada
28	I 3	North Sea, Atlantic Ocean
36	D 6	North Uist, United Kingdom
146	D 6	North West Cape, WA, Australia ▶
36	E 7	North West Highlands, United Kingdom ▲
146	E 9	Northam, WA, Australia
37	I 13	Northampton, United Kingdom
27	I 3	Northeast Pacific Basin, Pacific Ocean
151	L 9	Northern Cook Islands, Cook Islands
23	J 2	Northern Dvina, Europe
37	D 10	Northern Ireland, United Kingdom
151	L 7	Northern Line Islands, Kiribati
151	K 3	Northern Mariana Islands, United States ⊡
56	D 6	Northern Plain, Italy ◇
146	H 6	Northern Territory, Australia, Australia
28	D 2	Northwest Atlantic Mid-Ocean Channel, Atlantic Ocean ≋
26	F 2	Northwest Pacific Basin, Pacific Ocean
74	E 6	Northwest Territories, Canada □
32	D 4	Northwind Plain, Arctic Ocean
32	C 3	Norton Sound, United States ≈
69	B 11	Norway, Europe □
32	D 10	Norwegian Basin, Arctic Ocean
32	E 9	Norwegian Sea, Arctic Ocean
37	J 12	Norwich, United Kingdom
61	J 9	Nos Emine, Bulgaria ▶
61	J 8	Nos Kaliakra, Bulgaria ▶
61	J 8	Nos Shabla, Bulgaria ▶
130	K 3	Nosapu-misaki, Japan ▶
141	N 6	Nosy Bé, Madagascar
141	N 7	Nosy Boraha, Madagascar
131	F 9	Noto-hantō, Japan ▶
75	J 9	Nottaway, Canada
37	H 12	Nottingham, United Kingdom
136	D 4	Nouâdhibou, Mauritania
136	D 4	Nouakchott, Mauritania
150	H 11	Noumea, New Caledonia
61	C 7	Nova Gradiška, Croatia
97	K 8	Nova Iguaçu, Brazil
40	B 9	Nova Lajes, Portugal
75	M 9	Nova Scotia, Canada □
56	B 6	Novara, Italy
104	F 4	Novaya Zemlya, Russia
61	E 8	Novi Pazar, Serbia and Montenegro
61	E 7	Novi Sad, Serbia and Montenegro
97	J 10	Novo Hamburgo, Brazil
104	G 9	Novokuznetsk, Russia
33	M 1	Novolazarevskaya, Russia
104	C 6	Novomoskovsk, Russia
104	B 7	Novorossiysk, Russia
104	G 9	Novosibirsk, Russia
141	I 8	Ntwetwe Pan, Botswana
137	L 4	Nubian Desert, Sudan ▲
89	J 4	Nueva Rosita, Mexico
90	E 6	Nueva San Salvador, Netherlands Antilles
88	H 3	Nuevo Casas Grandes, Mexico
89	K 5	Nuevo Laredo, Mexico
151	O 8	Nuku Hiva, French Polynesia
151	K 10	Nuku'alofa, Tonga
151	L 2	Nukuoro, Federated States of Micronesia
111	I 5	Nukus, Uzbekistan
146	G 8	Nullarbor Plain, WA, Australia ▲
74	G 6	Nunavut, Canada □
84	I 5	Nunivak Island, AL, United States
48	H 7	Nunspeet, Netherlands
57	C 11	Nuoro, Italy
53	F 10	Nuremberg, Germany
68	J 8	Nurmes, Finland
109	K 9	Nusaybin, Turkey
32	B 9	Nuuk, Greenland
32	C 8	Nuussuaq, Greenland
126	H 8	Nyainqêntanglha Shan, China ▲
137	K 6	Nyala, Sudan
69	C 15	Nyborg, Denmark
141	K 3	Nyeri, Kenya
64	H 9	Nyíregyháza, Hungary
126	H 8	Nyingchi, China
69	D 15	Nykøbing, Denmark
69	F 12	Nyköping, Sweden
147	K 8	Nyngan, NSW, Australia
65	I 5	Nyoman, Belarus
130	G 6	Nyūdō-zaki, Japan, ▶
136	E 6	Nzérékoré, Guinea

O

Page	Ref	Name
85	B 15	Oahu, HI, United States
84	D 5	Oak Harbor, WA, United States
85	C 12	Oakland, CA, United States
150	D 10	Oamaru, New Zealand
89	L 10	Oaxaca, Mexico
23	J 2	Ob', Europe
36	E 8	Oban, United Kingdom
123	L 8	Obi, Indonesia
130	I 3	Obihiro, Japan
104	G 6	Obskaya Guba, Russia ≈
65	N 10	Obytichna Kosa, Ukraine ▶
81	J 7	Ocala, FL, United States
28	E 4	Oceanographer Fracture Zone, Atlantic Ocean
85	F 15	Oceanside, CA, United States
81	J 5	Ocmulgee, United States
131	H 10	Odawara, Japan
108	C 8	Ödemiş, Turkey
69	C 14	Odense, Denmark
64	F 7	Oder, Europe
52	H 5	Oderhaff, Germany/Poland ≈
65	L 10	Odesa, Ukraine
83	E 12	Odessa, TX, United States
108	J 6	Of, Turkey
53	D 9	Offenbach, Germany
53	C 11	Offenburg, Germany
136	H 7	Ogbomoso, Nigeria
85	I 10	Ogden, UT, United States
65	I 3	Ogre, Latvia
22	D 4	Ohio, North America
78	H 8	Ohio, United States □
150	F 5	Ohura, New Zealand
49	G 9	Oirschot, Netherlands
131	C 13	Ōita, Japan
111	L 9	Okara, Pakistan
140	H 7	Okavango Delta, Botswana ◇
131	D 12	Okayama, Japan
131	G 11	Okazaki, Japan
105	M 8	Okhotsk, Russia
65	J 6	Okhtyrka, Ukraine
131	J 16	Okinawa, Japan
131	K 15	Okinawa, Japan
131	K 16	Okinawa-shotō, Japan
131	J 15	Okinoerabu-jima, Japan
131	J 15	Okino-shima, Japan
131	C 11	Oki-shotō, Japan
83	G 10	Oklahoma, United States □
83	G 10	Oklahoma City, OK, United States
104	D 7	Oktyabr'skiy, Russia
131	K 15	Oku, Japan
130	G 5	Okushiri-tō, Japan
69	F 14	Öland, Sweden
99	H 11	Olavarría, Argentina
57	C 10	Olbia, Italy
52	D 5	Oldenburg, Germany
48	K 7	Oldenzaal, Netherlands
37	H 11	Oldham, United Kingdom
79	K 7	Olean, NY, United States
65	L 8	Oleksandriva, Ukraine
105	J 6	Olenek, Russia
40	F 9	Olhão, Portugal
64	H 9	Olomouc, Czech Republic
123	J 4	Olongapo, Philippines
64	G 5	Olsztyn, Poland
60	I 8	Oltenița, Romania
84	D 6	Olympia, WA, United States
82	I 8	Omaha, NE, United States
84	E 5	Omak, WA, United States
115	M 7	Oman, Asia
137	L 5	Omdurman, Sudan
137	M 7	Omo Wenz, Ethiopia
105	N 6	Omolon, Russia
104	F 8	Omsk, Russia
127	L 3	Öndörhaan, Mongolia
119	A 15	One and a Half Degree Channel, Maldives ≋
79	K 6	Oneida Lake, NY, United States
119	E 12	Ongole, India
109	L 5	Oni, Georgia
136	H 7	Onitsha, Nigeria
146	D 6	Onslow, WA, Australia
81	M 3	Onslow Bay, NC, United States ≈
84	F 8	Ontario, OR, United States
75	I 9	Ontario, Canada □
41	L 7	Ontinyent, Spain
83	H 10	Oologah Lake, OK, United States
49	B 10	Oostende, Belgium
49	F 9	Oosterhout, Netherlands
49	D 9	Oosterschelde, Netherlands ≈
80	H 4	Opelika, AL, United States
83	J 12	Opelousas, LA, United States
64	F 7	Opole, Poland
150	G 6	Opotiki, New Zealand
60	F 5	Oradea, Romania
136	G 1	Oran, Algeria
45	K 9	Orange, France
147	K 9	Orange, NSW, Australia
140	G 10	Orange, Namibia/South Africa
28	J 8	Orange Cone, Atlantic Ocean
90	E 4	Orange Walk, Belize
81	K 4	Orangeburg, SC, United States
91	L 7	Oranjestad, Aruba
60	F 7	Oraviţa, Romania
57	E 9	Orbetello, Italy
33	J 1	Orcadas, Argentina
146	G 5	Ord, WA, Australia
108	I 6	Ordu, Turkey
69	E 12	Örebro, Sweden
84	D 8	Oregon, United States □
65	M 8	Orel, Ukraine
104	C 6	Orel, Russia
104	D 8	Orenburg, Russia
61	I 10	Orestiada, Greece
41	L 8	Orihuela, Spain
75	K 10	Orillia, ON, Canada
22	E 6	Orinoco, South America
57	B 12	Oristano, Italy
69	K 9	Orivesi, Finland
89	L 9	Orizaba, Mexico
36	F 5	Orkney Islands, United Kingdom
81	K 8	Orlando, FL, United States
45	I 5	Orléans, France
79	N 7	Orleans, MA, United States
123	K 5	Ormoc, Philippines
69	G 9	Örnsköldsvik, Sweden
151	M 1	Oroluk, Federated States of Micronesia
151	K 8	Orona, Kiribati
65	K 4	Orsha, Belarus
104	D 8	Orsk, Russia
44	G 10	Orthez, France
115	J 2	Orūmīyeh, Iran
98	F 5	Oruro, Bolivia
131	F 11	Ōsaka, Japan
31	I 5	Osborn Plateau, Indian Ocean
111	L 6	Osh, Kyrgyzstan
140	G 7	Oshakati, Namibia
75	K 10	Oshawa, ON, Canada
131	H 11	Ō-shima, Japan
78	H 6	Oshkosh, WI, United States
61	D 6	Osijek, Croatia
65	N 7	Oskol, Ukraine
69	C 11	Oslo, Norway
109	H 9	Osmaniye, Turkey
52	C 5	Osnabrück, Germany
99	E 12	Osorno, Chile
49	H 9	Oss, Netherlands
69	G 9	Östersund, Sweden
64	F 8	Ostrava, Czech Republic
64	G 5	Ostróda, Poland
104	G 4	Ostrov Belyy, Russia
105	I 4	Ostrov Bol'shevik, Russia
105	J 3	Ostrov Bol'shoy Begichev, Russia
105	L 5	Ostrov Bol'shoy Lyakhovskiy, Russia
105	O 10	Ostrov Iturup, Russia
105	O 7	Ostrov Karaginskiy, Russia
104	F 4	Ostrov Kolguyev, Russia
105	I 3	Ostrov Komsomolets, Russia
105	L 4	Ostrov Kotel'nyy, Russia
105	N 10	Ostrov Kunashir, Russia
105	L 4	Ostrov Novaya Sibir', Russia
105	I 3	Ostrov Oktyabr'skoy Revolyutsii, Russia
105	O 9	Ostrov Onekotan, Russia
105	O 9	Ostrov Paramushir, Russia
105	O 10	Ostrov Urup, Russia
104	F 5	Ostrov Vaygach, Russia
64	F 6	Ostrów Wielkopolski, Poland
131	B 15	Ōsumi-kaikyō, Japan ≋
131	B 15	Ōsumi-shotō, Japan
40	H 9	Osuna, Spain
150	C 10	Otago Peninsula, New Zealand ▶
150	F 6	Otaki, New Zealand
130	G 4	Otaru, Japan
84	E 6	Othello, WA, United States
150	D 8	Otira, New Zealand
140	G 8	Otjiwarongo, Namibia
150	F 4	Otorohanga, New Zealand
69	B 11	Otra, Norway
83	H 9	Ottawa, KS, United States
75	K 10	Ottawa, ON, Canada
75	I 7	Ottawa Islands, NU, Canada
82	I 8	Ottumwa, IA, United States
136	F 6	Ouagadougou, Burkina Faso
136	F 5	Ouahigouya, Burkina Faso
136	H 2	Ouargla, Algeria
140	G 2	Ouésso, Congo
136	G 1	Oujda, Morocco
68	I 8	Oulu, Finland
68	J 8	Oulujärvi, Finland
68	I 8	Oulujoki, Finland
68	H 6	Ounasjoki, Finland
40	F 3	Ourense, Spain
49	G 13	Ourthe, Belgium
37	H 11	Ouse, United Kingdom
36	C 7	Outer Hebrides, United Kingdom
99	E 9	Ovalle, Chile
140	G 7	Ovamboland, Namibia
40	F 4	Ovar, Portugal
49	F 12	Overijse, Belgium
83	H 9	Overland Park, KS, United States
75	J 10	Owen Sound, ON, Canada
85	F 13	Owens Lake, CA, United States
78	F 10	Owensboro, KY, United States
85	F 9	Owyhee, United States
37	H 13	Oxford, United Kingdom
150	D 8	Oxford, New Zealand
80	F 3	Oxford, MS, United States
85	E 14	Oxnard, CA, United States
131	H 9	Oyama, Japan
83	H 10	Ozark Plateau, United States, United States
26	G 7	Ozbourn Seamount, Pacific Ocean
111	M 4	Ozero Alakol', Kazakhstan
111	J 6	Ozero Aydarkul', Uzbekistan
111	M 3	Ozero Sasykkol, Kazakhstan
105	I 5	Ozero Taymyr, Russia
111	K 2	Ozero Tengiz, Kazakhstan
65	K 11	Ozero Yalpuh, Ukraine
111	N 3	Ozero Zaysan, Kazakhstan

P

Page	Ref	Name
119	H 9	Pabna, Bangladesh
89	L 8	Pachuca, Mexico
26	H 6	Pacific Ocean
26	G 10	Pacific-Antarctic Ridge, Pacific Ocean
122	F 8	Padang, Indonesia
52	D 7	Paderborn, Germany
56	E 6	Padova, Italy
78	E 10	Paducah, KY, United States
150	F 3	Paeroa, New Zealand
61	B 7	Pag, Croatia
123	K 6	Pagadian, Philippines
151	L 3	Pagan, Northern Mariana Islands ▶
85	I 13	Page, AZ, United States
151	K 9	Pago Pago, American Samoa
65	I 1	Paide, Estonia
69	I 10	Päijänne, Finland
85	I 13	Painted Desert, AZ, United States
41	K 2	País Vasco, Spain
111	K 9	Pakistan, Asia □
122	E 3	Pakokku, Myanmar
122	H 4	Pakxé, Laos
137	I 6	Pala, Chad
41	O 3	Palafrugell, Spain
41	O 3	Palamós, Spain
123	K 4	Palanan Point, Philippines ▶
151	J 2	Palau, Pacific Ocean □
26	D 6	Palau Trench, Pacific Ocean
123	I 6	Palawan, Philippines
123	I 6	Palawan Passage, Philippines ≋
26	C 5	Palawan Trough, Pacific Ocean
122	G 9	Palembang, Indonesia
41	I 3	Palencia, Spain
89	N 9	Palenque, Mexico
57	G 14	Palermo, Italy
119	D 14	Palghat, India
119	C 9	Pali, India
151	M 1	Palikir, Federated States of Micronesia
119	E 14	Palk Strait, India/Sri Lanka
85	F 15	Palm Springs, CA, United States
41	O 6	Palma, Spain
97	J 6	Palmas, Brazil
33	I 1	Palmer, United States
33	J 3	Palmer Land, Antarctica
146	G 3	Palmerston, NT, Australia
150	F 6	Palmerston North, New Zealand
57	I 13	Palmi, Italy
96	E 3	Palmira, Colombia
114	H 3	Palmyra, Syria
26	H 5	Palmyra Atoll, Pacific Ocean
123	I 8	Palu, Indonesia
45	I 10	Pamiers, France
111	L 6	Pamirs, Asia ▲
81	N 2	Pamlico Sound, NC, United States ≈
83	F 11	Pampa, TX, United States
99	G 11	Pampas, Argentina ◇
41	K 2	Pamplona, Spain
90	H 8	Panama, North America
27	M 5	Panama Basin, Pacific Ocean
90	H 8	Panama Canal, Panama ≋
80	H 7	Panama City, FL, United States
90	H 8	Panama City, Panama
123	K 5	Panay, Philippines
65	I 4	Panevėžys, Lithuania
122	G 8	Pangkalpinang, Indonesia
97	I 8	Pantanal, Brazil ◇
89	L 7	Pánuco, Mexico
89	K 7	Pánuco, Mexico
127	J 9	Panzhihua, China
151	M 10	Papeete, French Polynesia
147	L 2	Papua New Guinea, Oceania □
98	H 6	Paraguay, South America
98	I 7	Paraguay, Paraguay
136	G 6	Parakou, Benin
97	I 2	Paramaribo, Suriname
99	H 9	Paraná, Argentina
99	H 9	Paraná, South America
119	D 11	Parbhani, India
64	E 7	Pardubice, Czech Republic
123	J 9	Parepare, Indonesia
61	E 11	Parga, Greece
97	I 4	Parintins, Brazil
45	I 4	Paris, France
83	H 11	Paris, TX, United States
79	I 9	Parkersburg, WV, United States
147	K 9	Parkes, NSW, Australia
56	D 6	Parma, Italy
97	L 4	Parnaíba, Brazil
97	K 6	Parnaíba, Brazil
65	I 2	Pärnu, Estonia
61	H 13	Paros, Greece
61	H 13	Paros, Greece
32	C 6	Parry Islands, Canada
97	I 4	Paru, Brazil
74	G 9	Pas, The, MB, Canada
83	G 13	Pasadena, TX, United States
85	F 14	Pasadena, CA, United States
80	F 6	Pascagoula, MS, United States
60	I 5	Pașcani, Romania
84	E 7	Pasco, WA, United States
108	K 7	Pasinler, Turkey
111	J 11	Pasni, Pakistan
99	F 13	Paso de Indios, Argentina
74	F 4	Passage Point, NT, Canada ▶

≈ Bay ≋ Channel □ Country ⊡ Dependent Territory ▲ Desert ⋮⋮ Geographic Area ▶ Headland ☀ Island 🌴 Island Group ∿ Lake ▲ Mountain

53	H 11	Passau, Germany
97	J 10	Passo Fundo, Brazil
96	E 4	Pasto, Colombia
99	F 14	Patagonia, Argentina/Chile
119	B 9	Patan, India
57	H 14	Paterno, Italy
79	L 8	Paterson, NJ, United States
118	D 6	Pathankot, India
82	D 8	Pathfinder Reservoir, WY, United States
118	D 7	Patiala, India
61	I 13	Patmos, Greece
119	G 9	Patna, India
108	L 7	Patnos, Turkey
78	F 9	Patoka Lake, IN, United States
97	K 8	Patos de Minas, Brazil
61	F 12	Patra, Greece
44	G 10	Pau, France
56	C 6	Pavia, Italy
111	L 2	Pavlodar, Kazakhstan
65	N 8	Pavlohrad, Ukraine
99	I 9	Paysandú, Uruguay
108	E 6	Pazarbaşı Burnu, Turkey ▶
61	G 9	Pazardzhik, Bulgaria
61	A 7	Pazin, Croatia
22	D 3	Peace, North America
74	E 8	Peace River, AB, Canada
80	E 5	Pearl, United States
61	E 9	Peć, Serbia and Montenegro
104	E 5	Pechora, Russia
104	E 5	Pechorskoye More, Russia,
83	E 12	Pecos, TX, United States
83	E 12	Pecos, NM, United States
64	F 10	Pécs, Hungary
98	I 7	Pedro Juan Caballero, Paraguay
52	H 5	Peene, Germany
150	E 8	Pegasus Bay, New Zealand ≈
122	F 4	Pegu, Myanmar
122	F 7	Pegunungan Barisan, Indonesia ▲▲
123	N 9	Pegunungan Maoke, Indonesia ▲▲
61	G 13	Peiraias, Greece
122	G 8	Pekanbaru, Indonesia
74	H 5	Pelly Bay, NU, Canada
97	J 10	Pelotas, Brazil
122	F 7	Pematangsiantar, Indonesia
141	L 6	Pemba, Mozambique
141	L 4	Pemba Island, Tanzania
75	K 10	Pembroke, ON, Canada
41	I 2	Pena Prieta, Spain ▲
123	I 8	Penambo Range, Indonesia/Malaysia ▲▲
84	F 7	Pendleton, OR, United States
99	F 16	Península Brecknock, Chile ▶
90	H 9	Península de Azuero, Panama ▶
99	G 16	Península Mitre, Argentina ▶
96	E 7	Península Paracas, Peru ▶
99	E 14	Península Tres Montes, Chile ▶
99	G 12	Península Valdés, Argentina ▶
99	H 11	Península Verde, Argentina ▶
75	J 6	Péninsule d'Ungava, QC, Canada ▶
37	G 10	Pennines, United Kingdom ▲▲
79	J 8	Pennsylvania, United States ⬛
146	H 8	Penong, SA, Australia
80	G 6	Pensacola, FL, United States
33	L 3	Pensacola Mountains, Antarctica ▲▲
104	C 7	Penza, Russia
37	E 15	Penzance, United Kingdom
78	E 8	Peoria, IL, United States
146	F 6	Percival Lakes, WA, Australia
96	E 3	Pereira, Colombia
99	H 10	Pergamino, Argentina
69	H 9	Perhonjoki, Finland
75	K 8	Peribonca, Canada
44	H 8	Périgueux, France
99	F 13	Perito Moreno, Argentina
104	E 7	Perm', Russia
28	H 7	Pernambuco Abyssal Plain, Atlantic Ocean ▬
28	G 7	Pernambuco Seamounts, Atlantic Ocean ▬
61	G 9	Pernik, Bulgaria
89	L 8	Perote, Mexico
45	J 11	Perpignan, France
83	F 10	Perryton, TX, United States
115	K 5	Persian Gulf, Asia
36	F 8	Perth, United Kingdom
146	E 9	Perth, WA, Australia
31	K 6	Perth Basin, Southern Ocean
65	E 5	Peru, South America ⬛
27	M 7	Peru Basin, Pacific Ocean ▬
27	M 5	Peru-Chile Trench, Pacific Ocean ▬
56	F 8	Perugia, Italy
49	D 12	Peruwelz, Belgium
65	L 9	Pervomays'k, Ukraine
104	E 7	Pervoural'sk, Russia
57	G 9	Pescara, Italy
111	L 8	Peshāwar, Pakistan
61	E 10	Peshkopi, Albania
111	K 4	Peski Muyunkum, Kazakhsta ▲
49	I 15	Pétange, Luxembourg
78	E 5	Petenwell Lake, WI, United States
22	E 10	Peter I Island, Antarctica
37	I 12	Peterborough, United Kingdom
147	I 9	Peterborough, SA, Australia
75	K 10	Peterborough, ON, Canada
79	K 10	Petersburg, VI, United States
89	P 8	Peto, Mexico
78	G 5	Petoskey, MI, United States
111	K 1	Petropavlovsk, Kazakhstan
105	O 8	Petropavlovsk-Kamchatskiy, Russia
60	G 7	Petroşani, Romania
104	D 5	Petrozavodsk, Russia
53	D 10	Pforzheim, Germany
122	H 5	Phan Thiêt, Vietnam
80	H 5	Phenix City, AL, United States
79	L 8	Philadelphia, PA, United States
49	F 13	Philippeville, Belgium
26	D 5	Philippine Basin, Pacific Ocean ▬
26	D 4	Philippine Sea, Pacific Ocean
123	K 3	Philippine Sea, Asia
26	D 4	Philippines Trench, Pacific Ocean ▬
122	G 5	Phnom Penh, Cambodia ◆
85	I 15	Phoenix, AZ, United States ⬚
151	J 8	Phoenix Islands, Kiribati
122	F 6	Phuket, Thailand
56	C 6	Piacenza, Italy
60	I 5	Piatra Neamț, Romania
98	E 6	Pica, Chile
40	B 9	Pico, Portugal
40	C 11	Pico de las Nieves, Spain ▲
40	B 10	Pico del Teide, Spain ▲
99	F 13	Pico Truncado, Argentina
97	L 5	Picos, Brazil
150	E 6	Picton, New Zealand
89	K 4	Piedras Negras, Mexico
69	K 9	Pielinen, Finland
82	F 7	Pierre, SD, United States ⬚
141	J 10	Pietermaritzburg, South Africa
141	J 9	Pietersburg, South Africa
89	N 10	Pijijiapan, Mexico
78	H 10	Pikeville, KY, United States
64	F 5	Piła, Poland
99	H 10	Pilar, Argentina
98	I 8	Pilar, Paraguay
98	H 7	Pilcomayo, Paraguay
118	E 8	Pilibhit, India
61	F 11	Pineios, Greece
127	L 7	Pingdingshan, China
151	M 1	Pingelap, Federated States of Micronesia
127	N 10	P'ingtung, Taiwan
127	M 9	Pingxiang, China
65	J 6	Pinsk, Belarus
56	D 8	Piombino, Italy
64	G 7	Piotrków Trybunalski, Poland
97	J 9	Piracicaba, Brazil
53	C 10	Pirmasens, Germany
61	F 8	Pirot, Serbia and Montenegro
56	D 7	Pisa, Italy
64	E 8	Pisek, Czech Republic
56	D 7	Pistoia, Italy
151	P 11	Pitcairn Island, Pitcairn Islands
151	P 11	Pitcairn Islands, United Kingdom ⬛
68	H 8	Piteå, Sweden
60	H 7	Pitești, Romania
79	J 8	Pittsburgh, PA, United States
79	M 7	Pittsfield, MA, United States
96	D 5	Piura, Peru
65	L 9	Pivdennyy Buh, Ukraine
85	D 11	Placerville, CA, United States
83	F 11	Plainview, TX, United States
140	G 6	Planalto do Bié, Angola ◆
141	K 6	Planalto Moçambicano, Mozambique ◆
40	H 5	Plasencia, Spain
140	H 5	Plateau du Kasai, Democratic Republic of Congo ◆
136	G 3	Plateau du Tademaït, Algeria ◆
23	L 4	Plateau of Tibet, Asia ◆
82	F 8	Platte, NE, United States
79	L 5	Plattsburgh, NY, United States
53	G 9	Plauen, Germany
52	G 5	Plauer See, Germany
64	D 8	Plechý, Czech Republic ▲
61	H 8	Pleven, Bulgaria
64	G 6	Płock, Poland
60	I 7	Ploiești, Romania
61	I 12	Plomari, Greece
61	H 9	Plovdiv, Bulgaria
37	D 10	Plymouth, United Kingdom
79	N 7	Plymouth, MA, United States
91	N 5	Plymouth, Montserrat ⬛
64	D 7	Plzeň, Czech Republic
56	D 6	Po, Italy
56	F 6	Po Delta, Italy
85	I 9	Pocatello, ID, United States
97	K 8	Poços de Caldas, Brazil
61	D 9	Podgorica, Serbia and Montenegro
61	E 10	Pogradec, Albania
127	P 6	P'ohang, South Korea
151	M 1	Pohnpei, Federated States of Micronesia
85	C 11	Point Arena, CA, United States ▶
85	D 14	Point Arguello, CA, United States ▶
85	D 14	Point Conception, CA, United States ▶
119	E 14	Point Pedro, Sri Lanka ▶
85	C 12	Point Reyes, CA, United States ▶
85	B 9	Point St George, CA, United States ▶
78	G 5	Point Sturgeon, WI, United States ▶
78	H 6	Pointe Aux Barques, MI, United States ▶
91	N 5	Pointe-à-Pitre, Guadeloupe
140	F 4	Pointe-Noire, Congo
44	A 6	Poitiers, France
64	G 5	Poland, Europe ⬛
108	F 7	Polatlı, Turkey
65	J 4	Polatsk, Belarus
123	J 9	Polewali, Indonesia
41	O 6	Pollença, Spain
65	M 8	Poltava, Ukraine
61	I 10	Polykastro, Greece
52	H 4	Pommersche Bay, Germany ≈
85	F 14	Pomona, CA, United States
81	L 10	Pompano Beach, FL, United States
57	H 11	Pompei, Italy ✶
83	G 10	Ponca City, OK, United States
91	M 5	Ponce, Puerto Rico
119	E 14	Pondicherry, India
40	G 2	Ponferrada, Spain
97	L 8	Ponta da Baleia, Brazil ▶
40	C 9	Ponta Degada, Portugal
97	J 9	Ponta Grossa, Brazil
45	L 6	Pontarlier, France
40	F 3	Ponte da Barca, Portugal
40	F 3	Ponteareas, Spain
40	F 3	Pontevedra, Spain
122	H 8	Pontianak, Indonesia
45	I 3	Pontoise, France
65	J 6	Ponya, Belarus
37	H 14	Poole, United Kingdom
150	F 2	Poor Knights Islands, New Zealand
96	E 3	Popayán, Colombia
83	J 10	Poplar Bluff, MO, United States
89	K 9	Popocatépetl, Mexico ▲
147	K 3	Popondetta, Papua New Guinea
56	F 5	Pordenone, Italy
61	A 7	Porec, Croatia
69	H 10	Pori, Finland
150	F 6	Porirua, New Zealand
33	O 7	Porpoise Bay, Antarctica ≈
68	H 8	Porsangen, Norway ≈
69	C 12	Porsgrunn, Norway
84	C 5	Port Angeles, WA, United States
83	I 13	Port Arthur, TX, United States
147	I 8	Port Augusta, SA, Australia
150	C 10	Port Chalmers, New Zealand
81	J 11	Port Charlotte, FL, United States
141	I 11	Port Elizabeth, South Africa
136	H 7	Port Harcourt, Nigeria
74	C 9	Port Hardy, BC, Canada
146	E 6	Port Hedland, WA, Australia
78	H 6	Port Huron, MI, United States
83	H 13	Port Lavaca, TX, United States
147	I 9	Port Lincoln, SA, Australia
141	O 8	Port Louis, Mauritius ⬛
147	K 3	Port Moresby, Papua New Guinea ◆
91	O 7	Port of Spain, Trinidad and Tobago ◆
147	I 9	Port Pirie, SA, Australia
137	L 2	Port Said, Egypt
137	M 4	Port Sudan, Sudan
150	H 10	Port Vila, Vanuatu ◆
37	D 10	Portadown, United Kingdom
74	H 10	Portage la Prairie, MB, Canada
40	F 6	Portalegre, Portugal
91	K 4	Port-au-Prince, Haiti ⬛
91	K 4	Port-de-Paix, Haiti
85	E 13	Porterville, CA, United States
140	E 3	Port-Gentil, Gabon
79	N 6	Portland, ME, United States
84	D 7	Portland, OR, United States
37	G 15	Portland Bill, United Kingdom ▶
40	F 6	Porto, Portugal
97	J 10	Porto Alegre, Brazil
28	B 8	Porto Inglês, Cape Verde
28	A 7	Porto Novo, Cape Verde
40	D 9	Porto Santo, Portugal
57	B 11	Porto Torres, Italy
96	G 6	Porto Velho, Brazil
90	H 8	Portobelo, Panama
56	D 7	Portoferraio, Italy
136	G 7	Porto-Novo, Benin ⬛
96	D 4	Portoviejo, Ecuador
36	D 7	Portree, United Kingdom
37	I 14	Portsmouth, United Kingdom
78	H 9	Portsmouth, OH, United States
79	N 6	Portsmouth, NH, United States
79	K 11	Portsmouth, VI, United States
40	E 9	Portugal, Europe ⬛
69	I 11	Porvoo, Finland
98	I 8	Posadas, Argentina
60	A 6	Postojna, Slovenia
57	I 11	Potenza, Italy
109	K 5	P'ot'i, Georgia
79	K 9	Potomac, United States
98	G 6	Potosí, Bolivia
52	G 6	Potsdam, Germany
150	H 4	Poverty Bay, New Zealand ≈
40	F 6	Póvoa de Varzim, Portugal
82	D 7	Powder, MT, United States
127	M 8	Poyang Hu, China
89	L 8	Poza Rica, Mexico
61	C 7	Požarevac, Serbia and Montenegro
61	C 7	Požega, Croatia
64	F 6	Poznań, Poland
98	I 7	Pozo Colorado, Paraguay
64	F 7	Prague, Czech Republic ◆
28	B 8	Praia, Cape Verde ⬛
56	E 7	Prato, Italy
80	H 5	Prattville, AL, United States
119	J 12	Prepari Island, India
89	N 10	Presa de la Angostura, Mexico
89	J 9	Presa del Infiernillo, Mexico
85	I 14	Prescott, AZ, United States
98	I 7	Presidencia Roque, Argentina
79	O 3	Presque Isle, ME, United States
37	G 11	Preston, United Kingdom
141	I 9	Pretoria, South Africa ◆
61	E 12	Preveza, Greece
84	H 5	Pribilof Islands, AL, United States
85	J 11	Price, UT, United States
61	E 8	Prijepolje, Serbia and Montenegro
61	F 10	Prilep, Macedonia
74	F 9	Prince Albert, SK, Canada
74	F 4	Prince Albert Peninsula, NT, Canada ▶
75	I 5	Prince Charles Island, NU, Canada
33	O 3	Prince Charles Mountains, Antarctica ▲▲
30	D 9	Prince Edward Fracture Zone, Indian Ocean ▬
30	E 9	Prince Edward Islands, Southern Ocean
75	M 8	Prince Edward Island, Canada ⬛
74	D 8	Prince George, BC, Canada
147	J 3	Prince of Wales Island, QLD, Australia
74	G 4	Prince of Wales Island, NU, Canada
74	C 8	Prince Rupert, BC, Canada
33	O 4	Princess Elizabeth Land, Antarctica ◆
140	E 3	Príncipe, São Tomé and Príncipe
65	J 6	Pripet, Belarus
65	J 6	Pripet Marshes, Belarus/Ukraine ◆
61	F 9	Priština, Serbia and Montenegro
45	K 8	Privas, France
61	E 9	Prizren, Serbia and Montenegro
123	I 10	Probolinggo, Indonesia
97	I 3	Professor Van Blommestein Meer, Suriname
89	O 7	Progreso, Mexico
32	D 4	Proliv Longa, Arctic Ocean ≈
45	L 10	Provence, France ◆
79	N 7	Providence, RI, United States ⬚
85	I 10	Provo, UT, United States
84	J 4	Prudhoe Bay, AL, United States
64	G 6	Pruszków, Poland
65	L 7	Pryluky, Ukraine
64	H 8	Przemysl, Poland
61	H 12	Psara, Greece
104	C 5	Pskov, Russia
61	F 11	Ptolemaïda, Greece
65	J 5	Ptsich, Belarus
96	E 6	Pucallpa, Peru
89	L 9	Puebla, Mexico
83	D 9	Pueblo, CO, United States
99	E 13	Puerto Aisén, Chile
89	L 10	Puerto Ángel, Mexico
96	G 3	Puerto Ayacucho, Venezuela
96	B 7	Puerto Ayora, Ecuador
96	B 7	Puerto Baquerizo Moreno, Ecuador
90	E 5	Puerto Barrios, Guatemala
90	G 6	Puerto Cabezas, Nicaragua
96	G 2	Puerto Carreño, Colombia
99	E 13	Puerto Cisnes, Chile
90	G 8	Puerto Cortés, Costa Rica
40	C 10	Puerto del Rosario, Spain
89	L 10	Puerto Escondido, Mexico
90	G 6	Puerto Lempira, Honduras
99	G 12	Puerto Madryn, Argentina
96	F 6	Puerto Maldonado, Peru
99	E 12	Puerto Montt, Chile
99	E 15	Puerto Natales, Chile
91	K 4	Puerto Plata, Dominican Republic
123	J 6	Puerto Princesa, Philippines
91	M 5	Puerto Rico, United States ⬛
28	D 6	Puerto Rico Trench, Atlantic Ocean ▬
99	F 14	Puerto San Julián, Argentina
98	I 6	Puerto Suárez, Bolivia
89	I 8	Puerto Vallarta, Mexico
96	A 7	Puerto Villamil, Ecuador
41	I 7	Puertollano, Spain
84	C 5	Puget Sound, WA, United States ≈
150	F 3	Pukekohe, New Zealand
61	A 7	Pula, Croatia
151	K 1	Pulap, Federated States of Micronesia
123	N 10	Pulau Dolak, Indonesia
151	K 1	Pulawat, Federated States of Micronesia
84	F 6	Pullman, WA, United States
151	I 2	Pulo Anna, Palau
151	K 1	Pulusuk, Federated States of Micronesia
98	F 7	Puna de Atacama, Argentina ▲▲
98	G 5	Punata, Bolivia
123	N 9	Puncak Jaya, Indonesia ▲
119	C 11	Pune, India
118	D 7	Punjab, India/Pakistan
96	F 7	Puno, Peru
57	J 12	Punta Alice, Italy ▶
40	H 10	Punta Almina, Spain ▶
99	H 11	Punta Alta, Argentina
99	F 15	Punta Arenas, Chile
99	G 12	Punta Bermeja, Argentina ▶
57	B 10	Punta Caprara, Italy ▶
96	E 3	Punta Chirambirá, Colombia ▶
99	F 15	Punta de Arenas, Chile ▶
41	J 10	Punta de las Entinas, Spain ▶
88	H 8	Punta de Mita, Mexico ▶
90	G 7	Punta del Mono, Nicaragua ▶
88	E 4	Punta Eugenia, Mexico ▶
99	E 12	Punta Galera, Chile ▶
89	P 8	Punta Herrero, Mexico ▶
98	E 7	Punta Jorjino, Chile ▶

▲▲ Mountain Range   ▣ National Capital   ⟲ Ocean   Physical Feature   ▬ Polar Base   River   ≈ Sea   ✶ Special Feature   ⬚ State Capital   ▬ Underwater Feature

99　E 11　**Punta Lavapié**, Chile ▶
99　E 9　**Punta Lengua de Vaca**, Chile ▶
99　F 14　**Punta León**, Argentina ▶
99　G 14　**Punta Medanosa**, Argentina ▶
96　D 5　**Punta Negro**, Peru ▶
99　G 12　**Punta Ninfas**, Argentina ▶
96　D 5　**Punta Pariñas**, Peru ▶
99　H 12　**Punta Rasa**, Argentina ▶
88　G 5　**Punta Rosa**, Mexico ▶
96　E 7　**Punta Santa Maria**, Peru ▶
90　F 8　**Puntarenas**, Costa Rica
119　G 11　**Puri**, India
48　F 7　**Purmerend**, Netherlands
96　H 5　**Purus**, Brazil/Peru ᔓ
69　K 10　**Puruvesi**, Finland ᔓ
122　H 9　**Purwakarta**, Indonesia
127　P 6　**Pusan**, South Korea
98　E 5　**Putre**, Chile
150　A 11　**Puysegur Point**, New Zealand ▶
104　B 8　**Pyatigorsk**, Russia
122　E 3　**Pyè**, Myanmar
68　I 8　**Pyhäjoki**, Finland ᔓ
69　K 9　**Pyhäselkä**, Finland ᔓ
61　F 13　**Pylos**, Greece
127　O 5　**P'yŏngyang**, North Korea ▪
85　E 11　**Pyramid Lake**, NV, United States ᔓ
22　H 3　**Pyrenees**, Europe ▲
61　F 13　**Pyrgos**, Greece

Q

111　K 8　**Qalāt**, Afghanistan
115　I 8　**Qal'at Bishah**, Saudi Arabia
111　J 7　**Qal'eh-ye**, Afghanistan
127　I 8　**Qamdo**, China
111　L 6　**Qarokŭl**, Tajikistan ᔓ
115　L 6　**Qatar**, Asia ▫
137　K 2　**Qattâra Depression**, Egypt ◇
115　K 2　**Qazvīn**, Iran
137　L 3　**Qena**, Egypt
127　I 5　**Qilian Shan**, China ▲
127　N 6　**Qingdao**, China
127　J 6　**Qinghai Hu**, China ᔓ
127　M 5　**Qinhuangdao**, China
127　N 3　**Qiqihar**, China
115　L 3　**Qom**, Iran
127　N 9　**Quanzhou**, China
57　C 12　**Quartu Sant'Elena**, Italy
115　M 2　**Quchan**, Iran
75　J 8　**Québec**, Canada ▫
75　L 9　**Québec**, QC, Canada
74　C 8　**Queen Charlotte Islands**, BC, Canada ⚊
74　C 9　**Queen Charlotte Sound**, BC, Canada ≈
74　G 3　**Queen Elizabeth Islands**, NU, Canada ⚊
33　O 4　**Queen Mary Land**, Antarctica ⠿
33　L 2　**Queen Maud Land**, Antarctica ⠿
33　L 5　**Queen Maud Mountains**, Antarctica ▲
147　J 6　**Queensland**, Australia ▫
150　B 9　**Queenstown**, New Zealand
147　J 11　**Queenstown**, TAS, Australia
141　K 7　**Quelimane**, Mozambique
89　K 8　**Querétaro**, Mexico
111　K 9　**Quetta**, Pakistan
90　D 6　**Quezaltenango**, Guatemala
123　K 5　**Quezon City**, Philippines
122　H 5　**Qui Nhon**, Vietnam
96　E 3　**Quibdó**, Colombia
119　D 15　**Quilon**, India
99　E 10　**Quilpue**, Chile
44　E 4　**Quimper**, France
44　E 5　**Quimperlé**, France
78　D 8　**Quincy**, IL, United States
96　E 4　**Quito**, Ecuador ▪

R

68　I 8　**Raahe**, Finland
123　J 10　**Raba**, Indonesia
136　F 1　**Rabat**, Morocco ▪
147　L 2　**Rabaul**, Papua New Guinea

114　H 7　**Rābigh**, Saudi Arabia
122　G 6　**Rach Gia**, Vietnam
78　F 7　**Racine**, WI, United States
64　H 7　**Radom**, Poland
99　H 9　**Rafaela**, Argentina
115　J 5　**Rafḥā'**, Saudi Arabia
115　M 4　**Rafsanjān**, Iran
57　H 15　**Ragusa**, Italy
111　L 10　**Rahimyar Khan**, Pakistan
119　D 12　**Raichur**, India
119　F 10　**Raipur**, India
119　F 10　**Raj-Nandgaon**, India
119　F 12　**Rajahmundry**, India
119　D 14　**Rajapalaiyam**, India
118　C 8　**Rajasthan**, India ⠿
119　B 10　**Rajkot**, India
119　H 9　**Rajshahi**, Bangladesh
150　D 8　**Rakaia**, New Zealand ᔓ
81　L 2　**Raleigh**, NC, United States ▪
81　N 3　**Raleigh Bay**, NC, United States ≈
151　M 3　**Ralik Chain**, Marshall Islands ⚊
115　J 10　**Ramlat as Sab'atayn**, Yemen ▲
115　J 9　**Ramlat Dahm**, Yemen ▲
60　G 7　**Râmnicu Vâlcea**, Romania
118　E 8　**Rampur**, India
122　E 3　**Ramree**, Myanmar ⚊
37　K 14　**Ramsgate**, United Kingdom
119　D 9　**Rana Pratap Sagar**, India ᔓ
99　E 10　**Rancagua**, Chile
119　G 10　**Ranchi**, India
69　C 14　**Randers**, Denmark
150　D 8　**Rangiora**, New Zealand
122　F 4　**Rangoon**, Myanmar ▪
119　H 9　**Rangpur**, Bangladesh
119　A 9　**Rann of Kachchh**, India ◇
82　E 7　**Rapid City**, SD, United States
151　L 10　**Rarotonga**, Cook Islands ⚊
114　H 6　**Rās Abū Madd**, Saudi Arabia ▶
115　N 7　**Rās al Ḥadd**, Oman ▶
115　K 10　**Rās al Kalb**, Yemen ▶
115　M 6　**Ras al Khaimah**, United Arab Emirates
115　N 8　**Ras al Madrakah**, Oman ▶
115　K 5　**Rās az Zawr**, Saudi Arabia ▶
114　H 6　**Rās Baridī**, Saudi Arabia ▶
137　O 5　**Rās Caluula**, Somalia ▶
137　O 5　**Rās Caseyr**, Somalia ▶
137　M 5　**Rās Dashen**, Ethiopia ▲
115　L 9　**Rās Fartak**, Yemen ▶
115　I 10　**Rās 'Īsá**, Yemen ▶
114　H 6　**Rās Karkūmā**, Saudi Arabia ▶
137　M 5　**Rās Kasar**, Sudan ▶
115　M 9　**Rās Naws**, Oman ▶
136　D 4　**Rās Nouâdhibou**, Mauritania ▶
115　M 8　**Rās Şawqirah**, Oman ▶
115　M 9　**Rās Sharbithāt**, Oman ▶
115　K 5　**Rās Tanāqīb**, Saudi Arabia ▶
136　D 4　**Rās Timirist**, Mauritania ▶
137　O 6　**Rās Xaafuun**, Somalia ▶
115　K 2　**Rasht**, Iran
151　M 3　**Ratak Chain**, Marshall Islands ⚊
69　E 9　**Rätansbyn**, Sweden
119　D 9　**Ratlam**, India
119　B 12　**Ratnagiri**, India
69　H 10　**Rauma**, Finland
119　G 10　**Raurkela**, India
56　F 7　**Ravenna**, Italy
53　L 12　**Ravensburg**, Germany
146　F 9　**Ravensthorpe**, WA, Australia
111　L 9　**Ravi**, India/Pakistan ᔓ
115　I 3　**Rāwah**, Iraq
111　L 8　**Rawalpindi**, Pakistan
99　G 12　**Rawson**, Argentina
122　G 5　**Rayong**, Thailand
61　I 8　**Razgrad**, Bulgaria
37　I 14　**Reading**, United Kingdom
79　L 8　**Reading**, PA, United States
130　G 2　**Rebun-tō**, Japan ⚊
65　K 6　**Rechytsa**, Belarus
97　M 6　**Recife**, Brazil
98　H 8　**Reconquista**, Argentina
83　G 11　**Red**, OK, United States ᔓ
122　G 3　**Red**, Vietnam ᔓ
85　C 10　**Red Bluff**, CA, United States
74　E 9　**Red Deer**, AB, Canada
23　J 4　**Red Sea**, Africa/Asia ≈
82　I 7　**Red Wing**, MN, United States
85　C 10　**Redding**, CA, United States
97　J 6　**Redenção**, Brazil

84　D 8　**Redmond**, OR, United States
150　D 7　**Reefton**, New Zealand
108　I 7　**Refahiye**, Turkey
53　G 10　**Regensburg**, Germany
56　D 6　**Reggio**, Italy
57　I 14　**Reggio di Calabria**, Italy
74　G 10　**Regina**, SK, Canada
111　J 9　**Registan**, Afghanistan ▲
140　G 8　**Rehoboth**, Namibia
37　I 14　**Reigate**, United Kingdom
45　J 3　**Reims**, France
74　G 8　**Reindeer Lake**, MB/SK, Canada ᔓ
41　I 2　**Reinosa**, Spain
52　C 6　**Remscheid**, Germany
78　E 10　**Rend Lake**, IL, United States ᔓ
44　F 4　**Rennes**, France
74　H 10　**Rennie**, MB, Canada
85　E 11　**Reno**, NV, United States
96　H 4　**Represa de Balbina**, Brazil ᔓ
97　I 9　**Represa de Itaipu**, Brazil/Paraguay ᔓ
97　J 8　**Represa Porto Primavera**, Brazil ᔓ
97　J 8　**Represa São Simão**, Brazil ᔓ
97　K 8　**Represa Três Marias**, Brazil ᔓ
97　J 5　**Represa Tucurui**, Brazil ᔓ
74　H 5　**Repulse Bay**, NU, Canada
75　K 9　**Réservoir Cabonga**, QC, Canada ᔓ
75　J 8　**Réservoir la Grande Deux**, QC, Canada ᔓ
75　J 8　**Réservoir la Grande Trois**, QC, Canada ᔓ
75　J 8　**Réservoir Manicouagan**, QC, Canada ᔓ
98　H 8　**Resistencia**, Argentina
60　F 7　**Reşiţa**, Romania
32　C 6　**Resolute**, Canada
150　A 10　**Resolution Island**, New Zealand ⚊
75　K 5　**Resolution Island**, NU, Canada ⚊
61　H 15　**Rethymno**, Greece
30　G 5　**Réunion**, France ⚊
141　O 8　**Réunion**, France ▫
53　D 11　**Reutlingen**, Germany
22　C 5　**Revillagigedo Islands**, North America ⚊
119　F 9　**Rewa**, India
84　I 8　**Rexburg**, ID, United States
28　G 2　**Reykjanes Basin**, Atlantic Ocean
28　G 2　**Reykjanes Ridge**, Atlantic Ocean ▲
68　B 6　**Reykjavík**, Iceland ▪
89　K 5　**Reynosa**, Mexico
65　J 3　**Rēzekne**, Latvia
52　C 6　**Rheine**, Germany
22　H 3　**Rhine**, Europe ᔓ
79　N 7　**Rhode Island**, United States ▫
61　J 14　**Rhodes**, Greece ⚊
45　K 7　**Rhône**, France ᔓ
37　G 11　**Ribble**, United Kingdom ᔓ
40　E 2　**Ribeira**, Spain
40　C 2　**Ribeira Grande**, Portugal
97　J 8　**Ribeirão Preto**, Brazil
98　F 3　**Riberalta**, Bolivia
65　K 9　**Ribniţa**, Moldova
81　J 4　**Richard B. Russell Lake**, GA, United States ᔓ
150　E 7　**Richmond**, New Zealand
78　H 10　**Richmond**, KY, United States
79　K 10　**Richmond**, VI, United States
85　F 13　**Ridgecrest**, CA, United States
65　I 3　**Rīga**, Latvia ▪
33　N 1　**Riiser-Larsen Peninsula**, Antarctica ▶
29　J 12　**Riiser-Larsen Sea**, Atlantic Ocean ≈
61　A 7　**Rijeka**, Croatia
48　J 7　**Rijssen**, Netherlands
56　F 7　**Rimini**, Italy
69　D 14　**Ringsted**, Denmark
68　G 4　**Ringvassøy**, Norway ⚊
96　G 6　**Rio Branco**, Brazil
99　G 9　**Rio Cuarto**, Argentina
97　K 9　**Rio de Janeiro**, Brazil
99　F 15　**Rio Gallegos**, Argentina
99　F 15　**Rio Grande**, Argentina
97　J 11　**Rio Grande**, Brazil
22　D 4　**Rio Grande**, North America ᔓ
89　J 6　**Rio Grande**, Mexico
89　I 7　**Rio Grande de Santiago**, Mexico ᔓ
29　G 9　**Rio Grande Fracture Zone**, Atlantic Ocean
29　F 9　**Rio Grande Rise**, Atlantic Ocean ▲
99　F 13　**Rio Mayo**, Argentina

97　J 7　**Rio Verde**, Brazil
89　K 7　**Rio Verde**, Mexico
96　E 4　**Riobamba**, Ecuador
96　F 1　**Riohacha**, Colombia
41　N 3　**Ripoll**, Spain
130　G 2　**Rishiri-tō**, Japan ⚊
90　F 7　**Rivas**, Nicaragua
22　F 8　**River Plate**, South America ᔓ
99　I 9　**Rivera**, Uruguay
85　F 14　**Riverside**, CA, United States
75　J 7　**Rivière aux Feuilles**, Canada ᔓ
75　L 9　**Rivière-du-Loup**, QC, Canada ᔓ
65　J 7　**Rivne**, Ukraine
56　A 6　**Rivoli**, Italy
115　K 6　**Riyadh**, Saudi Arabia ▪
108　J 6　**Rize**, Turkey
91　M 4　**Road Town**, British Virgin Islands ▪
45　K 7　**Roanne**, France
79　J 10　**Roanoke**, VI, United States
81　O 2　**Roanoke Island**, NC, United States ⚊
140　H 11　**Robben Island**, South Africa ⚊
98　H 5　**Robore**, Bolivia
99　J 10　**Rocha**, Uruguay
44　G 7　**Rochefort**, France
79　K 6　**Rochester**, NY, United States
82　I 7　**Rochester**, MN, United States
81　K 3　**Rock Hill**, SC, United States
91　I 2　**Rock Sound**, The Bahamas
82　C 8　**Rock Springs**, WY, United States
28　H 3　**Rockall Bank**, Atlantic Ocean ▲
28　H 3　**Rockall Trough**, Atlantic Ocean ▲
78　E 7　**Rockford**, IL, United States
147　L 6　**Rockhampton**, QLD, Australia
81　M 2　**Rocky Mount**, NC, United States
22　C 4　**Rocky Mountains**, North America ▲
45　I 9　**Rodez**, France
30　G 5　**Rodrigues Island**, Indian Ocean ⚊
49　I 10　**Roermond**, Netherlands
49　C 11　**Roeselare**, Belgium
83　I 10　**Rogers**, AR, United States
27　L 8　**Roggeveen Basin**, Pacific Ocean
118　D 8　**Rohtak**, India
83　I 9　**Rolla**, MO, United States
147　K 7　**Roma**, QLD, Australia
60　I 6　**Romania**, Europe ▫
57　F 9　**Rome**, Italy ▪
80　H 3　**Rome**, GA, United States
65　M 7　**Romny**, Ukraine
40　H 9　**Ronda**, Spain
97　I 7　**Rondonópolis**, Brazil
151　M 2　**Rongelap Atoll**, Marshall Islands ⚊
151　M 3　**Rongrik**, Marshall Islands ⚊
69　E 15　**Rønne**, Denmark
33　K 3　**Ronne Ice Shelf**, Antarctica ◇
49　E 9　**Roosendaal**, Netherlands
33　L 6　**Roosevelt Island**, Antarctica ⚊
69　D 9　**Røros**, Norway
65　K 8　**Ros'**, Ukraine ᔓ
99　H 9　**Rosario**, Argentina
88　E 4　**Rosarito**, Mexico
78　H 5　**Roscommon**, MI, United States
91　N 6　**Roseau**, Dominica ▪
84　C 8　**Roseburg**, OR, United States
137　L 6　**Roseires Reservoir**, Sudan ᔓ
53　G 12　**Rosenheim**, Germany
150　C 8　**Ross**, New Zealand
80　E 4　**Ross Barnett Reservoir**, MS, United States ᔓ
33　L 6　**Ross Ice Shelf**, Antarctica ◇
33　M 6　**Ross Island**, Antarctica ⚊
26　H 11　**Ross Sea**, Southern Ocean ⊃
136　D 4　**Rosso**, Mauritania
52　G 4　**Rostock**, Germany
104　B 7　**Rostov-na-Donu**, Russia
83　D 11　**Roswell**, NM, United States
151　L 5　**Rota**, Northern Mariana Islands ⚊
123　K 11　**Rote**, Indonesia ⚊
33　I 3　**Rothera**, United Kingdom ▪
37　H 11　**Rotherham**, United Kingdom
150　F 4　**Rotorua**, New Zealand
48　F 8　**Rotterdam**, Netherlands
45　J 1　**Roubaix**, France
44　H 3　**Rouen**, France
68　I 7　**Rovaniemi**, Finland
56　E 6　**Rovigo**, Italy
123　K 5　**Roxas**, Philippines
44　G 7　**Royan**, France
150　B 11　**Ruapuke Island**, New Zealand ⚊

150　H 4　**Ruatoria**, New Zealand
115　J 8　**Rub' al Khālī**, Saudi Arabia ▲
104　G 9　**Rubtsovsk**, Russia
111　J 2　**Rudnyy**, Kazakhstan
99　G 10　**Rufino**, Argentina
37　H 12　**Rugby**, United Kingdom
36　D 7　**Rum**, United Kingdom ⚊
140　H 7　**Rundu**, Namibia
61　I 8　**Ruse**, Bulgaria
104　H 7　**Russia**, Asia/Europe ▫
33　K 6　**Russkaya**, Russia ▪
109　M 5　**Rust'avi**, Georgia
141　I 9　**Rustenburg**, South Africa
83　I 12　**Ruston**, LA, United States
141　L 5　**Ruvuma**, Mozambique/Tanzania ᔓ
141　J 3　**Rwanda**, Africa ▫
104　C 6　**Ryazan'**, Russia
33　J 4　**Ryberg Peninsula**, Antarctica
104　D 5　**Rybinsk**, Russia
64　F 8　**Rybnik**, Poland
131　J 15　**Ryukyu Islands**, Japan ⚊
26　D 4　**Ryukyu Trench**, Pacific Ocean ▪
64　H 8　**Rzeszów**, Poland

S

52　F 8　**Saale**, Germany ᔓ
53　B 10　**Saarbrücken**, Germany
64　H 2　**Saaremaa**, Estonia ⚊
52　D 7　**Šabac**, Serbia and Montenegro
41　N 4　**Sabadell**, Spain
123　J 7　**Sabah**, Malaysia ⠿
137　I 3　**Sabhā**, Libya
89　J 4　**Sabinas**, Mexico
89　K 5　**Sabinas Hidalgo**, Mexico
115　M 2　**Sabzevār**, Iran
85　C 11　**Sacramento**, CA, United States
85　C 10　**Sacramento**, United States ᔓ
130　G 8　**Sadoga-shima**, Japan ⚊
69　D 12　**Säffle**, Sweden
85　K 15　**Safford**, AZ, United States
136　F 2　**Safi**, Morocco
131　B 13　**Saga**, Japan
122　E 3　**Sagaing**, Myanmar
131　H 10　**Sagami-nada**, Japan ≈
119　E 9　**Sagar**, India
78　H 6　**Saginaw**, MI, United States
41　L 6　**Sagunto**, Spain
22　H 5　**Sahara**, Africa ▲
118　D 7　**Saharanpur**, India
22　H 5　**Sahel**, Africa ◇
111　L 9　**Sahiwal**, Pakistan
31　L 5　**Sahul Shelf**, Southern Ocean
114　H 3　**Saïda**, Lebanon
119　H 9　**Saidpur**, Bangladesh
69　J 10　**Saimaa**, Finland ᔓ
37　I 13　**St Albans**, United Kingdom
79　I 9　**St Albans**, WV, United States
81　K 7　**St Augustine**, FL, United States
75　K 11　**St Catharines**, ON, Canada
82　H 6　**St Cloud**, MN, United States
78　D 4　**St Croix**, United States ᔓ
37　E 13　**St David's Head**, United Kingdom ▶
53　D 12　**St Gallen**, Switzerland
147　K 7　**St George**, QLD, Australia
85　H 12　**St George**, UT, United States
91　N 7　**St George's**, Grenada ▪
37　D 13　**St George's Channel**, Ireland/United Kingdom ⚊
37　E 13　**St Govan's Head**, United Kingdom ▶
28　I 8　**St Helena**, Atlantic Ocean ⚊
140　H 11　**Saint Helena Bay**, South Africa ≈
28　G 8　**Saint Helena Fracture Zone**, Atlantic Ocean
37　G 11　**St Helens**, United Kingdom
37　H 16　**St Helier**, United Kingdom
78　G 4　**St Ignace**, MI, United States
75　L 9　**St John**, NB, Canada
75　N 7　**St John's**, NL, Canada
91　N 5　**St John's**, Antigua and Barbuda ▪
83　H 9　**St Joseph**, MO, United States
91　N 5　**St Kitts and Nevis**, North America ▫
22　E 3　**St Lawrence**, North America ᔓ
32　D 3　**St Lawrence Island**, United States ⚊

≈ Bay　⚊ Channel　▫ Country　▪ Dependent Territory　▲ Desert　⠿ Geographic Area　▶ Headland　⚊ Island　⚊ Island Group　ᔓ Lake　▲ Mountain

▲ Mountain Range   ▬ National Capital   ৴ Ocean   Physical Feature   ▬ Polar Base   ৲ River   ৴ Sea   ★ Special Feature   ⌂ State Capital   ▬ Underwater Feature

85	J 14	**Show Low**, AZ, United States
83	I 12	**Shreveport**, LA, United States
37	G 12	**Shrewsbury**, United Kingdom
127	O 3	**Shuangyashan**, China
84	I 6	**Shumagin Islands**, AL, United States ☀
61	I 8	**Shumen**, Bulgaria
111	K 5	**Shymkent**, Kazakhstan
65	I 3	**Šiauliai**, Lithuania
61	B 8	**Šibenik**, Croatia
104	F 7	**Siberia**, Russia ▦
122	F 8	**Siberut**, Indonesia ⌃
60	G 6	**Sibiu**, Romania
123	I 7	**Sibu**, Malaysia
127	K 8	**Sichuan Basin**, China ◇
57	E 14	**Sicilian Channel**, Italy ⊠
57	G 14	**Sicily**, Italy ⌃
57	J 13	**Siderno**, Italy
136	G 1	**Sidi Bel Abbès**, Algeria
61	G 10	**Sidirokastro**, Greece
82	E 5	**Sidney**, MT, United States
64	H 6	**Siedlce**, Poland
52	C 8	**Siegen**, Germany
122	G 5	**Siem Reap**, Cambodia
56	E 8	**Siena**, Italy
99	G 12	**Sierra Grande**, Argentina
136	E 6	**Sierra Leone**, Africa ◻
28	H 6	**Sierra Leone Basin**, Atlantic Ocean ◣
89	J 9	**Sierra Madre del Sur**, Mexico ▲
88	G 3	**Sierra Madre Occidental**, Mexico ▲
89	J 4	**Sierra Madre Oriental**, Mexico ▲
40	G 8	**Sierra Morena**, Spain ▲
85	D 11	**Sierra Nevada**, CA, United States ▲
88	E 2	**Sierra San Pedro Martir**, Mexico ▲
85	J 16	**Sierra Vista**, AZ, United States
61	H 13	**Sifnos**, Greece ⌃
49	I 12	**Signal de Botrange**, Belgium ▲
33	I 1	**Signy**, United Kingdom ⊟
136	E 6	**Siguiri**, Guinea
109	K 9	**Siirt**, Turkey
118	C 8	**Sikar**, India
136	F 6	**Sikasso**, Mali
83	J 10	**Sikeston**, MO, United States
105	M 11	**Sikhote-Alin'**, Russia ▲
119	J 9	**Silchar**, India
109	G 10	**Silifke**, Turkey
118	H 8	**Siliguri**, India
126	G 7	**Siling Co**, China ⌇
69	E 11	**Siljan**, Sweden ⌇
108	K 8	**Silvan Baraji**, Turkey ⌇
122	E 7	**Simeulue**, Indonesia ⌃
65	M 11	**Simferopol'**, Ukraine
147	I 6	**Simpson Desert**, NT/SA, Australia ⣿
74	H 5	**Simpson Peninsula**, NU, Canada ▶
96	E 2	**Sincelejo**, Colombia
40	E 8	**Sines**, Portugal
122	G 8	**Singapore**, Singapore ♠
122	G 8	**Singapore**, Asia ◻
122	H 8	**Singkawang**, Indonesia
108	G 5	**Sinop**, Turkey
108	G 5	**Sinop Burnu**, Turkey ▶
40	E 7	**Sintra**, Portugal
127	N 5	**Sinŭiju**, North Korea
53	C 13	**Sion**, Switzerland
82	G 8	**Sioux City**, IA, United States
82	G 7	**Sioux Falls**, SD, United States
127	N 4	**Siping**, China
33	K 6	**Siple Island**, Antarctica ⌃
122	F 8	**Sipura**, Indonesia ⌃
147	I 4	**Sir Edward Pellew Group**, NT, Australia ☀
69	B 12	**Sira**, Norway
115	M 4	**Sīrjān**, Iran
109	L 9	**Şirnak**, Turkey
118	C 7	**Sirsa**, India
137	I 2	**Sirte**, Libya
61	B 7	**Sisak**, Croatia
40	H 5	**Sistema Central**, Spain ▲
41	J 3	**Sistema Ibérico**, Spain ▲
41	I 9	**Sistemas Béticos**, Spain ▲
118	E 8	**Sitapur**, India
61	I 15	**Siteia**, Greece
41	N 4	**Sitges**, Spain
84	K 6	**Sitka**, AL, United States
122	F 4	**Sittang**, Myanmar ⌇
122	E 3	**Sittwe**, Myanmar
108	H 7	**Sivas**, Turkey
109	J 9	**Siverek**, Turkey
137	K 3	**Siwa**, Egypt
69	C 14	**Sjaelland**, Denmark ⌃
69	B 13	**Skagerrak**, Denmark ⊠
68	G 8	**Skellefteå**, Sweden
69	D 11	**Ski**, Norway
61	G 11	**Skiathos**, Greece
69	C 12	**Skien**, Norway
136	H 1	**Skikda**, Algeria
61	G 12	**Skopelos**, Greece
61	F 9	**Skopje**, Macedonia ♠
36	D 7	**Skye**, United Kingdom ⌃
61	H 12	**Skyros**, Greece
61	H 12	**Skyros**, Greece ⌃
69	C 14	**Slagelse**, Denmark
60	H 7	**Slatina**, Romania
74	F 7	**Slave**, Canada ⌇
61	C 7	**Slavonski Brod**, Croatia
37	B 10	**Sligo**, Ireland
61	I 9	**Sliven**, Bulgaria
60	I 7	**Slobozia**, Romania
65	I 5	**Slonim**, Belarus
37	I 13	**Slough**, United Kingdom
64	G 8	**Slovakia**, Europe ◻
60	B 6	**Slovenia**, Europe ◻
65	N 8	**Slov''yans'k**, Ukraine
65	J 7	**Sluch**, Ukraine ⌇
65	J 6	**Slutsk**, Belarus
37	A 11	**Slyne Head**, Ireland ▶
75	L 7	**Smallwood Reservoir**, NL, Canada ⌇
61	E 7	**Smederevska Palanka**, Serbia and Montenegro
69	C 9	**Smøla**, Norway
104	C 5	**Smolensk**, Russia
61	H 10	**Smolyan**, Bulgaria
33	J 4	**Smyley Island**, Antarctica ⌃
85	G 9	**Snake**, United States ⌇
85	H 9	**Snake River Plain**, ID, United States ◇
48	H 5	**Sneek**, Netherlands
64	E 7	**Sněžka**, Czech Republic/Poland ▲
37	F 12	**Snowdon**, United Kingdom ▲
137	L 6	**Sobat**, Sudan ⌇
97	L 5	**Sobral**, Brazil
104	B 8	**Sochi**, Russia
151	M 10	**Society Archipelago**, French Polynesia ☀
83	C 11	**Socorro**, NM, United States
115	M 10	**Socotra**, Yemen ⌃
68	I 6	**Sodankylä**, Finland
69	F 10	**Söderhamn**, Sweden
69	F 12	**Södertälje**, Sweden
61	G 9	**Sofia**, Bulgaria
69	A 10	**Sogna Fjord**, Norway ≈
137	L 3	**Sohâg**, Egypt
28	E 4	**Sohm Abyssal Plain**, Atlantic Ocean ◣
45	J 2	**Soissons**, France
108	C 8	**Söke**, Turkey
109	J 5	**Sokhumi**, Georgia
136	G 6	**Sokodé**, Togo
136	H 6	**Sokoto**, Nigeria
119	C 10	**Solapur**, India
104	E 6	**Solikamsk**, Russia
52	C 8	**Solingen**, Germany
150	H 8	**Solomon Islands**, Pacific Ocean ◻
147	M 3	**Solomon Sea**, Pacific Ocean ◢
141	I 6	**Solwezi**, Zambia
30	E 4	**Somali Basin**, Indian Ocean ◣
137	O 7	**Somalia**, Africa ◻
78	G 10	**Somerset**, KY, United States
74	G 4	**Somerset Island**, NU, Canada ⌃
68	D 7	**Sømna**, Norway ⌃
119	F 9	**Son**, India ⌇
122	G 3	**Son La**, Vietnam
90	H 9	**Soná**, Panama
141	K 5	**Songea**, Tanzania
122	F 6	**Songkhla**, Thailand
111	J 11	**Sonmiani Bay**, Pakistan ≈
88	F 4	**Sonora**, Mexico ⌇
85	G 15	**Sonoran Desert**, AZ/CA, United States ▲
105	O 7	**Sopka Klyuchevskaya**, Russia ▲
75	K 9	**Sorel**, QC, Canada
108	G 7	**Sorgun**, Turkey
41	K 3	**Soria**, Spain
151	J 1	**Sorol**, Federated States of Micronesia ⌃

123	M 8	**Sorong**, Indonesia
68	H 4	**Sørøya**, Norway ⌃
141	I 9	**Soshanguve**, South Africa
64	G 7	**Sosnowiec**, Poland
61	I 10	**Soufli**, Greece
114	G 3	**Soûr**, Lebanon
141	I 10	**South Africa**, Africa ◻
119	J 14	**South Andaman**, India ⌃
146	H 8	**South Australia**, Australia ◻
31	K 7	**South Australian Basin**, Southern Ocean ◣
31	M 8	**South Australian Plain**, Southern Ocean ◣
78	G 7	**South Bend**, IN, United States
81	K 3	**South Carolina**, United States ◻
26	C 4	**South China Sea**, Pacific Ocean ◢
82	E 7	**South Dakota**, United States ◻
147	K 11	**South East Cape**, TAS, Australia ▶
26	G 7	**South Fiji Basin**, Pacific Ocean ◣
33	N 5	**South Geomagnetic Pole**, Antarctica ◇
29	F 11	**South Georgia**, United Kingdom ⌃
26	E 5	**South Honshu Ridge**, Pacific Ocean ◣
119	B 16	**South Huvadhu Atoll**, Maldives ⌃
31	L 10	**South Indian Basin**, Southern Ocean ◣
150	D 8	**South Island**, New Zealand ⌃
127	O 6	**South Korea**, Asia ◻
85	G 11	**South Lake Tahoe**, CA, United States
119	A 14	**South Maalhosmadulu Atoll**, Maldives ⌃
119	B 14	**South Male Atoll**, Maldives ⌃
119	B 14	**South Miladunmadulu Atoll**, Maldives ⌃
29	F 11	**South Orkney Islands**, Atlantic Ocean ☀
82	E 8	**South Platte**, NE, United States ⌇
33	M 4	**South Pole**, Antarctica ◇
29	G 11	**South Sandwich Islands**, Atlantic Ocean ☀
29	G 11	**South Sandwich Trench**, Atlantic Ocean ◣
22	F 9	**South Shetland Islands**, Antarctica ☀
29	D 12	**South Shetland Trough**, Atlantic Ocean ◣
37	H 9	**South Shields**, United Kingdom
150	E 5	**South Taranaki Bight**, New Zealand ≈
26	F 9	**South Tasman Rise**, Pacific Ocean ◣
36	D 7	**South Uist**, United Kingdom ⌃
150	B 11	**South West Cape**, New Zealand ▶
37	H 14	**Southampton**, United Kingdom
75	I 6	**Southampton Island**, NU, Canada ⌃
30	H 7	**Southeast Indian Ridge**, Indian Ocean ◣
27	J 10	**Southeast Pacific Basin**, Pacific Ocean ◣
37	J 13	**Southend-on-Sea**, United Kingdom
150	B 9	**Southern Alps**, New Zealand ▲
151	L 10	**Southern Cook Islands**, Cook Islands ☀
151	M 9	**Southern Line Islands**, Kiribati ☀
23	L 9	**Southern Ocean** ⌀
37	F 9	**Southern Uplands**, United Kingdom ▲
30	E 8	**Southwest Indian Ridge**, Indian Ocean ◣
26	H 8	**Southwest Pacific Basin**, Pacific Ocean ◣
64	H 4	**Sovetsk**, Russia
141	I 8	**Sowa Pan**, Botswana ⌇
141	I 9	**Soweto**, South Africa
130	G 2	**Sōya-wan**, Japan ≈
65	L 5	**Sozh**, Belarus ⌇
41	K 6	**Spain**, Europe ◻
91	I 4	**Spanish Town**, Jamaica
85	E 11	**Sparks**, NV, United States
81	J 3	**Spartanburg**, SC, United States
147	I 9	**Spencer Gulf**, SA, Australia ≈
36	F 7	**Spey**, United Kingdom ⌇
53	D 10	**Speyer**, Germany
29	I 11	**Spiess Seamount**, Atlantic Ocean ◣
32	E 8	**Spitsbergen**, Svalbard ⌃
61	B 8	**Split**, Croatia

84	F 6	**Spokane**, WA, United States
61	G 12	**Sporades**, Greece ☀
78	G 8	**Springfield**, OH, United States
79	M 7	**Springfield**, MA, United States
78	E 8	**Springfield**, IL, United States ⌂
83	I 10	**Springfield**, MO, United States
84	C 8	**Springfield**, OR, United States
150	D 7	**Springs Junction**, New Zealand
147	K 6	**Springsure**, QLD, Australia
79	J 9	**Spruce Knob**, WV, United States ▲
37	I 11	**Spurn Head**, United Kingdom ▶
150	E 7	**Spy Glass Point**, New Zealand ▶
119	E 15	**Sri Jayewardenepura Kotte**, Sri Lanka
119	E 15	**Sri Lanka**, Asia ◻
118	C 6	**Srinagar**, India
83	J 9	**St. Louis**, MO, United States
48	K 5	**Stadskanaal**, Netherlands
37	G 12	**Stafford**, United Kingdom
64	H 7	**Stalowa Wola**, Poland
79	M 7	**Stamford**, CT, United States
99	H 15	**Stanley**, Falkland Islands
105	K 8	**Stanovoy Khrebet**, Russia ▲
105	J 9	**Stanovoye Nagor'ye**, Russia ◇
48	I 6	**Staphorst**, Netherlands
61	H 9	**Stara- Zagora**, Bulgaria
64	E 5	**Stargard- Szczeciński**, Poland
80	F 4	**Starkville**, MS, United States
104	C 6	**Staryy Oskol**, Russia
79	K 8	**State College**, PA, United States
81	K 5	**Statesboro**, GA, United States
32	D 8	**Station Nord**, Greenland
79	J 10	**Staunton**, VI, United States
69	A 12	**Stavanger**, Norway
104	B 8	**Stavropol'**, Russia
82	D 8	**Steamboat Springs**, CO, United States
48	I 6	**Steenwijk**, Netherlands
74	G 4	**Stefansson Island**, NU, Canada ⌃
52	F 6	**Stendal**, Germany
83	G 12	**Stephenville**, TX, United States
82	E 8	**Sterling**, CO, United States
78	H 6	**Sterling Heights**, MI, United States
104	D 7	**Sterlitamak**, Russia
78	E 5	**Stevens Point**, WI, United States
150	B 11	**Stewart Island**, New Zealand ⌃
53	I 11	**Steyr**, Austria
69	F 12	**Stockholm**, Sweden ♠
37	H 11	**Stockport**, United Kingdom
85	D 12	**Stockton**, CA, United States
37	G 12	**Stoke-on-Trent**, United Kingdom
37	G 14	**Stonehenge**, United Kingdom ✶
69	C 14	**Store Baelt**, Denmark ⊠
69	D 9	**Støren**, Norway
74	F 4	**Storkerson Peninsula**, NU, Canada ▶
36	D 6	**Stornoway**, United Kingdom
69	E 9	**Storsjön**, Sweden ⌇
68	F 8	**Storuman**, Sweden
37	J 13	**Stour**, United Kingdom ⌇
37	C 10	**Strabane**, Ireland
57	B 10	**Strait of Bonifacio**, Italy/France ⊠
136	F 1	**Strait of Gibraltar**, Morocco/Spain ⊠
115	M 6	**Strait of Hormuz**, Asia ⊠
99	E 15	**Strait of Magellan**, Chile ⊠
122	F 6	**Strait of Malacca**, Indonesia/Malaysia ⊠
57	I 14	**Strait of Messina**, Italy ⊠
90	G 2	**Straits of Florida**, Caribbean Sea ⊠
52	G 4	**Stralsund**, Germany
37	E 10	**Stranraer**, United Kingdom
45	M 4	**Strasbourg**, France
150	E 5	**Stratford**, New Zealand
69	F 9	**Strömsund**, Sweden
61	G 9	**Struma**, Bulgaria ⌇
61	F 10	**Strumica**, Macedonia
65	I 8	**Stryy**, Ukraine
53	D 11	**Stuttgart**, Germany
65	I 7	**Styr**, Ukraine ⌇
61	E 6	**Subotica**, Serbia and Montenegro
60	I 5	**Suceava**, Romania
98	G 6	**Sucre**, Bolivia ♠
65	N 11	**Sudak**, Ukraine
75	J 10	**Sudbury**, ON, Canada
137	K 7	**Sudd**, Sudan ◇
41	L 6	**Sueca**, Spain
137	L 2	**Suez**, Egypt

137	L 2	**Suez Canal**, Egypt ⊠
115	M 6	**Şuḩār**, Oman
52	F 8	**Suhl**, Germany
127	L 7	**Suizhou**, China
122	H 10	**Sukabumi**, Indonesia
111	K 10	**Sukkur**, Pakistan
131	D 13	**Sukumo**, Japan
111	K 9	**Sulaiman Ranges**, Pakistan ▲
123	J 9	**Sulawesi**, Indonesia ⌃
96	D 5	**Sullana**, Peru
123	J 7	**Sulu Archipelago**, Philippines ☀
123	J 6	**Sulu Sea**, Philippines ◢
33	L 6	**Sulzberger Bay**, Antarctica ≈
122	G 8	**Sumatra**, Indonesia ⌃
123	J 10	**Sumba**, Indonesia ⌃
123	J 10	**Sumbawa**, Indonesia ⌃
141	J 5	**Sumbawanga**, Tanzania
109	O 6	**Sumqayit**, Azerbaijan
81	K 3	**Sumter**, SC, United States
65	M 7	**Sumy**, Ukraine
147	J 10	**Sunbury**, VIC, Australia
127	O 6	**Sunch'ŏn**, South Korea
26	C 5	**Sunda Shelf**, Pacific Ocean ◣
122	G 9	**Sunda Strait**, Indonesia ⊠
37	H 10	**Sunderland**, United Kingdom
69	F 10	**Sundsvall**, Sweden
85	C 12	**Sunnyvale**, CA, United States
147	L 7	**Sunshine Coast**, QLD, Australia ▦
68	J 8	**Suomussalmi**, Finland
131	C 13	**Suŏ-nada**, Japan ≈
78	D 4	**Superior**, WI, United States
108	L 8	**Süphan Daglari**, Turkey ▲
115	J 4	**Sūq ash Shuyūkh**, Iraq
127	M 7	**Suqian**, China
115	N 7	**Şūr**, Oman
123	I 10	**Surabaya**, Indonesia
123	I 10	**Surakarta**, Indonesia
119	B 10	**Surat**, India
122	F 6	**Surat Thani**, Thailand
49	H 14	**Sûre**, Luxembourg ⌇
119	B 10	**Surendranagar**, India
147	L 8	**Surfers Paradise**, QLD, Australia
104	G 7	**Surgut**, Russia
123	K 6	**Surigao**, Philippines
97	I 3	**Suriname**, South America ◻
131	H 7	**Suruga-wan**, Japan ≈
56	A 6	**Susa**, Italy
85	D 10	**Susanville**, CA, United States
84	C 8	**Sutherlin**, OR, United States
111	L 9	**Sutlej**, India/Pakistan ⌇
151	I 10	**Suva**, Fiji ♠
64	H 5	**Suwałki**, Poland
131	B 16	**Suwanose-jima**, Japan ⌃
127	O 5	**Suwon**, South Korea
127	N 7	**Suzhou**, China
127	M 7	**Suzhou**, China
131	F 11	**Suzuka**, Japan
32	E 8	**Svalbard**, Norway ◻
69	E 10	**Sveg**, Sweden
69	E 9	**Svenstavik**, Sweden
64	F 8	**Svitavy**, Czech Republic
65	K 6	**Svyetlahorsk**, Belarus
140	G 8	**Swakopmund**, Namibia
37	F 13	**Swansea**, United Kingdom
141	J 9	**Swaziland**, Africa ◻
69	E 13	**Sweden**, Europe ◻
83	F 12	**Sweetwater**, TX, United States
74	F 10	**Swift Current**, SK, Canada
37	H 13	**Swindon**, United Kingdom
53	D 13	**Switzerland**, Europe ◻
147	L 9	**Sydney**, NSW, Australia ▦
75	M 8	**Sydney**, NS, Canada
65	O 8	**Syeverodonets'k**, Ukraine
104	E 6	**Syktyvkar**, Russia
119	J 9	**Sylhet**, Bangladesh
33	O 2	**Syowa**, Japan ⊟
57	I 15	**Syracuse**, Italy
79	K 6	**Syracuse**, NY, United States
111	K 5	**Syrdar'ya**, Kazakhstan ⌇
114	H 3	**Syria**, Asia ◻
114	H 3	**Syrian Desert**, Asia ▲
61	H 13	**Syros**, Greece ⌃
104	D 7	**Syzran'**, Russia
65	E 5	**Szczecin**, Poland
64	G 10	**Szeged**, Hungary
64	F 9	**Székesfehérvár**, Hungary
64	F 10	**Szekszárd**, Hungary
64	G 10	**Szolnok**, Hungary
64	E 9	**Szombathely**, Hungary

≈ Bay　⊠ Channel　◻ Country　◻ Dependent Territory　▲ Desert　▦ Geographic Area　▶ Headland　⌃ Island　☀ Island Group　⌇ Lake　▲ Mountain

T

141 J 4 Tabora, Tanzania
115 J 1 Tabrīz, Iran
114 H 5 Tabūk, Saudi Arabia
123 K 5 Tacloban, Philippines
96 F 8 Tacna, Peru
84 D 6 Tacoma, WA, United States
99 I 9 Tacuarembó, Uruguay
127 O 6 Taegu, South Korea
127 O 6 Taejŏn, South Korea
28 H 4 Tagus Abyssal Plain, Atlantic Ocean ■
127 N 1 Tahe, China
151 N 10 Tahiti, French Polynesia ⚓
136 G 5 Tahoua, Niger
127 N 9 T'aichung, Taiwan
150 C 10 Taieri, New Zealand ⤳
150 F 5 Taihape, New Zealand
147 I 9 Tailem Bend, SA, Australia
127 N 10 T'ainan, Taiwan
127 N 9 Taipei, Taiwan
122 F 7 Taiping, Malaysia
127 O 10 Taiwan, Asia ▫
127 N 10 Taiwan Strait, China/Taiwan ≈
127 L 6 Taiyuan, China
127 N 8 Taizhou, China
115 J 10 Ta'izz, Yemen
111 L 6 Tajikistan, Asia ▫
40 H 6 Tajo, Spain ⤳
131 D 12 Takamatsu, Japan
131 F 9 Takaoka, Japan
150 F 3 Takapuna, New Zealand
131 H 9 Takasaki, Japan
131 F 11 Takatsuki, Japan
23 L 4 Taklimakan Desert, Asia ▲
136 F 7 Takoradi, Ghana
111 L 5 Talas, Kyrgyzstan
41 I 5 Talavera de la Reina, Spain
99 E 10 Talca, Chile
99 E 11 Talcahuano, Chile
111 M 4 Taldykorgan, Kazakhstan
123 K 8 Taliabu, Indonesia ⚓
81 I 6 Tallahassee, FL, United States ⟁
65 I 1 Tallinn, Estonia ■
98 E 7 Taltal, Chile
136 F 6 Tamale, Ghana
136 H 4 Tamanrasset, Algeria
37 F 14 Tamar, United Kingdom ⤳
89 K 8 Tamazunchale, Mexico
136 D 5 Tambacounda, Senegal
104 C 7 Tambov, Russia
81 J 8 Tampa, FL, United States
81 J 9 Tampa Bay, FL, United States ≈
69 I 10 Tampere, Finland
89 L 7 Tampico, Mexico
147 L 8 Tamworth, NSW, Australia
68 I 4 Tana Bru, Norway
146 H 5 Tanami Desert, NT, Australia ▲
99 H 11 Tandil, Argentina
131 C 15 Tanega-shima, Japan ⚓
141 L 4 Tanga, Tanzania
136 F 1 Tangier, Morocco
126 G 7 Tangra Yumco, China ⚓
127 M 5 Tangshan, China
123 I 8 Tanjung, Indonesia
122 H 9 Tanjung Bugel, Indonesia ▶
122 G 9 Tanjung Cina, Indonesia ▶
123 N 8 Tanjung d'Urville, Indonesia ▶
123 G 10 Tanjung Guhakolak, Indonesia ▶
122 G 9 Tanjung Lumut, Indonesia ▶
123 L 7 Tanjung Sopi, Indonesia ▶
123 N 10 Tanjung Vals, Indonesia ▶
123 J 7 Tanjungredeb, Indonesia
137 L 2 Tanta, Egypt
141 J 4 Tanzania, Africa ▫
136 F 4 Taoudenni, Mali
127 N 9 T'aoyüan, Taiwan
89 N 11 Tapachula, Mexico
97 I 5 Tapajós, Brazil ⤳
61 D 8 Tara, Serbia and Montenegro ⤳
123 I 7 Tarakan, Indonesia
41 J 6 Tarancón, Spain
57 J 11 Taranto, Italy
96 E 5 Tarapoto, Peru
45 K 7 Tarare, France
151 I 7 Tarawa, Kiribati ⚓

111 L 5 Taraz, Kazakhstan
44 H 10 Tarbes, France
146 H 8 Tarcoola, SA, Australia
147 L 9 Taree, NSW, Australia
60 H 7 Târgoviște, Romania
60 G 7 Târgu Jiu, Romania
60 H 6 Târgu Mureș, Romania
98 G 6 Tarija, Bolivia
126 F 5 Tarim Basin, China ◇
126 F 4 Tarim He, China ⤳
123 N 8 Taritatu, Indonesia ⤳
123 J 4 Tarlac, Philippines
64 G 8 Tarnów, Poland
41 N 4 Tarragona, Spain
109 O 8 Tarsus, Turkey
65 J 2 Tartu, Estonia
114 H 3 Tarṭūs, Syria
56 H 3 Tarvisio, Italy
111 K 5 Tashkent, Uzbekistan ■
111 L 5 Tash-Kömur, Kyrgyzstan
122 G 7 Tasik Kenyir, Malaysia ⚓
26 F 9 Tasman Basin, Pacific Ocean ■
150 E 6 Tasman Bay, New Zealand ≈
26 F 8 Tasman Sea, Southern Ocean ⚓
147 J 11 Tasmania, Australia ⚓
136 H 3 Tassili n'Ajjer, Algeria ◇
64 F 9 Tatabánya, Hungary
105 M 9 Tatarskiy Proliv, Russia ≈
108 K 3 Tatvan, Turkey
37 G 14 Taunton, United Kingdom
150 G 4 Taupo, New Zealand
64 H 4 Tauragė, Lithuania
150 F 4 Tauranga, New Zealand
150 E 2 Tauroa Point, New Zealand ▶
23 I 4 Taurus Mountains, Europe ▲
109 D 9 Tavas, Turkey
122 F 5 Tavoy, Myanmar
122 F 5 Tavoy Point, Myanmar ▶
119 D 10 Tawa Reservoir, India ⚓
89 K 9 Taxco, Mexico
36 H 5 Tay, United Kingdom ⤳
40 F 9 TaÛira, Portugal
104 H 6 Taz, Russia ⤳
109 M 6 T'bilisi, Georgia ■
64 G 6 Tczew, Poland
150 F 4 Te Kuiti, New Zealand
89 N 9 Teapa, Mexico
109 M 5 Tebulosmt'a, Georgia/Russia ▲
89 I 9 Tecomán, Mexico
89 K 10 Técpan, Mexico
111 I 7 Tedzhen, Turkmenistan
37 G 10 Tees, United Kingdom ⤳
90 F 6 Tegucigalpa, Honduras ■
115 L 2 Tehran, Iran ■
89 L 9 Tehuacán, Mexico
89 M 10 Tehuantepec, Mexico
108 C 6 Tekirdağ, Turkey
114 G 3 Tel Aviv-Jaffa, Israel
37 G 12 Telford, United Kingdom
64 H 3 Telšiai, Lithuania
123 K 9 Teluk Bone, Indonesia ≈
122 H 7 Teluk Datu, Malaysia ≈
123 M 9 Teluk Kamrau, Indonesia ≈
123 K 8 Teluk Tomini, Indonesia ≈
111 L 3 Temirtau, Kazakhstan
85 I 15 Tempe, AZ, United States
83 G 12 Temple, TX, United States
99 E 11 Temuco, Chile
119 J 14 Ten Degree Channel, India ≈
81 J 10 Ten Thousand Islands, FL, United States ⚓
119 E 12 Tenali, India
136 H 4 Ténéré du Tafassâsset, Niger ▦
40 B 11 Tenerife, Spain ⚓
146 H 5 Tennant Creek, NT, Australia
80 G 2 Tennessee, United States ▫
80 G 2 Tennessee, United States ⤳
68 I 6 Tenniöjoki, Finland ⤳
68 I 5 Tenojoki, Finland ⤳
97 L 7 Teófilo Otôni, Brazil
89 K 8 Teotiuacan, Mexico ✶
89 I 7 Tepic, Mexico
64 C 7 Teplice, Czech Republic
89 J 8 Tequila, Mexico
57 G 9 Teramo, Italy
40 B 9 Terceira, Portugal ⚓
97 K 5 Teresina, Brazil
111 K 7 Termez, Uzbekistan
49 D 10 Terneuzen, Netherlands
57 F 9 Terni, Italy

65 I 8 Ternopil', Ukraine
33 M 7 Terra Nova Bay, Italy ▬
57 F 10 Terracina, Italy
78 F 9 Terre Haute, IN, United States
48 G 4 Terschelling, Netherlands ⚓
41 L 5 Teruel, Spain
130 G 2 Teshio, Japan ⤳
141 J 7 Tete, Mozambique
65 K 7 Teteriv, Ukraine ⤳
61 E 9 Tetovo, Macedonia
83 I 11 Texarkana, TX, United States
83 F 12 Texas, United States ▫
48 F 5 Texel, Netherlands ⚓
122 H 3 Thai Nguyên, Vietnam
122 F 4 Thailand, Asia ▫
115 M 9 Thamarit, Oman
37 H 13 Thames, United Kingdom ⤳
150 F 3 Thames, New Zealand
119 B 11 Thane, India
122 H 3 Thanh Hoa, Vietnam
119 E 14 Thanjavur, India
23 K 5 Thar Desert, Asia ▲
61 G 10 Thasos, Greece ⚓
122 F 4 Thaton, Myanmar
85 J 14 Theodore Roosevelt Lake, AZ, United States ⚓
61 G 10 Thessaloniki, Greece
82 G 5 Thief River Falls, MN, United States
45 J 7 Thiers, France
136 D 5 Thiès, Senegal
119 B 13 Thiladhunmathee Atoll, Maldives ⚓
118 I 8 Thimphu, Bhutan ■
45 L 3 Thionville, France
61 H 14 Thira, Greece
61 G 12 Thiva, Greece
81 I 6 Thomasville, GA, United States
74 H 8 Thompson, MB, Canada
45 L 6 Thonon-les-Bains, France
33 M 1 Thorshavnheiane Mountains, Antarctica ▲
127 K 8 Three Gorges Dam, China ⤳
150 D 1 Three Kings Island, New Zealand ⚓
49 E 13 Thuin, Belgium
32 C 7 Thule, Greenland
53 C 13 Thun, Switzerland
75 I 10 Thunder Bay, ON, Canada
36 F 5 Thurso, United Kingdom
33 J 5 Thurston Island, Antarctica ⚓
126 F 4 Tian Shan, China ▲
127 M 5 Tianjin, China
127 K 7 Tianshui, China
137 I 4 Tibesti, Chad ▲
126 G 6 Tibet, China ▫
89 O 8 Ticul, Mexico
136 E 4 Tidjikja, Mauritania
127 O 3 Tieli, China
127 N 4 Tieling, China
23 L 4 Tien Shan, Asia ▲
49 F 11 Tienen, Belgium
69 F 11 Tierp, Sweden
99 F 16 Tierra del Fuego, Argentina ▫
97 J 8 Tietê, Brazil ⤳
81 J 6 Tifton, GA, United States
65 K 10 Tighina, Moldova
96 E 4 Tigre, Peru ⤳
23 I 4 Tigris, Asia ⤳
88 D 2 Tijuana, Mexico
90 E 5 Tikal, Guatemala ✶
27 J 6 Tiki Basin, Pacific Ocean ■
115 J 3 Tikrīt, Iraq
49 G 9 Tilburg, Netherlands
61 J 14 Tilos, Greece ⚓
150 D 9 Timaru, New Zealand
136 F 5 Timbuktu, Mali
60 F 6 Timișoara, Romania
75 J 9 Timmins, ON, Canada
123 K 10 Timor, Asia, ⚓
31 L 5 Timor Sea, Indian Ocean ≈
69 F 10 Timrå, Sweden
136 F 3 Tindouf, Algeria
151 L 5 Tinian, Northern Mariana Islands ⚓
61 H 13 Tinos, Greece
61 H 13 Tinos, Greece ⚓
118 K 8 Tinsukia, India
61 E 10 Tirana, Albania ■
65 K 10 Tiraspol, Moldova
36 D 8 Tiree, United Kingdom ⚓
150 F 4 Tirua Point, New Zealand ▶
119 E 14 Tiruchchirappalli, India

119 D 15 Tirunelveli, India
119 E 13 Tirupati, India
119 D 14 Tiruppur, India
119 E 13 Tiruvannamalai, India
136 H 1 Tizi Ouzou, Algeria
89 P 7 Tizimin, Mexico
89 I 8 Tlaquepaque, Mexico
136 G 1 Tlemcen, Algeria
141 N 7 Toamasina, Madagascar
91 O 7 Tobago, Trinidad and Tobago ⚓
111 J 2 Tobol, Kazakhstan
104 F 7 Tobol'sk, Russia
137 K 2 Tobruk, Libya
136 G 6 Togo, Africa ▫
131 G 11 Tōkai, Japan
131 B 16 Tokara-rettō, Japan ⚓
131 E 13 Tokasiki-jima, Japan ⚓
108 H 7 Tokat, Turkey
151 K 8 Tokelau Islands, New Zealand ▫
130 I 4 Tokkachi, Japan ⤳
150 G 4 Tokoroa, New Zealand
131 K 14 Toku-no-shima, Japan ⚓
131 K 14 Tokunoshima, Japan
131 E 12 Tokushima, Japan
131 C 12 Tokuyama, Japan
131 H 10 Tokyo, Japan ■
41 I 6 Toledo, Spain
78 H 7 Toledo, OH, United States
83 I 12 Toledo Bend Reservoir, LA/TX, United States ⚓
141 L 8 Toliara, Madagascar
60 A 6 Tolmin, Slovenia
41 K 2 Tolosa, Spain
89 K 9 Toluca, Mexico
104 D 7 Tol'yatti, Russia
78 E 5 Tomah, WI, United States
130 H 4 Tomakomai, Japan
80 G 5 Tombigbee, United States ⤳
104 G 8 Tomsk, Russia
123 K 8 Tomini, Indonesia
118 D 8 Tonk, India
122 G 5 Tônlé Sap, Cambodia ⚓
85 F 12 Tonopah, NV, United States
69 C 12 Tønsberg, Norway
85 I 10 Tooele, UT, United States
147 L 7 Toowoomba, QLD, Australia
146 H 4 Top Springs, NT, Australia
83 H 9 Topeka, KS, United States ⟁
115 N 2 Torbat-e Heydarīyeh, Iran
115 N 2 Torbat-e Jām, Iran
49 C 11 Torhout, Belgium
68 G 5 Torneälven, Sweden ⤳
68 H 7 Tornio, Sweden
40 H 4 Toro, Spain
75 K 10 Toronto, ON, Canada ⟁
37 F 15 Torquay, United Kingdom
85 E 14 Torrance, CA, United States
41 I 2 Torrelavega, Spain
89 I 6 Torreón, Mexico
40 F 6 Torres Novas, Portugal
147 J 3 Torres Strait, QLD, Australia ≈
40 E 6 Torres Vedras, Portugal
82 E 8 Torrington, WY, United States
64 G 5 Toruń, Poland
131 D 13 Tosa-wan, Japan ≈
131 H 11 To-shima, Japan ⚓
98 G 4 Tostado, Argentina
131 D 11 Tottori, Japan
45 L 4 Toul, France
45 L 10 Toulon, France
45 I 10 Toulouse, France
45 J 1 Tourcoing, France
49 C 12 Tournai, Belgium
44 H 5 Tours, France
130 H 6 Towada-ko, Japan ⚓
147 K 5 Townsville, QLD, Australia
130 H 4 Tōya-ko, Japan ⚓
131 F 10 Toyama, Japan
131 F 9 Toyama-wan, Japan ≈
131 G 11 Toyohashi, Japan

131 G 11 Toyota, Japan
109 L 5 Tqibuli, Georgia
108 K 7 Trabzon, Turkey
37 B 12 Tralee, Ireland
33 L 4 Transantarctic, Antarctica ▦
23 L 10 Transantarctic Mountains, Antarctica
30 D 7 Transkei Basin, Indian Ocean ■
60 F 6 Transylvania, Romania ▦
60 F 7 Transylvanian Alps, Romania ▲
57 F 14 Trapani, Italy
53 I 11 Traun, Austria
78 G 5 Travers City, MI, United States
99 J 10 Treinta y Tres, Uruguay
99 F 12 Trelew, Argentina
37 I 12 Trent, United Kingdom ⤳
56 E 5 Trento, Italy
79 L 8 Trenton, NJ, United States ⟁
56 F 5 Treviso, Italy
53 B 9 Trier, Germany
56 G 5 Trieste, Italy
61 F 11 Trikala, Greece
119 E 15 Trincomalee, Sri Lanka
99 I 10 Trinidad, Uruguay
98 G 4 Trinidad, Bolivia
83 E 10 Trinidad, CO, United States
91 O 7 Trinidad, Trinidad and Tobago ⚓
91 O 7 Trinidad and Tobago, North America ▫
61 F 13 Tripoli, Greece
114 G 3 Tripoli, Lebanon
137 I 2 Tripoli, Libya ■
29 I 9 Tristan da Cunha, Atlantic Ocean ⚓
29 G 9 Tristan da Cunha Fracture Zone, Atlantic Ocean ■
119 D 15 Trivandrum, India
75 L 9 Trois-Rivières, QC, Canada
69 D 12 Trollhättan, Sweden
68 G 5 Tromsø, Norway
69 D 9 Trondheim, Norway
80 H 5 Troy, AL, United States
79 L 6 Troy, NY, United States
45 J 4 Troyes, France
40 H 6 Trujillo, Spain
96 E 6 Trujillo, Peru
90 F 5 Trujillo, Honduras
75 M 9 Truro, NS, Canada
61 J 9 Tsarevo, Bulgaria
140 I 7 Tshikapa, Democratic Republic of Congo
131 F 11 Tsu, Japan
131 I 10 Tsuchiura, Japan
130 G 5 Tsugaru-kaikyō, Japan ≈
140 G 7 Tsumeb, Namibia
130 H 7 Tsuruoka, Japan
131 A 12 Tsushima, Japan ⚓
151 N 9 Tuamotu Archipelago, French Polynesia ⚓
27 J 7 Tuamotu Fracture Zone, Pacific Ocean ■
85 J 13 Tuba City, AZ, United States
53 D 11 Tübingen, Germany
85 J 15 Tucson, AZ, United States
83 E 11 Tucumcari, NM, United States
41 K 3 Tudela, Spain
27 I 2 Tufts Abyssal Plain, Pacific Ocean ■
123 K 4 Tuguegarao, Philippines
74 C 6 Tuktoyaktuk, NT, Canada
104 C 6 Tula, Russia
89 L 8 Tulancingo, Mexico
85 E 13 Tulare, CA, United States
60 J 7 Tulcea, Romania
83 H 10 Tulsa, OK, United States
119 D 13 Tumkur, India
61 I 9 Tundzha, Bulgaria ⤳
119 D 12 Tungabhadra Reservoir, India ⚓
137 I 1 Tunis, Tunisia ■
137 I 1 Tunisia, Africa ▫
96 F 3 Tunja, Colombia
80 F 3 Tupelo, MS, United States
98 G 6 Tupiza, Bolivia
23 K 4 Turan Lowland, Asia ◇
114 H 4 Turayf, Saudi Arabia
110 J 6 Turbat, Pakistan
60 G 6 Turda, Romania
61 I 8 Tŭrgovishte, Bulgaria
41 L 6 Turia, Spain ⤳
56 B 6 Turin, Italy
111 K 5 Turkestan, Kazakhstan

▲▲ Mountain Range ■ National Capital ⚓ Ocean   Physical Feature ▬ Polar Base ⤳ River ≈ Sea ✶ Special Feature ⟁ State Capital ■ Underwater Feature

GAZETTEER 173

108 H 8 **Turkey**, Asia/Europe ▢
108 G 11 **Turkish Republic of Northern Cyprus**, Asia/Europe ▢
110 H 6 **Turkmenbashi**, Turkmenistan
111 I 6 **Turkmenistan**, Asia ▢
91 K 3 **Turks and Caicos Islands**, United Kingdom ▢
91 K 3 **Turks Islands**, Turks and Caicos Islands ☷
69 H 11 **Turku**, Finland
49 F 10 **Turnhout**, Belgium
126 H 4 **Turpan**, China
23 L 4 **Turpan Depression**, Asia ◇
80 G 4 **Tuscaloosa**, AL, United States
56 D 7 **Tuscan Archipelago**, Italy ☷
56 D 8 **Tuscany**, Italy ▦
119 D 15 **Tuticorin**, India
151 K 9 **Tutuila**, American Samoa ☪
151 I 8 **Tuvalu**, Pacific Ocean ▢
89 I 8 **Tuxpan**, Mexico
89 L 8 **Tuxpan**, Mexico
89 L 9 **Tuxtepec**, Mexico
89 N 10 **Tuxtla Gutiérrez**, Mexico
108 F 8 **Tuz Gölü**, Turkey ☪
61 D 7 **Tuzla**, Bosnia-Herzegovina
104 C 5 **Tver'**, Russia
37 G 9 **Tweed**, United Kingdom ☪
85 H 9 **Twin Falls**, ID, United States
64 G 7 **Tychy**, Poland
83 H 12 **Tyler**, TX, United States
61 H 15 **Tympaki**, Greece
105 K 9 **Tynda**, Russia
37 G 9 **Tyne**, United Kingdom ☪
61 G 11 **Tyrnavos**, Greece
45 O 11 **Tyrrhenian Sea**, France/Italy ☶
104 F 8 **Tyumen'**, Russia

u

41 J 8 **Úbeda**, Spain
97 J 8 **Uberaba**, Brazil
97 J 8 **Uberlândia**, Brazil
122 G 4 **Ubon Ratchathani**, Thailand
96 E 5 **Ucayali**, Peru ☪
130 H 4 **Uchiura-wan**, Japan ≈
119 C 9 **Udaipur**, India
69 D 12 **Uddevalla**, Sweden
56 G 5 **Udine**, Italy
27 I 10 **Udintsev Fracture Zone**, Pacific Ocean ▰
122 G 4 **Udon Thani**, Thailand
141 I 2 **Uele**, Democratic Republic of Congo ☪
137 K 8 **Uele**, Somalia ☪
52 E 6 **Uelzen**, Germany
104 D 7 **Ufa**, Russia
141 J 2 **Uganda**, Africa ▢
140 G 5 **Uíge**, Angola
151 J 1 **Uithi**, Federated States of Micronesia ☪
151 M 3 **Ujae**, Marshall Islands ☪
119 D 10 **Ujjain**, India
123 J 9 **Ujung Pandang**, Indonesia
104 E 6 **Ukhta**, Russia
85 C 11 **Ukiah**, CA, United States
65 I 4 **Ukmergė**, Lithuania
65 I 8 **Ukraine**, Europe ▢
127 K 3 **Ulaanbaatar**, Mongolia ♣
127 I 2 **Ulaangom**, Mongolia
126 H 6 **Ulan Ul Hu**, China ☪
105 J 10 **Ulan-Ude**, Russia
127 L 2 **Uldz**, Mongolia ☪
119 C 11 **Ulhasnagar**, India
53 E 11 **Ulm**, Germany
127 P 6 **Ulsan**, South Korea
151 L 1 **Ulul**, Federated States of Micronesia ☪
74 F 4 **Uluqsaqtuuq**, NT, Canada
146 H 7 **Uluru**, NT, Australia ▲
104 D 7 **Ul'yanovsk**, Russia
65 K 8 **Uman'**, Ukraine
69 G 9 **Umeå**, Sweden
68 G 8 **Umeälven**, Sweden ☪
32 C 7 **Ummannaq**, Greenland
84 I 5 **Umnak Island**, AL, United States ☪
61 B 7 **Una**, Bosnia-Herzegovina ☪
75 K 6 **Ungava Bay**, QC, Canada ≈

80 F 1 **Union City**, TN, United States
79 J 8 **Uniontown**, PA, United States
115 L 7 **United Arab Emirates**, Asia ▢
37 G 10 **United Kingdom**, Europe ▢
36 H 3 **Unst**, United Kingdom ☪
151 J 9 **Upolu**, Samoa ☪
150 F 6 **Upper Hutt**, New Zealand
85 D 9 **Upper Klamath Lake**, OR, United States ☪
82 H 5 **Upper Red Lake**, MN, United States ☪
69 F 11 **Uppsala**, Sweden
110 H 2 **Ural**, Kazakhstan/Russia ☪
23 J 2 **Ural Mountains**, Asia ▲
110 H 2 **Ural'sk**, Kazakhstan
131 H 10 **Urawa**, Japan
111 J 5 **Urgench**, Uzbekistan
111 K 6 **Uroteppa**, Tajikistan
89 K 9 **Uruapan**, Mexico
97 I 10 **Uruguai**, Argentina/Uruguay ☪
99 I 10 **Uruguay**, South America ▢
22 F 8 **Uruguay**, South America ☪
126 H 4 **Ürümqi**, China
60 I 7 **Urziceni**, Romania
108 D 8 **Uşak**, Turkey
99 F 16 **Ushuaia**, Argentina
105 I 9 **Usol'ye-Sibirskoye**, Russia
45 I 7 **Ussel**, France
105 M 11 **Ussuriysk**, Russia
105 J 9 **Ust-Ilimsk**, Russia
111 M 2 **Ust'-Kamenogorsk**, Kazakhstan
111 I 5 **Ustyurt Plateau**, Uzbekistan ◇
89 N 9 **Usumacinta**, Mexico ☪
85 I 11 **Utah**, United States ▢
85 I 10 **Utah Lake**, UT, United States ☪
65 I 4 **Utena**, Lithuania
79 L 6 **Utica**, NY, United States
48 G 8 **Utrecht**, Netherlands
151 N 3 **Utrik**, Marshall Islands ☪
131 H 9 **Utsunomiya**, Japan
83 F 13 **Uvalde**, TX, United States
127 I 2 **Uvs Nuur**, Mongolia ☪
131 D 13 **Uwajima**, Japan
98 F 6 **Uyuni**, Bolivia
111 J 5 **Uzbekistan**, Asia ▢
64 H 9 **Uzhhorod**, Ukraine
61 E 8 **Užice**, Serbia and Montenegro

v

23 I 8 **Vaal**, Africa ☪
49 I 12 **Vaals**, Luxembourg
69 H 9 **Vaasa**, Finland
119 C 10 **Vadodara**, India
53 E 12 **Vaduz**, Liechtenstein ♣
151 J 9 **Vaiaku**, Tuvalu ♣
83 D 9 **Vail**, CO, United States
41 J 7 **Valdepeñas**, Spain
99 D 11 **Valdivia**, Chile
29 I 9 **Valdivia Seamount**, Atlantic Ocean ▰
75 J 9 **Val-d'Or**, QC, Canada
81 J 6 **Valdosta**, GA, United States
45 K 8 **Valence**, France
41 L 6 **Valencia**, Spain
96 G 2 **Valencia**, Venezuela
45 J 2 **Valenciennes**, France
65 I 2 **Valga**, Estonia
61 E 8 **Valjevo**, Serbia and Montenegro
49 H 10 **Valkenswaard**, Netherlands
41 I 4 **Valladolid**, Spain
89 P 8 **Valladolid**, Mexico
96 F 2 **Valledupar**, Colombia
85 C 12 **Vallejo**, CA, United States
98 C 8 **Vallenar**, Chile
57 H 16 **Valletta**, Malta ♣
91 N 4 **Valley, The**, Anguilla ♣
41 M 4 **Valls**, Spain
65 I 2 **Valmiera**, Latvia
119 D 14 **Valparai**, India
99 E 10 **Valparaíso**, Chile
108 L 8 **Van**, Turkey
146 H 3 **Van Diemen Gulf**, NT, Australia ≈
109 M 6 **Vanadzor**, Armenia
74 D 9 **Vancouver**, BC, Canada
74 D 9 **Vancouver Island**, BC, Canada ☪
69 D 12 **Vänern**, Sweden ☪

147 J 1 **Vanimo**, Papua New Guinea
44 F 5 **Vannes**, France
69 I 11 **Vantaa**, Finland
151 J 10 **Vanua Levu**, Fiji ☪
150 H 10 **Vanuatu**, Pacific Ocean ▢
119 F 9 **Varanasi**, India
68 I 4 **Varanger Fjord**, Norway ≈
61 C 6 **Varaždin**, Croatia
69 D 13 **Varberg**, Sweden
61 F 10 **Vardar**, Macedonia ☪
69 B 14 **Varde**, Denmark
56 C 5 **Varese**, Italy
69 J 9 **Varkaus**, Finland
61 J 8 **Varna**, Bulgaria
60 I 6 **Vaslui**, Romania
57 H 9 **Vasto**, Italy
69 F 12 **Västerås**, Sweden
69 E 10 **Västerdalälven**, Sweden ☪
69 F 13 **Västervik**, Sweden
57 F 9 **Vatican City**, Vatican City ♣
57 F 9 **Vatican City**, Europe ▢
68 C 6 **Vatnajökull**, Iceland ◇
69 E 12 **Vättern**, Sweden ☪
83 D 11 **Vaughn**, NM, United States
69 E 13 **Växjö**, Sweden
48 H 8 **Veenendaal**, Netherlands
68 D 7 **Vega**, Norway ☪
28 E 6 **Vema Fracture Zone**, Atlantic Ocean ▰
99 H 10 **Venado Tuerto**, Argentina
44 H 5 **Vendôme**, France
96 F 2 **Venezuela**, South America ▢
28 D 6 **Venezuelan Basin**, Atlantic Ocean ▰
56 F 6 **Venice**, Italy
49 I 10 **Venlo**, Netherlands
64 H 3 **Venta**, Lithuania ☪
56 A 7 **Ventimiglia**, Italy
64 H 2 **Ventspils**, Latvia
85 E 13 **Ventura**, CA, United States
99 H 9 **Vera**, Argentina
89 L 9 **Veracruz**, Mexico
119 B 10 **Veraval**, India
56 B 6 **Vercelli**, Italy
23 L 2 **Verkhoyanskiy Khrebet**, Asia ▲
82 I 5 **Vermilion Lake**, MN, United States ☪
79 M 6 **Vermont**, United States ▢
33 I 2 **Vernadsky**, Ukraine ▤
85 J 10 **Vernal**, UT, United States
83 F 11 **Vernon**, TX, United States
74 E 9 **Vernon**, BC, Canada
61 F 10 **Veroia**, Greece
56 E 5 **Verona**, Italy
45 I 4 **Versailles**, France
49 I 12 **Verviers**, Belgium
45 L 5 **Vesoul**, France
68 E 5 **Vest Fjord**, Norway ≈
68 E 5 **Vesterålen**, Norway ☪
57 H 10 **Vesuvius**, Italy ▲
64 F 10 **Veszprém**, Hungary
49 B 11 **Veurne**, Belgium
40 E 3 **Viana do Castelo**, Portugal
56 D 7 **Viareggio**, Italy
57 I 13 **Vibo Valentia**, Italy
69 C 14 **Viborg**, Denmark
41 N 3 **Vic**, Spain
56 E 5 **Vicenza**, Italy
45 J 7 **Vichy**, France
80 E 5 **Vicksburg**, MS, United States
147 K 10 **Victoria**, Australia ▢
146 G 5 **Victoria**, NT, Australia ☪
83 H 13 **Victoria**, TX, United States
74 D 10 **Victoria**, BC, Canada ☐
141 I 7 **Victoria Falls**, Zimbabwe
141 I 7 **Victoria Falls**, Zambia/Zimbabwe ☪
74 C 15 **Victoria Island**, NT/NU, Canada ☪
33 M 6 **Victoria Land**, Antarctica ☪
75 L 9 **Victoriaville**, QC, Canada
99 G 12 **Viedma**, Argentina
53 J 11 **Vienna**, Austria ♣
122 G 4 **Vientiane**, Laos ♣
45 I 5 **Vierzon**, France

122 H 4 **Vietnam**, Asia ▢
44 G 11 **Vignemale**, France ▲
40 F 3 **Vigo**, Spain
119 F 12 **Vijayawada**, India
68 D 8 **Vikna**, Norway ☪
69 B 10 **Vikøyri**, Norway
28 B 7 **Vila da Ribeira Brava**, Cape Verde
28 B 7 **Vila da Sal Rei**, Cape Verde
28 B 8 **Vila do Tarrafal**, Cape Verde
28 A 8 **Vila Nova Sintra**, Cape Verde
40 F 4 **Vila Nova de Gaia**, Portugal
40 F 4 **Vila Real**, Portugal
40 G 2 **Vilalba**, Spain
68 F 8 **Vilhelmina**, Sweden
65 I 2 **Viljandi**, Estonia
99 G 9 **Villa María**, Argentina
98 F 6 **Villa Martín**, Bolivia
98 G 6 **Villa Montes**, Bolivia
41 J 8 **Villacarrillo**, Spain
53 H 13 **Villach**, Austria
89 N 9 **Villahermosa**, Mexico
41 L 7 **Villajoyosa**, Spain
41 J 7 **Villanueva de los Infantes**, Spain
98 I 8 **Villarrica**, Paraguay
96 F 3 **Villavicencio**, Colombia
40 H 1 **Villaviciosa de Asturias**, Spain
98 G 6 **Villazon**, Bolivia
41 L 7 **Villena**, Spain
65 I 4 **Vilnius**, Lithuania
105 K 8 **Vilyuy**, Russia ☪
105 J 7 **Vilyuyskoye Vodokhranilishche**, Russia ☪
99 E 9 **Viña del Mar**, Chile
41 M 5 **Vinarós**, Spain
78 F 9 **Vincennes**, IN, United States
33 P 5 **Vincennes Bay**, Antarctica ≈
119 C 10 **Vindhya Ranges**, India ▲
122 H 4 **Vinh**, Vietnam
65 K 8 **Vinnytsya**, Ukraine
33 K 4 **Vinson Massif**, Antarctica ▲
91 M 4 **Virgin Islands**, United States ▢
79 J 10 **Virginia**, United States ▢
82 I 5 **Virginia**, MN, United States
79 L 11 **Virginia Beach**, VI, United States
61 C 6 **Virovitica**, Croatia
49 H 15 **Virton**, Belgium
61 B 8 **Vis**, Croatia ☪
85 E 13 **Visalia**, CA, United States
69 G 13 **Visby**, Sweden
74 F 4 **Viscount Melville Sound**, NU, Canada ≈
40 F 5 **Viseu**, Portugal
119 F 12 **Vishakhapatnam**, India
64 G 6 **Vistula**, Poland ☪
57 E 9 **Viterbo**, Italy
151 I 10 **Viti Levu**, Fiji ☪
23 L 3 **Vitim**, Asia ☪
97 L 8 **Vitória**, Brazil
97 L 7 **Vitória da Conquista**, Brazil
28 F 8 **Vitoria Seamount**, Atlantic Ocean ▰
41 J 2 **Vitoria-Gasteiz**, Spain
65 K 4 **Vitsyebsk**, Belarus
119 F 11 **Vizianagaram**, India
61 F 9 **Vladičin Han**, Serbia and Montenegro
104 C 6 **Vladimir**, Russia
105 M 11 **Vladivostok**, Russia
48 K 5 **Vlagtwedde**, Netherlands
48 F 4 **Vlieland**, Netherlands ☪
49 D 10 **Vlissingen**, Netherlands
45 L 8 **Voiron**, France
96 A 6 **Volcán Darwin**, Galapagos Islands ▲
96 A 7 **Volcán La Cumbre**, Galapagos Islands ▲
98 F 7 **Volcán Licancábur**, Bolivia/Chile ▲
98 F 7 **Volcán Llullaillaco**, Argentina/Chile ▲
96 A 6 **Volcán Wolf**, Galapagos Islands ▲
23 J 3 **Volga**, Europe ☪
104 C 7 **Volgograd**, Russia
104 D 5 **Vologda**, Russia
61 G 11 **Volos**, Greece
136 F 6 **Volta**, Ghana ☪
104 F 5 **Vorkuta**, Russia
104 C 6 **Voronezh**, Russia
65 I 2 **Võrtsjärv**, Estonia ☪
65 I 2 **Võru**, Estonia
45 L 5 **Vosges**, France ▲

33 N 5 **Vostok**, Russia ▤
61 G 8 **Vratsa**, Bulgaria
61 F 7 **Vršac**, Serbia and Montenegro
96 F 3 **Vuaupés**, Brazil/Colombia ☪
61 D 7 **Vukovar**, Croatia

W

49 G 9 **Waal**, Netherlands ☪
49 G 9 **Waalwijk**, Netherlands
78 F 9 **Wabash**, United States ☪
83 H 12 **Waco**, TX, United States
137 L 5 **Wad Medani**, Sudan
137 I 3 **Waddān**, Libya
48 G 5 **Waddenzee**, Netherlands ≈
137 L 4 **Wadi Halfa**, Sudan
114 G 4 **Wadi Rum**, Jordan ◇
131 J 15 **Wadomari**, Japan
147 K 9 **Wagga Wagga**, NSW, Australia
146 E 9 **Wagin**, WA, Australia
111 L 8 **Wah**, Pakistan
123 L 9 **Wahai**, Indonesia
85 B 15 **Wahiawa**, HI, United States
150 B 10 **Waiau**, New Zealand ☪
123 M 8 **Waigeo**, Indonesia ☪
150 F 3 **Waihi**, New Zealand
123 J 10 **Waikabubak**, Indonesia
150 F 4 **Waikato**, New Zealand ☪
85 C 15 **Wailuku**, HI, United States
150 D 9 **Waimate**, New Zealand
85 C 15 **Waimea**, HI, United States
150 F 5 **Waiouru**, New Zealand
150 G 5 **Waipawa**, New Zealand
150 E 7 **Wairau**, New Zealand ☪
150 G 5 **Wairoa**, New Zealand
150 E 3 **Waitakere**, New Zealand
150 C 9 **Waitaki**, New Zealand ☪
150 E 3 **Waiuku**, New Zealand
131 E 10 **Wakasa-wan**, Japan ≈
131 E 12 **Wakayama**, Japan
130 G 2 **Wakkanai**, Japan
64 F 7 **Wałbrzych**, Poland
37 F 13 **Wales**, United Kingdom ▢
147 K 8 **Walgett**, NSW, Australia
85 E 11 **Walker Lake**, NV, United States ☪
84 F 7 **Walla Walla**, WA, United States
31 J 5 **Wallaby Plateau**, Indian Ocean ▰
151 J 9 **Wallis**, Wallis and Futuna Islands ☪
151 J 9 **Wallis and Futuna Islands**, France ▢
80 H 5 **Walter F. George Reservoir**, AL, United States ☪
30 E 7 **Walters Shoal**, Indian Ocean ▰
140 G 8 **Walvis Bay**, Namibia
29 I 9 **Walvis Ridge**, Atlantic Ocean ▰
150 C 9 **Wanaka**, New Zealand
32 D 7 **Wandel Sea**, Arctic Ocean ▰
150 F 5 **Wanganui**, New Zealand
150 F 5 **Wanganui**, New Zealand ☪
147 J 9 **Wangaratta**, VIC, Australia
119 E 11 **Warangal**, India
119 E 10 **Wardha**, India ☪
49 C 11 **Waregem**, Belgium
147 L 6 **Warginburra Peninsula**, QLD, Australia ▶
150 F 2 **Warkworth**, New Zealand
79 J 7 **Warren**, PA, United States
78 H 7 **Warren**, MI, United States
136 H 7 **Warri**, Nigeria
37 G 13 **Warrington**, United Kingdom
147 J 10 **Warrnambool**, VIC, Australia
64 G 6 **Warsaw**, Poland ♣
64 F 6 **Warta**, Poland ☪
147 L 8 **Warwick**, QLD, Australia
79 N 7 **Warwick**, RI, United States
37 I 12 **Wash, The**, United Kingdom ≈
0 K 9 **Washington**, DC, United States ♣
84 D 6 **Washington**, United States ▢
79 M 7 **Waterbury**, CT, United States
37 D 13 **Waterford**, Ireland
82 I 7 **Waterloo**, IA, United States
79 K 6 **Watertown**, NY, United States
82 G 6 **Watertown**, SD, United States
37 I 13 **Watford**, United Kingdom
85 D 12 **Watsonville**, CA, United States
81 I 2 **Watts Bar Lake**, TN, United States ☪

137	K 7	Wau, Sudan
78	F 7	Waukegan, WI, United States
78	F 6	Waukesha, WI, United States
78	E 5	Wausau, WI, United States
49	F 12	Wavre, Belgium
75	J 10	Wawa, ON, Canada
81	J 6	Waycross, GA, United States
29	F 12	Weddell Abyssal Plain, Atlantic Ocean
99	H 15	Weddell Island, Falkland Islands
29	F 13	Weddell Sea, Atlantic Ocean
49	H 10	Weert, Netherlands
127	M 6	Weifang, China
52	F 8	Weimar, Germany
84	F 8	Weiser, ID, United States
80	H 3	Weiss Lake, AL, United States
49	I 14	Weiswampach, Luxembourg
150	D 6	Wekakura Point, New Zealand
141	I 9	Welkom, South Africa
147	I 4	Wellesley Islands, QLD, Australia
150	F 7	Wellington, New Zealand
85	G 10	Wells, NV, United States
53	H 11	Wels, Austria
84	E 6	Wenatchee, WA, United States
151	L 1	Weno, Federated States of Micronesia
127	N 8	Wenzhou, China
49	H 13	Werbomont, Belgium
52	E 8	Werra, Germany
52	B 7	Wesel, Germany
52	D 6	Weser, Germany
147	I 3	Wessel Islands, NT, Australia
33	K 4	West Antarctica, Antarctica
150	A 10	West Cape, New Zealand
26	E 5	West Caroline Basin, Pacific Ocean
99	H 15	West Falkland, Falkland Islands
151	K 1	West Fayu, Federated States of Micronesia
48	F 4	West Frisian Islands, Netherlands
81	L 9	West Palm Beach, FL, United States
29	D 12	West Scotia Ridge, Atlantic Ocean
23	K 3	West Siberian Plain, Asia
79	I 9	West Virginia, United States
146	F 7	Western Australia, Australia
65	J 3	Western Dvina, Belarus/Latvia
119	C 11	Western Ghats, India
136	E 3	Western Sahara, Morocco
49	D 10	Westerschelde, Netherlands
37	B 11	Westport, Ireland
150	C 7	Westport, New Zealand
123	L 10	Wetar, Indonesia
147	J 1	Wewak, Papua New Guinea
37	D 13	Wexford, Ireland
74	G 10	Weyburn, SK, Canada
150	G 4	Whakatane, New Zealand
150	E 2	Whangarei, New Zealand
31	I 5	Wharton Basin, Indian Ocean
80	G 3	Wheeler Lake, AL, United States
79	I 8	Wheeling, WV, United States
78	F 9	White, United States
85	G 12	White, United States
150	G 3	White Island, New Zealand
83	I 13	White Lake, LA, United States
23	I 5	White Nile, Africa
104	D 4	White Sea, Russia
136	F 6	White Volta, Burkina Faso/Ghana
37	F 10	Whitehaven, United Kingdom
74	D 6	Whitehorse, YT, Canada
83	C 11	Whitewater Baldy, NM, United States
147	K 5	Whitsunday Group, QLD, Australia
147	I 9	Whyalla, SA, Australia
83	G 10	Wichita, KS, United States
83	G 11	Wichita Falls, TX, United States
36	G 5	Wick, United Kingdom
85	I 14	Wickenburg, AZ, United States
53	K 11	Wiener Neustadt, Austria
53	C 9	Wiesbaden, Germany
147	J 8	Wilcannia, NSW, Australia
52	C 5	Wilhelmshaven, Germany
79	K 7	Wilkes Barre, PA, United States
33	O 6	Wilkes Land, Antarctica
85	J 15	Willcox, AZ, United States
91	L 7	Willemstad, Netherlands Antilles
84	C 8	Williamette, United States
79	K 7	Williamsport, PA, United States
82	E 5	Williston, ND, United States
82	H 6	Wilmar, MN, United States
81	M 3	Wilmington, NC, United States
79	L 8	Wilmington, DE, United States
140	E 8	Windhoek, Namibia
75	J 11	Windsor, ON, Canada
91	O 6	Windward Islands, Caribbean Sea
91	J 4	Windward Passage, Caribbean Sea
75	I 8	Winisk, Canada
85	H 10	Winnemucca, NV, United States
85	E 10	Winnemucca Lake, NV, United States
74	H 10	Winnipeg, MB, Canada
85	J 14	Winslow, AZ, United States
81	K 1	Winston Salem, NC, United States
48	J 8	Winterswijk, Netherlands
53	D 12	Winterthur, Switzerland
150	B 10	Winton, New Zealand
147	J 6	Winton, NSW, Australia
78	E 5	Wisconsin, United States
52	F 5	Wismar, Germany
52	F 6	Wittenberge, Germany
64	G 6	Włocławek, Poland
64	F 7	Wodzisław Śląski, Poland
151	K 1	Woleai, Federated States of Micronesia
53	I 13	Wolfsberg, Austria
52	F 6	Wolfsburg, Germany
74	G 3	Wollaston Lake, SK, Canada
74	F 5	Wollaston Peninsula, NU, Canada
147	K 9	Wollongong, NSW, Australia
48	I 5	Wolvega, Netherlands
37	G 12	Wolverhampton, United Kingdom
127	O 5	Wŏnsan, North Korea
78	E 4	Woodruff, WI, United States
150	F 6	Woodville, New Zealand
79	N 7	Worcester, MA, United States
37	F 10	Workington, United Kingdom
82	C 7	Worland, WY, United States
53	D 10	Worms, Germany
37	I 14	Worthing, United Kingdom
82	H 7	Worthington, MN, United States
151	M 3	Wotho, Marshall Islands
151	N 3	Wotje, Marshall Islands
105	N 4	Wrangel Island, Russia
32	E 3	Wrangel Sea, Arctic Ocean
64	F 7	Wrocław, Poland
127	K 5	Wuhai, China
127	M 8	Wuhan, China
127	N 7	Wuhu, China
52	C 8	Wuppertal, Germany
53	E 9	Würzburg, Germany
127	N 7	Wuxi, China
127	K 6	Wuzhong, China
127	L 10	Wuzhou, China
37	G 13	Wye, United Kingdom
146	G 4	Wyndham, WA, Australia
82	C 7	Wyoming, United States

X

109	O 5	Xaşmaz, Azerbaijan
141	K 9	Xai-Xai, Mozambique
89	L 8	Xalapa, Mexico
122	G 3	Xam Hua, Laos
109	N 7	Xankändi, Azerbaijan
61	H 10	Xanthi, Greece
41	L 7	Xátiva, Spain
127	N 9	Xiamen, China
127	L 7	Xi'an, China
127	L 7	Xiangfan, China
127	L 8	Xiangtan, China
127	K 7	Xianyang, China
127	N 2	Xiao Higgan Ling, China
126	G 8	Xigaz, China
127	M 4	Xilinhot, China
127	M 6	Xingtai, China
97	J 5	Xingu, Brazil
127	J 6	Xining, China
127	M 6	Xintai, China
127	L 6	Xinxiang, China
127	M 7	Xinyang, China
127	M 7	Xuchang, China
127	L 11	Xuwen, China
127	M 7	Xuzhou, China

y

61	G 8	Yablanitsa, Bulgaria
98	G 6	Yacuiba, Bolivia
137	I 2	Yafran, Libya
29	D 11	Yaghan Basin, Atlantic Ocean
127	M 2	Yakeshi, China
84	E 6	Yakima, WA, United States
131	C 16	Yaku-shima, Japan
105	L 7	Yakutsk, Russia
65	M 11	Yalta, Ukraine
130	H 8	Yamagata, Japan
131	C 12	Yamaguchi, Japan
104	G 5	Yamal Peninsula, Russia
61	I 9	Yambol, Bulgaria
136	F 7	Yamoussoukro, Côte d'Ivoire
126	H 8	Yamzho Yumco, China
105	L 6	Yana, Russia
127	L 6	Yan'an, China
114	H 6	Yanbu' al Baḥr, Saudi Arabia
111	K 6	Yangiyul, Uzbekistan
127	L 6	Yangquan, China
127	J 9	Yangtze, China
127	M 7	Yangzhou, China
127	O 4	Yanji, China
82	G 7	Yankton, SD, United States
127	N 6	Yantai, China
137	I 8	Yaoundé, Cameroon
151	J 1	Yap, Federated States of Micronesia
123	N 8	Yapen, Indonesia
88	G 4	Yaqui, Mexico
109	D 10	Yardimci Burnu, Turkey
37	J 12	Yare, United Kingdom
150	H 7	Yaren, Nauru
126	F 5	Yarkant He, China
75	L 9	Yarmouth, NS, Canada
104	D 6	Yaroslavl', Russia
108	I 6	Yasun Burnu, Turkey
131	B 14	Yatsushiro, Japan
119	E 11	Yavatmal, India
115	L 4	Yazd, Iran
80	E 4	Yazoo City, MS, United States
104	E 7	Yekaterinburg, Russia
36	H 3	Yell, United Kingdom
127	K 5	Yellow, China
127	N 6	Yellow Sea, China
74	F 7	Yellowknife, NT, Canada
82	C 6	Yellowstone, MT, United States
82	C 7	Yellowstone Lake, WY, United States
111	I 7	Yeloten, Turkmenistan
115	J 10	Yemen, Asia
122	E 3	Yenangyaung, Myanmar
104	H 7	Yenisey, Russia
104	H 8	Yeniseyskiy Kryazh, Russia
37	G 14	Yeovil, United Kingdom
109	M 7	Yerevan, Armenia
109	N 6	Yevlax, Azerbaijan
65	M 11	Yevpatoriya, Ukraine
127	K 8	Yibin, China
127	L 8	Yichang, China
127	O 2	Yichun, China
127	K 6	Yinchuan, China
127	N 5	Yingkou, China
126	G 4	Yining, China
127	L 8	Yiyang, China
122	H 10	Yogyakarta, Indonesia
131	F 11	Yokkaichi, Japan
131	H 10	Yokohama, Japan
131	I 10	Yokosuka, Japan
131	D 11	Yonago, Japan
127	N 9	Yong'an, China
79	M 8	Yonkers, NY, United States
37	I 11	York, United Kingdom
79	K 8	York, PA, United States
147	I 9	Yorke Peninsula, SA, Australia
74	G 9	Yorkton, SK, Canada
131	K 15	Yoron-tō, Japan
104	D 6	Yoshkar-Ola, Russia
79	I 8	Youngstown, OH, United States
85	C 9	Yreka, CA, United States
111	M 5	Ysyk-Köl, Kyrgyzstan
127	J 9	Yuan, China
85	D 11	Yuba City, CA, United States
89	O 7	Yucatan Channel, Mexico
89	O 8	Yucatan Peninsula, Mexico
127	L 8	Yueyang, China
105	N 5	Yukagirskoye Ploskogor'ye, Russia
22	C 2	Yukon, North America
74	D 6	Yukon Territory, Canada
127	L 10	Yulin, China
127	L 6	Yulin, China
85	H 15	Yuma, AZ, United States
127	I 5	Yumen, China
27	L 7	Yupanqui Basin, Pacific Ocean
131	J 14	Yuwan-dake, Japan
105	N 10	Yuzhno-Sakhalinsk, Russia
65	L 9	Yuzhnoukrayinsk, Ukraine

Z

48	F 7	Zaandam, Netherlands
64	F 7	Zabrze, Poland
89	J 7	Zacatecas, Mexico
61	B 8	Zadar, Croatia
40	G 7	Zafra, Spain
61	B 6	Zagreb, Croatia
23	J 4	Zagros Mountains, Asia
115	N 4	Zāhedān, Iran
61	E 13	Zakynthos, Greece
61	E 13	Zakynthos, Greece
64	E 10	Zalaegerszeg, Hungary
127	N 3	Zalantun, China
110	H 5	Zaliv Kara-Bogaz-Gol, Turkmenistan
105	N 7	Zaliv Shelikhova, Russia
60	G 5	Zalău, Romania
23	I 7	Zambezi, Africa
141	I 6	Zambia, Africa
123	K 6	Zamboanga, Philippines
40	H 4	Zamora, Spain
89	J 8	Zamora de Hidalgo, Mexico
64	H 7	Zamość, Poland
79	I 9	Zanesville, OH, United States
115	K 2	Zanjān, Iran
141	L 4	Zanzibar, Tanzania
127	M 6	Zaozhuang, China
104	G 9	Zapadnyy Sayan, Russia
99	F 11	Zapala, Argentina
29	G 9	Zapiola Seamount, Atlantic Ocean
65	M 9	Zaporizhzhya, Ukraine
108	I 7	Zara, Turkey
111	K 6	Zarafshon, Tajikistan
41	L 4	Zaragoza, Spain
111	J 9	Zaranj, Afghanistan
111	K 8	Zarghün Shahr, Afghanistan
136	H 6	Zaria, Nigeria
48	G 8	Zeist, Netherlands
64	G 4	Zelenogradsk, Russia
61	D 8	Zenica, Bosnia-Herzegovina
105	L 9	Zeyskoye Vodokhranilishche, Russia
127	O 4	Zhangguangcai Ling, China
127	M 5	Zhangjiakou, China
127	N 9	Zhangzhou, China
127	L 10	Zhanjiang, China
126	G 7	Zhari Namco, China
127	L 7	Zhengzhou, China
127	N 7	Zhenjiang, China
111	K 3	Zhezkazgan, Kazakhstan
65	K 5	Zhlobin, Belarus
33	P 3	Zhongshan, China
127	M 8	Zhuzhou, China
110	H 2	Zhympity, Kazakhstan
65	K 7	Zhytomyr, Ukraine
127	M 6	Zibo, China
127	M 8	Zigong, China
136	D 5	Ziguinchor, Senegal
89	J 9	Zihuatanejo, Mexico
141	I 7	Zimbabwe, Africa
136	H 6	Zinder, Niger
115	J 10	Zinjibār, Yemen
104	E 7	Zlatoust, Russia
64	F 8	Zlín, Czech Republic
137	I 2	Zlīṭan, Libya
48	F 8	Zoetermeer, Netherlands
108	E 6	Zonguldak, Turkey
136	E 3	Zouérat, Mauritania
115	L 9	Ẕufār, Oman
53	D 12	Zug, Switzerland
53	F 12	Zugspitze, Germany
48	I 4	Zuidhorn, Netherlands
127	K 9	Zunyi, China
61	D 7	Županja, Croatia
53	D 12	Zürich, Switzerland
48	I 7	Zutphen, Netherlands
136	E 7	Zwedru, Liberia
52	G 8	Zwickau, Germany
48	I 7	Zwolle, Netherlands
111	N 2	Zyryanovsk, Kazakhstan

▲▲ Mountain Range   ■ National Capital   Ocean   Physical Feature   Polar Base   River   Sea   Special Feature   State Capital   Underwater Feature

Acknowledgments

Key

t=top; l=left; r=right; tl=top left; tc=top center; tr=top right; cl=center left; c=center; cr=center right; b=bottom; bl=bottom left; bc=bottom center; br=bottom right

AA = The Art Archive

AAA = The Ancient Art & Architecture Collection Ltd

AAP = Australian Associated Press

AFP = Agence France-Presse

AMNH = American Museum of Natural History

APL/Corbis = Australian Picture Library/Corbis

AVA = The Advertising Archive Ltd

BA = Bridgeman Art Library (www.bridgeman.co.uk)

GC = The Granger Collection

GI = Getty Images

KC = Kobal Collection

MEPL = Mary Evans Picture Library

APL/MP = Australian Picture Library/Minden Pictures

N_G = NASA/Great Images in NASA

N_J = NASA/Jet Propulsion Laboratory

N_T = NASA/Total Ozone Mapping Spectrometer

NASA = National Aeronautics and Space Administration

PD = Photodisc

PE = PhotoEssentials

SML = The Science Museum, London

TPL = photolibrary.com

TPL/SPL = photolibrary.com/Science Photo Library

Illustrators: Susanna Addario; Paul Bachem; Graham Back; Anne Bowman; Gregory Bridges; Danny Burke; Fiammetta Dogi; Simone End; Christer Eriksson; Chris Forsey; John Crawford Fraser; Mark A. Garlick/space-art.co.uk; Jon Gittoes; Mike Gorman; Lorraine Hannay; Robert Hynes; INKLINK; David Kirshner; Frank Knight; Mike Lamble; Iain McKellar; James McKinnon; Marlene McLoughlin; Rob Mancini; Peter Mennim; Moonrunner Design Ltd.; Nicola Oram; Peter Bull Art Studio; Evert Ploeg; Tony Pyrzakowski; Oliver Rennert; John Richards; Edwina Riddell; Barbara Rodanska; Trevor Ruth; Claudia Saraceni; Michael Saunders; Peter Schouten; Marco Sparaciari; Roger Swainston; Steve Trevaskis; Thomas Trojer; Guy Troughton; Glen Vause; Rod Westblade; Ann Winterbotham; Murray Zanoni.

Bernard Thornton Artists UK: Tony Gibbons, Adam Hook, Christa Hook, Richard Hook, Stephen Seymour.

Illustrationweb.com: Andrew Beckett, Steinar Lund, Sharif Tarabay.

Wildlife Art Ltd: Robin Carter, Tom Connell, Ray Grinaway, David Hardy, Philip Hood, Ian Jackson, Ken Oliver, Michael Langham Rowe, Myke Taylor.

8b Craig Mahew/Robert Simmon/NASA/GSFC tc NASA/GSFC/METI/ERSDAC/JAROS & US/Japan Aster Science Team **9**tl NASA/GSFC/METI/ERSDAC/JAROS & US/Japan Aster Science Team tr Restec Japan/TPL/SPL **10**b NASA Goddard Space Flight Center/Reto Stöckli/Robert Simmon/ MODIS/USGS/Defense Meteorological Satellite Program tc N_G **11**tl NASA/TPL/SPL tr N_T **12**bl N_J br Adastra/GI cl APL/Corbis cr The Image Bank/GI tc NASA/TPL/SPL **13**br SRTM Team/ NASA/JPL/NIMA c NASA/GSFC/MITI/ERSDAC/JAROS & US/Japan Aster Science Team tl NASA/ GSFC/METI/ERSDAC/JAROS & US/Japan Aster Science Team tr Jacques Descloitres/MODIS Rapid Response Team/NASA/GSFC **16**c Shin Yoshino/APL/MP c Jim Brandenburg/APL/MP **17**c, cr APL/ Corbis cr Mitsuaki Iwogo/APL/MP tr Norbert Wu/APL/MP **18**bc Tom Owen Edmunds/GI bc Connie Coleman/GI cl APL/Corbis **19**cr APL/Corbis **38**br, cl, cr, tr APL/Corbis **39**bc Belvoir Castle, Leicestershire, UK/BA bl, br, c, cl, cr APL/Corbis c Paul Maeyaert/BA cl Lambeth Palace Library, London, UK/BA cl Christie's Images/BA tr Ashmolean Museum, Oxford, UK/BA **42**bc AFP bl APL/Corbis **43**bc AA/Museo Picasso Barcelona/Dagli Orti c, cl, cr BA tl Rafael Macia/photolibrary.com **46**cl APL/Corbis tr PD tr TPL/David Barnes **47**bc TPL bl APL/Corbis br AA/Bibliotheque Nationale Paris c Lauros/Giraudon/BA cr GI/BA/Rossetti tr AVA **50**bc, bl APL/Corbis **51**bc, br, c, cl, cr, tr APL/Corbis c, tc AFP tl Graphische Sammlung Albertina, Vienna, Austria/BA **54**c APL/Corbis **55**bl AVA br, cl APL/Corbis cl Germanisches National Museum, Nuremberg, Germany/BA tl Lauros/Giraudon/BA tr Christie's Images/BA **58**bl, br APL/Corbis c Peter Johnson, **59**bc, tr APL/Corbis bc Alessi cl Valerie Martin **62**cl APL/Corbis **63**bc, cl, cr APL/Corbis bc AA/Nicolas Sapieha tl GC **66**bc, bl, cl APL/Corbis tr GI/Taxi/Dan Sams **67**bc, bl, br, c, tr APL/Corbis c Tretyakov Gallery, Moscow, Russia/BA cl BA/Archives Charmet tc Museo Civico di Storia ed Arte, Modena, Italy/Alinari/BA **70**bl, br APL/Corbis **71**bc, cr, tc, tr APL/Corbis br Polar Music/Reg Grundy Prods/KC cl AA/Nasjonal Gallericht, Oslo/Album/Joseph Martin **75**tr AMNH **76**bl, c APL/Corbis tr AA/Tate Gallery, London **77**bc, bl, br, c, tr APL/Corbis cr AA/National Trust Quebec House/Eileen Tweedy cr AVA **86**c APL/Corbis tr Angela Handley **87**bc, bl, c, tl, tr APL/Corbis br PE **92**br, cr, tr APL/Corbis **93**bc, c, cl, cr, tc, tr APL/Corbis c Andrew Furlong **100**bl, br Angela Handley cl PD **101**bc, c, cl, cr, t, tl APL/Corbis br AFP br Bibliotheque Nationale, Paris, France/BA cr American Museum of Natural History, New York, USA/BA **106**br, c, cl, tc APL/Corbis **107**bc, c, cl, cr, tr APL/Corbis tc Mark Gallery/London, UK/BA tl Museum of Tropinin & His Contemporaries, Moscow, Russia/BA **112**bc APL/Corbis View bl APL/Corbis cl Persian School/British Museum London, UK/BA **113**bc, bl, br, c, tc, tr APL/ Corbis cr Topkapi Palace Museum, Istanbul, Turkey/BA **116**bl David W. Hamilton/GI cr APL/ Corbis **117**bc MEPL bl, br, cl, cr, tc APL/Corbis **120**cr APL/Corbis **121**bc, br, c, cl, tl APL/Corbis cl AA/Bodleian Library Oxford/The Bodleian Library cr Victoria & Albert Museum, London/BA tr British Library, London, UK/BA **124**c Digital Vision/GI cr APL/Corbis tc MEPL **125**bc, bl, c, cr, tc APL/Corbis tr Bushnell/Soifer/GI **128**br AAP Image/Xinhua Photo/Du Huajau **129**bc, c, tc APL/ Corbis bl Bibliotheque Nationale, Paris, France/BA bl SML (Science & Society Picture Library) tr Paul Freeman/BA **132**br, cr Japan National Tourist Organisation c Chris Shorten cl, tr APL/ Corbis **133**bc, bl, br, tc, tr APL/Corbis **138**bc, bl, tc APL/Corbis **139**bc, c APL/Corbis br PE c AAA tl APL/Zefa **142**br APL/Corbis **143**bl, br, c, cr, tc, tr APL/Corbis c Pascal Goetgheluck/TPL/SPL **148**bl, c APL/Corbis **149**bc, br, c, tl APL/Corbis c AAP Image cl By permission of the National Library of Australia cr Allport Library and Museum of Fine Arts, State Library of Tasmania tr By permission of the South Australian Museum **152**bl, br, cl APL/Corbis **153**bc, bl, br, c, cr APL/Corbis bl AAP Image/AP c PE tl La Trobe Picture Collection, State Library of Victoria

THE ARCTIC
32

GREENLAND
32

ALASKA
84

Iceland
68

CANADA
74

Azores
40

Madeira
40

UNITED STATES
OF AMERICA
78

THE ATLANTIC OCEAN
28

Canary
Islands
40

MEXICO
88

CENTRAL AMERICA AND
THE CARIBBEAN
90

Hawaii
84

Cape
Verde
28

THE PACIFIC OCEAN
26

Galapagos
Islands
96

NORTHERN
SOUTH AMERICA
96

THE PACIFIC ISLANDS
150

SOUTHERN
SOUTH AMERICA
98